Time Out

Sydney

timeout.com/sydney

Penguin Books

PENGUIN BOOKS

Published by the Penguin Group
Penguin Books Ltd, 80 Strand, London WC2R ORL, England
Penguin Books USA Inc., 375 Hudson Street, New York, New York 10014, USA
Penguin Books Australia Ltd, 250 Camberwell Road, Camberwell, Victoria 3124, Australia
Penguin Books Canada Ltd, 10 Alcorn Avenue, Toronto, Ontario, Canada M4V 3B2
Penguin Books (NZ) Ltd, cnr Rosedale and Airborne Roads, Albany, Auckland, New Zealand

Penguin Books Ltd, Registered Offices: 80 Strand, London WC2R ORL, England

First published 1997
Second edition 2000
Third edition 2001

Fourth edition 2004
10 9 8 7 6 5 4 3 2 1

Colour reprographics by Icon, Crowne House, 56-58 Southwark Street, London SE1 1UN
Printed and bound by Cayfosa-Quebecor, Ctra. de Caldes, Km 3 08 130 Sta, Perpètua de Mogoda, Barcelona, Spain

Edited and designed by
Time Out Guides Limited
Universal House
251 Tottenham Court Road
London W1T 7AB
Tel + 44 (0)20 7813 3000
Fax + 44 (0)20 7813 6001
Email guides@timeout.com
www.timeout.com

Editorial

Editor Cath Phillips
Consultant Editor Juliet Rieden
Copy Editors Christi Daugherty, Janice Fuscoe, Hugh Graham
Listings Checkers Sarah Craske, Miranda Herron
Proofreader John Pym
Indexer Jonathan Cox

Editorial/Managing Director Peter Fiennes
Series Editor Ruth Jarvis
Deputy Series Editor Lesley McCave
Guides Co-ordinator Anna Norman
Accountant Sarah Bostock

Design

Art Director Mandy Martin
Acting Art Director Scott Moore
Acting Art Editor Tracey Ridgewell
Acting Senior Designer Astrid Kogler
Designer Sam Lands
Junior Designer Oliver Knight
Digital Imaging Dan Conway
Ad Make-up Charlotte Blythe

Picture Desk

Picture Editor Jael Marschner
Deputy Picture Editor Kit Burnet
Picture Researcher Ivy Lahon
Picture Desk Assistant/Librarian Laura Lord

Advertising

Sales Director Mark Phillips
International Sales Manager Ross Canadé
International Sales Executive James Tuson
Advertising Sales (Sydney) Uptime Marketing Australia
Advertising Assistant Lucy Butler

Marketing

Marketing Manager Mandy Martinez
US Publicity & Marketing Associate Rosella Albanese

Production

Guides Production Director Mark Lamond
Production Controller Samantha Furniss

Time Out Group

Chairman Tony Elliott
Managing Director Mike Hardwick
Group Financial Director Richard Waterlow
Group Commercial Director Lesley Gill
Group Marketing Director Christine Cort
Group General Manager Nichola Coulthard
Group Art Director John Oakey
Online Managing Director David Pepper
Group Production Director Steve Proctor
Group IT Director Simon Chappell

Contributors

Introduction Juliet Rieden. **History** Juliet Rieden. **The Other History** Miranda Herron. **Sydney Today** Juliet Rieden.
Where to Stay Juliet Rieden. **Sightseeing Introduction** Juliet Rieden. **Central Sydney** Juliet Rieden. **Eastern Suburbs** Katie Ekberg. **Inner West** Prue Rushton (*Sacred sites* Miranda Herron). **North Shore** Juliet Rieden. **Northern Beaches** Katie Ekberg.
Parramatta & the West Ed Gibbs (*What's in a name?* Miranda Herron). **The South** Prue Rushton (Bundeena Marc Llewellyn).
Sydney's Best Beaches Katie Ekberg. **Cafés, Bars & Pubs** Pat Nourse. **Restaurants** Pat Nourse. **Shops & Services** Katie Ekberg (Fashion, Fashion accessories, Health & beauty, *Only in Oz, Home groan* Juliet Rieden). **Festivals & Events** Juliet Rieden. **Children** Deborah Dickson-Smith. **Film** Juliet Rieden. **Galleries** Tim Benzie. **Gay & Lesbian** Katie Ekberg. **Music** Ed Gibbs. **Nightlife** Prue Rushton. **Sport & Fitness** Sue Crowe. **Theatre & Dance** James Waites. **Short Trips** Marc Llewellyn (*Protest point* Miranda Herron). **Trip Planner** Marc Llewellyn. **Directory** Katie Ekberg.

Maps JS Graphics (john@jsgrahics.co.uk). **Map on page 315** reproduced with the kind permisson of Claire Sadler at Sydney Ferries. **Map on page 316** reproduced with the kind permission of Claudette Duckworth at State Rail Authority of NSW.

Photography Chris Ivin, except: pages 6, 8 Hulton Getty; pages 11, 12, 14, 16, 21, 22, 195, 228, 243 Newspix; pages 57, 103 PhotoLibrary.com; pages 191, 250 Greg Barret; page 203 Front Row/Miramax; pages 215, 219 Mazz Images; pages 240, 259 Corbis; page 249 Julian Watt; page 257 Alamy; page 266 Roberto Rinaldi/Bluegreen Pictures.
The following images were supplied by the featured establishments/artists: pages 51, 184, 185, 196, 203, 253.

Aboriginal flag on page 17 reproduced with the kind permission of Harold Thomas, author and owner of copyright ©1971.

The Editor would like to thank Russell Mills at Tourism New South Wales, Kim Salt at Michels Warren, Steven Gargano at Southern Cross Suites, Louise Owens at the Russell Hotel, Annabel Porter at BridgeClimb, Mike Harrison, and the Culross family.

Contents

Contents

Introduction

The secret has been out for quite a while now – Sydney rocks. The largest of Australia's cities boasts one of the world's most beautiful harbour settings, endless beaches, verdant parks, innovative and affordable restaurants, kicking nightlife, lots of pretty people and a carefree charm that's insatiably addictive. Sure, it's a long way from everywhere, but the marvels of international travel have whittled away at flight times and costs, making Australia, and especially Sydney, a genuinely viable option for all international tourists.

For decades, Sydney was the first port of call for visitors doing the big Australia tour, before heading off to Queensland and the Great Barrier Reef, the Red Centre and Uluru or the Top End and Kakadu's crocs. But these days travellers come just for the Emerald City itself. It's not so much that the place has changed, but that events such as the 2000 Olympics and the 2003 Rugby World Cup have thrown the city into the world spotlight and, like the showgirl it is, Sydney sparkled in the limelight.

Of course, Sydney has changed immeasurably over the years and continues to evolve in surprising directions. While the Opera House and the Harbour Bridge remain the city's icons, the CBD with all those skyscrapers can come as a bit of a shock. The latest spire, World Tower, a retail and residential complex a stone's throw from Chinatown, has 75 storeys with views from the top that stretch for miles. Indeed, apartment blocks are quickly dominating the city's real estate (and skyline), with more and more of the glass and concrete beasts popping up every year. And while weekly residential rents compare favourably with London, New York, Paris and Tokyo, there's no such thing as a real estate bargain. Sydney's median house price just hit half a million dollars and the only way it's heading is up.

Also on the up is Sydney's population, currently pitched at four million. The city boasts multicultural residents from 180 different nations, all hoping that its streets will be paved with gold. Whether their wishes are granted depends a lot on the will of the individual, but golden rays are a given. Sydney has an enviable climate offering long warm summers with blue skies, and mild winters when temperatures rarely drop below 12°C (54°F). Consequently, most of the city's popular activities are outdoors – lazing on the beach, throwing some prawns on the barbie, yachting and swimming in the harbour, eating and drinking al fresco, surfing in the ocean, playing cricket, even watching movies and opera.

Culturally, the city still has a way to go, but a vibrant contemporary arts scene, a growing movie industry inspired by the international success of many home-grown actors, and the annual Gay & Lesbian Mardi Gras Festival, the city's biggest tourist pull, are making inroads. One thing is certain, they don't have to pay people to come here any more!

ABOUT TIME OUT GUIDES

This fourth edition of the *Time Out Sydney Guide* is one of an expanding series of Time Out City Guides, produced by the people behind London and New York's successful listings magazines. Our guides are all written and updated by resident experts who have striven to provide you with all the most up-to-date information you'll need to explore the city or read up on its background, whether you're a local or a first-time visitor.

THE LOWDOWN ON THE LISTINGS

Above all, we've tried to make this guide as useful as possible. Addresses, telephone numbers, websites, transport information, opening times, admission prices and credit card details are all included in our listings. And, as far as possible, we've given details of facilities, services and events, all checked and correct as we went to press. However, owners and managers can change their arrangements at any time. Before you go out of your way, we'd advise you to phone and check opening times, ticket prices and other particulars. While every effort has been make to ensure the accuracy of the information contained in this guide, the publishers cannot accept responsibility for any errors it may contain.

PRICES AND PAYMENT

We have noted where venues such as shops, hotels and restaurants accept the following credit cards: American Express (AmEx),

Australia & New Zealand Bank Card (BC), Diners Club (DC), MasterCard (MC) and Visa (V). Many shops, restaurants and attractions will also accept other cards, including JCB, as well as travellers' cheques issued by a major financial institution (such as American Express).

The prices we've supplied should be treated as guidelines, not gospel. If prices vary wildly from those we've quoted, please write and let us know. We aim to give the best and most up-to-date advice, so we always want to know if you've been badly treated or overcharged.

THE LIE OF THE LAND

Sydney is a sprawling mass of suburbs clustered around a compact city centre, and at first the sheer number of suburbs can be baffling. The central area, however, is much easier to fathom, and small enough to explore on foot. Alternatively, public transport, in the form of ferries, buses, CityRail trains, LightRail and the Monorail, is excellent and accessible. Travelling to and from the suburbs is also easily done on public transport, and we've included full transport details with each listing. The options given are the most direct routes, but other routes may also be possible.

TELEPHONE NUMBERS

The international dialling code for Australia is 61, and the code for Sydney is 02 (drop the zero if calling from overseas). Standard Sydney phone numbers have eight digits. The 02 area encompasses the whole of New South Wales, and if you're calling from within NSW you don't need to use the area code. Call rates depend on distance – the further away you're phoning, the more it will cost. Generally, calls to within a 25-kilometre (16-mile) radius are charged at local rate, and anything further afield at long-distance rates.

1800 numbers are free when dialled within Australia, but are not necessarily accessible countrywide, and cannot be dialled from abroad. 13 and 1300 numbers are charged at the local rate or less throughout Australia.

ESSENTIAL INFORMATION

For all the practical information you might need for visiting the city, including visa and customs information, advice on disabled facilities and access, emergency telephone numbers and local transport, turn to the Directory chapter at the back of the guide. It starts on page 277.

MAPS

The map section at the back of this guide includes useful orientation and overview maps of the country and city. The maps start on page 303. Street maps to the centre of Sydney are on pages 308-313; map references indicate the page number and square on those maps. There's also a street index on page 314. On page 315 you'll find a map showing the routes of the Sydney Ferries, and on page 316 is a map of the CityRail train network in suburban Sydney.

LET US KNOW WHAT YOU THINK

We hope you enjoy the *Time Out Sydney Guide* and we'd like to know what you think of it. We welcome tips for places that you consider we should include in our future editions, and take note of your criticism of our choices. There's a reader's reply card at the back of this book for your feedback – or you can email us on sydneyguide@timeout.com.

There is an online version of this book, along with guides to 45 other international cities, at **www.timeout.com**.

In Context

Features

History

Sydney's journey from Aboriginal hunting ground to Olympic city.

People have inhabited the area now known as Sydney for tens of thousands of years. When Captain James Cook turned up in 1770, after being issued with orders that he should 'with the consent of the natives take possession of convenient situations in the name of the king', he noted that the Aborigines 'appear to be the most wretched people on earth. But in reality they are far happier than we Europeans'. Not surprisingly, the first words the Europeans ever heard from the Aborigines in the Sydney area were 'Warra! Warra!' – meaning 'Go away!'

On 29 April 1770 Cook landed at Botany Bay, which he named after discovering scores of plants hitherto unknown to science. Turning northwards, he passed an entrance to a harbour where there appeared to be safe anchorage. Cook called it Port Jackson after the Secretary to the Admiralty, George Jackson.

Back in Britain, King George III was convinced that the east coast of the island, which had been claimed for him and called New South Wales, would make a good colony. For one thing it would help reduce Britain's overflowing prison population. For another, a settlement in the region would be convenient both as a base for trading in the Far East, and in case of a war with the French or Dutch.

THE FIRST FLEET

On 13 May 1787 Captain Arthur Phillip's ship, *Sirius*, along with three provisions ships, two warships and six vessels of convicts, set sail from Portsmouth. On board were some 300 merchant seamen, their wives, children and servants and nearly 800 convicts. Thirty-six weeks later, on 18 January 1788, after stops in Tenerife, Rio de Janeiro and the Cape of Good Hope, the *Sirius* arrived at Botany Bay. The rest of the First Fleet arrived a couple of days later. Fewer than 50 passengers had perished en route – not a bad rate for the period.

At this time of year, Botany Bay turned out to be a grim site for the new colony: there was little water and it was exposed to strong winds and swell. One plus was that the naked 'Indians' seen running up and down the beach 'shouting and making many uncouth signs and gestures' turned out to be relatively friendly. Eager to make a good impression, Phillip and a small party of frock coats took a rowing boat to meet their new subjects. The meeting went well: the British exchanged a looking glass and beads for a wooden club.

Probably relieved that his first contact with the locals had not gone amiss – when William Jansz of the Dutch East India Company had met Aboriginal Australians in 1606 he reported back that they 'killed on sight' – Phillip decided to search for Port Jackson. He returned with glowing reports: it was 'one of the finest harbours in the world, in which a thousand sail of the line might ride in perfect security'. This is one of the earliest descriptions of Sydney Harbour.

That same day, Phillip's men caught the improbable sight of two ships approaching from the sea. These were the French frigates *La Boussole* and *L'Astrolobe*, commanded by Jean-François de Galaup, Count de la Pérouse, who was on a voyage of discovery through the southern hemisphere. Surprised by their old enemy, Phillip decided to up-anchor the whole fleet the following morning and lead it to Sydney Cove – named after Viscount Sydney, the minister responsible for the colony.

> ## 'Epidemics fuelled a belief among white settlers that the Aboriginal peoples were doomed to extinction.'

The First Fleeters set to as soon as they arrived. Trees were felled, marquees erected, convict shacks constructed from cabbage palms, garden plots dug and a blacksmith's forge set up. On 7 February the settlers gathered to hear Phillip declared the first governor of the state of New South Wales and its dependencies. His residence, Old Government House, still stands in Parramatta. It wasn't long, though, before convicts started to disappear. Several were found clubbed or speared to death, probably in revenge for attacks on the locals. Food ran dangerously low, scurvy took hold and the settlers' small herd of cattle began to diminish.

During the next few weeks the animosity between the settlers and the Aboriginal people came to a head, and the disappearance of several more convicts and a marine provoked Governor Phillip to try to capture some natives in a bid to force talks. Two boats were sent to Manly (named after the 'manly' nature of the undaunted Aborigines seen there). Following courteous overtures, the settlers suddenly grabbed an Aboriginal man, called Arabanoo, and rushed him to a boat under a hail of stones and spears. His hair was cut, his beard shaved

and he was bathed and dressed in European clothes. But despite attempts by the settlers to persuade him to tell his compatriots that they meant no harm, no ground was gained on the path to friendship.

In those early days, capturing Aborigines to turn them into honorary white men was all the rage. Two such captives, Bennelong and Colbee, were rough-and-ready types, scarred from warfare and smallpox. Colbee soon bolted, but Bennelong stayed for five months and eventually, dressed in top hat and tails, travelled to London to have tea with the royal family. He gave his name to the point of land where a hut was built for him – and on which the Sydney Opera House now stands.

Early in 1789 the local Aborigines began to succumb to smallpox contracted from the British or from sailors on the French vessels that had put in at Botany Bay. Hundreds were soon dead, among them Arabanoo. The epidemics fuelled a belief among white settlers, then and later, that the Aboriginal peoples were doomed to extinction.

THE SECOND FLEET AND THE RUM CORPS

If conditions were bad for the settlers at first, they got worse as the seasons progressed. Two years and two months after the First Fleet had sailed, Britain sent its first relief to Sydney. Carrying a small stock of provisions, the *Lady Juliana* arrived in 1790 with more than 200 convicts on board. Most were women, and almost all were too weak to work. This Second Fleet also brought a regiment known as the New South Wales Corps (NSWC), which had been formed to replace the marines. They found the settlement short of clothes, while rations were so meagre that it was feared that everyone might starve to death.

Both soldiers and convicts were so frail through lack of food that the working day had to be shortened. Thefts became commonplace and penalties for stealing increased. Meanwhile, the Aboriginal peoples were prospering on the food that grew, leaped or swam all around them. But the first settlers were so bound by the diet of the mother country that they would rather have starved than 'eaten native'.

By the end of June 1790, four more ships had sailed into Port Jackson, carrying with them a stock of convicts transported in abominable conditions. Some 267 people died en route and of the 759 who landed, 488 suffered from scurvy, dysentery or fever. Between 1791 and 1792, the death rate matched London's at the height of the Great Plague. Those remaining alive were forced to struggle on. Men faced a lashing from the cat-o'-nine-tails if they didn't work hard. The women had it little easier and were forced into long hours of domestic work or kept busy weaving in sweatshop conditions.

Finally, though, the arrival of yet more transports from England, bringing with them convicts, free settlers and supplies, meant that life in the colony began to pick up. In October 1792 Phillip reported that nearly 5,000 bushels of maize had been harvested and around 1,700 acres were under cultivation. In December that year, Phillip returned to England convinced the settlement would last.

It was almost three years before another governor arrived to take Phillip's place. The commanders of the NSWC used this interim period to their advantage by granting officers rights to work the land and employ convicts. Thanks to a shortage of money, rum rapidly became common currency and the NSWC ruled the rum trade, which led to it becoming known as the 'Rum Corps'.

Things progressed slowly until 1808, when Governor William Bligh (of *Mutiny on the Bounty* fame) was deposed in a military coup d'état. Bligh's evil temper and his attempts to deal with the corruption of the NSWC, which had bullied Bligh's predecessors through their control of the colony's rum, led to his downfall. The Rum Corps arrested Bligh and imprisoned him for a year. It is the only time in Australian history when an established government was overthrown by force.

The Corps ruled until Bligh was sent back to England and a new governor, Lachlan Macquarie, arrived. Macquarie later wrote that on his arrival he found the colony 'barely emerging from a state of infantile imbecility, and suffering from various privations and disabilities: the country impenetrable beyond 40 miles from Sydney.' A great planner, Macquarie oversaw the building of streets and the widening of others. He named three of the largest streets: George Street, after the king, and Pitt Street, after the prime minister; the grandest of all he named Macquarie Street. With the help of convict architect Francis Greenway, he set about building a city to be proud of, with a hospital, several churches, a sandstone barracks and Macquarie Lighthouse (still on South Head) to guide ships into the harbour.

With the discovery of the fertile hinterland beyond the Blue Mountains in 1813, the colony advanced in earnest. The flow of migrants increased after the end of the Napoleonic Wars in 1815, and soon farms and settlements dotted the regions around Sydney and Parramatta. In 1822, Macquarie was forced from the colony by powerful landowners (he died in London in 1824).

There still remained the issue of defence. Sydney was seen as prey to any passing foe. The city's vulnerability and its isolation from the protection of the distant motherland was confirmed in 1830 when its citizens woke to find that, in the night, four American frigates

How the white settlers viewed contact with the Aborigines, circa 1870.

had passed through the Heads and sailed up to Sydney Cove without anyone noticing. Since that day, Australia has been paranoid about attack, whether from the Russians during the Crimean War, Yankee privateers or the Spanish.

Fear of an invasion from Asia has been a constant undertone of government policy in more recent times. It was generally agreed that Sydney needed to be defended and, until 1870, the imperial garrison town stuck to its guns.

THE NEXT WAVE OF IMMIGRANTS

Finding transportation ruinously expensive, the British government sought to have the infant colony subsidise the cost. Convict labour was increasingly used to generate income. As in all slave societies, the workforce was inefficient, and the colony soon became the dumping ground for England's unemployed working classes rather than her criminals. Most of these free immigrants were bonded to their colonial employers, their passage paid for by the sale of land. In 1840 transportation of convicts to New South Wales was abolished. A total of 111,500 convicts – of whom just 16,000 were women – had arrived in NSW and Tasmania.

'The squalid conditions were perfect for rats and the bubonic plague they carried.'

By 1849 the population of convicts was outnumbered by free settlers. A new type of vessel, the clipper ship, had cut the sailing time from England to Australia by 49 days, to just 91. In the 1850s gold was discovered in New South Wales and Victoria, and prospectors rushed to Australia from all over the world. During the 1880s more than 370,000 arrived, mostly of British or Irish descent. Rich British businessmen poured money into the country and mine owners and farmers profited.

Governor Phillip had ensured as far back as 1790 that some physical distance was maintained between the government precinct to the east and the soldiers' barracks and convict quarters to the west of what is now known as Circular Quay. Built into the steep sandstone cliffs, this area – now known as the Rocks – quickly became as degenerate as the worst of London's slums. Tiers of narrow streets and sandstone stairs crammed with makeshift shacks and washing lines led up from riverside pubs and cheap lodging houses to comfortable terraced houses inhabited by sea captains and stevedores. The massive influx of immigrants in the mid 1800s meant housing was scarce, a problem exacerbated by many inner-city homes being converted into storehouses and offices.

By the late 19th century, the Rocks was known as Sydney's den of iniquity. Prostitution, drunkenness, theft and street gangs were rife. Sailors coming ashore after months at sea were robbed of everything they owned or press-ganged straight on to another vessel. The increasingly squalid area and the build-up of rubbish, silt and sewage made conditions in the Rocks perfect for rats and the bubonic plague carried by their fleas. In the first nine months of 1900 the plague killed 103 people. Crowds stormed the Board of Health's offices demanding a share of the colony's meagre supply of anti-plague medicine. The Rocks and Darling Harbour were quarantined and in 1902 the Sydney Harbour Trust was set up to clean up the harbour, and it announced that it had pulled from the water 2,524 rats, 1,068 cats, 283 bags of meat, 305 bags of fish, 1,467 fowl, 25 parrots, 23 sheep, 14 pigs, one bullock, nine calves and nine goats.

In the 1880s Sydney's remaining Aboriginal inhabitants were rounded up into a camp at Circular Quay and given government rations in a bid to keep them off the streets. In 1895 an Aboriginal reserve was set up at La Perouse, and located far from the centre of the city, near Botany Bay. By the end of the 19th century most of the area's original inhabitants were restricted to living on reserves or in missions, where they were introduced to the 'benefits of Christianity and European civilisation'.

By this time it was apparent that, though the Aboriginal population was in decline, the mixed-descent population was increasing. The fact that the latter group had some European blood meant that there was a place for them – albeit a lowly one – in society. Many children of mixed race were forcibly separated from their parents and placed in segregated 'training' institutions before being sent out to work. Girls were sent to be domestics to satisfy the nation's demand for cheap labour. It was also held that long hours and exhausting work would also curb their supposed promiscuity.

The Commonwealth of Australia came into existence on 1 January 1901. The country had 3.8 million inhabitants, and more than half a million of them crowded on to the streets of Sydney to celebrate the inauguration of the nation. The Aboriginal peoples weren't recorded in the census, however. They had to wait until 1967, when 90 per cent of the public voted voted to make new laws relating to Aboriginal people. This led the way for them to be recognised as Australian citizens, and to be included in the census of 1971.

THE NEW CENTURY AND WAR

After a lull following the 1890s depression, migration revived. In the years leading up to 1914, 300,000 mainly British migrants arrived, half of whom came on an assisted-passage scheme. In 1908 a Royal Commission set up to advise on the improvement of Sydney concluded that workers should be moved out of the slums to the suburbs. Six years later, though, World War I broke out. Around 10,000 volunteers in Sydney queued to go on the 'big adventure'. Most were sent to Gallipoli – a campaign that became synonymous in the Australian collective memory with British arrogance, callousness and incompetence. By the time the Allied forces were withdrawn in January 1916, the combination of lacklustre Allied leadership and stiff Turkish resistance inspired by the future president of Turkey, Kemal Ataturk, meant that casualties were well above 50 per cent, with little to show for thousands of lost lives. After Gallipoli, Australia was not going back to a subservient colonial role: the nation had come of age.

With the end of World War I it was reasoned that to defend Australia properly the country needed more people. A further 300,000 migrants arrived in the 1920s, mostly from England and Scotland, a product of the 'White Australia' policy. The origins of the policy can be traced to the mid 19th century when white miners' resentment towards Chinese diggers culminated in violence. The Immigration Restriction Act of 1901 placed 'certain restrictions on immigration and to provide for the removal from the Commonwealth of prohibited immigrants'; for example, applicants were required to pass a written test in a specific, usually European, language – with which they were not necessarily familiar. It was not until 1974 that Australia eliminated racial discrimination from its immigration policy.

Australia's vulnerability to attack came back to haunt it during World War II. On 31 May 1942, three Japanese midget submarines powered through the Heads and into Sydney Harbour. The first got tangled in a boom net across the harbour mouth, but the second slipped past. The third midget was spotted and attacked, which gave the second sub the chance to fire two torpedoes at the US cruiser *Chicago*. Both missed, but one struck the depot ship HMAS *Kuttabul*, killing 19 Australian and two British naval ratings asleep on board. Except for Aboriginals and settlers killed in early skirmishes, they were the only victims of enemy action on home ground in Sydney's history.

With the end of hostilities, Australia once again decided it needed to boost the size of its population. The slogan 'Populate or Perish' was coined and a new immigration scheme organised. In 1948, 70,000 migrants arrived from Britain and Europe. By the late 1950s most migrants were coming from Italy, Yugoslavia and Greece.

In 1951 the concept of assimilation, which had as its goal 'that all persons of Aboriginal descent will choose to attain a similar manner and standard of living to other Australians', was officially adopted as national policy. Eradication of Aboriginal culture was stepped up during the 1950s and 1960s, when even greater numbers of Aboriginal children were removed from their families. Many Aboriginal babies were adopted at birth, and were told that their true parents had died. The removal of children from their parents was halted in the 1970s, but the scars remain. The 'stolen generations' became the subject of fierce debate in Australia and expat director Phillip Noyce's *Rabbit-Proof Fence* – the story of three stolen children who run away from a camp and attempt to walk home over 1,000 miles of inhospitable country – brought the story to the world (*see p202* **Into the outback**).

In 1964 Australian troops joined their US counterparts in action in Vietnam. As in the States, anti-Vietnam War sentiment became a hot issue, and tens of thousands of Australians blockaded the streets of the major cities. A new Labor government, led by Gough Whitlam, came to power in 1972 after promising a fairer society and an end to Australia's involvement in the war. Within months the troops were brought home. Not long afterwards 'Advance Australia Fair' replaced 'God Save the Queen' as the national anthem, the Queen's portrait was removed from post office walls and her insignia on mailboxes painted out. Land rights were granted to some Aboriginal groups, and in 1974 the government finally put an end to the White Australia policy that had largely restricted black and Asian immigration since 1901. Two years later the official cord to Britain was cut when the Australian Constitution was separated from that of its motherland.

Ties with Britain loosened further in 1975 during a messy political wrangle, when the Conservative opposition moved to block the government's supply of money in the upper house. Without a budget, the Whitlam government was unable to govern, so on 11 November, Governor-General John Kerr sacked the government and made opposition leader Malcolm Fraser prime minister. There was fury that an Australian-elected government could be dismissed by the Queen's representative and resentment towards Britain flared.

INTO A THIRD CENTURY

Immigration continued throughout the 1980s and '90s, but now there were quite a few new faces among the crowds hoping for a better life in the 'lucky country'. Hundreds of thousands of migrants began coming in from Asia. Today, on average, around 90,000 people emigrate to Australia each year, from more than 150 countries. Of immigrants arriving in 2001 and 2002, most were born in New Zealand (17.6 per cent), the UK (9.8 per cent), China (7.5 per cent), South Africa (6.4 per cent), India (5.7 per cent) and Indonesia (4.7 per cent). With such a multicultural mix you'd think it was time to reconsider the 'self-governing republic' option. But you'd be wrong. In a close-run national referendum in 1999, 55 per cent of the electorate voted to keep the Queen as head of state – for the time being at least.

Some 460,000 Aborigines and the ethnically distinct people from the Torres Strait Islands off northern Queensland live in Australia today, but a rift still exists between them and the rest of the population. Aboriginal life expectancy is 20 years lower than that of other Australians; the infant mortality rate is higher; the ratio of Aboriginal people to other Australians in prisons is disproportionately high, and many are still restricted to the fringe of society.

In 1992 the 'Mabo decision' marked a breakthrough in Aboriginal affairs: the High Court declared that Australia was not *terra*

Terror in Bali

On 12 October 2002, Australia experienced its own 9/11. At around 11.20pm (local time), a pair of bombs destroyed two nightspots in Kuta, Bali, killing 202, including 88 Australians. The pretty holiday island had been Australia's most popular foreign tourist destination; Kuta had been its beer-and-surf heaven. But the terrorists responsible for this horrific act aimed to punish Bali for its tolerant courting of Western decadence, and to send a chilling wake-up call to America's ally, Australia. The bombs were placed in vehicles parked along Kuta's busiest entertainment strip and sent fireballs through the two clubs, which at the time were packed with hundreds of late-night revellers. Many survivors suffered horrific burns, and the bodies of some of those who died were too charred to be identified. One eyewitness told a *Sydney Morning Herald* reporter that 'there were so many people in the street, burned, injured or dead. One woman had lost the whole bottom half of her body. A man was crawling up the lane. He had no feet.'

The bombings sent shockwaves through Australia, but they didn't come entirely out of the blue. Official travel warnings at the time had outlined a heightened risk throughout Indonesia. And it was no secret that many Indonesians were angry with Australia for its involvement in East Timor's fight for independence in 1999. Just days after the attack occurred, Prime Minister John Howard was severely criticised for ignoring intelligence information about the threat posed by the Jemaah Islamiah terrorist group, a fundamentalist Islamic organisation with close links to Al-Qaeda.

The trial of the suspects began in Indonesia in July 2003. Amrozi bin Nurhasyim, dubbed the 'smiling assassin' after he joked with

police, was sentenced to death, along with his brother Muklas and operations chief Imam Sumadra. In January 2004 Amrozi lost an appeal to Indonesia's highest court, leaving a presidential clemency request as his last hope of escaping the death penalty (at the time of writing, a decision was expected shortly). Muklas, alias Ali Ghufron, has also lodged an appeal against his sentence. Twenty-six others have been sentenced to between three years and life in connection with the attack, which has been blamed on the Jemaah Islamiah group.

A four-metre (12-foot) sculpture (pictured) of three interconnecting 'figures' leaning towards each other in a gesture of grief and support was erected as a permanent memorial at Coogee Beach in October 2003. The site was renamed Dolphins Point in honour of the Coogee Dolphins rugby league club, which lost six of its team in the blast. Twenty people from Sydney's eastern suburbs died in the bombings; their names are on a nearby plaque.

Children from the notorious **Woomera detention centre**, 2002.

nullius ('empty land') as it had been termed since the British 'invasion'. This decision resulted in the 1993 Native Title Act, which allowed Aboriginal groups and Torres Strait Islanders to claim government-owned land if they could prove continual association with it since 1788. Later, the Wik decision determined that Aboriginal people everywhere could make claims on government land that was leased to agriculturists. But Prime Minister John Howard's Liberal coalition government, under pressure from farming and mining interests, curtailed these rights.

In response, Aboriginal groups threatened (but did not mount) major demonstrations during the 2000 Olympics. The opening ceremony paid tribute to the country's Aboriginal origins, and the flame was even lit by Aboriginal runner Cathy Freeman. To outsiders it seemed that Australia was embracing its past rather than marginalising it, but indigenous Australians were less impressed. John Howard, in particular, has come in for harsh criticism for his refusal to apologise for the actions of past generations.

With the reconciliation issue bubbling in the background, Howard's government turned its attentions to stemming the influx of refugees. In the late 1990s asylum seekers from Iraq and Afghanistan landed in Australia only to face a grim, prison-like existence in detention centres in the middle of the South Australian desert – most notoriously, Woomera (now closed). Processing their cases has taken years and many are still in virtual incarceration, with their future prospects unresolved.

In 1999 when victims of Yugoslavia's war-ravaged Kosovo came knocking, the Australian government was slow to respond. Eventually, local and international pressure forced Howard's hand and the refugees were admitted, but only for a short respite on newly created 'safe haven'

(ie temporary) visas. In August 2001 Howard played tough guy once again, turning away a Norwegian cargo ship carrying 400 Afghan and Iraqi asylum seekers, whom the captain had rescued from a leaky ferry. As the ship neared Australian shores, Howard – with one eye firmly on the voters – steeled himself for a showdown. 'I believe it is in Australia's national interests that we draw a line on what is increasingly becoming an uncontrollable number of illegal arrivals in this country,' he asserted.

Much unseemly to-ing and fro-ing followed. At one point, the government claimed that the refugees were blackmailing the Australian Navy into rescuing them by throwing their children overboard. Later – after Howard had won the November 2001 election – it was revealed that the pictures that had been flashed across the news had been taken a day later and were actually shots showing the bona fide rescue of the asylum seekers after their boat had sunk. Ultimately, the refugees weren't allowed to set foot on Australian soil; most ended up on the tiny Pacific island of Nauru.

Although heavily criticised internationally, Howard's strong-arm – and, according to many, racist – policies proved popular at the ballot box and he won a third term in office in 2001, sending the opposition Labor party into freefall.

Australia may be geographically removed from the centre of world affairs, but it is still increasingly involved in some of the 21st century's key issues. Australian troops led the UN peacekeeping force in East Timor (1999) and were heavily involved in George W Bush's 'war on terror', both in Afghanistan and Iraq. The nation has also suffered from such involvement; the 2002 Bali bombing (*see p11* **Terror in Bali**) underlined its vulnerability and sparked antagonism towards its Muslim communities, which doesn't bode well for the future of the country's multicultural melting pot.

Key events

40,000BC The Aboriginal Dharug tribal group occupy the area that is now Sydney.
29 April 1770 James Cook and Joseph Banks sail the *Endeavour* into Botany Bay.
26 January 1788 Settlement of the First Fleet at Sydney Cove.
1789 Smallpox epidemic among local Aboriginal people.
1808 NSWC officers, known as the 'Rum Corps', overthrow Governor William Bligh.
1810-21 Governor Macquarie instils order.
1813 WC Wentworth, George Blaxland and William Lawson are the first Europeans to cross the Blue Mountains.
1840 The transportation of convicts to NSW is outlawed by the British government.
1842 The city of Sydney is officially incorporated; the first councillors are elected.
1851 A gold rush begins and Sydney's population rises to 96,000 by 1861.
1855 The colony's first steam railway, the Sydney to Parramatta line, is completed.
1858 Men are granted the vote in NSW.
1878 Seamen begin a six-week strike over the use of Chinese labour, setting in motion a movement that would lead to the White Australia policy.
1900 Bubonic plague in Sydney. More than 100 people die in eight months.
1901 Ceremony of united Commonwealth of Australia and independent Monarchy in the British Commonwealth in Centennial Park. Edmund Barton is sworn in as prime minister.
1902 Women get the vote in NSW state elections.
1906 The world's first surf lifesaving club is founded at Bondi. Laws banning daylight beach bathing are scrapped.
1908 Canberra becomes Australia's capital.
1914-18 Of the 330,000 Australians sent to fight in World War I, 60,000 perish.
1922-30 The Empire Settlement Scheme moves thousands of working-class families from the industrial towns of Britain to Sydney.
1932 Sydney Harbour Bridge is opened.
1942 Three Japanese subs steal into Sydney Harbour and torpedo a ferry with Allied naval officers on board, killing 19.
1960-64 Aboriginal peoples are granted the vote and included in census figures.
1965-72 Australian troops sent to Vietnam.
1972 The Australian Labor Party gains power.
1973 Sydney Opera House is opened by the Queen and declared a wonder of the world.

1975 Governor-General Sir John Kerr, the Queen's representative, sacks the country's Labor government. The seeds of a serious Australian republican movement are sown.
1978 Hundreds of thousands of Vietnamese refugees enter the country; the first arrivals are illegal, stealing into Darwin by boat. The first Gay & Lesbian Mardi Gras ends in violence after police attack 1,000 marchers.
1985-86 A gang war for control of Sydney's prostitution, gambling and drug rackets rages. A web of business connections between Sydney's underworld and the police force is exposed.
1988 One million celebrate bicentennial at Sydney Harbour. Aboriginal peoples protest.
1992 Sydney Harbour Tunnel opens. The Mabo Case inserts the legal doctrine of native title into Australian law allowing Aborigines to claim traditional rights to land.
1993 'Sid-er-nee' wins the bid to stage the 2000 Olympics. Over 100,000 revellers party at Circular Quay until dawn.
1996 Liberal coalition government under John Howard wins power, ousting Labor Party.
1998 John Howard's coalition government narrowly wins a second term.
1999 Australian troops spearhead a peacekeeping force in East Timor. Referendum proposals to make Australia a republic are defeated.
2000 Aboriginal runner Cathy Freeman opens the Olympic Games at Homebush Bay.
2001 Australia's greatest cricketer, Sir Donald Bradman, dies at the age of 92. Centenary of Federation celebrations across Australia. A Norwegian ship carrying rescued refugees is refused entry to Australia and sent to a remote Pacific island. John Howard elected prime minister for a third term.
2002 Bombs explode in Bali nightclubs killing 202, including 88 Australians. Australian troops join UN peacekeeping forces in Afghanistan.
2003 NSW Premier Bob Carr's Labor government is re-elected for a third successive term. Australian Governor-General, Anglican archbishop Dr Peter Hollingworth, stands down following rape allegations. Australian troops form part of the 'coalition of the willing' (with the US and the UK) in the Iraq war. Australia sends peacekeeping troops to the Solomon Islands to quell a rebellion.

The Other History

The story of indigenous Australia is finally being told.

For many years the impact of European settlement on the indigenous Australians – Aboriginal and Torres Strait Islanders – has been glossed over, with historians and popular folklore celebrating the heroism and tenacity of explorers and early settlers as they tamed a harsh continent. In this version of history, the few hapless natives were swept away quietly on a tide of progress, and it is only relatively recently that Australians have been forced to confront their violent and oppressive past in relation to indigenous people.

Nowadays, it's a controversial and hotly debated topic. The arrival of Europeans is variously called invasion, colonisation or settlement, and fierce academic debate rages over the use of terms like genocide and war. Taunts of political correctness and a victim mentality are met with accusations of revisionism and whitewashing.

Some, including Prime Minister John Howard, say there is too much emphasis on the unsavoury aspects of the past. Dubbing this 'the black armband view of history', they call for people to stop navel-gazing and just get on with it. Others, particularly indigenous Australians, have demanded acknowledgement and action, including an apology from the

Commonwealth Government, land rights, compensation and reconciliation. The vitriol aside, at least there is now a debate.

IN THE BEGINNING
It's estimated that the first people arrived in Australia 50,000 to 70,000 years ago, travelling by foot from the north across land bridges and later by boat. Australian Aboriginals have one of the oldest continuous cultures and religions, but there was no unified nation or state; instead an estimated 500 clans or tribes, speaking some 250 complex individual languages, lived a mainly nomadic life.

One of the hardest things for the individualist, capitalist Europeans and their system of law to understand when they colonised Australia – and even today – is the indivisible interrelationship of land, spirituality and culture to Aboriginal people. According to indigenous traditional laws, no individual can own, sell or give away land. Land belongs to all members of the community and they in turn belong to the land. Ownership of a particular region was established during the Dreaming or Dreamtime – the time of creation. The details differ across the country, but the shared thread of creation stories tell of spiritual ancestors who came from the sky or earth, creating the world, giving life to animals and people, and establishing the laws of the Aboriginal societies. Within this tradition, geographic features and animals, and the stories associated with them, all acquired huge significance.

As custodians of a particular region, tribe members have a responsibility to maintain the stories, songs and rituals – also called the Dreaming – that signify ownership. Chants and songs 'map' the land, identifying natural features and defining its tribal boundaries. Knowledge of law and culture is passed on over the years, from elders down to initiated men and women; there are also special, secret areas of knowledge, and sacred locations that are maintained and entered only by the initiated.

The first Europeans saw the indigenous Australians as hopelessly backward and barbaric because they did not grow crops, use metal or make pottery. What they could not see was the complex and environmentally sensitive way Aboriginal people had adapted to the vagaries of the climate: travelling light with portable tools and weapons to the best hunting and gathering grounds; managing grassland with fire to keep tracks clear and to promote plant growth and pasture, thereby attracting animals; and harvesting the abundant seafood in coastal areas. Far from scrabbling a mean existence, they had a far more diverse diet than the Europeans did at that time, and there was time left over from the daily essentials for artistic and cultural pursuits.

THE ARRIVAL OF THE EUROPEANS

Since the 16th century, Australia briefly hosted various unenthused European visitors – the Portuguese, the Dutch, the French – but it was the British who stole the prize. Explorer Captain James Cook extensively mapped the east coast of Australia in the 1770s, and on 26 January 1788 Captain Arthur Phillip, with the French breathing down his neck, grabbed the eastern half of the continent for the British Crown.

As the settlement of Sydney staggered through its first years, the local indigenous population was almost wiped out by imported European diseases such as smallpox. Those who survived were then caught in a cycle of dispossession, violence and armed resistance – a pattern that continued as settlers spread across the continent. The best farmland was also the best hunting area. With restricted ability to hunt and gather, Aboriginals took livestock. Farmers retaliated brutally. Aboriginals retaliated brutally. Troops were sometimes called and outbreaks of guerrilla war ensued, with bloodshed on both sides.

The Aboriginals used their superior bush skills to evade the white settlers, but in the end the gun, the force of numbers, the help provided by Aboriginal trackers and in some areas an Aboriginal police force, plus disease, infertility and malnutrition, decimated populations.

The conflict didn't go unnoticed by the authorities and humanitarians. Evangelical Christian groups in England petitioned the government, and in the 1830s and '40s various edicts regarding the protection and rights of Aboriginals were issued. However, at the lawless frontier, where squatters simply took whatever land they wanted without either any payment or government consent, such ideals were largely ignored.

'In 1901 there were 76,000 Aboriginals, down from between 500,000 to a million in the 1780s.'

Such murderous hostility was not universal. Aboriginals became crucial to the farming industry and were exploited as a source of cheap and skilful labour, particularly as stockmen. By the 1880s it is estimated that they represented half the workforce. In many cases, the workers' extended families were allowed to remain on their traditional lands, working as domestic servants in return for rations.

But most indigenous Australians lived in a state of physical and legal limbo. Those who had been forced off their land were relocated to reserves. Some were able to cultivate food and make a basic living; others languished in dismal conditions on the edge of settlements. Religious missions were also set up to protect, educate and 'civilise'. The founding of the Commonwealth of Australia in 1901 almost completely ignored Aboriginal people by excluding them entirely from the national census.

From the early days of settlement it was widely assumed that indigenous Australians were doomed as a race. In 1901 it was estimated that there were 76,000 Aboriginal people, down from a population of between 500,000 to a million in the 1780s. By the 1930s, however, it became apparent that, remarkably, indigenous people had resisted extinction. A new strategy had to be devised. In 1939, assimilation became federal government policy, aiming to raise the status of indigenous people so they could live as whites did. The paternalistic protection boards that administered this policy also controlled every aspect of life – where people lived, their employment, who they married, their freedom of movement.

The most heartbreaking and controversial aspect was the forcible removal by the state of children, now known as the 'stolen generations'. Using skin colour as a guide, Aboriginal 'half-castes' were seen as having more potential for improvement than 'full bloods'. And so began what has been described as a policy of cultural genocide: removing children, particularly those of mixed race and with lighter skin, from their families and placing them in institutions or fostering them out to white homes. The cruel irony was that Aboriginal women, who were often victims of sexual exploitation by white males, were doubly punished by having their light-skinned children removed.

The impact on the cultural and social fabric was devastating – and the effects are still being felt today. Children were divorced from their home, culture and language, often losing contact completely with their family. Many were not even aware of their Aboriginal background. Poor records make it impossible to give precise numbers, but it is thought that 100,000 people were affected, that between one in three and one in ten of all Aboriginal children were separated from their families from 1910 to the 1970s, when the policy was halted.

Although indigenous people were expected to abandon their own culture and fit into white society, they still faced entrenched legal and social discrimination, which kept them marginalised, disenfranchised and trapped in a cycle of poverty.

FIGHTING BACK

During the 18th and 19th centuries, many indigenous Australians pursued campaigns of armed resistance. The 20th century was marked by the growth of political activism, which finally led, in the last quarter of the century, to an acknowledgement of the past and the beginning of a process of reconciliation.

Aboriginal communities in the 1920s and 1930s, particularly in south-eastern Australia, organised towards abolition of the paternalistic protection system. Actions of dissent – such as an Aboriginal elder protesting at the opening of Parliament House in Canberra in 1927, and the establishment in Sydney of a Day of Mourning on 26 January 1938, while Australia celebrated 150 years of white settlement – were the beginning of a movement that would gain more and more momentum.

In the 1950s, as the appalling conditions endured by many Aboriginal people became known, sympathetic white Australians, church groups, unions and advancement organisations opened a public debate. The Freedom Rides across rural New South Wales in 1965, and the press coverage they received, exposed the unofficial but prevalent exclusion of Aboriginals from schools, shops, bars, swimming pools and cinemas. The following year, the Gurindji people at Wave Hill cattle station in the Northern Territory went on strike for better wages and conditions. This turned into demands for land rights and self-determination, and is seen as the beginning of the modern land rights movement. When the Aboriginal Tent Embassy (*see p272* **Protest point**) was set up in 1972 outside Parliament House in Canberra and the newly designed Aboriginal flag (*see p17* **Flying colours**) was adopted, it became apparent to white Australia that the days of put up and shut up were over.

SORRY BUSINESS

After years of activism and lobbying the attitude of society and government slowly, and often reluctantly, began to shift. In 1967, more than 90 per cent of Australians voted in a national referendum to empower the federal government to make legislation in the interests of indigenous people, and to count them as citizens in the census.

In 1987, Prime Minister Bob Hawke set up a Royal Commission into Aboriginal Deaths in Custody in response to the disproportionate scale of indigenous incarceration and death in prison. It became the most comprehensive investigation of Aboriginal experience in

The **Walk for Reconciliation**. *See p18.*

AbOriginal Flying colours

Among the rather unremarkable flags flown on official buildings around Sydney, travellers may notice a striking red, black and yellow standout. It is the work of Harold Thomas, an Aboriginal artist originally from Alice Springs and the first Aboriginal to graduate from an Australian art school.

In the early 1970s, when the land rights movement was gaining momentum, Thomas recognised the need for an image that signified the national identity and unity of Aboriginal people, which would also make a strong visual statement at protest marches. The original design used more earthy colours, but, as Thomas said, 'the flag sprung from passionate  times', so they were replaced with bold black, red and yellow. The black represents the Aboriginal people, the red symbolises the earth and a spiritual relation to the land, and the yellow the life-giving sun.

First flown in Adelaide on 12 July 1971 as part of National Aboriginal Day, the flag was later adopted as the official standard of the Aboriginal Tent Embassy in Canberra (*see p272* **Protest point**). But it wasn't until 1995 that it was recognised as an official

Australian flag by the federal government. One year earlier, the flag and its place in the process of reconciliation between black and white Australia had been thrust into the international spotlight by champion sprinter Cathy Freeman at the Commonwealth Games in Victoria, Canada. As the first Aboriginal to represent Australia at the Olympic games, Freeman spurned the official Australian flag after her victorious 400-metre run and instead draped herself in the black, red and yellow. This caused a furore back home where conservative commentators condemned the political gesture. However, as is the Australian way, the raising of the prickly issue of indigenous issues was forgiven by a sports-mad public always ready to embrace a winner.

When Freeman won gold in the 400 metres at the 2000 Sydney Olympics, she ran with both an Australian and Aboriginal flag. This simple gesture was a bright and unifying moment in an otherwise troubled process of reconciliation, and demonstrated the powerful and complicated position the Aboriginal flag occupies in the Australian consciousness.

Australia's history. The resulting 1991 report made 339 recommendations, one of which was the establishment of a formal process of reconciliation between indigenous and other Australians through the Council for Aboriginal Reconciliation.

The idea of reconciliation was fine for most Australians, but it was a different story when it came to land rights. The Mabo decision in 1992 sent shockwaves through Australian society. The British had claimed Australia without treaty or payment because they categorised it as *terra nullius* – land belonging to nobody. Mabo had recognised for the first time that the indigenous Australians were the original inhabitants of the land, and British settlement did not necessarily extinguish their native title or ownership. This precedent gave farmers and mining interests the heebie-jeebies and a scare

campaign insinuated that everything from the Sydney Opera House to the family home could be clawed back. The 1993 Native Title Act allowed indigenous people to claim government land, excluding freehold title, if they could prove continuous connection with it since 1788.

Fear and uncertainty about potential land claims intensified in 1996 when another high court decision, known as Wik, indicated that native title could co-exist with pastoral leases, meaning native title claims could be lodged on some farmland. Under pressure from commercial interests, the Howard government (which took power the same year) watered down these rights. To the relief of many Australians, the complex, expensive and restricted nature of land claims has meant that cases are tied up in court for years, and the feared tidal wave of land grabs has never materialised.

In 1997, the National Enquiry into the Separation of Aboriginal and Torres Strait Islander Children from their Families produced a report, 'Bringing Them Home', a startling and controversial examination of the Stolen Generations. The response by the federal government was decidedly lukewarm. Unwilling to risk compensation claims, and reflecting the contemporary wave of racially inflammatory nationalism, Prime Minister Howard declined to apologise. Instead he issued a statement of regret. The government did, however, cough up an initial reparations package of $63 million.

Despite this limited response, many Australians were shocked and shamed, and a wave of pro-reconciliation activity ensued. In 1998 over a million signatures were collected around the country in thousands of Sorry Books and the first national Sorry Day was set up on 26 May. Two years later, the People's Walk for Reconciliation saw an unprecedented 300,000 people march across the Sydney Harbour Bridge to demonstrate their own desire for reconciliation. The Sydney Olympic Games in the same year showcased indigenous culture in its opening and closing ceremonies, and Aboriginal sprinter Cathy Freeman lit the Olympic cauldron and wowed the nation with a gold medal in the women's 400-metre race.

THE WAY FORWARD

It was, everyone agreed, all very warm and fuzzy. But what has actually been achieved? While there is greater awareness of indigenous issues, some see such public outpourings as a trite assuaging of white middle-class guilt, achieving few tangible outcomes.

The statistics speak for themselves. Despite the recommendations of the Deaths in Custody report, the number of indigenous Australians in prison has increased, with a rate of juvenile incarceration 21 times greater than for non-indigenous young people. Aboriginals also suffer high levels of unemployment, poor living conditions and a life expectancy 20 to 25 years shorter than the rest of the population. Lack of transport and limited access to employment, education, health facilities and social services in remote areas exacerbates the situation, leading to chronic poverty.

While there is still resentment of the special benefits indigenous people receive, much has changed for the better in recent years. It's usual that public events are prefaced by an acknowledgement of the traditional owners of the area, and some important sites, such as Uluru (formerly Ayer's Rock), have been handed back to their traditional owners. Indigenous people are now represented in

most walks of life, from sport to politics. The richness and antiquity of indigenous culture is widely celebrated. All are small steps in the right direction.

Within the indigenous community there are varied and often contradictory voices on the way ahead, with claims that there has been too much of an emphasis on land rights and not enough on economic self-determination. The argument that simply accepting government handouts ('sit-down money') only perpetuates the problems has gained ground, emphasising the need for financial resources and long-term solutions. Such thinking has encouraged communities to become alcohol-free, and seen a move to shift Aboriginal offenders out of the mainstream legal system, to be dealt with according to traditional law instead.

On a national level this response largely depends on the federal government. Issues of national security after September 11, the Tampa refugee crisis and the war in Iraq allowed the Howard government to let the agenda drift away from those divisive and difficult-to-solve indigenous problems. As a result, the reconciliation movement has almost ground to a halt on a national level.

'Aboriginals suffer high unemployment, poor living conditions and a much shorter life expectancy.'

However, a night of rioting in the inner Sydney suburb of Redfern in February 2004, sparked by the death of an Aboriginal teenager, put indigenous disadvantage momentarily back on the agenda. As usual, opinion was sharply divided. The police were accused of being soft on the rioters – and soft on crime in Redfern in general – because they are hamstrung by political correctness. For others, the resentment and hopelessness of the angry young people is a result of persistent police harassment, on top of problems of poverty and drugs.

Many ask, why does it take a riot for people to notice a community in crisis? And does this indicate the complete failure of reconciliation? Despite the deep and complex problems, there is hope, says Fred Chaney, the co-chairman of Reconciliation Australia. He believes that inflammatory media coverage of high-profile problem areas shouldn't diminish lower-profile 'pockets of success in reconciliation'.

'No one has all the answers,' he says. 'But what we do recognise better today is that we need to be asking the right questions about what's going wrong.'

Sydney Today

The brash, beautiful teenager of world cities is facing some very adult problems.

It's undeniably ironic that Sydney, named by Captain Arthur Phillip after his boss, the British Home Secretary Lord Sydney, began life as a convict settlement, a place for punishment and exile. Now the joke's on the mother country, for, while crowded grey Britain reeks with discontent, Sydney is one of the most liveable cities in the world, besieged by immigrants desperate to share its riches.

And what riches! The sparkling crenellated harbour, so clean that whales, penguins and dolphins play in its waters, numerous sandy beaches, peacock blue skies, more annual sun than an Englishman can shake his brolly at, a relaxed – some might say irresponsible – joie de vivre, and a relatively high standard of living. This, at least, is the city's tanned exterior; dig deeper and you'll find that even paradise has problems, and a city literally built on the bones of its Aboriginal ancestors can't help but have issues of identity.

Sydney is Australia's largest city, its developed metropolitan area stretching across 4,000 square kilometres (1,500 square miles), surrounded by a further 8,000 square kilometres (3,000 square miles) of largely natural parklands. One in five Australians live in or around the city – that's a population of four million, and increasing. The often bristling rivalry with the nation's second-largest metropolis, Melbourne, is usually depicted in terms of the brash, naughty, fun-loving teenager (Sydney) joshing for supremacy with its older, wiser, more sophisticated sibling (Melbourne) – and there are grains of truth to the metaphor. Sydney is a fickle town, hooked on the latest fad, obsessed with its glittery looks and always after a good time, while Melburnians like to think they're serious, cerebral folk with a love of the arts and fine food and a history based on businessmen and pastoralists rather than roguish convicts.

But times they are a changing. Sure, the beach and sport still rule Sydney's leisure time, but the city's arts scene is gaining ground too, most recently with the Sydney Theatre

Company's shiny new venue. The film industry, backed by Rupert Murdoch's Fox Studios, has put the Emerald City on the world movie map, and a host of top chefs are bringing pzazz to the restaurant scene. Gay Sydney is an accepted part of the city's make-up, and generates its own special culture with the annual Mardi Gras festival, the city's biggest tourist magnet. As for the bratty teenage analogy, adult realities such as immigration, drug abuse, gang crime and conservation are forcing Sydney to grow up fast.

MULTICULTURAL MELTING POT
The tourist board likes to boast that Sydney is one of the world's most multicultural cities, with inhabitants from 180 nations speaking 140 languages. In recent years, migrants from New Zealand and China have displaced the British as the largest national groups coming to NSW. But the inference that they all live in one big happy melting pot is not always reflected on the streets. Australians from a white British background still have the upper hand in society and, despite decades of Asian immigration, fear of the 'yellow peril' lurks in the hearts of many older Caucasians, and some younger ones too. In 2003 a disturbing survey of people in NSW and Queensland by Sydney academic Dr Kevin Dunn revealed that Australia had a 'hardcore of racists', the worst found in pockets of Sydney's working classes.

> **'All subjects are fair game for a spot of ribbing – it would be positively "unAustralian" to take oneself too seriously.'**

Immigrants currently in the firing line are Muslims and people from the Middle East. According to the 2001 census, Australia has just over 281,500 Muslims, half of whom live in NSW. Following September 11 and the Bali bombings, 54 per cent of those surveyed by Dr Dunn said they would be concerned if their relative married a Muslim, 45 per cent said some cultural groups did not belong in Australia and 12 per cent admitted to being prejudiced. The reality for Sydney's Muslims, who mainly reside in the city's south-west, is that they are at best viewed with suspicion and at worst abused and discriminated against.

To the visitor the casual use of racist terms and the adoption of racial stereotypes in the newspapers, on TV, in bus queues, on the radio and in pubs can be a bit of a shock. But the reality is not always as bad as it seems.

Underpinning the Australian psyche is an abhorrence of political correctness, resulting in almost all subjects being fair game for a spot of ribbing; after all, it would be positively 'unAustralian' to take oneself too seriously. The fact that one man's humour is another man's persecution often gets lost in the moment.

ADVANCE AUSTRALIA FAIR
There's one subject (after sport) that's sacrosanct, and that's being Australian and what that entails. Wherever you're from originally, being a 'proud Australian' must come first. Such fervent nationalism is the country's bedrock and is never more evident than at the frequent citizenship ceremonies that take place all over Australia, and especially in Sydney. Encouraged by TV advertising, new citizens are welcomed into the fold for who they are and can be. In accordance with the nation's surface championing of tolerance and diversity, new citizens are not expected to shed their cultural identity. They are, however, asked to pledge allegiance to Australia. The most patriotic ceremonies take place on Australia Day (26 January).

Cynics say it's all a pantomime and once everyone's back on the streets old prejudices creep back, but one unifying element is a belief that Australia is 'the lucky country'. Or, in the words of former Test cricket captain, Sydneysider and 2003's Australian of the Year, Steve Waugh: 'Being Australian means to me that we're lucky because this is the best country in the world. It's about looking after your mates, taking care of your family, being able to have a laugh at yourself. But really it's about making the most of the opportunity that Australia offers. You can do whatever you want to, you can achieve what you want and you can realise your dreams.'

This combination of optimism, self-confidence and 'no worries' levity is at the heart of Sydney culture, and one of its most appealing traits. Locals live for the long summer when many take a month or more off work to enjoy the outdoors. Head to Bondi or Manly on any weekday summer's evening, you'll find the beaches lined with personal trainers and their clients, business executives in wetsuits learning to surf, joggers galore and hundreds taking an end-of-the-day dip in the sea. Remember – those iconic lifesavers are actually volunteers, who choose to spend their weekends patrolling the city's beaches.

CITY NIGHTMARES
When night falls, however, Sydney's wholesome, health-conscious exterior begins to crack. From Thursday to Sunday the inner city converts

Burning issues

Dramatic footage of larrikin Aussie firefighters bravely battling banks of swirling flame has become an all-too-familiar sight on world news. And whatever the cause – El Niño, urban sprawl, global warming, youthful pyromaniacs – there's no doubt that Australian bushfires are becoming more common, and deadly, than ever before.

New South Wales has been badly hit in the past decade, and in the annual build-up to the summer holidays suburban Sydneysiders pray that this won't be the year they lose their house. In 1994, 400 homes were damaged in summer fires, while on Christmas Day 2001, the mother of all firestorms rolled across the Blue Mountains, burning perilously close to the city. Over the next ten days a ring of fire – more than 100 blazes – circled Sydney. Black embers showered the city, and helicopters carrying thousands of litres of water filled the skies. In 2002, the fires came earlier, in October, prompted by the worst drought in a century.

Of course, bushfires are nothing new. They have always been part of Australian life. Aborigines would clear areas using fire and were accustomed to lightning-sparked blazes across their dry homeland. Fires would burn until they were spent; it was part of the ecosystem. But as bushland has given way to urban sprawl, the natural balance has been upset.

It's not, however, all the fault of man's concrete jungles; the real jungles provide fuel for the flames too. In particular, the waxy leaves of Australia's famed eucalyptus trees are incredibly combustible. One possible solution is regular land clearing, but state governments faces huge resistance from local greenies. To compound the problem, many of the recent fires were started deliberately by vandals, or sparked by cigarette butts tossed from cars.

In December 2002, after decades of sitting back and coping as best they could, the Australian government unveiled a $110m package to create a Bushfire Cooperative Research Centre. Opened in Melbourne in December 2003, the centre brings together scientists, academics and fire authorities from across the country to share information and research about bushfires and how to control them. Many states, including NSW, are implementing preventative measures in preparation for the bushfire season, and the NSW government has introduced tough penalties for people who start fires, deliberately or by discarding cigarettes.

Needless to say, the recent disasters have offered opposition spokesmen a new opportunity for knocking the government: 'If [NSW premier] Bob Carr wants to fight the war on terror, it is about time Bob Carr, his ministers and his government got serious about the terror that faces Sydney every fire season, and the damage that is being done to homes and properties.'

into party central. But it's not all innocent fun: behind the festivities is an out-of-control drug crisis, a growing gambling problem, teenage drinking and spiralling crime. In 2003, a rush of gang-related shootings in Sydney's south-west left the police throwing up their hands in disbelief, while the eastern suburbs' million-dollar converted terraces are defaced with window bars and alarms to guard against the daily burglaries, many by junkies desperate for money to pay for their next fix.

Sydney's longstanding heroin problem is finally being addressed by the country's first medically supervised, legal injecting room, which opened in Kings Cross in 2001. In its first two years the centre managed 550

NSW Premier **Bob Carr** and wife Helena.

overdoses and referred 1,800 users to drug treatment, health, rehabilitation or welfare services. Reporting of injection in public places has decreased, with 42 per cent of those interviewed saying that if the centre had not been available their next hit would have been on a beach, in a park or in a public toilet.

> **'The death of an Aboriginal teenager in 2004 sparked one of Sydney's worst nights of rioting.'**

In the nightclubs, other drugs have moved centre stage. In 2003 a controversial UN survey on ecstasy and amphetamines claimed that the use of drugs in Australia was a 'serious phenomenon'. Meanwhile, Aussies' famous love of beer has developed into a nationwide alcohol problem. Sydney police were called to more than 120,000 alcohol-related incidents in 2002, including offensive behaviour, street assaults, drink-driving and malicious damage. And despite a reduction in the number of poker machines in pubs and hotels, Sydneysiders just can't seem to kick the habit, pouring more money than ever into the beasts.

Adding to all these problems, the death of an Aboriginal teenager in February 2004 sparked one of the worst nights of rioting ever seen in Sydney. Although confined to a few streets in Redfern, the clash involved bricks, bottles and Molotov cocktails being hurled at police by up to 100 Aboriginal youths. Redfern rail station and a car were torched, and the images swiftly flashed around the world, dampening Sydney's glossy image as a tourist haven.

BOB CARR'S SYDNEY

NSW Premier Bob Carr (Labor) has all these issues in his sights. Federal Prime Minister John Howard (Liberal) may live in Sydney's most coveted mansion (Kirribilli House) with the best view in town, but it's Bob in his chic modern house in untrendy Maroubra with his Malaysian-born wife Helena that Sydneysiders see as their saviour. In 2003, the book-loving, bushwalking ex-journalist won a landmark fourth term as state premier, making him a firm favourite for federal politics in years to come. But while his roots are socialist, there's some common ground between Howard and Carr. Like Howard, Carr is anti-immigration and has made many speeches declaring the evils of too many migrants. He's also strong on law and order, and has toughened sentencing and increased the prison population. Such rightist policies have strong support in limply conservative Sydney. To be fair, Carr is also renowned for his passion for the environment and his unfailing support for public education, the arts and women in the workplace.

Environment issues hit a chord with locals, who, after years of poor town planning, cavalier attitudes to sewage and waste disposal and reduction of green spaces, are ready to take their city in hand. Rules banning smoking in restaurants are in place, and many hope they will soon stretch to bars, clubs and even beaches. The annual nationwide Clean Up Australia Day, when volunteers clear the rubbish from streets, beaches and parks, is a sign of how much locals want their country to stay lucky.

People wanting to hang on to Sydney include Nicole Kidman and Russell Crowe, who despite working predominantly overseas, still retain homes in the city and proudly so. The brain-drain of earlier decades – think Germaine Greer and Clive James – is no longer an issue. But it isn't just celebrities who want to stay in Sydney, as a booming economy driven by sky-high house prices shows how attractive the city is. Could it be that Sydney's inner culture is at last matching up to its external beauty?

Where to Stay

Where to Stay

In between the sightseeing you'll have to do some sleeping.

The ill-advised building boom that saw too many top-class hotels dominating Sydney's hotel market came to a sudden end in the early Noughties. The problem wasn't just a lack of tourists, but a lack of the right kind of tourists – those happy to shell out $200 or more a night. During the Olympics the city bulged with corporate business types and cashed-up holiday makers, but 9/11, the Bali bombing, the Iraq war and the SARS epidemic all took their toll. Many of the larger hotel blocks were sold and converted into apartments.

At the other end of the scale, however, the budget market is going gangbusters, with a new type of backpacker leading the charge. The threadbare days of the hippy trail are long gone, and the savvier tourist industry players are tailoring their products to suit the mobile phone-carrying, designer shades-wearing, gold credit card-touting modern traveller. Hostels have had to sharpen up their act and hotel groups are realising that although such visitors won't pay top dollar, they will pay a little more for good looks and a private bathroom.

What this means is that, finally, Sydney has rooms to suit every pocket. Accommodation ranges from ultra-deluxe five-star palaces to boutique zones of 'cool', slick and convenient serviced apartments, clean and contemporary mid-range hotels and a host of budget options. If you want to stay in one of YHA Australia's hostels (there are nine in the Sydney area), note that rates are cheaper for members and you have to be a member to stay in the twin/double rooms – but instant annual membership is available ($35 for overseas visitors).

Many of the four-star-plus hotels are strung around the Rocks, Circular Quay, George Street, Hyde Park and Darling Harbour. A swag of backpacker joints congregate around Kings Cross, nearby Potts Point and Darlinghurst, and at Elizabeth Bay. Staying in these areas means you have access to plenty of restaurants and bars, but if you want to see the tourist sights you'll need to catch a CityRail train back into town.

The inner west suburbs, such as Newtown and Glebe, are a short train or bus ride from the city centre, and have the advantage of good pubs and a student atmosphere. Newtown's bustling King Street can be noisy and traffic-polluted, but that's just part of its charm.

If you fancy staying near the beach, you can't go wrong with Bondi, Coogee or Manly. The bus journey from Bondi and Coogee into the city can be a pain, but the beach atmosphere is fabulous. If you stay in Manly (a popular option with British visitors), you're limited by the ferry service from the city, which stops around midnight. For the full seaside experience, head for the northern beaches, such as Newport or the stunning but pricey Palm Beach.

The best Hotels

For cut-price glamour
Head for the stylish **Kirketon** (*see p35*) or **Hotel Altamont** (*see p37*), both in Darlinghurst.

For creature comforts
Dive Hotel. Pets come with the designer furniture in the coolest dive in town, located on Coogee Beach. *See p42.*

For extremely free sports
Attack the waves or head off on a mountain bike for free using the kit at **Indy's Bondi Beach Backpackers**. *See p42.*

For beer and a barbie
Try your Aussie skills skulling a schooner and whacking a steak on the barbie at the **Newport Arms** (*see p45*) and the **Coogee Bay Hotel** (*see p42*).

For an unusual harbour view
The **Sebel Pier One** on Circular Quay has a glass floor in its foyer. *See p30.*

For the most talented night porter
Dubbed Sir Victor by his appreciative employers, the piano-playing veteran at the **Hughenden Hotel** knows how to roll up his green sleeves. *See p38.*

For a wild encounter
Look out for wallabies, kookaburras and possums while staying at the remote and beautiful **Pittwater YHA**. *See p46.*

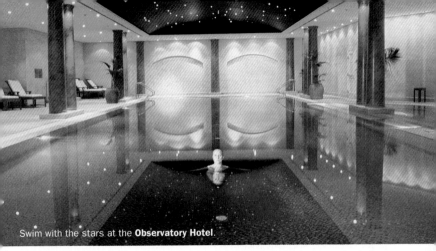
Swim with the stars at the **Observatory Hotel**.

In the end, though, where you stay may depend on when you come. The busiest tourist times are between November and May. The beach areas are packed from mid December to late January, when the school holidays are in full swing. If you want a room over Mardi Gras (February) or a harbour view at New Year, you'll have to book well in advance.

For assistance with finding the right place at the right price, *see p27* **Helping hand**.

KEEP IN MIND

● Room prices vary greatly, but in general Sydney is less expensive than many European cities, and you should be able to get a decent double room in the city for around $150 a night.

● In Australia a 'hotel' can also mean a pub. Many pubs have rooms at reasonable prices, but standards are mixed, so ask to see the accommodation first. Also check that there is adequate soundproofing.

● Despite increased government intervention, there are still numerous illegal backpacker hostels operating all over Australia. Their flyers are pasted on to lamp-posts or pinned to backpacker bulletin boards. While the prices may be tempting, these places can be cramped fire-traps that flout accommodation laws. For an up-to-date list of recommended legal hostels, see **www.hostelaustralia.com**, **www.visit nsw.com.au** or **www.yha.com.au**.

ABOUT THE LISTINGS

Unless stated otherwise all hotels listed below are air-conditioned. Rates quoted are for a double room, unless specified otherwise; these are rack rates, which are often higher than what you'll pay. It's always worth asking for standby prices, weekly rates or special deals; you may well get them, even in the peak season. Top hotels also often offer discounts at weekends, when business people with a life are sleeping

in their own beds. A ten per cent Goods & Services Tax (GST) applies to all hotels and hostels (as well as tours, internal airfares and restaurant meals) and by law it has to be part of the advertised price.

The CBD & the Rocks

Deluxe

InterContinental Sydney

117 Macquarie Street, at Bridge Street, CBD, NSW 2000 (9253 9000/1800 221 335/fax 9240 1240/www.sydney.intercontinental.com). CityRail/ ferry Circular Quay. **Rooms** 509. **Rates** $680-$830 single/double; $1,390-$6,160 suite. **Credit** AmEx, BC, MC, V. **Map** p310 C2.
The heritage-listed sandstone Treasury Building dates from 1851. It was converted into a hotel in 1985, and since then has undergone a series of major renovations, resulting in a 31-floor, five-star hotel that successfully combines its heritage credentials with contemporary design flair. Rooms have window seats, chaise longues and a genuinely workable desk, along with harbour and city views: the more you pay, the better the view, of course. For serious money you can get a vast suite, complete with kitchen and grand piano. The vistas from the top over Sydney Harbour are spectacular, and available to all guests from the indoor pool on the 31st floor. **Hotel services** *Babysitting. Bars. Beauty salon. Business centre. Concierge. Disabled: adapted rooms. Gym. No-smoking floors. Parking ($25). Pool (indoor). Restaurants. Sauna/spa.* **Room services** *Dataport. Room service (24hr). Safe. TV: cable/pay movies.*

Observatory Hotel

89-113 Kent Street, between Argyle & High Streets, Millers Point, NSW 2000 (9256 2222/fax 9256 2233/www.observatoryhotel.com.au). CityRail/ferry Circular Quay. **Rooms** 100. **Rates** $705-$745 single/double; $915-$2,000 suite. **Credit** AmEx, BC, DC, MC, V. **Map** p310 B1/2.

Owned by Orient-Express, this award-winning hotel works hard to keep its wealthy customers satisfied. It has the feel of a refined historic hotel, although it was only built in 1992; it underwent a million-dollar revamp in 2002. Rooms are decorated in an early colonial style, with mahogany furniture, tapestry drapes and tassels – although the marble bathrooms, stereo TVs, CD players and videos are utterly 21st century. Most have views of Observatory Hill or Walsh Bay. The hotel's dreamy spa – with its superb heated indoor pool, with the southern hemisphere constellations in lights on the ceiling – is marvellously OTT. You could stay here for weeks, if the trust fund allows.

Hotel services *Babysitting. Bar. Beauty salon. Business centre. Concierge. Disabled: adapted rooms. Gym. Limousine service. No-smoking floors. Parking ($30 overnight). Pool (indoor). Restaurant. Safe. Sauna/spa. Tennis court.* **Room services** *Dataport. Minibar. Room service (24hr). TV: cable/pay movies.*

Park Hyatt Sydney

7 Hickson Road, The Rocks, NSW 2000 (9241 1234/fax 9256 1555/www.sydney.park.hyatt.com). CityRail/ferry Circular Quay. **Rooms** 158. **Rates** $465-$555 single/double; $675-$6,195 suite. **Credit** AmEx, BC, DC, MC, V. **Map** p310 C1.

When this place opened in 1990 it was the only spot visiting celebrities and rich Americans would stay. Other hotels have since caught up, but it's still in the top few. The main draw is its fabulous location on the west side of the Harbour, with in-your-face views of the Opera House and Bridge, and a flotilla of extras that include 24-hour butler service. All rooms have marble bathrooms, shower and bath; some have balconies. There's also a heated rooftop pool

and luxury spa. The hotel makes full use of its setting; the chic harbourkitchen&bar restaurant (*see p142*) has floor-to-ceiling glass doors that let in the gentle sound of lapping water. Book well ahead for New Year, but be prepared for big price hikes.

Hotel services *Babysitting. Bars. Business centre. Concierge. Gym. No smoking. Parking (free). Pool (outdoor). Restaurants. Roof terrace. Sauna/spa.* **Room services** *Dataport. Minibar. Room service (24hr). Safe. TV: cable/DVD/pay movies/satellite.*

Shangri-La Hotel

176 Cumberland Street, between Essex & Argyle Streets, The Rocks, NSW 2000 (9250 6000/1800 801 080/fax 9250 6250/www.shangri-la.com/ sydney). CityRail/ferry Circular Quay. **Rooms** 563. **Rates** $460-$670 single/double; $950-$4,900 suite. **Credit** AmEx, BC, DC, MC, V. **Map** p310 B1/2.

The Shangri-La was undergoing refurbishment at the time of writing. It has a prime position between the Sydney Opera House and the Harbour Bridge, and all the rooms have fab views through their floor-to-ceiling windows; the corner rooms offer stunning panoramas, especially from the 20th floor up. On the 36th floor, Unkai, the main restaurant, serves Japanese food, while the Horizons bar (*see p133*) is ideal for a wrap-around gaze over Sydney.

Hotel services *Babysitting. Bar. Beauty salon. Business centre. Concierge. Disabled: adapted rooms. Gym/spa. No-smoking floors. Pool (indoor). Restaurants.* **Room services** *Dataport. Hi-fi. Room service (24hr). Safe. TV: cable.*

Sheraton on the Park

161 Elizabeth Street, between Market & Park Streets CBD, NSW 2000 (9286 6000/1800 073 535/ fax 9286 6686/www.sheraton.com/sydney). CityRail

Everyone's talking about celeb fave the **Establishment**. *See p29.*

Helping hand

Just about every visitor could use a little advice and assistance when it comes to finding a room for the night. A real asset is the **Sydney Visitor Centre** (9667 6050) in the arrivals hall of the international terminal at Sydney Airport. They'll negotiate last-minute room deals, and can get as much as 50 per cent chopped off standard rates. All the ticketing is done on the spot; you just present a voucher at the hotel. The **Tourism NSW Visitor Information Line** (13 2077) is another option for room-hunting.

Bargain-hungry backpackers can try the board adjacent to the **Sydney Visitor Centre** (*see p292*) in the Rocks, which offers a direct line to more than 50 establishments. Or contact **YHA Australia** (422 Kent Street, Sydney, NSW 2001, 9261 1111, fax 9261 1969, www.yha.com.au) for a free information pack with membership details and a list of Australian youth hostels.

Campers will find many options in the heart of the bush or on the beach, most with cheap, fully equipped cabins or villas. The airport's **Sydney Visitor Centre** (*see above*) can provide a list of cabins and campsites, but staff can't book for you. Also check out the official government website (**www.visitnsw.com.au**) and the National Roads & Motorists' Association's excellent camping and caravanning guides (**www.nrma.com.au**). The National Parks & Wildlife Service publishes a comprehensive booklet on NSW National Parks; to get one, visit **Cadman's Cottage** (*see p292*).

Many universities open their doors to casual visitors at low rates during the holidays. Dates of semester breaks vary, but are usually late November to late February, during Easter and in June and July; most also have short breaks around the end of September and October. Try the **University of New South Wales** (9385 4985, www.housing.unsw.edu.au) or the **University of Sydney** (9036 4000, www.suv.com.au).

If you're interested in short-term shared accommodation, contact **Sleeping with the Enemy** (9211 8878, www.sleepingwith theenemy.com). They offer rentals in houses around Sydney's fringe from $120 per week for a minimum one-month stay. There's no deposit and all furniture is provided.

St James. **Rooms** 557. **Rates** $520-$650 single/double; $780-$2,630 suite. **Credit** AmEx, BC, DC, MC, V. **Map** p311 C3.
Instead of the usual harbour views, this handsome branch of the worldwide chain looks out over the lush foliage of Hyde Park. The staircases and marble pillars of the grand lobby lead to luxurious rooms fitted with black marble and granite bathrooms and various deluxe amenities. The suites are quite something, and some have private terraces. The Botanica Brasserie is known for its weekend seafood buffet, or there's I'm Angus on the Park for Aussie fare. Cocktails are served late into the night in the Conservatory Lounge.
Hotel services Babysitting. Bar. Beauty salon. Business centre. Concierge. Disabled: adapted rooms. Gym. No-smoking floors. Parking ($35). Pool (indoor). Restaurant. Sauna/spa. **Room services** Dataport. Minibar. Room service (24hr). Safe. TV: cable.

The Westin Sydney

1 Martin Place, between Pitt & George Streets, CBD, NSW 2000 (8223 1111/1800 656535/fax 8223 1222/www.westin.com/sydney). CityRail Martin Place. **Rooms** 416. **Rates** $525-$625 single/double; $900-$3,500 suite. **Credit** AmEx, BC, DC, MC, V. **Map** p310 B/C2.
Located in the heart of the Central Business District, the Westin is an integral part of the redevelopment of the General Post Office (*see p67*). The heritage-listed building was constructed in 1887, although part of the hotel is in a new building adjacent. You pay a bit more for rooms in the heritage part, but unless you crave high ceilings and period detail, the Tower rooms are actually better, with striking city views. The 'heavenly beds' are deservedly famous, and the marble bathrooms have sunken baths and separate showers. There's a good gym with classes and personal trainers, but the lap pool is rather disappointing: even guests have to pay $20 a visit – yes, that's 20 bucks just for a quick dip.
Hotel services Babysitting. Bar. Business centre. Concierge. Disabled: adapted rooms. Gym. No-smoking rooms. Parking ($32). Pool (indoor). Restaurant. Spa. **Room services** Dataport. Minibar. Room service (24hr). Safe. TV: cable/pay movies.

Expensive

Avillion Hotel

389 Pitt Street, at Liverpool Street, CBD, NSW 2000 (8268 1888/1800 838 830/fax 9283 5899/www.avillion.com.au). CityRail Central or Town Hall/Monorail World Square/LightRail Central. **Rooms** 445. **Rates** $350-$410 twin/double; $460 family; $570-$790 suite. **Credit** AmEx, BC, DC, MC, V. **Map** p311 C3.

Within walking distance of Darling Harbour, Chinatown and the QVB, the Avillion is a large, convenient four-star hotel. It features original artwork of Sydney and the Australian bush, and the rooms are comfortably furnished with the working exec clearly in mind: each has voicemail, fax facilities and an internet terminal. There's no swimming pool, but the gym is spacious. A retail plaza in the lower lobby includes a newsagent, car rental office and a health and beauty salon. The hotel restaurant, Avery's, is worth a try on Friday nights, when it presents live jazz along with a seafood smorgasbord. Next door, at 111 Liverpool Street, are popular cocktail lounges V Bar and Uber. It often offers good-value deals; check the website for details.

Hotel services *Bars. Business centre. Concierge. Conference facilities. Disabled: adapted rooms. Gym. No-smoking floors. Parking ($26). Restaurant.* **Room services** *Dataport. Minibar. Room service (24hr). Safe. TV: cable/pay movies/satellite.*

The Blacket

70 King Street, at George Street, CBD, NSW 2000 (9279 3030/fax 9279 3020/www.theblacket.com). CityRail Martin Place or Wynyard. **Rooms** 42. **Rates** $210-$250 single/double; $385-$410 apartment. **Credit** AmEx, BC, DC, MC, V. **Map** p310 B2.

Another in Sydney's growing collection of boutique hotels, the Blacket may be more discreet than the rest, but it's just as groovy. It opened in 2001 in an 1850s bank building designed by city architect Edmund Blacket. The only remnants of the heritage property are the original staircase and two suites with soaring ceilings, polished floors, claw-foot baths and heavy drapes; otherwise, the hotel is ultra-modern, decked out in subdued black, brown and neutral tones with the odd flash of colour. There are five room types; the deluxe two-bed apartment is a good deal if there are three or four of you. Perks include the well-known Mediterranean Minc restaurant and cocktail bar, with a glass roof and views over George Street, and the basement Minc Lounge bar, housed in the former bank vault.

Hotel services *Bar. Concierge. Conference facilities. No-smoking rooms. Parking ($25). Restaurant. Safe.* **Room services** *Hi-fi. Room service (5.30-10.30pm). TV.*

Country Comfort Sydney Central

Railway Square, corner of George & Quay Streets, Haymarket, NSW 2000 (9212 2544/1300 650 464/ fax 9281 3794/www.countrycomfort.com.au). CityRail/LightRail Central. **Rooms** 113. **Rates** $260 single/double; $290 suite. **Credit** AmEx, BC, DC, MC, V. **Map** p311 B4.

Country Comfort is a large chain of three-star hotels throughout NSW and Queensland that aims to create the 'real Australian experience'. This translates into genuinely helpful staff in relaxed surroundings, with all the usual hotel services at prices that won't break the bank. Rooms are comfortable if drab (exposed brick walls and lots of brown), but the extras are all here – minibar, TV, pool, sauna, 24-hour reception – along with a so-so restaurant and

bar. The location opposite Central Station is handy, though not very pretty. But Chinatown and Darling Harbour are nearby, and a ten-minute bus ride will whisk you to Circular Quay.

Hotel services *Bar. Concierge. Laundry. No-smoking floors. Parking ($15). Pool (outdoor). Restaurant. Roof terrace. Sauna.* **Room services** *Minibar. Room service (24hr). TV: cable/pay movies.*

Establishment

5 Bridge Lane, at George Street, CBD, NSW 2000 (9240 3100/3110/fax 9240 3101/www. establishmenthotel.com). CityRail Wynyard or Circular Quay/ferry Circular Quay. **Rooms** 33. **Rates** $330-$399 single/double; $920-$1,050 penthouse. **Credit** AmEx, BC, DC, MC, V. **Map** p310 B2.

The large black entrance that merges into its dusty surrounds down a back alley hides the most talked-about hotel in Sydney. It may not have a view or a pool, but it's the place celebs (Robbie Williams, Kylie Minogue, Keanu Reeves, Bill Gates) choose to hang out. The Establishment complex was conceived by Sydney fashionistas Justin and Bettina Hemmes, so the decor and ambience reflect that. There are 33 sizeable rooms plus two penthouse suites. Bathrooms feature white terrazzo or limestone floors and Philippe Starck taps, and delicious extras include Bulgari toiletries, bathrobes, Bose stereo systems, Loewe TVs and DVD players. Most locals know the Establishment for the other spaces in the complex, which stretches right through to George Street; these include trendy nightclub Tank (*see p236*), pricey restaurant est. (*see p142*) and the exclusive Hemmesphere bar (*see p132*).

Hotel services *Bar. Business centre. Concierge. Gym. No-smoking floor. Restaurants.* **Room services** *Dataport. Hi-fi. Room service (6am-11pm). Safe. TV: cable/DVD. Workstation.*

Four Points by Sheraton

161 Sussex Street, at Market Street, CBD, NSW 2000 (9290 4000/1800 074 545/fax 9290 4040/ www.fourpoints.com). CityRail Town Hall/Monorail Darling Park. **Rooms** 631. **Rates** $360-$490 single/ double; $540-$2,360 suite. **Credit** AmEx, BC, DC, MC, V. **Map** p311 B3.

Part of the US-based Starwood hotel group – other properties in Sydney are the Westin (*see p27*), W (*see p34*) and Sheraton on the Park (*see p26*) – Four Points hotels are aimed at middle-management business types and holidaymakers. This means they claim to have all the features of a five-star establishment at a much lower cost. Certainly, this one overlooking Darling Harbour is good value. Rooms are uncluttered, with simple but functional furniture, and cable TV. There's also a fitness centre, a handy shopping arcade and the Corn Exchange restaurant for al fresco dining. Or you can grab a beer and basic grub at the historic Dundee Arms pub.

Hotel services *Babysitting. Bar. Business centre. Concierge. Disabled: adapted rooms. Gym. No-smoking floors. Parking ($29.50). Restaurant.* **Room services** *Room service (24hr). Safe. TV: cable/pay movies.*

Walk on water at **Sebel Pier One**.

The Grace Hotel

*77 York Street, at King Street, CBD, NSW 2000
(9272 6888/1800 682 692/fax 9299 8189/
www.gracehotel.com.au). CityRail Martin Place or
Wynyard.* **Rooms** 382. **Rates** $410-$450 single/
double; $585 suite; extra $49.50 per person for triple.
Credit AmEx, BC, DC, MC, V. **Map** p310 B2.

Modelled on the art deco Tribune Building in
Chicago and opened in 1930, this handsome, 11-
storey corner block was once the headquarters of the
Grace Bros department store. During World War II
it became HQ for General MacArthur's South Pacific
operations, but it is as a hotel that the space ultimately found its niche. Many of the original features,
such as the lifts, stairwells, marble floors and
pressed-metal ceilings, have been retained and
restored. Rooms are large with simple furnishings;
those with numbers ending 16 have a separate bath
and shower. There is an airy fitness centre, as well
as a rooftop sun terrace with glimpses of the water
at King Street Wharf. The indoor heated lap pool is
a bit cramped, but there are also jacuzzis, a sauna
and a steam room. It has a collection of average
eateries, a noisy Irish theme pub and the quieter
Grace Lounge bar.
Hotel services *Babysitting. Bar. Beauty salon.
Concierge. Disabled: adapted rooms. Gym.
No-smoking floor. Parking ($30). Pool (indoor).
Restaurant. Roof terrace. Sauna/spa.* **Room
services** *Dataport. Room service (24hr). Safe.
TV: pay movies.*

Sebel Pier One

*11 Hickson Road, on Dawes Point, Walsh Bay,
Sydney, NSW 2000 (8298 9999/1800 780 485/
fax 8298 9777/www.mirvac.com.au). CityRail/
ferry Circular Quay/bus 430.* **Rooms** 161. **Rates**
$440-$520-$600 single/double; $760 suite. **Credit**
AmEx, BC, DC, MC, V. **Map** p310 C1.

This stylish new boutique hotel is in a historic wharf
warehouse over the water at the end of the Rocks,
just steps from the Harbour Bridge. The first thing
you'll notice when you walk in is the glass floor in
the lobby, which reveals the harbour water below –
quite spectacular. Rooms have Harbour or Bridge
views, and decor is a fusion of the latest contemporary look and restored heritage details. The Front
restaurant and wine bar offers water views.
Hotel services *Babysitting. Bar. Business centre.
Concierge. Disabled: adapted rooms. Gym.
No-smoking rooms. Parking ($25). Restaurant.
Spa.* **Room services** *Dataport. Minibar. Room
service (24hr). Safe. TV: cable/pay movies.*

Moderate

Central Park Hotel

*185 Castlereagh Street, at Park Street, CBD, NSW
2000 (9283 5000/fax 9283 2710/www.central
park.com.au). CityRail Town Hall/Monorail Galeries
Victoria.* **Rooms** 35. **Rates** $185 single/double; $220
studio; $325 suite. **Credit** AmEx, BC, DC, MC, V.
Map p311 C3.

This compact corner hotel, located above a busy bar, restaurant and gaming room complex, features surprisingly spacious, two-storey, New York-style loft apartments (sleeping up to six), popular with long-stay corporate clients and honeymooners. There are also standard en suite rooms, and studios with an additional double sofa bed and a spa bath in the granite bathroom. The noise from busy Park and Castlereagh Streets down below is kept to a minimum by efficient window seals.
Hotel services *Concierge. Disabled: adapted room. No-smoking floors. Parking ($30). Safe.* **Room services** *Dataport. Refrigerator. TV: cable.*

Lord Nelson Brewery Hotel

19 Kent Street, at Argyle Street, Millers Point, NSW 2000 (9251 4044/fax 9251 1532/www.lordnelson. com.au). CityRail/ferry Circular Quay. **Rooms** 9. **Rates** $120 double shared bath; $180 double en suite.* **Credit** AmEx, BC, DC, MC, V. **Map** p310 B1.
Dating from 1841, the Lord Nelson holds prime position overlooking Observatory Hill. It claims to be the oldest pub in the city, and has nine Victorian-style guest rooms complete with the original bare sandstone walls to keep them cool. These days, of course, there's air-conditioning too. Not all rooms are en suite, so specify what you want when you book. A pretty brasserie on the first floor looks out over a large expanse of exposed sandstone towards the Harbour Bridge. The atmospheric bar downstairs (*see p133*) brews its own beer.
Hotel services *Bar. No smoking. Parking ($15). Restaurant. Safe.* **Room services** *Refrigerator. TV.*

Palisade Hotel

35 Bettington Street, at Argyle Street, Millers Point, NSW 2000 (9247 2272/fax 9247 2040/ www.palisadehotel.com). CityRail/ferry Circular Quay. **Rooms** 11. **Rates** $115-$125 single/double. **Credit** AmEx, BC, DC, MC, V. **Map** p310 B1.
Situated on the edge of the Rocks, the heritage-listed Palisade Hotel, built in 1916, was the place where many a young digger had his last drink before heading off to war in a troop ship from Millers Point or Circular Quay. Nowadays, the pub, with its crackling log fires in winter, is a popular meeting point, and its upmarket restaurant (*see p142*) pulls in the city slickers, both for the food and the view. The hotel has the feel of a friendly B&B: all the pleasantly furnished rooms have shared bathrooms; some have large balconies overlooking the working end of the harbour. None has air-conditioning.
Hotel services *Bar. No smoking. Payphone. Restaurant. Safe.* **Room services** *No phone.*

The Russell

143A George Street, between Alfred & Argyle Streets, The Rocks, NSW 2000 (9241 3543/fax 9252 1652/www.therussell.com.au). CityRail/ferry Circular Quay. **Rooms** 29. **Rates** $140-$195 double shared bath; $235-$290 double en suite; $320 suite. **Credit** AmEx, BC, DC, MC, V. **Map** p310 C1/2.
Located slap bang in the middle of the Rocks, behind the MCA, the Russell is a small, homely hotel housed

in a turreted 1840s building. Most of the rooms (18 en suite, 11 with shared bathrooms) are doubles, and all are decorated differently, in a cosy, old-fashioned style. If feels more like a country B&B than a city-centre hotel. There's a tiny rooftop garden and the pleasant, yellow-walled Boulders restaurant on the ground floor doubles as the breakfast room. It's the kind of place that attracts a lot of repeat business, so book well in advance.
Hotel services *Bar. No smoking. Parking ($25). Restaurant. Safe.* **Room services** *TV.*

Budget

Footprints Westend

412 Pitt Street, between Goulburn & Campbell Streets, CBD, NSW 2000 (9211 4588/1800 013 186/fax 9211 5312/www.footprintswestend.com.au). CityRail Central or Museum/LightRail Central. **Rooms** 90. **Rates** $21-$30 dorm; $69 twin; $85 double. **Credit** BC, MC. V. **Map** p311 B3/4.
This excellent, award-winning budget option opened in July 2002. It's a five-minute walk from Central Station, and the rooms are clean and modern, all (even the dorms) with en suite – a rarity in this price range. Linen and quilts are provided, and there's a night security, luggage lockers, a commercial-grade kitchen, a pool table and a popular TV/video lounge. Most rooms have air-conditioning, but it can't be guaranteed; if not, electric fans are available.
Hotel services *Café. Disabled: adapted room. Kitchen. Laundry. No smoking. Payphone. Safe. TV room. 24hr reception.* **Room services** *No phone.*

Railway Square YHA

8-10 Lee Street, at Railway Square, Haymarket, NSW 2000 (9281 9666/fax 9281 9688/www.yha. com.au). CityRail/LightRail Central. **Rooms** 64. **Rates** $27-$33 dorm; $78 twin shared bath; $88 twin en suite.* **Credit** BC, MC, V. **Map** p311 B4.
At the time of writing, a new YHA hostel is due to open in Railway Square, very near the company's Central hostel (*see below*). Built in a former parcels shed, the open-plan communal area incorporates a real disused railway platform (very Harry Potter), and some of the dorms are replicas of train carriages, on the original tracks (bathrooms are in the main building adjacent). Mod cons include a pool and air-conditioning. Most dorms have four beds, and there are some twin rooms. Extras include a large kitchen, lots of comfy communal areas (including a bridge on the second floor with a bird's-eye view of what's going on) and an internet café. It's bound to be popular, so book ahead.
Hotel services *Disabled: adapted rooms. Internet café. Kitchen. Laundry. No smoking. Payphone. Pool (outdoor). Safe. TV room.* **Room services** *No phone.*

Sydney Central YHA

11 Rawson Place, at Pitt Street, CBD, NSW 2000 (9281 9111/fax 9281 9199/www.yha.com.au). CityRail/LightRail Central. **Rooms** 151. **Rates**

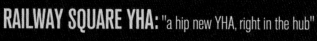

$27-$33 dorm; $82 twin shared bath; $94 twin/double en suite. **Credit** BC, MC, V. **Map** p311 B4.
YHA Australia's flagship Sydney hostel is in an imposing heritage-listed building opposite Central Station. It's popular, and it's easy to see why – the place has everything. It opened in 1997 and, despite high usage, still looks slick and new. Facilities include a small heated rooftop pool, a sauna, kitchens, barbecue equipment, laundry, TV rooms, a dining room, internet access and even a mini super-market. There's also a bistro-style café and a base-ment bar, Scubar. There are 54 twin rooms, some en suite, but most people stay in the dormitories, which have four to eight beds.
Hotel services *Bar. Café/restaurant. Disabled: adapted rooms. Internet café. Kitchen. Laundry. No smoking. Parking (limited, $12). Payphone. Pool (outdoor). Roof terrace. Safe. Sauna. TV rooms.* **Room services** *No phone.*

wake up!

509 Pitt Street, at George Street, Haymarket, NSW 2000 (9288 7888/1800 800 945/fax 9288 7889/ www.wakeup.com.au). CityRail/LightRail Central. **Rooms** 500 beds. **Rates** $25-$30 dorm; $79 twin/ double shared bath; $88 twin/double en suite. **Credit** MC, V. **Map** p311 B4.
This in-your-face, thoroughly modern backpackers' hotel opposite Central Station opened in 2002 and has proved a surefire hit with twentysomethings who just wanna have fun. The air-conditioned dorms with bunk beds sleep four, six, eight or ten (some of the smaller rooms are for women only). There are also double and twin rooms, some with private showers. Rules are minimal, but include no smoking in the rooms and no sleeping bags. The large reception area has comfy sofas, loads of internet booths and a well-used bar and café. There's 24-hour check-in, and security is keen, with lockers in the rooms and swipe-card access to each floor.
Hotel services *Bar. Café/restaurant. Disabled: adapted rooms. Internet café. Kitchen. Laundry. No smoking. Payphone. Safe. TV room. 24hr reception.* **Room services** *No phone.*

Y on the Park Hotel

5-11 Wentworth Avenue, at Liverpool Street, CBD, NSW 2010 (9264 2451/1800 994 994/ fax 9285 6288/www.ywca-sydney.com.au). CityRail Museum. **Rooms** 121. **Rates** $33 dorm; $72-$118 single; $88-$130 double/twin; $98-$149 triple. **Credit** AmEx, BC, MC, V. **Map** p311 C3.
The YWCA started life as a sanctuary for Christian women, mainly country girls coming to the city for the first time. Today it's a very different place: any-one is welcome and the accommodation options have moved with the times. The Y offers everything from four-bed dorms to deluxe en suite doubles, often used by business travellers. All are clean and contempo-rary and have basic furniture; the en suite rooms have fridges, TVs and phones. Rates include break-fast. The best thing about the Y is its location – just south of Hyde Park – and the fact that hotel profits support projects run by the YWCA across NSW.

Hotel services *Café. Disabled: adapted rooms. Internet access. Laundry. No smoking. Payphone. Safe. TV room.* **Room services** *No phones in dorms.*

Darling Harbour & Pyrmont

Deluxe

Star City Hotel

80 Pyrmont Street, between Jones Bay Road & Union Street, Pyrmont, NSW 2009 (9657 8393/ 1800 700 700/fax 9657 8345/www.starcity.com.au). CityRail Town Hall then 15mins walk/ferry Darling Harbour/LightRail Star City/Monorail Harbourside/ bus 443, 888. **Rooms** 481. **Rates** $390-$525 single/double; $550-$1,020 apartment; $550-$4,000 suite. **Credit** AmEx, BC, DC, MC, V. **Map** p310 A2.
Six years after opening in a blaze of glitz and glam-our, this OTT hotel above the Star City casino (*see p71*) is still going strong. The emphasis is on feel-ing like a star, so the suites offer 24-hour butler ser-vice. There are 306 standard rooms, 43 suites and two penthouses, while the apartment complex has 130 fully serviced apartments. Facilities include a new spa, a popular health club and a 25m pool with panoramic views of the city. There are 13 restau-rants and bars and two theatres in the casino/hotel. Be warned: it's very hard to go anywhere in the com-plex without encountering the casino and its miles and miles of poker machines.
Hotel services *Babysitting. Bar. Beauty salon. Business centre. Concierge. Disabled: adapted rooms. Gym. No-smoking floors. Parking ($24). Pool (outdoor). Restaurants. Sauna/spa.* **Room services** *Dataport. Minibar. Room service (24hr). Safe. TV: cable/pay movies/satellite.*

Expensive

Novotel Sydney on Darling Harbour

100 Murray Street, at Allen Street, Darling Harbour, NSW 2009 (9934 0000/1300 656 565/fax 9934 0099/www.novotel.com). CityRail Town Hall/ Monorail/LightRail Convention. **Rooms** 525. **Rates** $400-$425 single/double; $450-$600 suite. **Credit** AmEx, BC, DC, MC, V. **Map** p311 B3.
Situated next door to Sydney's Convention Centre, this chain hotel is aimed mainly at business trav-ellers. Thus it has two business centres, three board-rooms and even a poolside marquee for functions. The rooms (including 16 suites) are conservative in style, but spacious and with terrific city and harbour views. The location is excellent for sightseeing; it's next to Darling Harbour's numerous attractions, and just minutes via the Monorail to the CBD. The hotel also has a bar, a brasserie, a pool and, unusually for Sydney, a tennis court.
Hotel services *Babysitting. Bar. Business centres. Concierge. Disabled: adapted rooms. Gym. No-smoking floors. Parking ($20). Pool (outdoor). Restaurant. Safe. Tennis court. Terrace.* **Room services** *Dataport. Minibar. Room service (24hr). TV: cable/pay movies.*

Moderate

Hotel Ibis Darling Harbour

70 Murray Street, at Allen Street, Darling Harbour,
NSW 2009 (9563 0888/1300 656 565/fax 9563
0899/www.accorhotels.com.au). CityRail Town Hall/
Monorail/LightRail Convention. **Rooms** 256. **Rates**
$149 city view; $175 harbour view. **Credit** AmEx,
BC, DC, MC, V. **Map** p311 B3.
The Ibis brand is essentially a no-frills, 'people's
price' chain, so don't expect fancy taps or chocs on
the pillow. This branch is probably the best-value
hotel in the area, offering smart, simple, compact
accommodation right in the centre of Darling
Harbour. Half the smallish rooms have city views
across Darling Harbour, the others have views over
Pyrmont. The Skyline bar and restaurant has an outdoor terrace, and guests can use the sporting facili-
ties at the Novotel next door (*see p33*).
Hotel services *Bar. Disabled: adapted rooms.*
No-smoking floors. Parking ($15). Restaurant.
Safe. 24hr reception. **Room services** *Dataport.*
Refrigerator. TV.

Kings Cross, Potts Point & Woolloomooloo

Deluxe

W

6 Cowper Wharf Road, opposite Forbes Street,
Woolloomooloo, NSW 2011 (9331 9000/1800 025
525/fax 9331 9031/www.whotels.com). Bus 311,
312. **Rooms** 104. **Rates** $550-$580 single/double;
$650-$1,950 loft. **Credit** AmEx, BC, DC, MC, V.
Map p312 D2.
'Walking into W Sydney is like walking inside the
latest edition of *Wallpaper** magazine' – at least,
that's what their PR department claims. To be fair,
the reality is not far off. Occupying the front portion
of the Woolloomooloo finger wharf development, the
W retains much of the warehouse's echoey charm.
Opened in April 2000, it's the first W venture outside North America. Style is everything here: in the
chocolate-brown leather sofas, giant ottomans,
Philippe Starck lamps and sumptuous, gadget-
stuffed guest rooms. There's a well-equipped fitness
centre, indoor pool and the popular Water Bar (*see*
p137), but no restaurant (although there are plenty
of trendy eateries alongside the wharf).
Hotel services *Babysitting. Bar. Business centre.*
Concierge. Disabled: adapted rooms. Gym.
No-smoking floors. Parking ($30). Pool (indoor).
Spa. **Room services** *Dataport. Hi-fi. Minibar.*
Room service (24hr). Safe. TV: cable/pay movies.

Moderate

Simpsons of Potts Point

8 Challis Avenue, at Victoria Street, Potts Point,
NSW 2011 (9356 2199/fax 9356 4476/
www.simpsonshotel.com). CityRail Kings Cross.
Rooms 12. **Rates** $145 single; $175-$215 double;
$325 suite. **Credit** AmEx, BC, MC, V. **Map** p312 D2.
This well-restored 19th-century mansion is in one of
Potts Point's leafier streets, an oasis just minutes
from the madness of Kings Cross. The house was
built in the 1890s for John Lane Mullins, a member
of the NSW colonial parliament. Its grand rooms
were recently refurbished; in the winter there are
fires in the grates and complimentary sherry and
port on the hearth. All rooms are en suite and air-
conditioned, and the 'cloud suite' has lovely views
of the gardens and its own private spa. Continental
breakfast is served in the airy conservatory.
Hotel services *No alcohol licence. No smoking.*
Parking (limited, free). Safe. 24hr reception.
Room services *Dataport. Refrigerator.*

Victoria Court Hotel

122 Victoria Street, between Orwell & Hughes
Streets, Potts Point, NSW 2011 (9357 3200/1800
630 505/fax 9357 7606/www.victoriacourt.com.au).
CityRail Kings Cross. **Rooms** 22. **Rates** $75-$176
single/double; $150-$250 deluxe single/double.
Credit AmEx, BC, DC, MC, V. **Map** p312 D3.
Formed from two 1881 terraced houses, this hotel is
ideal if you love Victorian excess – chandeliers, four-
poster beds, fireplaces, antiques, rich fabrics. No
two rooms are the same. The more expensive have
marble fireplaces and wrought-iron balconies overlooking Victoria Street, the main gastronomic strip.
In its heyday the area was favoured by wealthy
merchants who liked to be near to the harbour –
these days it's a little less salubrious, just a street
away from the Cross's sex and drug dens. All rooms
have private bathrooms, and breakfast is served in
the beautiful, glass-roofed conservatory.
Hotel services *Courtyard. No smoking. Parking*
($11). **Room services** *Dataport. Safe. TV.*

Budget

Eva's Backpackers

6-8 Orwell Street, at Victoria Street, Kings Cross,
NSW 2011 (9358 2185/1800 802 517/fax 9358
3259/www.evasbackpackers.com.au). CityRail Kings
Cross. **Rooms** 28. **Rates** from $22 dorm; $55 double.
Credit MC, V. **Map** p312 D3.
This friendly, family-owned backpackers' hotel is a
firm favourite among travellers – so book well in
advance. It has twin, double and multi-shared
rooms, some en suite, some with air-conditioning.
Extras include free breakfast, a laundry room with
free washing powder, free tea and coffee, travel info,
wake-up calls, luggage storage facilities, broadband
internet access and, best of all, a rooftop terrace and
barbecue area with views over Sydney. Located at
the Potts Point end of Kings Cross, it's on a quiet
street, but close to all the amenities. Winner of a five-
rucksack rating from the NRMA.
Hotel services *BBQ. Internet access. Kitchen.*
Laundry. No smoking. Payphone. Roof terrace.
Safe. TV room. **Room services** *No phone.*

Y on the Park Hotel: budget luxe. *See p33.*

O'Malley's Hotel

228 William Street, at Brougham Street, Kings Cross, NSW 2011 (9357 2211/1800 674 631/ fax 9357 2656/www.omalleyshotel.com.au). CityRail Kings Cross. **Rooms** 15. **Rates** from $66 single/ double; from $88 triple/suite. **Credit** BC, MC, V. **Map** p312 D3.

Irish bar O'Malley's has been a popular music venue for ten years. The 1907 building has been faithfully restored, so the rooms (all en suite) have delightful period touches and a slightly chintzy feel of the good old days. Situated bang in the middle of Kings Cross – one block down from the famous red and white Coca-Cola sign – it's also just two minutes from the rail station, offering great links to the airport, CBD and interstate trains. All rooms are no-smoking, and the 'harbour view suite' has its own kitchen. On Sunday nights between 7.30pm and 8.30pm, try the 'toss the boss' competition: if you guess the flip of a coin right, the drinks are on O'Malley's.
Hotel services *Bar. No smoking. Parking ($13.50). Payphone. Safe.* **Room services** *Refrigerator. TV: cable.*

V Backpackers

144 Victoria Street, between Orwell & Earl Streets, Potts Point, NSW 2011 (9357 4733/1800 667 255/ fax 9357 4434/www.vbackpackers.com). CityRail Kings Cross. **Rooms** 27. **Rates** $24-$26; $55 twin/ double. **Credit** AmEx, BC, DC, MC, V. **Map** p312 D3.

This newly renovated hostel is favoured by party-ing travellers who like their beer. Rooms are clean, comfy and not too cramped, and come in three-, four- and six-bed dorms, plus twins and doubles. All bath facilities are shared, but the twins/doubles have their own TVs. There's a kitchen, pizzeria and coffee lounge, communal room with cable TV and big couches, and laundry facilities. On Mondays and Fridays you get a free (yes, free) barbecue meal along with a beer voucher for the much-loved nearby local, the Old Fitzroy Hotel (*see p137*).
Hotel services *Courtyard. Kitchen. Laundry. No smoking. Payphone. Restaurant. Safe. TV room.* **Room services** *No phone.*

Darlinghurst

Expensive

Medusa

267 Darlinghurst Road, between Liverpool & William Streets, Darlinghurst, NSW 2010 (9331 1000/ fax 9380 6901/www.medusa.com.au). CityRail Kings Cross. **Rooms** 18. **Rates** $270-$385 single/double. **Credit** AmEx, BC, DC, MC, V. **Map** p312 D3.

The first of Terry and Robert Schwamberg's bou-tique hotels, the Medusa opened in 1998. It's a quiet and intimate haven in a heritage-listed Victorian mansion. You can't miss it: the exterior is pink. Inside, it's uniquely decorated with lots of bright colour (the entrance hall is lipstick pink), a camp flourish or two and attention to detail. If you can afford it, splash out on one of the huge Grand Rooms, with high ceilings, period fireplace, funky chaise longue and sitting area. All rooms are en suite, with kitchenette, CD player and minibar. The urban-chic courtyard at the back has a water feature and sitting area. A great extra for canine-loving Australian visitors is that dogs are welcome.
Hotel services *Business centre. Courtyard. No smoking.* **Room services** *Dataport. Hi-fi. Minibar. Room service (7am-10pm). Safe. TV: cable/VCR.*

Moderate

Kirketon

229 Darlinghurst Road, between Farrell & Tewkesbury Avenues, Darlinghurst (9332 2011/ fax 9332 2499/www.kirketon.com.au). CityRail Kings Cross. **Rooms** 40. **Rates** $129-$179. **Credit** AmEx, BC, DC, MC, V. **Map** p312 D3.

The Kirketon sits on cosmopolitan Darlinghurst Road, surrounded by cafés and restaurants, and a stone's throw from the Cross's red-light district. This is the place for design-hungry visitors who like to be in the thick of it. Originally the love child of Sydney style couple Terry and Robert Schwamberg, who also run Medusa (*see above*), in December 2003 it was taken over by Paul Fischmann and his dynamic Eight Hotels group. Following on his suc-cess with the nearby Hotel Altamont (*see p37*), Fischmann slashed prices and increased occupancy. But while the prices have dropped by up to $90, not much else has changed: the customised furniture and mohair throws are intact, and style still rules. Downstairs you'll find trendy Salt restaurant (*see p149*) and cocktail bar.

Hotel services *Bar. Concierge. No smoking.*
Parking (limited, $15). Restaurant. **Room services**
Dataport. Hi-fi. Minibar. Refrigerator. Room service
(6-11pm). Safe. TV: cable/VCR.

Budget

Deluxe

Hotel Altamont

207 Darlinghurst Road, between Liverpool &
William Streets, Darlinghurst, NSW 2010 (9360
6000/1800 991 110/fax 9360 7096/www.altamont.
com.au). CityRail Kings Cross. **Rooms** 14. **Rates**
$109 double; $129 loft suite. **Credit** AmEx, BC,
MC, V. **Map** p312 D3.

A luxury budget hotel? You better believe it. This
former colonial Georgian mansion was renovated a
few years ago by award-winning architect Furio
Valich to provide boutique-style accommodation
that melds heritage elements with a postmodern
edge. The results are stunning – it's comfortable but
elegant, with custom-made furniture and designer
bathrooms. Mick Jagger is one of its more famous
guests. Rooms range from an airy loft suite with
soaring ceilings and walk-in wardrobe to dorm
rooms with bunk beds. There are four of the latter,
sleeping six or eight, all with private bathrooms, air-
conditioning and a TV. The ornate roof terrace is
lovely, and there's a reasonably priced lounge bar.
Unsurprisingly, the hotel is hugely popular, so book
ahead. Operations manager Alan Morris says he'll
drop the prices further if you rock up on the day and
want to haggle, and there are special deals for stays
of a week or longer.
Hotel services *Bar. Lounge. No-smoking rooms.*
Parking ($10). Roof terrace. Safe. **Room services**
Dataport. TV: cable/DVD.

Stamford Plaza Double Bay

33 Cross Street, between Bay Street & New South
Head Road, Double Bay, NSW 2028 (9362 4455/
1800 301 391/fax 9362 4744/www.stamford.com.au).
Ferry Double Bay/bus 323, 324, 325, 326, 327.
Rooms 140. **Rates** $500-$550 single/double;
$1,250-$3,500 suite. **Credit** AmEx, BC, DC, MC, V.
Map p312 F3.

This hotel attracted unwelcome notoriety under its
previous owners (the Ritz-Carlton group) as the
place where INXS frontman Michael Hutchence
ended his life. These days, such bad memories are
gone, replaced by tales of more recent famous
guests, including Bill Clinton and John Travolta
(who supposedly couldn't get enough of the hotel
restaurant's chocolate cake). It's a stylish place in an
over-the-top way, with an Italianate private courtyard and lots of frills and flounces . Rooms are large,
with expensive, traditional furniture and balconies
overlooking either the courtyard or the yachts in
Double Bay. There's a heated rooftop swimming
pool and sundeck, and high tea in the antiques-filled
lobby lounge is a very chic affair. The BayGrill
restaurant offers fine dining.
Hotel services *Babysitting. Bar. Business centre.*
Café. Concierge. Courtyard. Disabled: adapted rooms.
Health club. Kosher kitchen. No-smoking floors.
Parking ($16.50). Pool (outdoor). Restaurant.
Room services *Dataport. Room service (24hr).*
Safe. TV: cable/pay movies.

Medusa: the height of urban chic. *See p35.*

Home from home

The serviced apartment started as an idea to net corporate hotel business, but in the past few years has exploded into something that both suits and holidaymakers can't get enough of. What the apartments have over hotels is more space, more flexibility, in-built kitchens and other homely facilities, such as washing machines. These are some of Sydney's more interesting options.

Harbourside Apartments

2A Henry Lawson Avenue, McMahons Point, NSW 2060 (9963 4300/fax 9922 7998/ www.harbourside-apartments.com.au). Ferry McMahons Point. **Apartments** 82. **Rates** $225-$295 studio; $270-$340 1-bed; $395 2-bed. **Credit** AmEx, BC, DC, MC, V. These can be a tad dingy in a sort of faded chintz way, but the large windows (ask for one on the harbour side) offer sweeping views of the Bridge and Opera House. Apartments have fully equipped kitchens, and the waterfront pool is heated from September to May.

Medina Executive, Sydney Central

2 Lee Street, at George Street, Haymarket, NSW 2000 (8396 9800/fax 8396 9752/ www.medinaapartments.com.au) CityRail/ LightRail Central. **Apartments** 98. **Rates** $275 studio; $340 1-bed; $450 2-bed. **Credit** AmEx, BC, DC, MC, V. **Map** p311 B4.

The busy, family-owned Medina group has 18 apartment complexes across Oz, with two more due to open in 2004. This property, housed in the heritage-listed Parcel Post building, is a clever piece of restoration – outside grandly urban, but inside modern, warm and quiet, thanks to double-glazing. Most of the spacious apartments have full kitchens and laundries. There's also a grocery delivery service, gym, sauna and large pool.

O'Briens Lane Serviced Apartments

5 O'Briens Lane, at Palmer Street, Darlinghurst, NSW 2010 (9380 5388/ fax 9984 1966/www.obrienslane.com.au). CityRail Kings Cross. **Apartments** 7. **Rates** $115-$285. **Map** p311 C3.

Behind an 1840s Georgian façade sit seven modern apartments, hidden in a quiet lane, a short walk from the bustling gay clubs of Oxford Street. Rooms go from basic and spartan one-beds to the two-bedroom penthouse. All are clean and contemporary, with cable TV and dataports, but those on the upper floors are much lighter.

Quay Grand Suites Sydney

61 Macquarie Street, East Circular Quay, NSW 2000 (9256 4000/fax 9256 4040/ www.mirvachotels.com.au). CityRail/ferry

Hotel services *Babysitting. Business centre. Disabled: adapted rooms. No smoking. Parking ($15). Pool (indoor). Sauna/spa.* **Room services** *Dataport. Room service (7am-midnight). TV: cable/pay movies.*

Expensive

Sir Stamford Double Bay

22 Knox Street, at New South Head Road, Double Bay, NSW 2028 (9363 0100/1300 301 391/ fax 9327 3110/www.stamford.com.au). Ferry Double Bay/bus 323, 324, 325, 326, 327. **Rooms** 72. **Rates** $350 double; $420 loft; $630-$770 suite. **Credit** AmEx, BC, DC, MC, V. **Map** p312 F3.

Sir Stamford is best known for its incredibly popular courtyard café and restaurant. Located on the Knox Street side of the Cosmopolitan shopping mall, this is where Double Bay dames dressed up to the nines sit and watch their beautiful world go by. At the time of writing, there were plans to revamp the shopping centre and turn the hotel into residential apartments. Meanwhile, it's business as usual. Rooms are above the shopping mall: some are sleek, New York-style lofts; others are highly ornate, with four-poster beds. The indoor rooftop pool has a spa, sauna and gym, all open 24 hours. Look out for prints by the late Australian artist Norman Lindsay, and for dramatic Beidermeier furniture in the foyer.

Moderate

Hughenden Hotel

14 Queen Street, at Oxford Street, Woollahra, NSW 2025 (9363 4863/1800 642 432/fax 9362 0398/ www.hughendenhotel.com.au). Bus 378, 380, L82. **Rooms** 36. **Rates** $128 single; $148-$258 double. **Credit** AmEx, BC, DC, MC, V. **Map** p313 E5.

Sisters Elisabeth and Suzanne Gervay bought this crumbling grand 1870s mansion at auction in 1992 and embarked on the mammoth task of turning it into a heritage hotel. Today it has 36 rooms, all en suite, each furnished differently. Furniture is in keeping with the grand Victorian style, and any period detail that could be kept has been. The place is awash with original artwork, as Elisabeth is an artist who uses the hotel as a gallery for local talent. There's a comfortable lounge, an old-fashioned bar with a baby

Circular Quay. **Apartments** 67. **Rates** $520-$800. **Credit** AmEx, BC, DC, MC, V. **Map** p310 C1.

Bang next to the Opera House, this five-star complex of one- and two-bedroom apartments delivers what it should – spacious suites with balconies and lovely views, en suite bathrooms, equipped kitchens, two TVs etc. The ECQ Bar downstairs has a spectacular harbour view, while the adjacent Quadrant restaurant offers contemporary Australian cuisine. There's a fully equipped gym and heated indoor pool.

Regents Court Hotel

18 Springfield Avenue, off Darlinghurst Road, Potts Point, NSW 2011 (9358 1533/ fax 9358 1833/www.regentscourt.com.au). CityRail Kings Cross. **Rates** $220-$255. **Credit** AmEx, BC, DC, MC, V. **Map** p312 D3.

Dubbed by UK's *Tatler* magazine as 'Blake's without the pretention or price tag', this modern boutique hotel of studio suites is favoured by young actors and filmbiz types. Based in a restored 1920s building in a leafy cul-de-sac near Kings Cross, it's furnished with 1920s and '30s design classics by the likes of Le Corbusier and Eames. All suites have kitchens, and staff are keen. The verdant rooftop terrace is a popular venue for celebrity interviews.

Saville 2 Bond Street

Corner of George & Bond Streets, CBD, NSW 2000 (9250 9555/fax 9250 9556/ www.savillesuites.com.au). CityRail Wynyard. **Apartments** 169. **Rates** $340 studio; $365 1-bed; $490 2-bed; $1,300 penthouse. **Credit** AmEx, BC, DC, MC, V. **Map** p310 B2.

This stylish place (partly owner-occupied) is in the heart of the financial area, so apartments have full business services, including fax and voicemail, as well as excellent, well-equipped kitchens. There's a small rooftop pool, spa and gym, and buzzy Nelson's Café in the lobby.

Southern Cross Suites Sydney

Corner of Wentworth & Goulburn Streets, Surry Hills, NSW 2000 (9277 3388/1800 888 116/fax 9277 3399/www.southern crosssuites.com.au). CityRail Museum. **Apartments** 120. **Rates** $145 studio; $155 1-bed; $230 2-bed. **Credit** AmEx, BC, DC, MC, V. **Map** p311 C3.

The apartments here (mostly one-bedders) aren't as well provisoned as some places (the kitchenettes are tiny) and tend to the bland in design, but they're brilliantly located – just south of Hyde Park within striking distance of the CBD and Darling Harbour. Also, rates are very reasonable and the staff always friendly.

grand piano and a first-floor sun terrace. Quaife's restaurant (named after the original owner, founder of the colony's medical association) offers indoor and outdoor dining. Three rooms have recently been designated as 'pet friendly'.

Hotel services *Bar. Disabled: adapted rooms. Courtyard. No smoking. Parking (limited, free). Restaurant. Safe. 24hr reception.* **Room services** *Dataport. Refrigerator. TV.*

Sullivans Hotel

21 Oxford Street, between Greens Road & Verona Street, Paddington, NSW 2021 (9361 0211/ fax 9360 3735/www.sullivans.com.au). Bus 378, 380, L82. **Rooms** 64. **Rates** $130-$145 single/ double; $160-$195 family. **Credit** AmEx, BC, DC, MC, V. **Map** p311 D4.

A friendly, family-run hotel right in the heart of Paddo, with cinemas, shops, cafés, art galleries and the market on its doorstep. All rooms have private bathrooms, and family rooms are also available. There's a solar-heated pool and a new fitness room. Free secure parking and bicycle hire are added attractions. Sullivans also offers a free walking tour

of Paddington to help you get your bearings, and complimentary in-house movies and chocs at night. A spacious breakfast café on the ground floor looks out on to Oxford Street.

Hotel services *Café. Disabled: adapted rooms. Courtyard. Gym. No-smoking rooms. Parking (limited, free). Pool (outdoor). Safe.* **Room services** *Dataport. Refrigerator. TV.*

Vibe Rushcutters

100 Bayswater Road, next to Rushcutters Bay Park, Rushcutters Bay, NSW 2011 (8353 8988/1800 835 300/fax 8353 8999/www.vibehotels.com.au). CityRail Edgecliff or Kings Cross. **Rooms** 245. **Rates** from $165 twin/double; from $265 suite. **Credit** AmEx, BC, DC, MC, V. **Map** p312 D3.

This Rushcutters Bay hotel suffered post-2000, but is hoping to restore its glory under the ownership of the new Vibe hotel chain. Brainchild of the Medina apartments group, Vibe aims to plug the market gap for reasonably priced contemporary accommodation with a stylish, finger-on-the-pulse, well, vibe. This is the group's first acquisition, and at time of writing another was about to open in North Sydney. Rooms

Enjoy Victorian splendour at affordable prices at the **Hughenden Hotel**. *See p38.*

have all the usual facilities – minibar, dataport, TV – but attention is also paid to extras such as large fitness rooms and business suites. Guests are expected (or 'empowered') to do things for themselves – use the baggage trolleys to carry their own bags, and access hotel information via the in-room plasma screens. The rooftop pool is smallish and a little exposed on windy days, but the view is quite something. The restaurant, Curve, serves tapas-style food in the day and à la carte meals in the evening. **Hotel services** *Bar. Business centre. Concierge. Disabled: adapted rooms. Gym. No-smoking floors. Parking ($16.50). Pool (outdoor). Restaurant. Roof terrace. Sauna/spa.* **Room services** *Dataport. Minibar. Room service (24hr). TV: cable/pay movies.*

Budget

Golden Sheaf Hotel

429 New South Head Road, at Knox Street, Double Bay, NSW 2028 (9327 5877/fax 9327 8581/ www.goldensheaf.com.au). Ferry Double Bay/bus 323, 324, 325, 326, 327. **Rooms** 8. **Rates** from $88. **Credit** AmEx, BC, MC, V. **Map** p312 F3.

A recent refurbishment to this art deco pub has produced a clutch of impressive rooms at incredibly reasonable prices – a rarity in Double Bay. The rooms (all en suite) are slick and minimalist in design, with brown and cream tones. Some of the original details remain, though, and the contemporary additions blend in inoffensively. The Golden Sheaf is known as Double Bay's rowdiest pub, with a pumping beer garden, live entertainment and the excellent upstairs Soda Bar, so be prepared for noise.

Hotel services *Bar. Courtyard. No-smoking rooms. Restaurant.* **Room services** *Refrigerator. TV: cable.*

Bondi & Coogee Beaches

Expensive

Swiss-Grand Hotel

Corner of Campbell Parade & Beach Road, Bondi Beach, NSW 2026 (9365 5666/www.swissgrand. com.au). CityRail Bondi Junction then bus 380, 381, L82/bus 380, L82. **Rooms** 203. **Rates** $308-$352 single/double; $396-$418 ocean view/spa; $462 family room; $627-$1,650 suite. **Credit** AmEx, BC, DC, MC, V. **Map** p83.

This all-suite hotel, with its kitsch white columns and flamboyant rooftop bars, dominates the north end of Campbell Parade. It's a pretty cool place to stay – if you can afford it. Reception is on the first floor; the entrance is on Campbell Parade through a shopping arcade and up the lifts or stairs. Look up and you'll see galleries of rooms above, serviced by a couple of gaudily lit glass lifts. Most suites have balconies (those at the front have a great Bondi Beach vista), as well as two TVs, a minibar, separate bath and shower and all the usual goodies. There's a rooftop pool and an indoor lap pool, as well as the excellent Samsara Day Spa with its Balinese treatments. In the early evening, head for the popular Garden Terrace to watch the sun sink into the waves.

Hotel services *Babysitting. Bar. Beauty salon. Business centre. Concierge. Disabled: adapted rooms. Gym. No-smoking rooms. Parking (free).*

Pools (indoor & outdoor). Restaurants. Roof terrace. Sauna/spa. **Room services** *Dataport. Minibar. Room service (24hr). Safe. TV: cable/pay movies.*

Moderate

Bondi Beachside Inn

152 Campbell Parade, at Roscoe Street, Bondi Beach, NSW 2026 (9130 5311/fax 9365 2646/www.bondi inn.com.au). CityRail Bondi Junction then bus 380, 381, L82/bus 380, L82. **Rooms** 70. **Rates** $120-$140. **Credit** AmEx, BC, DC, MC, V. **Map** p83.

In a super-sunny location right opposite Bondi Beach, this modern, family-friendly, seven-storey inn has 70 rooms. Some have ocean views; all are en suite, with balconies, air-conditioning and kitchenettes. There's daily maid service, plus luggage storage and wake-up calls, and, most importantly in this busy, busy place, 24-hour free secure parking. Booking is essential in high season.

Hotel services *No smoking. Parking (free). Safe.* **Room services** *Cooking facilities. Refrigerator. TV.*

Coogee Bay Hotel

Corner of Arden Street & Coogee Bay Road, Coogee Beach, NSW 2034 (9665 0000/1800 211 805/fax 9664 1576/www.coogeebayhotel.com.au). Bus 372, 373, 374. **Rooms** 27 Heritage; 51 Boutique. **Rates** $130-$200 Heritage; $220-$280 Boutique. **Credit** AmEx, BC, DC, MC, V.

This pub hotel keeps on winning awards – and deservedly so. It combines a warm, laid-back pub atmosphere with the sort of slick, stylish accommodation you'd expect to find in an upmarket hotel. The modern Boutique wing is pitched around the four-star mark: rooms are huge, with marble bathrooms, balconies, VCRs and, in some, kitchenettes. The Heritage wing in the main part of the pub is a tad less impressive. The brasserie at the front overlooks the beach and has a huge patio; there's an à la carte menu, or you can go for the cook-your-own-steak option. The hotel is also a popular drinking hole (*see p137*).

Hotel services *Bar. Brasserie. Disabled: adapted room. No-smoking floor. Parking (free). Payphone. Safe. 24hr reception.* **Room services** *Dataport. Minibar. TV: cable/VCR.*

Dive Hotel

234 Arden Street, opposite the beach, Coogee Beach, NSW 2034 (9665 5538/fax 9665 4347/ www.divehotel.com.au). Bus 372, 373, 374. **Rooms** 14. **Rates** $165 standard; $180 balcony; $210 ocean view. **Credit** BC, MC, V.

Terry Bunton and Mercedes Mariano have transformed what was once a dingy, run-down guesthouse into an oasis of style. The best rooms in the house are the two large ones at the front, with a view of the sea. All are en suite, with a microwave, fridge, TV and VCR. The bathrooms are chic (if sometimes cramped), decked out in stainless steel and tiny blue tiles. Bed linens come in crisp black and white, while blocks of bold colour brighten up the look. At the

back is a terrace with leafy bamboo and trailing bougainvillea. Despite its 'cool' status, Dive is a friendly place, helped by the presence of the owner's pets, Babe the poodle and Stella the husky.

Hotel services *No air-conditioning. Courtyard. Laundry. No smoking. Safe.* **Room services** *Dataport. Hi-fi. Refrigerator. TV: cable/VCR.*

Hotel Bondi

178 Campbell Parade, at Curlewis Street, Bondi Beach, NSW 2026 (9130 3271/fax 9130 7974/ www.hotelbondi.com.au). CityRail Bondi Junction then bus 380, 381, L82/bus 380, L82. **Rooms** 50. **Rates** $50-$75 single; $95-$150 double; $125-$160 suite; $170-$220 family suite. **Credit** AmEx, BC, MC, V. **Map** p83.

It may be a heritage-listed Bondi landmark, but today the Hotel Bondi boasts a glitzy gaming room, nightclub, big-screen TV sports, DJ bar, bottle shops and every diversion imaginable. Many rooms have views of the beach, others have verandas, and some are en suite. Most also have air-conditioning, or there's usually an electric fan. The decor is a tad kitsch and motel-like, but it's a clean and comfortable place. The five bars include the BomBora Bar screening sporting events and the Sand Bar for pool nuts. The Starfish Café serves steaks and seafood in an al fresco setting. Fun, fun, fun all night long – but fear not, the rooms upstairs are soundproofed.

Hotel services *Bar. Beer garden. Payphone. Restaurant. Safe.* **Room services** *No air-conditioning (some rooms). Refrigerator. TV.*

Ravesi's

118 Campbell Parade, at Hall Street, Bondi Beach, NSW 2026 (9365 4422/fax 9365 1481/ www.ravesis.com.au). CityRail Bondi Junction then bus 380, 381, L82/bus 380, L82. **Rooms** 16. **Rates** $125-$230 double; $295 beachfront double; $260-$450 suite. **Credit** AmEx, BC, MC, V. **Map** p83.

A recent refurbishment has given Ravesi's clutch of designer rooms a new cool status. The Street Bar downstairs– with its glass frontage and groovy fold-back doors – has become the place for Bondi's pretty people to hang out. Upstairs, the guest rooms have a similar vibe. All have private bathrooms and are impeccably furnished and decorated, continuing the hotel's white and brown theme. Best are the six split-level suites, each with its own private terrace and awesome sea views.

Hotel services *Bars. Disabled: adapted rooms. No smoking. Parking ($8 each entry). Restaurant.* **Room services** *Dataport. Minibar. Room service (noon-10pm). Safe. TV: cable/DVD.*

Budget

Indy's Bondi Beach Backpackers

35A Hall Street, between Gould & O'Brien Streets, Bondi Beach, NSW 2026 (8300 8802/fax 9365 4994/www.indysbackpackers.com.au). CityRail Bondi Junction then bus 380, 381, L82/bus 380, L82. **Rooms** 27. **Rates** $23-$26 dorm; $65 twin. **Credit** BC, MC, V. **Map** p83.

Go on, take the plunge at friendly, beachside **Dive Hotel**. *See p42.*

This exuberant hostel (open since 1995) runs on adrenalin – of both the staff and their guests. The place caters for sports lovers, and anyone keen to take on the waves. It can supply free beach equipment, including bodyboards, fins, masks, snorkels and fishing rods. For landlubbers there are free mountain bikes and rollerblades. A small fee is charged for surfboards and wetsuits. Dorms come with six, eight or ten beds, and there are also 16 rooms in a nearby annex on Campbell Parade, which can be configured into doubles or triples. Other facilities include a fully equipped kitchen, laundry service and air-conditioned TV room, with 400 movies on DVD/video and a wide-screen TV.
Hotel services *No air-conditioning. Courtyard. Kitchen. Internet access. Laundry. No smoking. Payphone. TV room.* **Room services** *No phone.*

Lamrock Lodge

19 Lamrock Avenue, at Consett Avenue, Bondi Beach, NSW 2026 (9130 5063/fax 9300 9582/www.lamrock lodge.com). CityRail Bondi Junction then bus 380, 381, L82/bus 380, L82. **Rooms** 54. **Rates** $18 dorm; $50 twin/double. **Credit** AmEx, BC, MC, V. **Map** p83.
Just two minutes from Bondi Beach, this popular, three-storey hostel pulls in the backpackers with its TVs, microwaves and fridges in every room. Choose from four-share dorms, triples, doubles and singles; rates are better the longer you stay. Furniture is minimal, basic and generally clean, and bed linen, quilts and pillows are supplied. There are lots of vending machines for midnight snacks, plus 24-hour security and laid-back staff keen to offer you the lowdown on Bondi.
Hotel services *No air-conditioning. Courtyard. Internet access. Kitchen. Laundry. No smoking. Payphone. Safe.* **Room services** *Microwave. Refrigerator. TV: cable. No phone.*

Moderate

Tricketts Luxury B&B

270 Glebe Point Road, opposite Leichhardt Street, Glebe, NSW 2037 (9552 1141/fax 9692 9462/ www.tricketts.com.au). Bus 431. **Rooms** 7. **Rates** $176-$198. **Credit** AmEx, BC, DC, MC, V.
A wealthy merchant's house in the 1880s, a boys' home in the 1920s and then a children's courthouse, 270 Glebe Point Road had something of an institutional feel when owner Liz Tricketts set about transforming it into a B&B. It took three months to restore the cedar staircase alone, but her painstaking work was worth it. The seven guest rooms (one king-, five queen- and one twin-bedded room), all with antiques and Persian rugs covering the polished floors, are decorated in different styles. All are en suite, and the house has air-conditioning and central heating. In summer, breakfast is served on the rear deck; in cooler months it is in the conservatory.
Hotel services *Garden. Internet access. No smoking. Parking (free). Safe.* **Room services** *TV.*

Budget

Alishan International Guesthouse

100 Glebe Point Road, between Mitchell Street & St Johns Road, Glebe, NSW 2037 (9566 4048/ fax 9525 4686/www.alishan.com.au). Bus 431, 432, 433. **Rooms** 19. **Rates** $27-$33 dorm; $88-$99 single; $99-$115 double; $154 family. **Credit** AmEx, BC, MC, V. **Map** p311 A4.
This airy, plant-filled, century-old mansion house is popular with overseas travellers and business folk. The spacious dining room/lounge has a cool black

Ravesi's: for Bondi views. *See p42.*

This luxury hostel and motel easily deserves its five-star backpacker rating. Set just off Newtown's lively main strip, it prides itself on being a centre for the arty crowd (Sydney Uni, the School of Dramatic Arts and Enmore Theatre are all nearby). The place is spotless, and the rooms (with ceiling fans, but no air-con) make much use of natural materials: pine bunks, exposed brick walls, terracotta floors. Some rooms have TVs and refrigerators. There is a large modern kitchen, laundry, indoor and outdoor dining areas, TV common room and free activities, such as ping-pong, billiards and some gym equipment. It's a sociable place to hang your sun hat, so expect to join in the free wine and cheese nights, pool comps and soccer and rugby matches.
Hotel services *Garden. Internet access. Kitchen. Laundry. No smoking. Parking ($5). Payphone. Pool (outdoor). Safe. TV room.* **Room services** *No air-conditioning. No phone.*

Wattle House
44 Hereford Street, between Glebe Point Road & Walsh Avenue, Glebe, NSW 2037 (9552 4997/ fax 9660 2528/www.wattlehouse.com.au). Bus 431, 432, 433. **Rooms** 9. **Rates** $27 dorm; $40 per person twin/double. **Credit** MC, V.
The Wattle House's owners have slowly but surely restored this lovely old building to its original (c.1877) Victorian grandeur. Spotless, tidy and friendly, it's both non-smoking and alcohol-free. Free tea, hot chocolate and soup is offered in the self-catering kitchen, and each guest is given their own kit of crockery and cutlery. All linens and towels are provided, there are dressing gowns in the twin and double rooms, and plenty of storage space. The house also has a reading room with 200 books, a laundry, a TV/video lounge and beautiful landscaped gardens. Don't be surprised if you find a teddy bear on your bed; the owner is a collector and likes to put her bears to work. Advance booking is advisable, especially in summer.
Hotel services *No air-conditioning. Garden. Kitchen. Laundry. No smoking. Payphone. Safe. TV room.* **Room services** *No phone.*

stone floor and rattan furnishings, and there's a huge, well-equipped kitchen. There are dorms, simple single, double and family rooms, plus a special Japanese-style twin room with low beds and tatami mats on the floor. All rooms have private bathrooms, but there is no air-conditioning or in-room phones.
Hotel services *No air-conditioning. Disabled: adapted room. Garden. Internet access. Kitchen. Laundry. No smoking. Parking ($5). Payphone. Safe. TV room.* **Room services** *No phone.*

Australian Sunrise Lodge
485 King Street, between Camden & Alice Streets, Newtown, NSW 2042 (9550 4999/fax 9550 4457). CityRail Newtown. **Rooms** 18. **Rates** $59-$79 single; $69-$89 double; $79-$129 triple; $99-$179 family. **Credit** AmEx, BC, DC, MC, V. **Map** p93.
Located in Newtown's King Street (turn left from the station), this is a small, quiet, family-run place with a motel feel. The guest rooms (many with balconies overlooking a courtyard) are well-equipped, although they lack telephones and air-conditioning (there are ceiling fans, and electric fans are available on request). Some rooms are en suite. There is also a communal kitchen and lounge. The lodge is recommended by Sydney University for off-campus accommodation, so expect a studenty clientele.
Hotel services *Courtyard. Disabled. No smoking. Parking (free). Payphone.* **Room services** *No air-conditioning. Refrigerator. TV. No phone.*

Billabong Gardens
5-11 Egan Street, at King Street, Newtown, NSW 2042 (9550 3236/fax 9550 4352/www.billabong gardens.com.au). CityRail Newtown. **Rooms** 34. **Rates** $20-$23 dorm; $49 single; $66-$88 double. **Credit** BC, MC, V. **Map** p93.

North Shore

Expensive

Rydges North Sydney
54 McLaren Street, between Miller & Walker Streets, North Sydney, NSW 2060 (9922 1311/1800 251 565/fax 9922 4939/www.rydges.com.au). CityRail North Sydney. **Rooms** 166. **Rates** $285-$300 double; $335-$385 suite. **Credit** AmEx, BC, DC, MC, V.
Essentially a business hotel, this branch of the Rydges chain is located just over the Harbour Bridge, close to North Sydney's busy business and shopping district. All rooms have a private bath and shower, and many of the deluxe rooms/suites have a spectacular harbour view. There are also 18 'I Rooms' with computer systems designed to run like an office network, as well as executive boardrooms,

video conference facilities and even a conference concierge service. The Gnomes bar and restaurant is a tad dull, but serves breakfast, lunch and dinner. **Hotel services** *Babysitting. Bar. Business centre. Disabled: adapted rooms. No-smoking floors. Parking ($10). Restaurant. Safe.* **Room services** *Dataport. Minibar. Room service (6.30am-midnight). TV: cable/pay movies.*

Budget

Glenferrie Lodge

12A Carabella Street, at Peel Street, Kirribilli, NSW 2061 (9955 1685/fax 9929 9439/www.glenferrie lodge.com). Ferry Kirribilli. **Rooms** 70. **Rates** $35 dorm; $65 single; $95-$125 double; $145 family. **Credit** BC, MC, V.

A handsome, cavernous house located on Sydney Harbour in the wealthy suburb of Kirribilli, Glenferrie Lodge has huge verandas and charming, landscaped gardens. Rooms are not air-conditioned, but have ceiling fans. Some have TVs. The shared facilities are clean if basic, and there are ample bathrooms throughout. The guest lounge offers cable TV and internet access, and the dining room serves breakfast and dinner five nights a week. **Hotel services** *Internet access. Laundry. No smoking. Payphone. TV room.* **Room services** *No air-conditioning. No phone. Refrigerator.*

Northern Beaches

Deluxe

Jonah's

69 Bynya Road, between Norma & Surf Road, Palm Beach, NSW 2108 (9974 5599/fax 9974 1212/www.jonahs.com.au). Bus L90. **Rooms** 11. **Rates** *Mon-Thur, Sun* $399 double; $499 penthouse. *Fri, Sat* $650 double; $750 penthouse. **Credit** AmEx, BC, DC, MC, V.

Jonah's smart restaurant (*see p163*) is well known in Palm Beach as the place to dine and be seen to dine. In February 2004, eight more rooms were added to the existing three, including a super-deluxe penthouse. All are very luxurious and contemporary in style, with ocean views from private balconies, king-sized beds, TV, CD/DVD player and limestone bathrooms with jacuzzi spas. Weekend prices are always per couple and include an evening meal and breakfast. From Sunday to Thursday you can book just the room. **Hotel services** *Babysitting. Bar. Garden. Parking (free). No smoking. Restaurant. Safe.* **Room services** *Dataport. Refrigerator. Spa. TV: DVD/VCR.*

Expensive

Manly Pacific Sydney

55 North Steyne, between Raglan & Denison Streets, Manly, NSW 2059 (9977 7666/fax 9977 7822/www.accorhotels.com.au). Ferry Manly.

Rooms 159. **Rates** $350-$400 double; $650 suite. **Credit** AmEx, BC, DC, MC, V. **Map** p104.

Formerly the Manly Pacific Parkroyal, this fairly standard four-star hotel on the beach is now part of the multinatonal Accor chain. It has 159 rooms, all with balconies, over six floors. There's one restaurant and two bars, one looking out over the ocean. The Charlton Bar attracts a pub crowd with its pool tables and music. If the beach over the road is too crowded, there's always the heated rooftop pool, plus a spa, sauna and gym. **Hotel services** *Babysitting. Bars. Concierge. Courtyard. Disabled: adapted rooms. Gym. Parking ($11). Pool (outdoor). Restaurant. Safe. Sauna/spa.* **Room services** *Dataport. Minibar. Room service (24hr). TV: cable.*

Moderate

The **Newport Mirage** (Queens Parade, Newport, NSW 2106, 9997 7011, fax 9997 5217, www.newportmirage.com.au) opposite the **Newport Arms Hotel** (*see below*) has 47 rooms ($187 double), great facilities and is very popular with wedding parties.

Barrenjoey House

1108 Barrenjoey Road, opposite Palm Beach Wharf, Palm Beach, NSW 2108 (9974 4001/ fax 9974 5008/www.barrenjoeyhouse.com.au). Bus L90. **Rooms** 7. **Rates** $100-$195. **Credit** AmEx, BC, DC, MC, V.

A boutique guesthouse since 1923, this place is a central meeting point for visitors and locals. Three rooms are en suite, four have shared bathrooms, all are spotless and comfortable. The best rooms are the ones at the front with water views. Decor is cool and white, with beach house-style furniture: wooden stepladders used as towel rails, side tables draped in white tablecloths and pretty bowls of flowers. **Hotel services** *Bar. No smoking. Restaurant. Terrace. TV room.* **Room services** *No air-conditioning. No phone.*

Newport Arms Hotel

2 Kalinya Street, at Queens Parade, Newport, NSW 2106 (9997 4900/fax 9979 6919/www.newport arms.com.au). Bus L88, L90. **Rooms** 9. **Rates** $130 double; extra $30 per person family room. **Credit** AmEx, BC, DC, MC, V.

About a 40-minute drive from the CBD, the Newport Arms is on the shores of Pittwater, overlooking Church Point, Scotland Island and Ku-ring-gai Chase National Park. There are eight doubles, all with basic furniture and private bathrooms, and one family room that sleeps six. The hotel is also one of the most popular pubs in the area: its 'Saturday night at sunset' is a huge local night out, with cheap drinks and music from 8pm until late. The garden has the northern beaches' largest outdoor TV screen, which shows Fox Sports daily. **Hotel services** *Bar. Bistro. No-smoking. Parking (free). Payphone. Restaurant. Safe.* **Room services** *No phone. TV: cable.*

Periwinkle Guest House

18-19 East Esplanade, at Ashburner Streeet, Manly, NSW 2095 (9977 4668/fax 9977 6308/ www.periwinkle.citysearch.com.au). Ferry Manly. **Rooms** 18. **Rates** $99-$152 single; $130-$185 double. **Credit** BC, MC, V. **Map** p104.

This 1895 Federation building, with its iron-lace verandas and period charm, has been likened in style to the French Quarter of New Orleans, but the owners are adamant 'it's Aussie to the core'. Its position on the inner harbour beach of Manly Cove couldn't be better, within easy reach of Manly ferry wharf and such attractions as Oceanworld. Bedrooms have traditional ceiling fans, fireplaces and cane furniture; most are en suite. Heaters and electric blankets are provided in winter. Guests can use the kitchen and the laundry, and there's a court-yard with seating and an outdoor barbecue.
Hotel services *Kitchen. Laundry. No smoking. Parking (limited, free). Payphone. Safe. TV room.* **Room services** *No air-conditioning. No phone. Refrigerator. TV.*

Budget

Pittwater YHA

Morning Bay, Pittwater, NSW 2105 (9999 5748/ fax 9999 5749/www.yha.com.au). Ferry/water taxi Halls Wharf then 10mins walk. **Rooms** 8. **Rates** $23 dorm; $60 twin/double. **Credit** BC, MC, V.

If you only stay in one YHA, make it this one. You can't get here by car, which is probably the reason it's remained so special. It's an hour's bus journey from Sydney to Church Point, then a ferry ride to Halls Wharf, followed by a steep, ten-minute climb through the bush. If you arrive after dark, bring a torch. But it's worth it. The stone and wooden hill-side lodge sits hidden in the trees in Ku-ring-gai Chase National Park overlooking Morning Bay. The wildlife is breathtaking: red and green rosellas flit through the branches, and most visitors see at least one laughing kookaburra, as well as wallabies, possums running along the roof at night and goannas baking in the sun. There are boats and canoes for guests' use, and you can swim in the nearby bay or take off on a bush walk. It's a small place, with just 32 beds in eight rooms. You'll need to bring all your food – there are no shops – and bedding.
Hotel services *BBQ. Kitchen. Laundry. Lounge. No smoking. Payphone. Safe.* **Room services** *No air-conditioning. No phone.*

Sydney Beachhouse YHA

4 Collaroy Street, at Pittwater Road, Collaroy, NSW 2097 (9981 1177/fax 9981 1114/ www.yha.com.au). Bus 155, 156, L88, L90. **Rooms** 56. **Rates** $26 dorm; $65-$84 twin/double; $104 family. **Credit** BC, MC, V.

This YHA hostel has a reputation as one of the best, and is brilliantly located in the heart of the northern beaches – not in the millionaire's part, but in back-packer-friendly Collaroy, right opposite the beach. Rooms are bright, clean and basic; most sleep four in bunk beds and have shared bathrooms, but there are also twins and family rooms. Surfboards, boo-gie boards and pedal bikes are free for guests, and there's a smallish, solar-heated outdoor pool, a games and pool room, and a lounge with a log fire for chilly winter nights. If you don't like kids, steer clear in the school hols when interstate and country families pile in for their seaside sunshine breaks.
Hotel services *BBQ. Disabled: adapted room (family). Internet café. Kitchen. Parking (free). Payphone. Pool (outdoor). TV room.* **Room services** *No phone.*

The South

Expensive

Novotel Brighton Beach

Corner of the Grand Parade & Princess Street, Brighton-le-Sands, NSW 2216 (9597 7111/1300 656 565/fax 9597 7877/www.accorhotels.com.au/ novotel). CityRail Rockdale then bus 475, 478, 479. **Rooms** 296. **Rates** $294 double; $334-$374 bay view; $714 penthouse. **Credit** AmEx, BC, DC, MC, V.

Five minutes from Sydney International Airport and 25 minutes from the CBD, the Novotel has all that a stopover traveller requires, including an overhead walkway to the beach. With a shopping plaza, pool, fitness centre, beauty salon and nearby golf courses, everything is here – except for Sydney proper, of course. The uninspiring rooms all have private bath-rooms and balconies with views inland or over Botany Bay. There are three bars and a restaurant.
Hotel services *Babysitting. Bars. Beauty salon. Business centre. Concierge. Disabled: adapted rooms. Gym. No-smoking floors. Parking ($10). Pool (indoor & outdoor). Safe. Sauna/spa.* **Room services** *Dataport. Minibar. Room service (24hr). TV: pay movies.*

Rydges Cronulla

20-26 The Kingsway, at Gerrale Street, Cronulla, NSW 2230 (9527 3100/fax 9523 9541/ www.rydges.com.au). CityRail Cronulla. **Rooms** 84. **Rates** $280 double; $380 suite; $460 penthouse. **Credit** AmEx, BC, DC, MC, V.

This imposing boutique hotel, part of the Rydges chain, offers clean and comfortable rooms with spectacular ocean views. All rooms have en suite bathrooms and at least one balcony, plus a desk and workstation area, TV and free in-house movies. Numerous facilities include a pool, sauna and spa, and an aromatherapy, massage and reflexology clinic. The Raffles restaurant is open daily for breakfast, lunch and dinner, and there's an al fresco dining space on a terrace overlooking Cronulla Beach. A good choice if you enjoy the beach life, and the Royal National Park is nearby.
Hotel services *Bar. Beauty salon. Disabled: adapted rooms. Garden. No-smoking floors. Parking (free). Pool (outdoor). Restaurant. Safe. Sauna/spa.* **Room services** *Dataport. Minibar. Room service (6.30am-10pm). TV.*

Sightseeing

Introduction

Before you start, get your bearings here.

Fame follows function:
Sydney Opera House.

Although the centre of Sydney is relatively small and easy to navigate, the city does sprawl. Add in the complications provided by that stunning harbour and many lose the plot. But it's not as hard as it looks – honestly. The Harbour Bridge separates the north from the south, east and west, while the much newer suspension bridge, the Anzac Bridge, connects the city with the western suburbs.

Arranged by area, our Sightseeing chapters start with **Central Sydney**. This stretches from Circular Quay and the Rocks area, through the CBD with its high-rise spires, shops and historic sights, to Chinatown, family-friendly Darling Harbour, gay central Darlinghurst and neighbouring Surry Hills, colourful and seedy Kings Cross, smarter Potts Point and Woolloomooloo with its slick wharf conversion. Next are the **Eastern Suburbs**, the glamour home to the city's movers, shakers and just plain rich. Here you can shop till you drop in the boutiques of Paddington, Double Bay and Woollahra and eat and drink yourself silly in a plethora of the hippest bars, cafés and restaurants. The area extends via picturesque harbourside suburbs all the way to South

Head and also includes Bondi Beach, the closest ocean beach to the city and a unique combination of city frenzy and 'no worries' seaside languor.

Moving west is the **Inner West**, home to one-time slums renovated into quaint cottages in waterfront Balmain, new-age chic in Glebe, a feisty Italian quarter in Leichhardt and gay, studenty, innovative Newtown.

On the north side of the Harbour Bridge is the **North Shore**, including well-heeled Kirribilli, Milsons Point and McMahons Point with their 'dress circle' views of the Bridge and Opera House, and the high-end suburbs of Cremorne, Mosman and Balmoral. North Sydney, the city's second business district, is also here. Manly is the start of the **Northern Beaches**, a string of glorious ocean beaches, inaccessible by train, running all the way up to Palm Beach, playground of millionaires.

Parramatta & the West heads out into greater Sydney and the geographic centre of the city, Parramatta. There are a few historic sites here, thanks to its status as the country retreat for the colony's first governors. Sports fans will be more interested in the Olympic

Park complex, eight kilometres (five miles) east in Homebush Bay. Next comes the **South**, where you'll find historic Botany Bay, the site of James Cook's landfall in 1770. But today's gem of the south is Cronulla, a burgeoning seaside suburb with the feel of a Queensland sunshine resort.

Finally comes **Sydney's Best Beaches**, a chapter devoted to the pick of the city's surfing, swimming and sunbathing spots.

WHERE TO START

If you've come by plane, you may already have glimpsed the Opera House majestically bobbing on Sydney's crenellated harbour. If you're one of the chosen few arriving on a ritzy cruise ship, you'll probably wake up slap bang next to it. In any case, it is this icon that most visitors gravitate towards first and, fortuitously, it is a good place to find your bearings.

The Opera House is on the east side of Circular Quay and next to the main entrance to the Royal Botanic Gardens. From Circular Quay you can catch ferries over to the north shore and Manly with its ocean beach, or other destinations on the south side of the harbour, including Darling Harbour, Balmain and Watsons Bay. The cute gold and green ferries are a great way to see the city; tickets cost a little more than the bus or train, but the journey is a delight. Also at Circular Quay is a CityRail station for trains, and numerous bus stops for routes throughout the city.

The best way to start your exploration, though, is on foot, around the Quay and into the Botanic Gardens, and over to the Quay's west side where you'll find the Museum of Contemporary Art, the Overseas Passenger Terminal with its cool bars and restaurants and, behind, the historic area of the Rocks, to buy the more obvious souvenirs and visit the Harbour Bridge. Next jump on a harbour cruise – there are numerous options – to get a good idea of the layout of the harbour and spot some of the city's ritzier waterfront homes (is that Nicole Kidman vacuuming her drapes?).

Now you can dive into the CBD. From Circular Quay a series of parallel roads – serviced by buses and trains, and at some points by the Metro Monorail (an expensive, tourist-oriented service that circles the CBD at first-floor level, but also easily walkable – lead through Sydney's commercial and shopping areas to Town Hall. A slowish walk including a bit of window shopping from the Quay to the Town Hall will take about 30 minutes. From here you can walk west to the bustling and very touristy Darling Harbour or catch a train or bus to Kings Cross, the city's sinful heart, or a host of other suburbs.

TRANSPORT AND INFORMATION

The CityRail system is, in general, easy to understand, and services most of the main points of interest – apart from Manly (best reached by ferry or JetCat) and Bondi Beach (by bus from Bondi Junction or Circular Quay). Better, though, are the buses, partly because you get to look out of the window (much of the train line is underground) and partly because they go everywhere and are more frequent. The driver or other passengers will be more than happy to tell you where you need to get off; just ask – Sydneysiders like nothing more than showing off their city. The ferries are the best – and most fun – way to get to the north shore and other harbourside spots.

There are lots of good-value travel passes covering a combination of transport types or specific areas or journeys. If you're pressed for time, consider one of the two **Sydney Explorer** buses (see p51); with these you can visit most of the sights in quick succession, and pile a lot into a day. A **SydneyPass** (see p51) offers even more options. For details on all methods of public transport, see p279.

It's also worth arming yourself with as much practical information as you can. Start with a map – available at the information desk at Circular Quay next to the CityRail station, or at the **Sydney Visitor Centre** (see p292) in the Rocks. While you're there you can find more information about tours. Another port of call should be **Cadman's Cottage** (see p292), where you can learn about Sydney's impressive national parks.

Tours

Tickets for many tours are available from **Australian Travel Specialists** (9317 3402, www.atstravel.com.au), which has outlets at Wharf 6 at Circular Quay and the Harbourside Festival Marketplace at Darling Harbour. The **Opera House** (see p60) runs its own guided tours. For a look at Sydney's seamier side, try an evening walking tour through the Rocks with **Ghost Tours** (9240 8788/ www.ghosttours.com.au) or a drive in a 1960s Cadillac hearse with **Destiny Tours** (9555 2700/www.destinytours.com.au).

General

See Sydney & Beyond Smartvisit Card

1300 661 711/9247 6611/www.seesydneycard.com. **Rates** *1-day* $65/$80. *2-day* $109/$145. *3-day* $139/$195. *7-day* $199/$265. Concessions for 5-15s. This swipe card plus guide booklet gives you free entry to over 40 attractions across Sydney and the

Blue Mountains. It's certainly handy, but you'll need to cram in a lot to make it worth it, so check details first. The higher-priced rates also include free transport on ferries, buses and CityRail. Available from various outlets, including the visitor centres. There are similar cards for Melbourne and Tasmania.

On foot

Aboriginal Experiences

Depart from Aboriginal Art Shop, Sydney Opera House, Bennelong Point, Circular Quay (8509 5931/ margretc@optusnet.com.au). CityRail/ferry Circular Quay. **Tickets** $30-$65; $25.50-$55.25 concessions. **No credit cards. Map** p310 C1.
Margret Mhuragun Campbell and her husband offer tours that explore the history of the local Gadigal Aborigines and their relationship to the harbour and foreshores, and the use of native foods and medicines. The tours (one hour or two-and-a-half hours) traverse the area around the Opera House, Botanic Gardens and the Rocks. It's best to book 48 hours in advance.

The Rocks Pub Tour

Depart from Cadman's Cottage, 110 George Street, at Argyle Street, The Rocks (1800 067 676/ www.therockspubtour.com). CityRail/ferry Circular Quay. **Tours** 5.45pm Mon-Sat. **Tickets** $29.50. **Credit** BC, MC, V. **Map** p310 C1.
A civilised alternative to a pub crawl, this two-hour tour pops into some of Sydney's heritage pubs for a cleansing ale and a dose of local history.

The Rocks Walking Tours

Depart from Shop K4, Kendall Lane, off Argyle Street, The Rocks (9247 6678/www.rockswalking tours.com.au). CityRail/ferry Circular Quay. **Tours** 10.30am, 12.30pm, 2.30pm Mon-Fri; 11.30am, 2pm Sat, Sun. **Tickets** $18; $10.50-$14 concessions; $46.50 family. **Credit** BC, MC, V. **Map** p310 C1.
Explore the picturesque heritage area of Sydney on lively 90-minute guided tours.

Sydney Architecture Walks

Depart from Museum of Sydney, corner of Bridge & Phillip Streets, CBD (9518 6866/www.sydney architecture.org). CityRail/ferry Circular Quay. **Tours** 10.30am Wed, Sat **Tickets** (incl entry to the Museum of Sydney) $20; $15 concessions. **Credit** AmEx, BC, MC, V. **Map** p310 C2.
Operated by the Historic Houses Trust, these two-hour tours conducted by young architects reveal the diversity of Sydney's architecture, from its gritty industrial past to controversial contemporary

Action stations

Whether you climb over it, speed through its waters or fly high above it, Sydney's famous harbour is licensed to thrill.

Aussie Duck

Depart from corner of Argyle & Harrington Streets, The Rocks (9251 7774/ www.aussieduck.com). CityRail/ferry Circular Quay. **Tours** 10.30am, 12.30pm, 2.30pm, Thur-Sun. **Tickets** $49; $29-$37 concessions; $136 family. **Credit** AmEx, BC, MC, V. **Map** p310 C1.
Originally designed for military use, the very odd-looking, tank-like amphibious duck has been adapted as a civilian pleasure vehicle with air-conditioning and toilets. On the 90-minute tour the Aussie Duck weaves through the heart of Sydney on huge wheels, then transforms itself into a sea-going vehicle as two roof-mounted pontoons are lowered by hydraulic arms. You even get a free duck quacker to wave out of the window.

BridgeClimb

5 Cumberland Street, between Argyle & George Streets, The Rocks (9240 1100/ 8274 7777/www.bridgeclimb.com). CityRail/ferry Circular Quay. **Tickets**
$155-$225; $100-$175 concessions. No under-12s. **Credit** AmEx, BC, DC, MC, V. **Map** p310 B/C1.
The three-and-a-half-hour climb to the top of the Sydney Harbour Bridge (pictured) is, thankfully, less arduous and much safer than it appears. At 134 metres (440 feet) above sea level, the views from the top of the arch are stunning, and the commentary on the history of the bridge is fascinating. It's hugely popular so book well ahead, especially for night and weekend climbs. Revellers should note that all climbers are breath-tested and must have a blood alcohol level under 0.05%. Climbs leave every ten to 20 minutes daily from early morning to night, with dawn climbs during the summer.

Harbour Jet

Depart from Convention Jetty, between the Convention Centre & Harbourside Shopping complex, Darling Harbour (1300 887 373/ www.harbourjet.com). LightRail/Monorail Convention. **Tickets** from $60; $40 concessions. **Credit** AmEx, BC, DC, MC, V. **Map** p311 B3.
If you haven't whizzed about on a 420hp jet boat before then be prepared for some

Sightseeing

structures. There are two regular tours ('Sydney' on Wed, 'Utzon & the Sydney Opera House' on Sat), plus two others held intermittently; call for details.

By bus

Sydney Buses

13 1500/www.sta.nsw.gov.au.
The government-run Sydney Buses offer a great range of tourist services. For more information on travelling by bus, *see p279.*
DayTripper *1-day* $15; $7.50 concessions.
This one-day pass gives you access to regular rail, bus and ferry services, but not premium services (such as the Explorer buses and Manly JetCat).
Red Sydney Explorer *1-day* $30; $15 concessions; $75 family.
This red bus offers unlimited travel around the highlights of Sydney. The route covers Sydney Cove, the Opera House, Royal Botanic Gardens, Mrs Macquarie's Chair, the Art Gallery of NSW, Kings Cross, Chinatown, Powerhouse Museum, Star City Casino, Darling Harbour, under the Harbour Bridge, Queen Victoria Building, the Rocks – and more. Jump on and off as you please. Services (approximately every 18 minutes) start at Circular Quay, but

can be picked up at any of the red stops en route. The full circuit takes about 100 minutes. You can buy tickets from the driver (no credit cards).
Blue Bondi Explorer *1-day* $30; $15 concessions; $75 family.
This blue bus concentrates on the eastern side of town, stopping at Kings Cross and Rose Bay Convent before hitting the beaches of Bondi, Bronte, Clovelly and Coogee. A short run northwards takes in Watsons Bay and the Gap. The bus departs daily every 30 minutes from Circular Quay, but you can board anywhere along the route. Buy tickets from the driver (no credit cards). There's also a two-day twin ticket ($50; $25 concessions; $125 family), allowing unlimited travel on the Sydney Explorer and the Bondi Explorer for any two days in a seven-day period.
SydneyPass *3-day* $90; $45 concessions; $225 family. *5-day* $120; $60 concessions; $300 family. *7-day* $140; $70 concessions; $350 family.
The SydneyPass is the best-value package if you want to pack in a lot; available for three, five or seven days, it gives unlimited access to the Red Sydney Explorer, the Blue Bondi Explorer and all Sydney Ferry cruises, as well as regular bus, ferry and CityRail services and return travel on the AirportLink train.

serious high-speed fun, pumped up with rock music. Choose from a 35-minute Jet Blast Adventure departing several times each afternoon; a 50-minute Sydney Harbour

Adventure spin leaving twice daily; and an 80-minute Middle Harbour Adventure departing daily; call for exact times. Life jackets are provided for the wild (and wet) ride.

Ocean Extreme

Depart from Cockle Bay Marina, Wheat Road, Darling Harbour (0414 800 046/ www.oceanextreme.com.au). CityRail Town Hall/Monorail Darling Park. **Tickets** $80-$100. **Credit** AmEx, BC, MV, V. **Map** p311 B3.
Take a spin around the harbour in a rigid inflatable, Australia's only commercially operated Special Forces vessel. There are usually two tours daily (40 or 60 mins), with room for eight passengers.

Sydney Harbour Parasailing

Depart from near Manly Wharf, Manly (9977 6781/www.parasail.net). Ferry Manly. **Tickets** $65 solo; $110 tandem. **Credit** AmEx, BC, MC, V. **Map** p104.
Sightseeing with a rush of adrenalin – get strapped into a harness and flung 150 metres (490 feet) above Sydney Harbour while being towed along by a speed boat for ten minutes. The season is from October to May, and there are several departures a day.

By coach

Australian Pacific Touring

Depart from Coach Interchange, Lower Level, Star City Casino, Pirrama Road, Pyrmont (1 300 655 965/www.aptouring.com.au). CityRail Town Hall then 15min walk/LightRail Star City/bus 443, 888. **Tickets** from $52. **Credit** AmEx, BC, DC, MC, V. **Map** p310 A2.

APT's numerous trips include half-day Sydney and beaches tours, a night tour and 4WD day trips to the Blue Mountains.

Gray Line Tours

Depart from Wharf 4, Circular Quay (9252 4499/ www.grayline.com.au). CityRail/ferry Circular Quay. **Tickets** from $48. **Credit** AmEx, BC, DC, MC, V. **Map** p310 C2.

Gray Line offers a variety of sightseeing tours in and around Sydney, including one combined with a wildlife park sortie, where you can cuddle a roo.

Sydney by Diva

Depart from outside Oxford Hotel, Taylor Square, at Oxford Street, Darlinghurst (9360 5557/ www.sydneybydiva.com). Bus 378, 380, 382. **Tours** 5pm Sun. **Tickets** $60 economy; $80 first-class. **Credit** AmEx, BC, MC, DC, V. **Map** p311 C4.

Climb aboard a luxury coach for an outlandish and memorable three-hour comedy tour of Sydney's tourist spots, hosted by one (or two) of the city's top drag queens. If you choose the economy option, be prepared for wisecracks.

By boat

Perhaps Sydney's greatest attraction is its harbour, and the best way to see it is from the water. For more on travelling by ferry, *see p280.*

Sydney Ferries

Depart from Circular Quay (13 1500/www.sta. nsw.gov.au). CityRail/ferry Circular Quay. **Credit** AmEx, BC, MC, V. **Map** p310 C2.

Sightseeing cruises *Morning Harbour Cruise* $15; $7.50 concessions; $37.50 family. *Afternoon Harbour Cruise* $22; $11 concessions; $55 family. *Evening Harbour Lights Cruise* $19; $9.50 concessions; $47.50 family.

The cheapest sightseeing cruises are aboard the NSW state government-operated Sydney Ferries. On offer are a one-hour morning cruise (10.30am daily), a two-and-a-half-hour afternoon cruise (1pm weekdays, 12.30pm weekends and public holidays) – the best option for seeing most of the harbour – and a 90-minute evening cruise (8pm Monday to Saturday), which travels east as far as Double Bay and west to Goat Island.

Parramatta RiverCat $7; $3.50 concessions.

A comfortable hour-long run inland aboard a sleek catamaran that heads past unspoiled bays, old industrial areas, untouristy suburbs and the site of the 2000 Olympics. The last stop is Parramatta.

Captain Cook Cruises

Depart from Wharf 6, Circular Quay (9206 1111/ www.captaincook.com.au). CityRail/ferry Circular Quay. **Tickets** $20-$396. **Credit** AmEx, BC, DC, MC, V. **Map** p310 C2.

One of the biggest cruise operators, Captain Cook has been in business for over 30 years. There are 20 sightseeing and dining tours departing daily, from the basic Coffee Cruise (10am and 2.15pm, $39) to the Opera Afloat Dinner Cruise ($99) and a two-night cruise where you stay on board. The boats are huge and modern, but offer a less-intimate experience than the old-fashioned Sydney ferries.

Matilda Cruises

Depart from Jetty 6, Circular Quay (9264 7377/ www.matilda.com.au). CityRail/ferry Circular Quay. **Tickets** from $22. **Credit** AmEx, BC, DC, MC, V. **Map** p310 C2.

Matilda's unrestricted get-on/get-off sightseeing tours run eight times daily. The one-hour Rocket Harbour Express stops at Darling Harbour, Circular Quay, the Opera House, Watsons Bay and Taronga Zoo, while the 35-minute Manly Rocket Express stops at Darling Harbour, Circular Quay and Rose Bay on the way to Manly. There are also coffee, lunch and dinner cruises plus combined tickets for a cruise and a visit to the zoo or aquarium. Or you can charter various boats, including sailing catamarans.

By air

Cloud Nine Balloons

1300 555 711/www.cloud9balloonflights.com. **Tickets** from $240; $25 breakfast; $25 transfer from city. **Credit** AmEx, BC, MC, V.

Lifting off at dawn (weather permitting) from Parramatta Park, enjoy a tranquil two-hour balloon ride over the city followed by a champagne breakfast. Other tours are available.

Seaplane Safaris

1300 732 247/9371 3577/www.seaplanesafaris. com.au. **Tickets** $89-$520. **Credit** AmEx, BC, MC, V.

Travel in style by seaplane: take a short spin over the harbour for an aerial squiz at Sydney's icons or upgrade to a gourmet picnic, restaurant safari or an overnight dinner-and-accommodation package. Departures are from Rose Bay.

Sydney by Seaplane

1300 656 787/www.sydneybyseaplane.com. **Tickets** $145-$620. **Credit** AmEx, BC, MC, V.

Choose from a 15-minute joyride over Sydney Harbour, a spin up the coast to Palm Beach, a 90-minute tour from Sydney to the Blue Mountains or a fly-dine package with three-course lunch. Departures are from Rose Bay or Palm Beach.

Sydney Heli

9317 3402/www.avta.com.au. **Tickets** from $150. **Credit** AmEx, BC, DC, MC, V.

Flit above Sydney Harbour in a helicopter for 20 minutes, take a 30-minute tour over the harbour, Bondi Beach and the northern beaches, or enjoy a 25-minute dusk flight as far as Bondi. Other tempting but pricey options are available. Departures are from Sydney (Kingsford Smith) Airport, but they can collect you from your hotel.

By motorbike

Eastcoast Motorcycle Tours

9544 2400/www.eastcoast-mc-tours.com.au. **Tickets** $95 for 1hr-$265 for 4hrs. **Credit** AmEx, BC, DC, MC, V.

The way to see Sydney close up – the wind in your face and a throbbing Harley between your legs, while you clutch the waist of a manly Aussie. There are various options, including a one-hour zip around the city's main sights, a two-hour tour to the lovely northern beaches, and a four-hour trip to the Royal National Park and the south coast. Gear is provided and they pick you up from your hotel.

Easy Rider Motorbike Tours

1300 882 065/www.easyrider.com.au. **Tickets** $35 for 15mins-$900 for a 2-day outback adventure. **Credit** BC, MC, V.

Cruise on a classic Harley-Davidson around the CBD or Bondi, or take a longer trip to explore the northern beaches, Ku-ring-gai National Park, the Royal National Park, Kangaroo Valley or the Blue Mountains. Departures are from the Easy Rider stall in the Rocks Market, George Street (at weekends) or from outside the Santos Café on the corner of George Street and Hickson Road (at other times), although they will also collect clients from within a 5km/three-mile radius of the Rocks.

Sightseeing

Top ten Highlights

Sydney Harbour Bridge

The 'Coathanger' (*see p57*) took eight years to build and its opening in 1932 transformed Sydney life. Look at it, walk or take a car or train across it or even climb to the top of it (*see p50* **BridgeClimb**).

Sydney Opera House

Take in a performance in its hallowed theatres, join a daytime tour or simply marvel at its amazing structure. The off-white sails of this architectural icon are rightly among every tourist's holiday snaps. *See p60.*

Ferry to Manly

Jump on one of the double-ended green and golders for a half-hour ferry trip across the harbour to Manly (*see p103*). Hop off at the wharf, amble through the crowds on the Corso and lay down your towel on Manly Beach or hit the surf.

Bondi to Coogee clifftop walk

Go on the ultimate beach crawl on this incredible coastal walk, starting at Bondi Beach and winding past Tamarama Beach, Bronte Beach, Clovelly Bay, Gordons Bay and Coogee Beach. *See p85* **Walkabout 1.**

Mardi Gras Parade

Buy some feathers, pull on pair of sparkly shorts and nab a prime spot on the route of Sydney's famous (and televised) gay parade – the culmination of the Mardi Gras festival. For full details, *see p214* **Welcome to New Mardi Gras**.

Fruit bats

Move over, Dracula, these furry guys are so cute. See them hanging head down and stretching their wings in the fig trees of the **Royal Botanic Gardens** (*see p65*) during the day and then filling the skies at dusk as they go in search of food.

Palm Beach

If money's no object, fly in on a seaplane – otherwise catch the 190 bus for a great ride up the sandy necklace of the northern beaches to its jewel: Palm Beach. Go on a weekday and you'll be surprised at how empty it is. *See p107.*

Sydney Aquarium

It seems crazy to visit an aquarium when you're so close to the real thing – but it's a safe way to get close to a shark. It's also a great introduction to the hundreds of species that hug the Great Barrier Reef. *See p71.*

Al fresco cinema

In Sydney everything great happens outdoors – even the movies. In summer catch your favourite film either in Centennial Park with a picnic at **Moonlight Cinema** or in the Domain with the harbour as a backdrop at **Open-Air Cinema**. For both, *see p204.*

Yabbies & Balmain bugs

They're very tasty and so Sydney. Go to the **Sydney Fish Markets** (*see p72*), buy some yabbies (freshwater crayfish) and Balmain bugs (crustaceans) and have a feast. So much more exciting than prawns.

Gidday Mate!

Oz Experience

Welcome to Sydney. Oz Experience is an adventure travel network that links some of Australia's best destinations with some of the most unique attractions. To celebrate YOUR arrival into Sydney, and our 10 yrs in the business we have some great Aussie deals for you.

GREAT AUSSIE DEAL ❶

BLUE MOUNTAINS DAY TRIP

See the the magnificent 3 sisters in their splendour, take a photo of a koala, feed a kangaroo, or try the world's steepest railway ride. We take you on the most scenic route to the mountains so you don't miss a thing.

Includes lunch, 3 sisters, scenic railway
Worth $85 - cost $75*
*conditions apply

GREAT AUSSIE DEAL ❷

BLUE MOUNTAINS DAY TRIP + A SYDNEY HARBOUR CRUISE

For the adventurous ones, we have the blue mountains day trip with a wonderful Sydney harbour cruise that you can take a whole day to hop on-hop off. From the Opera house to Manly and under the Sydney Harbour bridge, this trip is a great way to see all of Sydney.

Includes lunch, 3 sisters, scenic railway, Sydney Harbour day cruise
worth $107 Cost $95*
*conditions apply

TO BOOK CONTACT YOUR LOCAL TRAVEL AGENT OR CALL 9213-1766 IN SYDNEY OR 1300-300-028 EVERYWHERE ELSE OR CLICK www.ozexperience.com

---

Get $20 off* a 5 Day Rental with Avis

Rent a Group C (Toyota Corolla Sedan or similar) through to a Group E (Holden Commodore or similar) for 5 days or more and you will get $20 off the daily time and kilometre charge. Please quote coupon number MPLA024 when booking. Valid until 28th February 2006.

Offer available from:

Artarmon	(02) 9439 3733
Bankstown	(02) 9792 1714
Circular Quay	(02) 9241 1281
Kings Cross	(02) 9357 2000
Parramatta	(02) 9630 5877
Star City	(02) 9660 7666
Sydney Airport	(02) 8374 2847
World Square	(02) 9261 0750

AVIS

We try harder.

For all other bookings please call Avis reservations on 136 333

*Cars subject to availability. Blackout periods 7th April 2004 - 17th April 2004, 20th December 2004 - 5th January 2005, 23rd March 2005 - 10th April 2005, 20th December 2005 - 05th January 2006. An advance reservation is required. Not transferable and not refundable. May not be used in conjunction with any other offer, promotion or coupon. Renter must meet Avis age, driver and credit requirements. Petrol, taxes, surcharges, optional insurances, vehicle registration fee, concession recovery fee, miscellaneous items and GST on these items are extra. Subject to the terms and conditions of the Avis rental agreement.
W.T.H. Pty. Limited - ACN 000 165 855 - Avis Licensee. CT4565

Central Sydney

Welcome to the city's fast-beating heart.

In the early days of the colony the east side of Sydney Cove was the place to find its power brokers – the governor's residence, government offices and parliament. In stark contrast, the west side was an unruly place where convicts built their tumbledown cottages in the Rocks and sailors fresh from months at sea caroused in seedy drinking dens. Governor Lachlan Macquarie (1810-21) was responsible for most of the grand buildings of the early convict period, and thanks to him, the city slowly grew more prosperous. The tracks hewn by convicts through the bushland that had been home to the Cadigal clan of the Eora tribe of Aboriginals now form main thoroughfares.

As with everything in this relatively young country, Sydney's centre is constantly evolving and the past decade has seen a lot of toil and hard cash thrown at transforming the city centre into what former mayor Frank Sartor liked to call a 'living city'. The results have been mixed. Many object to the towering apartment blocks that have sprouted – some of them dreadful, others exceptional works of architecture – but much of the slum housing has been demolished or refurbished, and the centre has certainly been injected with a new lease of life. Previously something of a morgue when the shops closed, now restaurants, bars and nightclubs pull in bright young (and not-so-young) things. At New Year, or when major festivals and sporting events are staged, this is *the* party area.

Central Sydney begins at the harbour, at Circular Quay. For many, it's the Bridge, rather than the Opera House, that anchors them to the city – it has an endearing habit of appearing when you least expect it; over a rise, or at the end of a tunnel of office blocks. Of course, both edifices are 20th-century additions and it's in the Rocks, around the wharves and along Macquarie Street, that you'll find remnants of settler history. To go further back to Aboriginal times, head for the **Museum of Sydney** (*see p60*) where a permanent exhibition honours the Cadigal people.

Beyond the CBD – aka Central Business District – lie the tourist attractions of Darling Harbour, the gay haven of Darlinghurst, the eateries of increasingly gentrified Surry Hills, and seedy Kings Cross and its smarter neighbours Potts Point and Woolloomooloo.

The CBD

Transport *Ferry Circular Quay/CityRail Circular Quay, Town Hall, Wynyard, Martin Place, St James or Museum/Monorail City Centre, Galeries Victoria, World Square, Garden Plaza or Haymarket/LightRail Capitol Square or Haymarket.*

The Rocks & around

In January 1788, after an eight-month voyage from Plymouth, England, the First Fleet stumbled ashore (after a short visit to Botany Bay) at Sydney Cove. Their brief was to 'build where you can, and build cheap'. Hence, the Rocks. Named after its rough terrain, the area survived as a working-class district for almost two centuries, until the 1960s, when it was nearly demolished to create an Australian Manhattan. Civic protest saved the day and the 'birthplace of the nation' was finally restored for posterity in the mid 1970s. Now safe under the wing of the Sydney Harbour Foreshore Authority, the Rocks still has to pay its own way, and many historic buildings have been turned to commercial use.

The resulting combination of period buildings, tourist shops, restaurants and pubs, along with harbourside vistas, has made the Rocks one of the city's major sightseeing attractions. As a result, locals have tended to shun the area, writing it off as a place filled with noisy boozers and tacky souvenirs neatly packaged for tour groups. But a clutch of good restaurants, the development of the Walsh Bay finger wharves, and the installation of groovier retailers are now attracting Sydneysiders.

Head first for the **Sydney Visitor Centre** (106 George Street – *see p292*), in what was in 1864 a home for sailors. You'll find information about Sydney and its surrounds, as well as two floors of exhibits: one with artefacts from an archaeological dig on Cumberland Street, the other telling the story of the Rocks. Pick up a copy of the 'Rocks Self-Guided Tour' ($4.95). Next door is **Cadman's Cottage**, probably the nation's oldest house; now home to the **Sydney Harbour National Park Information Centre** (*see p292*), it's the place for info on the Harbour's islands (*see p65* **Pick an island**).

In the Argyle Stores on Argyle Street, fashion designer **Alistair Trung** (*see p172*), and vintage clothing store **RoKit** (*see p179*) are

Sightseeing

well worth a visit. The **Rocks Market** (*see p170*) appears like magic every weekend, with puppeteers and other street performers. For a top Sydney meal, there's Neil Perry's **Rockpool** and David Thompson's **Sailors Thai** (for both, *see p143*), as well as the hip Overseas Passenger Terminal with its bars, eateries and fine harbour vistas. If you'd like

The best Viewpoints

Blues Point Reserve

Hundreds of tourist buses pull up here every day to see the 'dress circle' view of the Bridge and Opera House. Brilliant at sunset. *See p97.*

Jonah's

It's not just for the food that clued-up visitors head to Jonah's restaurant at Palm Beach. The uninterrupted view over Whale Beach and the wide ocean beyond have to be seen to be believed. *See p163.*

Mrs Macquarie's Chair

Mrs Macquarie, wife of one of NSW's most influential governors, had good reason to love this spot – the view over the Harbour with the Opera House next door and the Bridge in front is awesome. *See p61.*

Observatory Hill

Up behind the Rocks with the Harbour Bridge so near you feel you could touch it, Observatory Hill offers some wonderful harbour views. Go at night when everything twinkles. *See p56.*

Rose Bay

The lookout at the junction of Bayview Hill and New South Head Road opens up stunning views over the waving masts of boats in Rose Bay, with the Bridge in the background. *See p86.*

Sydney Harbour Bridge

You don't have to do the BridgeClimb (*see p50*) to get a view, though it really is priceless from the top. Alternatively, climb the Pylon Lookout or stay roadside, on the pedestrian path over the Bridge. *See p57.*

Sydney Tower

Right in the middle of the CBD and 250 metres (820 feet) above street level, the Sydney Tower offers a panoramic view over the city. For the ultimate thrill, try the new Skywalk. *See p68.*

a cocktail with your view, try the **Horizons Bar** (*see p133*) on the 36th floor of the Shangri-La Hotel on Cumberland Street.

Historic buildings include the **Garrison Church** (9247 1268, open 9am-6pm daily), on the corner of Argyle and Lower Fort Streets. The colony's first military church, it's still used today by the Australian Army and includes a free museum. You can also take a peek at how 19th-century working-class families lived at **Susannah Place** (*see p57*), a row of four brick terraces on Gloucester Street.

Still, much has been lost. The site of Sydney's first hospital, which struggled to care for 500 convicts who disembarked from the Second Fleet in 1790 suffering from typhoid and dysentery, is now an unprepossessing row of shops. A gallery now stands on the site of the **Customs Naval Office** (100 George Street) where one of the colony's most flamboyant customs officers, Captain John Piper, made money mismanaging taxes. He went on to build Sydney's finest mansion of its day at Eliza Point – now Point Piper – where he held extravagant parties until his maladministration came to light. In true Piper style, he had his crew row him beyond the Heads and play a Highland lament as he threw himself overboard. To his embarrassment, they dragged him from the sea and he died, impoverished, in 1851.

Off the main drag, under the thundering Bradfield Highway that feeds the **Sydney Harbour Bridge** (*see p57*) and towards Walsh Bay and Millers Point, the area has a quieter and gentler feel, with tiny cottages, working wharves and a few pubs vying for the honour of Sydney's oldest: the **Lord Nelson** (*see p133*) on Kent Street, the **Hero of Waterloo** on Lower Fort Street and the **Palisade** on Bettington Street, which also has a fine restaurant (*see p142*). The delightful **Glover Cottages** (124 Kent Street) – built by stonemason and surveyor Thomas Glover in the 1820s – were the first example of terraced housing in the colony. The charming Victorian **Sydney Observatory** (*see p58*), perched on the hill of the same name, offers views of the heavens above and the harbour below.

From Windmill Street, walk down the Windmill Steps to Hickson Road and you'll reach **Walsh Bay**, where the first wharves were built by a South Sea Islands trader in 1820. The area's grandest vision was realised by the Sydney Harbour Trust from 1901-22 when Hickson Road was carved through the sandstone, a massive seawall was built and buildings and piers were erected. As shipping methods changed, however, the Walsh Bay wharves became obsolete and were finally

The centre of the action: Sydney Harbour and its beloved Bridge.

abandoned in the 1970s. Revitalisation started with the development of Piers 4/5 to house various cultural institutions, including the **Sydney Theatre Company** (*see p250*).

Plans to create a public boardwalk all the way from Pier 1 (where the **Sebel Pier One** hotel (*see p30*) has prime position) to Piers 8/9, finally took shape in 2003. Construction is not yet complete, but it's a great walk from Circular Quay past the **Museum of Contemporary Art** (*see below*), behind the Overseas Passenger Terminal, in front of the Hyatt Hotel, under the Harbour Bridge, around Dawes Point Park (where you can see remains of the **Dawes Point Battery**, *see below*), and along the waterfront.

Of course, as soon as the First Fleet pitched its tents in the Rocks, traditional Aboriginal life started to dissolve. Archaeological evidence suggests that the area had been inhabited by Aboriginal people for at least 20,000 years, but the indigenous population succumbed rapidly to the European gift of smallpox. To learn more about the area's indigenous history, take a tour with **Aboriginal Experiences** (*see p50*).

Dawes Point Battery

Dawes Point, beneath south end of Harbour Bridge. CityRail/ferry Circular Quay. **Map** p310 C1.
Sydney's first permanent fortification was built in 1790 against a feared Spanish invasion, rebuilt in 1820 by pioneer architect Francis Greenway and renovated in the 1850s and '60s. The battery was demolished in 1925 when the Harbour Bridge was built, but excavation has uncovered some remains. These include the floor of the original powder magazine, the circular battery with evidence of four gun emplacements, underground magazines, a stone ramp and the footings of the officers' quarters.

Museum of Contemporary Art

140 George Street, between Argyle & Alfred Streets, The Rocks (9252 4033/24hr recorded information 9241 5892/www.mca.com.au). CityRail/ferry Circular Quay. **Open** 10am-5pm daily. *Tours* 2pm Mon-Fri; 11am, noon, 1.30pm Sat, Sun. **Admission** free. **Credit** AmEx, BC, DC, MC, V. **Map** p310 B/C1.
The MCA is the only major gallery in Sydney with a serious interest in contemporary art. Shows include selections from the permanent collection of international and Australian art (including some fine Aboriginal works), touring overseas shows and curated temporary displays. Funding has been an ongoing problem and in early 2001 the future looked grim indeed, but after much public wrangling the state government came to the rescue. The MCA is currently going through something of a renaissance under director Elizabeth Macgregor, who has staged a fascinating string of exhibitions. The MCA Café (*see p126*) is worth a look.

Susannah Place Museum

58-64 Gloucester Street, The Rocks (9241 1893/ fax 9241 2608/www.hht.nsw.gov.au). **Open** *Jan* 10am-5pm daily. *Feb-Dec* 10am-5pm Sat, Sun. **Admission** $7; $3 concessions. **Map** p310 B2.
Built in 1844, this terrace of four houses, including a corner shop, original brick privvies and open laundries, gives an idea of what 19th-century community living was really like. You can top off your visit with a purchase from the recreated shop.

Sydney Harbour Bridge & Pylon Lookout

Bridge & Pylon Lookout accessible via stairs on Cumberland Street (9240 1100/www.pylonlookout. com.au). **Open** 10am-5pm daily. **Admission** $8.50; $3 concessions; free under-7s. **Credit** AmEx, BC, DC, MC, V. **Map** p310 C1.
Long before the Opera House was built, Sydney had 'the Coathanger'. Now an elderly structure, it was once the world's largest single-span bridge. Locals

Sydney's icons. *See p57 and p60.*

and the ceremony resumed. The bridge was declared 'one of the seven wonders of the modern world'.

The recently refurbished Pylon Lookout, in the south-east pylon, is well worth a visit. Climb 200 steps past three levels of exhibits celebrating the history of the bridge and its builders. Stained-glass windows feature a painter, riveter, stonemason, rigger, concreter and surveyor. Original bridge memorabilia from the 1930s is also on display; more up-to-date souvenirs are available in the shop. And the views from the top are magnificent. The more intrepid can take a guided tour to the top of the bridge itself (*see p50* **BridgeClimb**), with only a harness between you and a plunge into the harbour.

Sydney Observatory

Watson Road, off Argyle Street, Observatory Hill, The Rocks (9217 0485/www.phm.gov.au/observe). CityRail/ferry Circular Quay. **Open** *Museum* 10am-5pm daily. *Night tours* phone for details. **Admission** *Museum & gardens* free. *Day tours* $6; $4 concessions; $16 family. *Night tours* $15; $10-$12 concessions; $40 family. **Credit** BC, MC, V. **Map** p310 B1.

Built in 1858, Sydney Observatory gained international recognition under Henry Chamberlain Russell, government astronomer 1870-1905, who involved Sydney in the International Astrographic Catalogue, the first complete atlas of the sky. The Sydney section alone took 80 years to complete and filled 53 volumes. Air pollution turned the observatory into a museum in 1982. It's been revamped recently, and a new exhibition celebrates the long tradition of Australian astronomy, including the use by Aboriginals, over thousands of years, of southern constellations to navigate land and sea, and for ceremonial use. Interactive displays include a virtual reality tour over the surfaces of Venus and Mars, and there are lessons on how telescopes work. Night viewings (booking essential) include a talk and tour, 3-D Space Theatre session and viewing through a state-of-the-art 40cm (16in) mirror telescope.

Circular Quay

Circular Quay is the hub of Sydney's ferry system, where the charming green and yellow vessels (*see p61* **Sydney's ferrytale**) leave for all points around the harbour. Commuters and day-trippers board and disembark from a constant stream of ferries, JetCats, RiverCats and water taxis, while tourists and teenagers idle in the cafés drinking cappuccinos, listening to buskers and admiring the view. Fastfood kiosks abound, but you'll also find **City Extra** (9241 1422), one of the few 24-hour restaurants in town. Information stands proffer free literature, and sightseeing cruises and tours, by bus as well as boat, leave from here. The view is particularly lovely at night, when the Opera House, the Bridge, the Overseas Passenger Terminal and Fort Denison are lit up.

had dreamed for decades of a bridge to link the north and south harbour shores before construction of the 'All Australian Bridge' began in 1924, by which time Sydney's ferries were struggling to carry 40 million passengers a year. The winning design came from English firm Dorman, Long & Co, but used Australian steel, stone, sand and labour. Families within the path of the new bridge and its highways were displaced without compensation – 800 houses were demolished. A total of 1,400 workers toiled on the structure which is 134m (440ft) high and 1,149m (3,770ft) long. It took eight years to build, and workers grafting without safety rails took great risks: 16 of them died. The opening ceremony in 1932, broadcast around the world, was interrupted by a lone horseman – disaffected Irishman Francis de Groot – who galloped forward and slashed the ribbon with his sword, declaring the bridge open in the name of 'the decent citizens of New South Wales'. After the police had removed him (he was fined £5), the ribbon was retied,

Circular Quay at night, looking back from the Opera House.

The newly renovated **Overseas Passenger Terminal** on the west side of the quay, where the international cruise liners moor, is not only an award-winning piece of architecture, it's one of the city's coolest night-time hangouts with its clutch of restaurants and bars, including Mod Oz supremo **Quay** (*see p143*), buzzy **Wildfire** (8273 1222, www.wildfiresydney. com), mega **Cruise** (9251 1188, www.cruise restaurant.tv) and seafood specialist **Doyle's at the Quay** (9252 3400, www.doyles.com.au).

On the opposite (east) side of the Quay is **Opera Quays** with the much-shouted-about **Toaster building**, a rather ugly apartment block for those with more money than taste. While the development on this side of the Quay has somewhat ruined the complete Bridge/Opera House view, the restaurants, shops and **Dendy Opera Quays** cinema (*see p201*) inject razzamatazz to this tourist hub.

As you walk around the Quay, look out for a series of round metal plaques set into the promenade, each one dedicated to a famous writer. Forming **Writers' Walk**, these offer brief quotations on Sydney and human nature. Many (but not all) of the writers are Australians – Germaine Greer, Peter Carey, Barry Humphries, Clive James.

Sydney Opera House (*see p60*), the city's icon, is on Bennelong Point on the tip of the eastern side of Circular Quay. All the photos in the world cannot prepare you for how stunning it is. The site is where Governor Phillip provided a hut for Aboriginal Bennelong in 1790. Phillip had captured Bennelong – one of the governor's more foolish moves – and planned to use him as a mediator. Some of the key events in Bennelong's sorry life are depicted in a series of paintings by Donald Friend on display in the Opera House.

Behind the Quay, across Alfred Street, is the **Customs House** (*see below*), which has just undergone the latest in a series of refurbishments. Two blocks over on the corner of Albert and Phillip Streets is the **Justice & Police Museum** (*see p60*). Look up and you'll spy the terracotta spine of the 41-storey **Aurora Place**. Designed by Italian architect Renzo Piano, it's worth a peek inside, if only for its artworks. Opposite Aurora Place is **Chifley Tower** on one corner, and **Governor Phillip Tower** on the other. Architecturally, these are three of the more interesting late 20th-century additions to the skyline and, sitting so close together, are a reminder that this is the so-called 'big end' of town. Governor Phillip Tower stands on the site of the first Government House. Inside is Trevor Weeke's towering bust of Governor Macquarie. The excellent and informative **Museum of Sydney** (*see p60*), which also has a very good shop, is next door.

Customs House

31 Alfred Street, between Loftus & Young Streets, Circular Quay (9265 9333/www.cityofsydney.nsw. gov.au). CityRail/ferry Circular Quay. **Map** p310 C2. Built in 1885, Customs House was one of government architect James Barnet's finer works. Its double-pillared colonnade, wrought-iron panels and long clean lines give it a sense of space and majesty, underlined by the open area in front. The building is heritage-listed, but its use continually changes. The latest revamp has seen the City of Sydney lavish $18 million on an internal refurbishment due to be finished in 2004. The ground and first floors will house the City of Sydney Library, including a 'living' scale model of the city, updated under glass, it is updated as the real streets and landscape change. Fashionable eaterie Café Sydney (*see p227*) retains its enviable location on level five, with amazing views.

Justice & Police Museum

Corner of Albert & Phillip Streets, Circular Quay (9252 1144/www.hht.nsw.gov.au). CityRail/ferry Circular Quay. **Open** *Jan* 10am-5pm daily. *Feb-Dec* 10am-5pm Sat, Sun. **Admission** $7; $3 concessions; $17 family. **Credit** (over $10) BC, MC, V. **Map** p310 C2.

Fittingly, the Justice & Police Museum has been a Water Police Court (1856), Water Police Station (1858) and plain old Police Court (1886). Death masks of some of Australia's more infamous crims are on display, as well as mugshots, assorted deadly weapons and newspaper reports of sensational wrongdoings. Also on view is a recreated 1890s police charge room, a dark and damp remand cell, and a restored Court of Petty Sessions with its notorious communal dock, which could hold up to 15 prisoners at a time.

The museum is one of 11 houses and museums managed by the Historic Houses Trust. If you're planning to visit a few of these, consider buying a Ticket Through Time ($23, $10 concessions, $40 family), which permits unlimited entry to all properties for three months from the date of purchase. The Trust's events calendar (9518 6866) has details of new exhibits, historic walks and other activities.

Museum of Sydney

Corner of Bridge & Phillip Streets, CBD (9251 5988/www.hht.nsw.gov.au). CityRail/ferry Circular Quay. **Open** 9.30am-5pm daily. **Admission** $7; $3 concessions; $17 family. **Credit** AmEx, BC, MC, V. **Map** p310 C2.

This modern building stands on one of the most historic spots in Sydney, site of the first Government House, built in 1788 by Governor Arthur Phillip and home to the first nine governors of NSW. In 1983 archaeologists unearthed the original footings of the house, which had remained preserved since the building's 1846 demolition; the remains are a feature at the museum. Run by the Historic Houses Trust and opened in 1995, the MOS offers a mix of state-of-the-art installations and nostalgic memorabilia. A giant mouse spine spans the full height of the building and charts the physical development of the city; elsewhere a trade wall features goods on sale in Sydney in the 1830s. This area was the first point of contact for the indigenous Cadigal people and the First Fleet, so the museum also explores colonisation, invasion and contact. The Cadigal Place gallery honours the clan's history and culture, while, outside the museum, the *Edge of the Trees* sculpture by Fiona Foley and Janet Laurence symbolises that first encounter as the Cadigal people hid behind trees and watched officers of the First Fleet struggle ashore.

Sydney Opera House

Bennelong Point, Circular Quay (box office 9250 7777/information 9250 7111/tours 9250 7250/ www.sydneyoperahouse.com). CityRail/ferry Circular Quay. **Open** *Box office* 9am-8.30pm Mon-Sat; 2hrs before show time. *Tours* every 30mins 9am-5pm daily. **Tour tickets** $20; $14 concessions; $55 family. **Credit** AmEx, BC, DC, MC, V. **Map** p310 C1.

Set in a heavenly harbour, its cream wings reminiscent of the sails of the First Fleet, the Sydney Opera House is the city's most famous icon. It took 14 troubled years and $102 million to build – $95 million more than was anticipated. In true Aussie style, the shortfall was met by lotteries. The cultural cathedral has never been visited by its creator, Danish architect Jørn Utzon, who resigned halfway through the project following a clash with the Minister of Public Works. On its opening night in 1973, an impromptu appearance was made onstage by two small possums.

In its five auditoria the Opera House holds 2,400 opera, concert, theatre, film and dance performances a year, attended by some 1.5 million people. The accolade of 'first performer' belongs to Paul Robeson who, in 1960, at the invitation of the militant builders' union, sang *Old Man River* at the construction site. The building is currently undergoing a 'venue improvement programme' under the guidance of Utzon and his architect son and partner Jan, and in December 2003 was (finally) listed on the State Heritage Register.

Attend a performance if you can; otherwise, take one of the daily guided tours. It's also a great place to while away a few hours. Eateries range from the haute-cuisine (and haute-priced) Guillaume at Bennelong (*see p142*) to the very stylish Opera Bar (*see p134*), with indoor and outdoor seating and live entertainment, and the Sidewalk Café. *See also p230.*

Macquarie Street, Hyde Park & College Street

Tree-lined Macquarie Street – named after Lachlan Macquarie, the great reformist governor of NSW, who served from 1809 to 1821 – is the closest thing the CBD has to a boulevard. It fairly drips with old money and resonates with history: on one side you'll find Sydney's main public buildings, on the other handsome apartment blocks belonging to medicos, the well-heeled and the 'squatocracy' (a sarcastic term for Australia's 'landed gentry').

To the west of Macquarie Street, the **Royal Botanic Gardens** (*see p65*) – which contain **Government House** (*see p63*), the home of NSW governors – form a green and pleasant rump to the city, leading down to the water at **Farm Cove**. In summer, a huge screen rises from the water on the cove's eastern side and seating is erected in the gardens so that locals can catch a movie – with the Opera House and Harbour Bridge in the background – at the **Open-Air Cinema** (*see p204*).

South of the Botanic Gardens is another spacious green retreat, the **Domain**. Home to Sunday soap-box orators, the Domain has long been the place for civic protest: huge crowds gathered in 1917 to protest against World War I conscription, in 1931 more than 100,000 demonstrated against the governor's dismissal of Premier Jack Lang, and in 2003 up to 50,000 demonstrated against the invasion of Iraq. The Domain is also where you'll find the **Art Gallery of New South Wales** (*see p63*) and memorials to poets Robert Burns and Henry Lawson. The park itself is rather dull, but hold your breath for the final sensational view: **Mrs Macquarie's Chair** overlooking the harbour. The Domain used to be Governor Macquarie's own private park, and its tip was

the favourite spot of his wife Elizabeth. A seat has been shaped in the rock – hence the name – and the view is still one of Sydney's finest. On the Woolloomooloo Bay side of the Domain is **Andrew (Boy) Charlton Pool** (*see p63*), a popular outdoor lap pool for city workers, and a favoured sunbaking spot for trim gay men.

At Macquarie Street's southern end, between Elizabeth and College Streets, is gracious **Hyde Park**, named after its much larger London counterpart. It used to have a rowdy reputation,

Sydney's ferrytale

Sydney's ferry tradition dates back to convict times when the *Rose Hill Packet*, a convict-built ship also known as 'the Lump', ran between Sydney Cove and Parramatta. The round trip, powered by sail and oar, often took up to a week. Steamships arrived in 1831, but the beginnings of the modern-day ferry system dates from 1861, when the North Shore Ferry Company began the first commuter-style service across the harbour. Then fewer than 1,000 people lived on the north shore, and it was this service that created the middle-class commuting suburbs of Manly and Mosman.

In 1878 the firm added 'Steam' to its name and began to use double-ended, propeller-driven ferries – an innovative design retained in some of today's fleet. Until 1932, when the Harbour Bridge opened, the northern suburbs were all dependent on ferries. The building of the Bridge, and the motor car, led to a period of decline, with 40 million passengers a year dropping to 14 million.

Today, the ferries are still loved by commuters and, especially, visitors. The modern fleet is subdivided into Freshwater

ferries, SuperCats, Lady Class, First Fleet, RiverCats and HarbourCats. The large, double-ended Manly ferries offer a gateway to the northern beaches, while the old-style green-and-golders are supplemented by speedy catamarans serving the inner harbour, Parramatta and Manly. Some are named after animals, such as *Gannett* and *Platypus*; others have Aboriginal derivations: *Karingal* ('happy home') and *Kara Kara* ('full moon'). Newer names combine sporting heroes (Evonne Goolagong, Dawn Fraser) with historical figures from history, such as Australia's only saint Mary MacKillop, and Sydney suburbs such as Narrabeen.

But the ferries are facing problems, among them poor patronage, declining fare revenue and unsatisfactory timetables that fail to reflect public needs. In mid 2004 they are to be removed from the jurisdiction of the State Transit Authority – which also looks after Sydney's buses – and run as a state-owned corporation. It's a controversial move, but for ferry fans it offers the chance that the vessels will be restored to their former glory. As one enthusiast says, 'This is one of the world's most sublime journeys to work.'

The many faces of the **Sydney Opera House**. *See p60.*

and was more a venue for sideshows, wrestling and boxing matches than a park; until the late 1820s it also served as Sydney's racecourse. Now it's a tranquil green space and fitting home to elegant Australian memorials, including the famous 1934 art deco **Anzac Memorial**, honouring those who have served Australia in war, and the graceful **Archibald Fountain**, commemorating the Australian-French Alliance of 1914-18. During the **Sydney Festival** (*see p194*) in January, the park erupts with free entertainment and, in summer, office workers flop down on the grass, while ibis pick their long-legged way around the supine bodies. Hyde Park is a fine sight at night, with fairylights in the trees and possums scampering up trunks and foraging among the plants. The main avenue of Hills fig trees running north through the park is especially striking.

At the north end of the park on Macquarie Street is the **Hyde Park Barracks Museum**

(*see p63*) adjacent to the Old Mint. Next door stands **Sydney Hospital** (*see p66*), flanking **Parliament House** (*see p65*); on the other side is the **State Library of New South Wales** (*see p66*). Notable churches in the area include **St James'** (corner of King and Phillip Streets, 9232 3022), designed by Francis Greenway and the oldest church in Sydney (completed 1824), and **St Stephen's Uniting Church** (197 Macquarie Street, 9221 1688, www.ststephenschurchsydney.org.au).

Opposite the south-eastern corner of the park is the block-long **Mark Foy's Building**, with its distinctive gold trim and green turrets. Once a department store, completed in 1917, it was converted to a court complex in 1991. Francis Foy, one of the seven siblings who established the original store, took his architect to look at department stores around the world before settling on the design. The lower levels are made of a special glazed brick shipped from

62 Time Out Sydney

Scotland. Unable to decide whose name the store should carry, the siblings settled the dispute by naming it after their father, Mark Foy.

On the College Street side of the park are **St Mary's Cathedral** (*see p66*), the **Australian Museum** (*see below*) and **Cook & Phillip Park** (*see p241*), a $35-million aquatic and sports centre opened in 1999. Even if you don't fancy a dip, at least pop in to see Wendy Sharpe's wonderful murals above the 50-metre pool depicting the life of 19th-century swimming star Annette Kellerman, who went on to become Australia's first Hollywood movie star.

Andrew (Boy) Charlton Pool

Mrs Macquarie's Road, The Domain (9358 6686). **Open** 6.30am-7pm/8pm daily. **Admission** $5; $3.50 concessions. **Map** p312 D2.

A recent $10-million refurbishment has made this harbourside pool *the* place for inner-city summer swimming. It was a popular bathing spot long before the British arrived, and public sea baths first opened here in 1860. In the early 1920s famous Aussie swimmer Andrew 'Boy' Charlton achieved many of his triumphs here – including, as a 16-year-old, beating European champ Arne Borg, setting a new world record in the process. Today, the baths offer an eight-lane 50m heated pool, learners' and toddlers' pools, sundeck and café. The pool's harbourside edges are glazed, allowing swimmers unparalleled views across the sparkling bay.

Art Gallery of New South Wales

Art Gallery Road, The Domain (9225 1700/ www.artgallery.nsw.gov.au). CityRail Martin Place or St James. **Open** 10am-5pm Mon, Tue, Thur-Sun; 10am-9pm Wed. **Admission** free; charges apply for some exhibitions. **Credit** AmEx, BC, MC, V. **Map** p310 C2.

New South Wales' main art gallery moved to its present site in the Domain in 1885. It includes a solid collection of 19th- and 20th-century Australian artists, as well as Aboriginal and Torres Strait Islander art, European masters and international contemporary artists, plus a fine Asian art collection. There are regular blockbuster touring shows from overseas galleries. One of its most popular, and controversial, exhibitions is the annual Archibald Prize, a portraiture competition, which is complemented by the Wynne (landscape and sculpture) and Sir John Sulman competitions (best 'subject/genre paintings' and murals). Wednesday is late-opening night, with free talks, debates and performances, and there are regular events for kids. Tours of the general collection are held two to three times a day.

Australian Museum

6 College Street, CBD (9320 6000/www.austmus. gov.au). CityRail Museum, St James or Town Hall. **Open** 9.30am-5pm daily. **Admission** $8; $3-$4 concessions; $19 family ticket. **Credit** AmEx, BC, MC, V. **Map** p311 C3.

Established in 1827, this museum houses the nation's most important animal, mineral, fossil and anthropological collections, and prides itself on its innovative research into Australia's environment and indigenous cultures. Displays cover the Pacific Islands, Asia, Africa and the Americas, with items ranging from Aboriginal kids' toys to a tattooed chalk head from the Solomon Islands. Any serious museum-tripper should see a few of the local stuffed animals, and the displays here should answer all your questions about Australian mammals. If you're at all interested in Aboriginal culture and beliefs, visit the Indigenous Australia section, which tackles such contentious issues as 'the stolen generation', deaths in custody and problems facing indigenous people today. The museum also holds around 1,000 Aboriginal objects of a secret/sacred nature separate from the main collections; access to these can be arranged through the Aboriginal Heritage Unit.

Government House

Macquarie Street, CBD (9931 5222/www.hht.nsw. gov.au). CityRail/ferry Circular Quay. **Open** *House* 10am-3pm Fri-Sun. *Garden* 10am-4pm daily. *Tours* every 30mins 10.30am-3pm Fri-Sun. **Admission** free. **Map** p310 C2.

Designed in 1834 by William IV's architect, Edward Blore, the plans for Government House (the official residence of the NSW governor) had to be modified to take account of local conditions, such as the Australian sun being in the north rather than the south. However, the original Gothic Revival concept remained, and today's visitors can still enjoy the crenellated battlements and detailed interiors. Past governors have dabbled in redecorating and extensions with rather weird results, but the marvellously restored State Rooms are now the best example of Victorian pomp in the country. The current governor doesn't live here, but it's still used for state and vice-regal functions. Don't miss the exotic gardens.

Hyde Park Barracks Museum

Queens Square, corner of Macquarie Street & Prince Albert Road, CBD (9223 8922/ www.hht.nsw.gov.au). CityRail Martin Place or St James. **Open** 9.30am-5pm daily. **Admission** $7; $3 concessions; $17 family. **Credit** BC, MC, V. **Map** p310 C2.

Designed by convict architect Francis Greenway, the Barracks were completed in 1819 to house 600 male convicts, who were in government employ until 1848. Subsequently used as an immigration depot and an asylum for women, it eventually metamorphosed into a museum. The top level houses recreated convict barracks: rough hammocks hang side by side in the dormitories, while recorded snippets of conversation surround you. A computer database allows you to follow the official records of various convicts, from conviction via much flogging to, in some cases, eventual rehabilitation. The women's section on level two is no less thought-provoking – these (mostly Irish) women were escaping an awful existence to start what must have been an equally burdensome new

life in a harsh colony. The Greenway Gallery on the ground floor has temporary shows, usually related to Australian social history.

Parliament House

6 Macquarie Street, opposite Hunter Street, CBD (9230 2111/tours 9230 3444/www.cityofsydney. nsw.gov.au). CityRail Martin Place. **Open** 9.30am-4pm daily. *Tours Non-sitting days* 9.30am, 11am, 12.30pm, 2pm, 3pm. **Admission** free. **Map** p310 C2.
Known to locals as the 'Bear Pit', the NSW Parliament is said to be the roughest, toughest parliament in the country. Its impressive sandstone home was built between 1811 and 1814 as the northern wing of the Rum Hospital, but was commandeered in 1829 to house the new colony's decision makers. Only the Legislative Assembly (Lower House) existed until the 1850s, when the parliament became bicameral. The Legislative Council (Upper House) meets in a building originally intended for use as a church; the cast-iron prefab was being shipped from Glasgow to Victoria when it was diverted mid-voyage to Sydney. The parliament is largely modelled on its mother house in London. There's a Speaker and Black Rod, and even the colour scheme follows the British tradition of green for the lower chamber and red for the upper. Legislative sessions are open to the public with viewing from the public gallery, and booking is essential for the tours.

Royal Botanic Gardens

Mrs Macquarie's Road, CBD (9231 8111/weekends 9231 8125/www.rbgsyd.nsw.gov.au). CityRail/ ferry Circular Quay. **Open** *Park* 7am-sunset daily. *Sydney Tropical Centre* 10am-4pm daily. **Admission** *Park* free. *Sydney Tropical Centre* $2.20; $1.10 concessions. **Credit** (shop only) AmEx, BC, MC, V. **Map** p310 C/D2.

Pick an island

Port Jackson, as Sydney Harbour is properly called, is sprinkled with islands, all of them under the auspices of the National Parks & Wildlife Service (NPWS). You can cast yourself away on some, or take a historical tour.

The easiest to get to are **Fort Denison** (pictured), near Mrs Macquarie's Point, and **Goat Island**, off Balmain, both accessible by guided tour. Fort Denison (tours 11.30am-3.15pm Mon-Fri, 2.30pm-5.15pm Sat, Sun, $22, $18 concessions) originally served as an open-air prison and was called Pinchgut Island after the starvation rations served to its inmates (bread and water for a week). Its first resident, Thomas Hill, was marooned for seven days in 1788 as punishment for taking biscuits. In 1862 a fort, along with the distinctive Martello tower, were added and it was renamed Fort Denison after then-governor William Denison.

Due to its central location and large size, Goat Island was the site of a 19th-century water police station, a gunpowder depot and

barracks and, later, the nerve centre for port operations. The current afternoon and evening tours are under review, so call for the latest information.

Shark Island, off Point Piper, **Clark Island**, near Darling Point, and **Rodd Island**, west of the Harbour Bridge in Iron Cove, are open to day-trippers year-round, with a $5 landing fee per person. Visitor numbers are limited and you must book in advance with NPWS and arrange your transport by private boat, chartered ferry or water taxi from the NPWS list of licensed operators. Boats are allowed to drop off and pick up at the island wharfs, but not to tie up. There's also a weekend ferry service to Shark Island run by NPWS in conjunction with **Matilda Cruises** (9264 7377, www.matilda.com.au). Toilets and picnic tables are provided, but you must take your rubbish home. Swimming is not recommended, except from Shark's sandy beach (there's no lifeguard).

For more details, visit the National Park info centre at **Cadman's Cottage** (*see p292*).

Sightseeing

The 30 broad green hectares (74 acres) of the Royal Botanic Gardens (established 1816) include the site of Australia's first vegetable patch. You can still see the spot where, two centuries ago, Governor Arthur Phillip first planted his big yams. The Domain surrounds the gardens; in colonial times this land acted as a buffer between the governor's home and the penal colony, but by 1831 roads and paths had been built to allow public access. It has remained a people's place ever since. Highlights include the Sydney Tropical Centre, spectacular rose gardens, the colony of fruit bats near the Palm Grove visitor centre, and the prehistoric Wollemi Pine, one of the world's rarest species, discovered in 1994 by a ranger in the Blue Mountains. There are free guided walks (10.30am daily) and tours (1pm weekdays) – or you can take the 'trackless train' ($10), which stops at areas of interest, ending up at the Opera House. To learn more about Aboriginal life in the area, visit the Cadi Jam Ora garden with its indigenous display; groups of five or more can book a walk with an Aboriginal guide (details on 9231 8134/8050, $17 per person).

St Mary's Cathedral

Corner of College Street & Cathedral Square, CBD (9220 0400/www.sydney.catholic.org.au). CityRail St James. **Open** 6.30am-6.30pm Mon-Fri, Sun; 8am-6.30pm Sat. *Tours* noon Sun; also by arrangement. **Admission** free. **Map** p311 C3.

St Mary's is the seat of the Roman Catholic archbishop of Sydney (currently the controversial Cardinal George Pell) and stands on the site of Australia's first Catholic chapel. William Wilkinson Wardell's design replaced the original cathedral, ruined by fire in 1865. Constructed from local sandstone, it's the largest Gothic cathedral in the southern hemisphere – 106m/348ft long with a 46m/150ft central tower – dwarfing many of the European models from which it took inspiration. Wardell's original twin spires, never originally erected due to funding problems, were lowered into place by helicopter in 1999.

State Library of New South Wales

Corner of Macquarie Street & Cahill Expressway, CBD (9273 1414/www.slnsw.gov.au). CityRail Martin Place. **Open** *Library* 9am-9pm Mon-Fri; 11am-5pm Sat, Sun. *Exhibitions* 9am-5pm Mon-Fri; 11am-5pm Sat, Sun. Closed *Mitchell Wing* Sun. *Tours* 11am Tue; 2pm Thur. **Admission** free. **Map** p310 C2.

The State Library is essentially two libraries in one: the modern General Reference Library (GRL) provides access to five million books, CD-Roms and other media stored over five floors below ground, while the historic Mitchell Wing (1910) holds the world's greatest collection of Australiana, including James Cook's original journals and the log book of Captain Bligh. The latter wing has fine bronze bas-relief doors depicting Aboriginal peoples and European explorers, a grand mosaic and terrazzo vestibule, stained-glass windows and extensive amounts of Australian stone and timber. Its Shakespeare Room is a fine example of mock-Tudor style, with a ceiling modelled on Cardinal Wolsey's

closet in Hampton Court and stained glass windows depicting the Seven Ages of Man. The GRL's very popular Family History Service offers free courses to help trace your family history, and changing exhibitions highlight the library's large and fascinating collection of historical paintings, manuscripts, photos and rare books. There are guided tours of both libraries.

Sydney Hospital & Sydney Eye Hospital

8 Macquarie Street, opposite Martin Place, CBD (9382 7111/www.sesahs.nsw.gov.au/sydhosp). CityRail Martin Place. **Open** *Museum* 10am-3pm Tue. **Admission** $6. *Historic tour* $8 (book 2wks in advance). *Tour & museum* $12. **Map** p310 C2.

Originally known as the Rum Hospital, because its construction was met with government-controlled rum sales, Sydney Hospital is the city's only early institutional building still performing its original function. The current structure is a grandiose, late Victorian edifice, which thoughtlessly replaced the centre of what was once an eye-catching trio; cast your eyes to Parliament House (*see p65*) on one side and the Mint on the other to get an idea of what the hospital originally looked like. Outside stands the *Il Porcellino* bronze boar sculpture, a copy of the famous original in Florence; its snout is shiny from people rubbing it for good luck. Inside, the marble floors, magnificent windows and colour scheme have been carefully restored. The lobby lists those who donated to the construction and the respective amounts – Dame Nellie Melba kicked in £100, as much as some of the business giants of the day.

You can't walk in off the street, but you can book two weeks ahead for guided tours. The Lucy Osburn-Nightingale Foundation Museum is open to the public on Tuesdays. But the courtyard is open to everyone and has a very good café (9382 7359), with views over the Domain and an elaborate and colourful cast-iron fountain commemorating British comedian Robert Brough, who endeared himself to Australian audiences in the 19th century.

Martin Place & around

The pedestrian boulevard of **Martin Place**, running west from Macquarie Street down to George Street, is the home of the grand **General Post Office** (*see p67*), and where crowds gathered to celebrate the end of two world wars. The largest non-garden open space in the CBD, it houses the **Cenotaph** – which commemorates Australian lives lost in World War I – and, in December, a Christmas tree wilting in the Sydney sun. At the other end, lunchtime concerts and a fountain make this an outdoor mecca for office workers, and huge screens are often erected here during big sporting events and cultural occasions.

The very fine Victorian GPO has been renovated and its ground floor sacrificed to

Sydney's seemingly insatiable food obsession, with a gourmet greengrocer, a butcher, fishmonger and wine bar, as well as a steakhouse, cafés and a sushi outlet. The upper floors contain showy retail outlets, and a rather formal luxury/business hotel, the **Westin Sydney** (*see p27*). The sandstone banks and office buildings erected along the southern edge of Martin Place during the economic boom of wool and wheat now jostle with modern monstrosities and the odd elegant skyscraper. The newly refurbished **MLC Centre** (*see p169*) houses a huge electrical store and some great outdoor cafés.

Sydney's core of commerce is bordered by Circular Quay, King, York and Phillip Streets. Suits and secretaries, cycle couriers and company cars do the capitalist crawl from the foyers of luxury hotels to the legal district around Phillip Street, where you may catch sight of a bewigged barrister, robes flapping, scurrying across the street.

At night this area used to be quite dull, but twenty- and thirtysomething hangouts like the **Establishment** complex – home of **Tank** nightclub (*see p236*), **Hemmesphere** cocktail bar (*see p132*), **est.** restaurant (*see p142*) and a swanky hotel (*see p29*) – and the bars and bistro of **Hotel CBD** (75 York Street, 8297 7000) have introduced a fresh after-hours vigour, while upmarket steakhouse **Prime** (*see p140*), inside the GPO, and **Wine Banc** (*see p134*), with its vast international wine list, keep rich tourists and city folk fed and oiled.

General Post Office

1 Martin Place, CBD (9229 7700). CityRail Martin Place or Wynyard. **Open** *Shops* 9am-6pm Mon-Fri; 10am-4pm Sat. **Map** p310 B/C2.

The GPO's foundations were laid in 1865, but workers' strikes and complications from building over the Tank Stream (the colony's first water supply) meant that it didn't open until 1874. The grand clock tower was added in 1891, its chimes based on London's Big Ben, with both the clock mechanism and bells made in England. The building's Italianate flourishes dominated the young city's skyline for decades before it fell into neglect; by 1989 the building was no longer adequate for the needs of Australia Post and in 1990 it was boarded up. A deal between the city fathers and the Westin Hotel group rescued the building, restoring the original cast-iron staircase, clock tower and two ballrooms, and transforming the offices into hotel guestrooms. The GPO hall is now a light-drenched atrium that forms part of the hotel lobby, and leads down to a food emporium modelled after the one in London's Harrods. The colonnaded Martin Place entrance is flanked by upmarket shops. Much of the GPO's beauty is in the details: the stencilling on the walls, the Moderne windows, and the gold leaf ceiling patterned with

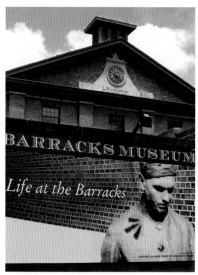

Hyde Park Barracks Museum. *See p63.*

leaves – spot the English rose and the Irish shamrock, as well as the Australian wattle and gum. The Tank Stream viewing room is open daily to visitors.

Centrepoint area

The main shopping district of the CBD – roughly bounded by Hunter, Elizabeth, George and Park Streets – takes as its epicentre Sydney's two department stores, thoroughly modern **Grace Bros** and majestic **David Jones** (for both, *see p166*). Nearby are the grandiose **State Theatre** (*see p253*) and the stately **Queen Victoria Building** (*see p68*). Pedestrianised **Pitt Street Mall** is always packed with shoppers and has lots of buskers, but never enough seats.

The **Sydney Tower** (*see p68*), also known as Centrepoint or AMP Tower, rises 250 metres (820 feet) above a shopping centre between Pitt Street Mall and Castlereagh Street. Despite its spindly appearance, the tower, which is held in place by 56 cables, is capable of withstanding earthquakes and extreme wind conditions – as the publicity blurb goes, 'if the strands of these cables were laid end to end, they would reach from Sydney to New Zealand'. Now do you feel safe? In 2004 the tower underwent a glitzy revamp, adding **Skytour**, a virtual reality adventure tour, and **Skywalk**, a heart-thumping open-air walk around the roof. In nearby Castlereagh Street sits the incredibly elaborate **Great Synagogue** (*see p68*).

Sydney Tower viewed from Hyde Park.

and gamely survived, long periods of neglect; demolition threats were finally quashed in the 1980s when a $75-million budget restored the building to its former grandeur. It now houses 200 outlets, including shops, cafés and restaurants. Of particular note are the coloured lead-light wheel windows, the cast-iron circular staircase, and the original floor tiles and lift. The magnificent ballroom on the third floor is now the Tea Room (*see p127*). On the hour, shoppers gather on gallery two to watch the Royal Automata Clock display a moving royal pageant. The execution of Charles I goes down a storm. *See also p169*.

Sydney Tower, Skytour & Skywalk

Podium Level, 100 Market Street, CBD (9222 9502/www.sydneyskytour.com.au/www.sydney skywalk.com.au). **Open** *Tower & Skytour* 9am-10.30pm Mon-Fri, Sun; 9am-11.30pm Sat. *Skywalk* 9am-9.30pm daily. **Admission** *Skytour* $22; $15.85 concessions; $39-$67 family; free under-5s. *Skywalk* $85; $68 concessions. **Map** p311 B3.

The turret of this well-known city symbol can hold 960 people and includes two levels of restaurants, a coffee lounge and an observation deck with 360° views. Three high-speed lifts take approximately 40 seconds to travel from bottom to top. If the lift fails you've got 1,504 stairs to climb back down. There are two new tourist attractions for 2004: Skytour offers a simulated ride through Australia's cultural history and geography, including climbing Uluru, a game of Aussie Rules footie and a tussle with a saltie (saltwater crocodile), while the Skywalk, due to open in mid 2004, promises a 75-minute wander around the roof of the tower – vertigo sufferers, this is *not* for you. Harnessed to a range of skyways and viewing platforms, participants will have the whole of Sydney at their feet; they'll be able to see the city's Harbour, beaches and, on a clear day, as far as the Blue Mountains. The viewing platforms are accessible to wheelchairs.

Great Synagogue

166 Castlereagh Street, between Park & Market Streets, CBD (9267 2477/www.greatsynagogue. org.au). CityRail Town Hall or St James. **Open** *Services* 5.30pm/6.15pm Fri; 8.45am Sat. *Tours* noon Tue, Thur. **Admission** $5. **Map** p311 C3.

Sydney's Jewish history dates back to convict times – there were around 16 Jews on the First Fleet – and the Great Synagogue, consecrated in 1878, is deemed the mother congregation of Australian Jewry. Designed by Thomas Rowe, the building is a lavish confection of French Gothic with large amounts of Byzantine thrown in. The superb front wheel window repeats the design of the wrought-iron gates outside, while, inside, the cast-iron columns holding up the balcony where the women sit are capped with intricate plaster designs. The ceiling, deep blue with gold-leaf stars, depicts the Creation. Twice-weekly tours include a short video about the history of the synagogue and Australia's Jewish community. A small museum is also open before and after tours.

Queen Victoria Building (QVB)

455 George Street, between Market & Druitt Streets, CBD (information 9265 6855/tours 9265 6864/ www.qvb.com.au). CityRail Town Hall/Monorail Galeries Victoria. **Open** 9am-6pm Mon-Wed, Fri; 9am-9pm Thur; 9am-5pm Sat; 11am-5pm Sun. **Map** p311 B3.

Designed by George McRae to resemble a Byzantine palace, the QVB occupies an entire block on George Street, and once dominated the Sydney skyline with its dramatic domed roof – an inner glass dome encased by a copper-sheathed outer dome. Completed in 1898 to celebrate Queen Victoria's golden jubilee, it originally housed street markets. It has suffered,

Town Hall

Thanks to a lengthy but successful revamp, Town Hall CityRail station and its surrounding underground shopping mall is no longer the purgatory it used to be. The refurbishment has widened walkways, introduced the odd water feature and generally smartened up shopfronts. This place is something of a crossroads, connecting Bathurst Street, the Queen Victoria Building, the chic **Galeries Victoria** shopping mall (*see p167*), the train station and **Sydney Town Hall** (*see p69*) – and is invariably crowded. During the day, office workers and students gather on the Town Hall steps to chat, eat lunch and wait for buses. Next door is the Anglican **St Andrew's Cathedral** (*see p69*).

The area south of the Town Hall above Chinatown has also been spruced up, but there's still an air of urban disquiet, especially at night. The multiplex cinemas on George Street draw hordes of office workers and suburbanites into town to catch a movie and ingest some popcorn, and the surrounding burger bars and late-night pubs keep folk hanging out well into the early hours. Be prepared to jostle with teenagers streaming in to play video games at the many amusement arcades, and rowdy backpackers and boozers heading for drinking dens such as **Cheers Bar & Grill** (561 George Street, 9261 8313) and the always lively Irish bar **Scruffy Murphy's Hotel** (43 Goulburn Street, 9211 2002). The latter is open 24 hours a day, seven days a week, offering bands, big-screen sports and even drag karaoke on some nights.

But there are areas of more genuine interest, including some quirky comics and record shops and discount stores. In the 'Spanish quarter', the tiny stretch of Liverpool Street between George and Sussex Streets, you can have tapas and a *cerveza* at the **Spanish Club** (No.88, 9267 8440). To take home genuine Spanish chorizo, olives and Rioja, dive into **Torres Cellars & Delicatessen** (No.75, 9264 6862).The area used to be quite down at heel, but a clean-up has encouraged previously lacklustre restaurants to lift their game; best of the crop is the upmarket **Don Quixote** (545 Kent Street, 9264 5129).

The newest addition to the area, and one that is certain to shape its future, is Sydney's tallest residential building, **World Tower**, on the corner of George and Liverpool Streets. This glass and steel structure soars 75 levels, offering swanky, state-of-the-art city living on top of its very own shopping arcade. Running slap bang along the front of the building is the futuristic-looking **Monorail**, so the whole scene resembles something out of *Blade Runner*.

St Andrew's Cathedral

Sydney Square, corner of George & Bathurst Streets, CBD (9265 1661/www.sydney.anglican.asn.au). CityRail Town Hall. **Open** 9am-5pm Mon, Tue, Fri; 8am-8pm Wed; 9am-6.30pm Thur; 10am-4pm Sat; 7.30am-8pm Sun. *Tours* by arrangement daily. **Admission** free. **Map** p311 B3.

This huge late-Gothic edifice, the oldest cathedral in Australia, was started with astonishing confidence by Governor Macquarie (who named it after the Scottish saint) when Sydney was still the size of a small village. The first stone was laid in 1819, and it was finally consecrated in 1868. Three architects contributed to it, the most notable being Edmund Blacket, city architect 1849-54. Special elements link the cathedral to the motherland, including a marble floor from Canterbury Cathedral and two stones from the Palace of Westminster. Military commemorations honour the landings at Gallipoli and the prison camp at Changi in Singapore. Recent conservation work has restored the interior (altered in the 1950s) to its orginal glory.

Sydney Town Hall

Corner of George & Druitt Streets, CBD (9265 9189/concert details 9265 9007/www.sydneytown hall.com.au). CityRail Town Hall. **Open** 8am-6pm Mon-Fri. **Admission** free. **Map** p311 B3.

Built on a graveyard and completed in 1889, Sydney Town Hall is an impressive High Victorian building, topped by a clock tower with a two-ton bell. It has retained its original function and interiors, including the Council Chamber and Lord Mayor's offices. The Vestibule, its colourful domed ceiling hung with a huge crystal chandelier, has some of the earliest examples of Australian-made stained glass, and is stunning. Behind it, the Centennial Hall is dominated by a magnificent 8,000-pipe organ; with a capacity of 2,048, it was once the largest concert hall in the world. It's still used for organ recitals and other musical events.

Chinatown & Haymarket

The Chinese have been a positive presence in Sydney since the First Fleet landed in 1788: two of the ships' cooks were said to be Chinese. By 1891 the Chinese population had reached 14,000, but dwindled to 4,000 as the 'White Australia' policy peaked in the 1950s. Today, Chinese migrants make up the third-largest group of immigrants coming to New South Wales. Vietnamese refugees (including many of Chinese descent) arrived in the wake of the Vietnam War, while dissident students sought asylum after China's 1989 Tiananmen Square debacle. In the years leading to the handover of Hong Kong to China many Hong Kong Chinese left for Australia.

When you hit Chinatown, the vitality and energy of the Chinese community is obvious. Sino-Sydneysiders do not live in a ghetto: there are also established suburban enclaves in Strathfield, Willoughby and Ashfield, and many are simply integrated into the community. But Chinatown is the commercial and culinary hub; once confined to Dixon Street, a somewhat tacky mall created in the early 1980s, it continues to expand and change at a phenomenal rate. It now extends well into Haymarket, over Hay Street, down Thomas and Ultimo Streets, and across George Street.

Around the ornate gates in Dixon Street, soil, sand and rock from Guangdong province has been buried. For the Chinese, it symbolises that Australia is their home and they can be buried there. Sussex Street has now taken over from Dixon Street as the main strip; the brightly lit section from Goulburn Street to Hay Street (where **Paddy's Market** resides *– see p170*) bustles with activity from early morning to late at night. There are restaurants, shops, supermarkets, Chinese-language cinemas and some well-hidden gambling spots, and this is one of the few places in Sydney where you can get a meal and a drink at 2am.

In daylight hours, chic shops sell (real and ersatz) Agnès B and Katharine Hamnett watches, Versace and Romeo Gigli perfumes, Jean-Paul Gaultier bags and a range of bewilderingly hip gear. The Chinese community is not only growing in size, it's also increasingly affluent. The days of wall-to-wall sweet and sour pork have been left far behind. Little Chinatown diners serve Peking-style dumplings, while others specialise in handmade noodles, barbecued duck or seafood. Grand Hong Kong-style dining rooms with over-the-top chandeliers are always packed with Chinese and Anglos choosing delicacies from yum cha (dim sum) trolleys.

Darling Harbour, Pyrmont & Ultimo

Transport Darling Harbour *Ferry Darling Harbour/CityRail Central or Town Hall/Monorail Darling Park, Harbourside, Convention or Exhibition Centre/LightRail Exhibition or Convention/bus 888.* **Pyrmont** *Ferry Pyrmont Bay/LightRail Star City, Convention or Pyrmont Bay/bus 888.* **Ultimo** *CityRail Central/Monorail Haymarket/LightRail Haymarket or Exhibition.*

The reclaimed waterfront of Darling Harbour, on the west side of the CBD, boasts some acclaimed modern architecture (courtesy of architect Phillip Cox) and a huge retail complex (courtesy of global greed). So many attractions are here – the gaudily tacky **Star City** casino (*see p71*), the **Sydney Aquarium** (*see p71*), the **Chinese Garden** (*see p71*), the **Australian National Maritime Museum** (*see below*), **Sydney Entertainment Centre** (*see p223*) and the **IMAX** cinema (*see p203*) – that it's easy to overlook the most basic one: the view from the Pyrmont side of Darling Harbour of the western cityscape – one of the best in Sydney. And it's free. There's also the **Harbourside** shopping centre (*see p167*), good for classy, if pricey, souvenirs.

Darling Harbour hosts a stream of free festivals, concerts and other events on weekends and school holidays throughout the year. New Year's Eve and Australia Day, in particular, are occasions for giant parties. More details from the **Darling Harbour Information Line** (1902 260 568, www.darlingharbour.com.au).

Cockle Bay Wharf (named because of its abundance of shellfish), on Darling Harbour's eastern shore, houses an array of cafés, restaurants and clubs spread across an epic space designed by populist American architect Eric Kuhne, who also designed the public areas in adjoining **Darling Park** (and the enormous Bluewater development in Kent, England). Initially written off by many as a failure, Cockle Bay has become a hugely successful entertainment precinct and a fun place to dine and hang out. During the day, it's a haven for teens and families; at night, tourists and twentysomethings move in, many heading for the sail-like glass building of mega nightclub **Home** (*see p235*).

Further north, past the Sydney Aquarium, the party continues along the newly created **King Street Wharf** at yet more restaurants, cafés and a clutch of waterside apartments. The current place to be on a hot summer's night, if you're under 30, is the **Cargo Bar/ Lounge** (*see p234*), a rowdy outdoor venue with pumping music and great waterside views.

Pyrmont, to the west of Darling Harbour (reached by the pedestrian Pyrmont Bridge), was once a mix of working-class cottages, refineries, quarries and engineering works. Now it is filling with apartment buildings and office blocks (including Rupert Murdoch's pay TV station, Foxtel) as the city spreads ever westward. It's also home to Star City, Sydney's casino – a vulgar, Las Vegas-like creation (also by Phillip Cox) with a recently refurbished deluxe hotel (*see pxxx*).

Pyrmont's biggest draw is **Sydney Fish Markets** (*see p72*), one of the best in the world. From its auction rooms premium-grade tuna goes to Japan, and a dozen or more outlets sell fresh-off-the-boat seafood. Browse among enticing mounds of salmon, snapper and yabbies (freshwater crustaceans), then pick up some rock oysters and find a sunny wharfside seat at which to picnic – but watch out for the pelicans: they're partial to seafood too.

Ultimo – south of Pyrmont and west of Chinatown, which is creeping towards it – has evolved into a strange meeting place of media, academic and museum life. Once notorious for some of Sydney's most squalid housing, and later the site of the municipal markets, it's now home to the sprawling **University of Technology**, the headquarters of the **Australian Broadcasting Corporation** and the masterfully converted **Powerhouse Museum** (*see p71*).

Australian National Maritime Museum

2 Murray Street, Harbourside, Darling Harbour (9298 3777/www.anmm.gov.au). Ferry/LightRail Pyrmont Bay/Monorail Harbourside/bus 443, 888. **Open** *Jan* 9.30am-6pm daily. *Feb-Dec* 9.30am-5pm daily. **Admission** free (fee for special exhibits). **Credit** AmEx, BC, DC, MC, V. **Map** p310 A2.

For a city whose history has always been entwined with its harbour, the sea and water travel, it comes as no surprise that this museum is one of the finest and most unabashed when it comes to maritime treasures. The biggest exhibits are the vessels themselves, among them *The Spirit of Australia*, the world's fastest boat, designed by Ken Warby on his kitchen table and built in his backyard in 1974. Other craft include 1888 racing yacht *Akarana*, 1950s naval destroyer HMAS *Vampire* and traditional Vietnamese junk *Tu Duo* ('Freedom'), which sailed into Darwin in 1977 with 39 refugees. A new exhibition tracing the history of the Royal Australian Navy opened in late 2003. The Yots Café offers fine open-air eating on the water's edge, there's an innovative shop and, if you really want to splash out, sailing packages with qualified skippers. During January the museum stages Wetworld – a wet fun centre for kids aged five to 12.

Chinese Garden

Corner of Pier & Harbour Streets, Darling Harbour (9281 6863/www.citysearch). CityRail Town Hall or Central/Monorail/LightRail Haymarket. **Open** 9.30am-5.30pm daily. **Admission** $6; $3 concessions. **No credit cards. Map** p311 B3.

Unless you're prepared to arm-wrestle for your share of tranquil spots, avoid this place at the weekend when it's full of grimly determined tourists. Designed in Sydney's sister city, Guangzhou, China, to celebrate the bicentenary in 1988, the Garden of Friendship symbolises the bond between the two. The dragon wall features two dragon heads, one in gold for Guangzhou, one in blue for NSW, with a pearl in between. There are waterfalls, weeping willows, water lilies, 'wandering galleries' and wooden bridges. Head up to the teahouse balcony, order a cup of *shui-hsien* tea and enjoy the best view of all: the entire park reflected in the Lake of Brightness, stuffed full of chubby carp. Not surprisingly, the Garden is a big hit with brides, so be prepared to be muscled aside by a wedding party.

Powerhouse Museum

500 Harris Street, between Henry & Macarthur Streets, Ultimo (9217 0111/www.phm.gov.au). CityRail Central/Monorail Haymarket/LightRail Haymarket or Exhibition/bus 501. **Open** 10am-5pm daily. **Admission** $10; $4-$5 concessions; $24 family. **Credit** AmEx, BC, DC, MC, V. **Map** p311 B3.

This former power station opened as a fun and funky museum in 1988 and is the largest, and probably best, in Australia, with a collection of 385,000 objects, 22 permanent and five temporary display spaces, and more than 250 interactive exhibits. It covers science, technology, creativity, decorative arts and Australian popular culture, resulting in exhibitions on such diverse topics as Tokyo street style and childhood memories of migration. Taking a fresh, hands-on approach, with banks of computers and interactive video screens, the Powerhouse is a joy to visit – the KIDS (Kids Interactive Discovery Spaces) will keep under-8s involved for hours.

Eats and treats in **Chinatown**. *See p69.*

Star City

80 Pyrmont Street, at Foreshore Road, Pyrmont (9777 9000/www.starcity.com.au). CityRail Town Hall then 15mins walk/LightRail Star City/Monorail Harbourside/bus 443, 888. **Open** 24hrs daily. **Map** p310 A2.

It's easy to get lost at this huge casino complex – though that's probably a deliberate ruse to keep you gambling. Opened in 1997, Star City is both slick and tacky – marble toilets, cocktails, champagne, fine dining, then fish and chips, beer and miles of pokies. There are 1,500 slot machines, a huge sports betting lounge and sports bar and 200 gaming tables featuring everything from blackjack and roulette to Caribbean stud poker. Elsewhere are invitation-only private gaming rooms for the high rollers, many flown in from Asia. The Lyric Theatre (*see p251*) and Showroom cabaret venue stage glittery shows (recently, *The Lady Boys of Bangkok*) and the revamped luxury hotel with its impressive spa (*see p33*) means you don't ever have to leave – or, in other words, you're trapped.

Sydney Aquarium

Aquarium Pier, Wheat Road, Darling Harbour (9262 2300/www.sydneyaquarium.com.au). Ferry Aquarium/CityRail Town Hall or Wynyard/Monorail Darling Park/bus 443. **Open** 9am-10pm daily. *Seal sanctuary* 9.30am-sunset daily. **Admission** $24; $12-$16 concessions; $29-$64 family. **Credit** AmEx, BC, DC, MC, V. **Map** p310 B2/3.

This fantastic aquarium comprises a main exhibit hall, two floating oceanariums – one dedicated to the Great Barrier Reef (and the largest collection of sharks in captivity), the other a seal sanctuary – and two touch pools. Watch out for the saltwater crocs in the northern river section and those elusive platypus in the southern river section. In 2003 the aquarium unveiled its $2.25-million seal sanctuary refurbishment, with water pumped direct from Sydney Harbour. Underwater viewing tunnels mean visitors can watch the seals powering and frolicking close up. Allow at least a half day to appreciate everything. A new café sells above-average meals and sarnies, but you might prefer to bring a picnic.

Sydney Fish Markets

Corner of Pyrmont Bridge Road & Bank Street, Pyrmont (9004 1100/www.sydneyfishmarket. com.au). LightRail Fish Market. **Open** from 5.30am for auctions; 7am-4pm daily for the public. **No credit cards. Map** p311 A3.

This working fishing port – with trawlers in Blackwattle Bay, wholesale and retail fish markets, shops (including a bakery, deli, florist and bottle shop), a variety of indoor and outdoor eateries and picnic tables on an outdoor deck – is well worth the trek to Pyrmont. To enjoy the full experience, get up early and catch the noisy wholesale fish auctions; they start at 5.30am, but as long as you arrive by 7am you'll get the gist. The largest market of its kind in the southern hemisphere, and the world's second-largest in terms of variety outside Japan, it trades more than 100 species a day and over 15 million kilos of fish a year. There's even the Sydney Seafood School (9004 1111), which offers classes (from $70) in handling and cooking seafood – everything from sushi to sashimi, tapas to paella.

East Sydney & Darlinghurst

Transport Kings Cross side *CityRail Kings Cross/bus 311, 312, 324, 325, 326, 327.* **Oxford Street side** *CityRail Museum/bus 378, 380, 382.*

Stand with your back to Hyde Park at Whitlam Square facing down Oxford Street towards Paddington, and you're on the edge of the CBD and the inner city. Although not as dangerous or seedy as Kings Cross, the lower end of **Oxford Street** attracts a steamy mix of junkies, down-and-outs and all-night hedonists. Nearer to Taylor Square, it's also the main gay hub of eastern suburbs Sydney, and as night falls the street fills with crowds of perfectly pumped boys in regulation tight tees, and high-haired drag queens flitting between shows in the huddle of pubs and clubs along 'the Strip'. Restaurants and takeaways serve from nasi goreng, sushi, tandoori chicken and chips. This area is lively well into the early hours and can get a little edgy, so watch your back – although there's always someone willing to help if you do find yourself in trouble.

As with the rest of Sydney, modern apartment blocks are forever popping up between the trad Victorian terraces and with them an influx of cashed-up DINKs (double

income no kids). Consequently, the previously drab shops have perked up – the clothes shops are more innovative and you can buy candles and minimalist homeware. But Darlinghurst and East Sydney are not yet a second Paddington or Double Bay – the wonderful queer-central **Bookshop Darlinghurst** (*see p171*) proudly stamps its identity on the Strip, as do the wig and fetish wear shops and tattoo parlours.

Some consider **Taylor Square** to be the heart of gay Sydney (*see p212-220*), and the epicentre of the Strip, but there's not a lot to see here. After 18 months of scaffolding, drilling and dust, the revamped square was unwrapped in late 2003. The results were a tad disappointing, but the upgrade has achieved wider, safer pavements and generally cleaner streets, helped by a row of pavement-level water squirts that surprise night-time revellers. Plans are also afoot to upgrade Oxford Street, including sparkly new granite paving, trees, public art and cycle paths, to be completed in time for the 2005 Mardi Gras Festival.

Just beyond Taylor Square, on the north side of Oxford Street, **Darlinghurst Road** begins its downhill run to Kings Cross. The Victorian and art deco mansions here give a good idea of what the area used to be like. Take the time to wander through the old **Darlinghurst Gaol**, a magnificent collection of sandstone buildings dating from the 1820s, now a campus for the Sydney Institute of Technology and one of the city's best art schools. Incongruously, it also houses a butchery school, so don't be surprised to see arty types one minute and men in bloodied aprons the next. The jail was built on a hill as a conspicuous reminder to all that Sydney was a penal colony. Drop into the library and they'll give you a handout on the jail's history.

Back then, instead of negotiating the hustling hordes and screeching traffic of Darlinghurst Road, you'd have reached the Cross by scrambling through scrub and sand drifts, past farms and sandstone quarries, before finally clambering down wooden ladders to Woolloomooloo Bay. Along the Darlinghurst ridge, where the Coca-Cola sign now stands at the top of William Street, was once the site of the city's important windmills. Walk past on a blustery August day and you'll see why. Another place worth visiting is the **Sydney Jewish Museum** (*see p73*). Jewish immigrants have played a vital part in Australia's history and their story is told here.

Running roughly parallel to Darlinghurst Road on its east side is **Victoria Street**, a lively mix of cafés, restaurants, shops and a few residential homes. The restaurants here

Catch the Monorail to the tourist-friendly attractions of **Darling Harbour**. *See p70*.

and on Darlinghurst Road are generally better than those on Oxford Street. For a great French night out, head to **Sel et Poivre** (No.263, 9361 6530). For ice-cream and sorbet, queue up at the rightfully popular **Gelato Messina** (No.241, 8354 1223): one spoonful and you're hooked. To find the beautiful people, seek out the tiny but oh-so-cool cocktail bar at the back of **Will & Toby's Bistro & Bar** (No.292, 9356 3255). A stone's throw from each other on Darlinghurst Road are the stylish boutique hotels **Medusa** and **Kirketon** (for both, *see p35*), the latter also home to hip Mod Oz restaurant **Salt** (*see p149*).

Sydney Jewish Museum

148 Darlinghurst Road, at Burton Street, Darlinghurst (9360 7999/www.sydneyjewish museum.com.au). CityRail Museum or Kings Cross/bus 378, 380, 389. **Open** 10am-4pm Mon-Thur, Sun; 10am-2pm Fri. **Admission** $10; $6-$7 concessions; $22 family. **Credit** (shop only) BC, MC, V. **Map** p311 D3.

In the aftermath of World War II, over 30,000 survivors of the Holocaust emigrated to Australia, settling mainly in Sydney and Melbourne. This museum opened in 1992 in Maccabean Hall, built to commemorate the Jews of NSW who had served in World War I. The hall has been the centre of Jewish life in Sydney ever since, so it was apt to transform it into a permanent memorial to victims of both world wars. There are two permanent displays – 'Culture and Continuity' and 'The Holocaust' – plus excellent touring exhibitions.

Surry Hills & Redfern

Transport Surry Hills *CityRail Central/ bus 301, 302, 303.* **Redfern** *CityRail Redfern/ bus 305, 309, 310.*

Crown Street, the first major thoroughfare to cross Oxford Street, runs south to the ever-so-slightly tumbledown terraces of Surry Hills. Crown Street is an interesting mix of the very cool and the tatty. At night the vibe is heady and laid-back, with restaurants, cafés and bars to suit every taste and pocket. The Oxford Street end tends to be more chic; witness the recently renovated **Dolphin on Crown** pub (No.412, 9331 4800) complete with its very acceptable kerbside restaurant. Opposite is **Medina on Crown**, a smart, serviced apartment block popular with short-stay business types. There's a hub of trendy hangouts, including Cantonese restaurant **Billy Kwong** (*see p146*), **MG Garage** (*see p147*), which has sports cars amid the tables, and its more reasonably priced sister eaterie, **Fuel** (No.488, 9383 9388). The **Clock Hotel** (*see p237*), with its dining room and wrap-around balcony, is very popular with a youthful set who are as keen on their cocktails and designer beer as they are on the pool tables.

Also worth noting are Thai curio shop **Mrs Red & Sons** (No.427, 9310 4860) and **Mondo Luce** (No.439, 9690 2667), one of number of modish lighting shops. The fire-engine-red

Shell out at **Sydney Fish Markets**. *See p72.*

causing mass overcrowding. In the decades
that followed, government programmes (some
helpful, some definitely not) have disseminated
the area's Aborigines and today it's undergoing
intensive reinvention, with some pockets
hurtling upmarket. But the central patch of
run-down terraces in a one-hectare area
bounded by Eveleigh, Vine, Louis and Caroline
Streets – which make up 'the Block', the
beleaguered heart of a black-run Aboriginal
housing co-operative – remains.

The area's problems – poverty, drugs and
alcoholism – boiled over in February 2004
after the death of a 17-year-old Aboriginal
youth sparked some of the worst street riots
Sydney has ever seen. The Redfern Aboriginal
community blamed the police for Thomas
Hickey's death (he was impaled on a fence).
Up to 100 youths threw bricks, bottles and
Molotov cocktails at the ill-prepared police.
Forty police officers were injured, and
Redfern's train station and a car were torched.
At the time of writing, several investigations
were under way.

In neighbouring **Waterloo**, a mini town is
under development. If all goes to plan (and it's
a 20-year plan), **Green Square Town
Centre**, focused on the sparkly new Green
Square train station and bordered by Botany
Road and Bourke Street, will house 4,500 people
in 2,500 new apartments and houses, plus
parks, shops and recreation centres. 'Affordable
housing' is promised, as is 'acknowledgement of
the social and architectural history of the site'
inhabited 8,000 years ago by indigenous people.
How the project develops remains to be seen.

Trinity Hotel (9319 6802) on the corner of
Devonshire Street, with its covered outdoor
tables and chairs, sports screens and lounge
bar, buzzes from early evening, while tiny café
La Passion du Fruit (*see p128*) is a haven
for discerning foodies.

All this activity is gradually and inevitably
gentrifying Surry Hills, as has happened to
previously funky Paddington, now too chichi
for words. Surry Hills peters out in the west at
Central Station (just beyond the rag trade centre
on and around Foveaux Street) and in the south
at **Cleveland Street**, the border with Redfern.

Aboriginal people from rural areas started
moving into Redfern in the 1920s because of its
proximity to Central Station, cheap rents and
local workshops offering regular work. More
arrived during the Depression of the 1930s, and
by the 1940s the area had become synonymous
with its indigenous population. Following
the 1967 national referendum, which gave
indigenous people citizenship rights, Redfern's
Aboriginal population increased to 35,000,

Brett Whiteley Studio

*2 Raper Street, between Crown & Bourke Streets,
Surry Hills (9225 1881/www.brettwhiteley.org).
CityRail Central/bus 301, 304.* **Open** 10am-4pm Sat,
Sun. **Admission** $7; $5 concessions. **Credit** AmEx,
BC, MC, V. **Map** p311 C5.

Brett Whiteley was one of Australia's most exciting
artists. In 1985 he bought a warehouse in Surry Hills
and converted it into a studio, art gallery and living
space. Following Whiteley's death in 1992 – in the
motel room he was rumoured to have used for his
drug and alcohol habit – the studio was converted
into a museum. Managed by the Art Gallery of
NSW, it offers a singular insight into the artist
through photos, personal effects, memorabilia and
changing exhibitions of his work.

Kings Cross

Transport *CityRail Kings Cross/bus 311, 312, 324.*

Kings Cross (the cross is formed by the
intersection of Darlinghurst Road and Victoria
Street) is Soho's little sister, with a thick scab

Sightseeing

of fairly standard sleaze – Porky's Nite Spot, the Love Machine, Kinks Adult Shop, ad nauseam – concentrated on 'the Strip', stretching along **Darlinghurst Road** from William Street to the picturesque El Alamein fountain. This area has long been the city's vice quarter and today is dominated as much by drugs as by prostitution. It's the site of Australia's first legal 'shooting gallery', a monitored, fully staffed injecting room opened in 2001. Despite much controversy, the centre has just been granted a second term, and many in the know say it has reduced the number of heroin deaths in the area, and provided desperately needed support for the growing number of users.

Today's Cross is a fading glittery hangover from the R&R days of the Vietnam War, when thousands of US soldiers descended with fistfuls of dollars and a desire to party the horrors of war out of their consciousness. Their appetites tended towards the carnal, and the dreary parade of seedy strip clubs and massage parlours – now frequented mostly by suburbanites, out-of-towners and international sailors – is evidence of how they got their kicks. But whatever the state of life on the streets, the Cross's neon lights still pull in hordes of backpackers, sustained by a network of hostels, internet cafés and cheap and cheerful restaurants.

However, the Cross is due for a change: a drastic and controversial clean-up project is under way (*see p76* **A Cross to bear**). The good news for tourists is that there are plenty of police on the beat, and when the night turns ugly, as it inevitably does for some, you needn't get caught in the crossfire.

At the beginning of the Cross, the inconspicuous **Crest Hotel** (111 Darlinghurst Road, 9358 2755) has perhaps the only bona fide straight sauna in the area – the **Ginseng Bathhouse** (*see p188*), a traditional Korean bathhouse with an impressive range of therapeutic treatments. It also has the **Goldfish Bowl** bar, recently liberated from its sleazy image by a cool revamp that includes heavy-duty doormen.

Another place that has succumbed to the ubiquitous glass and white refurb is the **Bourbon** (24 Darlinghurst Road, 9358 1144). Previously the legendary Bourbon & Beefsteak Bar, it used to be the chosen watering hole for stalwart locals, sailors and some of the area's more colourful characters, but is now aiming for the youth style set. The somewhat rocky transition has seen the old crowd turned away by zealous doormen and the media running with their cause. Is this a sign of things to come in the Cross?

Potts Point & Woolloomooloo

Transport *CityRail Kings Cross/bus 311, 312.*

In contrast to the Kings Cross Strip's wall-to-wall neon lighting, **Macleay Street**, with its columns of cool plane trees, is made for slow strolling and offers genuine architectural and culinary pleasures. Tall, impregnable apartment buildings such as the neo-Gothic **Franconia** (No.123) offer a glimpse of the grandeur of the old Cross. Orwell Street, running west off Macleay, houses one of Sydney's finest art deco buildings, the old Minerva theatre – now called the **Metro** and, fittingly, home to Kennedy Miller Productions, which brought the world *Mad Max* and *Babe*.

This quarter, known as Potts Point, has many fine eateries – try **jimmy liks** (*see p151*), the **Yellow Bistro** (*see p152*) or **Fratelli Paradiso** (*see p151*) – and a good selection of coffee shops. It's a far cry from the desperate world of the Strip – you could be on another planet, one populated by chic, wealthy Sydneysiders. If you turn off Macleay Street and into Challis Avenue (also dotted with cafés), you'll soon come to the northern end of **Victoria Street** and a handful of the grand 19th-century terraces that formerly made it one of the city's most elegant thoroughfares. Victoria Street backs on to a cliff that drops down to Sydney's oldest suburb, Woolloomooloo, which stands partly on land filled with scuttled square riggers, and is now a mix of public housing, incorporating many original buildings, and swish new developments.

You can walk down from Victoria Street via Horderns, Butlers or McElhone Stairs. Alternatively, Italian restaurant **Mezzaluna** (123 Victoria Street, 9357 1988) offers a spectacular view over Woolloomooloo Bay to the city skyline. **Embarkation Park**, built atop a Navy carpark at the corner of Victoria Street and Challis Avenue, affords an equally magnificent vista, particularly midweek around twilight when the office towers are lit up.

Macleay Street becomes **Wylde Street**, which runs out of puff at the **Garden Island Naval Base** on Woolloomooloo Bay, where you are greeted by the surreal sight of the Royal Australian Navy's fleet moored by the side of the road. The US Navy also regularly docks here, disgorging fodder for the strip joints and massage parlours of the Cross.

Jutting into the bay is **Cowper Wharf**, constructed in 1910 as a state-of-the-art wool and cargo handling facility. Over the years the wharf fell into disuse, and it seemed destined to crumble into the harbour until Premier Bob Carr slapped a conservation order on the site.

Sightseeing

As the largest remaining timber-pile wharf in Australia, and a rare example of industrial Federation architecture, it had to be saved.

In 2000, a stylish mix of eateries, apartments, the upmarket **W** hotel (*see p34*) and private marinas opened. Those who can't afford to eat in the restaurants that line the finger wharf (including the much-talked-about **Otto** – *see p151*) promenade on the boardwalk in the sun. At the foot of the wharf is **Artspace** (*see below*), an extraordinary government-run art gallery. Nearby on Cowper Wharf Road is **Harry's Café de Wheels**, Sydney's most famous pie cart, here since World War II.

Opposite the wharf, on the corner of Bourke Street, is **Woolloomooloo Bay Hotel** (9357 1177). This large traditional pub with outdoor seating, restaurants, a balcony and bands is always lively, and from Thursday nights on it's packed with old neighbourhood faces and rowdy youngsters who don't care for the W hotel bar peacocks over the road. Indeed, this clash of cultures has become something of a problem: tussles between incoming yuppies and grass-roots locals occur with alarming regularity. Visitors should stick to the main streets, especially at night when the winding roads leading back towards Potts Point and the Cross tend to become drug alleys.

Artspace

The Gunnery, 43-51 Cowper Wharf Road, between Forbes & Dowling Steets, Woolloomooloo (9368 1899/www.artspace.org.au). Bus 311, 312. **Open** 11am-6pm Tue-Sat. **Admission** free. **Credit** BC, MC, V. **Map** p312 D2.

This government-funded contemporary art gallery presents edgy, experimental and challenging work. Five large galleries and 12 studios (for local and international artists) are housed in the historic Gunnery building. Prepare to be 'shocked, stimulated, inspired and entertained' – or so they claim.

A Cross to bear

Kings Cross with no sex and drugs – is such a thing possible? Probably not, but in 2003, then Lord Mayor Lucy Turnbull announced her intentions to de-ghettoise the area – sparking equal measures of outrage and approval. Ladies of the night, dens of naughtiness and colourful characters living on society's edge have given the Cross its special ambience, argue aficionados, and are part of its unique boho history. Meanwhile, if the red-light area and its attendant drug industry are moved from the Cross, where will they turn up next?

It's a complex issue and one undeniably fuelled by the existence of Sydney's only government-sponsored legal injection room, in the heart of the Darlinghurst Road strip. Turnbull steers clear of discussing the injection room, but is worried that new residents – those who have paid top dollar for glitzy apartments in the rash of new buildings – are being forced to shop, wine, dine and socialise elsewhere.

The Mayor hopes to close any sex premises breaking the law and, through stringent planning restrictions, prevent new brothels and strip clubs, which will make room for other types of business – chichi cafés and food emporiums, no doubt. The council has also committed $15 million for the upgrade of Darlinghurst Road itself: improving footpaths, lighting and removing graffiti. Whether such moves represent the start of a puritanical purge or a genuine desire to

prevent the Cross from becoming a no-go ghetto remains to be seen. For the moment though, the sex and drugs are still very much intact, albeit under the watchful eye of the ever-present police.

Eastern Suburbs

Those in the know head east.

What was once a mix of shifting marshes and scrub, rocky harbourside terrain and windswept ocean headlands is today the much primped location of Sydney's most affluent. Some areas in the eastern suburbs have always attracted wealthy patronage – Rose Bay, Double Bay, Vaucluse, Woollahra and Point Piper all have the stamp of early colonial extravagance, with elegant mansions, English-style gardens and summer houses. But what has happened to Paddington and Bondi Beach is synonymous with Sydney's own glittering rise. In Paddington yuppies and the middle classes have driven out any skerrick of the slum dwellings that existed before, while Bondi Beach is no longer just a working-class seaside enclave, but is now a playground for the new rich, the youthful cool set and those who just wanna have fun.

The seemingly unstoppable rise in real estate prices and ongoing gentrification has led to an increasing number of glass edifices around Bondi Beach, Tamarama, Bronte, Coogee and even as far out as Maroubra. Locals bemoan the loss of sea views, but, to be fair, the rather dull, red-brick bungalows and units of yesterday have been replaced by often-impressive, one-off palaces with wrap-around views and all the latest comforts. Sure, they crowd the coastline, but there's no shortage of people prepared to pay top dollar to move in.

In Paddington cleverly renovated Victorian terrace houses are fetching more than a million dollars. They're still narrow, dark, cold in the winter and on tiny plots, but pull out the back, drop in some glass, install a spiral staircase and you'll begin to see the light. These houses with their iron-lace-trimmed balconies have an old-fashioned charm that is much prized in this relatively young country.

For the super-rich, of course, there are the distinguished established residences that flank Centennial Park and are also found in Double Bay, Rose Bay, Elizabeth Bay, Woollahra and Vaucluse. Some are Victorian, while many of the more interesting mansions – such as Boomerang in Elizabeth Bay, a flamboyant Spanish Mission-style creation – date from the 1920s and '30s and have a 'golden age of Hollywood' aura.

For the visitor, with all this prime property comes a plethora of great shops, restaurants, bars and cafés. The needy new residents ensure that good places are well patronised and bad ones go out of business fast. At weekends the eastern suburbs attract a multitude of characters. Whether it be glamorous boys walking their pooches down Oxford Street, fevered cyclists in Centennial Park, the doof-doof set in their mobile disco cars on Bondi's Campbell Parade, leggy beauties combing Paddington's size-fascist boutiques or tourists trailing round the market, well-coiffured ladies lunching in Double Bay or families picnicking in Nielsen Park, everyone gravitates towards the east at some point.

Paddington

Transport *Bus 378, 380, L82.*

Paddington gets its unique blend of urban chic, arty intellectuals and monied style from its position, protected from the city to the west by the more edgy burbs of Darlinghurst and Surry Hills and bordering old-money Woollahra and Centennial Park to the east and south. Walking along the main drag, **Oxford Street**, with the city behind you, you pass the heart of gay Sydney at Taylor Square; Paddington proper starts around the Puma concept store (formerly the Albury Hotel, a legendary drag venue). The scene gets straighter, but no less fashionable, the further you climb up the hill until you reach the wide green open spaces of **Centennial Park** (*see p80*). Bookstores, cinemas and clothes shops line the way, interspersed with numerous cafés, pubs and cocktail bars, each filled with a slightly different crowd.

Across the road from the Puma store are two of Sydney's art house cinemas, the **Academy Twin** (*see p201*), and the **Verona** (*see p203*). Next door is the city's best **Mambo** outlet (*see p178*) and nearby are two great bookstores, open late and perfect for pre- and post-cinema browsing: **Berkelouw Book Sellers** and **Ariel** (for both, *see p171*) across the road.

Halfway up Oxford Street on the left-hand side, with the garish, boudoir-esque **Alannah Hill** fashion boutique (*see p172*) on its corner, is the beginning of **Glenmore Road**. This long, winding residential street is peppered with art galleries, the odd café, a noisy Irish pub and some of the area's most expensively refurbished Victorian terraces. At just about its

Some like it cold

A strange, uniquely Australian ritual occurs
at Bondi Beach every year on the first Sunday
in May. Members of the iconic Bondi Icebergs
winter swimming club gather at their open-air
ocean pool and throw blocks of ice into
the water to remember deceased members
of the club. They then proceed to swim in the
freezing water – as they will every Sunday
throughout the Australian winter until the
end of September.

The club was formed in 1929 by a small
group of stalwart swimmers and pioneering
lifesavers who wanted to stay fit during the
winter by indulging in their favourite pastime:
swimming. They would meet at the rocks at
the southern end of Bondi Beach (hence their
original name, the Rock Spiders) and swim in
the sea there in what is known as the Bogey
Hole. Later they took over the Bondi Baths
(opened in 1890). 'The gatherings were full
of fun, and novelty events were the keynote
of the Icebergs competitions. Handicap races
were held for undisclosed prizes such as a
tin of worms. To become a member one had
to walk around the baths fully clothed and
be pushed into the pool,' one club veteran,
Andy Cleland, recalled.

The Icebergs Club has always been about
loyalty, dedication – and rules. The Twenty-
niners drew up a constitution, elected office
bearers and the original rule – that you must
swim three out of every four Sundays during
the winter, over a period of five years, to
maintain membership or face dismissal – is
still upheld. The Icebergs 'family' was always
cared for, and a hat would be passed around
meetings for benevolent causes.

For a club formed in 1929 – think talkies
snuffing the silent movies and Donald
Bradman scoring centuries – membership
was, of course, restricted to men; it wasn't
until 1994 that women were finally admitted.
In 1932 a weatherboard club room for the

Icebergs was erected adjacent to Bondi
Baths; it was rebuilt and expanded in 1955.
In the old days the social side was limited
to a few bottles of beer and pickled onions
out of a hat, but 75 years on it's only the
rule book that's familiar. Today the four-storey
Bondi Icebergs Club houses one of Sydney
top eateries after a multi-million dollar

midpoint is the popular, villagey **Five Ways**,
which is actually at the junction of five roads.
If you stand on Heeley Street or have a bite at
the popular, slightly overpriced but very good
Gusto deli (9361 5640) on the corner of Heeley
and Broughton streets, you can see the water
of Rushcutters Bay glimmering, and the masts
of the Cruise Yachting Club of Australia.

Also here are a clutch of eateries: **Tapenade**
(2B Heeley Street, 9360 6191), a tapas bar with a
lovely outdoor courtyard; French bistro **Vamps**

(227 Glenmore Road, 9331 1032); the excellent
Eat Thai@Five Ways (229 Glenmore Road,
9361 6640), upmarket fish 'n' chips den **A Fish
Called Paddo** (239 Glenmore Road, 9326
9500); plus **...and the dish ran away with
the spoon** (226 Glenmore Road, 9361 6131),
a favourite hangover stop for organic burgers
and roast chook. Overseeing the lot is the
majestic **Royal Hotel** (*see p138*), built in 1888
in a grand classical style. On the ground floor
is a busy pub with pokies and TV screens;

refurbishment in 2002 by Sydney ad supremo John Singleton. He stepped in when the club's lease had expired and it was about to lose its licence.

A magnificent pool, gym, sauna and deck (all open to the public) were built on the ground floor; the first floor became the national HQ for Surf Life Saving Australia and its small museum; the Icebergs took over the second floor; and the Icebergs Dining Room & Bar, with panoramic views over the beach, now occupies the third floor. There is also the Sundeck Café, a more informal eatery.

But it's the swimming that really matters: every Sunday in winter at 10am the men and women who are proud to wear the Icebergs polar bear logo gather for their ritual plunge. There are now around 940 members; to qualify for life membership you need to notch up an incredible 40 years of club membership. As for the next generation of Icebergs, they're called the Icecubes; formed in 1985 for nine- to 18-year-olds, they swim the same season as the adults. Go the Bergs, go the Cubes!

Bondi Icebergs Club

1 Notts Avenue, Bondi Beach (café 9130 3120/gym 9365 0423/museum 9130 7370/pool 9130 4804/www.icebergs. com.au). CityRail Bondi Junction then bus 380, 381, L82/bus 380, L82. **Open** *Bar* 10am-midnight Mon-Thur; 8am-midnight Fri, Sat; 8am-10pm Sun. *Café* 10am-10pm Mon-Fri; 8am-10pm Sat, Sun. *Gym* 6am-8.30pm Mon-Fri; 8am-5pm Sat, Sun. *Museum* 10am-3pm Mon-Fri. *Pool* 6am-8pm Mon-Fri; 6.30am-6.30pm Sat, Sun. **Admission** *Gym* $15. *Museum* free. *Pool* $3.80; $2.20 concessions; $1 spectators; family $9. **Map** p83.

upstairs there's a restaurant with a wrap-around balcony, which gets packed, especially on Australian high days and holidays.

If you continue down Glenmore Road you'll eventually pass **White City Tennis Club** on the left, currently the subject of controversial development proposals that have pitched some NIMBY locals against both councillors and businessmen. Further down is **Trumper Park** with its cricket oval. Behind is native bushland and a fairly steep and mosquito-ridden walkway

up to Edgecliff on the left and Woollahra, via tennis club Palms, on the right. For a fabulous bird's-eye view of Paddington head for the bench by courts five and six.

Back at the beginning of Glenmore Road and on the other side of Oxford Street is **Victoria Barracks** (*see p80*). Built by convicts to house soldiers and their officers (some of the contemporary NCO housing is visible in nearby Underwood Street), the complex pre-dates most of Paddington and its strict Georgian lines are more than a little at odds with the area's current cosmopolitan atmosphere.

From the Barracks to Centennial Park, Paddington is a feverishly trendy, constantly opening and folding mix of the latest fashion, homeware and gift shops, plus much-used cafés, bars and pubs that spill out on to the street. Both **Paddington Town Hall** (built in 1891) on the corner of Oatley Road and **Paddington Post Office** (1885) opposite look resplendent in the sunlight. They're a reminder of halcyon days when these grand Victorian buildings – the Town Hall in typical Classical Revival style with a 106-foot (32.5-metre) clock tower – dominated the skyline and steam trams rattled up Oxford Street.

Next to the Post Office is the enchanting **Juniper Hall** (c1820), probably the oldest surviving villa in Australia. It was built as a family home for gin distiller Robert Cooper, its name originating from the berry used to make gin. Cooper, nicknamed 'Robert the Large' for his size, was a colourful character, a convict who smuggled wine from France, fathered 28 children and founded Sydney College, which later became Sydney Grammar School. In 1984 the property was restored by the National Trust and is now privately leased to local businesses, including a prominent agency.

Crowded **Paddington Market** (*see p170*), on the corner of Oxford and Newcombe Streets, is the highlight of the area every Saturday. You'll find a hotchpotch of local crafts, good, reasonably priced clothing (a number of Sydney designers started out here), fortune-tellers, masseurs, candlesticks made out of dinner forks and just about every other money-spinning wheeze imaginable.

The **Paddington Inn** (338 Oxford Street, 9380 5277) is the area's best-known pub. It has good bar-bistro food and a heaving mix of locals, tourists and the transitory overseas population that washes through Paddo. To see some of Sydney's best local female fashion designers duck down William Street, north off Oxford Street just before the Paddington Inn, and check out **Collette Dinnigan** (*see p172*), **Leona Edmiston** (*see p173*) and **Sylvia Chan** (No.20, 9380 5981).

Victoria Barracks

*Oxford Street, between Greens & Oatley Roads
(9339 3170). Bus 378, 380, L82.* **Open** *Museum*
10am-1.30pm Thur; 10am-3pm Sun. *Tour* 10am
Thur. Closed early Dec-early Feb. **Admission** *Tour*
free. *Museum* $2; $1 concessions. **Map** p313 D4.

Built with local sandstone between 1841 and 1849,
the Georgian Regency-style Victoria Barracks were
designed by Lieutenant Colonel George Barney, who
also built Fort Denison and reconstructed Circular
Quay. Sydney's first barracks had been at Wynyard
Square, where the soldiers of the 11th (North
Devonshire) Regiment of Foot had been able to enjoy
all the privileges of living in the city – the pubs, the
eating houses, the brothels. So there were groans of
despair when they were uprooted to the lonely outpost that was Paddington. The site had been chosen
because it had bore water and was on the line an
attacker from the east might use, but in reality it was
scrub: heath, swamp and flying sand from the
adjacent dunes, which caused conjunctivitis (known
as 'Paddington pink-eye'). And while the imperial
main building and majestic parade ground were
(and still are) quite stunning, the soldiers' quarters
were cramped, and British regiments dreaded being
posted to Australia. Nowadays, the barracks are used
as a military planning and administration centre.

The museum is housed in the former 25-cell jail,
also home to a ghost, Charlie the Redcoat, who
hanged himself while incarcerated for shooting his
sergeant. There are uniforms, guns and medals
galore, and helpful, friendly staff. Well worth a visit.

Centennial Park & Moore Park

Transport Centennial Park *Bus 352, 355, 378,
380, L82.* **Moore Park** *Bus 339, 373, 374, 376,
377, 391, 392, 393, 395, 396.*

Where Oxford Street heads off towards Bondi
Junction, you hit **Centennial Park** (*see below*).
The most popular breathing space and picnic
spot in the eastern suburbs, this sizeable park
is an oasis of fields, artificial lakes, bridle paths
and cycle tracks. It's a lovely place to ride horses
and the **Centennial Parkland Equestrian
Centre** (*see p241*) can easily sort you out for
an afternoon in the saddle. Reaching all the
way down to **Randwick Racecourse**
(*see p245*) and across to **Queens Park** and
Moore Park, Centennial Park was created in
the 1880s on the site of the Lachlan Swamps
as part of the state celebrations to mark the
centenary of the landing of the First Fleet. The
three parks (Centennial, Moore and Queens)
encompass 385 hectares (951 acres) and are
collectively known as Centennial Parklands.

The **Royal Agricultural Society
Showground**, on the west side of Centennial
Park (Cook Road), was formerly the site of the

annual Sydney Royal Easter Show in April,
but was controversially and expensively
redeveloped by **Fox Studios Australia**
(*see below*) into a film studio and entertainment
complex. Next to the showground (approached
from Moore Park Road or Driver Avenue)
the huge white doughnuts that form **Sydney
Cricket Ground** (aka Aussie Stadium) and
Sydney Football Stadium (for both, *see
p243*) light up the skyline for miles around
at night. South of the cricket ground, **Moore
Park Golf Course** (*see p239*) is one of the
most popular and high-quality public golf
courses in the city.

Centennial Park

*Between Oxford Street & Alison Road (9339 6699/
www.cp.nsw.gov.au). Bus 352, 355, 378, 380, L82.*
Open *Pedestrians* 24hrs daily. *Vehicles Nov-Feb*
6am-8pm daily. *Mar, Apr, Sept, Oct* 6am-6pm daily.
May-Aug 6.30am-5.30pm daily. Car-free days last
Sun in Feb, May, Aug, Dec. **Admission** free.
Map p313 E5.

In late 2003 Centennial Parklands announced plans
to develop a code of conduct on 'bunch cycling' following complaints from the public about packs of
as many as 60 cyclists not obeying the 30km speed
limit and displaying aggressive behaviour. 'The
park is not a velodrome,' says the parklands administration. Certainly, a Sunday afternoon trip to
Centennial Park provides a fine example of local
Australians at leisure – and that means some sort of
activity, be it horse-riding, cycling, rollerblading,
jogging, dog-walking or kite-flying... watch out
where you walk, there's plenty to bump into. The
parklands are vast and extremely beautiful. There
are statues, lakes, fish-life and native Australian
flowers aplenty, plus a spacious, conservatory-style
restaurant and café, a popular weekday meeting
place for well-heeled local young mums. Ranger-led
walks include Tree Tours, Frog Pond Workshops
and the excellent night-time Spotlight Prowl.

Fox Studios Australia

*Driver Avenue, Moore Park (9383 4333/www.fox
studios.com.au). Bus 339, 373, 374, 376, 377, 391,
392, 393, 395, 396/shuttle bus from various hotels.*
Open *Backlot* 10am-5pm daily. *Shops, restaurants,
cinema & other entertainment venues* times vary.
Admission *Backlot* $24.95; $14.95-$19.95 concessions.
Bent Street free. **Credit** AmEx, BC, DC, MC, V.
Map p313 D5.

Fox Studios opened as professional working studios
in May 1998 and to the public in late 1999. Since then
proud Sydneysiders have become used to welcoming a host of US stars to their city, and some, such
as Keanu Reeves and Tom Cruise, back like old mates
as they return to film sequels to the *The Matrix* and
Mission: Impossible blockbusters. The studios have
eight stages, film-editing, sound-recording and
mixing facilities, purpose-built orchestral recording
stage, casting, travel and freight facilities and special effects equipment. If you fancy yourself as the

Sightseeing

Lovely, leafy **Woollahra Library**. *See p86.*

next Russell Crowe, head for Central Casting (9380 2844) at the back of the main precinct, where the studios cast hundreds of extras.

Regrettably, Australia's first (and still its only) Hollywood-style film studios are not open to the public, even for tours. What you get instead is a super-slick shopping complex, with 16 cinemas, 15-plus eateries – including the very popular Sports Central with three bars, four ten-pin bowling alleys, seven pool tables, 45 TV screens and two super-screens – and some huge entertainment spaces. It's a pretty good place to shop, with the likes of RM Williams, Stussy, Esprit, General Pants Co and a huge Dymocks bookshop. Kids will have a ball at the two state-of-the-art playgrounds, seasonal ice-skating rink popular Bungy trampoline. Channel V, Australia's first interactive TV studio, is based here; teenagers can watch live recordings from Tuesday to Saturday afternoons and even get involved.

And if you're into fresh produce and global food-stuffs, visit the Farmers' Market on Wednesday and Saturday. Farmers from all over NSW come to Fox to sell their meat, fruit and veg (most of it organic) direct to the public. Everything's here in abundance, for every taste – from pies and pâté to strawberries, waffles and even a Chinese massage in between stalls.

Woollahra

Transport *Bus 200, 327, 389.*

Leading off Oxford Street, opposite the Paddington Gates at Centennial Park, **Queen Street** is the closest thing in eastern Sydney

to an old-fashioned English high street. This 'village' of expensive antique shops, galleries, delis, homeware stores and boutiques marks the beginning of the salubrious (but terribly twee) suburb of Woollahra. The antique shops are incredibly expensive but surprisingly rich in wares – there's everything here from a Louis XVI mantel clock to delicious art deco jewellery and late Ming dynasty furniture.

Turn left at the traffic lights into Moncur Street, walk past the posh deli, **Jones the Grocer** (*see p183*), and round to the right into Jersey Road and you'll come to the **Lord Dudley Hotel** (No.236, 9327 5399), which oozes English pubdom from its ivy-clad exterior down to its cosy bar with British beer on tap. It's exceptionally popular with older monied locals and revellers from the nearby **Palms Tennis Centre** (Quarry Street, Trumper Park, 9363 4955) and **Paddington Bowling Club** (2 Quarry Street, 9363 1150), who meet there for a leisurely post-match schooner.

A walk from the east end of Queen Street via Greycairn Place and Attunga Street to Cooper Park – which runs east into Bellevue Hill – is a pleasure in the jacaranda season (late November to December), when the area is awash with vivid purple blossoms. From the eastern end of Cooper Park, across Victoria Road, you'll find small **Bellevue Park**, which has truly knockout views down to the harbour.

The eastern suburbs, from Woollahra to Double Bay, Bellevue Hill, Bondi Junction and Bondi, are home to Sydney's Jewish community. On Friday evenings and Saturday mornings the streets are alive with the faithful walking to and from the various synagogues dotted through the area, including the liberal **Temple Emanuel** in Woollahra (7 Ocean Street, 9328 7833) and the beautifully designed **Central Synagogue** in Bondi Junction (15 Bon Accord Avenue, 9329 5622).

Bondi Junction

Transport *CityRail Bondi Junction/bus 200, 352, 355, 378, 380, L82.*

Inexperienced visitors beware: there are really four Bondis. Bondi Junction is the bustling, suburban transport and shopping interchange bordering Paddington, Woollahra and Queens Park on the west side and Bondi on the east. Bondi is essentially the area around Bondi Road, which is the commercial street linking the Junction with the beach. Then there's Bondi Beach proper, around Campbell Parade, and going north from the beach, heading towards Bondi Golf Course, is North Bondi. The one most visitors usually want is Bondi Beach,

A famous stretch of sand: **Bondi Beach**.

but thanks to a rush of high-rise apartment blocks in Bondi Junction, many people may find themselves staying here instead. In any case, most people get to the beach via a train to Bondi Junction, followed by a bus, or by a brisk 30-minute walk.

In the past few years Bondi Junction has been plagued with a building boom that has left residents living in a huge building site. It's still not quite finished, but with the late 2003 opening of the revamped David Jones department store in the promising **Westfield Bondi Shopping Centre** (*see p170*), the area is improving. Completion is set for mid 2004, which is when the Junction may finally come into its own. A combination of sensational views, proximity to the city (ten minutes to the west), the beach (ten minutes to the east) and Centennial Park (five minutes to the south) and the construction of some vast ritzy apartment blocks has contributed to the real estate price hikes. Neighbouring **Queens Park** has less concrete and is leafier, with low-rise, older-style homes along streets that rival Paddington and Woollahra for beauty.

From the Junction, there are two roads to Bondi Beach. One is **Old South Head Road**, which turns away from the ocean and leads to Watsons Bay – so take the turn-off at O'Brien Street or Curlewis Street. Better for the beach itself is **Bondi Road**, which leads through Waverley into the suburb of Bondi (which is increasingly called 'Bondi Heights' by estate agents keen to exploit its growing trendiness). Bondi Road is an eclectic stretch of shops that

includes the well-stocked **Kemeny's Food & Liquor** (No.137, 9389 6422), the popular takeaway seafood shop **The One That Got Away** (No.163, 9389 4227), an assortment of junk shops, travel agents, grocers and most of Sydney's kosher food outlets.

Bondi Beach & around

Transport Bondi Beach *CityRail Bondi Junction then bus 380, 381, L82/bus 380, L82.* **Coogee** *CityRail Bondi Junction then bus 313, 314/bus 372, 373, 374.*

Bondi Beach is, above all, a city beach, the beauty of which is not always apparent on first viewing. Don't expect the tranquillity or natural loveliness of the northern beaches. Bondi Beach is overdeveloped, overcrowded, noisy, dirty and hyped. It's also a wonderful beach and a non-stop buzz, the closest thing most Sydneysiders have to a sacred site.

In recent years the faded 1920s charm of the suburb has been resurrected into a post-Paddo, post-Darlo trendiness. The rash of cafés and restaurants (covering all price ranges, but increasingly more in the upper bracket) lining the main thoroughfare of Campbell Parade, along with surf and souvenir shops, are usually packed at the weekend, with post-beach casuals and some seriously beautiful people. Among the restaurants, **Hugo's**, **Sean's Panaroma** (for both, *see p155*) and top chef Luke Mangan's new venture **Moorish** (*see p153*) are almost as typical of Bondi these days as the famous beach

Bondi really scores is on location: it's the city's closest ocean beach, and is easily accessible by bus.

The four lanes of **Campbell Parade** and the green swathe of Bondi Park separate the shops and houses from the beach. A recent glass and steel revamp of local pub **Ravesi's** (118 Campbell Parade, 9365 4422) on the corner of and Hall Street has made it a magnet for the area's pretty people. **Hall Street** is the 'villagey' heart of Bondi, with a good bookshop, hardware store, banks, post office and a few cafés. Most of the area's popular backpackers' accommodation is on or around Campbell Parade, Hall Street and nearby Lamrock Avenue and Roscoe Street. Heading north, the famous **Bondi Hotel** (9130 3271) on the corner of Campbell Parade and Curlewis Street is extremely popular with visiting Poms.

Up at the north end of the beach is another cluster of cafés and restaurants, and just below it there's an outdoor gym where you'll probably see a lot of well-honed muscles and tanned flesh, preening and posing. In fact, this end of the beach has recently replaced nearby Tamarama as the number one spot for tanning, posing and mutual admiration among Sydney's gay population. Further on is the pricey Ben Buckler headland and the shops of North Bondi. Beyond the headland is the dinky little **Bondi Golf Course**, site of some Aboriginal rock engravings, and **Williams Park** next to

itself. Summer nights bring in punters by the carload, particularly around Christmas and on New Year's Eve, when Bondi is best given a wide berth. There are plenty of places to hire wetsuits and surfboards along Campbell Parade; good ones include **Bondi Surf Co** and **Surfworld** (for both, *see p178*). For info on surfing lessons, *see p240* **Make a splash**.

As for the beach itself, there are plenty of others quite near the city that provide Sydneysiders with a regular dose of sun, surf and R&R. But this spectacular golden sweep has become a national institution – spiritual home of the famous all-weather **Bondi Icebergs Swimming Club** (*see p78* **Some like it cold**) and regular haunt of Sydney surfers. Its fame can't be said to rest only on aesthetic grounds, as there are many cleaner beaches all along the coastline, and ones with fewer souvenir shops and less traffic as well. The fact is, that where

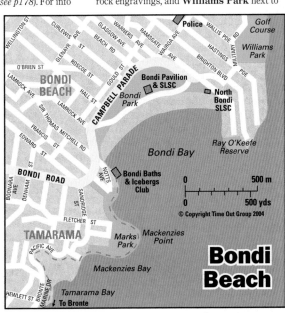

Extravagant **Elizabeth Bay House**.

league club, and 20 from the eastern suburbs. Bronte and Coogee have both enjoyed a small renaissance and are now littered with budget hostels, which often offer better quality and value for money than touristy Bondi.

Elizabeth Bay & Rushcutters Bay

Transport *CityRail Kings Cross/bus 200, 311, 312, 323, 325.*

Back on Sydney Harbour, Elizabeth Bay begins beyond Fitzroy Gardens at the southern end of Macleay Street. Here, instead of backpackers and rubberneckers, there are uncrowded streets lined with attractive apartments, dating from the 1930s to the present day, tumbling down to the harbour. Worth seeking out are **Elizabeth Bay House** (*see below*) and **Boomerang**, on the corner of Ithaca Road and Billyard Avenue, a 1930s Alhambra-esque fantasy that has been home to some of Sydney's highest fliers – and fastest fallers. On the edge of Elizabeth Bay is **Beare Park**, one of those little green havens of tranquillity that dot the harbourside.

The next inlet east is the romantically named Rushcutters Bay, so called because of the convicts who really did cut rushes here: two of them were the first Europeans to be killed by the local Aboriginal inhabitants, in May 1778. Now there is a large and peaceful park lined by huge Moreton Bay figs. The bay is home to the **Cruising Yacht Club of Australia** (CYCA) on New Beach Road; its marinas are a frenzy of activity every January when the club is the starting point for the blue-water classic **Sydney Hobart Yacht Race** (*see p194*). If you fancy trying your hand at some sailing, or simply want to sit back, glass of wine in hand while a skipper steers you around the harbour, **Eastsail** (d'Albora Marinas, New Beach Road, 9327 1166) close to the CYCA is well worth investigating.

Elizabeth Bay House

7 Onslow Avenue, Elizabeth Bay (9356 3022/www. hht.nsw.gov.au). CityRail Kings Cross/bus 311, 312. **Open** 10am-4.30pm Tue-Sun. **Admission** $7; $3 concessions; $17 family. **Credit** (over $10) BC, MC, V. No expense was spared on this handsome Greek Revival villa, designed by John Verge for NSW colonial secretary Alexander Macleay in 1839: it boasted the first two flushing toilets in Australia, the finest staircase in Australian colonial architecture and breathtaking views of Elizabeth Bay and the harbour. But Macleay's extravagance proved fatal and his debt-ridden family were forced to move out. Over the years the grand old house was vandalised, partly demolished and finally divided into

it, which, over the years has become Sydney's favourite place to come after a long night out on the town to watch the sunrise.

The chimney further up the headland is something of a landmark, but few realise that its elevated position is in contrast to a more lowly role: it's a sewage treatment plant. The sandstone promontory is honeycombed with a vast network of tunnels and canals that processes the gunk from the eastern suburbs and pumps it to an outlet five kilometres (three-and-a-half miles) into the ocean.

On the southern rim of the cove is the Bondi Icebergs complex and, beyond it, a stunning walk along the cliffs to **Tamarama Beach**, **Bronte Beach** and Waverley Cemetery (*see p85* **Walkabout 1**). The walk gets very crowded during the annual **Sculpture by the Sea** exhibition (*see p192*) in late October or early November. The views are fabulous from Bondi's southern headland, which turns inwards to show off Bondi Beach in all of its glory. Past the cemetery, the coastal walk continues south to lovely **Clovelly Beach** and then on to dramatic **Coogee Beach**, with its historic Wylie's Baths and the deservedly popular women's pool. Overlooking Coogee Beach on Dunningham Reserve is a sculpture by Sasha Reid, erected in October 2003 in commemoration of all those who died in the 2002 Bali bombings (*see p11* **Terror in Bali**). Two plaques nearby list the victims from Sydney: six from the local Dolphins rugby

15 studio flats, garrets for the artists who flocked to Kings Cross. From 1928 until 1935 it acted as a kind of cheap boarding house for the Sydney 'Charm School' artists, who included Wallace Thornton, Rex Julius and Donald Friend. The 22-hectare (54-acre) gardens, on which Macleay lavished so much love, have long since gone to property developers, but this beautiful house still breathes noblesse, wealth and good taste – and a good sniff of decadence to boot. Rooms are furnished as they would have been in its heyday, 1839-45. Don't miss it.

Darling Point & Double Bay

Transport Darling Point *Ferry Darling Point/ bus 324, 325, 326, 327.* **Double Bay** *Ferry Double Bay/bus 324, 325, 326, 327.*

Bordered by Rushcutters Bay Park to the west and Edgecliff to the south, Darling Point is another of Sydney's most exclusive suburbs, commanding spectacular views – the best of which can be sampled free from **McKell Park** at the northern tip of Darling PointRoad. Head south down the street to the corner of Greenoaks Avenue to see **St Mark's Church**, designed by the acclaimed Gothic Revival architect Edmund Blacket and consecrated in 1864, and still de rigueur for showy society, showbiz and arriviste weddings.

The next suburb to the east from here is Double Bay, which is also known as 'Double Pay', as it is Sydney's luxury shopping precinct. Migration after World War II turned 'the Bay' into a sophisticated European village of cafés, restaurants, delicatessens and ritzy boutiques. Looks are important in this enclave, so don't venture here in your tracky daks unless you're immune to scornful looks and titters. It's also worth noting that cosmetic surgeons prosper in the area – take a look at the high-gloss ladies who lunch and you'll see why. Nevertheless, it's still a good place to grab a coffee or a bite to eat amid the pretty streets and lanes. The stunning purple blooms of the jacaranda tree set Double Bay ablaze in springtime – and for good reason: Michael Guilfoyle, one of the area's earliest professional gardeners, whose own nursery of exotic plants could be found on the corner of Ocean Avenue in the mid 1800s, was solely responsible for first acclimatising the Brazilian species to Australia's weather.

New South Head Road is the main thoroughfare through the Bay. The **Golden Sheaf Hotel** at No.429 (9327 5877) has had a serious and successful renovation, and now is even more of a popular watering hole with both young and old. Its very good bistro and beer garden is especially busy on Sunday afternoons when (very loud) bands perform. At the western end of New South Head Road

Walkabout 1

Bondi to Coogee
Character Dramatic beach views.
Length 5km (3 miles) one way.
Difficulty Easy; uphill climbs.
Start at Bondi Beach. Head south and take the steps to Notts Avenue, past the Bondi Icebergs clubhouse, following the signposted path to MacKenzie's Bay (also known as 'dog beach' – you'll see why). The clifftop walk bends around to Tamarama Bay, then climbs over the headland to Bronte. You pass Waverley Cemetery then descend to the tranquil flatwater coves of Clovelly Bay and Gordons Bay and, from there, around the barren Dunningham Reserve headland, past the memorial to the Coogee Dolphin rugby league players who died in the 2002 Bali bombing – to Coogee Beach. At weekends, whatever the weather, this is a hugely popular walk attracting a mixture of tourists, joggers and the Sunday gossip crowd. For a quieter stroll, opt for an early evening during the week and catch a pretty sunset as well.

South Head
Character Stately old fishing villages and a naval base.
Length 4km (2.5 miles) loop.
Difficulty Easy.
Start at the northern end of Cliff Street in Watsons Bay. Walk north along Camp Cove beach and climb the wooden stairs to the track to Lady Bay Beach, the city's designated nudist beach. From there, you can walk all the way to the Hornby Lighthouse on the tip of South Head and look back up through the guts of the harbour to the city. Turn around and head back the same way; at Camp Cove, instead of heading right along Cliff Street, go left on the path through Sydney Harbour National Park and along the clifftop away from South Head to the Gap, Sydney's prime suicide (and sometimes murder) spot. From here, climb down the hill, join Military Road and complete the circle to Watsons Bay.

you'll find real estate agents, upmarket tea specialist **Taka Tea Garden** (*see p186*) and **Lesley McKay's Bookshop** (Queens Court, 118 Queen Street, 9328 2733). There are also two beaches at Double Bay, but only one of them is suitable for swimming. The beach next to Steyne Park and the Sailing Club wharf is not, but it's a nice place to promenade and always bustling with yachties. On summer weekends you can see the famous 18-footer sailing boats that compete in the annual Sydney to Hobart race, rigging up and practising their moves, ready for battle. The Double Bay ferry service was suspended at the end of 2003, but should be running again by the April 2004.

If you want to swim, walk east for ten minutes on New South Head Road to **Redleaf Pool** (a netted swimming area) and **Seven Shillings Beach**. This sweet little harbour beach is well hidden from the road, has a lovely garden setting and attracts a good mix of people. Behind the beach next to Blackburn Gardens is the handsome Woollahra municipal council building, recently refurbished and boasting all sorts of designer touches. On the other side of the gardens is **Woollahra Library** (548 New South Head Road, 9391 7100), undeniably the quaintest library in Sydney, set on two levels with views of the harbour and surrounded by English cottage-style gardens. It's also a good place to read the newspapers for free.

Point Piper, Rose Bay, Vaucluse & Watsons Bay

Transport Point Piper *Bus 323, 324, 325.* **Rose Bay** *Ferry Rose Bay/bus 323, 324, 325.* **Vaucluse & Watsons Bay** *Ferry Watsons Bay/bus 323, 324, 325, 386, 387.*

These picturesque harbourside suburbs are a blend of serious new and ageing money, with a beautiful foreshore that is open to everyone and easily enjoyed on the cheap. By ferry from Circular Quay you can take in Darling Point, Rose Bay and Watsons Bay (not every ferry stops at every destination, there's no service to Darling Point at the weekends and the Rose Bay service has been temporarily suspended, so check the latest info before you leave).

From Double Bay, small harbour beaches dot the shorefront up to Point Piper. Point Piper all high-walled mansions, but you can enjoy the panoramic views that cost millions from tiny **Duff Reserve** on the edge of the harbour; it's reached by very steep steps near the end of Wolseley Road, and is a good picnic spot if you manage to beat the crowds.

Lyne Park in Rose Bay is where the city's seaplanes land (for flights, *see p278*). Or you can just watch them from the comfort of top-notch bayside restaurants **Catalina** (*see p154*) and **Pier** (*see p155*). On the other side of New South Head Road is **Woollahra**

Golf Course; unlike the very toffy Royal Sydney Golf Course right next door, it's open to the general golfing public.

The streets from Rose Bay to Vaucluse feature yet more millionaire mansions; for the jealously inclined, the hidden jewels of the Hermitage Foreshore Reserve and an arm of Sydney Harbour National Park, which run around the peninsula, come as compensation. They are reached by a walking track that starts at Bayview Hill Road, below the imposing stone edifice of **Rose Bay Convent**, and offer fine views of the Harbour Bridge, as well as picnic spots aplenty and glimpses of the lifestyles of the rich and incredibly comfortable. The walk emerges at **Nielsen Park** (*see p87*), off Vaucluse Road, where there is an enclosed bay, **Shark Beach**, which is particularly beautiful on a summer evening, and a popular restaurant, the **Nielsen Park Kiosk** (9337 1574).

Further along, on Wentworth Road, the estate that became **Vaucluse House** (*see p87*) was bought by newspaperman and politician William Charles Wentworth in 1827. It's open to the public, along with its fine tearooms. Next to Vaucluse Bay, **Parsley Bay** is a lesser-known verdant picnic spot popular with families.

It is claimed that Watsons Bay was the country's first fishing village. Now largely the province of **Doyles on the Beach** seafood restaurant (9337 2007) and rowdy weekend pub **Doyles Palace Hotel** (*see p137*) – both owned by one of the bay's original fishing families – it has stunning views (particularly at night) back across the harbour to the city, and retains vestiges of its old charm, including original weatherboard houses and terraces. These are best seen by walking north to the First Fleet landing spot at Green Point Reserve, and on to Camp Cove and Lady Bay beaches, South Head and the Hornby Lighthouse.

On the far (ocean) side of the peninsula from Watsons Bay beach is the bite in the sheer cliffs that gives the **Gap** its name – and from which many have jumped to their death. Gap Park is the start of a spectacular cliff walk that runs south back into Vaucluse. Along the way, hidden high above the approach to Watsons Bay at the fork of the Old South Head Road, is another fine Blacket church, **St Peter's** (331 Old South Head Road, 9337 6545), which is home to Australia's oldest pipe organ, dating from 1796, and once loaned to the exiled Napoleon. The church gates commemorate the Greycliffe ferry disaster of 1927 when 40 people (including many schoolchildren) died in a mid-sea collision.

You can hire putt putt boats for a spot of fishing, or just messing around, from **Jimmy's Boat Hire** (11 Marine Parade, 0407 462 738).

A nun's-eye view – the harbour panorama from **Rose Bay Convent**. *See p86.*

Nielsen Park

Greycliffe Avenue, Vaucluse. Bus 324, 325.
Open 5am-10pm daily.
Generations of Sydneysiders have been flocking to Nielsen Park for family get-togethers since the early 1900s, to sit on Shark Beach or the grassy slopes behind or to climb the headlines either side of the beach for a great view across the harbour. With its abundance of shady trees, gentle waters, panoramic views and the excellent Nielsen Park Kiosk (serving à la carte meals plus snacks and ice-creams), it's the perfect picnic spot. Nestled in the grounds to the rear of the grassy slopes lies Greycliffe House, a Gothic-style mansion built in 1862 as a wedding gift from the co-founder and first editor of *The Australian* newspaper, William Charles Wentworth, for his daughter Fanny and husband John Reeve. In 1913 it became a baby hospital, then a home for new mothers. Nowadays it's a NSW National Parks & Wildlife Service (NPWS) office, providing info on parks throughout the state. Watch out for the sea-planes that take off in neighbouring Rose Bay and begin their ascent just over the waters of Shark Bay.

Vaucluse House

Wentworth Road, Vaucluse (9388 7922/ www.hht.nsw.gov.au). Bus 325. **Open** *House* 10am-4.30pm Tue-Sun. *Grounds* 10am-5pm Tue-Sun. **Admission** $7; $3 concessions; $17 family. **Credit** (over $10) BC, MC, V.
The oldest 'house museum' in Australia nestles prettily in a moated 19th-century estate, surrounded by ten hectares (25 acres) of prime land, with its own sheltered beach on Vaucluse Bay. From 1827-53 and 1861-2 this was the opulent home of William Charles Wentworth, one of the most influential Australian-born colonists. The house originally stood in a vast, 209-hectare (516-acre) estate, and 26 servants were required to look after the master's seven daughters and three sons, not to mention his vineyards,

orchards and beloved racehorses. The Historic Houses Trust has endeavoured to keep the place as it was when the Wentworths lived there. In the kitchen a fire burns in the large grate and hefty copper pans line the walls; a tin bath, taken on European travels, still displays its sticker from London's Victoria Station; the drawing room is sumptuously furnished, and has a door that hides a secret (just ask a guide to open it).

Randwick & Kensington

Transport Randwick *Bus 314, 316, 317, 371, 372, 373, 374, 376, 377.* **Kensington** *Bus 391, 392, 393, 394, 396, 397, 399.*

Randwick has long been synonymous with **Royal Randwick racecourse** (*see p245*) on Alison Road bordering Centennial Park. The University of NSW campus lies south of it, while, across the road, the **National Institute of Dramatic Art** (NIDA) – alma mater of such stars as Nicole Kidman and Mel Gibson – has its headquarters and also a new whizz-bang theatre (*see p251*).

Anzac Parade is one long highway, but it does have a scattering of highlights, including one of Sydney's most eccentric eateries, the **Grotta Capri Seafood Restaurant** (Nos.97-101, 9662 7111) – where the food is no better than passable, but the decor is truly a kitsch masterpiece – and some of Sydney's finest Indonesian and Malaysian restaurants. Just up the road, and well worth a visit, is the bubblegum-pink **Peter's of Kensington** (*see p167*). This maze-like department store attracts long queues at sale times and in the long build-up to Christmas.

Inner West

Head across the 'other' bridge to discover a funky, multicultural world.

It's quite strange that passing through the arches of the Anzac Bridge – city gateway to the inner west – can produce such a uniformly profound effect. Some describe it as 'almost spiritual'; others 'a thing of great beauty'. What lies directly beyond the bridge is not so immediately inspiring – lots of dead-end construction – and has, until recently, largely gone unnoticed by those from the other side of the city. But one more year of work on the Cross City Tunnel (which will link Kings Cross to Darling Harbour, and promises to cut journey times), and the east-meets-west experience will be complete.

Since the 2000 Olympics registered something west of Darling Harbour in the mind maps of the eastern suburbs' elite, many foodies have been making their own pilgrimage across the bridge, to the delis, bakeries, cafés and restaurants of Balmain, Rozelle, Glebe, Leichhardt and Haberfield. Meanwhile, Newtown has become known as one of Sydney's most eclectic and interesting neighbourhoods, while Marrickville has its own special feel, thanks to a mix of Greek and Vietnamese communities.

Those who actually have mortgages in these areas are likely to be found at home saving pennies for paint and screws. It is entirely possible that the explosion of DIY home makeover shows on TV is being driven by Sydney's inner west, which can't seem to down tools. Only in the more classic white-bread area of Balmain do locals seem to have the kind of dosh that fuels an ever-burgeoning foodie scene. Yet, despite the shimmer the inner west has received recently, it remains at heart the domain of a bohemian and multicultural mix.

Balmain, Birchgrove & Rozelle

Transport Balmain *Ferry Balmain, East Balmain or Balmain West/bus 442, 443, 434.* **Birchgrove** *Ferry Birchgrove/bus 441.* **Rozelle** *Bus 432, 433, 434, 440, 441, 442, 500.*

Snuggled in the inner west's harbour, a six-minute ferry ride from Circular Quay or a 20-minute bus trip from the city centre, Balmain was settled in the 1830s by boatbuilders; today it's increasingly home to on-the-make, monied types. **Darling Street** – the spine of this area – starts at the **Balmain East Wharf** (where the ferries dock) and curves up past the sandstone **Watch House** (once the police lock-up and now headquarters of the Balmain Historical Society). Once this strip earnestly sprouted natural therapies and good bookshops; now it heaves with an impossible number of food joints and homeware shops. Such has been the Balmain surge on food that Starbucks and other large franchises are starting to sneak into the area – despite howls of protest from the locals.

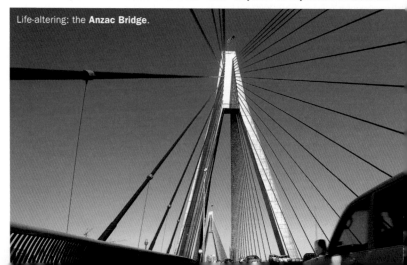

Life-altering: the **Anzac Bridge**.

It's an easy place to try out a range of food styles. **Go Bungai** (333 Darling Street, 9818 8810) does its own cheeky take on Japanese; **Kazbah on Darling** (No.379, 9555 7067) transports you to Morocco; **Tuk Tuk Real Thai** (No.350, 9555 5899) offers fast and funky Thai; **Blue Ginger** (No.241, 9818 4662) makes you realise just how far modern Asian cuisine has come in this country; **Simmone Logue** (No.341, 9555 1422) brings you back home with glamour comfort food; and **Circle Café** (No.344, 9555 9755) reminds you of Balmain's more simple, eccentric '70s period; it houses a Uniting Church service on Sunday mornings. For a simpler outing, go to **Dockside Seafood** (No.314, 9810 6587), order mandarin scallops or spicy prawns, then catch a bus back down the road to the wharf to eat in the park overlooking the Harbour Bridge.

Today, pubs are still the lifeblood of Balmain. Glamour couples head for the refined surrounds of the **London Hotel** (234 Darling Street, 9555 1377) or the **Exchange Hotel**, which also has comedy nights. Ageing funsters patronise the **Unity Hall Hotel** (292 Darling Street, 9810 1331), while the **Town Hall Hotel** (No.366, 9818 8950) hovers oddly between pleasing pool sharks and house music lovers. Sit-down musos will find a mix of bands at the **Cat & Fiddle Hotel** (*see p225*) or cool jazz at the **Sackville Hotel** (*see p228*).

For an old-fashioned pub, head to Birchgrove on the northern side of Darling Street. The ramshackle **Sir William Wallace Hotel** (31 Cameron Street, 9555 8570) features a large autographed poster of a kilted Mel Gibson in *Braveheart* mode and wears a similar styled emblem over its front door. Locals claim that Gibson, who lived in the area as an up-and-coming actor, was first inspired by the Scottish patriot while drinking at their bar. On Sundays, the owners still throw a free barbecue lunch. There's also the **Riverview Hotel** (29 Birchgrove Road, 9810 1151), for years owned by the legendary Olympic gold medal-winning swimmer Dawn Fraser; her name lives on at the carefully restored outdoor, seawater **Dawn Fraser Pool** at the edge of the very charming, harbourside **Elkington Park**.

Another park can be found at the harbour end of the narrow finger of Louisa Road, which is lined with half-hidden, multi-million-dollar homes. The peninsula was originally an abattoir of sorts, where Aboriginal people used to kill kangaroos. Its name was officially changed from Long Nose Point to **Yurulbin Point** in 1994 to reflect its Aboriginal heritage, but most people still refer to it by its former name. The wharf at its end is where the Birchgrove ferries arrive.

Balmain Market (*see p170*), held on Saturdays at St Andrew's Church on the corner of Darling Street and Curtis Road, is worth a browse. Meet at St Andrew's front gate at 11am on Saturdays (or by arrangement) for a guided tour of the area by Balmain Historical Society member Kath Hamey (details on 9818 4954, www.balmainassociation.homestead.com).

Continue west along Darling Street to reach Rozelle. If you're driving, let the overall-clad lads fill 'er up at Balmain's oldest service station, **Bill's Garage** (418 Darling Street), established in 1915 and still with its original fixtures. At the weekend **Rozelle Market** (*see p170*) seasoned bargain hunters can ferret through stalls of discount CDs, plants, ceramics and collectibles. Also along this stretch is a smattering of cafés, nurseries, antiques stores and gift shops, including fancy chocolatier **Belle Fleur** (*see p182*). To the north is the **Balmain Leagues Club** (138-152 Victoria Road, 9556 0400), one of two venues belonging to local rugby battlers the Wests Tigers (formerly known as the Balmain Tigers) and a good place for a cheap steak and beer.

Head deeper into Rozelle along Darling Street and you'll see the strained legacy of Tetsuya, the internationally renowned Japanese chef who for years had his first restaurant here. The **Barn Café & Grocery** (731 Darling Street, 9810 1633) hulks like a monolith to modern cuisine, selling top-notch (and expensive) produce. For more home-grown authenticity, head to **Orange Grove Farmers Market**, held each Saturday at Orange Grove Public School at the junction of Darling Street and Balmain Road. The organic produce and multinational cuisines (Ethiopian, Japanese, Dutch) are good – and cheap – enough to lure Bondi dwellers across town.

Glebe

Transport *Bus 431, 432, 433, 434, 468/ LightRail Glebe.*

Directly to the west of central Sydney and shaped by its proximity to **Sydney University** on Parramatta Road, Glebe is an incongruous but atmospheric mix of grand, turn-of-the-20th-century mansions flanking quaint terraces and drab 1970s flat lets, with most streets still sporting their original rusty street signs. There are more holistic therapists and chiropractors here than anywhere else in town, as well as an overpowering aroma of curries and fresh Thai food.

All the action can be found along **Glebe Point Road**. The southern end joins up with the snarling traffic of Parramatta Road,

AbOriginal Sacred sites

While Sydney is a centre for contemporary Aboriginal art and culture – from visual arts and dance to native cuisine – there is less evidence of pre-colonial indigenous culture. Many sites have been destroyed or built over, or, in the case of rock engravings and paintings, have faded away when the owners, who had responsibility for maintaining them over the centuries, died or were forced from their lands. Engravings have huge sacred significance and represent social and spiritual life, recording information about hunting and past events, real or mythical. Access was often restricted to men or women only, or to those who had been initiated into the secret cultural knowledge.

Some of Sydney's main roads, such as George and Oxford Streets, were originally established Aboriginal tracks, and over the years artefacts have been discovered all over the city. Some ended up in museums, but many have been lost. The quarrying of sandstone for building and ballast for ships also destroyed much history. However, there are several accessible sites – thought to be between 200 and 5,000 years old – which give an idea of what once was. These sites are extremely fragile and nothing should be touched or stepped on.

For more information, pick up the STA brochure 'Sydney's Aboriginal Sites by Bus and Ferry', or Melinda Hinkson and Alana Harris's book *Aboriginal Sydney*. An excellent history of indigenous Sydney can be found at www.cityofsydney.nsw.gov.au/barani.

Balls Head Reserve
CityRail Waverton then 10mins walk to end of Balls Head Road.
From the car park follow the track on the left-hand side and look for a white wooden fence, which encloses an engraving of a six-metre (20-foot) whale with a man inside, first recorded in the 1890s. Further along the path is the Midden Walk, which takes in a sandstone shelter with fabulous views of the city. Archaeologists in the 1960s, who discovered remains of shellfish, mammals and 450 stone artefacts, concluded that the area was used by men to make and maintain

while the northern end tails off at Rozelle Bay overlooking the Anzac Bridge in Pyrmont. Here, at **Jubilee Park**, locals play touch football and walk dogs at sunset. There's always a plethora of travellers around, thanks to several budget hotels, including the large and leafy **Glebe Village Backpackers** hostel (256 Glebe Point Road, 9660 8133, www.bakpak group.com/glebevillage). Play pool with a young crowd at **Toxteth Hotel** (No.345, 9660 2370) and, for a cheap night out, dine in boho comfort at the **Craven Café** (No.166, 9552 2656) on everything from outsized focaccia to Moroccan lemon chicken. Afterwards, duck next door to the art deco **Valhalla** (*see p202*), a landmark art house cinema. Glimpses of glamour are starting to creep into the retail landscape, with the likes of café/patisserie **Stephen Baker** (95 Glebe Point Road, 9692 9692), **Sonoma Woodfired Baking Co** (No.215, 9660 2116), modern Italian café/ restaurant **Rosso Nero** (No.407, 9660 2646) and the upmarket florist **Verdant Flower Merchants** (166 St Johns Road, 9518 7385).

Bibliophiles should head for **Gleebooks** (*see p171*), which is something of a literary institution. For indigenous culture, turn off Wigram Road to **Tranby Aboriginal Co-operative College** (13 Mansfield Street,

9660 3444). Housing books, music, reference material, clothing and artifacts, the college also runs a mail-order service. For sleek and interesting gifts, visit **Interim: The Design Gift Store** (47 Glebe Point Road, 9552 2559): it sells everything from Alessi to clever Room products from Melbourne. For a more eclectic choice, take a ramble through sprawling **Glebe Market** (*see p170*) on a Saturday.

You'll never go hungry in Glebe – but expect competent rather than amazing food. There is an overwhelming battery of Indian, Chinese, Vietnamese and Thai eateries battling each other down to tiny $4-$8 pricings. Traditional pubs include the **Nag's Head Hotel** (*see p138*), and Irish pub the **Friend in Hand Hotel** (58 Cowper Street, 9660 2326) which hosts live crab races every Wednesday night. As well as having the **No Names Restaurant** (9660 9200) under its roof, the pub is stuffed with street signs, number plates and even a surfboat hanging from the roof in one room. For a more upmarket take, try Italian institution the **Mixing Pot** (178 St Johns Road, 9660 7449) or the superb **Boathouse on Blackwattle Bay** (*see p158*), which serves expensive signature seafood to match its waterside view. A different kind of evening's entertainment is on offer at nearby **Wentworth Park Greyhound**

hunting gear while subsisting on shellfish gathered by the women. Early colonial glass remains also indicate Aboriginals inhabited this shelter after colonisation.

Berry Island Reserve

CityRail Woolstonecraft then 10mins walk to end of Shirley Road.

The Gadyan interpretive track, named after the local word for the Sydney cockle, takes in Sydney redgums and other native species and gives an idea of what the city would have been like before colonisation. A sandstone platform has evidence of a tool grinding site, a rock hole that would have stored water, and an engraving, thought to be of a fish and probably 700 years' old. The tip of the island is a large shell midden, an area where shells have built up over hundreds of years.

Bondi Golf Course

CityRail Bondi Junction then bus 380, 381, L82/bus 380, L82.

This site – thought to have been a ceremonial ground – is on the sea side of the golf course, in an area cordoned with a chainlink fence

near a brick chimney. It has carved images of a whale with a shark superimposed; a man holding a fish; and two fish and a boomerang. In the 1880s about 87 figures were recorded, mainly marine animals including a seal and a dolphin, but these are now buried under turf. Closer to the edge of the cliff the hull of a ship can be discerned; thought to have been carved with a metal chisel, the style of the boat suggests it was made during British colonisation. Other engravings can be seen at nearby Ray O'Keefe Reserve off Ramsgate Avenue, and at Mackenzies Point in Marks Park, Tamarama.

Grotto Point

Ferry Manly then bus 132, 133.

Follow the walking track from Cutler Road into picturesque Sydney Harbour National Park. Head towards Castle Rock Beach, and then take a flight of steps down to a seat on the right-hand side. A railway sleeper to the left of the track marks the entrance to the site, which is known for its unusual and well-maintained engravings that include images of kangaroos, sharks and fish.

Track (*see p245*), Sydney's premier dog-racing venue, which has meets every Monday and Saturday night. If you want a feel of what Sydney used to be like before money took over, it's a great night out (there are bars and a bistro). The betting ring here is about the only place where you'll still see pork-pie hats worn without a trace of irony.

For guided walking tours of the area, contact Maureen Fry at **Sydney Guided Tours** (9660 7157, http://members.ozemail.com.au/~mpfry); she also runs similar informative tours in Balmain, Rozelle and Annandale.

Annandale

Transport *Bus 436, 437, 438, 439, 440, 470.*

Annandale was once earmarked as a 'model township' – hence broad, tree-lined Johnston Street (named after Lieutenant George Johnston, the first man to step ashore in 1788, albeit on the back of a convict). Located between Leichhardt and Glebe, it soon became a predominantly working-class district. It is best known today for its period architecture. A particularly fine example is the beautiful sandstone **Hunter Baillie Memorial Presbyterian Church** (80 Johnston Street), the spire of which is visible

from the air as you fly into Sydney. There's ornate wrought ironwork on the **Goodwin Building** (corner of Johnston Street and Parramatta Road), while the towering pillars outside Annandale Primary School once guarded George Johnston's house. Along Johnston Street stand three huge homes with distinctive tall towers; they're known as the **Witches' Houses** because they resemble witches' hats from a distance. Local memoirist John Clare quite famously claims that they were also once home to covens.

Like Leichhardt, Annandale has a mix of long-time residents and more recent gentrifiers who have chosen the inner west as an affordable spot for buying and renovating quaint terraced houses. Bisected by broad paved roads, peaceful Annandale lacks the brashness of Glebe, the self-consciousness of Balmain and the lively ethnicity of Leichhardt, but it has a discernible village feel. Adding to the pull of the area are restaurants like **Three Clicks West** (*see px158*) serving modern Australian cuisine, and **Zenith on Booth** (37 Booth Street, 9660 6600), serving southern Italian. Relax before or after with drinks at the **North Annandale Hotel** (9660 7452), on the corner of Booth and Johnston Streets. Also check out the **Annandale Hotel** (*see p224*) – the legendary live music pub that

Take a ramble through eclectic **Glebe Market**. *See p90.*

launched many of Australia's best bands – or chill out to some of Sydney's best jazz at **Side On Café** (*see p229*).

Leichhardt

Transport *Bus 436, 437, 438, 439, 440, 445, 470.*

Further to the south-west lies **Leichhardt**. Formerly the 'Little Italy' of the west, it has now outgrown that title, and its 'dykeheart' subset of lesbians has also been overrun with squadrons of new home renovators. The suburb's main thoroughfare, **Norton Street**, pumps to a whole new nightlife vibe, while still retaining some of the old. It's studded with coffee shops, delis, Italian restaurants and Thai takeaways.

Serious ice-cream heads can't go past **La Cremeria Sorbetteria** (106 Norton Street, 9564 1127), where Luigi de Luca makes what many consider the best gelato in town, although **Glace** around the corner (27 Marion Street, 9569 3444) is luring interlopers from the east with sexy offerings like champagne sorbet. Grab a quick caffeine fix at **Bar Sport** (2A Norton Street, 9569 2397) or head to **Bar Italia** (*see p131*) at the northern end for sit-down cappuccino, focaccia or spaghetti – all cheap. Nearby **Café Gioia & Pizzeria** (126A Norton Street, 9564 6245), housed in a renovated service station, is fun for families, while those wanting a sophisticated modern take on Italian will find it at **Alio** (*see p147*) and the expansive **Grappa** (*see p157*).

A cluster of local Australian heritage buildings includes the two-storey **Leichhardt Town Hall** (107 Norton Street), built in 1888, which often hosts visiting art exhibitions; the former **Post Office** (No.109); and **All Souls Anglican Church** (No.126). However, it's the recently built **Italian Forum** (*see p167*) at the southern end of Norton Street that impacts with its Italianate architecture. This giant retail, residential and commercial development centres around a colonnaded piazza, with outdoor cafés, restaurants and bars, and a fountain featuring a statue of Dante. Italians swear it reminds them of home, although Australians haven't quite clicked into its style.

Down the road is Palace's **Norton Street Cinema** (*see p202*), a four-screen art house with a very good licensed bar and restaurant called **Martini**, a café, a bar, a CD shop and yet another giant retail development. Readers should look to **Berkelouw Book Sellers** (*see p171*) across the road for a great selection of titles, and a café to read them in.

Haberfield

Transport *Bus 436, 437, 438, 439, 440, 445, 470.*

Situated to the west of Leichhardt, Haberfield is the latest 'Little Italy' in the west – 'little' being the operative word. So far it's managed to maintain its homeland authenticity without giving itself over to the new glamour that's stifling Leichhardt. Foodies make a beeline for its main thoroughfare, **Ramsay Street**, where you'll find **Paesanella** delicatessen (No.88, 9799 8483) for perhaps the best antipasti and cheeses in Sydney; **Haberfield Bakery** (No.153, 9797 7715) for bread (17 to choose from) and fresh pasta; and **A&P Sulfaro Pasticceria** (No.119, 9797 0001) for gelati, biscotti and other yummy desserts.

Also on Ramsay Street, the ultra-stylish **Lanzafàme** (*see p157*) is Haberfield's newest, and priciest, 'deeply Italian' restaurant. And while the thin pizza and slick surrounds of

La Disfida (*see p157*) still entice outsiders, locals will point you to the first-class pizzas at **Il Goloso** (No.104, 9716 4344). Around the corner is old favourite **Napoli in Bocca** (73 Dalhousie Street, 9798 4096), which offers trad trattoria-style pizza and pasta in a setting of terracotta tiles and checked cloths.

Newtown, Erskineville & Enmore

Transport Newtown *CityRail Newtown/ bus 422, 423, 426, 428, 352.* **Erskineville** *CityRail Erskineville.* **Enmore** *CityRail Newtown/ bus 428, L28.*

You can throttle it with renovators and young families; you can trick up the rough edges with smart shops, but Newtown somehow manages to remain stubbornly (and comfortably) down at heel, like an old drag queen in her glitter rags. Lying to the south of Annandale and Glebe, Newtown has it all: few other areas accommodate so many subcultures – grungy students from the nearby University of Sydney, young professional couples, black-draped goths, punks, gays and lesbians – and in such apparent harmony.

You could easily spend a day wandering along the main drag, **King Street** (and it's faster to stroll than drive, since the traffic can be notoriously bad). Intriguing and often eccentric specialist shops include one dedicated solely to buttons, another to ribbons and braids, another to arty candles. A major player in the area is the **Dendy Newtown** four-screen cinema (*see p201*); next door is a good dance and alternative music shop, **Fish Records** (*see p189*), which opens late, as does bookshop **Better Read Than Dead** (No.265, 9557 8700). There's also **Goulds** (*see p171*), one of the largest and most popular second-hand bookshops in the city. Maybe it's because of the wild mix of humanity that makes up Newtown, but it's the perfect place to find anything for anyone. **Pentimento** (No.249, 9565 5591) has an exquisite range of books, homewares and handbags, while **Eastern Flair** (No.319, 9565 1499) offers exotic jewellery and homewares. For divine teas, visit **Tea Too** (No.173, 9550 3044), while funky bags of all kinds are available at **Crumpler** (No.305, 9565 1611).

You'll have no trouble finding somewhere to linger over a cappuccino – every second shopfront is a café or restaurant, and new places seem to open every week. Particularly numerous are Thai eateries, often with joke names like Thai-Foon; one of the best is **Thai Pothong** (294 King Street, 9550 6277). **The Old Fish Shop Café** (No.239A, 9519

4295) is a popular open-sided café with strings of garlic and chilli hanging from the roof. Also try **Bacigalupo** (No.284, 9565 5238) for organic coffee, or **El Basha Café** (No.233, 9557 3886) for Lebanese sweets and pastries.

Newtown has no shortage of pubs, each with its own distinctive slant. Check out bands at the recently revived **Sandringham Hotel** (*see p226*), still adorned with original green and yellow tiles. New on the block for jazz and blues is the **Vanguard** (*see p226*) – more of a music club than a pub. The **Newtown Hotel** (*see p216*), remains an ever-popular gay haunt, but has tarted itself up with a lounge bar on the first level. Most hotels have a restaurant tucked away at the back, often with an open-air courtyard. Recommended is **Sumalee Thai** restaurant at the **Bank Hotel** (*see p213*), adjacent to Newtown train station. The decor is simple, with green plastic tables and long green railway station benches, still marked with station names. For new all-hours comfort, try **Zanzibar** (No.323, 9519 1511); with pool downstairs and a cushion room upstairs, it relies on low lighting and beads to pump its name's exotic promise.

The bottom end of King Street, south of the rail station, has always been heaven for fans of antiques, junk and second-hand clothes, but edgy fashion shops are now beginning to

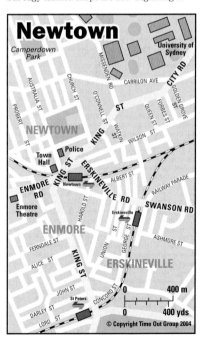

Sightseeing

predominate – look for **Dragstar** (No.535A, 9550 1243), the **Raglab** (No.537, 9557 0955) and **Zukini** (No.483, 9519 9188). Many of the shops are vacant, but there are still some interesting places to explore, including such Pacific produce merchants as **Island Food Supplies** (No.567, 9519 1141) and **Fiji Market** (No.591, 9517 2054), which also has cheap sari fabrics and fabulously gaudy Hindu icons and posters.

While in Newtown it's also worth ducking off King Street to the two E suburbs: Erskineville and Enmore. To reach the former – which is rapidly expanding as its own crowd-puller – turn off King Street at Erskineville Road and keep walking. You may recognise the landmark deco **Imperial Hotel** (*see p215*) from the movie *Priscilla, Queen of the Desert*. If drag shows are your gig, you can head here on Thursday to Sunday nights to see one of the best.

On Swanson Street – which is a continuation of Erskineville Road – is the jazz club the **Rose of Australia** (*see p228*). For well-priced, good all-round food (and soy and dandelion lattes, of all things), try the **Big Boys Café** (106 Erskineville Road, 9557 9448) before heading down for a seriously strong espresso at **Café Sofia** (7 Swanson Street, 9519 1565).

If it's food that you're looking for, it's worth walking a little further down the road (which changes its name again, to Copeland Street) for the gourmet deliciousness of the breakfast and lunch café **Bitton** (*see p131*). Despite its somewhat off-the-beaten-track location, Bitton has thrived under French-born chef David Bitton and his Indian wife, Sohani. Try the one-pan bacon and eggs with Turkish bread or the fresh salad of lamb, marinated in Bitton's own dressings. You can buy sauces, dressings and oils to take home, and David also offers private dinners and cooking classes.

To get to Enmore, return to Newtown and then turn off of King Street on to Enmore Road. The best reason to come here is to check out the **Enmore Theatre** (*see p222*), a renovated deco-style theatre popular with quality rock bands (local and international) and stand-up comedy acts. For a pre-gig dinner, you can't go wrong by tryin the excellent food at the **Banks Thai Restaurant** (91 Enmore Road, 9550 6840) with its raised, cushioned seating. If you're still hungry after the gig, though, more food can be found at late-opening **Saray Turkish Pizza** (18 Enmore Road, 9557 5310). In fact, there's no need to stop there, as there's still more dining options among the cluster of high quality Lebanese restaurants on the street, among them **Emma's on Liberty** and **Fifi's** (for both *see p158*). The **Duke of Edinburgh Hotel** (148 Enmore Road, 9550 3452) is also great for cheap food, drinks and a game of pool.

Marrickville

Transport CityRail Marrickville/bus 423, 426.

To the south-west of Enmore is Marrickville, a suburb that gives an indication of the true multicultural and multiracial future of Australia. Originally a 19th-century working-class suburb, Marrickville has benefited from all the trends in post-war migration to Australia. In the 1950s and '60s it was a signficant Greek enclave, and there is still a superb Greek deli, **Lamia Supa Deli** (278 Marrickville Road, 9560 2440) and a collection of upstairs 'coffeehouses' where old Greek men go to play cards (and never, ever gamble), but more recently it has become home to a large Vietnamese community. It also has a growing gay and lesbian presence, along with young 'n' funky Anglos fleeing Newtown and Enmore's ridiculous rents.

In Marrickville, food is all. For lunch, you can enjoy the ubiquitous pork roll (pâté, fish sauce, three different types of pork, carrot, shallots and mayo on a crusty roll) for $2-$3 – any Marrickville Road bakery will make you one in seconds. For something more substantial, try a steaming bowl of phô, the chunky, odoriferous, sinus-clearing Vietnamese rice noodle soup. If you're after a more advanced Vietnamese repast, the best in Marrickville is **Thanh Huong** (358 Illawarra Road, 9558 0657). The management here also own next-door **Thanh Huong 2** (No.356). At both you'll find a menu of more than 300 Vietnamese, Chinese and Thai dishes; if you've ever wanted to try a kangaroo jungle curry or a crocodile mussaman curry, you need look no further.

Marrickville also boasts one of Sydney's best – and best-value – yum cha (dim sum) joints: **Hung Cheung** (338 Marrickville zRoad, 9560 4681). Yum cha starts at 9am daily, and you'll have to queue after midday on weekends. They also do superb chilli mud crab. Lovers of trad Greek food cannot go past the **Corinthian Rotisserie** (283 Marrickville Road, 9569 7084), a rustic taverna that offers one of the best takeaway dinners in town. The eat-in meals are enormous, the atmosphere authentic and you can get beer, wine and retsina.

Fans of tack, camp and over-the-top glitz should experience the **Marrickville RSL** (359 Illawarra Road, 9559 1555), a fascinating cultural collision between the old-guard Returned Services League and the gambling-loving Vietnamese community. The poker machines are always busy, the drinks are dirt cheap and the entertainment (karaoke, singing competitions) is free, and usually bizarre: imagine the worst variety acts possible, and a decor that makes you think you're tripping.

North Shore

Head north for stunning views, verdant foreshore and established money.

Prime Minister John Howard's humble abode, **Kirribilli House**. *See p96.*

Wealthy Sydneysiders face a terrifying decision: the edgy glamour of the eastern suburbs or the sedate sophistication of the north shore? Many of them start with the former and then feel the comfortable pull of the latter, poor lambs. To be fair, the north shore has much to offer. Its waterside suburbs boast the best views in town – think the Opera House and Harbour Bridge in one frame from your living room, or kookaburras and rainbow lorikeets nestled in weeping figs along the Cremorne foreshore in another. Add to this a clutch of pretty harbour beaches, numerous delis, cafés and coffee shops, and family homes echoing with federation heritage and the appeal is obvious.

The 'north shore' is not actually an officially designated area, rather a term used to lump together the suburbs on the north side of the harbour up to the northern beaches. Many of these suburbs are not actually on the shore, nor are they especially interesting to tourists, being suburban enclaves. Those that are worth visiting – Kirribilli, North Sydney, McMahons Point, Milsons Point, Mosman, Balmoral, Cremorne – are all on the water. The loosely termed 'northern suburbs' link the north shore with the western suburbs, and include middle-class areas such as Cheltenham, Epping, Beecroft and North Ryde. The north shore stops at Hornsby in the north, Lane Cove in the west and Belrose in the east. It is punctuated by the sprawling commercial-retail centres at places like North Sydney, Chatswood and Hornsby.

Getting around the north shore is not easy. Its size and sprawl mean that you're best off in a car and many of its hidden beaches can only be reached by car (or on foot if you're prepared for the hills). But there is public transport available in the form of the north shore CityRail train line from North Sydney to Hornsby, a wide range of buses and the green-and-gold ferries from Circular Quay. The latter offer the most picturesque way to travel and capture the area's true atmosphere, visiting the lower north shore suburbs. Take a seat outside at the front or back of the ferry and ogle the waterfront houses and foreshore flora and fauna. Each of these suburbs has a centre, usually boasting clusters of cafés and speciality shops, plus stunning harbour views and harbourfront walks. The region is also home to Taronga Zoo, a famous Sydney landmark and the world's only harbourside zoo.

Today the north shore is largely the homeland of Sydney's well-heeled whites, and while the multicultural landscape is slowly changing with Japanese, Chinese, Korean and South African immigrants moving in, the original Aboriginal population is long gone. The early north shore settlers in the first decades of the 1800s were land grantees, among them Billy Blue, James Milson and Edward Wollstonecraft, and its development into a place of white estates and family homes stems from that time. The Cammeraygal and Wallumedegal tribes who inhabited the area when the First Fleet arrived in Sydney Cove in 1788 had largely been driven out of the region by the 1860s.

The Cammeraygal, recorded as being a powerful and numerous tribe, 'most robust and muscular', lived along the foreshore, in the bushland and cliffs, and in rock shelters. Places such as Berry Island, Balls Head, Kirribilli, Cremorne and Cammeray are dotted with cultural remains of the Cammeraygal.

Kirribilli

Transport *Ferry Kirribilli.*

The north shore starts at Kirribilli and Milsons Point, tiny suburbs nestled on either side of the Harbour Bridge and boasting sweeping vistas of the city and the Opera House, dubbed 'dress circle views' by real estate agents. Despite the apartment blocks that have sprung up in between the old houses, both suburbs are Victorian in feel with many original buildings still standing. The southern tip of Kirribilli is home to the official Sydney residences of the prime minister – **Kirribilli House** – and the governor-general – **Admiralty House**, where British royals and other foreign dignitaries stay. The latter is the most impressive, a classic colonial mansion built in 1844-5 by the Collector of Customs, Lieutenant-Colonel Gibbes. Originally called Wotonga, in 1885 the place was bought by the NSW government to house admirals of the fleet, hence its name today.

Kirribilli House next door with its rolling, manicured lawns was built in 1855 in a Gothic Revival style by a rich local merchant; after a series of owners it was acquired by the government in 1956 for use by the prime minister, his family and important guests. Since taking office in 1996, John Howard has used the house as his principal home, rather than the official prime ministerial residence, the Lodge in Canberra. It's a choice that opposition parties claim is costing the tax

North Sydney Olympic Pool. *See p98.*

payer dearly, but Mr Howard is not about to give up his harbour view – and when you see it you'll understand why. To get the best views of Kirribilli House and Admiralty House, hop on a ferry from Circular Quay.

There's a distinct village feel to Kirribilli and its good-life residents continue to fill the cafés and restaurants around the hub of Fitzroy, Burton and Broughton Streets. Try the laid-back **Freckle Face** (32 Burton Street, 9957 2116), smart restaurant **Cloudstreet** (34 Burton Street, 9922 1512), run by chef Julianne Lever, formerly of 'it crowd' hangout Catalina in Rose Bay, **Randolph's on Fitzroy** (Shop 4, 12 Fitzroy Street, 9955 3738) and the renowned **Kirribilli Hotel** (35 Broughton Street, 9955 1415) with its outdoor terrace. The famous **Ensemble Theatre** (*see p251*), built over the water at Careening Cove, serves up new and classic theatre.

A particularly good time to visit Kirribilli is on the fourth Saturday of the month when one of Sydney's oldest markets is held on the former Kirribilli Bowling Club site (on the corner of Burton and Alfred Streets). All sorts of stuff is on sale, but it's best known for upmarket bric-a-brac and antiques.

Despite appearances, not everyone in Kirribilli is rolling in cash. In among the million-dollar mansions and swank apartment blocks lurk some Housing Commission blocks and older, cheaper homes. It's not quite a case of rich and poor rubbing shoulders, though, since the shoulder pads around the big homes tend to stretch some distance, but it does mean that the area retains a modicum of balance of old-world character and modern reality.

Milsons Point, McMahons Point & North Sydney

Transport Milsons Point *CityRail/ferry Milsons Point.* McMahons Point *Ferry McMahons Point.* North Sydney *CityRail North Sydney.*

On a sunny day, treat yourself to a ferry trip from Circular Quay's Jetty 4 gliding past the Opera House to Milsons Point wharf (Alfred Street South). From here, you can take the harbourside walk in either direction; if you do it early when the PM's in town, you might well pass him on his morning power walk flanked by bodyguards. The ferry pulls up right in front of the grinning face and huge staring eyes of the newly reopened **Luna Park** funfair (*see p100* **Luna tunes**). To the right (with your back to the water) is the revamped **North Sydney Olympic Pool** (*see p98*), perhaps the most stunningly located swimming pool in the world: it's on the edge of the water, beneath the underbelly of the Harbour Bridge.

The pool also houses a couple of snazzy eateries popular with the media and advertising crowd who work in North Sydney. The less-formal **Ripples** (corner of Alfred Street and Olympic Drive, 9929 7722) is bang next to the pool and has outdoor tables. On the other side, in a glass box overlooking the pool, is the pricey **Aqua Dining** (*see p161*). Run by the same people, both restaurants are open for lunch and dinner.

If you walk along the boardwalk in front of the pool, you can peek in through the glass-sided bay windows at the swimmers and sunbathers. The colourful art deco façade has fabulous mouldings of frogs and cockatoos. Carry on under the Bridge and continue past the green lawns of **Bradfield Park** with the rather ugly brown *Australian Angel*, the Swiss cultural contribution to an exhibition of sculpture and graphic art at the Sydney 2000 Olympics. There's also a plaque commemorating

the deaths of 51 people from typhus aboard the quarantined ship *Surry*, which was anchored here in 1814. Third mate Thomas Raine was the only officer to survive and his grandson Tom Raine founded the wealthy Sydney estate agents Raine & Horne – a fitting north shore tale. The foreshore walk ends at **Mary Booth Lookout**, a patch of green with a fabulous view that's perfect for picnicking.

In the other direction from Luna Park the foreshore walk winds around **Lavender Bay**; it's especially dazzling at sunset when the city lights shimmer in the golden glow. Walk up the Lavender Bay Wharf steps to Lavendar Street, turn left and after another couple of minutes you'll reach **Blues Point Road**, which slices down from North Sydney through the heart of McMahons Point. It's one of Sydney's great people-watching strips. There are numerous cafés, pubs, delis and restaurants from which to take in the view; try **Blues Point Café** (No.135, 9922 2064) or the popular and sometimes rowdy **Commodore Hotel** (No.206, 9922 5098, www.commodorehotel.com.au) with its large outdoor terrace. Allow time to walk down to **Blues Point Reserve**, a swathe of open parkland at the southern tip of Blues Point that provides a great photo op for that obligatory Sydney Harbour holiday snap.

The northern end of Blues Point Road merges into Miller Street, dominated by North Sydney office blocks. A little way up on the left-hand side of Miller Street is Mount Street and the bizarre **Mary MacKillop Place** (*see p98*). This homage to Australia's only saint stands on the site of her former convent and is worth a visit, if only for its zany exhibition. To get a sense of the history of the area, visit the **Don Bank Museum** (*see below*), located inside one of North Sydney's oldest houses.

The heart and main commercial centre of the lower north shore is **Military Road**, a low-slung, seemingly endless and faceless strip of shops, cafés and restaurants that heads east through Neutral Bay to Balmoral. At No.118, in Neutral Bay, the popular **Oaks** pub (*see p138*) with its tree-covered courtyard, is a hangout for local movers and shakers, who order steaks and fish by the kilo and then make for the outdoor barbecue to cook up a storm.

Don Bank Museum

6 Napier Street, off Berry Street, North Sydney (9955 6279). CityRail North Sydney. **Open** noon-4pm Wed; 1-4pm Sun. **Admission** $1. **No credit cards.**
It's not known exactly when this house was built, but parts are thought to date from the 1820s. Originally called St Leonards Cottage (most of North Sydney, as it now is, was once called St Leonards) it was part of the Wollstonecraft Estate, 212 hectares (524 acres) granted to Edward Wollstonecraft in

Sightseeing

Walkabout 2

Cremorne Point

Character Great water views and bushland.
Length 3km (2 miles) loop.
Difficulty Easy.

The track from Bogota Avenue (walkable from Neutral Bay ferry wharf or on the 225 bus) to Cremorne Point and round to Mosman Bay is hardly taxing, but the spectacular vistas are quite breathtaking. The path takes you along Shell Cove to the fenced, harbourside MacCallum Pool with its uninterrupted views across to the city. Continue past Cremorne wharf and head into the pretty bushland up to Robertsons Point where you'll see the whitewashed lighthouse. From here you can look west to Kurraba Point, Kirribilli and Shell Cove Bay, south to the city, Woolloomooloo and Pinchgut Island and east to Double Bay and Watsons Bay, looking over Taronga Zoo. There are toilets, a children's play area and picnic tables here.

Follow the signs along the foreshore to Mosman Bay. You'll pass the stunning Lex & Ruby Graham Gardens, lovingly maintained by this local couple and now taken on by the National Trust. You may also see kookaburras, magpies, lizards and rainbow lorikeets. Watch out for 'The Laurels', a huge house set back from the bushland; it's one of Sydney's best examples of the Federation Arts and Crafts style, an early 20th-century movement that aimed to combine informality and homeliness with craftsmanship and art. At the Mosman Bay marina either climb the steps and follow signs back to the track's starting point, or walk round to the wharf where you can catch a ferry.

1825. The house was bought by North Sydney Council in the late 1970s and restored with assistance from heritage groups. It is now a community museum. As well as visiting exhibitions, its permanent displays include kitchen objects from the times of the early settlers and other historical items. The building itself is significant, being one of the few surviving examples of an early timber-slab house.

Mary MacKillop Place

7 Mount Street, between Edward & William Streets, North Sydney (8912 4878/www.marymackillop place.org.au). CityRail North Sydney. **Open** 10am-4pm daily. **Admission** $7.50; $3-$5 concessions; $15 family. **Credit** BC, MC, V.

Mary MacKillop (1842-1909) was the founder of the Sisters of St Joseph, an order initially devoted to educating poor Australian children. Often referred to as 'the people's saint', MacKillop's pioneering work lead to her beatification in 1995 when the Pope visited and blessed the site, giving Australia its first – and only – saint to date. She died on 8 August and the eighth day of each month has traditionally become a day of pilgrimage to the museum for devout Catholics. The Place includes MacKillop's home, Alma Cottage, and the chapel housing her tomb. A curious mix of humble 19th-century artefacts and high-tech wizardry, the displays of MacKillop's possessions – including crucifixes, rosary beads, figurines and scraps of her habits – are jazzed up with talking dioramas, videos and other surprisingly cool special effects, all of which take you on a journey through the saint's life.

North Sydney Olympic Pool

Alfred Street South, at the foreshore, Milsons Point (9955 2309/www.northsydney.nsw.gov.au). CityRail/ferry Milsons Point. **Open** 5.30am-9pm Mon-Fri; 7am-7pm Sat, Sun. **Admission** *Pool* $4.40; $2.10-$3.60 concessions; free pensioners. *Gym* $12.50. *Sauna & spa* $5.50. **Credit** AmEx, BC, DC, MC, V.

This unique outdoor swimming pool, situated on the harbour between the Bridge and Luna Park, holds a special place in Sydneysiders' hearts. Built on the site where much of the construction work for the Sydney Harbour Bridge was carried out, it opened in 1936. Hailed as the 'wonder pool of Australasia' because of the high standard of its facilities and the sophistication of its filtration system – at the time one of the most advanced in the world – the building boasts wonderful, still-intact art deco styling and decorative plasterwork. A total of 86 world records have been set here by such swimming greats as Jon Konrads, Shane Gould and Michelle Ford. Thanks to a revamp in the early 2000s, a 25m indoor pool, state-of-the-art gym, spa and sauna have been added to the famed 50m heated outdoor pool.

Cremorne, Mosman, Balmoral & the Spit Bridge

Transport Cremorne *Ferry Cremorne Point/bus L88 to Neutral Bay then bus 225.* **Mosman** *Ferry South Mosman, Old Cremorne or Mosman Bay/CityRail Milsons Point then bus 228, 229, 230.* **Balmoral** *Ferry Taronga Zoo then bus 238/CityRail Milsons Point then bus 229.*

If you continue east along Military Road (an extension of the busy main route that links the suburbs of the lower north shore), you will arrive at some of Sydney's richest suburbs: Cremorne, Mosman and Balmoral, where the heavily monied live in conspicuous splendour.

Cremorne Point, a sliver of a peninsula, offers one of the finest panoramas of Sydney Harbour. It's the perfect setting for a scenic harbourside stroll (*see p98* **Walkabout 2**), or you can take the ferry to Cremorne Point wharf and walk south to Robertsons Point, with its lighthouse and unbelievable views across to the Opera House and the eastern suburbs.

You can then hop back on the ferry to Mosman Bay wharf, where an uphill walk or bus will take you into Mosman village (alternatively, the Cremorne Point walk leads around Mosman Bay). Stop at the friendly **Rowers Restaurant** (3 Centenary Drive, 9953 7713, www.mosmanrowers.com) for lunch, dinner or (on Sundays) breakfast. Part of the Mosman Rowing Club, it's right on the water with a great outdoor seating area and reasonably priced DIY barbecue options.

Further east lies **Taronga Zoo** (*see below*), which occupies a splendid vantage point overlooking Bradleys Head. Catch the ferry from Circular Quay to Taronga Zoo (Athol) wharf and board the Sky Safari cable car, which takes you up to the main zoo compound where there are yet more splendid panoramic views across the harbour to the city.

North of the zoo, Mosman's commercial centre runs along Military Road and is a good place to people-watch and shop (if your wallet can cope). All the chainstores are here, plus a clutch of Australian designers, plenty of 'shabby chic' homeware shops and endless delis and coffee shops.

Beyond Mosman is Balmoral, one of Sydney's prettiest harbour suburbs. Boasting not one but two beaches, lots of green space, a Romanesque bandstand (which is the venue for many local events) and a couple of excellent restaurants – **Watermark** (2A The Esplanade, 9968 3433, www.watermarkrestaurant.com.au) and **Bathers' Pavilion** (*see p161*) – plus a pretty decent fish and chip shop for a promenade snack, Balmoral offers a more relaxed version of north shore life. The two arcs of sand, Edwards and Balmoral Beaches, are separated by Rocky Point, and part of Edwards is protected by a shark net. If you come on a Saturday before 10am and you're likely to spy members of the Spit Amateur Swimming Club pounding the water. This family-friendly club is a local institution and has been using Balmoral's outdoor baths since 1916.

Head further north and you hit the **Spit Bridge**, the beautiful bottleneck faced by those wanting to head further up the northern shore. The view driving down Spit Road from Military Road is one of Sydney's most delicious, with boats bobbing in the marina either side of the narrow bridge causeway and million-dollar mansions clinging to the rocky cliffs. Traffic comes to a thrilling halt when the bridge lifts to let boats pass beneath.

Taronga Zoo

Bradleys Head Road, Mosman (9969 2777/ www.zoo.nsw.gov.au). Ferry Taronga Zoo/bus 247. **Open** 9am-5pm daily. **Admission** *Zoo only* $25; $13.50-$17.50 concessions; $65 family; free under-4s. *Zoopass* $31.70; $15.70 concessions. **Credit** AmEx, BC, DC, MC, V.

Only 12 minutes by ferry from Circular Quay, the 'zoo with a view' covers 30 hectares (74 acres) on the western side of Bradleys Head. The zoo moved here from Moore Park in Sydney's eastern suburbs in 1916. The animals arrived by ferry; the story goes that Jessie the elephant actually walked from Moore Park to Circular Quay before gingerly climbing aboard ship. The zoo contains 380 species (currently 2,200 animals); best of all, especially for foreigners, are the native species including koalas, kangaroos, platypus (twins were born recently), echidnas, Tasmanian devils and lots of colourful, screechy birds (follow the Wild Australia Walk to see them all). Visitors are no longer allowed to cuddle koalas, but a 'koala encounter' (11am-3pm) lets you have your photo taken beside one of the sleepy critters.

Other highlights include the Free Flight Bird Show, the Capral Seal Show, Giraffes in Focus – meet the giraffes face to face, listen to a keeper talk and grab a close-up photo – the huge Komodo dragon and the gorilla forest. New exhibits include Backyard to Bush, a journey from an Aussie backyard through an adventure-packed farmyard into the wilderness of the bush, and construction is currently under way on the Asian Elephant Rainforest (opening late 2004), Great Southern Oceans and African Safari.

The zoo is on a hill, so if you're coming by ferry, take the cable car to the top and then walk back down to the wharf – and get a Zoopass, which covers the return ferry trip, cable car and admission. It's a huge place and tricky to find your way around (the free map is pretty poor), so allow at least three to four hours for a visit. There are several cafés, but it's more agreeable to take your own picnic.

Waverton & Wahroonga

Transport Waverton *CityRail Waverton.* **Wahroonga** *CityRail Wahroonga.*

While it's true that the north shore's most spectacular vistas are found on the harbour foreshore, there are a couple of other areas worth visiting for something a little different. A train ride across the Harbour Bridge to Waverton (one stop past North Sydney) will deliver you to **Balls Head Reserve**, a thickly wooded headland overlooking the start of the Parramatta River. Turn left out of the station down Bay Road, which runs into Balls Head Road; it's a five- to ten-minute walk. From here you can look west to Gladesville, south to the city, Balmain and Goat Island and east to McMahons Point and beyond. Until 1916

Sightseeing

Luna tunes

Behind the wide-mouthed grin and bulging eyes of Luna Park's gaudy entrance face on the Milsons Point foreshore lies a story of ups and downs, highs and lows, thrills and spills, but, ultimately, a tale of nostalgia pulling through in the end. Sydney's kitsch, colourful amusement park is set to reopen in April 2004 and will then echo again with the whoops of delight of new generations as its

fairground rides twist and turn, soar and dip, spin and sail – though only a few years ago it looked as if the lights of Luna Park had been switched off forever.

The park's origins lay in South Australia, where Luna Park Glenelg ran for five years before it was relocated in 1935 to Sydney, next to the northern pylon of the Harbour Bridge. The Lavender Bay site was historic

this area was the home of a local Aboriginal community (*see p90* **Sacred sites**), but during World War I the Australian Army claimed the land and a Quarantine Depot (which is still standing) was then established. Wildlife is abundant and on summer nights you might see flying foxes feeding on the Port Jackson fig trees, dragon lizards, geckos, brush-tailed possums and up to 68 species of bird. There are free gas barbecues, so you can take your own steak or prawns and dine out at one of the finest window seats in Sydney.

West of Balls Head, around the next cove, **Berry Island Reserve** is the best place to see remnants of the north shore's Aboriginal heritage (*see p90* **Sacred sites**). The island was originally a camping area for Aboriginal communities, and evidence of their way of life,

including shell middens and axe grindings, are still visible. In the early 19th century Edward Wollstonecraft attached the island over mud flats (now reclaimed as lawns) to his land by building a stone causeway; the area became a public nature reserve in 1926.

Wahroonga is a quiet, leafy suburb on the north-west fringe of the north shore, and the place where you'll find **Rose Seidler House** (*see p101*). This was the first building that the Viennese-born architect Harry Seidler designed in Australia. He went on to become one of Sydney's most celebrated architects, and his unusual buildings around the city continue to provoke admiration and controversy in equal measure. The house itself is impressive enough on its own, but you must also check out the amazing panoramic views of Ku-ring-gai in itself, having been the Dorman Long workshops, used for the construction of the Bridge. Pivotal in the move was star performer and showman Ted 'Hoppy' Hopkins; he soon became the new park's maintenance engineer, a crucial role that involved supervising the safe running of all of the park's rides.

The park's heyday lasted until well into the 1950s, and it became an iconic and much-loved fixture on the harbour. Thousands came to scream on the Big Dipper rollercoaster and other classic rides, such as Coney Island, the Ghost Train, the Spider, the Ferris Wheel, the Dodgems, River Caves, Tumblebug and Tango. The famous face has always been there, but has changed over the years from austere to feminine to grotesque to clown-like to the rather sinister current version. A slow decline into the '70s not only brought inflation but new rides, which meant demolishing old rides and a cessation of the old habit of closing the park for regular winter maintenance schedules. This proved to be a fatal mistake. In 1979 a fire on the ghost train killed a man, his two sons and three of their Sydney classmates. The smile was wiped off the face of Luna Park and its doors were slammed shut. It looked like the end.

But it's hard to keep a good park down. Between 1981 and 1988 the funfair opened sporadically, until full-blown reconstruction began in 1992. At that point, a number of the original rides were refurbished and a boardwalk connecting Luna Park to Lavender Bay was constructed. The park reopened in

1995, but only lasted a matter of months. Furiously bad weather kept crowds away, but when they did bowl up and clamber on to the Big Dipper, Luna Park's biggest moneyspinner, the 'whoosh factor' proved too much for the local residents who complained in droves about the deafening screams of delight. A 'noise restriction' order severely limiting the ride's operating hours meant it was no longer financially viable to keep the park open. The Big Dipper was sold to a funfair in Queensland.

Then, in 2000 a new development plan was approved and, finally, it appears that Luna Park will live again, this time as a performance venue and a 1930s-style fun park. Some of the park's old traditional rides are still around, as are many of its old-fashioned sideshow games as Laughing Clowns, Goin' Fishin' and Milkcan. Modern additions include the 2,000-seat Luna Pavilion arena, the refurbishment of Crystal Palace as a banqueting venue, a new café and a basement car park.

As the park's old motto goes, it's time again 'Just for Fun'.

Luna Park Sydney

1 Olympic Drive, at the foreshore, Milsons Point (9922 6644/www.lunaparksydney.com). CityRail/ferry Milsons Point. **Open** *(from Apr 2004) 11am-6pm Mon-Thur, Sun; 11am-midnight Fri; 10am-midnight Sat.* **Admission** *Admission free. Rides individual rides vary; $35 unlimited ride pass; $95 family unlimited ride pass.* **Credit** *AmEx, BC, DC, MC, V.*

National Park from almost every window. Those sweeping views help explain why Seidler chose this location in the first place.

Rose Seidler House

71 Clissold Road, at Devon Street, Wahroonga (9989 8020/www.hht.nsw.gov.au). CityRail Wahroonga. **Open** *10am-5pm Sun; and by appointment.* **Admission** *$7; $3 concessions; $17 family.* **No credit cards**.

Harry Seidler built this house, his first commission, in 1948-50 for his parents, Rose and Max. The ambitious architect came over from New York, where he had been working for Bauhaus guru Marcel Breuer, specifically to build the house; it was the first local instance of 'mid-century modern' domestic architecture, and consequently subject to much debate. In basic terms, Rose Seidler House is a cube with a section cut away below, and another cut from the

centre to form the sun deck. Here the solid walls of a traditional house are replaced by glass and the entire structure is anchored to the ground by slender columns. Inside, the open-plan interior is divided into two distinct zones: the living or public areas, and the sleeping or private areas. The original 1950s colour scheme has been restored and the furniture and furnishings, by important postwar designers such as Charles Eames and Eero Saarinen, are arranged as designed by Seidler. The kitchen had all 1950 mod cons – the very latest refrigerator, stove and dishwasher plus a waste-disposal unit and exhaust fan – all of which were then utterly new to Australia, and added to the house's allure locally. The architect's parents, Max and Rose Seidler, lived in the house until 1967, when Rose died and Max was moved into a retirement home. Guided tours of the building are available on request.

Northern Beaches

Oh, we do like to be beside the seaside.

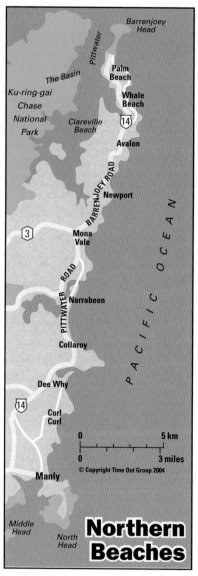

Barrenjoey
Head

Pittwater

The Basin

Palm
Beach

Ku-ring-gai
Chase

Whale
Beach

National
Park

Clareville
Beach

14

Avalon

BARRENJOEY ROAD

Newport

3

Mona
Vale

PITTWATER ROAD

Narrabeen

Collaroy

Dee Why

14

Curl
Curl

0   5 km

0   3 miles

© Copyright Time Out Group 2004

Manly

Middle
Head

North
Head

**Northern
Beaches**

PACIFIC OCEAN

Think of a Sydney beach and most will come
up with Bondi or Manly. But the real surfie
heart of the city lies beyond the city reaches,
over Spit Beach, past Manly and further up the
northern coastline. It's also where you'll find
the most beautiful of Sydney's beaches. Here
lies a string of stunning golden sand and surf,
with many beaches all but empty on weekdays
– just you, the sea, the sun and your board.

The northern beaches officially start at
busy, touristy Manly, but it is the more distant
suburbs such as Collaroy, Narrabeen, Newport
and Avalon that set the tone for the area.
The secret of the northern beaches' character
(dubbed the 'insular peninsula' by some) lies
in their relative inaccessibility: there's no
suburban train line that goes to the area. This
means that residents of the northern beaches
must either drive to the city in the crawling
rush-hour traffic, sit on a sweaty bus or charter
their own boat. While Australians are happy
long-distance drivers, hellish daily commutes
are another matter. This prospect has largely
kept city workers away from the northern
beaches, and allowed the area to develop in a
special way: it's a unique blend of genuine
locals with not too much spare cash, and
nouveau northern beachers (think Kerry
Packer) who breeze in and snap up the prime
property sites – the ones with eye-popping
ocean views and space for a helipad. The
presence of rich folk has encouraged the
opening of a smattering of cool restaurants,
upmarket shops and classy businesses, while
the locals have fought to preserve the beaches,
parklands and countrified atmosphere.

But the bad news is that the tide is turning.
Real-estate hikes have put pressure on every
Sydney suburb and as the city's urban sprawl
seeps further out even the northern beaches
have succumbed to the invasion of apartment
blocks and shopping centres that are the norm
elsewhere. Take the L90 bus from Wynyard
up Pittwater Road (the easiest way to tour
the northern beaches if you don't have a car)
and you'll immediately spot the changes –
family suburbs such as Dee Why, Narrabeen,
Mona Vale and Newport are awash with
imposing developments. Palm Beach became
a millionaires' playground long ago, and the
coastline is now cluttered with more and more
architect-designed palaces, while Avalon,

The swooping crescent of **Manly Beach**, a short ferry ride from Circular Quay.

always the protected heart of the northern beaches, is growing far quicker than the outspoken 'Save Our Avalon' locals would like; with its homeware shops, sushi and juice bars, it's in danger of turning into a mini Mosman.

For the tourists, though, the development is not all bad. There are far more places to stay than there used to be – cute B&Bs, pub-style accommodation, youth hostels and four-star hotels – and more choice of eating and watering holes. And while locals may whinge about the changes, this is still an undeniably stunning stretch of coastline.

Manly

Transport *Ferry Manly.*

A summery explosion of shops, restaurants, cafés, surfboards, people and colour, this famous beachside suburb nestles on its own peninsula, boasting both ocean and harbour beaches, and views from every corner. Since its first days as a resort in the 1920s, Manly's catchphrase has been 'seven miles from Sydney and a thousand miles from care' – actually an advertising slogan coined by the once-famous Port Jackson & Manly Steamship Company. Hearing it might cause the locals to cringe a little these days, but the sentiment still remains.

The suburb was given its name by Arthur Phillip the first governor of New South Wales, when he saw a number of 'manly' Aboriginal men of the Kay-ye-my clan on the shore of what he later called Manly Cove. Given that the area remains a centre for such macho pursuits as surf-lifesaving, bodysurfing, beach volleyball, kayaking and the Australian Ironman Championships, the name still fits. Appropriately enough, this is also where the

English rugby team chose to stay during their World Cup victory in November 2003.

Sydneysiders have mixed feelings about Manly, but its perennial holiday atmosphere and one-and-a-half kilometres (one mile) of tree-lined ocean beach is irresistible to visitors. The tourists who head for Manly are a curious mix of the well-heeled, who stay at the area's expensive hotels, a burgeoning (predominantly British) backpacker brigade holing up at cheap hostels and pubs, and day-trippers from the Sydney suburbs.

To get to Manly take one of the large Manly ferries (30 minutes) or the pricier but faster JetCats (15 minutes) from Circular Quay to Manly Wharf on secluded **Manly Cove**, where you'll find a peaceful patch of harbourside sand (though no surf, of course). The **Visitor Information Centre** (9977 1088, www.manly tourism.com, open 9am-5pm Mon-Fri; 10am-4pm Sat, Sun) is situated at the front of the wharf, and is the place to find brochures, bus timetables, free maps and the handy A5 pocket magazine *Manly Seaside Observer*. The recently upgraded **Manly Wharf Hotel** (*see p163*) with its outside deck is one of Sydney's finest waterside restaurants. Nearby, at the western end of the cove, is popular **Oceanworld Manly** (*see p105*), **Manly Art Gallery & Museum** (*see p104*) behind it and, further west, the start of a fine walk to **Spit Bridge** (*see p108* **Walkabout 3**).

The main pedestrian precinct, the **Corso**, links Manly Wharf with Manly Beach on the oceanfront, and is lined with restaurants, surf shops, fast-food joints and tourist shops. A recent influx of new businesses, including a clutch of high-street chains, plus cool clothing and footwear shops, has made this strip a popular shopping destination in its own right.

The Corso's amphitheatre is used regularly for live entertainment and has been known to draw enormous crowds, particularly for the fantastically popular **Manly International Jazz Festival** (*see p192*).

The main attraction is **Manly Beach** itself, a long, pale crescent of sand and surf, fringed by giant Norfolk pines, and a mecca for surfers, cyclists, in-line skaters and sunbathers. The pines were planted in the 1850s by Henry Gilbert Smith, a wealthy English immigrant who decided to turn Manly from a tiny fishing village into a resort for Sydneysiders. It was here too that local newspaper editor WH Gocher flouted the law prohibiting daylight bathing in 1902, a symbolic act that probably marked the beginning of Manly's – and Sydney's – love affair with sun, sea, sand and surf. Eddie and Joe Sly were the first lifesavers to patrol the beach after crowds failed to understand the danger of the surf. They staged a lifesaving demo in 1903 to raise money for their service.

Head south along the beachfront road to find a row of laid-back bars and cafés with lovely ocean views on South Steyne. Busy most of the time, they are perfect spots in which to enjoy a meal or coffee, or just watch the world cruise by. Popular spots include **Blue Water Café** (28 South Steyne, 9976 2051), **Zinc Café** (No.30-31, 9977 9199) and **Rouge Mediterranean Café** (No.33, 8966 9872). Or there's the chic **Manly Ocean Beach House** (Ocean Promenade, North Steyne, 9977 0566) slap bang in the middle of the beachside promenade, so close to the surfers you can almost touch them.

A must is the 15-minute walk to **Shelly Beach**. Walk south on the beachfront from Manly Beach to Marine Parade, and follow the winding path around the headland known as Fairy Bower, passing magnificent cliff-top homes along the way. Watch out for the beautiful, and carefully hidden, sea-themed sculptures along the Sculpture Walk. En route are a couple of eateries. The **Bower Restaurant** (7 Marine Parade, 9977 5451) is a good spot for breakfast, lunch or an early dinner, while, at Shelly Beach, the sandstone **Le Kiosk** (1 Marine Parade, 9977 4122/2956) is a smart restaurant with a cheaper takeaway kiosk next door.

Another must is the spectacular view from **North Head**, the northern half of the two Heads that form the gateway to Sydney Harbour. It's a five- to ten-minute drive via Darley Road (running south-east from the middle of the Corso) and North Head Scenic Drive. North Head is also home to the historic **North Head Quarantine Station** (*see p105*) and **North Fort** (*see p105*). You can take bus 135 from Wentworth Street, but be aware that the service operates in the daytime only.

Manly Art Gallery & Museum

West Esplanade (9949 1776). Ferry Manly. Open 10am-5pm Tue-Sun. **Admission** $3.50; $1.10 concessions. **No credit cards.** Map p104.

PACIFIC PARADE
North Steyne SLSC
Manly
PINE ST
NORTH STEYNE
SMITH ST
PITTWATER
0   400 m
0   400 yds
© Copyright Time Out Group 2004
BIRLEY ROAD
QUINTON RD
OCEAN RD
KANGAROO ST
WHISLER ST
DENISON ST
North Steyne Beach
RAGLAN STREET
ROAD
RAGLAN ST
TASMAN SEA
Ivanhoe Park
Manly Oval
CENTRAL AVE
SYDNEY ROAD
JAMES ST
SOUTH STEYNE
Manly Beach
Police
GILBERT ST
BELGRAVE ST
THE CORSO
Oceanworld Manly
WEST ESPLANADE
Pool
WENTWORTH ST
VICTORIA PDE
Manly SLSC
MARINE PARADE
To Shelly Beach
Ferry
i
EAST ESPLANADE
ASHBURNER ST
CLIFF ST
REDDALL ST
BOWER ST
Manly Wharf
DARLEY ROAD
Manly Cove
COVE AVE
OSBORNE ROAD
ADDISON ROAD
To North Head

Although Manly is not exactly synonymous with high culture, you could always pop into this small gallery/museum if all the surfer lingo starts to curdle your brain. The gallery, opened in 1930, boasts an 800-strong collection of paintings by Australian artists, an impressive ceramics display and edgy exhibitions by local students and photographers. The museum is devoted to the history of Manly and has a marvellously kitsch collection of beach memorabilia, including vintage swimming costumes.

North Fort

North Fort Road, off North Head Scenic Drive (9976 6102/www.northfort.org.au). Ferry Manly then bus 135. **Open** 11am-4pm Wed, Sat, Sun. **Admission** $8; $4-$5 concessions; $15 family. **No credit cards**.

The remote location of North Fort means its landscape has changed little since early colonial paintings. Wind-blown sand dunes cover the headland, with hanging swamps among the coastal shrub. Today it is home to the Royal Australian Artillery National Museum, once part of the School of Artillery, constructed between 1935 and 1938 in the shadow of war and the need to defend Sydney Harbour from naval attack. You can still tour the fortifications and underground tunnels and a memorial walkway is under construction.

North Head Quarantine Station

North Head Scenic Drive (bookings 9247 5033/ www.manlyquarantine.com). Ferry Manly then bus 135. **Open** (pre-booked tours only) *Public tour* 1.10-3.40pm Mon, Wed, Fri-Sun. *Adults' ghost tour* 7.30-10.30pm Wed, Fri-Sun. *Kids' ghost tour* 6-8pm Fri. **Admission** *Public tour* $11; $7.70 concessions. *Adults' ghost tour* $22 Wed; $22.50 Fri-Sun. *Kids' ghost tour* $13.20. **Credit** BC, MC, V.

The ghost tours at the North Head Quarantine Station are possibly the creepiest sightseeing you'll ever do. Built in 1828, the station was the prison – and burial place – of scores of unfortunate souls, who were quarantined here for a minimum of 30 days if their ship was suspected of carrying an infectious disease, such as smallpox, bubonic plague or influenza. The station was overcrowded, the treatment often degrading and many who died were buried in unmarked graves. Closed in 1972 (though, incredibly, it was used as emergency housing for Vietnamese orphans in 1975), the station is currently a top attraction for ghoulish tourists. They are led through its black streets, old fumigation rooms, shower blocks and cemetery by a guide with a kerosene lamp. Several visitors claim to have seen the resident ghosts – a mustachioed man in a three-piece suit and a stern matron; others have reported feeling nauseous after getting a whiff of putrid and inexplicable smells. If you take a night tour, bring a torch and wear flat shoes.

Despite its grim past the Quarantine Station is much revered by locals, and recent protests have prevented it from being leased to a private developer. It lies on the grounds of an ancient Aboriginal ceremonial site, and is home to many threatened species of flora and fauna: bandicoots nest at Spring Cove and it is the only breeding colony for fairy penguins on mainland New South Wales.

Oceanworld Manly

West Esplanade (9949 2644/www.oceanworld. com.au). Ferry Manly. **Open** 10am-5.30pm daily. **Admission** $16.50; $8.50-$12.50 concessions; $28-$39.90 family. 15% discount after 3.30pm. **Credit** AmEx, BC, DC, MC, V. **Map** p104.

Located a couple of hundred metres from Manly's ferry terminal, Oceanworld is about as good as aquaria get. The three-level attraction has a floor devoted to dangerous Australian animals (poisonous snakes, funnel web spiders, giant monitor lizards, crocodiles) and another to tropical fish, corals and venomous sea creatures. The main attraction, on the lower level, is the oceanarium, which holds the largest sharks in captivity in Australia, plus giant rays and sea turtles. You can view them via a 110m/360ft-long underwater viewing tunnel. Fish and sharks are fed at 11am on Mondays, Wednesdays and Fridays and there's a dangerous Australian animal show at noon, 1.30pm and 3pm daily. Other attractions include the 'touch pool' where you can get up close and personal with hermit crabs and starfish. For the really adventurous there's Shark Dive Xtreme ($150-$195), a chance to swim with huge grey nurse sharks.

Freshwater to Whale Beach

Transport Dee Why, Collaroy, Narrabeen, Warriewood & Mona Vale *Bus 155, 156, L88, L90.* Newport & Avalon *Bus L88, L90.* Whale Beach *Bus 193.*

From Manly, the other northern beaches stretch out like a golden necklace and the names – Freshwater, Curl Curl, Dee Why, Collaroy, Narrabeen, Newport and Avalon – slip off the tongue like a surfer on the crest of a wave. This is serious surf territory, where Sydney's pro-surfers choose to limber up. Here the air smells of sea salt and coconut oil, and every second teenager hides under a mop of matted bleached blond hair, with a surfboard in tow. Scattered communities of holiday homes are gradually turning into suburbs, as increasing numbers of Sydneysiders from all classes opt to work in the city and put up with the long drive home for the sybaritic pleasures of life on the northern beaches.

The best way to explore the northern beaches is by car, allowing you to stop, take in the view, and swim at leisure at whichever beach you fancy. Otherwise, the L90 bus from Wynyard will take you all the way to Palm Beach (the journey takes about 90 minutes if you don't stop), calling in at various beaches en route, with breathtaking views all the way.

Sightseeing

Last but not least: **Palm Beach**.

You can pick up the useful and informative **Sydney's Northern Beaches Map**, produced by the Northern Beaches Visitors Association, from Sydney Beachhouse YHA (4 Colloroy Street, Collaroy, 9981 1177) or any of the northern beaches visitor centres; much of the same information is on its website, www.sydneybeaches.com.au. Also take a look at www.northernbeaches.com.au.

If you want to try one of the best meat pies in Sydney head for **Upper Crust** (1003 Pittwater Road, 9971 5182) at the crest of the hill in Collaroy. Sylvia and Fran's legendary pies have amassed such a devoted following there's always a jostle for a parking spot outside the shop: be prepared to fight for your place in the queue with barefooted surfies who dash across the busy street for a bite between waves. Alternatively, there's the **Hog's Breath Café** (1066 Pittwater Road, 9972 3000, www. hogsbreath.com.au) right on the beach at Collaroy, a nighttime hot spot. If you crave a cold beer or have time for a leisurely lunch, stop at the **Newport Arms Hotel** in Newport (2 Kalinya Street, 9997 4900, www.newport arms.com.au), which also has rooms. Nestled on the shores of Pittwater, and boasting one of Sydney's most famous beer gardens, it's a great place to enjoy fabulous water views.

Visitors in a car can take a detour to **Garigal National Park** (9451 3479, www.national parks.nsw.gov.au), which links Sydney's north shore suburbs with the northern beaches. Covering more than 2,000 hectares (nearly 5,000 acres) of rugged bushland, sandstone outcrops and waterways, it's divided into various sections. The western section hugs Middle Harbour Creek, which leads into Sydney Harbour; a walking track by the creek offers historical interest (and four picnic areas), and some rare native ash and stringybark trees. Further north is the much larger **Ku-ring-gai**

Chase National Park (*see p108*) situated on the western shore of Pittwater. It has the classic Sydney mix of sandstone, bushland and water vistas, plus walking tracks, horse-riding trails and picnic areas.

The final must-stop before Palm Beach is **Avalon**, once something of a secret but now a thriving shopping centre and booming residential village – and getting bigger by the minute. It's approached via a slightly unnerving steep and winding road, which offers stunning and dramatic ocean views for whoever is in the passenger seat, but one hairy ride for the driver. On your right, you'll pass the jaw-droppingly steep decline that leads to **Bilgola Beach**. On the upward ascent into Avalon, look out for the traditional birthday and anniversary greetings that locals pin to the trees. **Avalon Beach** is down the hill on the right. This beautiful surf beach was once considered as a possible new location by the makers of *Baywatch*, but the locals weren't having any of it. Today Avalon surfies still jealously guard their turf; they're in their combies from dawn until dusk, waiting for that perfect wave.

The town itself has two main strips: Avalon Parade, which runs from the beach up towards the Pittwater side of the peninsula, and the Old Barrenjoey Road, which crosses Avalon Parade and leads to Palm Beach in one direction and Sydney in the other.

On Old Barrenjoey Road old favourite the **Ibiza Café** (No.47, 9918 3965) does a roaring trade; it's got an open pavement area for summer and a warm, friendly feel in winter. **Bookoccino** (No.37A, 9973 1244) is one of the best bookshops on the northern beaches with an excellent range of children's books, cookery, biographies, history, Australiana and much more; as the name suggests, there's a café here too. There's also the traditional and well-

established **Avalon Toy Shop** (No.33, 9918 9106). A range of new shops includes **Gem Palace** (No.45, 9918 4257) offering Indian-style gifts and clothing, a sushi bar and a juice bar. At the time of writing, a slick new shopping/ apartment complex was in the works, tentatively titled the Peninsula.

To get to the idyllic stretches of **Long Beach** and **Clareville Beach** on the calm shore of Pittwater, head up Avalon Parade with the post office on the left. Avalon Parade turns into Hudson Parade and hooks left to run parallel to Pittwater; when you reach the bottom of the hill, turn right into Delecta Avenue (20 minutes' walk from Avalon, a few minutes in the car). The sandy beach is not good for swimming, but it's popular with locals for meet-and-greet Sunday barbecues. Many also moor their boats here. **Clareville Kiosk** (27 Delecta Avenue, 9918 2727, www.clarevillekiosk.com.au), a delightful beach house-style restaurant, is open from Wednesday to Sunday for dinner and on Sunday for lunch. Be sure to book.

There's one more treasure to be seen before you reach Palm Beach, the end of the northern beaches road. For many locals, **Whale Beach** is closer to paradise than glitzier Palm. Its inaccessibility helps, making it a definite 'those in the know' bolt-hole. You can get here by bus – the 193 from Avalon Parade in Avalon – or by walking from Careel Head Road where the L90 bus stops. Head along Careel Head Road then turn left into Whale Beach Road and continue until you reach the beach itself; it's a long (at least half an hour) and hilly trek through residential roads lined with wonderful beach houses – but it's worth the effort. The pinky sand, rugged surf and rocky headland have a quality all their own, and there's an oceanside swimming pool.

Palm Beach & around

Transport *Bus L90.*

Finally to **Palm Beach**, the well-heeled tip of the northern beaches, where you'll find more million-dollar mansions than seagulls. It's worth at least a day's exploration. The community itself is reserved and somewhat quiet, although at the time of writing a smallish shopping complex on Ocean Road was about to be redeveloped.

If you haven't time for the road trip from the city, splash out and do it in style by seaplane. Planes fly from Rose Bay to Pittwater on the sheltered western side of the Palm Beach peninsula. Try **Sydney Harbour Seaplanes** (9388 1978, www.seaplanes.com.au). Its gourmet packages include one combining flights with a meal and/or overnight stay at the exclusive **Jonah's** restaurant and hotel (69 Bynya Road, Palm Beach, 9974 5599, www.jonahs.com.au – *see p163*) with its breathtaking views over Whale Beach.

Don't mistake **Palm Beach Wharf** on the western side of the peninsula for the main beach. Palm Beach proper is on the eastern, ocean side. At the southern end of the beach – the safest place to swim – the colonial-style buildings of the Palm Beach Surf Club and private Palm Beach Pacific Club sit majestically, their picturesque wooden balconies surrounded by stately palms. It was this beautiful corner of Australia that Governor Arthur Phillip first passed in his cutter before entering Broken Bay in 1788; a plaque commemorates his voyage.

Soap fans might want to head further up to **North Palm Beach**, where, if you're lucky, the kids from *Home and Away* will be filming by the **North Palm Beach Surf Club**. When the 'Summer Bay SLSC' sign is hanging on the side of the building, the Channel Seven crew are in business and you may well spot wily old Alf Stewart (aka actor Ray Meagher) ordering a latte from the kiosk or younger cast members learning their lines. Right at the top of the peninsula is **Barrenjoey Head** and its historic lighthouse, which can be reached by a short but steep walk (*see right* **Walkabout 3**). There are free guided tours of Barrenjoey Lighthouse every half hour from 11am to 3pm on the first Sunday of the month; there are plans to run these every Sunday.

If the sun gets too hot – there's not much shade, particularly on the southern end of the beach – head to the wharf and take a boat trip instead. The **Palm Beach Ferry Service** (9918 2747, www.palmbeachferry.com.au) runs every day (including Christmas Day) across Pittwater to the Basin, an area within **Ku-ring-gai Chase National Park** (*see below*), where you can walk to some excellent Aboriginal rock carvings. Cool off afterwards with a swim in the spookily dark and seriously deep bay that, thanks to its shape, gave the Basin area its name. **Palm Beach & Hawkesbury River Cruises** (0414 466 635, www.sydneyscenic cruises.com), offers a trip that crosses Pittwater into Broken Bay, stops at Patonga (a pleasant beach village) and then cruises up the beautiful lower Hawkesbury River into Cowan Waters, stopping at Bobbin Head for lunch. The boat leaves daily from Palm Beach at 11am or Patonga at 11.30am, returning to Palm Beach at 3.30pm, with more cruises at the weekend and during school holidays. Tickets cost $32; $16-$27 concessions. Alternatively, splash out on a **Peninsula Water Taxi** (0415 408831) for a bespoke cruise for up to six people.

Ku-ring-gai Chase National Park

NPWS office 9472 9300/www.nationalparks. nsw.gov.au. **Open** sunrise-sunset daily. **Admission** $3 per adult (arriving by boat/ferry); $10 per vehicle. **Map** p307.
Occupying nearly 15,000 hectares (37,000 acres) of dense forests, hidden coves and sheltered beaches where the Hawkesbury River meets the sea, Ku-ring-gai Chase was designated a national park in 1894. It is located in one of Sydney's wealthiest municipalities, stretching from the suburbs of St Ives North and Wahroonga in the south to Broken Bay in the north. Every visitor to Sydney should take in the West Head lookout, with its views over the mouth of the Hawkesbury, the beginning of the Central Coast, Barrenjoey Lighthouse and Palm Beach. Walking tracks lead to significant examples of Aboriginal rock art. Guided walks and canoe and boat tours can also be arranged. There are various routes into the park depending on where you want to go; contact the park office for more info.

Walkabout 3

Spit Bridge to Manly

Character Outback on the harbour.
Length 10km (6.25 miles) one way.
Difficulty Easy to moderate; some climbs.
Catch a bus from Wynyard to Spit Bridge (there are plenty, including the 180 or 248) or take bus 143 or 144 from Manly. You'll find the start of the track at the first right-hand exit north of the bridge (just before Avona Crescent). The clearly marked trail (look for blue signs to Manly) leads across Sandy Bay, past Clontarf Beach, up to Castle Rock and then across a patch of Sydney Harbour National Park, with its giant gum trees and rich bird life. It's a rollercoaster track, dropping deep into dense bushland before soaring to cliff-top escarpments with breathtaking views. You'll pass pockets of sub-tropical rainforest, Aboriginal archaeological sites and numerous harbour beaches. If you're feeling adventurous, you can clamber down to Reef Beach, or continue walking to Forty Baskets Beach, around North Harbour to Fairlight Beach and, finally, to Manly, where you emerge near Manly Wharf. You can, of course, do this walk in reverse.

Barrenjoey Lighthouse

Character Rugged bushland and incredible ocean views.
Length 2.5km (1.65 miles) one way.
Difficulty Moderate.
This is called a 'bush walk', probably because it's along a 4WD track. But don't let the shorter length mislead you – you'll work up quite a sweat. The starting point, at the northern end of Barrenjoey Beach (on the Pittwater side), is marked in paint on the side of a rust-coloured shed. Just head up towards the lighthouse, stopping when the views become too wonderful to ignore. The summit offers a spectacular, 360-degree vista that takes in the Pacific Ocean, Pittwater, Palm Beach and Lion Island, a deserted rocky outcrop that guards the entrance to Broken Bay. Visible 19 miles out to sea, the 1881 lighthouse was built from Hawkesbury sandstone.

▶ For more detail on some of the beaches mentioned here, *see pp118-124* **Sydney's Best Beaches**.

Parramatta & the West

Immigrants old and new have shaped Sydney's suburban heartland.

The western suburbs may not be top of your must-see list for Sydney, but they boast a more diverse mix of nationalities and cultures than anywhere else in the city. The so-called 'Westies' – all too often dismissed by their eastern suburb cousins as unsophisticated, with a voracious appetite for gambling and drinking – have much to smile about in their more spacious (and cheaper) surrounds. For a fuller picture of the Harbour City, head west.

Well before you've hit the natural lushness of the Blue Mountains, there's the blend of historic structures and modern-day success in Parramatta – the unofficial capital of the west – as well as the 'other-worldliness' of Asian centre Cabramatta, and plenty of family-friendly sites. Then there's the Olympic Park area in Homebush Bay, which is being redeveloped into a huge commercial and residential site. Adjacent Newington was used to house the athletes of the 2000 Games; now all the accommodation has been converted and sold and its residents are ready for their new suburb to flower and flourish. As well as a host of top-class sporting venues, there are shops, schools, health centres and entertainment for an estimated workforce of 10,000.

Greater Western Sydney was once a series of rural farming communities, which explains why some of the oldest white settlement buildings can still be found here. These days, the 'settlement' story is very different, of course. Not only do the western suburbs cover more than two-thirds of the metropolitan area, they also house nearly a third of the city's population (1.34 million), with a mix of blue-collar Aussies, Asians, East Europeans, Latinos and others. What's more, the melting pot attracts up to 75 per cent of the 50,000 people who migrate to Sydney each year, making it the fastest-growing area of the city, some 30 years after the original housing boom. According to local government estimates, the population will swell in the coming decades to top the two million mark.

Parramatta

Transport *RiverCat/CityRail Parramatta.*

To explore the 'other' half of Sydney, you should start with Parramatta, gateway to the west and the geographic centre of Sydney. You can get there by RiverCat from Circular Quay along the pristine Parramatta River (the most scenic route – just under an hour), by train (25-30 minutes) or by car (35-40 minutes).

Western Sydney belonged to the Dharug, Dharawal and Gandangara people before the white settlers took it from them, and the word Parramatta is Aboriginal in origin – as are many of Sydney's place names (*see p114* **What's in a name?**). The famous Aboriginal warrior Pemulwuy kept the people of Parramatta in fear of their lives for more than a decade before he was eventually killed in 1802 and his head sent to England. More than 1,000 descendants of the Dharug still live in western Sydney and altogether there are over 10,000 Aboriginal people in the district, many having moved in from rural areas.

As Australia's second-oldest white settlement, Parramatta's rich heritage makes it a unique destination. Also known as the 'Cradle City', it was the site of many of Australia's firsts: its first jail, land grant, successful farm (which saved the First Fleet in 1788 from starvation), orchard, train line to Sydney and woollen mill. Many of the original settlers were laid to rest in the city's **St John's Cemetery**, located on O'Connell Street between the cathedral and spacious **Parramatta Park**.

Parramatta also contains the state's second-largest business district (after the CBD to the east), and thus has a dynamic mix of old and new, with towering skyscrapers right next door to heritage-listed huts. **Elizabeth Farm** (*see p110*), built in 1793 by wool pioneer John Macarthur, and named after his wife, is the oldest home still standing in Australia. On the way there is **Experiment Farm Cottage** (*see p110*), a beautiful colonial cottage built on the site of Australia's first land grant. Also open for inspection is **Old Government House** (*see p110*), the oldest public building in Australia. Standing in the sprawling grounds of Parramatta Park, the spot was chosen by Governor Phillip within a few months of the establishment of the penal settlement at Sydney Cove in January 1788, and was used by NSW governors until the new government house opened in Sydney in 1845.

It's apt that Parramatta was the setting for Australia's first recorded race meeting and first legal brewery, as two things the people

Discover colonial history at **Old Government House**.

of western Sydney love are a beer and a bet.
Rosehill Gardens Racecourse (*see p246*)
on Grand Avenue is a citadel to both pursuits,
particularly during the Autumn Carnival when
the $2-million Golden Slipper – the world's
richest race for two-year-olds – is held.

Cultural attractions include the **Parramatta
Riverside Theatres** (*see p252*), which is also
used for events during the Sydney Festival
in January. **PJ Gallaghers Irish Pub** (74
Church Street; 9635 8811), formerly the General
Bourke Hotel, prides itself on being the finest
drinking hole and music venue in the west,
while other old Parramatta pubs with character
include the **Woolpack** (19 George Street, 9635
8043), the **Albion** (135 George Street, 9891
3288, www.albionhotel.com.au) and the
Commercial (2 Hassall Street, 9635 8342).

Those seeking retail therapy during their
tour of the west should head to **Westfield
Parramatta**, supposedly the second-largest
shopping centre in the southern hemisphere.
And for kids, in the nearby suburb of
Merrylands, just south of the Great Western
Highway, is the entertaining **Sydney
Children's Museum** (*see p197*).

Elizabeth Farm

*70 Alice Street, between Arthur & Alfred Streets,
Rosehill (9635 9488/www.hht.net.au). CityRail
Harris Park or Rosehill then 15mins walk.* **Open**
10am-5pm daily. **Admission** $7; $3 concessions;
$17 family. **Credit** BC, MC, V.
Elizabeth Farm is notable for two things. It became
the birthplace of the Australian wool industry when
John Macarthur imported merino sheep for breeding
at the site; and the farm's main building – with its
deep, shady verandas and stone-flagged floors –

became the prototype for the Australian homestead.
The original property now comprises only the main
building, restored to its 1830s condition, with a
recreated Victorian garden to match. Parts of the
original 1793 construction – the oldest surviving
European building in Australia – remain and the
interior has been furnished in period style.

Experiment Farm Cottage

*9 Ruse Street, Harris Park (9635 5655/www.nsw.
nationaltrust.org.au). CityRail/RiverCat Parramatta
then 10mins walk.* **Open** 10.30am-3.30pm Tue-Fri;
11am-3.30pm Sat, Sun. **Admission** *Experiment
Farm only* $5.50; $4 concessions; $14 family.
Experiment Farm & Old Government House $10;
$7 concessions; $25 family. **Credit** (over $20) BC,
MC, V.
This modest cottage is located on the site of the
colony's first land grant, which was given to convict
James Ruse – Australia's first private farmer – in
1792. Ruse then sold the land to a surgeon, John
Harris, who built the house the following year. It's
operated by the National Trust, and if you're planning to visit Old Government House, you can buy a
joint ticket for admission to both.

Old Government House

*Parramatta Park, Parramatta (9635 8149/www.
nsw.nationaltrust.org.au). CityRail/RiverCat
Parramatta then 15mins walk.* **Open** 10am-4pm
Mon-Fri; 10.30am-4pm Sat, Sun. **Admission**
Old Government House only $8; $5 concessions;
$17 family. *Old Government House & Experiment
Farm Cottage* $10; $7 concessions; $25 family.
Credit (over $20) BC, MC, V.
Previously a vice-regal residence and, at the turn
of the 20th century, a boarding house for a local
boys' school, Old Government House was built on
the foundations of Governor Arthur Phillip's 1790
cottage. Now restored to its former glory after a

110 Time Out Sydney

Telstra Stadium at **Sydney Olympic Park**.

multi-million-dollar revamp, it boasts the nation's most important collection of Australian colonial furniture. You can buy combined admission for here and Experiment Farm Cottage.

Homebush Bay

Transport *CityRail Olympic Park/RiverCat Homebush Bay.*

Sydney Olympic Park (*see below*) – host to the 'best ever' Olympic Games in 2000 – is in Homebush Bay, eight kilometres (five miles) east of Parramatta. The site features a huge range of sporting and entertainment facilities, including the mammoth **Sydney Superdome** (*see p224*) and the **Sydney Showground** (9704 1111, www.sydneyshowground.com.au), which plays host to the annual Big Day Out music festival and other large-scale events. If you've got the tiniest sporting spark in your body, or simply want to see what all the fuss was about, do visit – you'll go home impressed.

An arm of the Parramatta River, the bay is surrounded by 180 hectares (444 acres) of wetlands, woodland and grassland, which provide sanctuary for 160 bird species. Birdwatchers should head to **Bicentennial Park** (*see below*), the largest of five main parkland areas, and a pleasant spot for picnics.

Bicentennial Park

Park *Opposite Sydney Olympic Park, Homebush Bay.* **Visitor centre** *Off Australia Avenue, between Bennelong Road & Homebush Bay Drive (9714 7545/7888). CityRail Olympic Park/RiverCat Homebush Bay then bus 401.* **Open** *10am-4pm Mon-Fri; 9.30am-4.30pm Sat, Sun.* **Admission** free.

Bicentennial Park is one of the best places to go for specialist birdwatching excursions. A waterbird refuge and salt marsh are out on the water, with a fine viewing tower at their north-easterly tip. You may recognise the Brickpit, at the park's heart, as Mad Max's Thunderdome. Day and night nature tours are available.

Sydney Olympic Park

Visitor centre *1 Showground Road, at Herb Elliot Avenue, Homebush Bay (9714 7545/ www.sydneyolympicpark.nsw.gov.au). CityRail Olympic Park/RiverCat Homebush Bay then bus 401.* **Open** 8am-6pm daily.
Telstra Stadium *Olympic Boulevard (box office 8765 2000/tours 8765 2300/www.telstra stadium.com.au).* **Open** 10.30am-3.30pm daily. *Tours every 30mins.* **Admission** *30mins tour* $15; $7.50-$13 concessions; $42 family. *60mins tour* $26; $13-$19.50 concessions; $60 family. **Credit** BC, MC, V.

The most scenic way to get to Olympic Park is on the RiverCat from Circular Quay to Homebush Bay (30-40 minutes). Bus 401 meets the boat and takes you to the visitor centre. The park is big, but perfectly, and pleasantly, walkable if the weather isn't too hot. You can go on a guided walking tour (noon daily from the visitor centre), or explore the area on your own. If you prefer to travel by train, the station you want is Olympic Park not Homebush, but there are few direct CityRail services (unless an event is being staged); your best bet is to go to Lidcombe and pick up the Sprint train from there.

To see the various stadia and arenas rising out of the flat landscape as you approach is awe-inspiring in itself. The size and scope of the biggest – Telstra Stadium (formerly Stadium Australia) – dwarfs everything else in the vicinity. At the Sydney International Aquatic Centre (*see p243*) you can go for a dip, marvel at the indoor waterslides and get a faint tingle of what it must be like to perform before thousands of cheering spectators (swim meets continue to be held here). It's free to visit the Sports Centre (*see p243*) and stroll down the gallery's Hall of Champions, covering athletes from the 1890s to the present. To get into the other key venues, however, you'll need to take an organised tour (ask at the visitor centre). The Telstra Stadium tours, which last 30 or 60 minutes, depending on how much you want to see, are particularly good.

Blacktown & around

Transport *CityRail Blacktown.*

Blacktown, 11 kilometres (seven miles) north-west of Parramatta, earned its name from being home to the Native Institute, established by the early authorities to educate Aboriginal children. If you want to see lots of native animals, including a face-to-face encounter with a koala, visit the excellent, family-run **Featherdale Wildlife Park** (*see p112*).

Sightseeing

Aaah... **Featherdale Wildlife Park.**

For a unique insight into Australian taste through the years, head north of Blacktown to historic **Rouse Hill House** (*see below*). You can visit the house only on a guided tour, and it's wise to book in advance.

Western Sydney is often dubbed 'club land'. Leagues clubs, golf clubs, bowling clubs, workers' clubs, returned servicemen's clubs – they're absolutely everywhere, providing community services and cheap food, drink and entertainment, subsidised by row upon row of poker machines. Two of the biggest and the best are **Blacktown Workers Club** on Campbell Street (9830 0600, www.bwcl.com.au) and **Rooty Hill RSL Club** (9625 5500, www.rootyhillrsl.com.au) on the corner of Sherbrooke and Railway Streets, in Rooty Hill. Blacktown is also home to one of Sydney's last two remaining drive-in movie theatres, the **Greater Union Drive-In** (*see p203*).

Public transport is generally poorer in the west than in the east, so Westies tend to have a special attachment to their cars. The real rev-heads love **Eastern Creek Raceway** (Brabham Drive, Eastern Creek, 9672 1000, www.eastern-creek-raceway.com), Sydney's biggest automotive venue, which regularly hosts touring car, motorbike and drag races.

Featherdale Wildlife Park

217-229 Kildare Road, at Lynwood Avenue, Doonside (9622 1644/www.featherdale.com.au). CityRail Blacktown then bus 725. **Open** 9am-5pm daily. **Admission** $16.50; $8-$13 concessions; $42 family; free under-4s. **Credit** AmEx, BC, DC, MC, V.

Kangaroos, koalas and Tasmanian devils all feature in this well-kept wildlife park, which houses one of Australia's largest collection of native animals. The huge diversity of birds includes the bizarre cassowary (which lives in the rainforests in the tropical far north, but is rarely spotted by locals) and some scary-looking owls.

Rouse Hill House

Guntawong Road, Rouse Hill Regional Park, Rouse Hill (9627 6777/www.hht.net.au). CityRail Riverstone then bus 741R or taxi. **Tours** *Mar-Nov* every hr 10am-2pm Wed, Thur, Sun. Closed Dec-Feb. **Admission** $7; $3 concessions; $17 family. **Credit** BC, MC, V.

This two-storey Georgian house, set in a 15-hectare (37-acre) estate, was the home of the Rouse family for six generations. Free settler Richard Rouse built the original house in 1813-18, and the last direct descendant left in 1993. There are also some 20 outbuildings and a very early 'dry weather' garden.

Penrith

Transport *CityRail Penrith.*

At the foot of the Blue Mountains and perched on the banks of the Nepean River, Penrith is around 50 kilometres (31 miles) west of central Sydney. It's a sprawling modern suburb that boasts beautiful rural and bushland scenery as well as history and modern culture. At the heart of Penrith is **Panthers**, Australia's largest licensed club, and the rugby league team it supports. The huge **Panthers World of Entertainment** on Mulgoa Road (4720 5555, www.panthersworld.com.au) resembles an antipodean Butlins resort; you'll find not only a vast array of 24-hour bars, gaming facilities, restaurants, nightclubs and live music, but also a motel, swimming pools, water-skiing, waterslides, tennis courts, beach volleyball, a golf driving range and more. This staggering creation rakes in more than $100 million in revenue a year, with the profits being ploughed back into the rugby club and the community (the club is a non-profit organisation).

You might catch the Panthers training on winter weekends in **Penrith Park**, just opposite the club centre. Or try to attend one of their home games in the **Penrith Stadium** (4720 5555) against one of the western suburbs' three other first-class rugby league teams: the Parramatta Eels, the Bulldogs or the Tigers.

Penrith also offers dogs and trots at **Penrith Paceway** (corner of Station and Ransley Streets, 4721 2375, www.harness. org.au/penrith). On a more cultural note, there's the well-respected **Q Theatre** (corner of Belmore and Railway Streets, 4721 5735, www.railwaystreet.com.au), the **Joan**

Sutherland Performing Arts Centre
(597 High Street, 4721 5423) and the beautiful
Penrith Regional Art Gallery (86 River
Road, Emu Plains, 4735 1100).

On the river you'll find the historic
paddlewheeler **Nepean Belle** (The Jetty,
Tench Avenue, 4733 1274, www.nepeanbelle.
com.au), which offers lunch and dinner cruises
up the spectacular Nepean Gorge. The Penrith
area is also home to several vineyards, among
them **Vicary's Winery** in Luddenham (1935
The Northern Road, 4773 4161, www.vicarys
winery.com.au), which runs tastings and uses a
converted woolshed for weekend bush dances.

North of Penrith, the Nepean River becomes
the **Hawkesbury River**, which forms the
lifeline of another unique part of western
Sydney. For the historic towns of Richmond,
Windsor and Wilberforce and more on the
delights of the Hawkesbury, *see pp256-272.*

Cabramatta & Bankstown

Transport Bankstown *CityRail Bankstown.*
Cabramatta *CityRail Cabramatta.*

The city-suburbs of Cabramatta and Bankstown
and their neighbours are the country's
multicultural heartland. Sydney is the most
popular destination for immigrants entering
Australia, and the vast majority of those go
to live in the western suburbs. In some south-
western suburbs, more than half the population
was born overseas – in Italy, Greece, Vietnam,
Cambodia, the Philippines, China, Serbia,
Croatia, Poland, Latin America, Lebanon and
the Pacific Islands. Consequently, there's
quality, inexpensive dining to be had.

Cabramatta, in particular, has developed
a name for itself as the culinary centre of
the western suburbs. It also suffers from a
reputation as the heroin capital of Sydney,
thanks to the presence of the Asian 5T gang,
and tends to hit the headlines for its
preponderance of drug- and gang-related
deaths. For a grittily honest portrayal of
the lives of the homeless and disadvantaged
in the Asian centre of Sydney, check out local
director Khoa Do's raw, no-holds-barred film
The Finished People (2003).

But it's important to keep things in
perspective. True, as a casual tourist, you
should remain vigilant and savvy when
wandering about – and it's better to visit
during the day rather than after dark – but
if you like dining and shopping, don't miss the
area's exotic mix of Aussie suburbia, Saigon,
Shanghai and Phnom Penh.

From Cabramatta CityRail station, cross over
the road to Arthur Street and pass through the

Asian lifestyles in **Cabramatta**.

AbOriginal What's in a name?

Sydney has some exotic-sounding place names, a welcome (if sometimes challenging) relief from the monotony of replicated British names and unimaginative homages to politicians and royalty. Many are said to be derived from Aboriginal words – although it's a rather inexact science as early record-keeping was sketchy and some languages have died out. Below are some examples.

There is also a plan to dual-name 20 sites around Sydney Harbour. Traditional names have been workshopped by descendants of original Sydney tribes with reference to First Fleet records, which listed names but not meanings. Darling Harbour may also become Dumbalong, Sydney Cove Warrane, Shark Island Bowambillee and Farm Cove Wahganmuggalee.

Bondi: the sound of the waves breaking on the beach.
Cabramatta: from the words 'cabra', an edible freshwater grub, and 'matta', a point or jutting-out piece of land.

Cammeray: named after the Cammeraygal Aboriginal tribe, who were fierce fighters according to legend.
Coogee: from 'koojah', meaning 'a stinking place'.
Cronulla: from 'kurranulla', meaning 'the place of pink seashells'.
Curl Curl: 'lagoon'.
Mount Ku-ring-gai: named after the hunting ground of the Ku-ring-gai clan, whose name means 'the men'.
Narrabeen: possibly 'swan' or, more popularly, after an Aboriginal woman named Narrabin who supposedly helped in the apprehension of a band of bushrangers and Aborigines who murdered a settler family.
Parramatta: 'head of the river', 'place where the eels lie down' or a 'meeting of the waters'. The local rugby league team are the Eels.
Woollahra: 'meeting ground', 'a sitting-down place' or 'camp'.
Woolloomooloo: from 'walla-mulla', meaning young male kangaroo.

ornate Pai Lau Gate into Freedom Plaza, the main marketplace. It's like stepping into Asia, with the authentic flavours of Thai, Laotian, Cambodian, Filipino and Chinese cuisine on offer at numerous stalls. There's plenty of discount fabrics, clothing and jewellery too: on Park Road, John Street, Hughes Street and around the main plaza, direct importers and wholesalers ply their wares for all their worth in typical Asian bazaar fashion (haggling is the norm). Other attractions are the nearby Tien Hau and Kwan Zin Buddhist temples.

The best time to visit is when the Chinese and Vietnamese communities hold their New Year celebrations (around February), with wild dragon parades and more firecrackers than you can shake a match at. Some lucky visitors may experience the annual Moon Festival, held on the 15th day of the eighth lunar month – August or September, depending on the year.

Nearby Casula is also worth a look, if only for the **Casula Powerhouse** (*see below*).

Because of the high number of immigrants, soccer (or 'wog ball', as you may hear local rugby supporters disparagingly call it) is a bigger sport than rugby in this part of the city. Sydney soccer fans follow their teams with a sometimes fiery passion, based along ethnic lines, and the games can be boisterous and spectacular affairs. The Italian

community-backed **Marconi Stallions** team is the region's representative in the national soccer league, and **Club Marconi** (Prairie Vale Road, 9823 2222, www.clubmarconi.com.au) is the biggest licensed club in the area, with multicultural quirks such as facilities for playing bocce (lawn bowls).

Bankstown is also the home suburb of the famous cricketing Waugh brothers, and boasts a killer cricket team, which you can catch on summer weekends at the **Bankstown Oval** (Bankstown District Sports Club, 8 Greenfield Parade, 9709 3899, www.bankstownsports.com).

Casula Powerhouse

1 Casula Road, opposite CityRail station, Casula (9824 1121/www.casulapowerhouse.com). CityRail Casula. **Open** 10am-4pm daily. **Admission** free.
Casula Powerhouse, opened in 1994, is a converted electricity generating station transformed by art-works that are incorporated into the fabric of the building. It runs a lively exhibition programme with a strong emphasis on community and contemporary arts. The building is currently being revamped – with a new multi-purpose theatre and performance space, new exhibition spaces, arts business centre, artist studios and production spaces – with reopening planned for late 2004. Until then, the bulk of the exhibitions are on show in the Liverpool Regional Museum, on the corner of Hume Highway and Congressional Drive, Liverpool.

The South

Sun, surf and bush: welcome to Aussie living, soap opera-style.

About as close to the south as most inner-city types get is Sydney (Kingsford Smith) International Airport at Mascot. Perhaps it's because the view from the airport out over Botany Bay will reveal an oil refinery at Kurnell, an airport runway and container shipyards at La Perouse. This might also explain why the area south of the airport remains the domain of generations who have always lived there, seemingly trapped in a twilight zone of sun, sea and bush.

Brighton-le-Sands is home to a large Greek population, while Cronulla and its surrounding suburbs are full of whitebread Australians who were probably strapped to their surfboards, boats – and anything else that floats – as toddlers. With backyard pools upping the water quotient, the area is like TV's *Neighbours* and *Home and Away* rolled into one.

On weekends, families from the outer south and west suburbs catch the train in to picnic under the beachside trees – but that's about as far as the interloping goes. More appetising to those living east of the city is the former-artist-colony chic of Bundeena, across Port Hacking in the Royal National Park. Still, the southern locals aren't complaining – it just means they get to keep all the more private picnic and swimming spots to themselves.

Botany Bay

Transport Kurnell *CityRail Cronulla then bus 987.* **Brighton-le-Sands** *CityRail Rockdale then bus 475, 478, 479.*

When the British 'discovered' Sydney Harbour in 1770, they landed on the tip of the **Kurnell Peninsula**, in Botany Bay. Under the command of James Cook, and with botanist Joseph Banks leading a party of scientists, the crew of HMS *Endeavour* spent a week exploring the area and recording information on the flora and fauna they found (hence the bay's name). Eighteen years later, when the newly appointed governor of New South Wales, Captain Arthur Phillip, arrived with the First Fleet, he relinquished the base at Kurnell in favour of a deeper bay further north, which was named Sydney Cove. But Kurnell's historical significance was not forgotten, and in 1899 more than 100 hectares (250 acres) of land were set aside as a public area.

Captain Cook's Landing Place is now a regular stop on the school excursion circuit; on weekdays it's crowded with children visiting the Cook Obelisk, Cook's Well and Landing Rock. To find out more about the history of the area and the young colony, visit the **Discovery**

Sightseeing

Greek enclave **Brighton-le-Sands**. *See p116.*

Centre (Captain Cook Drive, Botany Bay National Park, 9668 9111, open 11am-3pm Mon-Fri, 10am-4.30pm Sat, Sun, $6 per car).

On the west side of Botany Bay, just below the airport, is **Brighton-le-Sands**, a grandiose name for a busy strip of cafés and restaurants dominated by an oversized, pyramid-shaped branch of the **Novotel** hotel chain. Anyone familiar with the coastline near Athens will understand why this stretch has been snapped up by the Greeks. On Friday and Saturday evenings and all day Sunday, the main drag, the **Grand Parade**, is choked with bumper-to-bumper traffic and crowds visiting the numerous eating and drinking establishments in 'Little Athens'.

On the Grand Parade itself, **Café Neptune** (No.87; 9567 8590) rivals next door's **Eurobay** (No.86; 9597 3300) for an ultra-smooth, Greco-Italian blend of food and style. A few doors down, restaurant/café **Kamari** (No.82, 9556 2533) is more rustic, with its whitewashed walls and terracotta floors. The cafés and restaurants along Bay Street around the corner attract a slightly older, more glam Greek crowd, sunning themselves in their Gucci shades. There's **Orea Grecian Cuisine** (No.376, 9599 5775) and snitchy **Zande Brasserie** (No. 376, 9567 6475), which has a dress code and insists that management approval is required for groups of more than six. The most upmarket restaurant is **Le Sands** (Grand Parade, 9599 2128) with its panoramic views of Botany Bay (never mind the planes landing to the left, and the pipes and towers of the Caltex oil refinery to the right). Former world champion boxer Jeff Fenech has just taken on **Enigma** (88 Grand Parade, 9556 3611) which touts, of all things, Greek yum cha with all-you-can-eat servings of dips, halloumi, dolmádes and other traditional Greek dishes.

The Bay itself is usually a kaleidoscope of colour as windsurfers and kitesurfers take advantage of the continuously near-cyclonic weather. To have a go yourself, contact **Long Reef Sailboards & Surf** (*see p242*).

Cronulla

Transport *CityRail Cronulla.*

A strange thing happens every Sunday to **Cronulla Beach** – the Bondi (some say the Surfers' Paradise) of the south. The surfers seem to flee to its northern end (Elouera, Wanda and Green Hills Beaches) and are replaced by multicultural families in vast numbers, who set about picnicking. Cronulla is a much longer beach than its more famous city counterparts (Bondi, Coogee, Clovelly and Maroubra). It takes at least four hours to walk its length

The view from **Bass & Flinders Point**.

from South Cronulla to Green Hills and beyond to the north – where, at weekends, 4WDs churn up what remains of the sand hills.

In fact, revs are big in these parts – especially on the water. Jetskis, speedboats and waterskiers create chaos on Port Hacking every weekend. For more water action, contact **Cronulla Surf School** (9544 0895, www.cronullasurfschool.com) for surfing lessons, and **Pro Dive** (9544 2200, www.prodivecronulla.com) to discover what lies beneath.

A quieter pursuit can be enjoyed on land along a walking track that starts at the end of South Cronulla and wends its way south around the cliff of Port Hacking, past sea pools to **Darook Park**, where you can swim in calm, clear water (on weekdays, at least). Halfway along the track is **Bass & Flinders Point**; from here you can stare across the water to Jibbon Beach on the edge of the Royal National Park (to visit the beach and park, catch a ferry from Cronulla to Bundeena).

In Cronulla itself, the pedestrianised strip in Cronulla Street is jammed with surf shops. For great coffee and corn fritters, duck into **Surfeit** (2 Surf Road, 9523 3873) – you might even see swimming supremo Ian Thorpe having breakfast here. If you like your food with a view, try **Sandbar** (corner of Gerrale Street and the Kingsway, 9544 3023), where you can get great breakfasts with Aussiefied names, such as 'Diggerdict' – English muffin, poached eggs, hollandaise sauce and hash browns.

Nearby are more view-tastic restaurants, such as the mid-market **Stonefish** (8-18 The Kingsway, 9544 3046), which offers pasta, stir-fries and steaks, as well as seafood, and **Joe's Fish Bar** (2 The Kingsway, 9544 5522). for bargain-priced fish and burgers.

At night, the upstairs balcony of **Sale di Mare** cocktail bar and restaurant (at Gerrale Street and the Kingsway, 9544 3133) is crammed with people enjoying one of the best views over the beach, while the famous, recently renovated **Northies-Cronulla Hotel** (at Elouera Street and the Kingsway, 9523 6866, www.northies.com.au) spills over with energy during the summer. For a slower vibe, try **Brass Monkey** (115A Cronulla Street, 9544 3844), where you can hear live jazz and blues. For a quick fix, head for Cronulla's best fish shop, **South Beach Seafoods** (20 Gerrale Street, 9544 0800) – load up on oysters and prawns, then scoff them by the beach.

Bundeena & around

Transport *CityRail Cronulla then ferry Bundeena.*

From Cronulla's Tonkin Street wharf you can take a 20-minute ferry ride across Port Hacking to Bundeena, a small village (population 2,700) nestling at the top of the north-eastern section of the **Royal National Park** (*see below*). It's a charming spot, increasingly sought after by stressed urbanites wanting to get away from it all. Established in 1879, the Royal was Australia's first national park (and the second in the world, after Yellowstone in the US). Covering 15,000 hectares (37,000 acres) on the southern boundary of the Sydney metropolitan area, it offers some stunning coastline, rainforest, open wetlands, estuaries and heath. You can spend days bushwalking, picnicking, swimming and birdwatching here. Bundeena is a handy gateway to its delights, especially as most of the park is best explored by car.

Bundeena, which means 'noise like thunder' in the local Aboriginal language, was named after the sound of the surf pounding on the east coast. The Aboriginal Dharawal people used the area as a camping ground, and were sometimes joined by other large clans for feasting and ceremonies. In the 1820s white settlers arrived in the 'village', as locals call Bundeena, to build a few fishing shacks. More came during the 1930s Depression, but it was only after World War II that a substantial number of permanent residences and holiday homes began to appear.

There are three main beaches, including two that fall into the national park. The main strip of sand is **Hordens Beach**, which you'll see to your right as you approach by ferry. Walk up the hill from the wharf to find a small supermarket, a newsagent, a couple of inexpensive cafés and a fish and chip shop.

To reach **Jibbon Beach**, walk left from the ferry, past a toilet block and the RSL club (which serves very cheap drinks and has a fabulous Chinese restaurant open Tuesday to Saturday). Follow the road to its end, turn downhill and through a cutting to the magnificent, forest-edged, orange-sand beach. At the far end, hop up the rocks and take the track through the bush to **Jibbon Head** (about 20 minutes), where there are awe-inspiring views out to sea. A sign en route points to Aboriginal rock engravings of whales and fish. From Jibbon Head you can walk further down the coast on a well-worn track; it's about a three-hour return walk to Marley Beach, six hours to Wattamolla. Take plenty of water, sunscreen and insect repellent in summer.

The third beach, **Bonnyvale**, is to the right just before you leave the village (you can walk to it in about 15 minutes via Bundeena Drive). Edged by swamp and ponds, it's an exceptionally long and pristine beach, with very shallow water that's great for kids.

The ferry to Bundeena leaves Cronulla every hour on the half-hour from 5.30am to 6.30pm weekdays (there's no 12.30pm service), returning on the hour from 6am to 7pm. On weekends, the first ferry leaves at 8.30am and the last returns at 7pm. It costs $4.50 each way. It's around a 20-minute drive to Bundeena through the national park if you come by road (about an hour in total from the city).

Royal National Park

9542 0649/www.nationalparks.nsw.gov.au. **Open** *Park* 9am-sunset daily. *Visitor centre* 8.30am-4.30pm daily. **Admission** $10 per vehicle.

You can get to the Royal by following walking paths from various nearby CityRail stations – Engadine, Heathcote, Loftus, Otford, Waterfall – but driving is the easiest way to explore its vast expanse. The park's nerve centre is at Audley, on the Hacking River – once the heart of the park's Victorian 'pleasure gardens' – where you'll find the main visitor centre, spacious lawns, an old-fashioned dance hall and a causeway. Hire a canoe or rowing boat from the Audley boatshed and head upstream to picnic spots at Ironbark Flat or Wattle Forest. If you're a surfer, Garie Beach provides the waves, while further south is Werrong Beach, located among isolated rainforest and the park's only authorised nude bathing spot. At secluded Wattamolla Beach you can often see migrating whales. Walking trails include Lady Carrington Drive, an easy 10km (six-mile) track along the Hacking River, and the more arduous 26km (16-mile) Coast Track, which hugs the coastline from Bundeena to Otford.

Sydney's Best Beaches

Your guide to the top swimming, surfing and sunbathing spots.

Who's afraid of a little melanoma? Nobody on **Bondi Beach**, that's for sure. *See p120.*

Summer, winter, after school, after work, with a bunch of mates or just plain solo, beaches are where Sydneysiders head to chill out. And with more than 50 beaches along Sydney's coastline, from posey Palm Beach in the north to family magnet Cronulla in the south, each one has its own character. The protected harbour beaches inside the Heads are smaller and have no surf, but are great for views and picnics; after heavy rain they're not ideal for swimming though, as pollution floats in through the storm pipes. Instead, locals often take their daily dip in the outdoor seawater pools cut into the rocks on many beaches – both harbour and ocean. The bigger, bolder ocean beaches attract hordes of surfers and serious swimmers.

From September to May nearly all Sydney's ocean beaches are patrolled at weekends by local volunteer lifesavers and during the week by lifeguards; hours vary with the beach and time of year. The famous surf lifesavers wear red and yellow uniforms and an unmistakeable skull cap. The council-paid lifeguards (who are sometimes also hired on harbour beaches)

wear different colours – usually a more sober blue or green – and in surfing hot spots such as Bondi and Manly work 365 days a year.

Rules on Sydney's beaches are stringent: alcohol and fires are banned, and on many beaches ball games, skateboards, rollerblades, kites and frisbees are also illegal. That said, rules are regularly flouted by 'no worries' regulars, especially off-season. Locals love to fish on the beach, but you need a licence and there are catch limits. Dropping rubbish is also an offence – 'Don't be a tosser, take your rubbish with you!' is the motto – and recycling a must in the provided bins. And don't expect to find deckchair touts, donkeys or even an ice-cream seller, because Sydneysiders are fiercely protective of their unspoilt beaches – and intend to keep them that way.

WATER TEMPERATURES

The water at Sydney beaches can turn icy without warning, so take the following as a guide only. As a general rule, the water temperature lags a couple of months behind the air temperature. So, when the weather is warming up in October and November, the sea is still holding its winter chill of 16-17°C (61-63°F). Only in December does the sea become a nicely swimmable 18-19°C (64-66°F). The ocean is a balmy 20-21°C (68-70°F) from February to April, sometimes until May. It can even reach 23-24°C (73-75°F) if there's a warm current running from the north.

Below are the best Sydney beaches; the harbour beaches are listed from east to west; the northern ocean beaches heading north; and the southern ocean beaches heading south. The number given for each beach corresponds to those on the **Sydney Harbour map** on pp308-9. There's also a map of the **northern beaches** on p102. For info on the latest surfing conditions, visit www.coastalwatch.com.

Harbour beaches

South

Shark Beach 34
Nielsen Park, Vaucluse Road, Vaucluse. Bus 325.
Locals swim in the smooth warm waters of this sheltered harbour inlet all year round. In summer it's as packed as an Australian beach can get, with families swarming the narrow 300m (1,000ft) beach or picnicking in the shade of the Moreton Bay fig trees on the grassy slopes. Part of leafy Nielsen Park, the beach also boasts fabulous views of Manly, Shark Island (hence its name) and, from the upper parklands, the Harbour Bridge. If you don't swim, you can watch the ferries, yachts, kayakers, seaplanes and oil tankers vie for space in the harbour, or you could just grab a bite to eat. Sergio and Lucia Lieto run the renowned Nielsen Park Kiosk, an Italian restaurant that's been here since 1914 and that boasts spectacular sunset views. During the summer its adjoining café serves bruschetta and home-made gelati to the chic children of Vaucluse.
Services *Café (closed winter Mon-Fri). Changing rooms. Child-friendly. No dogs. Parking. Picnic area. Restaurant. Shade. Shark net (Sept-May). Showers. Toilets.*

Parsley Bay 29
Horler Avenue, Vaucluse. Bus 325.
Since the 1970s Parsley Bay's expansive picnic lawn has been a popular venue for weddings; indeed, it's the grass, not the tiny beach, which is the big draw here. Nestled at the foot of a steep road of million-dollar mansions, the bay is part of a 14-acre nature reserve with its own ranger and an abundance of birds, fish and insects. It's great for small children who can play safely on the lawns and in the well-equipped recreation area, and there are excellent walks through the bush and even across a suspension bridge over the water. The small crescent-shaped beach (approx 70m/230ft long) leads into

what are often murky waters: after heavy rain, rubbish floats into the bay from storm pipes. Nevertheless, the millpond-like swimming area is popular with snorkellers and scuba divers, thanks to its array of tropical fish.
Services *Café. Changing rooms. Child-friendly (play area). No dogs. Parking. Picnic area. Shade. Shark net (removed for repairs 1mth winter). Showers. Toilets.*

Camp Cove 4
Victoria Street, Watsons Bay. Ferry Watsons Bay/bus 324, 325, L24, L82.
Serious sun-seekers love this 200m (650ft) strip of bright yellow sand, which runs in a thin curve against a backdrop of designer cottages. It's also a gay haven, which probably has more to do with its secluded ambience than its name. The beach is not great for surfing, but it's a fine place for a dip and provides fabulous views of the city skyscrapers. At the southern end of the upper grasslands is the start of the South Head Heritage Trail. Camp Cove has just one small kiosk, but plenty of parking spaces.
Services *Café (Oct-May). Lifesavers (Oct-May). No dogs. Parking. Toilets.*

Lady Bay Beach 22
Corner of Victoria & Cliff Streets, Watsons Bay. Ferry Watsons Bay/bus 324, 325, L24, L82.
Sydney's first nudie beach, Lady Bay Beach is just below South Head and a short walk along the South

Family-friendly **Whale Beach**. See p124.

Sightseeing

Head Heritage Trail from Camp Cove. Steep iron steps lead down to the 100m (330ft) beach, which is reduced to virtually nothing when the tide comes in; you're better off sunbathing on one of the rocks. It's popular as a pick-up place for gay men, but Lady Bay offers scenic thrills as well as sexual ones: namely, spectacular views of the city and, if you walk around the headland to Hornby Lighthouse, the open sea to the east. In fact, it's the last southern beach inside the harbour.

Services *No dogs. Toilets (on cliff top above beach).*

North

Balmoral Beach ❶
The Esplanade, Balmoral. Ferry South Mosman then bus 233/ferry Taronga Zoo then bus 238.
Home to Sydney's seriously rich, Balmoral has been a popular bathing spot since the late 1900s. Its beach promenade and Bathers' Pavilion (now one of Sydney's most sought-after eateries; see *p161*) were both built in the late 1920s and retain a genteel air from that era. Hundreds of families flock here at weekends to enjoy the sheltered waters of its two large sandy beaches, which together stretch for about 1.5km (one mile). The beaches are separated by Rocky Point, a tree-covered picnicking island accessible by a footbridge. To the south Balmoral Beach has an enclosed swimming area surrounded by boardwalks, excellent for kids. To the north, Edwards Beach is bigger and less protected, but has rock pools with shells, fish and anemones. You can hire boats from Balmoral Boathouse.

Services *Boat hire. Cafés. Changing rooms. Child-friendly (play area). Danger: underwater rocks. No dogs. Parking. Picnic areas. Restaurants. Shade. Shark nets. Shops. Showers. Toilets.*

Chinamans Beach ❻
McLean Crescent, Mosman. Bus 175, 178, 249.
A real Sydney secret, Chinamans Beach in Middle Harbour is stumbled upon through dunes on the edge of the Rosherville bushland reserve. It's a quiet paradise, with 300m (1,000ft) of beautiful sand, gently lapping waters and huge architect-designed homes perched in the hills above. Located right opposite busier Clontarf Beach, Chinamans has plenty of recreational facilities – a play area, picnic tables nestled under pepper trees, and rolling lawns where you can play ball games – but no shop, café or restaurant. Children love the mass of barnacle-encrusted rock pools at the southern end, but there's a $500 fine for taking any crustaceans home.

Services *Changing rooms. Child-friendly (play area). No dogs. Parking. Picnic area. Shade. Showers. Toilets.*

Clontarf Beach ❽
Sandy Bay Road, Clontarf. Bus 171, E71.
With around 600m (2,000ft) of great sand, a large grassy picnic area, an excellent playground, outdoor pool and all the facilities, Clontarf is a very popular family spot. It's situated right opposite the Middle

Harbour Yacht Club, so there are good views of the Spit Bridge with boats sailing underneath and cars racing over the top. And it's worth stopping at Balgowlah Heights en route to pick up a picnic – the fantastic Gourmet Deli on Beatrice Street is open from 7am to 7pm daily.

Services *Barbecues. Café. Changing rooms. Child-friendly (play area). No dogs. Parking. Picnic area. Pool. Restaurant (closed July). Shade. Shark net (Sept-May). Showers. Toilets.*

Ocean beaches

South

Bondi Beach ❷
Queen Elizabeth Drive, Bondi Beach. CityRail Bondi Junction then 380, 381, 382, L82 bus/bus 380, L82.
Australia's most famous beach, Bondi is believed to have been named after an Aboriginal word meaning 'the sound of breaking waves'. Certainly, its crashing breakers attract a huge fraternity of surfies as well as ubiquitous Britpackers and new-generation hippies strumming guitars on the sand. When the volleyball stadium for the 2000 Olympics was temporarily constructed on the beach, locals went bananas – but the pay-off has been a much-needed clean-up job. Today the elegant Bondi Pavilion, built in 1929 as a changing area, houses showers, toilets, a community centre and some cafés. Two lifesaving clubs patrol the 1km (0.65-mile) beach – 'Ready Aye Ready' is the motto of the North Bondi Surf Life Saving Club. The central area near the Pavilion is the safest swimming area; surfers favour the southern end, with its strong rips. Also at this end is a skateboard ramp and the famous Bondi Iceberg's pool and club (*see p78* **Some like it cold**). Be vigilant – 'Thieves go to the beach too' warn big NSW police signs. Lockers are available in the Pavilion – use them. *See p83* for a map.

Services *Barbecues. Cafés. Changing rooms. Lifeguards/savers. No dogs. Parking. Picnic area. Play area. Pool. Restaurants. Shark net (Sept-May). Shops. Showers. Toilets.*

Tamarama Beach ❹⓿
Pacific Avenue, Tamarama. CityRail Bondi Junction then bus 360, 361.
A 100m (330ft) sheltered cove, Tamarama is neither easy to get to by public transport nor to park at should you decide to drive there. Once you arrive, it's not particularly accessible either: you have to climb down 40 steep steps to reach the water. And with its tricky surf and deep rip, it's not a swimming spot. That said, it's got a serious fan base of macho surfers who like to surf dangerously, and dedicated sun-seekers (there's absolutely no shade to be found on the sand). The latter consist mostly of air stewards, who have dubbed the beach Glamarama. Britpackers play Sunday soccer matches on the large grassy picnic area. The small kids' play area with swings and slide is within eyeshot of the very

Macho surfers prefer **Tamarama Beach**. *See p120.*

excellent Tama café, which serves wonderful gourmet vegetarian and non-vegetarian sandwiches as well as refreshing power juices.

Services *Barbecue. Café (closed May-Sept Mon-Fri). Changing rooms. Danger: underwater rocks. Lifeguards/savers (Sept-May). No dogs. Parking. Picnic area. Play area. Shark net (Sept-May). Showers. Toilets.*

Bronte Beach ❸

Bronte Road, Bronte. CityRail Bondi Junction then bus 378.

Bronte is absolute bliss for local parents – pack the kids, the swimsuits and the boogie boards and this 300m (1,000ft) stretch of sand will babysit all day long. Though the water has a strong rip and is great for surfing, the outdoor Bronte Baths at the southern end – and the adjacent community centre – are the preserve of kids. There's plenty of shade under the sweeping sandstone rocks and scores of covered picnic benches (some with inlaid chessboards) to enjoy the traditional Aussie tucker served at the Bronte Kiosk – meat pies and hot chips aplenty.

Services *Barbecues. Cafés. Changing rooms. Child-friendly (play area). Danger: underwater rocks. Lifeguards/savers (Sept-May). No dogs. Parking. Picnic area. Pool. Restaurants. Shade. Shark net (Sept-May). Shops. Showers. Toilets.*

Clovelly Beach ❾

Clovelly Road, Clovelly. CityRail Bondi Junction then bus 360/bus 339, X39.

Once known as Little Coogee, tucked around the corner from the more famous Big Coogee (now simply Coogee), Clovelly is an idyllic spot, swathed in natural beauty. The tiny square of sand slopes into a long inlet of calm water, surrounded by a board-walk and a concrete promenade. It's a favourite with scuba divers and snorkellers, but it's the wheelchair access that weaves the real magic. Winner of the National Access Australia Awards in 1988, the Clovelly Bay boardwalk boasts specific entry points to the water with locking devices for a submersible wheelchair, on loan from the Beach Inspector's office (weekdays) or the SLSC (weekends). On the south promenade sits a chic 25m three-lane lap pool, built in 1962 and nicely revamped in 2002.

Services *Barbecues. Café. Changing rooms. Child-friendly. Lifeguards/savers (Sept-May). No dogs. Parking. Picnic area. Pool. Restaurant. Shade. Showers. Toilets. Wheelchair access.*

Coogee Beach ⓬

Beach Street, Coogee. CityRail Bondi Junction then bus 313, 314/bus 372, 373, 374, X73, X74.

This excellent family swimming beach is 400m (1,300ft) long, with old-fashioned pools carved into the rocks at both ends. It's not great for surfing, but at least you don't have to worry about getting munched: in 1929 it was declared Australia's first shark-proof beach when nets were introduced. There are plenty of fast-food restaurants, cafés and places to picnic, and it's very much a tourist attraction. In April 2003 the northern headland was renamed Dolphin Point, in memory of the six Coogee Dolphin rugby league players who were killed in the Bali bombings. Two memorial plaques, plastered with photographs, list the 26 victims from the local community (from a total Australian death toll of 88).

Services *Barbecues. Cafés. Changing rooms. Child-friendly. Lifeguards/savers. No dogs. Parking. Picnic area. Pools. Restaurants. Shade. Shark net (Sept-May). Shops. Showers. Toilets.*

Beach safety

rescued; don't fight the current by swimming toward shore.

SHARK THINKING

Despite what you might read in the papers, shark attacks are very rare. The last fatal attack in Sydney harbour was in 1963, while in the past 20 years only one person in NSW has died from a shark

TO THE RESCUE

Each year Sydney's famed surf lifesavers carry out countless rescue operations. A disproportionate number are of foreigners who have underestimated the 'rips' (currents) in the surf. Most of Sydney's ocean beaches are surf beaches, meaning that waves can be up to three or four metres (ten to 13 feet) high and conceal powerful rips. More often, the waves are less than one metre high; at Bondi and Manly, the waves are somewhere in the middle of the scale.

To be safe, always swim between the red and yellow flags that the lifesavers plant in the sand each day. If you stray outside the flags, they'll blow whistles and scream through megaphones at you. Another good rule is to stay within your depth. But don't be fooled into thinking shallow water is completely safe. 'Dumpers' are waves that break with force, usually at low tide in shallow water, and can cause serious injury. Anyone who has been dumped will never forget the powerful force that kept them pinned to the sand with the water swirling over them. Waves that don't break at all (surging waves) can knock swimmers over too and drag them out to sea. Finally, remember that 'alcohol and water don't mix' – most adults who drown in NSW are under the influence.

If you do get caught by a rip and you're a confident swimmer, the best advice is to try to swim diagonally across the rip. If you're not, stay calm, stick your hand in the air to signal to a lifeguard and float until you're

attack. It's true there have been more shark sightings in recent years, but this is because better sewage methods have made Sydney's beaches much cleaner, and the sharks love their new clean playground. That said, the closest most people get to a shark is at the city's aquaria.

A large number of Sydney's beaches are shark-netted – although this is not quite the impenetrable barrier that you might hope for. The nets, installed by NSW Fisheries, are 150 metres (490 feet) long and seven metres (23 feet) deep and are anchored to the ocean floor within 500m (1,640 feet) of the shore. You won't spot them because they are always dropped in ten metres (32 feet) of deep water ensuring a three- metre (ten-foot) clearance for swimmers and surfers. The nets are not so much a physical barrier to sharks, but prevent them establishing a habitat close to the shore. They are moved from time to time to ensure the sharks don't catch on.

Since beach swimming became popular, sharks have tended to shy away from the shore – believe it or not, most species are more scared of you than you are of them. Tiger sharks, hammerheads and bronze whalers are the most commonly seen sharks and, although potentially nasty, they are not naturally aggressive. White pointers – the mean machines – are rare.

If by some quirk of fate you do see a shark while swimming, try not to panic and swim calmly to shore. Admittedly, this is easier said than done, but keep in mind that sharks are attracted to jerky movements. But experts at Taronga Zoo advise: 'Any action you take may disrupt the attack pattern, such as hitting the shark, making sudden body movements, blowing bubbles, gouging at its eyes etc.'

Scared? Honestly, it hardly ever happens.

STINGERS

Two kinds of jellyfish are common on Sydney's beaches in summer. The jimble (a less potent southern relative of the deadly box jellyfish) is box-shaped with four pink tentacles. It is commonly found within the harbour beaches. On the ocean beaches you're more likely to come across bluebottle jellyfish (aka Portuguese Man-of-War), which has long blue tentacles and tends to appear only when an onshore wind is blowing.

Jimbles can deliver a painful sting but are not dangerous; bluebottles are nastier, causing an intense, longer-lasting pain, red, whip-like lesions and, occasionally, respiratory problems. Be aware that even dead bluebottles stranded on the beach can sting, so don't touch them.

Treatment for each is different. If stung by a jimble, wash the affected area with vinegar (lifeguards and lifesavers keep stocks of vinegar), gently remove any remaining tentacles (with tweezers or gloves) and apply ice to relieve the pain. If stung by a bluebottle, leave the water immediately, don't rub the skin and don't apply vinegar; instead use an icepack or anaesthetic spray.

DANGEROUS CURRENT

Maroubra Beach

Marine Parade, Maroubra. Bus 376, 377, 395, 396, X77, X96.

Maroubra was chosen as the new headquarters for Surfing NSW in July 2003, and this did not come as much of a surprise, since the waves are huge here and it's long been a top surf spot. All of the outfit's coaching, judging, educational and safety programmes are now conducted at the 1.1km (0.68-mile) beach, which also picked up the Keep Australia Beautiful 'cleanest beach' award in 2002. Much less touristy than neighbouring Coogee, it's also a favourite with joggers. There are a few local shops, recently refurbished showers and toilets, a well-equipped children's play area, plus a sizeable skateboard park (which is packed when school's out) situated next to the beach's windswept dunes.

Services *Barbecues. Cafés. Changing rooms. Child-friendly (play area). Lifeguards/savers. No dogs. Parking. Picnic area. Pool. Restaurants. Shark net (Sept-May). Shops. Showers. Toilets.*

Cronulla Beach

Mitchell Road, Cronulla. CityRail Cronulla.

A vast sandy beach more than 6km (3.75 miles) long, Cronulla is the south's most popular surfing and swimming spot. It has the feel of a big Queensland resort with its high-rise apartments and hotels, bars, steakhouses and car-loads of young rev-heads. The southern end, a half-moon patch of sand around 100m (330ft) long, is patrolled by a lifeguard all year round; with less of a rip, this is family territory to bathe, fossick in the rock pools or swim indoors at the Cronulla Sports Complex (located next to the life-saver's hut). The much longer northern end has a fiercer tow and views of a not-so-pretty oil refinery. There's a huge grassy picnic area with plenty of tables and an esplanade walkway. To get to Cronulla from the city, it takes about 50 minutes by train or an hour by car.

Services *Cafés. Changing rooms. Child-friendly (play area). Lifeguards/savers (south all year round; north Sept-May). No dogs. Parking. Picnic area. Pools. Restaurants. Shade. Shark net (Sept-May). Shops. Showers. Toilets.*

North

Shelly Beach 36

Marine Parade, Manly. Ferry Manly.

A ten-minute stroll south of Manly, Shelly Beach is a family delight with its 100m (330ft) of yellow sand, gentle waters and grassy picnic area. As you stroll south along the promenade from Manly, don't miss the Fairy Bower ocean pool, an excellent outdoor rock pool with spectacular views of the coastline. Set in Cabbage Tree Bay, Shelly Beach is best known for good swimming conditions, but is also popular with novice scuba divers testing the deep.

Services *Barbecue. Café. Changing Rooms. Child-friendly. No dogs. Parking. Picnic area. Restaurant (closed winter Sun-Mon). Shade. Showers. Toilets.*

Manly Beach ㉖

Manly. Ferry Manly.
Jumping aboard a Sydney ferry is a must and a trip to Manly is the perfect excuse. Take one of the trusty old yellow-and-green giants from Circular Quay to Manly Wharf in Manly Cove, where there's a small harbour beach (about 250m/820ft long) and a netted swimming area. To reach the open sea, head across busy pedestrianised street the Corso to the 1.5km crescent of sand known as Manly Surf Beach, but actually comprising Queenscliff in the north, followed by North Steyne, South Steyne and Manly beaches. A mecca for mums, surfies and international tourists, Manly has all the facilities of a big resort. And plenty of history: in 1903 it was one of the first beaches to permit daylight swimming, but the crowds didn't understand the danger of the surf – there are rips along the entire length of the beach – and fishermen Eddie and Joe Sly set up Manly's first lifesaving patrol. For a map, *see p104.*
Services *Cafés. Changing rooms. Child-friendly. Lifeguards/savers. No dogs. Parking. Picnic area. Pool (at Queenscliff). Restaurants. Shade. Shark net (Sept-May.) Shops. Showers. Toilets.*

Collaroy Beach

Pittwater Road, Collaroy. Bus 183, 184, 187, 188, 190, E83, E84, E86, E87, E88, E89, L88, L90.
North of Manly lies a stretch of magnificent surfing beaches with wonderfully ludicrous names: Curl Curl, Dee Why, Long Reef, Narrabeen. At Collaroy, which lies directly south of Narrabeen, there's a 1km (0.65-mile) stretch of honey-coloured sand pounded by huge waves. It's also got an excellent, large ocean pool, plus a toddler pool to the south. The Bruce Bartlett Memorial Playground to the rear is shaded and has masses of fun equipment. The Hog's Breath Café is right on the beach and so the whole area tends to get thumping at night.
Services *Barbecues (in play area). Cafés. Changing rooms. Child-friendly (play area). Danger: underwater rocks. Lifeguards/savers (Sept-May). Parking. Picnic area. Pools. Restaurants. Shark net (Sept-May). Shops. Showers. Toilets.*

Newport Beach

Barrenjoey Road, Newport. Bus 187, 188, 190, E87, L88, L90.
This 1km (0.65-mile) windswept beach offers good surf with easy access to a busy main road of shops, cafés and restaurants. Its accessibility makes it very popular with locals keen to catch a quick wave. There's a well-equipped, fenced-off play area in the grassland to the rear, but at dusk the beach can get rowdy and is no place for youngsters.
Services *Barbecues. Cafés. Changing rooms. Children's play area. Danger: underwater rocks. Lifeguards/savers (Sept-May). No dogs. Parking. Picnic area. Pool (south end). Restaurants. Shark net (Sept-May). Shops. Showers. Toilets.*

Avalon Beach

Barrenjoey Road, Avalon. Bus 190, 188, E88, E89, L88, L90.

Once considered as the new filming location for *Baywatch*, this sandy beach (about 1km/0.65 miles long) gets pretty busy in the summer, especially with surfies, who arrive by the carload to tackle the generous waves. There's also good swimming and an excellent ocean pool at the southern end, and the whole beach is backed by sand dunes. Newport is also a popular after-school hangout for local youths, who are attracted by its big skateboard park, which is located behind the car park.
Services *Barbecues. Changing rooms. Children's play area. Lifeguards/savers (Sept-May.) Parking. Picnic area. Pool. Shark net (Sept-May). Showers. Toilets.*

Whale Beach

The Strand, Whale Beach. Bus 190, E88, L90.
You'd better hurry to Whale Beach – the authorities have announced a five-year 'improvement programme' to its facilities, which means this 700m (2,300ft) stretch of salmon pink sand may no longer be such a peaceful bolt-hole. Approached via mind-bendingly steep roads, the beach offers big surf and a rugged coastline. There's a 25m ocean pool at the southern end – take care as the tide comes in: the waves crash over the pool and surrounding rocks.
Services *Barbecue. Café (closed July). Changing rooms. Child-friendly (play area). Danger: underwater rocks. Lifeguards/savers (Sept-May). Parking. Picnic area. Pool. Restaurants. Shade. Shark net (Sept-May). Showers. Toilets.*

Palm Beach

Barrenjoey Road, Palm Beach. Bus 190, L90.
Situated at the northernmost tip of the northern beaches peninsula, Palm Beach is a local paradise. Don't be fooled by Palm Beach Wharf, a busier beach on the west side which you come to first. Keep on driving up the hill and around the bend to get to the real deal on the east side: you won't be disappointed. Palm Beach is home to Sydney's rich and famous; colonial-style mansions set in palm-filled lawns possess breathtaking views of foaming ocean and nearly 2km (1.2 miles) of caramel-coloured sand. The southern end, known as Cabbage Tree Boat Harbour, is the safest spot to swim and surf. If you find the sea too daunting, there's the excellent Jack 'Johnny' Carter outdoor pool, named after the man who spent 50 years teaching local kids to swim. The Beachcomber café on North Palm Beach serves good tucker. And keep an eye out for young Aussie actors on a tea break – this is where the hit soap *Home and Away* is filmed.
Services *Barbecues (in play area). Café. Changing rooms. Child-friendly (play area in adjacent Governor Phillip Park). Lifeguards/savers (Sept-May). Parking. Picnic area. Pool. Restaurant. Shade. Shark net (Sept-May). Shops. Showers. Toilets.*

> ▶ To find out more information on many of the beaches listed here, see the relevant **Sightseeing** chapters.

Eat, Drink, Shop

Cafés, Bars & Pubs

From flat whites to schooners, this is a city that likes its drinks.

Danks Street Depot. *See p131.*

Cafés

This is a city obsessed by coffee. Sydneysiders can tell their arabica from their robusta, their macchiati from their ristretti, and have been known to follow their favourite barista from café to café. While the Italian terms have widespread currency, there are a few homegrown synonyms thrown in for good measure. The espresso is commonly referred to as a 'short black'; a 'flat white' is a milk coffee served not like a latte in a glass but in a coffee cup; and a 'long black' roughly translates into an Italian lungo – similar to a double espresso. The Italian influence isn't total, however: coffee drinkers in Sydney tend to sit and linger over their hit, even with the shorter drinks, whereas

their Florentine counterparts would toss their espresso back barely breaking stride.

Prices are the same whether you stand, sit inside or sit outside. Table service is the norm, and, unlike in other Australian states, most cafés aren't licensed to sell or serve alcohol. The Italian influence typically extends to the food, with sandwiches constructed in the Italian style and served on Italian bread (though baguettes and Turkish bread have become very popular), and light meals usually focus on pasta dishes. Asian dishes aren't uncommon, of course, and even in the less central suburbs you can find yourself nibbling turnip cake and a cup of pu-erh tea in a Taiwanese snack joint, picking over chai and chaat in an Indian sweet shop or savouring the taste of condensed milk in a thick Vietnamese coffee.

American mega-chain Starbucks is slowly wooing office workers in the CBD, but, thankfully, independent cafés still abound in café hubs such as Darlinghurst's Victoria Street, along Oxford Street, King Street in Newtown, and Glebe Point Road in Glebe.

Central Sydney

The CBD & the Rocks

GG Espresso

175 Pitt Street, between Martin Place & King Street, CBD (9221 1644). CityRail Wynyard or Martin Place. **Open** 7am-5pm Mon-Fri. **Unlicensed.** **Credit** AmEx, BC, DC, MC, V. **Map** p310 C2.
That's GG as in George Gregan. Not content with making his mark in the world of rugby union, the Wallabies' captain has set about making his initials synonymous with good coffee in the inner city. The food on offer is pretty basic, but the espresso has plenty of oomph.

MCA Café

Museum of Contemporary Art, Circular Quay (9241 4253). CityRail/ferry Circular Quay. **Open** 10am-4.30pm daily. **Licensed**. **Credit** AmEx, BC, DC, MC, V. **Map** p310 C1.
Once powered by the might of the Rockpool restaurant empire, the MCA caff is now under the stewardship of a less ambitious catering company, and the food shows far less panache. The Circular Quay location is divine, however, and the umbrella'd timber deck on the gallery's forecourt is a great place to meet friends for drinks.

The Tea Room

Level 3, QVB, 455 George Street, between Market & Druitt Streets, CBD (9269 0774). CityRail Town Hall/Monorail Galeries Victoria. **Open** 11am-5pm Mon-Fri, Sun; 11am-3pm Sat. **Licensed**. **Credit** AmEx, BC, DC, V. **Map** p311 B3.

High tea junkies take note: the QVB's Tea Room (at the Market Street end of the building) is the best place in town to come for a finger-sandwich fix. Soaring ceilings and luxurious fittings make it a popular spot for wedding receptions, while the rest of us can enjoy smart updates of bangers and Yorkshire pud, macaroni and cheese and, of course, a peerless selection of fine leaf teas.

Pyrmont

Concrete

224 Harris Street, at Pyrmont Bridge Road, Pyrmont (9518 9523). LightRail Fish Market or Wentworth Park. **Open** 7am-4pm Mon-Sat; 8am-4pm Sun. **Licensed/BYO**. **Credit** AmEx, BC, DC, MC, V. **Map** p311 A3.

Though the decor is as modern and industrial as the name suggests, there's nothing cold about Concrete. Dotcom types swing by for their fresh juices while pram-pushers seek out the superior scrambled eggs with goat's cheese. Laze away an afternoon with good coffee, smiling service and lots of magazines.

Darlinghurst

Bar Coluzzi

322 Victoria Street, between Liverpool & William Streets, Darlinghurst (9380 5420). CityRail Kings Cross. **Open** 5am-7pm daily. **Unlicensed**. **No credit cards**. **Map** p312 D3.

One of Sydney's caffeinated landmarks, Coluzzi has provided cups of high-quality, Italian-style espresso for decades. Thronged by locals and regulars, its wooden streetside seating sees almost as much primping and posing as it does good coffee.

bills

433 Liverpool Street, at West Street, Darlinghurst (9360 9631). CityRail Kings Cross/bus 389. **Open** 7.30am-3pm Mon-Sat. **BYO**. **Credit** AmEx, BC, MC, V. **Map** p312 D3.

Now at the heart of an ever-expanding empire of cookbooks and TV appearances, this café is still the finest of Bill Granger's achievements. Its communal table plays host to his famous creamy scrambled eggs, sunrise drink and toasted homemade coconut bread at breakfast, while lunch sees the simplicity of steak sandwich with garlic cream and chicken club sandwich with roasted tomatoes. Expect to wait, expect to be seduced. If you want similar food with (slightly) shorter queues, try sister restaurant bills 2 in Surry Hills; unlike the mothership, it's open for dinner (Monday to Saturday) as well as Sunday lunch, and it's licensed.

Other locations: bills 2 359 Crown Street, Surry Hills (9360 4762).

Ecabar

128 Darlinghurst Road, at Liverpool Street, Darlinghurst (9332 1433). CityRail Kings Cross. **Open** 7am-5pm Mon-Sat; 9am-4pm Sun. **BYO**. **No credit cards**. **Map** p312 D3.

It's all about the coffee. Not that the scrambled eggs with pesto or the sliced boiled egg with tomato and avocado on rye aren't great. And not to make light of the brilliant fresh pear, apple and lime juice. It's just that the coffee at this popular sunny sliver of a venue is really, really outstanding.

Latteria

320B Victoria Street, between Liverpool & William Streets, Darlinghurst (9331 2914). CityRail Kings Cross. **Open** 5.30am-7.30pm daily. **Unlicensed**. **No credit cards**. **Map** p312 D3.

Want a caffè just like mamma used to make? Check Latteria out. The coffee and panini are pure Italian, sure, but it's the incredible efficiency with which the space – or lack thereof – is used that really makes you think you're just off the Via Tornabuoni.

The best Drinks

Best for breakfast

Head to **bills** (*see left*) for ricotta hotcakes with honeycomb butter, coconut bread, legendary scrambled eggs... get in early and get into it.

Best for coffee

Good coffee isn't hard to find in Sydney, but for the very best go to **Toby's Estate** (*see p129*) in Woolloomooloo, **Ecabar** (*see above*) in Darlinghurst or **Allpress Espresso** (*see p132*) in Rosebery.

Best for cocktails

What mix master Marco Faraone at **Lotus** (*see p137*) doesn't know about cocktails probably isn't worth drinking. And **Longrain** (*see p135*) does the feistiest Bloody Mary – sorry, Bloody Longrain – in town.

Best beer gardens

Lounge in the sun, beer in hand, at the **Courthouse Hotel** (*see p138*) in Newtown or the **Coogee Bay Hotel** (*see p137*) overlooking Coogee Beach. Ah, bliss.

Best for drinks with a view

Gaze from any window at the **Bennelong Bar** (*see p132*) inside the Sydney Opera House – and swoon. Alternatively, clock a bird's-eye view from the **Orbit Bar** (*see p134*), a whopping 47 floors above the CBD.

Eat, Drink, Shop

Le Petit Crème

118 Darlinghurst Road, between Farrell Avenue &
Liverpool Street, Darlinghurst (9361 4738). CityRail
Kings Cross. **Open** 7am-3pm Mon-Sat; 8am-3pm
Sun. **BYO. No credit cards. Map** p312 D3.
'The small cream' from which this café takes its
name is better known by the Italian term, crema. But
everything here, from the crêpes to the coffee to the
'80s film posters, is pure Paris. Pull up a bentwood
chair and dive into an enormous Gallic breakfast
and BYO Gauloises.

Tropicana

227B Victoria Street, between William & Surrey
Streets, Darlinghurst (9360 9809). CityRail Kings
Cross. **Open** 5am-11pm daily. **BYO. No credit**
cards. Map p312 D3.
Forget agents and casting calls: this is where the
real business of Sydney's film and theatre industry
takes place. Against a background of reasonable
coffee, adequate café food and capable service, deals
are done and names are made. Immortalised in the
name of Tropfest (*see p204*), the country's leading
short film showcase, the Trop has an energy – and
a clientele – like no other.

Una's

340 Victoria Street, at Surrey Street, Darlinghurst
(9360 6885). CityRail Kings Cross. **Open** 7.30am-
10.30pm daily. **Licensed/BYO** (wine only).
No credit cards. Map p312 D3.
It's Heidi meets *Queer as Folk* every day at this
wood-panelled Victoria Street stayer. Lederhosen-
wearing waiters flit between tables of boys fuelling
up on the menu's big, meaty mainstays of schnitzel,
German sausages, stews and sauerkraut. Una's is
cheap, no one leaves hungry, and the little-known
upstairs bar is worth its weight in weird.

Surry Hills

Il Baretto

496 Bourke Street, at Arthur Street, Surry Hills
(9361 6163). CityRail/LightRail Central. **Open**
8am-3pm, 6-10pm Tue-Sat; 9am-3pm Sun. **BYO.**
No credit cards. Map p311 C4.
The popularity of the loud 'Little Bar' is such that
you'll often have to wait. The authentico carbonara,
gorgeous gnocchi with gorgonzola, and specials
such as duck ragu with house-made pappardelle or
brown butter and nettle ravioli, will have you licking your plate. Best for dinner.

La Passion du Fruit

Corner of Bourke & Devonshire Streets, Surry Hills
(9690 1894). CityRail/LightRail Central/bus 302.
Open 8am-midnight Mon-Sat; 10am-3pm Sun.
BYO. No credit cards. Map p311 C5.
After 30 years in fickle, novelty-obsessed Surry
Hills, you can be pretty sure that the Fruit fellas are
doing something right. The food is as fresh, simple
and primary-colourful as the paint job – and the
service isn't far behind.

Kings Cross, Potts Point & Woolloomooloo

Just down Cowper Wharf Road from the
revamped Woolloomoollo Wharf and the
W Hotel is shiny snack van **Harry's Café de**
Wheels. A much-loved Sydney institution,
it's been supplying late-night meat pies with
gravy, mash and mushy peas to locals, visitors,
overseas sailors, cab drivers and drunks for
more than 50 years.

Café Hernandez

60 Kings Cross Road, between Ward Avenue
& Roslyn Street, Kings Cross (9331 2343).
CityRail Kings Cross. **Open** 24hrs daily.
Unlicensed. No credit cards.
Map p312 D3.
A favourite among strong-coffee drinkers, this
Spanish-inflected, 24-hour establishment just off the
Kings Cross strip is also one of the few places in the
city where you'll find non-alcoholic entertainment
after the witching hour.

Spring Espresso

Corner of Challis Avenue & Macleay Street,
Potts Point (9331 0190). CityRail Kings Cross.
Open 6.30am-6.30pm daily. **Unlicensed.**
No credit cards. Map p312 D2.
A landmark on Potts Point's see-and-be-seen scene,
Spring, though tiny, bounces with as much energy
as the name suggests, and the menu, though brief,
can be relied upon for simple pleasures. The fit-out,
it must be noted, nearly out-glams the clientele. The
entrance is on Challis Avenue.

Quirky **Badde Manors**. *See p131.*

Toby's Estate

Corner of Cathedral & Palmer Streets, Woolloomooloo (9358 1196/www.tobysestate.com.au). CityRail Kings Cross. **Open** 7am-5.30pm Mon-Fri; 7.30am-4pm Sat. **Unlicensed. Credit** AmEx, BC, DC, MC, V. **Map** p311 C3.

Though Toby's beans are widely available, coffee obsessives come to this Cathedral Street roastery-cum-espresso bar to worship at the scant few tables that surround the roasting machinery. Textbook espresso is guaranteed.

Zinc

Corner of Macleay & Rockwall Streets, Potts Point (9358 6777). CityRail Kings Cross. **Open** 7am-5pm Mon-Sat; 8am-4pm Sun. **BYO. Credit** BC, MC, V. **Map** p312 D2/3.

Perhaps Zinc's popularity with the Beautiful People is connected to the prominent role that mirrors play in its design. Or maybe it's just that the city's beauties have a taste for just-squeezed blood orange juice, good coffee and lovely, fresh Italianate salads.

Eastern Suburbs

Brown Sugar

100 Brighton Boulevard, at Campbell Parade, North Bondi (9365 6262). CityRail Bondi Junction then bus 380, 381, L82/bus 380, L82. **Open** 7.30am-4pm Mon-Fri; 8am-4pm Sat; 9am-4pm Sun. **BYO. No credit cards.**

Yes, it makes grown men cry. Women too, when they have trouble finding a table on a sunny Saturday morning. Persevere for celeb-spotting, not to mention superior breakfasting on the likes of scrambled tofu.

Caffe Brioso

Corner of Oxford & Underwood Streets, Paddington (9358 5259). Bus 378, 380, L82. **Open** 7.30am-4.30pm daily. **BYO. No credit cards.** **Map** p313 D4.

Ah, Oxford Street. Just as there are lots of restaurants, but few that you'd really go out of your way for, Paddington's 'Golden Mile' also suffers from the 'cafés, cafés everywhere, but not a coffee to drink' syndrome. This well-hidden gem bucks the trend, with good beans, smart baristas and fair prices.

Flat White

Corner of Jersey Road & Holdsworth Street, Woollahra (9398 9922). Bus 380, 389. **Open** 7.30am-5pm daily. **Unlicensed. Credit** BC, DC, MC, V. **Map** p313 E4.

Gruyère and ham brioche toastie? Oh, yes. The space isn't huge (and, between you and me, neither are the portions), but everything at this relative newcomer – including the clientele – is skewed towards the perfectly formed.

Gertrude & Alice

40 Hall Street, at Consett Avenue, Bondi Beach (9130 5155). CityRail Bondi Junction then bus 380, 381, L82/bus 380, L82. **Open** 9.30am-10.30pm Mon-Fri; 8.30am-10.30pm Sat, Sun. **BYO. Credit** AmEx, BC, DC, MC, V. **Map** p83.

Borders and other big book chains be damned: Gertrude & Alice pairs a great range of second-hand books with the kind of hospitality you'd expect from its namesake authors (Stein and Toklas were famous for their Paris table – on a good day, that is). Breakfasts here are simple and pleasant, while the coffee is good all the time.

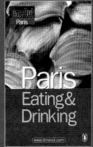

Inner West

Badde Manors

Corner of Glebe Point Road & Francis Street,
Glebe (9660 3797). Bus 370, 431, 432, 433, 434.
Open 8am-midnight Mon-Thur; 8am-1pm Fri-Sun.
BYO. No credit cards. Map p311 A4.
Maybe the waiters can't help themselves. Maybe it's
the name. Or maybe those tattoos and piercings
have unusual side-effects. Whatever the reason, their
manners can, at times, be a little 'eccentric'. But, just
like the staunchly veggie food, the funny wooden
booths and the gelato-vending window, they're just
part of this veteran café's charm. So deal with it.

Bar Italia

169 Norton Street, at Macauley Street, Leichhardt
(9560 9981). Bus 436, 437, 438, 440, 445, 470,
L38. **Open** 9am-11.30pm Mon-Thur, Sun; 9am-
12.30am Fri, Sat. **BYO. No credit cards.**
Many Sydneysiders got their first taste of gelato
within these very walls, and many more still make
the pilgrimage as soon as the weather gets even a
little warm. The savoury stuff is nothing special –
Bar Italia is all about the coffee, the vibe and the
double-scoop of pistachio and tiramisu trickling
down your fingers.

Bitton

37A Copeland Street, between Newton Street &
Mitchell Road, Alexandria. Open 7am-3pm Tue-Fri; 8am-3am Sat,
Sun. **Unlicensed. Credit** AmEx, BC, DC, MC, V.
A liberal splash of Gallic charm colours everything
in this friendly café, from the repartee of the waiters and kitchen staff to the divine crêpes with
orange jelly. Bitton also does a roaring trade in
jams, sauces, oils and pretty much anything else
that can be bottled or put in a jar.

Canteen

332 Darling Street, between Montague & Beattie
Streets, Balmain (9818 1521). Ferry Balmain/
bus 433, 434, 442, 445. **Open** 7am-late Mon-Sat;
8am-late Sun. **BYO. No credit cards.**
Soccer-mums, footie dads and dilettante creatives of
every stripe crowd this veteran of the Darling Street
café crush. The look is minimal, but, thankfully,
there's nothing spare about the food or the serves.

Danks Street Depot

2 Danks Street, at Young Street, Waterloo
(9698 2201). Bus 301, 302, 303, 305, 355.
Open 7.30am-5pm Mon-Fri; 8am-5pm Sat. Closed
Christmas-mid Jan Tue-Sat. **Licensed/BYO.**
Credit BC, MC, V.
'Melburnian' is a term oft-used in talk of this curi-
ously warm industrial space. One can extrapolate,
then, that Sydneysiders associate Melbourne with
good value, professional service and unpretentious
food cooked with a great deal of skill and plenty of
thought for flavour. The corned-beef Reuben can't
be beat. While here, be sure to visit some of the nine
galleries on the premises (*see p211*).

Vargabar

Corner of Wilson Street & Erskineville Road,
Newtown (9517 1932). CityRail Newtown. **Open**
7am-7pm Mon-Sat; 8am-7pm Sun. **Unlicensed.**
No credit cards. Map p93.
Forget café-laden King Street – the coolest coffee in
this part of the world is just off the beaten track.
Friendly staff serve thoughtful, interesting eats in
the mould of the American diner-style meatball
sandwich with grilled cheese, and hangover-helpers
such as the iced liquorice tea or Berocca frappé.

North Shore

Awaba

Corner of the Esplanade & Awaba Street, Balmoral
Beach (9969 2104). Bus 233, 238, 257. **Open**
7.30-11.15am, noon-3pm daily. **Licensed/BYO.**
Credit AmEx, BC, MC, V.
Sunglasses-on may be a very Sydney look, but in
this sunny space, it's almost a necessity. No need to
shield your eyes from the menu, however (though it
is quite bright): what's on offer is pretty upmarket
fare. The simple stuff tends to works best, and the
fish and chips is one of the finest going.

Northern Beaches

Avalon Beach Café

23 Avalon Parade, Avalon (9918 6999). Bus 190.
Open 7am-5pm daily. **Licensed/BYO. Credit**
AmEx, MC, V.
Corncakes with pancetta and rocket? Yes, please.
Lunch and dinner certainly aren't bad, but it's at
breakfast that the ABC really shines. Then again,
the house-made ice-cream is wonderful, particularly
the brown-bread version. A liberal attitude towards
the idea of ice-cream for breakfast makes for a neat
solution to this dilemma.

Ground Zero

18 Sydney Road, at Central Avenue, Manly
(9977 6996). Ferry Manly. **Open** 8am-6pm daily.
Licensed. Credit AmEx, BC, DC, MC, V.
Map p104.
Sun, surf and… short blacks? For some reason
Sydneysiders have recently come to think that a fun
day at the seaside isn't right unless it's capped off
with a cappuccino, or some other decent sort of coffee.
This loungey establishment, just a hop and a skip
from the sand of Manly Beach, is one of the best
places to get your java fix this side of the bridge.

Parramatta & the West

Mado Café

63 Auburn Road, between Mary & Beatrice Streets,
Auburn (9643 5299). CityRail Auburn. **Open**
8am-midnight daily. **Unlicensed. Credit** AmEx,
BC, DC, MC, V.
Unique in Sydney – and, as far as we know, the
whole country – the Mado Café adds another

dimension to the city's growing obsession with Middle Eastern flavours. The many flavours of house-made ice-cream are the order of the day, though the meals are good and cheap and the pastries and Turkish coffee very much the real deal.

The South

Allpress Espresso

58 Epsom Road, between Dunning & Mentmore Avenues, Rosebery (9662 8288). Bus 309, 310, 343, 345. **Open** 7am-3pm Mon-Fri; 8am-2pm Sat. **Unlicensed. Credit** BC, MC, V.
Allpress's interior provides a microcosmic reflection of the evolution of this neighbourhood, with industrial machinery (coffee-roasting and packing equipment) juxtaposed with the forces of gentrification in the form of its customers and the swish look of the café itself. The coffee is outstanding, while the breads and pastries, from sister company Brasserie Bread, are a must.

Bars & Pubs

Yes, Sydneysiders like a drink. Is it really so surprising in a city whose first currency was rum? Things have come along way in the last 200 years, of course, and thanks to plenty of labour exchanged between the bars of Sydney, Paris, New York and most especially London, and a general obsession with things we can put in our mouths, the standard of cocktails – not to mention wine – is generally very high.

Though Sydney's licensing laws have loosened marginally in recent years, they're still pretty draconian. It's difficult and expensive for individuals to obtain liquor licences, so most bars are started by consortia unwilling to risk their investment on dangerous things like character and individuality. Anyone who wants to have a drink in a restaurant or licensed café must, in most instances, establish their 'intention to dine'.

Meanwhile, pubs – confusingly known as 'hotels' for their additional accommodation past – continue to do a roaring trade. And whether they're of the million dollar-refit ilk or fragrantly unreconstructed, the primary trade will be in beer. Cold draught beer is bought in middies (a 285ml glass, close to a half-pint) and, more commonly, 425ml schooners. Boutique beers such as Coopers, James Boag's, Cascade and James Squire are increasingly popular, and imported brands are widely available, but the bulk of beer drunk tends to be the big domestic names. These were once divided fiercely down state lines, with Resch's and Toohey's beers being the big deal in Sydney and New South Wales, but

lately VB (Victoria Bitter) has become almost ubiquitous. Fosters, it should be mentioned, rarely gets a look-in. Except by tourists.

Central Sydney

The CBD & The Rocks

The Australian Hotel

100 Cumberland Street, at Gloucester Street, The Rocks (9247 2229). CityRail/ferry Circular Quay. **Open** 11am-midnight daily. **Credit** AmEx, BC, DC, MC, V. **Map** p310 B1.
Locals and tourists alike flock to this old-school pub just by the Harbour Bridge. There's no view to speak of, but the neighbourhood is very much olde Sydney town, while the range of local and imported beers on tap is seriously impressive.

Bennelong Bar

Sydney Opera House, Bennelong Point, Circular Quay (9241 1999). CityRail/ferry Circular Quay. **Open** 5.30pm-late daily. **Credit** AmEx, BC, DC, MC, V. **Map** p310 C1.
In a city where very expensively designed bars are becoming almost commonplace, the Bennelong Bar still stands out. Even if it weren't distinguished by its location, inside one of the sails of the Opera House overlooking the harbour, the high standards set by the bar staff, and the excellent oysters and crab sandwiches prepared in the kitchen of the adjoining flash restaurant (*see p142*), mark Bennelong as one of Sydney's great drinking experiences.

Ember

Overseas Passenger Terminal, Circular Quay West, The Rocks (8273 1204). CityRail/ferry Circular Quay. **Open** noon-1am Mon-Fri, Sun; 5pm-late Sat. **Credit** AmEx, BC, DC, MC, V. **Map** p310 C1.
It's all about the Manhattans. Quite fitting, really, for a bar that adjoins Wildfire, a big, brash, American-owned restaurant. Munch some popcorn shrimp while you peruse the selection of infused bourbons and the lengthy cocktail list. The Puska, a house drink made with Medos honey vodka and plenty of crushed ice, is a must for hot nights by the Quay.

Hemmesphere

Establishment Hotel, 252 George Street, between Bridge Street & Abercrombie Lane, CBD (9240 3000). CityRail Wynyard or Circular Quay/ferry Circular Quay. **Open** 6pm-late Tue-Sat. **Credit** AmEx, BC, DC, MC, V. **Map** p310 B2.
On the ground floor of the enormous Establishment building, lots of guys – and girls – in near-identical suits shout orders for pricey beers and stare blankly at the talent. Meanwhile, upstairs sees a considerably rosier picture: couples lounge around a high-ceilinged loft-style bar, sipping luxe cocktails and discussing the relative merits of the various absinthe drinks on offer. The downside is that it's wise to book in advance. First-floor restaurant est. (*see p142*) serves fabulous Mod Oz fare.

Eat, Drink, Shop

Nice ice, baby

Paris in the summertime sees many ice-cream shops closing. Because of the heat. Happily, no such weirdness is tolerated in Sydney, and the city's purveyors of cold confections, busy at the best of times (Australians are the third-largest consumers of ice-cream after New Zealand and the US), go into overdrive. Reliable chains **Gelato Messina** (9818 3141) and **Gelatissimo** (9211 4411) have stores dotted throughout the city and suburbs, and the following independent outfits are highly recommended.

Bar Italia

The site of many a Sydneysider's first encounter with the good stuff, Italia's gelato is still among the finest in the city. The zabaglione will rock your world. *See p131.*

Gelateria Caffe 2000

650 Darling Street, at Merton Street, Rozelle (9555 6032). Bus 433, 434, 442, 445. **Open** 7.30am-5pm Mon-Wed; 7.30am-9pm Fri, Sat. **Unlicensed. No credit cards.**
This family-run Rozelle store has a huge following for its flagship flavour, which gets its kick from home-made boysenberry jam.

De Luca

Bondi Pavilion, Bondi Beach (9300 8555). CityRail Bondi Junction then bus 380, 381, L82/bus 380, L82. **Open** 10am-7pm daily. **No credit cards.** **Map** p83.
One of very few ice-cream proprietors who make their own gelato from scratch, Luigi de Luca makes some of the best ice-cream outside Rome.
Other locations: La Cremeria Sorbetteria 106 Norton Street, Leichhardt (9564 1127).

Passion Flower

Harbourside, Darling Drive, Darling Harbour (9281 8022). CityRail Town Hall/ferry Darling Harbour/Monorail Harbourside or Convention/LightRail Convention. **Open** 9am-1am Mon-Fri; 8am-1pm Sat, Sun. **Credit** AmEx, BC, DC, MC, V. **Map** p311 B3.
Asian flavours are the draw here. Lychee or sticky rice and black sesame please all tastes, while the intrepid can sample wasabi, durian or chilli-chocolate.
Other locations: Capitol Theatre Centre, corner of Campbell & George Streets, Haymarket (9281 8322); 730-742 George Street, CBD (9281 8322).

Pompei's

Corner of Roscoe & Gould Streets, Bondi Beach (9365 1233). CityRail Bondi Junction then bus 380, 381, L82/bus 380, L82. **Open** 11am-late Tue-Sun. **Credit** AmEx, BC, MC, V. **Map** p83.
Giorgio Pompei sources the freshest and best ingredients for the gelati at his Bondi Beach store. The brilliant fruit flavours, like the exceptional white nectarine, speak of his commitment to quality.

Eat, Drink, Shop

Horizons Bar

36th Floor, Shangri-La Hotel, 176 Cumberland Street, between Essex & Argyle Streets, The Rocks (9250 6013). CityRail/ferry Circular Quay. **Open** noon-1am Mon-Thur; noon-2am Fri, Sat; noon-midnight Sun. **Credit** AmEx, BC, DC, MC, V. **Map** p310 B1/2.
So '80s they should make it a theme bar, the drinks at Horizons are expensive, the waiters are dressed in get-ups so hotel-silly they can barely keep straight

faces and the view goes on forever. It's definitely worth coughing up for a couple of Martinis to watch at least one sundown, and the drinks are made with a certain amount of finesse.

Lord Nelson Brewery Hotel

Corner of Argyle & Kent Streets, Millers Point (9251 4044/www.lordnelson.com.au). CityRail/ferry Circular Quay. **Open** 11am-11pm Mon-Sat; 11am-10pm Sun. **Credit** AmEx, BC, DC, MC, V. **Map** p310 B1.

Wine Banc: fine wines in a fine setting.

Real ale bores, rejoice – the Lord Nello is one of the best places to explore the joys of Sydney's varying microbrews. The rest of us will be over at the bar, admiring the pub's colonial stonework and hopping into the seriously hearty bar plate, pickled onions, cheese, pickles, door-stopper wedge of bread and all.

Opera Bar

Lower Concourse Level, Sydney Opera House, Bennelong Point, Circular Quay (9247 1666/ www.operabar.com.au). CityRail/ferry Circular Quay. **Open** 11.30am-late daily. **Credit** AmEx, BC, DC, MC, V. **Map** p310 C1.
One of those multi-purpose venues that actually gets it right. The Opera Bar offers 'better than it needs to be' lunch for quayside rubberneckers; a lovely environment for an afternoon beer; quick, reasonably priced dinners for the pre-theatre crowd; and then live music (*see p227*) and cocktails most nights for people looking to shake a little booty in the shadow of the Opera House.

Orbit Bar

Level 47, Australia Square, 264 George Street, between Hunter Street & Martin Place, CBD (9247 9777). CityRail Wynyard or Martin Place. **Open** 5pm-late daily. **Credit** AmEx, BC, DC, MC, V. **Map** p310 B2.
Do not adjust your set, and don't worry, your drink hasn't been spiked: it's the bar itself that's spinning. And, 47 floors up, you get a fat eyeful of the city in plush retro-modern surrounds. The drinks are decent and the cheese twists suitably twisty.

Posh

Overseas Passenger Terminal, Circular Quay West, The Rocks (9251 1188). CityRail/ferry Circular Quay. **Open** 5pm-late Mon-Fri; 6pm-late Sat. **Credit** AmEx, BC, DC, MC, V. **Map** p310 C1.
The prices certainly are up there, but so's the view. And the low leather sofas give you ringside seats for the play of traffic on the harbour. Be warned, however, that port-out-starboard-home privileges won't help you when a cruise liner is berthed by the windows, obscuring the vista. Better then to turn inwards, ignore the uninspiring bar menu and focus on the ritzy cocktail selection.

Wine Banc

53 Martin Place, entrance on Elizabeth Street, CBD (9233 5399). CityRail Martin Place. **Open** 4pm-late Mon-Fri; 6pm-late Sat. **Credit** AmEx, BC, DC, MC, V. **Map** p310 C2.
A jug of wine, some live jazz (*see p229*) and thou. OK, so the wine comes either in Riedel crystal by the glass or in pricey (if eye-catching) boutique bottles, but the rest is bang on. In addition to one of the city's most intriguing wine lists and a more-than-serviceable menu, this swank basement also does a fine line in cocktails and eaux de vie.

Darling Harbour

The Loft

King Street Wharf, Darling Harbour (9299 4770). CityRail Town Hall/ferry Darling Harbour/ Monorail Darling Park. **Open** 5pm-late Mon-Thur; noon-late Fri-Sun. **Credit** AmEx, BC, DC, MC, V. **Map** p310 B2.
You've gotta love the Baghdad iced tea – cucumber voddy, Bombay Sapphire gin, apple, mint, lime and jasmine tea – and there's much to love about the Loft in general. Local bar legends Mike Enright and Garth Foster are as dedicated to their craft as they are creative. Carved Moorish-styled ceilings, lots of squishy leather loungers and verandas opening out on to water views all conspire to keep you smiling.

East Sydney & Darlinghurst

For great people-watching, check out the large, second-floor balcony of **Kinselas Middlebar** (*see p215*), overlooking Taylor Square in the heart of gay Sydney. Also in Darlinghurst, the **Q Bar** (*see p235*) wears its age well. The drinks aren't that special, but the music can be great, the look is appealingly louche and the very-late-night crowd has much to commend it.

Burdekin Hotel

Corner of Oxford & Liverpool Streets, Darlinghurst (9331 3066). Bus 378, 380, 382. **Open** noon-midnight Mon-Wed; noon-2am Thur; noon-4am Fri; 5pm-6am Sat; 5pm-midnight Sun. **Credit** AmEx, BC, DC, MC, V. **Map** p311 C3.

One of the best Sydney bars of the early 1990s, the Burdekin may have aged, but it still has great bone structure. A range of upstairs rooms offers a world of dance options on the weekend, while the ground-floor bar feels like an upmarket pub. The tiny deco Dugout Bar in the basement, with its speakeasy cred, is a definite favourite.

Chicane

1A Burton Street, at Riley Street, Darlinghurst (9380 2121). CityRail Museum/bus 389. **Open** 5.30pm-midnight Tue-Sun. **Credit** AmEx, BC, DC, MC, V. **Map** p311 C3.

Any bar that can knock out a killer Negroni every time, replete with burnt-orange garnish, deserves praise. An aggressively chic fit-out with showpiece toilets, lots of smooth concrete, high-backed easy chairs and a Rothko-esque colour scheme also add weight to what is already a great place to sidle up to for cocktails.

Darlo Bar

Corner of Liverpool Street & Darlingurst Road, Darlinghurst (9331 3672). Bus 378, 380, L82. **Open** 10am-midnight Mon-Sat; noon-10pm Sun. **Credit** AmEx, BC, DC, MC, V. **Map** p312 D3.

More properly known as the Royal Sovereign Hotel, the Darlo Bar has been a local institution for the past decade: in gay-friendly Darlinghurst it's distinguished by its reputation for being the number-one straight pick-up joint. There's plenty of boy-boy, girl-girl action to be had over its pool tables, mismatched op-shop furniture and adequate drinks, but the ease with which happy young heteros hook up here is almost freakish.

East Sydney Hotel

Corner of Cathedral & Crown Streets, East Sydney (9358 1975). CityRail Kings Cross/bus 200. **Open** 10am-1am Mon-Fri; noon-midnight Sun. **Credit** BC, MC, V. **Map** p311 C3.

With signs proudly bearing the news that it's a poker machine-free establishment, the East Sydney Hotel marks itself out as a breed apart. And if the friendly bar staff, roaring darts tournaments and generally genial air of this old-fashioned pub are any guide, this is a breed that should most certainly be encouraged. The outdoor tables make for excellent, beer-enhanced people-watching.

Fix

Kirketon Hotel, 229 Darlinghurst Road, between Farrell & Tewkesbury Avenues, Darlinghurst (9332 2566). CityRail Kings Cross. **Open** 6pm-1am Tue-Sun. **Credit** AmEx, BC, MC, V. **Map** p312 D3.

Frequently described as bento-box this and cigar-box that, there's no escaping the fact that Fix, the exclusive back bar of the Kirketon Hotel (*see p35*), is small and windowless. But what a box! The intensely red palette recalls a French brothel, while the cocktail list and bar menu remind you that Fix is attached to one of the city's coolest hotels, not to mention one its most innovative restaurants, Luke Mangan's Salt (*see p149*).

Surry Hills

Hollywood Hotel

Corner of Foster & Campbell Streets, Surry Hills (9281 2765). CityRail Museum/bus 301, 302. **Open** 11am-midnight Mon-Wed; 11am-3am Thur-Sat. **No credit cards**. **Map** p11 C4.

Hooray for the Hollywood. One of the most personable pubs in town, it draws a busy mix of young and old, straight and gay, musical and less so, all under the commanding gaze of the great Doris Goddard. A former cabaret performer, Hollywood starlet and chanteuse, the formidable Ms Goddard puts all the charm and wit of her 70-plus years into maintaining an establishment that gives performance its due without losing the sense that it should ever be anything less than lots of fun.

Longrain

85 Commonwealth Street, at Hunt Street, Surry Hills (9280 2888). CityRail Central/bus 301, 302. **Open** noon-midnight Mon-Fri; 5.30pm-midnight Sat. **Credit** AmEx, DC, MC, V. **Map** p311 C4.

Now this is a bar. And a restaurant, for that matter, but the bar is so much part of the leading edge of

Get in the mood at **moogbar**. See p136.

Sydney nightlife that it commands equal footing with the famed Thai diner (*see p148*). Taste the greatness first in the Bloody Longrain – a winning mix of vodka, red chilli, nahm jim, cucumber and coriander – and then settle back on a low stool to contemplate the beauty of the converted warehouse and the freshness and zest that informs every aspect of the business.

Mars Lounge

16 Wentworth Avenue, between Oxford & Goulburn Streets, Surry Hills (9267 6440). CityRail Museum. **Open** 5pm-midnight Wed; 5pm-3am Thur-Fri; 7pm-3am Sat; 7pm-1am Sun. **Credit** AmEx, BC, DC, MC, V. **Map** p311 C3.
Sunday night is the new Saturday. Or at least it is in this neighbourhood. Fed up with Oxford Street and its surrounds being overrun by the suburban hordes on Fridays and Saturdays, many locals now save much of their partying for Sundays. Foremost among the Sunday-nighters, the dark and spacious Mars Lounge is famed for its mixed crowd and extensive selection of ultra-premium vodkas.

moogbar

413 Bourke Street, between Campbell Street & Church Lane, Surry Hills (9331 3602). Bus 378, 380, L82. **Open** 5.30pm-1am Wed-Sat; 5.30pm-midnight Sun. **Credit** AmEx, BC, MC, V. **Map** p311 C4.
Flair may be a dying art, but bar manager Steve Rodwell has the paddles out and is yelling 'Clear!' Part of what is alleged to be the world's first one-

suite hotel (yep, just one), this tiny bar is decorated in the kind of no-expense-spared style that makes you wish they're spared some of the expense. The tiger's eye-inlaid bar is cute, however, and though the drinks aren't cheap, they're made with consummate care – even if Steve does drop the occasional bottle mid-juggle.

Kings Cross, Potts Point & Woolloomooloo

The **Soho Bar** (*see p236*) combines a glam lounge bar with a throbbing club, and also offers lots of pre-dinner cocktail deals midweek.

Barons

5 Roslyn Street, between Darlinghurst Road & Ward Avenue, Kings Cross (9358 6131). CityRail Kings Cross. **Open** 6pm-late Mon-Thur, Sun; 6pm-6am Fri, Sat. **Credit** AmEx, BC, DC, MC, V. **Map** p312 D3.
Of course you intend to dine. Technically the bar for the Thai restaurant downstairs, the quirks of the liquor licensing laws mean that unless you're a diner, you're really not supposed to enjoy Barons' bizarre contrast of Teutonic hunting lodge-style (note the backgammon booths and open fires) and slice-of-late-nightlife patrons. So, of course you intend to dine, right?

Hugo's Lounge

Level 1, 33 Bayswater Road, between Ward Avenue & Kellett Street, Kings Cross (9357 4411). CityRail

Courthouse Hotel: the quintessential Sydney pub. *See p138.*

Kings Cross. **Open** 6pm-late Tue-Thur; 5pm-3am Fri, Sat; 7pm-3am Sun. **Credit** AmEx, BC, DC, MC, V. **Map** p312 D3.

Inner-city brother of chi-chi Bondi Beach restaurant Hugo's (*see p155*), the Lounge also does dinner, but most people come here for the drinks. The drinks and the babes, that is. Male and female, they tend towards the blonde, corn-fed, monied (or money-hungry) end of the spectrum and prowl the Lounge's broken-glass bar, dim banquettes and canopied veranda. Mere mortals come for the peerless fresh mango Daiquiris.

jimmy liks

188 Victoria Street, between Darlinghurst Road & Orwell Street, Potts Point (8354 1400). CityRail Kings Cross. **Open** 5-11pm daily. **Credit** AmEx, BC, DC, MC, V. **Map** p312 D3.

You've gotta love a list that features a drink called the Kyoto Protocol, especially when it also offers some of the finer Asian-accented cocktails in town. Chilli, saké, nahm jim, ginger and more find their way into jimmy liks' concoctions. Service is famously uneven, so arrive early, pull up a pew on the street or slide on to a stool at the long, elegant bar, and bat those lashes extra hard. *See also p151.*

Lotus

22 Challis Avenue, at Mcleay Street, Potts Point (9326 9000). CityRail Kings Cross. **Open** 6pm-late Tue-Sat. **Credit** AmEx, BC, DC, MC, V. **Map** p312 D2.

Small and, to some, perfectly formed, the decor of this small bar (adjoining popular Mod Oz restaurant Lotus) isn't the main drawcard. Sure, the banquettes are plush, the wallpaper attractively textured and retro, the lighting designed more attractively still – but the real reason you're here is standing behind the bar. Marco Faraone has won pretty much every major prize for bartenders since he was imported from Wine via London a few years back. Try one of his Old Fashioneds and find out why.

Old Fitzroy Hotel

129 Dowling Street, at Cathedral Street, Woolloomooloo (9356 3848). CityRail Kings Cross/bus 200. **Open** 11am-midnight Mon-Fri; noon-midnight Sat; 3-10pm Sun. **No credit cards**. **Map** p312 D3.

Theatre, laksa, beer. Not uncommon to encounter them all during a night on the town, but finding them all under the one roof – and a particularly comely roof, at that – is more of a talking point. Best of all? Even without the cheap and reasonable Asian noodle soups and the talents of the Tamarama Rock Surfers, one of the city's more daring theatre troupes, the pub has a rollicking charm rare for this neck of the woods. *See also p252.*

Tilbury Hotel

Corner of Nicholson & Forbes Streets, Woolloomooloo (9368 1955). Bus 311. **Open** 8.30am-11.30pm Mon-Sat; 8.30am-9.30pm Sun. **Credit** AmEx, BC, MC, V. **Map** p312 D3.

Now this is a pub renovation. The not particularly old innards of the Tilbury were scraped out in 2003 and replaced with a lovely open space that majors on polished timber, chrome trim and oodles of natural light. It ain't cheap, but then the city's most chi-chi beer garden didn't pay for itself. The mod-Italian restaurant is also well worth a look; *see p151.*

Water Bar

W Hotel, Woolloomooloo Wharf, Cowper Bay Road, opposite Forbes Street, Woolloomooloo (9331 9000). Bus 311. **Open** 4-10pm Mon, Sun; 4pm-midnight Tue-Sat. **Credit** AmEx, BC, DC, MC, V. **Map** p312 D2.

The bar at the W hotel (*see p34*) may be the size of a middling aircraft hangar, but the design and placement of its booths and ottomans is so clever that you get the sense of space without it feeling stark, cold or empty – in fact, quite the opposite. A 15-plus bottle selection of vodkas is just one virtue of the excellent bar, and this is the ideal place for smokers and non-smokers to mingle without fear of irritating one another.

Eastern Suburbs

Big, boisterous and full of life, the **Beach Road Hotel** (*see p234*) in Bondi Beach retains an indefinable splash of character in the face of tourists, blow-ins and various renovations.

Coogee Bay Hotel

Corner of Arden Street & Coogee Bay Road, Coogee (9665 0000/www.coogeebayhotel.com.au). Bus 372, 373, 374. **Open** *Beach Bar* 9.30am-late Mon-Sat; 9am-midnight Sun. *Sports Bar* 9am-3am Mon-Wed; 9am-5am Thur, Fri, Sat; 9am-10pm Sun. *Arden Bar & Arden Lounge (summer only)* noon-1am daily. *Hibiscus Lounge* 9pm-late Fri, Sat. **No credit cards**.

Seating 500, the Coogee Bay's beer garden is enormous, and with a cool ocean breeze waving the palms and Coogee Beach spread before you, it's a contender for the best of its ilk in town. Other bars within the pub itself – which is also enormous – offer sport, Top-40 DJs, cook-your-own steaks and live music, none of which come close to supplanting the allure of the outdoor areas. It's also got stylish and affordable rooms; *see p42.*

Doyles Palace Hotel

Corner of Military Road & Cliff Street, Watsons Bay (9337 5444). Bus 324, 325, L24, L82. **Open** 10am-10pm Mon-Fri, Sun; 10am-11pm Sat. **Credit** BC, DC, MC, V.

The fish and chips are so-so. The drinks aren't thrilling or cheap. But the Watto (as it's known) is still going to make most Sydneysiders' list of the city's top pubs. An eastern suburbs institution, there really is something to be said for watching the sun sink over the harbour from the comfort of the hotel's capacious veranda, surrounded by other beer-swilling day-trippers.

Icebergs Bar

*1 Notts Avenue, Bondi Beach (9365 9000).
CityRail Bondi Junction then bus 380, 381, L82/
bus 380, L82.* **Open** 10am-midnight Mon-Thur;
8am-midnight Fri, Sat; 8am-10pm Sun. **Credit**
AmEx, BC, DC, MC, V. **Map** p83.

There is no better time to enjoy the bar adjoining the
swank Icebergs Dining Room (*see p152*) than at
dusk. The rays of the dying sun swing across the
length of Bondi Beach, turning the Northern Heads
golden, while loved-up, cash-flashing punters kick
back on the bar's multi-level lounges and narrow
balconies, sipping from the Italianate cocktail list or
poppin' Cristal and crunching prosciutto-wrapped
grissini. One of the world's great bars. *See also p78*
Some like it cold.

Royal Hotel

*237 Glenmore Road, at Broughton Street,
Paddington (9331 2604). Bus 378, 380, L82.*
Open 10am-midnight Mon-Sat; 10am-10pm Sun.
Credit AmEx, BC, DC, MC, V. **Map** p313 D4.

Paddington is ground-zero for strapping lads and
lasses who love their rugby, and lots of them love
the Royal too. Three levels of well-heeled conviviality are divided between the ground-floor bar, the
quite reasonable Mod Oz restaurant on the first floor,
and the second floor's Elephant Bar, which is stuffed
with pachyderm knick-knacks and young upwardly
mobiles enjoying Cosmpolitans and Caipiroskas.

Inner West

Courthouse Hotel

*Corner of Australia & Lennox Streets, Newtown
(9519 8273). CityRail Newtown.* **Open** 10am-
midnight Mon-Sat; 10am-10pm Sun. **No credit
cards. Map** p93.

From the meal orders coming over the PA ('Number
14, number 14 – your T-bone is ready') to the beer
garden at the back, this is the epitome of all that's
good and right about drinking beer in Sydney. And
what a beer garden. Whiling away a summer's arvo
over a few shandies amid the nippers, mums and
Newtown scruffs under the frangipani trees has got
to be one of the great simple pleasures of living in
this town. A landmark. And a great place to spend
Anzac Day, by the by.

Leichhardt Hotel

*95 Norton Street, between Parramatta Road &
Marion Street, Leichhardt (9569 6640). Bus
435, 436, 437, 438.* **Open** noon-midnight Mon-
Wed, Sun; noon-3am Thur-Sat. **Credit** AmEx, BC,
DC, MC, V.

A two-storey-high reproduction of Caravaggio's
Bacchus makes the business of this ostentatiously
renovated open space all too clear. In the midst of
Norton Street's red-sauce merchants, the Leichhardt
is a shiny beacon of things done with an eye away
from the Old Country – Caravaggio notwithstand-
ing. Downstairs you'll find cheap Asian food,
upstairs darkness and layered shooters.

The Nag's Head Hotel

*Corner of St Johns Road & Lodge Street, Glebe
(9660 1591/www.nagshead.com.au). Bus 431,
432, 433, 434, 370.* **Open** 9.30am-midnight Mon-
Sat; noon-midnight Sun. **Credit** BC, MC, V.
Map p311 A4.

One of the closest approximations to a proper British
pub to be found in Sydney, the Nag's has what too
many wannabe boozers can't seem to manage:
charm. It's got all the ye olde glass, woody bits and
Mother Country draught beers that any real ale fan
could want, and its situation – away from the main
drag of Glebe Point Road – keeps the mix of young
students, old whippersnappers and locals fresh.

Town Hall Hotel

*326 King Street, between Newman & Wilson Streets,
Newtown (9557 1206). CityRail Newtown.* **Open**
9am-3am Mon; 9am-3.30am Tue-Thur; 9am-5am Fri,
Sat; 10am-midnight Sun. **No credit cards. Map** p93.

Along with the Zanzibar (née Oxford) and Bank
Hotel (*see p213*), the Town Hall forms what locals
affectionately refer to as the Devil's Triangle of pubs
near the juncture of King Street and Enmore Road.
All three are popular with students, the pierced, tattooed, dyed and branded, as well as the just plain
reckless, but there's a kind of mojo at work at the
Townie that sees its two floors of undistinguished
wooden furniture and framed train-wreck photos
play host to the sort of two-fisted drinking mayhem
that make it a thing of beauty unto itself.

North Shore

The Oaks

*Corner of Military & Ben Boyd Roads, Neutral Bay
(9953 5515). Bus 247, 263.* **Open** 10am-midnight
Mon-Wed; 10am-1.30am Thur-Sat; noon-midnight
Sun. **Credit** AmEx, BC, DC, MC, V.

Sydney's biggest pub? Quite possibly. A north
shore institution, the Oaks is beloved of locals
young and old, who are here, we suspect, because
this place has it all. The cook-your-own barbie may
or may not be regarded as a plus, but the huge
spreading namesake tree in the beer garden is lovely,
and the fireplaces, bistro, pizzas, innumerable bars
and various other hooks are put to good use.

Northern Beaches

Manly Wharf Hotel

*Manly Wharf, East Esplanade, Manly (9977 1266/
www.manlywharfhotel.com.au). Ferry Manly.* **Open**
11am-midnight Mon-Sat; 11am-10pm Sun. **Credit**
AmEx, BC, DC, MC, V. **Map** p104.

From the bamboo-screened cocktail bar to the public bar opening out on to the large timber deck and
the open-air jetty bar, the new Manly Wharf Hotel
is all about light, water and a fresh, contemporary
look. There's a good range of well-priced Margarita-
variants, summery stick drinks and classics. The
Mod Oz restaurant (*see p163*) is worth a gander too.

Restaurants

Sydney's dining scene just gets better and better.

The French might be proverbially fond of talking about what they're having for dinner while they're having lunch, but Sydney loves to talk about last night's dinner over breakfast. The city is obsessed by food and drink, particularly when it can be had at a slick new boîte or bar. Yes, Sydneysiders are in thrall to Manhattan Hot Restaurant Syndrome – a big opening or glowing review will see the glammed-up hordes descend on an unwitting establishment, jamming its phone lines, filling its reservation book and packing it to the rafters night after night. Then, often with breathtaking speed, the party shifts to a new locale, leaving the original owners dazed with a mixture of horror and relief.

That's the worst of it, anyway. The good news is that Sydneysiders are learning. Longevity is the new industry buzzword, and though Sydney dining is still a bit top-heavy (locals are irresistibly drawn to the new and shiny), it's the restaurants content to play the long game – serving quality food at reasonable prices to customers likely to return in the same year – that are attracting the most love.

The other words you'll hear pouring from the mouths of chefs and diners are 'seasonality' and 'regionality'. Like bills of fare in London or New York, Sydney menus are now swollen with discursions on the provenance of key ingredients – expect to see Coffin Bay scallops, Thirlmere poultry, Junee lamb, Yamba prawns and Bangalow sweet pork, just to name a handful of favourites. The detail can, at times, be a little much (not every diner wants to know the precise manner in which the snapper was rendered brain-dead prior to its date with the skillet), but the trend reflects the growing recognition that it's quality local produce that gives Sydney food much of its bounce and zing.

In terms of flavours, the tastes of the Middle East that enliven the top end of Melbourne dining have made some ground in Sydney, and local chefs are flirting with the popularity of Spanish cuisines, but Asia still rules the roost. Chinese cooking techniques are popular – steaming, red-braising, white-cooking, not to mention the careful manipulation of texture through twice- and even thrice-cooking – while ingredients common to Thai, Vietnamese, Malaysian and Japanese kitchens are always close to hand. Italian food is hugely popular, and despite raging debate about the authenticity of the local version, the standard of 'Oz-talian' is quite high – at least in terms of coffee-making. Modern Australian food borrows freely from Asian, European and Middle Eastern traditions, but, thankfully, the practice of incorporating all three on the one plate died out with the close of the 1990s, and the days of the blackbean beurre blanc are well behind us.

One flavour you won't get much of in Sydney restaurants is smoke. It's good news for some, a nightmare for others, but smoking is banned everywhere indoors that food is served. The fines are steep and the laws strictly enforced, so anyone keen to spark up after a meal had best find an outside table or partake of the Sydney smokers' ritual of huddling outside the door. Bars, too, are following this lead, so ensure an ashtray is handy before you reach for the cigs.

On the plus side, the BYO tradition is alive and kicking; many restaurants – including some of the high-flyers – will allow you to Bring Your Own. This often extends only to bottled wine, so call ahead if you plan to bring beer. A small corkage fee is usually charged. In the listings below we've indicated whether the restaurant is licensed, BYO, both or doesn't allow alcohol at all. We've also given the price range for main courses at dinner.

Tipping, meanwhile, is something Sydneysiders do to reward exceptional service, not to keep angry waiters at bay. Ten per cent on top of the bill is the local standard, but no one's likely to be offended if you up the ante.

The CBD & the Rocks

Asian

Azuma

Chifley Plaza, 2 Chifley Square, corner of Phillip & Hunter Streets, CBD (9222 9960). CityRail Martin Place. **Open** noon-2.30pm, 6-10pm Mon-Fri; 6-10pm Sat, Sun. **Main courses** $30-$40. **Licensed/BYO. Credit** AmEx, BC, MC, V. **Map** p310 C2. **Japanese**
The deluxe skyscraper setting will have you squinting and pretending you're in Roppongi Hills or some other monied Tokyo setting, but the lightness and boldness of the kitchen's way with traditional Japanese flavours will tell you otherwise. When Azuma-san suggests you try sashimi with a squeeze of lemon rather than the ubiquitous soy, follow his advice and experience raw fish perfection.

n't
miss

Dining

The Boathouse on Blackwattle Bay

Order a dozen or two of the best freshly shucked oysters from around the country. The champagne vinaigrette is optional; glasses of bubbly and slices of brown bread and good butter aren't. *See p158.*

East Ocean

This yum cha (dim sum) diner is great for families, groups of friends and the terminally hungover alike. *See p145.*

Guillaume at Bennelong

Boasting views of the Opera House is one thing. Running a restaurant inside one of its sails is entirely another. Try the full dining extravaganza (*see p142*) or indulge in a seductive supper of champers and crab sarnies in the bar (*see p132*).

Icebergs Dining Room

Picture being in a box floating over the crashing waves of Bondi Beach. Decorate that box with the city's glitterati, smart waiters and Karen Martini's chic Italian eats – and you have some idea of the magic of this unique restaurant. *See p152.*

Pier

In a city where quality fish is a religion, chef Greg Doyle is its highest-ranking cleric, preaching the gospel of absolute freshness at his waterside Rose Bay altar. Hallelujah. *See p155.*

Sean's Panaroma

A meal at Sean's is at once utterly casual yet entirely memorable for the simplicity of the food and the congeniality of the atmosphere. Plus all the waiters are drop-dead hotties. *See p155.*

Tetsuya's

Alongside France's Alain Ducasse, Spain's Ferran Adria, America's Charlie Trotter and fellow Japanese expat Nobu Matsuhisa, Tetsuya Wakuda is part of that elite club of chefs whose work drives the world of fine dining forward. *See p143.*

Sailors Thai Canteen

The Canteen offers some of the world's finest imperial Thai cuisine (à la David Thompson), in designer environs, at a price that will appeal to all palates. *See p143.*

Sushi-e

Level 4, Establishment Hotel, 252 George Street, between Bridge Street & Abercrombie Lane, CBD (9240 3041/www.merivale.com.au). CityRail Wynyard. **Open** 6-10pm Tue; noon-2pm, 6-10pm Wed; noon-2pm Thur; noon-2pm, 6.30-10pm Fri; 6.30-10pm Sat. **Main courses** $9.50-$45. **Licensed.** **Credit** AmEx, BC, DC, MC, V. **Map** p310 B2.
Japanese
White men may not be able to jump, but Sean Presland is living proof that they can certainly break into the rarefied world of Japanese sushi chefs. Tokyo-trained Presland turns out the classics with the best of them, but it's his innovations like the mirin and chive-dressed kingfish that really justify this restaurant's (not inconsiderable) expense.

Yoshii

115 Harrington Street, between Essex & Argyle Streets, CBD (9247 2566/www.yoshii.com.au). CityRail/ferry Circular Quay. **Open** 6-9.30pm Mon, Sat; noon-2pm, 6-9.30pm Tue-Fri. **Set menus** $80, $110. **Licensed. Credit** AmEx, BC, DC, MC, V. **Map** p310 C1/B2. **Japanese**
Ryuichi Yoshii is, hands-down, Sydney's best sushi chef, and to watch him work at the sushi bar is like witnessing some strangely delicious surgery. He's no slouch on the cooked stuff either; the smoked rudderfish with white miso, delivered in a smoking cedar parcel, is poetry on a plate. Better still, it all takes place in a room which marries contemporary cool with Japanese attention to detail.

American

Prime

Lower Ground Floor, Westin Hotel, 1 Martin Place, CBD (9229 7777). CityRail Martin Place. **Open** noon-3pm, 6-10pm Mon-Fri; 6-10pm Sat. **Main courses** $32-$44. **Licensed. Credit** AmEx, BC, DC, MC, V. **Map** p310 B/C2.
The closest Sydney gets to a big, New York-style steakhouse, this designer basement in the old GPO building is all about the blokey business of heavy stone, blockbuster reds, and meat – and lots of it. The red wine sauces are finger-lickin' great, and the knives are made from German surgical steel.

European

Aqua Luna

5-7 Macquarie Street, Opera Quays, East Circular Quay (9251 0311). CityRail/ferry Circular Quay. **Open** noon-3pm, 5.30-11pm Mon-Fri; 6-11pm Sat; 5.30-10pm Sun. **Main courses** $30-$36. **Licensed. Credit** AmEx, BC, DC, MC, V. **Map** p310 C1. **Italian**
Lovers of the River Café/Carluccio school of Anglo-Italian cooking will enjoy Irish chef Darren Simpson's menu of provincial favourites (plus a very respectable version of the roasted bone marrow with parsley salad familiar to patrons of London's St John's restaurant). Fans of smooth service and views of the Quay won't be disappointed either.

Eat, Drink, Shop

Guillaume at Bennelong. *See p142.*

Bilson's

Radisson Plaza Hotel, 27 O'Connell Street, at Pitt Street, CBD (8214 0496). CityRail Wynyard. **Open** noon-2.30pm, 6-9.30pm Mon-Fri; 6-9.30pm Sat. **Set prices** (2 courses) $55, $65. **Licensed.** **Credit** AmEx, BC, DC, MC, V. **Map** p310 C2. **French**

The Godfather of Australian cooking, Tony Bilson's love of French cuisine has transformed the way we eat in restaurants, leading a generation of chefs in their appreciation of haute cuisine and classical technique. Witness the clarity of the venison consommé, or the brick-red perfection of the carpaccio that accompanies it. This hotel dining room highlights everything that is good about the Old School of dining – not least the cheese platter and eaux de vie – with none of the fustiness.

Certo

340 Kent Street, between King & Market Streets, CBD (9241 1344/www.certo.com.au). CityRail Wynyard. **Open** noon-2.30pm, 6-9.30pm Mon-Fri; 6-9.30pm Sat. **Main courses** $18-$35. **Licensed.** **Credit** AmEx, BC, DC, MC, V. **Map** p310/311 B2/3. **Italian**

The less-than-special rumpus-room decor isn't the only thing unusual about this basement boîte: it's the only Italian restaurant in town run by an almost exclusively Japanese team, on both sides of the kitchen door. The whole menu is strong, but, somewhat unsurprisingly, lighter dishes and anything with seafood are the best bets, and the spaghetti with lobster is outstanding.

Modern Australian

Aria

1 Macquarie Street, East Circular Quay (9252 2555/ www.ariarestaurant.com.au). CityRail/ferry Circular Quay. **Open** 12.30-2.30pm, 5.30-11.30pm Mon-Sat; 5.30-10pm Sun. **Main courses** $38-$45. **Licensed.** **Credit** AmEx, BC, DC, MC, V. **Map** p310 C1.

It's easy to sing the praises of chef Matt Moran when you've got enough walnut and dark leather around and under you to outfit a fleet of BMWs, and the Opera House, Harbour Bridge and water are spread before you. Lamb from the farm of Moran's dad is a special worth looking out for, while Bangalow sweet pork finds a great partner in a crab boudin.

Edna's Table

204 Clarence Street, between Druitt & Market Streets, CBD (9267 3933/www.ednastable.com.au). CityRail Town Hall/Monorail Galeries Victoria. **Open** 6-10pm Tue, Wed, Sat; noon-3pm, 6-10pm Thur, Fri. **Licensed.** **Main courses** $28-$36. *Native tasting menu* $88; $135 with wine. **Credit** AmEx, BC, DC, MC, V. **Map** p311 B3.

If you want to try some native Australian foodstuffs – kangaroo, emu, crocodile, pepperberry, bush

Top treats at **Sailors Thai**.

tomatoes, lemon myrtle – this is the place. Chef Raymond Kersh and his sister Jennice at front of house are pioneers in the use of indigenous ingredients. Great all-Oz wine list too.

est.

Establishment Hotel, 252 George Street, between Bridge Street & Abercrombie Lane, CBD (9240 3010/www.merivale.com.au). CityRail Circular Quay or Wynyard/ferry Circular Quay. **Open** noon-3pm, 6-10pm Mon-Fri; 6-10pm Sat. **Main courses** $37-$41. **Licensed**. **Credit** AmEx, BC, DC, MC, V. **Map** p310 B2.

Despite the grandeur of the white-columned room, the innate professionalism of the staff and the light, seemingly effortless elegance of Peter Doyle's food, a meal at est. won't quite cost you the earth. One of the great chefs of Sydney, Doyle's dishes start French but end all his own, as in the case of the John Dory with sauce Jacqueline. Wine buffs and vegetarians are especially well catered for.

Forty One

Level 42, Chifley Tower, 2 Chifley Square, corner of Phillip & Hunter Streets, CBD (www.forty-one.com.au). CityRail Martin Place. **Open** noon-2pm, 7pm-late Mon-Fri; 7pm-late Sat. **Set menu** $120 3 courses. **Licensed**. **Credit** AmEx, BC, DC, MC, V. **Map** p310 C2.

Yes, we know: it's on level 42. The funny thing is, after chowing down on Dietmar Sawyere's Old Country-inflected Mod Oz menu (hello, the famous roasted crown of hare) and quaffing some Krug, no one seems to care. Or perhaps they're too busy talking about the men's toilet – how many other urinals offer these kind of views?

Guillaume at Bennelong

Sydney Opera House, Bennelong Point, Circular Quay (9241 1999/www.guillaumeatbennelong. com.au). CityRail/ferry Circular Quay. **Open** 5.30-

11.30pm Mon-Sat. **Main courses** $35. **Licensed**. **Credit** AmEx, BC, DC, MC, V. **Map** p310 C1.

Given the following that Guillaume Brahimi picked up while working with Joel Robuchon in Paris, it's tempting to call his food French, but there's a lightness to, for example, his signature dish of tuna infused with basil that is pure Sydney. Fitting then, that he plies his trade in a stellar restaurant located in the city's finest structure.

harbourkitchen&bar

Park Hyatt Hotel, 7 Hickson Road, The Rocks (9256 1660). CityRail/ferry Circular Quay. **Open** noon-2.30pm, 6-10pm daily. **Main courses** $32-$39. **Licensed**. **Credit** AmEx, BC, DC, MC, V. **Map** p310 C1.

Hotels can be tricky things for good chefs. Anthony Musarra has confidence and flair to burn in his kitchen – the only shame of the restaurant is the floor staff. Focus your attention instead on wall-to-wall views of the water. Ahhh. Now nip into the clubby-as-hell Club Bar for a snort of Laphroaig and a Cohiba. Double-ahhh.

Palisade Hotel

Corner of Bettington & Argyle Streets, Millers Point (9247 2272). CityRail/ferry Circular Quay/bus 308. **Open** noon-3pm Mon-Fri; 6-9.30pm Sat. **Main courses** $26-$33. **Licensed**. **Credit** AmEx, BC, DC, MC, V. **Map** p310 B1.

A hidden gem, the upstairs dining room in this lovely old pub is certainly worth the fossick. Brian Sudek crafts food that sings with freshness, balance and simplicity. Service can be as laid-back as the atmosphere, but that's not necessarily a bad thing. Be warned – the bridge-side location doesn't necessarily translate to views for all.

Pavilion on the Park

1 Art Gallery Road, opposite the Art Gallery of NSW, The Domain (9232 1322). CityRail Martin Place.

sailors thai

best waiters. Seafood is, unsurprisingly, handled with particular aplomb. Anything involving crab gets the thumbs-up, as does the 'Wild and Tame Abalone' and the 'Six Tastes of the Sea' (aka sashimi with a platinum AmEx).

Tetsuya's

529 Kent Street, between Bathurst & Liverpool Streets, CBD (9267 2900). CityRail Town Hall/ Monorail Galeries Victoria. **Open** 6-9.30pm Tue- Sat. **Set menu** $175 12 courses. **Licensed/BYO**. **Credit** AmEx, BC, DC, MC, V. **Map** p311 B3.
You must eat here. No arguments. Yes, it's a very large amount of money to pay for food. But it's cheap when you consider that you're really paying for a holiday – a break from everything you thought you knew about food and how good it could be. Though it's a fixed price for 12 dishes, each is so light and small you're guaranteed to leave groaning only with pleasure. And don't worry: everyone ends up eating the entire dish of butter whipped with black truffle and parmegiano that accompanies the bread. They'd worry if you didn't.

The Wharf

End of Pier 4, Hickson Road, Walsh Bay (9250 1761/www.thewharfrestaurant.com.au). CityRail/ferry Circular Quay then 15mins walk/ bus 430. **Open** noon-2pm, 6-10pm Mon-Wed; noon-2pm, 6-10.30pm Thur-Sat. **Main courses** $32. **Licensed**. **Credit** AmEx, BC, DC, MC, V. **Map** p310 B1.
Cavernous, isn't it? A diner could almost feel lost, were it not for Aaron Ross's capacity to create a menu that is at once down-to-earth and completely gripping. Asian flavours are particularly well handled, but there's pleasure – and excellent value – to be found throughout. The bar menu is perfect for pre-theatre diners (the Sydney Theatre Company is based here; *see p254*), and for the light of wallet.

South-east Asian

Sailors Thai

106 George Street, between Essex & Argyle Streets, The Rocks (9251 2466). CityRail/ferry Circular Quay. **Open** *Canteen* noon-10pm daily. *Restaurant* noon-2pm, 6-10pm Mon-Sat. **Main courses** *Canteen* $15-$25. *Restaurant* $24-$34. **Licensed**. **Credit** AmEx, BC, DC, MC, V. **Map** p310 C1/2. **Thai** Chef David Thompson now spends most of his time running Nahm, his superb Michelin-starred Thai restaurant in London. Here you can eat food every bit as dynamic and thrilling, but for a fraction of the cost. And if even the relative bargain of the down- stairs fine-diner is too rich for your blood, you can sacrifice a little comfort, service and range for food that is significantly cheaper yet no less impressive in the upstairs Canteen. The signature *som dtam* – nuggets of caramelised pork with peanuts, dried tiny shrimp, cherry tomatoes and a fiery sour salad of green mango – can be considered Authentic Thai Food 101 for newcomers to the cuisine.

Open *Café* 9am-5pm daily. *Restaurant* noon- 3.30pm Mon-Fri, Sun. **Main courses** *Café* $8-$16. *Restaurant* $28-$36. **Licensed**. **Credit** AmEx, BC, DC, MC, V. **Map** p310 C2.
There are definitely worse settings than this for restaurants. Prehistoric-looking Moreton Bay fig trees provide the backdrop for what must be one of the best places for a leisurely lunch. Breakfast at the adjoining Pavilion on the Park café is a must.

Quay

Upper Level, Overseas Passenger Terminal, Circular Quay West, The Rocks (9251 5600/ www.quay.com.au). CityRail/ferry Circular Quay. **Open** noon-2.30pm, 6-10pm Mon-Fri; 6-10pm Sat, Sun. **Main courses** $38-$46. **Licensed**. **Credit** AmEx, BC, DC, MC, V. **Map** p310 C1.
Did Peter Gilmore have too many blocks to play with as a kid, or not enough? The near-obsessive presentation of circles and squares on his plates could be a concern were they not constructed from such brilliantly original combinations of textures and flavours. Witness the quail raviolo with abalone and celeriac, the red-braised pork belly with seared scallops, or the legendary five-texture Valrhona chocolate cake. With some of Sydney's most intrigu- ing food on offer in an unquestionably luxe setting, this is our kind of geometry.

Rockpool

107 George Street, between Essex & Argyle Streets, The Rocks (9252 1888/www.rockpool.com). CityRail/ferry Circular Quay. **Open** 6-10pm Tue-Sat. **Main courses** $54. **Licensed**. **Credit** AmEx, BC, DC, MC, V. **Map** p310 C1/2.
Though he's one of the architects of Modern Oz food, chef Neil Perry is more frequently likened to a rock star. His flagship restaurant is the biggest big-night- out diner in the country, but despite the glamour and swish many simply come to enjoy innovative food with plenty of integrity served by some of the city's

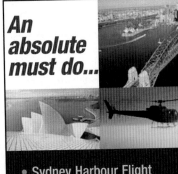

Chinatown & Haymarket

Asian

Chinese Noodle Restaurant

*8 Quay Street, at Thomas Street, Haymarket
(9281 9051). CityRail Central/
Haymarket/LightRail Capitol Square or Haymarket.*
Open 11am-9pm daily. **Main courses** $13-$20.
BYO. No credit cards. Map p311 B4.
North-western Chinese
Yes, those are plastic grape vines strung across the ceiling, and yes, this is definitely a Chinese restaurant. It's one of the best – and one of the cheapest – serving dishes from the north-western provinces. The noodles are handmade, the dumplings fresh and the atmosphere lively. 'Combination noodles' resembles a bizarre parallel universe spag bol, replete with cucumber julienne garnish. A must.

East Ocean

*88 Dixon Street, between Harbour & Sussex Streets,
Haymarket (9211 3674). City Rail/LightRail Central.*
Open 10am-midnight Mon-Fri; 9am-2am Sat, Sun.
Main courses $11.80-$16.80. **Licensed. Credit**
AmEx, DC, MC, V. **Cantonese**
After a recent revamp, East Ocean looks terribly slick (for a Hong Kong-style, barn-sized Cantonese diner, anyway), while the food is as pleasing as ever. Ignore the printed menu and have a chat with the waiters about how best to enjoy the live seafood. The pipis (clams) in XO sauce are the bomb, and the yum cha is among the finest. Tsingtao beer to wash them down is, of course, de rigueur.

Emperor's Garden BBQ & Noodles

*213 Thomas Street, between Ultimo & Quay
Streets, Haymarket (9281 9899). CityRail
Central/Monorail Haymarket/LightRail Capitol
Square or Haymarket.* **Open** 9.30am-11pm daily.
Main courses $9.50-$20. **Licensed. Credit** AmEx,
BC, DC, MC, V. **Map** p311 B4. **Cantonese**
There are other establishments in Chinatown that dispense barbecue that's nearly as good as the Emperor's, but the hardcore of roast and barbecue pork fanciers (and their pigeon and soy chicken brethren), Westerners and Cantonese alike, still only go to one place for their fix.

Golden Century

*393-399 Sussex Street, between Goulburn & Hay
Streets, Haymarket (9212 3901). CityRail Town
Hall/Monorail World Square or Garden Plaza/
LightRail Capitol Square.* **Open** noon-4am daily.
Main courses $15-$30. **Licensed. Credit** AmEx,
BC, DC, MC, V. **Map** p311 B3. **Cantonese**
Though the printed menu is great, many regulars bypass it completely and wave for some steamed fish with ginger and shallot, the salt-and-pepper prawns and the restaurant's top-notch signature Peking duck. After 10pm the restaurant switches down a gear, offering cheaper, one-bowl meals for owls, drunks, chefs and other miscreants. Midnight

congee (we favour the pork and preserved egg version) at the Golden C is a Sydney foodie institution.

Marigold Citimark

*683 George Street, between Hay Street & Ultimo
Road, Haymarket (9281 3388). CityRail Central/
LightRail Capitol Square.* **Open** 10am-3pm, 5.30-11pm daily. **Main courses** $15-$30. **Licensed.**
Credit AmEx, BC, DC, MC, V. **Map** p311 B4.
Cantonese
There's something in the local adage that Sydney is the place for yum cha, while Melbourne rules the roost when it comes to Cantonese by night. But the Marigold comes close to confusing the issue, cunningly offering a dazzling array of snacks at lunch, and then an equally impressive line-up after dark, not least the sizzling pepper oysters.

Musashi

*Corner of Pitt & Campbell Streets, Haymarket
(9280 0377). CityRail Central/LightRail Capitol
Square.* **Open** 11.45am-2.30pm, 5.30-10pm Mon-Fri;
5.30-10pm Sat. **Main courses** $5-$35. **Licensed.**
Credit AmEx, MC, V. **Map** p311 B4. **Japanese**
Fickle as the young Japanese cool crowd in Sydney may be, this downtown-glam *izakaya* seems to have some staying power in the fashionable restaurant stakes. The food's certainly pretty good for the low prices. The sashimi's OK, but the cooked stuff, such as the okonomiyaki – here thoughtfully translated as 'Japanese pizza' – is where it's at.

Chinese Noodle Restaurant: a handy spot.

Eat, Drink, Shop

ntrance on Little Hay Street,
8122). CityRail Central/Monorail
....ightRail Haymarket or Capitol Square.
Open 11.30am-3.30pm, 5.30-11pm daily. **Main courses** $15. **Licensed/BYO**. **Credit** AmEx, BC, DC, MC, V. **Map** p311 B3. **Sichuan**
Those who fear spice should abandon all hope now, for whether it comes in the form of the fresh or dried namesakes of the restaurant or the cool-burn of the chefs' native Sichuan pepper, it's very much the order of the day. One of only a handful of Sichuan places in the country, and one of the best. The lobster and crab dishes deserve their great popularity, and the treatment of the sea cucumber provides great thrills for texture-food fiends.

South-east Asian

Pasteur
709 George Street, between Ultimo Road & Valentine Street, Haymarket (9212 5622). CityRail Central/ LightRail Capitol Square. **Open** 10am-9pm daily. **Main courses** $6-$10. **BYO**. **No credit cards**. **Map** p311 B4. **Vietnamese**
There's not a lot going on here, decor-wise, and the blaring AM radio only adds to the auditory chaos. The only thing in the joint subject to any aesthetic order is the phô: hefty bowls of beef broth, slippery white rice noodles and meat – it's the business.

Thainatown
426 Pitt Street, between Goulburn & Campbell Streets, Haymarket (9281 3216). CityRail Museum/ Monorail World Square/LightRail Capitol Square. **Open** 10am-10pm daily. **Main courses** $9-$11. **BYO**. **No credit cards**. **Map** p311 B/C3. **Thai**
Picture a milkbar and a Thai restaurant getting into a fight. Picture the restaurant winning. Almost. Now imagine that the resulting booth-lined space served the most authentic, appealing and, above all, cheap Thai food in the nation. Check out the attention to detail in the pad kaprow – it's a riot of texture and taste, spiked with slices of red chilli, finely julienned kaffir lime leaf and chopped green beans.

Darling Harbour

Asian

Zaaffran
Level 2, 345 Harbourside, Darling Harbour (9211 8900/www.zaaffran.com.au). Monorail Harbourside. **Open** noon-2.30pm daily; 5.30-9.30pm Mon-Thur, Sun; 5.30-10.15pm Fri, Sat. **Main courses** $17.50-$25. **Licensed**. **Credit** AmEx, BC, DC, MC, V. **Map** p311 B3. **Indian**
The name, which means saffron, provides a clue: this polished, upmarket Indian restaurant specialises in complex and intriguing spice mixes. The lamb kebabs, for one, draw rave notices. Not cheap, but definitely interesting.

Seafood

Nick's Seafood
The Promenade, King Street Wharf, Darling Harbour (9264 1212/www.nicks-seafood.com.au). CityRail Town Hall/Monorail Darling Park. **Open** noon-3pm, 6-10pm Mon-Sat; noon-10pm Sun. **Main courses** $23-$28. **Licensed**. **Credit** AmEx, BC, DC, MC, V. **Map** p310 B2.
You can eat brilliantly at Nick's or you cannot. The trick is simple: order fish from the extensive selection (don't ever pass up an opportunity to eat red emperor) and get it cooked as simply as possible, with other basics – salads, mash and whatnot – on the side. Follow these simple instructions, add a sunny day and a chilled riesling, and you won't find a better al fresco seafood experience.

South-east Asian

The Malaya
39 Lime Street, King Street Wharf, Darling Harbour (9279 1170/www.themalaya.com.au). CityRail Town Hall/Monorail Darling Park. **Open** noon-3pm, 6pm-late daily. **Main courses** $22-$24. **Licensed**. **Credit** AmEx, BC, DC, MC, V. **Map** p310 B2. **Malaysian**
The Malaya looms large in the recent history of Sydney restaurants, having been responsible, over the course of 30-odd years and several changes of location, for introducing local palates to galangal, lemongrass and other Asian flavours. The latest incarnation is the slickest yet: an airy establishment boasting water views.

Surry Hills

Asian

Billy Kwong
355 Crown Street, between Albion & Foveaux Streets, Surry Hills (9332 3300). CityRail/LightRail Central. **Open** 6-10pm daily. **Main courses** $22-$38. **Licensed/BYO** (wine only). **Credit** AmEx, BC, MC, V. **Map** p311 C4. **Cantonese**
It's loud, you can't book, you eat elbow-to-elbow with other diners on three-legged stools – and it's utterly fabulous. Kylie Kwong (*see p159* **Take a wok**) takes the fold of her Cantonese ancestry and sexes it up, keeping the emphasis on freshness, flavour and levity. Stir-fries rock, the kingfish sashimi sings with sweet freshness and the crisp duck with blood plums has a well-deserved following.

Maya Dhaba
430 Cleveland Street, at Crown Street, Surry Hills (8399 3785). Bus 301, 302, 303, 372, 393, 395. **Open** 11am-3pm, 5.30-10.30pm daily. **Main courses** $13-$15. **BYO**. **Credit** BC, DC, MC, V. **South Indian**
Spawn of the city's increasingly common Maya Indian sweet shops (gulab jamin, anyone?), but

where the other Maya outlets typically only augment their dessert sales with the odd masala dosai, Dhaba has a full – and very attractive – menu of meaty delights from the subcontinent's south.

Sagar

423 Cleveland Street, between Crown & Bourke Streets, Surry Hills (9319 2170). Bus 301, 302, 303, 372, 393, 395. **Open** noon-10.30pm Tue-Sun. **Main courses** $11.50-$12.50. **BYO**. **Credit** AmEx, BC, DC, MC, V. **Indian**

It's pretty nondescript, yes, but what this narrow little room lacks in airs and graces it makes up for in chicken biriyani. That and scores of other daily Indian specials keep things fresh at Sagar – one day sees a range of meat thalis, another a wealth of vegetarian dosai. The uniting factor in all this? Every special represents a total bargain.

Uchi Lounge

15 Brisbane Street, between Goulburn & Oxford Streets, Surry Hills (9261 3524). CityRail Museum. **Open** 6.30-11pm Tue-Sat. **Main courses** $13.50-$16.50. **Licensed/BYO** (wine only). **Credit** AmEx, BC, MC, V. **Map** p311 C4. **Japanese**

Despite the fact that they're so hip they can barely see over their pelvises, the aggressively fashion-forward folk at this well-hidden restaurant are a surprisingly nice bunch of kids. The other surprise is how little they charge for their extremely stylish and edible mod Japanese eats, such as the kickin' sautée of enoki mushrooms or the outstanding agedashi tofu. Drinks in the bar downstairs will open your eyes – and your palate – to the idea of saké as the party drink of the future.

European

Alio

3-5 Baptist Street, at Cleveland Street, Surry Hills (8394 9368/www.alio.com.au). Bus 372, 393, 395. **Open** 6-10.30pm Mon-Sat. **Main courses** $25-$30. **Licensed/BYO** (Mon-Thur only). **Credit** AmEx, BC, DC, MC, V. **Italian**

You've gotta hand it to them, this gang of young chefs and restaurateurs are really making a fist of this nifty little Surry Hills eaterie. A good cut above the trattoria level, Alio nonetheless offers good value for its Italy-via-the-River-Café eats. Their bollito misto, for example, finds few competitors in Australia. And they're mates with Jamie Oliver. (That's a good thing, right?)

Bécasse

Corner of Albion & Mary Streets, Surry Hills (9280 3202/www.becasse.com.au). CityRail/LightRail Central. **Open** 6.30-10.30pm Mon-Sat. **Main courses** $30-$80 (dégustation menu). **Licensed**. **Credit** AmEx, BC, DC, MC, V. **Map** p311 C4. **French**

Justin North is one of a handful of chefs credited with keeping Sydney food real: using skills learned at various posh restaurants here and in London,

North creates culinary magic, turning out inventive, elegant, modern French-accented dishes for not very much money at all, bless his chequered trousers. The assiette of pigeon and foie gras is just a taste of the culinary fireworks this kid is capable of.

Café Mint

579 Crown Street, between Lansdowne & Cleveland Streets, Surry Hills (9319 0848). Bus 301, 302, 303. **Open** 7am-5pm Mon, Sat, Sun; 6-10.30pm Wed-Fri. **Main courses** $16-$22. **BYO**. **No credit cards**. **Mediterranean**

The modern takes on Mediterranean food that have been the talk of Melbourne for some years have yet to make real waves in Sydney, but there are a few noteworthy incursions, one of the best being this cool yet inexpensive caff-cum-restaurant down the uncool end of Crown Street. The food's great and the almond and grapefruit frappé is an exceptional hangover-buster.

Marque

355 Crown Street, between Albion & Foveaux Streets, Surry Hills (9332 2225). CityRail/LightRail Central. **Open** 6.30-10.30pm Mon-Sat. **Main courses** $32-$44. **Licensed/BYO**. **Credit** AmEx, BC, DC, MC, V. **Map** p311 C4. **French**

Michelin-starred chefs of Paris, beware! Mark Best knows your tricks, having worked hard in your kitchens, and is in danger of upstaging you with his small, chic, understated Surry Hills restaurant. Tremble before his globe artichoke millefeuille, gibber at the lightness of his boudin blanc and run screaming from his beetroot tart – he's coming for your jobs…

MG Garage

490 Crown Street, between Collins & Arthur Streets, Surry Hills (9383 9383/www.mggarage.com.au). CityRail Central. **Open** 6-9.30pm Mon, Sat; noon-2.30pm, 6-9.30pm Tue-Fri. **Main courses** $35-$42. **Licensed**. **Credit** AmEx, BC, DC, MC, V. **Map** p311 C4. **French**

Brit chef Jeremy Strode left his mark on Melbourne dining and is now in the process of wowing the foodies of Sydney with his mastery of classical technique and creative prowess. Never mind that the restaurant is also a sports car showroom – only rubes and motor nerds give that aspect a second thought. Specials at lunch and in the early evening democratise the delight.

Tabou

527 Crown Street, between Devonshire & Lansdowne Streets, Surry Hills (9319 5682/www.tabourestaurant.com.au). Bus 301, 302, 303. **Open** noon-2.30pm, 6.30-10pm Mon-Fri; 6-10.30pm Sat, Sun. **Main courses** $25-$30. **Licensed/BYO** (Mon-Thur, Sun only). **Credit** AmEx, BC, DC, MC, V. **Map** p311 C5. **French**

Lots of bistros in this town forget that a bistro, almost by definition, needs to be a boisterous affair. Thankfully, Tabou has that requirement in hand,

Eat, Drink, Shop

at almost undercut their elegance with ~~...~~ The upstairs bar, incidentally, is one ~~of the~~ best-kept secrets on Crown Street.

South-east Asian

Cochin

61 Fitzroy Street, at Bourke Street, Surry Hills (9358 5388). Bus 301, 302, 303. **Open** 6-10pm Tue-Sun. **Main courses** $18-$30. **BYO. Credit** BC, MC, V. **Map** p311 C4. **Vietnamese**
The name of this stark, yet warm little room alludes to the interplay of cuisines during the French occupation of Vietnam. Thus the menu sees cracked rice sitting side by side with baguettes. Asian-seasoned lamb cutlets come with a glossy reduction sauce, and the dessert menu is worth very much more than a cursory glance.

Longrain

Corner of Commonwealth & Hunt Streets, Surry Hills (9280 2888/www.longrain.com.au). CityRail Museum or Central/LightRail Central. **Open** noon-2.30pm, 6-10.30pm Mon-Fri; 6-10.30pm Sat. **Main courses** $28-$45. **Licensed. Credit** AmEx, BC, DC, MC, V. **Map** p311 C4. **Thai**
The restaurant's hip and gorgeous and so's the *Wallpaper**-reading crowd that frequents its communal tables. Think the food's going to have less depth and integrity than your waitress's lip-gloss? Think again. Marty Boetz takes authentic Thai flavours and techniques and dresses them up for a big night out. The braised shin of beef is curry gone glam, while the betel leaves with prawn, peanuts and pomelo are frequently ripped-off by other chefs, but seldom bested. The bar here is a must-visit too; *see p135.*

Red Lantern

545 Crown Street, between Lansdowne & Cleveland Streets, Surry Hills (9698 4355/www.redlantern. com.au). Bus 301, 302, 303. **Open** 12.30-3pm, 6.30-10.30pm Tue-Fri; 1-3pm, 6.30-10.30pm Sat, Sun. **Main courses** $16-$18. **Licensed. Credit** AmEx, DC, MC, V. **Vietnamese**
The chef might be a white guy, but the combination of his skills and the knowledge and experience of the restaurant's young Vietnamese owners raise Red Lantern above most other purveyors of the cuisine, while the funked-up look and democratic prices give it uncommon edge.

Turkish

Erciyes

409 Cleveland Street, between Crown & Bourke Streets, Surry Hills (9319 1309). Bus 301, 302, 303, 372, 393, 395. **Open** 11am-midnight daily **Main courses** $10-$20. **Licensed/BYO. Credit** AmEx, BC, MC, V. **Map** p311 C5. **Turkish**
Err-*chee*-ehs. It's really not that hard, but it seems to elude most non-Turkish speakers for some reason. But no one seems to have a problem wrapping their tongue around the spicy sausage-topped Turkish pizzas, the cabbage rolls or smoky kebabs. Hit the dips and breads hard and don't leave without a Turkish coffee. Saturdays see the ante upped by, uh-uh, belly dancers.

Darlinghurst & East Sydney

Asian

Oh! Calcutta!

251 Victoria Street, at Burton Street, Darlinghurst (9360 3650/www.ohcalcutta.com.au). CityRail Kings Cross. **Open** 6pm-midnight Mon-Sat. **Main courses** $16.90-$26.90. **Licensed. Credit** AmEx, BC, MC, V. **Map** p311 D4. **Indian**
Easily the most glamorous Indian in town, Oh! Calcutta!'s fit-out, by local design legends Burley Katon Halliday, marries comfort with edgy good looks in a manner that echoes the kitchen's gift for clarifying the tastes of the subcontinent and applying them to upmarket ingredients, as with the excellent crab salad with pooris. Basil Daniell is an engaging host, and keen to lead unwitting diners through the best the restaurant has to offer.

Rise

23 Craigend Street, at Royston Street, Darlinghurst (9357 1755/www.rise.com.au). CityRail Kings Cross. **Open** 6-10pm Tue-Sun. **Main courses** $25-$35. **Licensed. Credit** AmEx, BC, DC, MC, V. **Map** p311 D3. **Japanese**
Soft-shell tacos what? Gai-yang chicken huh? Fasten your seatbelt and make sure you've got a firm grip on your chopsticks: chef Raita Noda takes his native Japanese as the departure point for his food and then proceeds deftly to interweave international influences at a fierce rate of knots. Culinary high-flyers take note.

European

Pizza Mario

248 Palmer Street, between Liverpool & Burton Streets, East Sydney (9332 3633). CityRail Museum. **Open** 6-10pm Mon-Fri, Sun; noon-2pm, 6-10pm Sat. **Main courses** $12-$23. **Licensed. Credit** AmEx, BC, MC, V. **Map** p311 C3. **Pizza**
In a setting as swish as the Republic apartment complex, we can only interpret the chequered tablecloths as a stab at irony. Happily, no one is trying to be clever when it comes to the pizza: it's thin, crisp, wood-fired and, if you order the DOC version (you should), comes topped simply with tomato and buffalo mozzarella.

Ristorante Riva

379 Liverpool Street, at Darlinghurst Street, Darlinghurst (9380 5318). CityRail Kings Cross. **Open** 6.30-10.30pm Mon-Fri; 12.30-3pm, 6.30-10.30pm Sat. **Main courses** $33-$34. **Licensed. Credit** AmEx, BC, DC, MC, V. **Map** p312 D3. **Italian**

Fine dining, and a view too: **Icebergs Dining Room**. *See p152.*

Beverly Riva is the very model of everything you want from floor staff. Her charm is neatly matched by that of the creations of her husband. Chef Eugenio reinterprets classic *cucina* for the inner-city set, cleaning lines here, amping up flavours there, making for food that is at once seductive and full of integrity. The braised oxtail will have you sucking the bones and calling for a nice big Barolo.

Modern Australian

Onde

346 Liverpool Street, between Womerah Avenue & Victoria Street, Darlinghurst (9331 8749). CityRail Kings Cross. **Open** 5.30-11pm Mon-Thur; 5.30-11.30pm Fri, Sat. **Main courses** $17-$25. **Licensed**. **Credit** AmEx, BC, DC, MC, V. **Map** p312 D3.
Not so much a restaurant as the part-time dining room of half of swinging Darlinghurst, Onde is unpretentious, buzzy, well priced and friendly – in short, the epitome of the good neighbourhood restaurant. The steak frites with red wine butter and a sassy red will cure whatever may ail you.

Pello

71-73 Stanley Street, between Riley & Crown Streets, East Sydney (9360 4640). CityRail Museum. **Open** noon-3pm, 6-10pm Mon-Fri; 6-10pm Sat. **Main courses** $27-$32. **Licensed/BYO** (Mon-Thur only). **Credit** AmEx, BC, DC, MC, V. **Map** p311 C3.
In the sea of Stanley Street's red-sauce merchants, Pello stands out like a beacon of non-Italian goodness. The look is sharp and the pace is fast, but there are enough smiles from the staff and so much to engage you on chef Thomas Johns' menu that it never feels cold. A bowl of Pello's fiesty chilli crab linguine is perfect for lunch.

Salt

229 Darlinghurst Road, between Farrell & Tewkesbury Avenues, Darlinghurst (9332 2566/ www.saltrestaurant.com.au). CityRail Kings Cross. **Open** noon-3pm Mon; noon-3pm, 6-11pm Tue-Fri; 6-11pm Sat. **Main courses** $41.50-$44.50. **Licensed**. **Credit** AmEx, BC, DC, MC, V. **Map** p312 D3.
Luke Mangan runs three leading restaurants in Sydney – the other two are Bistro Lulu (*see p152*) and Moorish (*see p153*) – another in Auckland and barely a week goes by without his appearance in magazines and on TV. Yet somehow he seems always to be in the kitchen of his very chichi restaurant, pumping out his unique and innovative take on Mod Oz cuisine. Surely cloning is the only possible explanation – you'd need at least one of the many Lukes on the job full-time just to keep the tempura quail leg this close to perfection.

South-east Asian

Phamish

354 Liverpool Street, at Boundary Street, Darlinghurst (9357 2688). CityRail Kings Cross. **Open** 6-10pm Mon, Wed-Sun. **Main courses** $12.50-$17.50. **BYO**. **Credit** AmEx, BC, DC, MC, V. **Map** p311 D4. **Vietnamese**
Part of the movement to upgrade Vietnamese cuisine, Phamish takes lots of southern Vietnamese standards and places them in the context of a very buzzy, shiny, Darlinghurst no-bookings BYO. The food won't always knock your socks off (though the crunchy take on the rice paper roll is intriguing, and the chilli-tamarind prawns are fun), but it's never bad and the price is right for groups.

Kings Cross, Potts Point & Woolloomooloo

European

Base

31 Challis Avenue, at Macleay Street, Potts Point (9331 0008). CityRail Kings Cross. **Open** 7pm-late daily. **Main courses** $22-$25. **Licensed. Credit** AmEx, BC, DC, MC, V. **Map** p312 D2. **Pizza**

That would be the thin, crisp, attractively ember-charred foundations upon which these guys build their pizza perfection. The offerings here might not be as close to the ideal as those produced in the Italian enclaves of the city's inner west, but they're certainly within shouting distance, and more than enough to satisfy a 'real' pizza craving. The service ain't half bad, either.

Fratelli Paradiso

12-16 Challis Avenue, at Victoria Street, Potts Point (9357 1744). CityRail Kings Cross. **Open** 7am-11pm Mon-Fri; 7am-5pm Sat, Sun. **Main courses** $26. **Licensed. Credit** AmEx, BC, DC, MC, V. **Map** p312 D2. **Italian**

Gotta love that wallpaper: a pattern of big sexy lips sucking down some spaghetti strands. Expect to see a similar scene on the dials of your fellow diners – there's plenty in the way of both sexy pouts and good pasta in this dim, stylish diner. Calamari San Andrea is a favourite, while the Italian-style roast spring lamb is minimal and brilliant. If you're feeling less than flush, the adjoining bakery knocks out very decent Italian pastries and savouries.

Nove

9 Woolloomooloo Wharf, Cowper Bay Road, opposite Forbes Street, Woolloomooloo (9368 7599). Bus 311. **Open** noon-11pm Sun. **Main courses** $9-$26. **Licensed. Credit** AmEx, BC, DC, MC, V. **Map** p312 D2. **Pizza**

Buzz, buzz, buzz. What's that? Oh, it's a scene. Look one way and you'll see celebs and water views. Turn your head to the other for an eyeful of today's pizza (square-cut, Roman-style) and a blackboard full of clipped, thoughtful Italian treats. And it's not a bad spot for just a mid-afternoon Peroni or Aranciata Rosso.

Otto

8 Woolloomooloo Wharf, Cowper Wharf Road, opposite Forbes Street, Woolloomooloo (9368 7488/ www.otto.net.au). **Open** noon-3pm, 6pm-late daily. **Main courses** $29-$36. **Licensed. Credit** AmEx, BC, DC, MC, V. **Map** p312 D2. **Italian**

Don't ask to speak to Otto – it's actually Italian for 'eight', which is the number of this celeb-magnet. If you can fight your way through the air-kissing and attract the attention of the charming, but wildly inconsistent waiters, you might be in for some outstanding *cucina moderna*. Or you might not – it's that sort of place. But you'll have fun either way.

Tilbury Hotel

Corner of Nicholson & Forbes Streets, Woolloomooloo (9368 1955). Bus 311. **Open** noon-3pm, 6-10pm Tue-Sun. **Main courses** $23-$30. **Licensed. Credit** AmEx, BC, MC, V. **Italian**

Plagued as Sydney is by awful pub renovations, it's almost a shock to witness one done right. The Tilbury in Woolloomooloo is just such a beast, and the sharp, mod-Italian restaurant that nestles smack in the middle of it all gives the pub a civilised air, while feeding off its energy. A Bellini made with champagne and fresh nectarines segues nicely into roasted yabbies with limoncello and tarragon butter, which in turn gives way to perfectly pink calf's liver with house-made brioche, radicchio and balsamic vinegar. *See also p137.*

Seafood

Fishface

132 Darlinghurst Road, between Liverpool & Burton Streets, Kings Cross (9332 4803). CityRail Kings Cross. **Open** 6-11pm Mon-Sat. **Main courses** $22-$29. **BYO. No credit cards. Map** p312 D3.

Steve Hodges used to run half the show at Rose Bay's smart Pier restaurant, but now he's taking it to the people, making over this popular fish caff and taking the menu upmarket without putting the prices out of reach. The sashimi bar is top-notch, while the fish and chips must be tried to be believed; the note suggesting it be eaten with the fingers is entirely superfluous. There is no other way.

South-east Asian

Arun Thai

28 Macleay Street, at Rockwall Crescent, Potts Point (9326 9135). CityRail Kings Cross. **Open** 6-10.30pm daily. **Main courses** (casual dining) $7-$25; (fine dining) $20-$40. **Licensed. Credit** AmEx, BC, DC, MC, V. **Map** p312 D2/3. **Thai**

In a city full of really average Thai restaurants, anything that deviates from the dull and uniform norm is a boon. Enter Arun Thai: serving royal Thai food, this plush restaurant doesn't quite have the sophistication of Longrain (*see p148*) or Sailors Thai (*see p143*), but there's certainly lots to like, and its authenticity is solid.

jimmy liks

188 Victoria Street, at Darlinghurst Road, Potts Point (8354 1400). CityRail Kings Cross. **Open** 6-11pm daily. **Main courses** $24. **Licensed. Credit** AmEx, BC, DC, MC, V. **Map** p312 D3. **South-east Asian**

So much like its Surry Hills big bro Longrain (*see p148*) that its nickname is Shortgrain, jimmy liks has copped flak for not treating its customers particularly well. And in terms of service, it's a fair cop. But don't let that keep you from sampling the good cocktails (*see p137*) nor, for that matter, the full-flavoured takes on the street food of South-east Asia.

Eat, Drink, Shop

The hang lae curry of lamb shank with peanuts and pickled garlic is a killer, while the pad thai with scallops and garlic chives brings new glamour to an old takeaway favourite.

Modern Australian

Bayswater Brasserie

32 Bayswater Road, at Ward Avenue, Kings Cross (9357 2177/www.bayswaterbrasserie.com.au). CityRail Kings Cross. **Open** 5-11pm Mon-Thur, Sat; noon-11pm Fri. **Main courses** $18-$33. **Licensed. Credit** AmEx, BC, DC, MC, V. **Map** p312 D3.
In the 1980s, the Bayz was known by many Sydney business people as 'the Office'. Those long-lunching days of expense account excess may be long gone (sniff), but the air of cultured hedonism still remains at this exceedingly pleasant landmark. Don't go past the freshly shucked oysters, and indulgent snackers shouldn't miss the foie gras on toast.

The Yellow Bistro

57-59 Macleay Street, at Mcdonald Street, Potts Point (9357 3400). CityRail Kings Cross. **Open** 7.30-10.30pm Mon-Sat; 7.30am-3pm Sun. **Main courses** $26.50-$29.50. **Licensed. Credit** AmEx, BC, DC, MC, V. **Map** p312 D2.
George Sinclair is an exemplary bistro chef, while Lorraine Godsmark is a dessert chef with the golden whisk. Together, they make beautiful food. He serves feather-light gnocchi with fresh tomato and pesto, she makes the legendary date tart and superb macaroons. Not only can you sample their skills at breakfast, lunch and dinner, you can also get stuff to take home from Yellow's food store section.

Eastern Suburbs

Asian

Mu Shu

108 Campbell Parade, at Hall Street, Bondi Beach (9130 5400). CityRail Bondi Junction then bus 380, 381, L82/bus 380, L82. **Open** 6-11pm Mon-Sat; noon-3pm, 6-11pm Thur-Sat; noon-3pm, 6-10pm Sun. **Main courses** $20-$25. **BYO. Credit** AmEx, BC, DC, MC, V. **Map** p83. **Pan-Asian**
You know you're in flash territory when male diners return to the table unsure whether they've just relieved themselves in a designer urinal or done something terrible to a water feature. Mu Shu is as big and brash as its Bondi setting, with an ambitious pan-Asian menu. It could all be a bit much were it not for the shameless love-me attitude that is its saving grace. Don't miss the house-roasted Cantonese-style duck with feather-light pancakes or the fabulously gingery wok-fried whole snapper. Good cocktails too.

Wasavie

8 Heeley Street, at Glenmore Road, Paddington (9380 8838). Bus 380, L82. **Open** 6-10pm Tue-Sat. **Main courses** $20-$25. **BYO. Credit** AmEx, BC, DC, MC, V. **Map** p313 D4. **Japanese**

This minimal little local is living proof that good, cheap Japanese food isn't a paradox. You can sear your slices of raw fish on a hot stone for a bit of theatre, abandon yourself to the pleasures of the flesh in the form of the sumptuously sticky braised pork belly with hot mustard, or walk on the wilder side with Japanese-slash-Mod Oz experiments.

European

Bistro Lulu

257 Oxford Street, opposite William Street, Paddington (9380 6888/www.bistrolulu.com.au). Bus 378, 380, L82. **Open** 6-11pm Mon-Wed, Sun; noon-3pm, 6-11pm Thur-Sat. **Main courses** $28.50. **BYO. Credit** AmEx, BC, DC, MC, V. **Map** p313 D4. **French**
Bentwood chairs? Check. Specials written on the mirror? Check. Garlic bread and onion soup? Check. Menu written with an understanding of the true appeal of the bistro (ie big flavours handled with finesse and little pretension)? Check. Luke Mangan's Lulu is the best Oxford Street has to offer in smart-casual dining, interpreting the bistro brief broadly enough to offer the likes of duck liver parfait and sirloin with pommes frites alongside a salad of crisp pork belly and cuttlefish dressed with tamarind.

Buon Ricordo

108 Boundary Street, at Liverpool Street, Paddington (9360 6729/www.buonricordo.com.au). Bus 378, 380, 382. **Open** 6.30-11pm Tue-Sat. **Main courses** $30-$40. **Licensed. Credit** AmEx, DC, BC, MC, V. **Map** p311 D4. **Italian**
Armando Percuoco is hospitality on two legs. Watch him: clapping a back here, kissing a hand there, his big sandpaper voice booming one minute, conspiratorial the next. And yet he somehow runs a tight kitchen too, with Buon Ricordo's luxe fare earning it a swag of best-Italian awards over the past decade. Go all out with the tagliatelle alla tartfuovo, a rich explosion of house-made pasta with soft-poached truffled egg, or spare your arteries and delight your palate with the excellent seared beef carpaccio.

Buzo

Corner of Jersey Road & Windsor Street, Paddington (9328 1600). Bus 380, 389. **Open** 6.30pm-late Mon-Sat. **Main courses** $19.50-$25. **Licensed. Credit** AmEx, BC, DC, MC, V. **Map** p313 E4. **Italian**
The atmosphere of this classy osteria is fostered by the rustic simplicity of the chalkboard menu, the relatively modest pricing and the crush of locals who storm the place. Risotti are a highlight, as are faves such as the Sicilian roast lamb and the vincisgrassi, which interleaves porcini, prosciutto, pasta and truffle oil in a luxurious lasagne.

Icebergs Dining Room

1 Notts Avenue, Bondi Beach (9365 9000/ www.idrb.com). CityRail Bondi Junction then bus 380, 381, L82/bus 380, L82. **Open** noon-3pm 6.30-9.30pm Tue-Sun. **Main courses** $32-$34. **Licensed. Credit** AmEx, BC, DC, MC, V. **Map** p83. **Italian**

Bondi Beach-flavoured eye-candy is the order of the day at this roost for the see-and-be-seen crowd. Chef Karen Martini's stripped-back menu is presented in a room bursting with contemporary Italo-Bondi style. What better way to enjoy a strikingly fresh and simple salad of grilled lobster with green peas, fingerling potatoes, tarragon and mayo than with the deep blue at one elbow and a waiter discreetly pouring you a glass of Veuve at the other. The adjoining bar (*see p138*) is fabulous at dusk. The building also houses the famous Icebergs winter swimming club; *see p78* **Some like it cold**.

Lucio's

Corner of Windsor & Elizabeth Streets, Paddington (9380 5996/www.lucios.com.au). Bus 380, 382. **Open** 12.30-3pm, 6.30-11pm Mon-Sat. **Main courses** $32-$42. **Licensed. Credit** AmEx, BC, DC, MC, V. **Map** p313 E4. **Italian**
Love art and food? Lucio's – where the myth of the starving artist is exploded – is the answer. The walls are festooned with works by many of the foremost Australian painters of the past 50 years, while the plates come adorned with Timothy Fisher's modish Italian eats. The chilli crab linguine has acquired local-legend status.

Moorish

180-120 Ramsgate Avenue, at Campbell Parade, North Bondi (9300 9511). CityRail Bondi Junction then bus 380, 381, L82/bus 380, L82. **Open** noon-3pm, 6-11pm Mon-Fri; 10am-4pm, 6-11pm Sat; 10am-4pm, 6-10.30pm Sun. **Main courses** $28.50. **Licensed.** AmEx, BC, MC, V. **Map** p83.
Mediterranean
Locating a Moorish restaurant near this much sand seems to make sense; the ocean is merely a nice bonus. The major criticism levelled at this polished glass box (another of Luke Mangan's joints) is that the spicing falls somewhat short of the mark. But there's still a good deal in the contemporary North African/Spanish menu to delight, not least the tapas, the roast spatchcock with smoked paprika and aubergine, the spunky waiters and the Pedro Ximenez and raisin ice-cream. Moor, Moor, Moor.

Pompei

Corner of Roscoe & Gould Streets, Bondi Beach (9365 1233). CityRail Bondi Junction then bus 380, 381, L82/bus 380, L82. **Open** 11am-late Tue-Sun. **Main courses** $15.50-$17.90. **Licensed/BYO** (wine only). AmEx, BC, MC, V. **Map** p83. **Pizza**
It's a matter of fierce debate: is the greatest thing about Pompei the creamy, all-natural gelato (*see p133* **Nice ice, baby**) that comes in a range of drool-worthy flavours – or is it the pizza, Naples-thin and available topped with everything from seasonal delights, like the pizza bianca with fresh artichoke, to the timeless margherita? It's a question best examined in person, as frequently as possible.

Restaurant Balzac

Corner of Perouse Road & St Pauls Street, Randwick (9399 9660). Bus 372, 3763, 376. **Open** 6-10pm

Eat streets

Successive waves of immigration have been the key force shaping Sydney dining, and while Mod Oz borrows freely from all manner of cuisines, to sample the tastes of other cultures at their most authentic – and usually their cheapest – it's best to hit the suburbs and check out the ethnic enclaves, both old and new, that represent some of the most tempting eating in town.

Haberfield's **Ramsey Street** and Leichhardt's **Norton Street** provide two different slices of Sydney Italian life, while fans of Indian food are well served by the eateries that dot the length of **Cleveland Street**, dividing Redfern and Surry Hills. Vietnamese food is good and plentiful on **Marrickville Road** and **Illawarra Road** in Marrickville, but for a real slice of Saigon, head to **John Street**, Cabramatta. Petersham's **Little Audley Street** has the barbecued chickens and custard tarts of Portugal; the best Turkish pizzas and kebabs are found around **Auburn Road** in Auburn; the scent of *kimchi* announces the presence of a glut of Korean restaurants in **Campsie**; and **Hurstville, Ashfield** and **Chatswood** are home to Chinatowns that rival the city's original for bustle and diversity.

Wed, Thur, Sun; 5.30-10.30pm Fri, Sat. **Main courses** $26. **Licensed/BYO** (Tue-Thur only). **Credit** AmEx, BC, DC, MC, V. **French**
Oh, Balzac, how do we love thee? When counting the ways, factor in chef Matt Kemp's genius for combining and transforming cheaper ingredients into culinary gold, the loving service and the low-key refinement of the whole experience, from smart amuse-gueule soups to indulgent cheeses and dessert wines. The attention to detail in dishes such

Eat, Drink, Shop

as ballotine of rabbit foie gras and salsify with a salad of walnuts and sweetbreads is unflagging. Book well in advance – particularly if you're keen to try the super-cheap pre-cinema special: two courses and coffee for under $40 a head.

Modern Australian

Booker's

209 Glenmore Road, at Broughton Street, Paddington (9332 3328). Bus 380, L82. **Open** noon-3pm, 6.30-10pm Tue-Fri; 9am-3.30pm, 6.30pm-late Sat, Sun. **Main courses** $22-$29. **Licensed**. **Credit** AmEx, BC, DC, MC, V. **Map** p313 D4.
This newish addition to the neighbourhood is wholly dedicated to good food. Chef Jane Booth's dishes, such as the golden calves' sweetbreads with braised radicchio and hazelnuts, make Booker's the kind of place you'd like to eat at every day. And there's a great courtyard out the back too.

Bistro Moncur

Corner of Moncur & Queen Streets, Woollahra (9363 2519/www.woollahrahotel.com.au). Bus 378, 380, 382. **Open** 6-10.30pm Mon; noon-3pm, 6-10.30pm Tue-Sat; noon-3pm, 6-9pm Sun. **Main courses** $22.50-$39.90. **Licensed**. **Credit** AmEx, BC, DC, MC, V. **Map** p313 E4/5.
Bistro Moncur isn't as cheap as its name might suggest, but it is one of the finest examples of a smart-casual restaurant in Sydney that really gets it right, balancing near-boisterous conviviality with food that is as satisfying as it is seductive. Damien Pignolet is the god of (seemingly) simple things done well. Bistro classics such as Provençale fish soup with rouille, pork sausages with onions Lyonnaise

and sirloin steak with Café de Paris butter aren't just near-perfect – they're near-perfect every time.

Catalina

Lyne Park, off New South Head Road, Rose Bay (9371 0555/www.catalinarosebay.com.au). Ferry Rose Bay/bus 323, 324, 325. **Open** noon-11pm Mon-Sat; noon-6pm Sun. **Main courses** $25-$39. **Licensed**. **Credit** AmEx, BC, DC, MC, V.
Arriving by boat has a certain cachet, yes, but to really nail the sense of occasion nothing beats pulling up in a seaplane. Catalina is pricey, showy and not immune to occasional attitude attacks. That said, the juxtaposition of so-Sydney water views and superb wine is pretty special, and the food is pretty slick. Spanking-fresh slices of raw kingfish come dressed with sweet and sour onions, radish and pomegranate, while those troubled by the seafood bias will love the chargrilled beef tenderloin with potato rosti, bone marrow and red wine sauce.

Claude's

10 Oxford Street, between Queen Street & Jersey Road, Woollahra (9331 2325/www.claudes.org). Bus 380, L82. **Open** 7.30-9.30pm Tue-Sat. **Set menus** $125 3 courses; $150 8 courses. **Licensed/BYO**. **Map** p313 E4/5. **Credit** AmEx, BC, DC, MC, V.
Described by outsiders as Modern Australian and French, the type of cuisine served in this soigné, subdued terrace might better be termed Tim Pak Poy food for all the good it does the unfamiliar diner. The chef borrows freely from the Asian and European traditions he has mastered, yet never loses sight of each creation's internal logic. It's a parallel universe where grilled watermelon with mushrooms not only makes sense, but is sublimely appealing. Worth a visit.

The Boathouse on Blackwattle Bay.
See p158.

Eat, Drink, Shop

The Four in Hand Bistro

*Corner of Elizabeth & Sutherland Streets,
Paddington (9362 1999). Bus 380, L82.* **Open** 6.30-
10pm Mon-Thur; noon-2.30pm, 6.30-10pm Fri, Sat;
6.30-9pm Sun. **Main courses** $25. **Licensed**.
Credit AmEx, BC, DC, MC, V. **Map** p313 E4.
I SAID IT'S REALLY LOUD IN HERE, ISN'T IT?
That's one of the salient features of this pub dining
room. Another is the enormous painting of a squid
that takes up an entire wall. And the other is the food:
it's really outstanding, and much less expensive than
it should be. So there's the trade-off – divine eats or
easy conversation. We'll take the pigeon with salad
or the twice-cooked soufflé any day. Sign-language
has its advantages, right?

Hugo's

*70 Campbell Parade, at Lamrock Avenue, Bondi
Beach (9300 0900/www.hugos.com.au). CityRail
Bondi Junction then bus 380, 381, L82/bus 380,
L82.* **Open** 6.30pm-midnight Mon-Fri; 9am-4pm,
6.30pm-midnight Sat, Sun. **Main courses**
$30-$38. **Licensed**. **Credit** AmEx, BC, DC, MC, V.
Map p83.
Yes, it's him… and don't look now, but that's her
too. Yep, Hugo's is home to a capital-S scene. But
there is some substance under all that style: subtle-
ty isn't the kitchen's forte, but a little showiness is
to be expected with a clientele like this. Asian dishes, such as the Sichuan roasted duck and shiitake
omelette in duck broth, are definitely the way to go.
Also check out Hugo's Lounge (*see p136*), its sister
bar in Kings Cross.

The Light Brigade

*Corner of Oxford Street & Jersey Road, Woollahra
(9331 2930). Bus 380, L82.* **Open** 6pm-midnight

Tue-Thur; noon-3pm, 6pm-midnight Tue-Sat. **Main
courses** $26. **Licensed**. **Credit** AmEx, BC, DC,
MC, V. **Map** p313 E4/5.
The Light Brigade is definitely a leading example
of the renaissance of pub dining in this country. The
new pub bistro is all about simple food done well –
and is all the better for it. Start with oysters, natch,
then glide through entrées such as jasmine tea-
smoked trout, chorizo, boiled egg and baby cos
salad before hitting the well-priced mains, which
include excellent seared tuna with a bean cassoulet,
sausage and horseradish.

Sean's Panaroma

*270 Campbell Parade, at Ramsgate Avenue, Bondi
Beach (9365 4924). CityRail Bondi Junction then
bus 380, 381, L82/bus 380, L82.* **Open** noon-
3.30pm, 6.30-10pm Wed-Sat; noon-3.30pm Sun.
Main courses $37. **Licensed/BYO**. **Credit** BC,
MC, V. **Map** p83.
Picture an afternoon whiled away over a glass of
Viognier or three. A man striding through the small
tiled room in a dripping wetsuit barely causes a stir.
But the blackboard-menu special of lightly fried blue
swimmer crab with lime aïoli really sets tongues
wagging. Sean's is one of the most relaxed, charm-
ingly idiosyncratic restaurants in the world. Don't
miss it, and don't miss adjoining Aroma-to-Go,
which sells brilliant espresso and apple and rasp-
berry turnovers just like mum never made.

Seafood

Pier

*594 New South Head Road, opposite Cranbrook
Road, Rose Bay (9327 4187/www.pierrestaurant.
com.au). Bus 323, 324, 325.* **Open** noon-3pm,
6-10pm Mon-Sat; 6-9pm Sun. **Main courses** $37.
Licensed. **Credit** AmEx, BC, DC, MC, V.
Jutting into Rose Bay itself, Pier is so committed to
freshness that diners are submitted to a vaguely
alarming précis of preferred fish-killing techniques
on the menu. Those troubled by phrases like 'brain-
spiking' are best served by simply sampling chef
Greg Doyle's work. Witness, for example, the
incomparable texture of the salmon 'pastrami',
beautiful orangey-pink sheets of barely cured fillet
drizzled with oil and dotted with spice. And don't
miss dessert: the soufflés are a thing of beauty.

Inner West

African

Le Kilimanjaro

*280 King Street, between Erskineville Road & Brown
Street, Newtown (9557 4565). CityRail Newtown.*
Open 6-10pm Mon, Tue; noon-3pm, 6-10pm Wed-
Sun. **Main courses** $10-$12.50. **BYO**. **No credit
cards. Map** p104.
African food doesn't get a whole lot of play in
Sydney – quite possibly because it's usually done

very badly. But Le Kilimanjaro is one of the few restaurants well on its way to getting it right. Dishes come from all over the continent, but the cuisine – and decor – takes Senegal as its key cultural cue. And how often do you eat from wooden plates?

Asian

Dakhni
65 Glebe Point Road, between Francis & Cowper Streets, Glebe (9660 4887). Bus 413, 435, 436, 437, 438, 440, 461. **Open** 5-10.30pm Mon, Sun; noon-2.30pm, 5-10.30pm Tue-Thur; noon-2.30pm, 5-11.30pm Fri, Sat. **Main courses** $13.90-$16.90. **BYO. Credit** AmEx, BC, DC, MC, V. **Map** p311 A4. **South Indian**
Whether chatting over chaat or here to pay more attention to the warm spicing of dishes from the breadth of Tamil South India, diners are drawn to Dahkni's simple formula of homely food cooked with skill and served with care. Order the dosai – and the crunchy, yoghurty fun of the bel chaat, of course – and explore at will.

Faheem's Fast Food
196 Enmore Road, between Metropolitan & Edgware Roads, Enmore (9550 4850). CityRail Newtown. **Open** 5pm-midnight Mon-Sat; noon-midnight Sun. **Main courses** $4.90-$14. **Unlicensed. No credit cards. Indian/Pakistani**
Faheem may be the man, but we reckon it's Haleem that's responsible for all the repeat business. In a menu of brilliant halal and vegetarian subcontinental cheap treats, haleem – a Pakistani curry of four different kinds of lentils and boneless beef cooked to seriously flavoursome mush – still stands out. How many dishes earn a subtitle, much less one as high-falutin' as the King of Curries? Super cheap and open to midnight too.

European

La Disfida
109 Ramsay Street, at Kingston Road, Haberfield (9798 8299). Bus 436, 438, L38. **Open** 6-10.30pm Wed-Sun. **Main courses** $11-$15. **Licensed/BYO** (wine only). **Credit** BC, MC, V. **Pizza**
This is Sydney's best pizza restaurant. They don't suffer fools and their foolish ideas about pizza (half-and-halfs; thick crust; topping requests; anything involving pineapple) gladly, and their commitment to the shining and perfect idea of the thin, crisp, Neapolitan style of pizza is so strong that one bite will see bend you to their way of thinking.

Ecco
Drummoyne Sailing Club, 2 St Georges Crescent, at Drummoyne Wharf, Drummoyne (9719 9394/ www.ecco.com.au). Ferry Birkenhead Point/bus 506. **Open** noon-3pm, 6-10pm Tue-Sat. **Main courses** $23-$34. **Licensed. Credit** AmEx, BC, DC, MC, V. **Central Italian**
Slowly – very slowly – Australians are coming to understand that the food of Italy is not so much one cuisine, but an extremely diverse patchwork of inter-related provincial cultures, each with its own flavours and techniques. The tastes of central Italy are on offer in this authentic, waterside osteria, though they're interpreted freely. Thus the osso buco comes with gorgonzola-spiked pasta, while the stuffing for the zucchini flowers includes not only mozzarella but olives and sun-dried tomatoes.

Grappa
267-277 Norton Street, between William Street & City West Link, Leichhardt (9560 6090/ www.grappa.com.au). Bus 445, 446. **Open** 6-10pm Mon, Sat, Sun; noon-3pm, 6-10pm Tue-Fri. **Main courses** $19.50-$33. **Licensed/BYO** (wine only). **Credit** AmEx, BC, DC, MC, V. **Italian**
From toddlers sucking on strands of linguini with chilli and roasted tomato to couples exchanging looks over slices of pizza to tables of old whipper-snappers hoeing into the whole salt-baked snapper, punters of all ages and stripes find something to tempt on this barn-like restaurant's menu.

Lanzafàme
Corner of Ramsay & Dalhousie Streets, Haberfield (9716 9800). Bus 436, 437, 438. **Open** 6-10pm daily. **Main courses** $29-$35. **Licensed/BYO** (wine only). **Credit** BC, MC, V. **Southern Italian**
Haberfield is the latest inner-west European enclave to have been 'discovered' by the food hounds of the other suburbs. To the locals, the great Italian food isn't that much of a novelty. But what is new is a restaurant in the class of John Lanzafâme's elegant establishment. Pappardelle with rabbit? Yes! Guinea fowl with wild mushroom ragu? Hello. Consider the bar raised.

Peasant's Feast
121A King Street, between Missenden Road & Elizabeth Street, Newtown (9516 5998). CityRail Newtown. **Open** 6-10pm daily. **Main courses** $19.50-$25.50. **BYO. Credit** AmEx, V. **Map** p93. **Pan-European**
King Street's dining scene is a bit of a sham: restaurants, restaurants everywhere, but nothing good to eat. So it is that dining at the Feast comes as that much more pleasant a surprise: organic produce is brought to the fore, but flavour and presentation haven't become casualties to the kitchen's ideals. And it's well priced, too.

Perama
88 Audley Street, between New Canterbury Road & Trafalgar Street, Petersham (9569 7534/ www.perama.com.au). CityRail Petersham. **Open** 6-10pm Tue-Sat; 8am-3pm Sun. **Licensed/BYO**. **Main courses** $18-$28. **Greek**
The whitewash and retsina are all in place, yes, but there's something unusual about this Greek restaurant. That's right, it's the food: from Greek favourites such as falling-off-the-bone lamb or rabbit pie adventures in food history, like the Byzantine

original sense) specials, such as the honey-peppered figs, it's really interesting – and really good. Super-warm service, as well as the superb baklava ice-cream, seals the deal.

Il Piave

639 Darling Street, between Merton Street & Victoria Road, Rozelle (9810 6204). Bus 433, 434, 442, 445. **Open** 6-10pm Tue-Sat; noon-4pm Sun. **Main courses** $23.90-$28.90. **Licensed/BYO**. **Credit** AmEx, BC, DC, MC, V. **Northern Italian**
We think it might be Italian for 'clean lines and good service'. Or perhaps 'unpretentious food, full of life and good enough to eat every day'. Brush up on your Italian-language skills while grazing on the better-than-necessary bread and olives, then swoon over the fat scampi with radicchio and fennel, but be sure to leave some of the swooning and hand-waving for the outstanding desserts.

L'Unico

Corner of Darling & Elliott Streets, Balmain (9810 5466/www.lunico.com.au). Bus 433, 434, 442, 445. **Open** 6-10pm Mon, Tue, Sat; noon-3pm, 6-10pm Wed-Fri, Sun. **Main courses** $29-$38. **Licensed/ BYO** (Mon, Wed, Thur only). **Credit** AmEx, BC, DC, MC, V. **Italian**
How cool is this basement bar? And how cool too is Danny Russo's approach to Italian food. Richness is there for those who want it – yes, we're looking at you, zampone (stuffed pig's trotter) – while other dishes demonstrate the power of simplicity so central to many of Italy's great cuisines. *Molto bene.*

Zenith on Booth

37 Booth Street, at Nelson Street, Annandale (9660 6600). Bus 370, 470. **Open** 6.30-10.30pm Tue-Fri; noon-2.30pm, 6.30-10.30pm Sat. **Main courses** $29. **Licensed/BYO** (Tue-Thur only). **Credit** AmEx, BC, MC, V. **Italian**
So what if Mario Percuoco's dad Armando is one of the country's most famous (and mercurial) Italian restaurateurs. The people of Annandale have watched for too long while surrounding suburbs got all the great restaurants, and now that they've got one of their own they're not taking the pressure off for a second. They want their angel-hair pasta with asparagus and crab to be excellent every time, dammit. And Percuoco *fils*, it must be said, is giving them what they want.

Middle Eastern

Emma's on Liberty

Corner of Liberty & Gladstone Streets, Enmore (9550 3458). CityRail Newtown. **Open** 6-11pm Tue-Sat. **Main courses** $9-$14. **BYO. No credit cards.**

...ay which aspect of Emma's is ...he noise or the value. Smarter ...sted that the two may in fact be ...value of the Lebanese treats con-...' sense of conviviality, spurring

them to greater feats of volubility, not to mention volume. The dips here are a near religious experi-ence, and the *mjadra* has enough caramelised onion to do any Lebanese mum proud.

Fifi's

158 Enmore Road, between Metropolitan & Simmons Roads, Enmore (9550 4665). CityRail Newtown. **Open** 5.30pm-late Tue-Sun. **Main courses** $10-$15. **Licensed/BYO** (wine only). **Credit** AmEx, BC, DC, MC, V. **Lebanese**
It was sad to learn that Fifi's, so beloved of local couples and groups, had to discontinue its break-fast service. However, much as we miss the mind-altering coffee and the oh-so-refreshing slices of watermelon with halloumi, there's solace to be found in well-rendered classics in the cabbage roll, kebab and legume salad vein.

Modern Australian

Three Clicks West

127 Booth Street, between Johnston & Annandale Streets, Annandale (9660 6652/www.threeclicks west.com.au). Bus 370, 470. **Open** 6.30-10.30pm Mon-Sat. **Main courses** $28. **Licensed/BYO** (Mon-Wed only). **Credit** AmEx, BC, DC, MC, V.
That's three clicks from the city's centre – not that you'd be able to tell from such an urbane menu: the crystal-clear beef consommé with braised oxtail dumpling and black beignet effortlessly walks the tightrope between hearty and chic. Service and pricing definitely hint at the suburban location, but in a good way, being warmer and more reasonable, respectively, than what you'd expect in their east-ern counterparts.

Welcome Hotel

91 Evans Street, between Nelson & Merton Streets, Rozelle (9810 1323). Bus 432, 433, 434, 440, 500, 502, 504. **Open** noon-3pm, 6-10pm daily. **Main courses** *Bar* $13-$19.90; *Restaurant* $24-$29. **Licensed. Credit** AmEx, BC, DC, MC, V.
The chef's Irish, much of the beer is English, the food's modern Australian – and having a schooner and a bite under the trees in the tidy backyard beer garden is pure Sydney. Servings are big, the service friendly and prices fair to boot. Scallops with creamed leeks share a menu with Peking duck and coriander noodles as comfortably as the boys and girls at the bar lift their arms on a long afternoon.

Seafood

The Boathouse on Blackwattle Bay

Blackwattle Bay end of Ferry Road, Glebe (9518 9011/www.bluewaterboathouse.com.au). Bus 431, 432, 433, 434, 370. **Open** noon-3pm, 6.30-10.30pm Tue-Sun. **Main courses** $42-$45. **Licensed. Credit** AmEx, BC, DC, MC, V. **Map** p311 A3.
It's all about the oysters. Order lots of them – there are typically at least six kinds – and lash out on

Eat, Drink, Shop

Take a wok

'This girl likes small things,' says **Kylie Kwong**, sitting in the window seat of **Billy Kwong** (*see p146*), the modestly sized Surry Hills restaurant she opened in 1999. 'With Billy Kwong I wanted to make a little place that was run on heart and soul. It's about doing what you love and doing what you know you can do well, expressing all your passions. I want it to be on the cutting edge – I like originality and creativity, and I don't like to follow fads or fashions.'
Fashion, however, follows Kwong.

Thanks to a high-profile ABC TV series in 2003 (*Kylie Kwong: Heart and Soul*) and two cookery books, she's Australia's latest celebrity chef. A tall, striking woman in her mid 30s, Kwong is in many ways a typical Sydney success story. Born and bred in Sydney to a fourth-generation Chinese-Australian family, her laid-back but passionate approach has won her acclaim in one of the most male-dominated of professions – and she's named after the country's most famous export.

Her brand of urban Asian food is at once lighter and fresher than the old-school cuisines, yet true to its (mostly Cantonese) roots. 'All the dishes here are based on traditional Chinese recipes,' says Kwong, 'but they're termed modern because of my upbringing in Australia and the time I spent working with [famed Modern Australian chef] Neil Perry at Rockpool and with [leading Sydney Italian restaurateur] Stefano Manfredi.'

She cites the crisp-skinned duck with fresh orange sauce as a good example: 'The duck is treated in a very Cantonese way, marinated in Sichuan pepper and salt, then steamed and then deep-fried – that use of multiple cooking methods is very Chinese. Then it's teamed with this modern sauce, which is sort of Thai with fish sauce and lime juice, and then either oranges or

blood plums, and then back to Chinese with star anise and cinnamon.'

The best Sydney food, Kwong says, is all about spontaneity. 'We're surrounded by this great produce, and it results in a very fast, fresh style of food. You don't want to cover up flavours or cook the ingredients very much,' she explains. Certainly, Kwong – and her restaurant – make a fine example of the city at its best.

some quality bubbles. Now marvel at their freshness, their diverse tastes and textures, how well they go with brown bread and champagne – and at the unique glory of this most relaxing of top-tier Sydney restaurants. Crab, flown in fresh from the Northern Territory, gets minimal mucking about, cracked and tossed in a wok just long enough and with just enough salt, pepper and spring onion to bring out the meat's clean sweetness. Saturday lunches don't come much more pleasant than this.

South-east Asian

Bay Tinh
318 Victoria Road, at Marrickville Road, Marrickville (9560 8673). CityRail Marrickville or Sydenham.
Open 11.30am-2pm, 5.30-10.30pm Mon-Fri, Sun; 4.30-11pm Sat. **Main courses** $9.25-$11.70. **BYO.**
Credit BC, MC, V. **Vietnamese**
In his former line of work cooking for the prime minister of Vietnam, chef Tinh was no doubt accustomed

Hot stuff at **Bay Tinh**. *See p159.*

to serving big groups; a good thing, for the stunning value for money offered by his stalwart Marrickville restaurant is a magnet for groups, discerning and otherwise. All order the bonfire dishes (nothing makes the half-drunk happier than food that's on fire), all leave full of gullet and relatively fat of wallet.

WildEast Dreams

102 Norton Street, between Marion & Parramatta Road, Leichhardt (9560 4131/www.wildeast dreams.com). Bus 436, 437, 438, 440, 445, 470, L38. **Open** 6-10pm Tue-Fri; noon-3pm, 6-10pm Sat, Sun. **Licensed**. **Credit** AmEx, BC, DC, MC, V. **South-east Asian**
Irritating, early '90s name, it's true. But the name is kinda fitting, considering the nerve it took owner Albert Wong to open a glam South-east Asian restaurant in this most Italian of neighbourhoods. The restaurant also pulls off that rarest of tricks – the ginger soup with black sesame dumplings actually constitutes an Asian dessert worth ordering. Not only is the restaurant a hit, but lucky diners occasionally have the pleasure of witnessing Wong tinkling the ivories of the centrepiece grand piano.

Vegetarian

Iku Wholefood Kitchen

25A Glebe Point Road, between Parramatta Road & Francis Street, Glebe (9692 8720). Bus 370, 431, 432, 433, 434. **Open** 11.30am-9pm Mon-Fri; 11am-8pm Sat; noon-7.30pm Sun. **Main courses** $7-$9. **BYO**. **No credit cards**. **Map** p311 A4. **Vegan**
Vegetarians, vegans, macro-eaters and other diet-conscious individuals flock to Iku's sharp-looking establishments in search of nourishment that is entirely vegetable in origin. Pleasing tastes and textures don't always rule the day, but specialities such as the lime leaf curry laksa and the rice balls have dedicated followings.

Other locations: 62 Oxford Street, Darlinghurst (9380 9780); 168 Military Road, Neutral Bay (9953 1964); 279 Bronte Road, Waverley (9369 5022); 612A Darling Street, Rozelle (9810 5155).

Asian

Kam Fook Chatswood

Level 6, Westfield Shoppingtown, entrance on Help Street, Chatswood (9413 9388). CityRail Chatswood. **Open** 10am-11pm daily. **Main courses** $5.80-$24.80. **Licensed/BYO**. **Credit** DC, MC, V. **Cantonese**
Despite its size – being marginally smaller than a middling football stadium – the Kam Fook manages to offer personalised service that is so condescending to *gweilos* that you'll be tempted to salute their efficiency. Argue, instead, with your waiter, that you'd like to see the *real* specials list, and stand firm until they acquiesce and bring you some of the most authentic Cantonese food in the land.

Mino

521 Military Road, between Gurrigal & Harbour Streets, Mosman (9960 3351). Bus 143, 144, 151, 228, 289, 230, 243, 246, 247, 257. **Open** 6-10pm Tue-Sun. **Main courses** $24-$55. **Licensed/BYO**. **Credit** AmEx, BC, MC, V. **Japanese**
Military Road's many Japanese eateries range from very ordinary mass-market sushi joints to the well-hidden charms of this little restaurant. Not much to look at from the outside, Mino is nonetheless quite nice once you're through the door – and though the à la carte options are wide-ranging, regulars all seem happy to put their faith in the chef's *kaiseki* menu.

Nilgiri's

81-83 Christie Street, between Pacific Highway & Oxley Street, St Leonards (9966 0636/ www.nilgiris.com.au). CityRail St Leonards. **Open** noon-3pm, 6-10pm daily. **Main courses** $20-$26. **Licensed/BYO** (wine only). **Credit** AmEx, BC, MC, V. **Pan-Indian**
The recipient of the *Sydney Morning Herald's* award for best Indian restaurant 2004, Nilgiri's takes dishes from all over India and imbues them with the its trademark refinement and elegance of spicing. The owners' commitment to educating Sydneysiders in the best that Indian dining has to offer is to be heartily commended.

Sea Treasure

46 Willoughby Road, at Falcon Street, Crows Nest (9906 6388). Bus 257, 273, 288, 289, 290, 291, 292. **Open** 11am-3pm, 5.30-11pm Mon-Fri; 10am-3pm, 5.30-11pm Sat, Sun. **Main courses** $18.50-$32. **Yum cha** $3.80-$19.80. **Licensed/BYO**. **Credit** AmEx, BC, MC, V. **Cantonese**
Those tanks aren't there for show: seafood – surprise, surprise – is the Treasure's area of expertise. Fat Pacific oysters come steamed on the shell with XO sauce, flounder gets the salt-and-pepper treatment,

while Murray cod finds itself steamed delicately and doused in ginger and shallot. Wok that booty. Winner of the *SMH*'s best Chinese gong in 2004.

Ying's

270 Willoughby Road, between Bruce & Shirley Roads, Crows Nest (9966 9182). Bus 257, 273, 288, 289, 290, 291, 292. **Open** 11am-3pm, 6-11pm daily. **Main courses** $25-$35. **Licensed/BYO**. **Credit** AmEx, BC, DC, MC, V. **Cantonese**
One of the first Cantonese restaurants in Sydney to break the surly-waiter barrier, Ying's owes much of its success to owner Ying Tam's unerring sense of hospitality and willingness to concede that great Cantonese food needn't be served by tight-lipped automatons in garish yet run-down barns. The seafood banquet demonstrates the menu's highlights, including the pipis (clams) in Chiu Chow-style broth, and what appear to be the world's largest and most succulent salt-and-pepper prawns.

European

Brasserie Bit

12 Waters Lane, between Grosvenor Street & Grosvenor Lane, Neutral Bay (9953 9999). Bus 247, 263. **Open** noon-3pm, 6-10pm Mon-Sat. **Main courses** $16-$27. **Licensed/BYO**. **Credit** AmEx, BC, DC, MC, V. **German**
German beer is great, but the poor reputation of the food of the Fatherland has largely been maintained by the food of the Fatherland. Chef Lothar Winkler sees beyond the stodge, however, making the Teut accent sing in cured Tasmanian salmon with roe and avocado, the grilled Nurnburger sausages on rosti, not to mention the slow-roasted duck with cinnamon plums, red cabbage and cranberries. And the beer really is something.

Cala Luna

235 Spit Road, at Quakers Road, Mosman (9968 2426). Bus 169, 175, 178, L80. **Open** 6-9pm Tue-Sat. **Main courses** $25-$36. **Licensed/BYO** (wine only). **Credit** AmEx, BC, DC, MC, V. **Sardinian**
One of very few Italian restaurants in Sydney willing to specialise in the cuisine of a single region – in this case, Sardinia – what this bustling tratt doesn't have in the way of views and chichi interiors it more than makes up for with such Sardinian favourites as spaghetti alla bottarga and roast suckling pig.

Carabella

3 Broughton Street, at Bligh Street, Kirribilli (9954 6015). CityRail/ferry Milsons Point. **Open** 8am-4pm Mon, Sun; 8am-10pm Tue-Sat. **Main courses** $25-$55. **BYO**. **Credit** BC, MC, V. **Spanish**
Where most other Spanish restaurants in Sydney flounder in a slurry of cheap wine and cheaper and nastier tapas, Carabella is distinguished by the tastes of sherry vinegar, fine anchovies, *jamón* and other pleasures of Iberian cuisine. The decor is as fresh as the menu – the waiters only more so.

Modern Australian

Aqua Dining

North Sydney Pool, corner of Paul & Northcliff Streets, North Sydney (9964 9998/www.aqua dining.com.au). CityRail/ferry Milsons Point. **Open** noon-2.30pm, 6-10pm Sat; noon-2.30pm, 6-10.30pm Mon-Fri, Sun. **Main courses** $34-$42. **Licensed**. **Credit** AmEx, BC, DC, MC, V.
Aussies with childhood memories of standing barefoot and dripping by the deep end, while clutching a meat pie slathered in tomato sauce, may be thrown by the setting of this hip diner. But there's something very appealing about looking out over North Sydney's lovely Olympic pool and across the harbour as you dine. In place of chlorine-scented sausage rolls, Aqua Dining offers a Milanese-style veal cutlet on a salad of marinated feta, aubergine, olives, lemon and rocket, or breast of duck with potato gallette, chanterelles and savoy cabbage.

Bathers' Pavilion

4 The Esplanade, between Awaba Street & Mandolong Road, Balmoral Beach (9969 5050/ www.batherspavilion.com.au). Ferry Taronga Zoo then bus 238/ferry Mosman South then bus 233. **Open** *Restaurant* noon-2.30pm, 6.30-9.30pm daily. *Café* 7am-late daily. **Set menus** *Restaurant* $90 2 courses; $110 3 courses. **Main courses** *Café* $13-$20. **Licensed**. **Credit** AmEx, BC, DC, MC, V.
Serge Dansereau is one of the big men of Australian cuisine. Big, that is, in terms of his contribution to Sydney dining, helping to usher in the idea of seasonality and an Australian style of cooking (not to mention numerous individual ingredients) – and this beautiful beachside restaurant highlights the best of his philosophy. Seared scallops snuggle up to beef-cheek ravioli in a barely-there ginger-soy sauce, demonstrating Dansereau's light touch and mastery of Asian flavours, while the veal rack with wild mushrooms, pomme purée and spinach shows the part provincial European simplicity plays.

Milsons

Corner of Broughton & Willoughby Streets, Kirribilli (9955 7075/www.milsonsrestaurant.com.au). CityRail Milsons Point. **Open** noon-3pm, 6-9.30pm Mon-Thur; noon-3pm, 6-10.30pm Fri; 6-10.30pm Sat. **Main courses** $30-$36. **Licensed/BYO**. **Credit** AmEx, BC, DC, MC, V.
We've yet to see the prime minister duck in for a bite, but his residence is so close he'd be a fool (ahem) not to delve into this sexy restaurant to get a taste of what his more food-savvy constituents are spending their tax-breaks on. Seafood and Asian flavours are handled with particular grace.

Tables

1047 Pacific Highway, between Telegraph & Gandview Streets, Pymble (9983 1047). CityRail Pymble. **Open** noon-2.30pm, 6-9.30pm Mon-Fri; 6-9.30pm Sat. **Main courses** $27; $48 (2 courses). **Licensed/BYO** (wine only). **Credit** AmEx, BC, DC, MC, V.

Manly Wharf Hotel. *See p163.*

Our theory is that the creative energy the Tables team conserved coming up with the name, they wisely channelled into the menu. Slow-braised pork belly arrives with seared scallops, chilli jam and a pool of the beautifully aromatic, star anise-spiked braising liquor. The technicolour decor we can only put down to a rash burst of exuberance – happily, everything that appears on the plates exhibits a more even aesthetic temper.

Seafood

Garfish
Corner of Burton & Broughton Street, Kirribilli (9922 4322). CityRail/ferry Milsons Point. **Open** 7.30am-11am, noon-3pm, 6-9.30pm Mon-Thur; 7.30am-11am, noon-3pm, 6-10pm Fri, Sat; 7.30am-11am, noon-3pm, 6-8.30pm Sun. **Main courses** $22-$28. **Licensed/BYO** (wine only). **Credit** AmEx, BC, MC, V.
These guys are really into their fish. Working hand-in-hand with one of Sydney's leading seafood suppliers, the focus is on freshness. And it's great to see the fish choice going beyond the usual clichés of salmon and tuna. Try the likes of aromatic kingfish curry with aubergine pickle or choose one of the day's catch from the blackboard, select a cooking method and garnish and await satisfaction.

South American

Vera Cruz
314 Military Road, between Winnie & Langley Avenue, Cremorne (9904 5818). Bus 247, 263. **Open** 6-10pm Mon-Sat. **Main courses** $26.50. **Licensed/BYO**. **Credit** AmEx, BC, MC, V.
Mexican
'True Cross', maybe, but it's still not true Mexican cuisine – that great gap in the Australian culinary landscape. But the food on offer at this very-designer boîte isn't aiming for authenticity so much as a crowd-pleasing lightness and clarity of flavour – no bad thing, either. A couple of *cervezas, por favor*, don't go astray, for that matter.

Northern Beaches

Asian

Avalon Chinese Restaurant
74 Old Barrenjoey Road, at Avalon Parade, Avalon (9918 6319). Bus 190. **Open** 11am-3pm Mon-Sat; 5-10pm Sun. **Main courses** $12.80-$19.80. **Licensed/BYO**. **Credit** AmEx, BC, DC, MC, V.
Cantonese
Avalon is not the first place you'd go looking for a Cantonese restaurant, but once you've seen past the déshabillé arcade setting to the so-bad-it's-great, gold-and-red flocked Asian-print wallpaper, you won't look back. Nothing beats the salt-and-pepper squid after a big day in the surf.

European

Alhambra Cafe & Tapas Bar
54 West Esplanade, opposite Manly Wharf,
Manly (9976 2975). Ferry Manly. **Open** noon-3pm,
6-10.30pm Mon-Fri; noon-5pm, 6-10.30pm Sat, Sun.
Main courses $18-$24. *Tapas* $5-$10.50. **Licensed.**
Credit AmEx, BC, DC, MC, V. **Map** p104.
Moroccan/Spanish
Moorish by theme, moreish by nature, this loud, fun
restaurant in Manly does a kickin' line in tapas, as
well as richly spiced tagines, fluffy jewelled cous-
cous and luscious b'stilla (chicken pie). The outdoor
seating and wild flamenco on Saturday nights only
serve to up the ante.

Bistro Marlo
11 Wentworth Street, between South Steyne &
Darley Road, Manly (9976 0800). Ferry Manly.
Open 6-10pm Mon, Tue; noon-3pm, 6-10pm Wed-
Sun. **Main courses** $26.50-$29.50. **Licensed/BYO**
(wine only). **Credit** AmEx, BC, MC, V. **French**
Chef and restaurateur Mark Armstrong should, by
rights, have a street named after him for all the work
he's done at his previous restaurants to redress the
imbalance of fine food north and south of the bridge.
His latest enterprise is no less popular, turning heads
with its tender tripe and provincial salads.

Modern Australian

Jonah's
69 Bynya Road, between Norma & Surf Road,
Palm Beach (9974 5599/www.jonahs.com.au).
Bus 190, L90. **Open** noon-3pm, 6.30pm-late Mon-
Tue; 6.30pm-late Wed-Sun. **Main courses** $36.
Licensed. Credit AmEx, BC, DC, MC, V.
The room isn't super-special, but the setting, overlooking Whale Beach, is hard to beat. The smart
money is on renting a room (yes, it's a hotel too) with
an ocean view, ordering the barbecued king prawns
with fennel, aïoli and garlic toast, and maybe the
grilled snapper fillet with mussel and clam bouill-
abaisse, trawling your way through as much of the
excellent wine list as possible, and then retiring
upshtairsh for a well-earned resht. You can even fly
here by seaplane (*see p52*) if you have the dosh.

Manly Wharf Hotel
Manly Wharf, East Esplanade, Manly (9977 1266/
www.manlywharfhotel.com.au). Ferry Manly. **Open**
11am-12.30am Mon-Sat; 11am-10pm Sun. **Main**
courses $28. **Licensed. Credit** AmEx, BC, DC,
MC, V. **Map** p104.
The newly slick Manly Wharf development is a
divine place to meet for a drink (*see p138*), but it's
also a really lovely spot to rendezvous for more solid
sustenance. While the steaks and pastas are good,
the seafood is, fittingly enough for the waterside
location, a big highlight. You can choose from the
fish grill dishes – snapper with tomato, lemon and
basil, say – or just go the whole hog and opt for the
enormous seafood platter.

Parramatta & the West

Asian

Shun Tak Inn
Corner of Macquarie & Marsden Streets,
Parramatta (9635 8128). CityRail Parramatta.
Open 10am-midnight daily. **Main courses** $25-$30.
Licensed/BYO. Credit AmEx, BC, DC, MC, V.
Cantonese
Let's hear it for the Singapore-style crab. Not only
does it come in a beautifully tomatoey chilli sauce
that will have you licking your fingers, it is accom-
panied by the traditional steamed buns to sop up the
juices. Score! The yum cha, too, will have you in
thrall to the kitchen.
Other locations: 138 Church Street, Parramatta
(9635 8130).

Woodland's
67 George Street, between Horwood Place &
Parramatta Mall, Parramatta (9633 3838). CityRail
Parramatta. **Open** 11.30am-2.30pm, 6-9.30pm daily.
Main courses $11-$18. **Licensed/BYO. Credit**
AmEx, BC, DC, MC, V. **South Indian**
Consider the masala dosai: is there a bigger commonly available foodstuff? And why hasn't anybody
invented plates big enough not to be dwarfed by
these vast, crisp, southern Indian pancakes? You
may not find any answers here, but you will find
blissfully light examples of the dosai genre.
Other locations: 238 George Street, Liverpool
(9734 9949).

Middle Eastern

Summerland
457 Chapel Street, between Ricard & French
Streets, Bankstown (9708 5107). CityRail
Bankstown. **Open** noon-10.30pm daily. **Main**
courses $13-$18. **Licensed/BYO** (wine only).
Credit AmEx, BC, MC, V. **Lebanese**
Thirty-five bucks and a big appetite will take you
far at this most hospitable of Lebanese restaurants.
One of its many draw-cards (apart from the sheer
volume of food comprising its banquets) is a focus
on seafood. It goes well beyond the usual whitebait,
which is something not commonly seen in Lebanese
eateries in Australia, and an asset factor we'd love
to see emulated elsewhere.

South-east Asian

Pho An
27 Greenfield Parade, between Chapel Road & Neville
Lane, Bankstown (9796 7826). CityRail Bankstown.
Open 7am-9pm daily. **Main courses** $8.70-$10.40.
Unlicensed. No credit cards. Vietnamese
There's plenty of dissent over who does what best
in the world of Sydney Vietnamese restaurants. But
not when it comes to phô. The beef noodle soup (and
the chicken version, for that matter) dispensed at

Eat, Drink, Shop

this Bankstown landmark is the very coriander-accented nectar of the gods, and the toppings, from steak slices (prosaic) to wobbly bits (exciting), are without peer.

Tan Viet

95 John Street, between Railway Parade & Hill Street, Cabramatta (9727 6853). CityRail Cabramatta. **Open** 8.30am-7pm daily. **Main courses** $8.50-$9.50. **BYO. No credit cards.** Vietnamese

The poultry versions of phô, the great Vietnamese soup, tend to be overshadowed by the beef style that is the nation's lifeblood. But not here: chicken gets celebrated in soup as well as some very fine fried incarnations, while the duck phô is a rare treat.

Temasek

Roxy Arcade, 71 George Street, between Holwood Place & Smith Street, Parramatta (9633 9926). CityRail Parramatta. **Open** 11.30am-2.30pm, 5.30-9.30pm Tue-Sun. **Main courses** $10-$22. **BYO. Credit** AmEx, BC, DC, MC, V. **Malaysian**

Long held to be the purveyor of Sydney's finest curry laksa, this plastic-tableclothed palace also takes top honours in the beef rendang and Hainan chicken stakes. Call ahead for house specialities such as fish-head curry and chilli crab.

Thanh Binh

52 John Street, between Railway Parade & Smith Street, Cabramatta (9727 9729). CityRail Cabramatta. **Open** 9am-9pm daily, **Main courses** $8-$30. **BYO. No credit cards.** Vietnamese

John Street is full of buzzy Vietnamese restaurants, but Angie Hong's Thanh Binh is pretty much universally accepted as the mothership. The choice is typically broad, but, atypically, almost everything on the menu is interesting, with many dishes unique to this one establishment. The other branches fight the good fight, but the original is still best. **Other locations:** 111 King Street, Newtown (9557 1175); 33 Arthur Street, Cabramatta (9724 9633).

Turkish

Sahara

Burwood Shopping Plaza, 101 Burwood Road, Burwood (9747 5440). CityRail Burwood. **Open** 8am-midnight daily. **Main courses** $9-$28. **Licensed/BYO. Credit** AmEx, BC, DC, MC, V.

Is this the fanciest kebab shop in town? It's certainly the only one with textured walls and other glam architectural quirks. The kitchen's no slouch, either – there's not a lot that will be unfamiliar to dabblers in local Turkish fare, but the quality is top-notch.

Sofra

Corner of Auburn Road & Queen Street, Auburn (9649 9299). CityRail Auburn. **Open** 7am-midnight daily. **Main courses** $8-$16. **Unlicensed. No credit cards.**

In the very Turkish suburb of Auburn, on the very Turkish strip of Auburn Road, just a stone's throw from the mosque, is this very Turkish eaterie. Forget

rugs on the walls and bellydancers – the look here is tiles, backlit pictures of food and fluoro strips – Sofra's cred is down to its very good charcoal-grilled kebabs and fluffy pide. And the baklava rocks.

The South

Asian

Ocean King House

Corner of Princes Highway & English Street, Kogarah (9587 3511). CityRail Carlton. **Open** 11am-3pm, 5.30-10.30pm daily. **Main courses** $12-$28. **Licensed/BYO. Credit** AmEx, BC, DC, MC, V. **Cantonese**

The best yum cha, say many clued-up Sydneysiders, is no longer necessarily to be found in Chinatown, but in suburban restaurants like this. The stunning diversity of dishes on offer in this former mansion (the fried dough-stick in rice noodle sheets is tops) and their overall quality lends weight to that argument, while the juicy mud crab in XO sauce with vermicelli is an excellent reason to come after dark.

European

Chez Pascal

250 Rocky Point Road, at Ramsgate Road, Ramsgate (9529 5444). Bus 302, 303. **Open** 7-9.30pm Tue-Sat. **Main courses** $15.50-$24. **BYO. Credit** DC, MC, V. **French**

Hankering for some old-school French fun? Make a beeline for Chez Pascal: in a room decorated with murals of a can-can chorus line you can indulge in gloriously unreconstructed coq au vin, super-rich saucisson Lyonnaise and garlic-laden snails. Crêpes Normande to finish are, of course, mandatory.

Middle Eastern

La Roche

61-67 Haldon Street, Lakemba (9759 9257). CityRail Lakemba. **Open** 9am-10pm daily. **Main courses** $4-$11. **Unlicensed. No credit cards.** Lebanese

Right in the heart of Lebanese Sydney you'll find some very authentic eateries. Simplicity is the order of the day at La Roche (the name reflects Lebanon's high ratio of French speakers) and everything is cheap, fresh and, uh, cheap.

Modern Australian

Les Trois Freres

16 Princes Highway, between Belgrave Esplanade & Clare Street, Sylvania (9544 7609). Bus 477. **Open** 6-10pm Tue-Sat. **Main courses** $25-$27. **BYO. Credit** AmEx, BC, DC, MC, V.

The Three Brothers have been largely responsible for holding the culinary fort in this neck of the woods for several years. And what a job they do: the food isn't, as you may have thought, French in origin, but it is worth a detour, not least for the value.

Shops & Services

Spend, spend, spend – Sydney is serious about shopping.

Since the 2000 Olympics, downtown Sydney has undergone a shopping transformation. Gone are the dingy arcades and lacklustre shops, replaced by sophisticated revamps designed to keep Sydney's population of new trendsetters satisfied. The **CBD** is shopping central. A maze of arcades, both above and below ground, will take you from the corner of Bathurst and Kent Streets through to Town Hall Square and on, connecting George, Pitt and Market Streets. Each mall has its own character and style, but all are extremely busy. The major department stores are **David Jones** (see p166) and **Grace Bros** (see p166), both on Market Street. For traditional souvenirs, duty-free and a taste of historic Sydney, head for the **Rocks**, where shopping and sightseeing go hand in hand.

While out-of-towners may gravitate to the city, those in the know make for Oxford Street, **Paddington**, the true heart of Sydney's fashion scene. Paddo locals avoid their area on Saturdays because of the crowds visiting the popular crafts market. Further down Oxford Street, in **Darlinghurst**, the shops reflect the area's role as the centre of queer Sydney with fetish gear, wig shops and diverse bookshops. In Crown Street you'll find offbeat clothing stores and lots of restaurants.

The well-heeled eastern suburbs mob shop in **Woollahra**'s Queen Street for antiques and pastries, and **Double Bay** for middle-of-the-road designer fashion and a long lunch. On the north shore it's the Military Road stretch in **Neutral Bay** and **Mosman** where there are homewares, kids' clothes, classic fashion and everything a middle-class family could need.

On the west side of the CBD lie the suburbs of Balmain, Rozelle, Leichhardt and Glebe, all offering surprisingly different shopping experiences. The water-end section of Darling Street is **Balmain**'s main drag and caters for the area's funky, upwardly mobile young families. Further up the street in **Rozelle** the shops change gear with interesting bric-a-brac stores and organic produce. In **Leichhardt**, revel in Italian fashion on Norton Street and at the delightful new **Italian Forum** complex (see p167) of shops and eateries. Backpacker-friendly Glebe Point Road in **Glebe** has numerous second-hand booksellers amid cafés, pubs and health food shops. King Street in studenty, multicultural **Newtown** is home to quirky furniture shops, great vinyl outlets and loads of vintage clothing shops.

Over on **Bondi Beach** and **North Bondi**, the shopping vibe is very laid-back with an emphasis on surf gear, swimwear, body art and vintage clothing. Busy Oxford Street and its surrounding streets in nearby **Bondi Junction** is entirely different, and currently undergoing massive construction work. Shops here are geared towards budget-conscious families; this is the place to find cheap second-hand furniture and electrical goods.

International fashion is hugely popular, with many big names represented in Sydney. But don't miss some of the local talent – see p176 **Home goan**. Duty-free shopping abounds, particularly in the heart of the CBD. Head for the cavernous **Downtown Duty Free**, which occupies the whole basement level

The best Shops

For clothes that mamas and papas used to wear
Rokit (see p179); Puf'n Stuff (see p178).

For a novel way to take your latte
Berkelouw Book Sellers (see p171); Sappho Books (see p172); Kinokuniya (see p167 The Galeries Victoria).

For sounds for the cool set
Central Station Records (see p189); Red Eye (see p189).

For bags of style
bondi beach bag co (see p179); Quick Brown Fox (see p179); Skipping Girl (see p173).

For Eastern promise
Cambodia House (see p189); Ginseng Bathhouse (see p188); Made in Japan (see p187); Taka Tea Garden (see p186).

For tasty picnic treats
David Jones (see p166); Delicacies on King (see p182); Provedoré Pelagios (see p183).

Eat, Drink, Shop

Even the food is beautiful at **David Jones**.

of the Strand Arcade (*see p169*) – make sure you take your travel documents. For Australiana, *see p184* **Only in Oz**.

OPENING HOURS

Shops open between 9am and 10am and close between 5.30pm and 6pm Monday to Friday, except for Thursday when most mainstream shopping areas stay open until around 9pm. On Saturday most places tend to shut pretty sharpish between 5pm and 6pm. Sunday trading is the norm but hours vary quite a bit. Most shops tend to be open between 11am and 4pm, or 5pm in the summer.

Sale time is usually at the end of summer and winter, but department stores also hold sales to coincide with public holidays. The big ones to watch out for are David Jones's twice-yearly clearance at the end of June and after Christmas, and Grace Bros' Boxing Day sale.

What you see on the price tag is what you pay; it includes GST (Goods & Services Tax). For details of how to reclaim your GST when you fly out, *see p290*.

One-stop shopping

Department stores

David Jones

Market Street, at Castlereagh Street; Elizabeth Street, at Market Street, CBD (9266 5544/ www.davidjones.com.au). CityRail Martin Place, St James or Town Hall/Monorail City Centre.
Open 9.30am-6pm Mon-Wed, Fri; 9.30am-9pm Thur; 9am-6pm Sat; 11am-5pm Sun. **Credit** AmEx, BC, DC, MC, V. **Map** p311 C3.

Undoubtedly Sydney's most beautiful place to shop, DJ is the world's oldest department store still trading under its original name. It was opened in 1838, just 50 years after colonisation, by Welsh-born immigrant David Jones. It's famous for its stylish window displays, and locals like the natty black and white dogtooth-check carrier bags. The flagship city store is on two sites linked by a first-floor walkway. The Market Street store has three floors of men's wear, plus furniture, homewares and electrical goods. The food hall on the lower ground floor has just been revamped with fabulous results. Upmarket cosmetics and perfumes, together with jewellery and accessories, are on the ground floor of the Elizabeth Street store. Above are four floors of women's fashion, including international designers.
Other locations: Westfield Bondi Shopping Centre, 500 Oxford Street, Bondi Junction (9619 1111); Westfield Shopping Centre, Argyle & Marsden Streets, Parramatta (9841 3555); see website for other suburban locations.

Grace Bros

436 George Street, at Market Street, CBD (9238 9111/www.gracebros.com.au). CityRail St James or Town Hall/Monorail City Centre. **Open** 9am-6pm Mon-Wed, Fri, Sat; 9am-9pm Thur; 11am-5pm Sun. **Credit** AmEx, BC, DC, MC, V. **Map** p311 B3.

The addictive televison ad coos 'my store, Grace Bro-o-thers', which is exactly what this eight-floor department store in the heart of the CBD aims to be – something for every family member. It's not as exclusive as DJ's, but it's still a pretty slick opera-

tion. There are seven floors plus a mezzanine, and the perfume department is unrivalled. It also boasts a whole floor devoted to computers and gadgets. **Other locations**: Westfield Bondi Shopping Centre, 500 Oxford Street, Bondi Junction (9387 0222); 159-175 Church Street, Parramatta (9891 2222); see website for other suburban locations.

Peter's of Kensington

57 Anzac Parade, between Todman Avenue & Alison Road, Kensington (9662 1099/www.peters ofkensington.com.au). Bus 390, 391, 392, 393, 394, 395, 396, 397, 398, 399. **Open** 9.30am-5.30pm Mon-Fri; 9.30am-5pm Sat. **Credit** AmEx, BC, DC, MC, V.

Just look for the bubblegum pink building on Anzac Parade a couple of streets from Royal Randwick racecourse and you'll find an old-fashioned emporium of household items, quality collectibles, luggage, trad children's toys, mumsy European cosmetics (Crabtree & Evelyn) and even top-notch fountain pens and cigar cases. And prices are far lower than you'd expect in a classy city department store.

Shopping centres

Chifley Plaza

2 Chifley Square, corner of Hunter & Phillip Streets, CBD (9221 6111/www.chifleyplaza.com.au). CityRail Martin Place. **Map** p310 C2.

A chic, New York-style tower in the business district housing designer labels such as MaxMara, Pierucci, Leona Edmiston (*see p173*) – and the reason most people come here: Tiffany & Co. Food outlets include excellent Japanese restaurant Azuma.

The Galeries Victoria

500 George Street, at Park Street, CBD (9265 6888/ www.tgv.com.au). CityRail Town Hall/Monorail Galeries Victoria. **Map** p311 B3.

Designed by award-winning Sydney architects Crone Associates, the four-level Galeries Victoria is Sydney's newest shopping centre and has more than a whiff of trendy Tokyo about it. It's home to leading fashion and lifestyle brands (Polo Jeans, Mooks, L'Occitane), as well as a Fitness First gym and Kinokuniya, Sydney's largest cross-cultural bookshop with titles in English, Japanese and Chinese, and an in-store coffee lounge.

Harbourside

Darling Drive, Darling Harbour (9281 3999/ www.harbourside.com.au). CityRail Town Hall/ ferry Darling Harbour/Monorail Harbourside. **Map** p311 B3.

A glitzy shopping centre on the Pyrmont side of Darling Harbour. The shops, including a good clutch selling Australian products, are open until 9pm daily to attract as many tourists as possible after a day's sightseeing – but don't expect to nab a bargain.

Italian Forum

23 Norton Street, between Parramatta Road & Marion Street, Leichhardt (9518 3396/www.italian forum.com.au). Bus 435, 436, 437, 438, 440, L38, L39, L40.

Who'd have thought an attempt to recreate an Italian village complete with Romanesque piazza could be pulled off with such panache right slap in the middle of Sydney's west? This square of upmarket shops, restaurants, cafés and even stonewashed

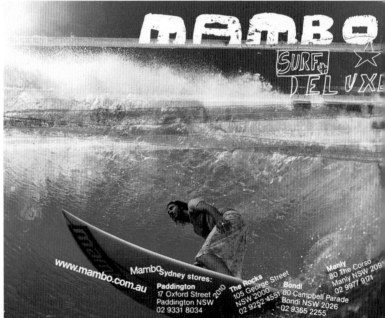

The unique **Italian Forum**. *See p167.*

apartments, which opened in April 2000, really does conjure up an authentic taste of Italy. You'll find Versace, stylish leather handbags at Florence Travel Goods, OshKosh, DKNY kids' wear and shoes to die for. There's also a beauty salon, classic jewellers, perfumerie and hairdresser. The shops are in a gallery overlooking the piazza where cafés and restaurants cluster around an old-fashioned carousel, a fountain and a statue of Dante (of course).

Mid City Centre

197 Pitt Street Mall, between King & Market Streets, CBD (9221 2422). CityRail Martin Place, St James or Town Hall/Monorail City Centre. **Map** p311 C3.
There's a big HMV, a large Rebel Sports and the fashion store Marcs at the front, and a den-like fast-food frenzy on the lower ground floor.

MLC Centre

Corner of King & Castlereagh Streets, CBD (9224 8333/www.mlccentre.com.au). CityRail Martin Place/ Monorail City Centre. **Map** p310 C2.
This established, but recently refurbished shopping arcade houses such top international names as Gucci and Cartier. The Theatre Royal is also part of the complex, as is a huge Harvey Norman Technology Shop with home theatre/cinema rooms. The outdoor cafés overlooking Martin Place get packed out with office workers at lunchtime.

Queen Victoria Building (QVB)

455 George Street, between Market & Druitt Streets, CBD (information 9265 6855/tours 9265 6864/ www.qvb.com.au). CityRail Town Hall/Monorail Galeries Victoria. **Map** p311 B3.
The airy Victorian halls of this historic building are perfect for shopping – if it weren't for the crowds. The 200 or so outlets include designer labels, fashion chainstores, beauty boutiques, florists and

chocolate shops on level one, leading contemporary commercial art space Quadrivium on level two and lots of Australiana gift shops. The lower ground level links through to the Town Hall Square shops and station along with the Galeries Victoria shopping centre. *See also p167.*

The Rocks Centre

10-26 Playfair Street, at Argyle Street, The Rocks (8267 0700/www.therocks.com). CityRail/ferry Circular Quay. **Map** p310 B1.
A shopping wonderland, purely aimed at the tourist, but with lots of good-quality souvenirs and gifts in a number of different outlets, at a range of prices. Australia does actually have natural, historic and interesting souvenirs and this is the best one-stop place to find them.
   The shop Spirit of Downunder (9251 0087) sells boomerangs, didgeridoos and painted miniature animals, as well as Aboriginal paintings that come with certificates of authenticity from the artists. Earth Chant (9241 1662) sells clothing and T-shirts with Aboriginal designs, as well as tribal jewellery, boomerangs and CDs. Rocks Merino (9251 5515) specialises in Australian sheepskin footwear (this is where to buy uggs); you can even get kangaroo leather and Australian saltwater crocodile skin products. Bonz on the Rocks (9247 8393) sells Australian-made leather, merino and mohair garments. Other outlets worth investigating include the Aussie Koala Shop (9247 6388), Oz Outback Style (9252 4322), the Original Macadamia Nut Shop (9251 7088), Opal Beauty (9241 4050) and Bushman's Gift (9247 2483).

Skygarden

77 Castlereagh Street, between Market & King Streets, CBD (9231 1811/www.skygarden.com.au). CityRail Martin Place or St James/Monorail City Centre. **Map** p310/311 C2/3.
A veritable maze of a mall, linking to Imperial Arcade and Glasshouse. Inside are Sportsgirl, a huge Borders bookshop and video café, stylish contemporary retro clothing store Anton's and a Starbucks.

Strand Arcade

412-414 George Street, between King & Market Streets, CBD (9232 4199/www.strandarcade.com.au). CityRail Martin Place or St James/Monorail City Centre. **Map** p311 C3.
Built in 1891, Strand Arcade is as beautiful as the QVB but a hundred times cooler. Don't be put off by the odd opal or koala sweater on the ground floor or the huge Downtown Duty Free (9233 3166) in the basement, because the best fashion and accessories are to be found upstairs. Check out especially boudoir-style Alannah Hill (*see p172*).

Sydney Central Plaza

450 George Street, at Market Street, CBD (8224 2000/www.westfield.com.au). CityRail Town Hall or St James/Monorail City Centre. **Map** p311 B3.
The jewel in the crown of Sydney Central Plaza is feisty department store Grace Bros (*see p166*), but there are plenty of other shops worth visiting.

Eat, Drink, Shop

Sydney designer Morrissey (*see p173*) is here, as well as Saba and the excellent chainstore Witchery (*see p177*). Cornucopia, the international food court on the lower ground floor, is the city's best, and open until 10pm on Thursdays.

Westfield Bondi Shopping Centre

500 Oxford Street, at Grosvenor Street, Bondi Junction (9947 8000/www.westfield.com.au). CityRail Bondi Junction/bus 380, L82. **Map** p313 F5.
At the time of writing a plush refurbished branch of David Jones, complete with huge family-friendly food hall (with kosher counter), is the sole retailer trading on this vast site, which will eventually comprise 330 shops. Completion is due mid 2004 when DJ will be joined by Grace Bros, two supermarkets, a discount department store, a cinema complex and lots of other shops, including top fashion labels Marcs, Wayne Cooper and Zimmermann. It's a huge project and will have parking for 3,300 and 62 escalators – all at a cost of $680 million.

Markets

Most Sydney markets are held in schools or church grounds. Be prepared to try things on in the toilets and leave the credit cards at home as cash is preferred and you're more likely to get a bargain that way.

Balmain

St Andrew's Church, corner of Darling Street & Curtis Road, Balmain (9555 1791). Ferry East Balmain or Balmain/bus 434, 442, 443.
Open 8am-4pm Sat.
Babywear and handmade homewares predominate here – a reflection of the area's yuppification – also crafts, second-hand books, plants and fruit and veg. There's a multicultural food hall in the church.

Bondi Beach

Bondi Beach Public School, corner of Campbell Parade & Warners Avenue, Bondi Beach (9315 8988). CityRail Bondi Junction then bus 380, 381, L82/bus 380, L82. **Open** *Summer* 9am-5pm Sun. *Winter* 9am-4pm Sun. **Map** p83.
A growing gathering place with a good choice of new, locally designed clothes and crafts, plus second-hand stuff and general bric-a-brac.

Glebe

Glebe Public School, Glebe Point Road, between Mitchell Street & Parramatta Road, Glebe (4237 7499). Bus 431, 432, 433. **Open** 9am-4pm Sat. **Map** p311 A4.
The most feral of all the markets and usually packed with bare-footed new age types. Second-hand clothes are good here and there's a big playing field for picnic lunches (and locals taking the weed).

Kings Cross Car Market

Kings Cross Car Park, Ward Avenue, at Elizabeth Bay Road, Kings Cross (9358 5000). CityRail Kings Cross. **Open** 9am-5pm daily. **Map** p312 D3.

This underground car park in Kings Cross contains an area for overseas travellers to buy and sell cars. There are no professional car dealers, only private sellers, and you can pick up a car, wagon, van or campervan right here – and they often come complete with camping gear as well.

Kirribilli

Bradfield Park, Alfred Street, at Burton Street, Milsons Point (9922 4428). CityRail/ferry Milsons Point. **Open** 7am-3pm 4th Sat of the mth.
This monthly market specialises in 'upmarket' bric-a-brac and antiques.

Paddington

Paddington Uniting Church, 395 Oxford Street, at Newcombe Street, Paddington (9331 2923/www.paddingtonmarket.com.au). Bus 378, 380, L82. **Open** *Summer* 10am-5pm Sat. *Winter* 10am-4pm Sat. **Map** p313 E4.
Many a big-name fashion designer began by selling to the crowds that swarm to Paddington market. There are also masses of jewellery makers, ceramicists and artisans selling their wares, plus multi cultural food stalls at the back. A word of warning: parking is impossible on Saturday, when packs of promenading fashion victims turn the footpath into a claustrophobic's worst nightmare.

Paddy's

Market City, corner of Hay & Thomas Streets, Haymarket (1300 361 589/www.sydneymarkets.com.au). CityRail Central or Town Hall/Light Rail/Monorail Haymarket. **Open** 9am-5pm Thur-Sun. **Map** p311 B4.
Paddy's has more of a mass-market angle, catering to bargain-hunting families from near and far. It's fully under cover in a large pavilion and sells clothing, shoes, CDs, electronics and fruit and veg – all at cheap, cheap prices.

The Rocks

George Street, at Playfair Street, The Rocks (Sydney Harbour Foreshores Authority 9240 8717/www.rocksmarket.com). CityRail/ferry Circular Quay. **Open** 10am-5pm Sat, Sun. **Map** p310 C1.
Here you'll find mainly quality arts, crafts, homewares, antiques and collectibles.

Rozelle

Rozelle Public School, Darling Street, between Victoria & Merton Streets, Rozelle (9818 5373). Bus 432, 433, 434, 440, 445. **Open** 9am-4pm Sat, Sun.
For the most part, this is a good, old-fashioned bric-a-brac market. Expect such second-hand market staples as clothes, music, books and plants.

Surry Hills

Shannon Reserve, Crown Street, at Foveaux Streets, Surry Hills (9361 4908). CityRail/Light Rail Central. **Open** 10am-5pm 1st Sat of the mth. **Map** p311 C4.
This is the hippest of all of the city's many weekend markets. You'll find lots here to catch the eye in the form of clothes, accessories, good junk, and a lot of interesting people as well.

Alistair Trung's nomadic designs. *See p172.*

Books

Along with the shops listed here, the all-purpose book chain **Dymocks** is also a good option, as it not only has books but excellent stationery and travel sections. You're never far from one of its shops, as it has branches all over town, including one at 424 George Street, CBD (9235 0155/www.dymocks.com.au).

Ariel

42 Oxford Street, between Barcom Avenue & West Street, Paddington (9332 4581/www.ariel books.com.au). Bus 378, 380, L82. **Open** 9am-midnight daily. **Credit** AmEx, BC, DC, MC, V. **Map** p313 D4.
Open late, this bookshop is a favourite hangout for the many arty types who seem to seep out of the NSW University College of Fine Arts opposite. Fittingly, Ariel stocks a lot of great (read: expensive) art, design, photography, fashion and contemporary culture books, which the laidback staff are happy for you to leaf through for as long as you like.
Other locations: 103 George Street, The Rocks (9241 5622).

Berkelouw Book Sellers

19 Oxford Street, between South Dowling Street & Greens Road, Paddington (9360 3200/ www.berkelouw.com.au). Bus 378, 380, L82. **Open** 9.30am-midnight daily. **Credit** AmEx, BC, DC, MC, V. **Map** p313 D4.
Berkelouw has an intriguing selection of new and antique Australiana and assorted rare books – many locked behind glass. It's a great place to while away half an hour while waiting to catch a movie at one of the nearby Palace art house cinemas; the café upstairs has a great view of Oxford Street.
Other locations: 70 Norton Street, Leichhardt (9560 3200).

The Bookshop Darlinghurst

207 Oxford Street, between Flinders & South Dowling Streets, Darlinghurst (9331 1103). Bus 378, 380, L82. **Open** 9.30am-11pm Mon-Sat; 11am-midnight Sun. **Credit** AmEx, BC, DC, MC, V. **Map** p313 C4.
Specialises in gay and lesbian material and also stocks a range of rare imported books. The staff are exceptionally knowledgeable.

Gleebooks

49 Glebe Point Road, between Cowper & Francis Streets, Glebe (9660 2333/www.gleebooks.com.au). Bus 431, 432, 433. **Open** 10am-9pm Mon-Fri, Sun; 9am-9pm Sat. **Credit** AmEx, BC, DC, MC, V. **Map** p311 A4.
Highly rated Gleebooks has two branches on Glebe Point Road. No.49 sells new titles while No.191 specialises in second-hand and children's books, as well as more esoteric works on the humanities.
Other locations: 191 Glebe Point Road, Glebe (9552 2526).

Map World

280 Pitt Street, between Park & Bathurst Streets, CBD (9261 3601/www.mapworld.net.au). CityRail Town Hall/Monorail Galeries Victoria. **Open** 8.30am-5.30pm Mon-Wed, Fri; 8.30am-6.30pm Thur; 10am-4pm Sat. **Credit** AmEx, BC, DC, MC, V. **Map** p311 C3.
Road maps for the whole of Australia, as well as travel guides, atlases and books about such outdoor activities as four-wheel driving and rock climbing.
Other locations: 136 Willoughby Road, Crows Nest (9966 5770).

Second-hand

In addition to those listed below, *see also above* **Berkelouw Book Sellers** and **Gleebooks**.

Goulds

32 King Street, between Queen & Georgina Streets, Newtown (9519 8947/www.gouldsbooks.com.au). Bus 422, 423, 426, 428, 352. **Open** 8am-midnight daily. **Credit** AmEx, BC, MC, V.
Around 3,000m (9,000ft) of books make this the largest second-hand bookshop in Sydney. It's a librarian's nightmare, but well worth the rummage – and it's open until midnight.

Eat, Drink, Shop

Sappho Books
165 Glebe Point Road, between St Johns Road &
Mitchell Street, Glebe (9552 4498). Bus 431, 432,
433. **Open** 9am-10pm daily. **Credit** AmEx, BC, DC,
MC, V. **Map** p311 A4.
A popular, friendly and immaculately catalogued
second-hand bookshop that really does offer something for everyone – from Australian first editions
and leather-bound tomes to art books and the latest
chick lit. There's also a comfortable café at the rear.

Cameras & photo developing
Bondi Beach One Hour
25 Hall Street, between Campbell Parade &
Gould Street, Bondi Beach (9300 9577).
CityRail Bondi Junction then bus 380, 381,
L82/bus 380, L82. **Open** 9am-6pm daily.
Credit AmEx, BC, MC, V. **Map** p83.
Basic photo develompent and other camera-related
services are provided at this handily located shop.
Want to send snapshots home that look like post-
cards? Photos processed here come with those nifty
old-fashioned white borders.

Fletcher's Fotographic
317 Pitt Street, between Park & Bathurst Streets,
CBD (9267 6146/www.fletchers.net). CityRail Town
Hall/Monorail Galeries Victoria. **Open** 8.30am-
5.30pm Mon-Wed; 8.30am-7.30pm Thur; 8.30am-6pm
Fri; 9am-2pm Sat. **Credit** AmEx, BC, DC, MC, V.
Map p311 C3.
This is Australia's camera superstore chain, with
branches all over town. It's a good place to start your
search for duty-free items, because you'll get the best
advice. It also has a professional department and
second-hand cameras.

Fashion
Sydneysiders love labels and get their regular
fix of Gucci or Chanel in a convenient enclave in
the CBD around Martin Place and Castlereagh,
Elizabeth and King Streets where all the top
designers have their boutiques. Designer
central is the are around the corner of King
and Castlereagh Streets. Budget-challenged
fashionistas are well catered for with **Voi** –
'Go Gucci, stay solvent' – (125 York Street,
9261 0526) and the regular **Fashion Designer
Warehouse** sales at Paddington Town Hall
(9331 4592); check newspapers for dates. For
a somewhat low-key yet no less enjoyable
shopping experience, check out William Street
in Paddington. Here you'll find **Collette
Dinnigan** (*see below*), **Sylvia Chan** (No.20,
9380 5981, www.sylviachan.com.au) and the
Corner Shop (*see p175*) for the latest styles,
second-hand designer clothes at **Di Nuovo**
(Nos.92-94, 9361 4221) and handmade shoes
by **Andrew McDonald** (No.58, 9358 6793,
www.andrewmcdonald.com.au).

Australian designers
Akira Isogawa
12A Queen Street, at Oxford Street, Woollahra
(9361 5221/www.akira.com.au). Bus 378, 380, L82.
Open 10.30am-6pm Mon-Wed, Fri; 10.30am-7pm
Thur; 10am-6pm Sat; noon-5pm Sun. **Credit** AmEx,
BC, MC, V. **Map** p313 E5.
Akira's multi-layering of transparent fabrics blurs
the lines of season and gender. His garments are sold
in all the world's fashion epicentres.

Alannah Hill
118-120 Oxford Street, at Glenmore Road,
Paddington (9380 9147). Bus 378, 380, L82.
Open 10am-6pm Mon-Wed, Fri, Sat; 10am-8pm
Thur; 11am-6pm Sun. **Credit** AmEx, BC, DC, MC, V.
Map p313 D4.
Alannah's style is glamorous yet naughty. You'll
find an abundance of rich fabrics and textures, com-
bining velvet trims with intricate lace, as well as a
variety of girly accessories.
Other locations: Strand Arcade, 412-414 George
Street, CBD (9221 1251).

Alistair Trung
Argyle Stores, 18-24 Argyle Street, at Playfair Street,
The Rocks (9252 8828/www.alistairtrung.com).
CityRail/ferry Circular Quay. **Open** 10am-6pm daily.
Credit AmEx, BC, DC, MC, V. **Map** p310 B1.
Alistair Trung was born in Vietnam and emigrated
when he was 11. His extraordinary women's wear
designs have a touch of Asia, but more noticeably
of nomadic hill tribe clothing and the layering of
Indian saris. Colours are mostly neutral and earthy
with the odd flash of red, blue or yellow.

Charlie Brown
178 Oxford Street, opposite Victoria Barracks,
Paddington (9360 9001/www.charliebrown
online.com). Bus 378, 380, L82. **Open** 10am-6pm
Mon-Wed, Fri, Sat; 10am-9pm Thur; 11am-5pm Sun.
Credit AmEx, BC, DC, MC, V. **Map** p313 D4.
American-born Charlie Brown has finally signed up
for Aussie citizenship. She now stocks Howard
Showers label as well as her own, but it's Charlie
fashion that's the drawcard. Her designs are flamboyant, innovative, very wearable – and affordable.
Best of all, sizes go up to 18. You'll also find vintage
accessories, exciting costume jewellery, cool hats, a
small children's collection and the 'Yes Mistress' cosmetics range.

Collette Dinnigan
33 William Street, off Oxford Street, Paddington
(9360 6691/www.collettedinnigan.com.au).
Bus 378, 380, L82. **Open** 10am-6pm Mon-Sat;
noon-4pm Sun. **Credit** AmEx, BC, DC, MC, V.
Map p312 D4.
Dinnigan's trademark is the use of vibrant fabrics
with exquisite beading and embroidery, resulting in
feminine clothes that are highly sensual. Her work
is loved by stick-thin celebs, and the prices are as
jaw-dropping as the designs.

Leona Edmiston

88 William Street, off Oxford Street, Paddington
(9331 7033/www.leonaedmiston.com.au). Bus 378,
380, L82. **Open** 10am-6pm Mon-Sat; noon-4pm Sun.
Credit AmEx, BC, DC, MC, V. **Map** p311 D4.
Having split with fellow designer Peter Morrissey
(*see below*), talented Sydneysider Leona Edmiston
has set up on her own with a fun and flirty collection
of pretty frocks. Feminine is the call here, with deli-
cate prints and flattering cuts. A favourite with local
'it' girls heading for the Spring Racing Carnival.
Other locations: Chifley Plaza, corner of Hunter &
Phillip Streets, CBD (9230 0322).

Lisa Ho

Corner of Oxford & Queen Streets, Woollahra
(9360 2345/www.lisaho.com.au). Bus 378, 380,
L82. **Open** 10am-6pm Mon-Wed, Fri, Sat; 10am-8pm
Thur; 11am-5pm Sun. **Credit** AmEx, BC, DC, MC, V.
Map p313 E5.
Thanks to actress Naomi Watts, who wore one of
Lisa Ho's creations to the Emmys, this Sydney-
based designer is at last being recognised overseas.
Her designs use lots of colour in stretch fabrics or
sheer chiffon, often with beaded detail. The clothes
are designed for normal-sized women (thank you)
and are rather more affordable than most of
Sydney's designers. Great swimwear too.
Other locations: Strand Arcade, 412-414 George
Street, CBD (9222 9711).

Morrissey

372 Oxford Street, between Elizabeth Street & Jersey
Road, Paddington (9380 7422). Bus 378, 380, L82.
Open 10am-6pm Mon-Wed, Fri, Sat; 10am-8pm
Thur; 11am-5pm Sun. **Credit** AmEx, BC, DC, MC, V.
Map p313 E4.
Peter Morrissey began his fashion career with Leona
Edmiston (*see above*), and they created the Morrissey
Edmiston label, successful for 14 years. They split
in 1997 and today Morrissey is owned by Oroton.
His designs have changed little though; he's still
producing wearable men's and women's fashion for
the funky and body-conscious.
Other locations: Sydney Central Plaza, 450 George
Street, CBD (9221 8002).

Scanlan & Theodore

443 Oxford Street, between Elizabeth Street &
Jersey Road, Paddington (9361 6722/www.scanlan
theodore.com.au). Bus 378, 380, L82. **Open** 10am-
6pm Mon-Wed, Fri; 10am-8pm Thur; 10am-5.30pm
Sat; noon-5pm Sun. **Credit** AmEx, BC, DC, MC, V.
Map p313 E4.
Definitely one of the better young Australian
women's wear designers: more original than most,
with good fabrics, colours and quality.

Skipping Girl

124A Roscoe Street, at Gould Street, Bondi Beach
(9365 0735/www.skippinggirl.com). CityRail Bondi
Junction then bus 380, 381, L82/bus 380, L82.
Open *Summer* 10am-6pm Mon-Wed, Sun; 10am-7pm
Thur-Sat. *Winter* 10am-6pm daily. **Credit** AmEx,
BC, MC, V. **Map** p83.

Claire Danes and Gwen Stefani are among the celeb
followers of local-girl-made-good Hayley Allen, who
turned a design based on a bag found in a south
Indian fruit and spice market into an internationally acclaimed business. Today Barneys (New York)
and Harvey Nichols (London) are among the stock-
ists of her cute bags with skipping rope handles, one-
off T-shirts and innovative footwear, including
delightful wellies adorned with clouds.

Zimmermann

24 Oxford Street, at Ocean Street, Woollahra
(9360 5769/www.zimmermannwear.com). Bus
378, 380, L82. **Open** 10am-6pm Mon-Wed, Fri,
Sat; 10am-8pm Thur; noon-5pm Sun. **Credit** AmEx,
BC, DC, MC, V. **Map** p313 E5.
Nicole Zimmermann started this label in 1990 and
was joined by her sister Simone in 1991. The duo's

Naughty **Wheels & Doll Baby**. *See p177.*

Don't bring problems into Australia.

To protect Australia's environment from pests a[nd] diseases that could be carried in food, plant or anir[mal] material from overseas, all luggage is screened or x-rayed [on] arrival. Declare all quarantine items. If you don't, you will [be] caught and could face fines over $60,000 and 10 ye[ars] imprisonment. Find out what you can and cannot bring i[nto] Australia from your Australian Embassy or High Commissi[on] or at **www.aqis.gov.au**

Declare or beware.

Quarantine Matters!

Australian Gover[nment]
Australian Quara[ntine]

success has been huge. Zimmermann's swimwear (at No.24) has always been its calling card, and is still brilliant with bright, bold and contemporary designs for hip bodies. In 2002 the label was hired by the UK's M&S to design a new swimwear line. But there's much more than bathers; lingerie, dresses, trousers and great tops are all available in their new shop further down Oxford Street.

Other locations: 387 Oxford Street, Paddington (9357 4700).

Boutiques

The incredibly popular US label **Diesel**, beloved by the young and relatively hip for its casual, sporty clothes, opened its first Australian concept store in Paddington in late 2003 at 408 Oxford Street, at Elizabeth Street (9331 5255).

Belinda

8 Transvaal Avenue, off Cross Street, Double Bay (9328 6288/www.belinda.com.au). Ferry Double Bay/bus 323, 324, 325, 326, 327. **Open** 10am-6pm Mon-Fri; 10am-5pm Sat. **Credit** AmEx, BC, DC, MC, V. **Map** p312 F3.

This shop offers the pick of the crop, both locally and from overseas, selected by the store's stylish namesake. This is the place for exquisite fashion enhanced with the perfect beautiful accessories and just the right sparkling jewellery.

Other locations: 29 William Street, Paddington (9380 8873); 39 William Street, Paddington (9380 8728); MLC Centre, corner of King & Castlereagh Streets, CBD (9233 0781).

Bracewell

274 Oxford Street, between Ormond & William Streets, Paddington (9331 5844/www.bracewell.com.au). Bus 378, 380, L82. **Open** 10am-6pm Mon-Wed, Fri, Sat; 10am-8.30pm Thur; 11.30am-5.30pm Sun. **Credit** AmEx, BC, DC, MC, V. **Map** p313 D4.

This sophisticated shop stocks mainly its own label, plus the hot jeans and denim label Saff & Bide, favoured by rock chicks and celebrities.

The Corner Shop

43 William Street, off Oxford Street, Paddington (9380 9828). Bus 378, 380, L82. **Open** 10am-6pm Mon-Wed, Fri, Sat; 10am-7pm Thur; noon-5pm Sun. **Credit** AmEx, BC, DC, MC, V. **Map** p311 D4.

For this eclectic fashion venture, the Belinda team (*see above*) scours the world's international fashion fairs to bring back the hippest and brightest of the up-and-coming designers.

D-PO

441 Oxford Street, between Queen & Elizabeth Streets, Paddington (9361 4339). Bus 378, 380, L82. **Open** 10am-6pm Mon-Wed, Fri, Sat; 10am-8pm Thur; 11am-5.30pm Sun. **Credit** AmEx, BC, DC, MC, V. **Map** p313 E4/5.

Urban groovers swarm here for the latest G-Star, Psycho Cowboy and Diesel. Cool. Very cool.

Idle Wild

52 Oxford Street, betweeen Barcom Avenue & Comber Street, Paddington (9360 1569). Bus 378, 380, L82. **Open** 10am-6pm Mon-Wed, Fri, Sat; 10am-8pm Thur; 11am-5pm Sun. **Credit** AmEx, BC, MC, V. **Map** p313 D4.

Idle Wild is a great Sydney label: soft colours in floaty skirts and pretty feminine shirts and tops. But this shop also stocks edgy Melbourne label Metallicus and the wonderful Yoshi Jones, a distinctive local designer who uses fabric from vintage Japanese kimonos in her Eastern-influenced skirts, wide pants and wraparound dresses.

JAG

19 Castlereagh Street, at Martin Place, CBD (9233 4366/www.jag.com.au). CityRail Martin Place. **Open** 10am-6pm Mon, Tue; 9am-6pm Wed, Fri; 9am-8pm Thur; 10am-5pm Sat. **Credit** AmEx, BC, DC, MC, V. **Map** p310 C2.

The JAG label was the brainchild of Melbourne designers Rob and Adele Palmer, who shot to success in the 1970s with their casual sportswear and sharp denim designs, attracting a worldwide following that included Steve McQueen, Jackie Onassis and Bianca Jagger. Today the company is owned by Brisbane footwear group Colorado and boasts a team of young funky designers. The range – for men, women and children – includes well-made smart basics in good-quality natural fabrics.

Jeremy

26 Oxford Street, between Barcom Avenue & West Street, Paddington (9332 1526/www.jeremyville.com). Bus 378, 380, L82. **Open** 10am-6pm Mon-Wed, Fri, Sat; 10am-8pm Thur; 11am-5pm Sun. **Credit** AmEx, BC, MC, V. **Map** p313 D4.

Art, graphic design and Andy Warhol are the influences for this edgy urban streetwear label, part of a bigger design company and something of a Sydney success story. The clothing label was launched in 1998 and has achieved minor cult status with its arty T-shirts, sporty bags and cute tracksuit tops.

Marcs

197 Pitt Street Mall, between King & Market Streets, CBD (9221 4583/www.marcs.com.au). CityRail Martin Place, St James or Town Hall/Monorail City Centre. **Open** 9.30am-6pm Mon-Wed, Fri; 9am-9pm Thur; 9am-5pm Sat; 11am-5pm Sun. **Credit** AmEx, BC, DC, MC, V. **Map** p310/311 C2/3.

The Marcs label first began back in the 1980s when a couple of designers had the idea to make men's shirts out of women's fabrics, and has since developed into a massively successful string of men's and women's clothes shops. The label was recently taken over by Oroton, which also owns Morrissey (*see p173*) and Polo Ralph Lauren. It offers cool fashion basics using lots of colour, plus imported labels including Diesel and Juicy Couture.

Other locations: 280 Oxford Street, Paddington (9332 4255); 118 Campbell Parade, Bondi Beach (9300 0436); 645 Military Road, Mosman (9968 1298); 31-33 Knox Street, Double Bay (9362 5977).

Eat, Drink, Shop

Home groan

Established in 1868, and located opposite the QVB, the chain store **Gowings** is an institution, promoting products made by Australians for Australians. It's mainly a men's wear shop, with good-quality basics, surf T-shirts, swimwear, lumberjack shirts and shoes, including Blundstones. But there's more – camping gear, toys, toiletries – and it's also become a firm favourite with the Sydney queer scene, as evident from many of the quirky gifts on sale – including the following.

● **Sydney City Hanky** ($15.95)
A neckerchief-sized hanky with a fully readable map of Sydney. Use it to find your way home after a night on the tiles.

● **Surfer Bob dashboard toy** ($14.95).
When the holiday's over, Bob will ride the waves on your dashboard.

● **Bonds undies** (from around $8.95)
Aussie supermodel Sarah O'Hare and former tennis champ Pat Rafter fronted Bonds' latest ad campaign, catapulting the sensible, old-fashioned (the company was founded in 1915) makers of 'Cottontails' to top of the fashion charts. Gowings has the full men's range, but for the divinely comfortable boxers for 'hard-working girls' in great colours, go to **Grace Bros** or **David Jones** (for both, *see p166*).

● **Coghlans Deluxe Mossie Head Net** ($8.95)
Forget hats with corks, this is the real deal. You may look like a beekeeper in this protective head net, but its main selling point is that it works – wear it and the mossies will leave you alone.

● **Nimbin Hemp Short** ($44.95)
No, you can't smoke them, but these Aussie-made shorts crafted from hemp are ecologically sound, and appropriately named after the famous NSW hippy community, Nimbin.

Gowings
Corner of George & Market Streets, CBD (9287 6394/www.gowings.com.au). CityRail Town Hall or St James/Monorail City Centre. **Open** 8.30am-6pm Mon-Wed, Fri; 8.30am-9pm Thur; 9am-6pm Sat; 10am-5pm Sun. **Credit** AmEx, DC, MC, V. **Map** p311 B3.
Other locations: 319 George Street, CBD (9262 1281); 82 Oxford Street, Darlinghurst (9331 5544).

Paablo Nevada
140 Curlewis Street, between Campbell Parade & Glenayr Avenue, Bondi Beach (9365 0165). CityRail Bondi Junction then bus 380, 381, L82/bus 380, L82. **Open** 9am-6.30pm Mon-Fri; 10.30am-6.30pm Sat; 11am-6.30pm Sun. **Credit** AmEx, BC, MC, V. **Map** p83.
A Sydney label combining urban-chic streetwear with a little bit of country: great pointy toed boots, plus sleek shirt dresses and smart stretch pants.
Other locations: 15 Cross Street, Double Bay (9362 9455)

Robby Ingham
424-28 Oxford Street, between Elizabeth Street & Jersey Road, Paddington (9332 2124). Bus 378, 380, L82. **Open** 10am-6pm Mon-Wed, Fri, Sat; 10am-8pm Thur; 11am-5pm Sun. **Credit** AmEx, BC, DC, MC, V. **Map** p313 D4.
What started out as a single men's shop is slowly building up into a small empire. Now there are individual Robbie Ingham shops catering to men, women and jeans' wearers. The attraction are its simple, good designs. Local labels include Helen Sherry and Sample, while imports are represented by Paul Smith and Comme des Garçons.
Other locations: MLC Centre, corner of King & Castlereagh Streets, CBD (9232 6466).

Ruby & Min
250 Darling Street, at Booth Street, Balmain (9818 3100). Ferry East Balmain/bus 443, 434, 442. **Open** 10am-6pm Mon-Wed, Fri; 10am-8pm Thur; 10am-5pm Sat; noon-5pm Sun. **Credit** AmEx, BC, MC, V.
Pretty, feminine and accessible women's wear with lots of reasonably priced accessories including bags, thongs, shoes and belts.
Other locations: 128 Queen Street, Woollahra (9328 0101).

Saba
Sydney Central Plaza, 450 George Street, at Market Street, CBD (9231 2436/9232 4666/www.saba. com.au). CityRail Town Hall or St James/Monorail City Centre. **Open** 9am-6pm Mon-Wed, Fri, Sat; 9am-9pm Thur; 11am-5pm Sun. **Credit** AmEx, BC, DC, MC, V. **Map** p311 B3.
Melbourne designer Joe Saba's label has always been synonymous with style and sophistication. But after a heart attack in 1999 and a personal rethink, the fashion legend sold his sprawling collection of shops. What remains still seems to conform to Joe's style – although it's not actually his designs any more. Expect hip denims, cosy knitwear and smart suits for men and women.
Other locations: 270 Oxford Street, Paddington (9331 2685); 39 Bay Street, Double Bay (9362 0281).

Swellstore
256 Oxford Street, between Ormond & William Streets, Paddington (9331 5822). Bus 378, 380, L82. **Open** 10am-6pm Mon-Wed, Fri; 10am-8.30pm Thur; 9.30am-5.30pm Sat; 11am-5pm Sun. **Credit** AmEx, BC, DC, MC, V. **Map** p313 D4.

Swellstore is one of the few places in Sydney that stocks Pinks shirts, Duffer of St George, Evisu, Fred Perry, Camper shoes and the clothes of the popular Melbourne designer Roy.

Wheels & Doll Baby

259 Crown Street, at Goulburn Street, Darlinghurst (9361 3286/www.wheelsanddollbaby.com). CityRail Museum/bus 373, 374, 377, 378, 380. **Open** 10am-6pm Mon-Wed, Fri, Sat; 10am-8pm Thur; noon-5pm Sun. **Credit** AmEx, BC, DC, MC, V. **Map** p311 C3.

Melanie Greensmith's vampy rock 'n' roll-inspired fashion label used to be renowned for its leather and lace, but she's recently shifted focus to Parisian polka dots and French florals. She dubs her line of posh punk frocks, customised Bonds knickers, naughty tees and shapely dresses, skirts and blouses 'clothes to snare a millionaire' – which is exactly what she's doing with customers such as Kelly Osbourne, Goldie Hawn and Kate Hudson.

Chainstores

Along with the shops listed below, other reliable women's wear chains to be found in and around Sydney include places like **Country Road** (142 Pitt Street, CBD, 9394 1818, www.countryroad.com.au), which is excellent for good basics; cheap and cheerful **Dotti** (356 Oxford Street, Paddington, 9332 1659, www.dotti.com.au); the funky, unique chain **Seduce** (163 King Street, Newtown, 9565 2022, www.seduce.com.au); and **Sportsgirl** (Skygarden, 77 Castlereagh Street, CBD, 9223 8255, www.sportsgirl.com.au), where many young girls spend their first pay cheque before graduating to the more grown-up **Elle B** and **David Lawrence**. **Witchery** (332 Oxford Street, Paddington, 9360 6934, www.witchery.com.au) offers well-priced designs that often copy the latest catwalk releases. For men and women try plain and practical **Rivers** (Town Hall Arcade, 464 Kent Street, CBD, 9264 3501, www.rivers.com.au), a sort of Aussie Gap. *See also p176* **Home groan**.

RM Williams

389 George Street, between King & Market Streets, CBD (9262 2228/www.rmwilliams.com.au). CityRail Martin Place, St James or Town Hall/Monorail City Centre. **Open** 8.30am-6pm Mon-Wed, Fri; 8.30am-9pm Thur; 8.30am-5pm Sat; 11am-4pm Sun. **Credit** AmEx, BC, DC, MC, V. **Map** p310/311 B2/3.

Don't fail to stop by this 'bushman's outfitters' for the real thing in moleskins and riding boots – accept no substitutes. RM Williams himself died in late 2003 at the grand old age of 95; an event that hit the front page of every newspaper in the country. *See also p184* **Only in Oz**.

Other locations: Chifley Plaza, corner of Hunter & Phillip Streets, CBD (9233 5608); 71 George Street, The Rocks (9247 0204); Fox Studios, Moore Park (9360 0289).

Children

There are an increasing number of Australian kids' labels – Bright Bots, Gumboots, Fred Bare, Mini Minors; look for them at **David Jones** and **Grace Bros** (for both, *see p166*). Or try the numerous markets (*see p170*) for something more original – Bondi, Balmain and Paddington are particularly good.

Fetish

House of Fetish

93 Oxford Street, between Crown & Riley Streets, Darlinghurst (9380 9042). Bus 373, 374, 377, 378, 380. **Open** 10am-7pm Mon-Wed, Fri, Sat; 10am-9pm Thur; 1-5pm Sun. **Credit** AmEx, BC, MC, V. **Map** p311 C3/4.

Leathers, feathers, masks and some cool skirts all perfect for the Sleaze Ball or Mardi Gras.

Reactor

433 King Street, between Whitehorse & Newman Streets, Newtown (9517 4500/www.rubber.com.au). CityRail Newtown. **Open** 10am-5pm Tue; 10am-6pm Wed-Sat; noon-5pm Sun. **Credit** AmEx, BC, MC, V. **Map** p93.

Australia's largest manufacturer and retailer of fetish clothing has been going for almost 30 years. You'll find designs for men by Jacques Tchong and for women by Medusa's Mistress, plus latex designs by Donna. Unsurprisingly, the online store is especially popular with rubber divas.

Tool Shed

Basement, 191 Oxford Street, at Taylor Square, Darlinghurst (9360 1100/www.toolshed.com.au). Bus 378, 380, L82. **Open** 10am-1am Mon-Thur, Sun; 10am-3am Fri, Sat. **Credit** AmEx, BC, DC, MC, V. **Map** p311 C4.

Should you feel the need for an extra sexual accessory, head for Tool Shed, which stocks a vast range of appliances, protuberances and fetish wear. **Other locations**: 81 Oxford Street, Darlinghurst (9332 2792); 196-198 King Street, Newtown (9565 1599).

Surfwear & swimwear

In addition to those listed below, *see also p173* **Zimmermann** and **Lisa Ho**.

Aussie Boys

102 Oxford Street, between Crown & Palmer Streets, Darlinghurst (9360 7011/www.aussieboys.com.au). Bus 373, 374, 377, 378, 380. **Open** 10am-6pm Mon-Wed, Fri, Sat; 10am-9pm Thur; 11am-5pm Sun. **Credit** AmEx, BC, DC, MC, V. **Map** p311 C3.

A fun, friendly store selling beach towels from the cute Aussie Boys label, Dolce & Gabbana bathers and Bonds T-shirts; there's even a hair stylist downstairs. A one-stop shop for all that the smart gay man needs at the beach.

Between the Flags

*Opera Quays, East Circular Quay (9241 1603).
CityRail/ferry Circular Quay.* **Open** 9am-9pm Mon-Fri; 10am-9pm Sat, Sun. **Credit** AmEx, BC, MC, V.
Map p310 C2.

Great sporty clothing and surfwear with 10% of the retail cost going to the Bondi Surf Bathers' Live Saving Club. The Opera Quays shop has some fantastic maritime memorabilia – a full-size upturned boat serves as the counter, and there's a paddle and photos – while the wood-lined Bondi branch has a ceiling in the shape of a boat hull.
Other locations: QVB, 455 George Street, CBD (9261 0960); Harbourside, Darling Drive, Darling Harbour (9212 5994); 152 Campbell Parade, Bondi Beach (9365 5611); Bondi Pavilion, Queen Elizabeth Drive, Bondi Beach (9365 4063).

The Big Swim

74 Campbell Parade, between Lamrock Avenue & Hall Street, Bondi Beach (9365 4457). CityRail Bondi Junction then bus 380, 381, L82/bus 380, L82. **Open** 9.30am-6pm daily. **Credit** AmEx, BC, DC, MC, V. **Map** p83.

Perhaps the best place in Sydney to buy swimwear: rack after rack of well-priced, practical one-pieces and fun bikinis in loads of different styles. And it's right opposite the beach.
Other locations: 51 The Corso, Manly (9977 8961); Warringah Mall, Brookvale (9907 3352).

Bondi Surf Co

72 Campbell Parade, between Lamrock Avenue & Hall Street, Bondi Beach (9365 0870). CityRail Bondi Junction then bus 380, 381, L82/bus 380, L82.
Open *Summer* 9am-7pm daily. *Winter* 9am-6pm daily. **Credit** AmEx, BC, MC, V. **Map** p83.

Sales, hire, repairs, surfboards, bodyboards and wetsuits for the serious surfer. Plus surfie clothing, sunglasses, watches and other accessories.

Mambo

17 Oxford Street, between Barcom Avenue & Glenmore Road, Paddington (9331 8034/ www.mambo.com.au). Bus 378, 380, L82. **Open** 10am-6pm Mon-Wed, Fri-Sun; 10am-8pm Thur.
Credit AmEx, BC, DC, MC, V. **Map** p313 D4.

Mambo celebrates its 20th birthday in 2004 and it's been quite a journey for founder Dare Jennings. With 20 stores worldwide, the once-alternative Mambo is now an institution, though its stable of flamboyant artists are still pulling out rabbits when it comes to innovative design. Reg Mombassa was the original artist whose fire-breathing fowl is now a classic in boardshort fabrics. Today there's much more than shorts and T-shirts – swimwear, sunnies (sunglasses), caps, wallets, postcards and posters.
Other locations: 80 Campbell Parade, Bondi Beach (9365 2255); 80 The Corso, Manly (9977 9171); 105 George Street, The Rocks (9252 4551).

Rip Curl

82 Campbell Parade, between Lamrock Avenue & Hall Street, Bondi Beach (9130 2660/www.rip curl.com.au). CityRail Bondi Junction then bus 380,

381, L82/bus 380, L82. **Open** *Summer* 9am-7pm Mon-Wed, Fri-Sun; 9am-9pm Thur. *Winter* 9am-6pm Mon-Wed, Fri-Sun; 9am-8pm Thur. **Credit** AmEx, BC, MC, V. **Map** p83.

If it's 'killer gear' you want to 'drag your carcass' to school in, this is the shop. Rip Curl's website pulls out all the superlatives to attract kids to buy for beach, the waves and school. Designs here tend to be innovative, irreverent and fun, and it's proud to be the manufacturer of the world's first stitchless boardshort. Don't ask us how they do it. This place has great stuff for girls too.
Other locations: 98-100 The Corso, Manly (9977 6622).

Surfworld

Swiss Grand Hotel, 180 Campbell Parade, between Curlewis Street & Beach Road, Bondi Beach (9300 0055). CityRail Bondi Junction then bus 380, 381 L82/bus 380, L82. **Open** 9am-10pm daily. **Credit** AmEx, BC, DC, MC, V. **Map** p83.

Step over the threshold on to the surfboard-shaped rug and you're in surfie heaven. Every big name is on sale here – Stussy, Roxy, Billabong, plus some cool Lonsdale shirts and tops. You'll find gear for the beach (swimmers, boardshorts) and the street (men's long-sleeved shirts, canvas wallets for girls). This is also an excellent place for hiring surf and bodyboards if you haven't got your own.
Other locations: 79 Gould Street, Bondi Beach (9300 8226).

Vintage, recycled & second-hand

Blue Spinach Recycled Designer Clothing

348 Liverpool Street, at Womerah Avenue, Darlinghurst (9331 3904/www.bluespinach.com.au). Bus 389. **Open** *Summer* 10am-6pm Mon-Wed, Fri, Sat; 10am-8pm Thur. *Winter* 10am-6pm Mon-Wed, Fri, Sat; 10am-7pm Thur. **Credit** AmEx, BC, DC, MC, V. **Map** p311 B3.

Opened in 1997 by Mark and Jayne Thompson this is the most innovative and upmarket recycled clothing joint in town. Clothes, shoes, handbags, ties, belts and sunglasses – usually no more than two seasons' old – from labels both local and international.

Jazz Garter

409 Pitt Street, between Goulburn & Liverpool Streets, CBD (9211 2404). CityRail Museum/ Monorail World Square/Light Rail Capitol Square. **Open** 10am-6pm Mon-Fri; 11am-2pm Sat. **Credit** BC, MC, V. **Map** p311 B/C3.

Opened more than 30 years ago, Jazz Garter was one of the first second-hand clothing stores in Sydney. It is large and crammed full of well-cared-for retro clothes, accessories and shoes.

Puf'n Stuff

96 Glenayr Avenue, at O'Brien Street, Bondi Beach (9130 8471). CityRail Bondi Junction then bus 380, 381, L82/bus 380, L82. **Open** 10am-6pm daily. **Credit** AmEx, BC, MC, V. **Map** p83.

Fun, funky staff front this popular second-hand clothes shop a short walk from Bondi Beach. But you have to be quick to snap up a 1950s or '70s original: the owners know their stuff and nothing stays on the rails for long. You'll find everything from Elvis T-shirts and denim jackets with original patches to strappy stilettos and floaty evening wear.
Other locations: Puf'n More Stuff 102 Glenayr Avenue, Bondi Beach (9130 8984).

The Rokit Gallery

Argyle Stores, 18-24 Argyle Street, at Playfair Street, The Rocks (9247 1332). CityRail/ferry Circular Quay. **Open** 10am-6pm daily. **Credit** BC, MC, V. **Map** p310 B1.
A treasure-trove of vintage clothing and jewellery in immaculate condition. Most of the stock is from the 1930s, '40s and '50s and ranges from dresses, coats, skirts and blouses to all necessary accoutrements – cigarette cases, magazines, watches. It looks more like a glittering museum than a second-hand clothes shop, and behind the counter you'll find a shop assistant made up in full '50s eye-liner and face powder with clothes to match. Wonderful.

Route 66

255-257 Crown Street, between Oxford & Campbell Streets, Darlinghurst (9331 6686/www.route66. com.au). Bus 373, 374, 377, 378, 380. **Open** 10.30am-6pm Mon-Wed, Fri; 10.30am-8pm Thur; 10am-6pm Sat; noon-5pm-Sun. **Credit** AmEx, BC, MC, V. **Map** p311 C3.
Rockabilly heaven. A huge range of second-hand Levi's, 1950s chintz frocks and more Hawaiian shirts than you can swing a hula skirt at.

Fashion accessories

Bags & luggage

bondi beach bag co

76 Campbell Parade, between Lamrock Avenue & Hall Street, Bondi Beach (9300 0826/www.bondi beachbagco.com.au). CityRail Bondi Junction then bus 380, 381, L82/bus 380, L82. **Open** 9.30am-6.30pm daily. **Credit** BC, DC, MC, V. **Map** p83.
Exactly what it says – bags for the beach in a shop opposite Bondi Beach. The colourful woven rattan bbbc beanies are famous and stocked by big department stores all over the country.

Quick Brown Fox

100 Oxford Street, between Hopewell & Comber Streets, Paddington (9331 3211). Bus 378, 380, L82. **Open** 10am-6pm Mon-Wed, Fri, Sat; 10am-8pm Thur; noon-5pm Sun. **Credit** AmEx, BC, MC, V. **Map** p313 D4.
Creations by some of the world's most obscure and cutting-edge young designers are to be found in this funky, singular store. One of its biggest attractions is the fact that most items here are one-offs.
Other locations: Mid City Centre, 197 Pitt Street Mall, CBD (9232 6666); 312 King Street, Newtown (9557 0811).

Decadent **Belle Fleur** chocs. *See p182.*

What
Londoners
take when
they
go out.

Hats

Strand Hatters

*Strand Arcade, 412-414 George Street, between
King & Market Streets, CBD (9231 6884/
www.strandhatters.com.au). CityRail Martin Place
or St James/Monorail City Centre.* **Open** 8.30am-6pm
Mon-Wed, Fri; 8.30am-8pm Thur; 9.30am-4.30pm
Sat; 11am-4pm Sun. **Credit** AmEx, BC, DC, MC, V.
Map p311 C3.
Need to fill shopping orders for Akubra hats? This
is the place to come. A specialist in hats for men.

Jewellery

Family Jewels

*46-48 Oxford Street, between West & Comber Streets,
Paddington (9331 6647/www.thefamilyjewels.com.au).*
Open 10am-6pm Mon-Wed, Fri,
Sat; 10am-7.30pm Thur; 11am-6pm Sun. **Credit**
AmEx, BC, DC, MC, V. **Map** p313 D4.
Silver jewellery from all over, plus fun designs from
hot local designers and sparkly costume jewellery.
Other locations: Sydney Central Plaza, 450 George
Street, CBD (9231 0009); 393A Oxford Street,
Paddington (9331 3888).

Victoria Spring

*110 Oxford Street, between Glenmore Road &
Hopewell Street, Paddington (9331 7862/www.
victoriaspringdesigns.com). Bus 378, 380, L82.*
Open 10am-6pm Mon-Wed, Fri, Sat; 10am-7pm
Thur; noon-4pm Sun. **Credit** AmEx, BC, MC, V.
Map p313 D4.
There was a time when Victoria stuck to just jew-
ellery. Not any more. Her found-object style now
includes flatware, candlesticks, chandeliers, textiles
and a stash of sumptuous cushions and embroidered
throws. The style is feminine and frilly, with no
shortage of sequins, lace and baubles.
Other locations: Strand Arcade, 412-414 George
Street, CBD (9238 0700).

Lingerie

In addition to the shop listed below, some
department stores also have excellent and
extensive selections of lingerie. *See p166*
David Jones and **Grace Bros**.

Jaye M Underfashion

*Strand Arcade, 412-414 George Street, between
King & Market Streets, CBD (9231 2796). CityRail
Martin Place or St James/Monorail City Centre.*
Open 9am-5pm Mon-Wed, Fri; 9.30am-6pm Thur;
9.30am-3pm Sat. **Credit** AmEx, BC, MC, V.
Map p311 C3.
Those who know come here for the best selection of
good-brand bras to be found in Sydney. All the regular makes are stocked and – more importantly – in
a full range of sizes and colours. Best of all, Jaye M
are size specialists and so they make sure that their
customers get a perfect fit.

Shoes

See also p166 **Department stores**.

Gary Castles Shoes

*Shop 30, Strand Arcade, 412-414 George Street,
between King & Market Streets, CBD (9232 6544/
www.garycastlessydney.com). CityRail Martin Place
or St James/Monorail City Centre.* **Open** 9.30am-6pm
Mon-Wed, Fri, Sat; 9.30am-8.30pm Thur; 11am-5pm
Sun. **Credit** AmEx, BC, DC, MC, V. **Map** p311 C3.
Gorgeous, original, sophisticated styles in great
colour combos at a shade under international
designer prices. The sales are especially enticing.
Other locations: 328 Oxford Street, Paddington
(9361 4560); 45A Bay Street, Double Bay (9327 5077).

Max's Shoes

*150 Campbell Parade, between Hall & Curlewis
Streets, Bondi Beach (9300 9838). City Rail Bondi
Junction then bus 380, 381, L82/bus 380, L82.*
Open 9am-6pm Mon-Wed, Fri, Sat; 9am-9pm Thur;
10am-7pm Sun. **Credit** AmEx, BC, DC, MC, V.
Map p83.
This popular shop offers a huge range of cool and
contemporary shoes, ranging from the bargain
specials out front to more expensive styles. Prices
are pleasingly reasonable.
Other locations: 462 Oxford Street, Bondi Junction
(9387 3187); 156 Belmore Road, Randwick (9399 7950).

Platypus Shoes

*47 The Corso, Manly (9977 1500/www.platypus
shoes.com). Ferry Manly.* **Open** 9am-6pm Mon-Wed,
Fri, Sat; 9am-7pm Thur; 10am-6pm Sun. **Credit**
AmEx, BC, DC, MC, V. **Map** p104.
Hip brands like Diesel, Royal and Birkenstock, at
reasonable prices. Plus loads of cool trainers and
Aussie Blundstones.
Other locations: Market City, corner of Hay
& Thomas Streets, Haymarket (9211 8499);
124 Campbell Parade, Bondi Beach (9365 0015);
385 Oxford Street, Paddington (9360 1218); 275 King
Street, Newtown (9557 4599).

Vendor

*229A King Street, between Missenden Road &
Church Street, Newtown (9557 1939). CityRail
Newtown/bus 422, 423, 426, 428.* **Open** 9.30am-6pm
Mon-Wed, Fri, Sat; 9.30am-9pm Thur; 10.30am-5pm
Sun. **Credit** AmEx, BC, DC, MC, V. **Map** p93.
Lots of sporty street shoes, including trainers,
loafers and an array of lace-up and slip-on plimsoles
in funky colours and designs.
Other locations: 108 Oxford Street, Paddington
(9331 8860).

Tattooing & piercing

Flesh FX

*78 Campbell Parade, between Lamrock Avenue &
Hall Street, Bondi Beach (0439 132779). CityRail
Bondi Junction then bus 380, 381, L82/bus 380,
L82.* **Open** noon-6pm daily. **No credit cards**.
Map p83.

Eat, Drink, Shop

Popular tattoo and body piercing parlour in a tiny arcade opposite the beach. There's a huge selection of designs, including great whale and dolphin art. If the tattooist doesn't think the tattoo will work – for health or artistic reasons – he won't do it. Prices start at $80 for a small tattoo and $90 for navel piercing.

The Piercing Urge

251 Crown Street, between Oxford & Goulburn Streets, Darlinghurst (9360 3179/www.thepiercing urge.com.au). Bus 352, 373, 374, 377, 378, 380. **Open** 11am-7pm Mon-Wed, Fri; 11am-8pm Thur; 11am-6pm Sat; noon-6pm Sun. **Credit** AmEx, BC, DC, MC, V. **Map** p311 C3/4.

Established in Melbourne in 1991, the Sydney studio opened in 1994. It's a clean and smart place offering full body, facial and genital piercing, plus custom-made jewellery. There's also a very good follow-up service, just in case you have any problems.

Wigs

Ahead In Wigs

125 Oxford Street, between Crown & Flinders Streets, Darlinghurst (9360 1230). Bus 352, 373, 374, 377, 378, 380. **Open** 10am-5pm Mon-Wed, Fri, Sat; 10am-8pm Thur. **Credit** BC, MC, V. **Map** p311 C4.

One of many wig shops along this strip, popular with the gay community and those after a new look.

Celebrity Wigs

167 Oxford Street, between Crown & Flinders Streets, Darlinghurst (9331 5240/www.celebritywigs. com.au). Bus 352, 373, 374, 377, 378, 380. **Open** 10am-5pm Mon-Wed, Sat; 10am-6pm Thur-Fri. **Credit** AmEx, BC, DC, MC, V. **Map** p311 C4.

A huge collection of wigs and hairpieces aimed at party girls, drag queens and hair extension addicts.

Food & drink

Butchers

Jim's Butchery

211 Oxford Street, between Taylor Square & South Dowling Street, Darlinghurst (9331 1678). Bus 352, 378, 380. **Open** 7am-5.30pm Mon-Fri; 7am-1pm Sat. **No credit cards**. **Map** p311 C4.

A good old-fashioned butcher reminiscent of the days when now-busy Darlinghurst was just a village, Jim's has been selling meat since 1962. If you're looking for a juicy steak or plump lamb chop to throw on your mate's barbie, this is the place.

T&R Gourmet Butchery

Cosmopolitan Centre, corner of Bay & Knox Streets, Double Bay (9327 6107). Ferry Double Bay/bus 324, 325, 327. **Open** 7am-5.30pm Mon-Fri; 7am-4pm Sat. **Credit** AmEx, BC, DC, MC, V. **Map** p312 E3.

It may seem crazy to head to Double Bay for a slab of steak for the barbecue, but folk go out of their way to buy their meat from this butcher. It specialises

in aged and grain-fed beef, continental-cut veal and pork, fresh poultry and home-made sausages. They'll also give you sound advice on cooking, and there's a free home-delivery service.

Chocolates

Belle Fleur

658 Darling Street, between Victoria Road & Nelson Street, Rozelle (9810 2690/www.bellefleur.com.au). Bus 500, 501, 502, 504, 505, 506, 507, 508. **Open** 9am-6pm Mon-Fri; 9am-4pm Sat; 10am-4pm Sun. **Credit** AmEx, BC, MC, V.

The window displays of Belle Fleur will stop you in your tracks – a 1m (3ft) carved fishing boat surrounded by the heads and fins of menacing sharks, a life-sized leather travelling case – all made of chocolate. But then Jan and Lynne ter Heerdt are third-generation chocolate makers from Belgium, who set up in Sydney 20 years ago. The chocolates are freshly made daily.

Max Brenner Chocolate by the Bald Man

447 Oxford Street, between Centennial Park & Elizabeth Street, Paddington (9357 5055). Bus 378, 380, L82. **Open** 10am-6pm Mon-Sat; 11am-6pm Sun. **Credit** AmEx, BC, MC, V. **Map** p313 E4/5.

There's a café out front and an upmarket shop out back. Max Brenner certainly knows his cocoa beans – in the café, drink frozen chocolate cocktails, thick steaming cups of hot choc or gorge on strawberries dipped in chocolate fondue; in the back, choose from the enormous array of chocolate squares, each a unique recipe, and build up your own bespoke box. **Other locations**: Chatswood Chase, 345 Victoria Avenue, Chatswood (9411 6962); Manly Wharf, Manly (9977 4931).

Delis & gourmet foods

Delicacies on King

257 King Street, between Enmore Road & O'Connell Street, Newtown (9557 4048). CityRail Newtown. **Open** 8am-7pm Mon-Wed, Fri; 8am-9pm Thur; 9am-6pm Sat, Sun. **Credit** BC, MC, V. **Map** p93.

A fabulous continental deli with such mouth-watering savouries as home-made moussaka, cheese pies and gourmet ravioli, as well as lots of imported products including cool tins of Dutch liquorice and little jars of Lebanese garlic.

the fine food store

595 Darling Street, between Victoria Road & Elliot Street, Rozelle (9810 2858). Bus 500, 501, 502, 504, 505, 506, 507, 508. **Open** 10am-7pm Mon-Fri; 9am-5pm Sat; 10am-4pm Sun. **Credit** AmEx, BC, MC, V.

The staff are surprisingly friendly and approachable in this chic gourmet food store whose motto is 'food is our passion'. This place does what it says on the lable, selling pasta, frozen dim sum, and tins of real English golden syrup. There's also a cheese room.

Eclectic **Punch Gallery**. See p187.

Jones the Grocer
68 Moncur Street, at Queen Street, Woollahra (9362 1222/www.jonesthegrocer.com.au). Bus 389. **Open** *Summer* 8.30am-6pm Mon-Fri; 8.30am-5.30pm Sat; 8.30am-4.30pm Sun. *Winter* 9am-6pm Mon-Fri; 9am-5.30pm Sat; 9am-4.30pm Sun . **Credit** AmEx, BC, DC, MC, V. **Map** p313 E4.
Known for fine cheeses, sausages, cakes and high-quality grocery items, Jones is also a great place to hang out and just have a coffee, surrounded by its good stocks of excellent foods.

Provedoré Pelagios
235 Victoria Street, between Liverpool & William Streets, Darlinghurst (9360 1011). CityRail Kings Cross/bus 389. **Open** 9am-8pm Mon-Sat; 10am-7pm Sun. **Credit** AmEx, BC, MC, V. **Map** p311 D3.
Established in 1926, this traditional Italian grocer prides itself on its knowledgeable and enthusiastic staff. The bread is divine and there are salads, cold cuts, cheese, organic veg and gourmet pasta. The chocolate counter at the checkout is especially tempting at Easter. You can also have a coffee in the small lounge area at the front.

Margaret Fulton's Kitchen
Queens Court, 118-122 Queen Street, at Moncur Street, Woollahra (9362 9177/www.margaret fultonskitchen.com.au). Bus 389. **Open** 10am-8pm Mon-Fri; 9am-6pm Sat; noon-5pm Sun. **Credit** AmEx, BC, MC, V. **Map** p313 C4/5.
Margaret Fulton was a celebrity chef before the term was invented. She's been bringing her good honest recipes into Australia's dining rooms for many years, and now has a chain of four shops selling ready-made meals, marmalades, jams and pickles. **Other locations**: 123 Norton Street, Leichhardt (9518 1444); The Grove, 166-174 Military Road, Neutral Bay (9904 4900); Metcentre, 273 George Street, CBD (9247 4440).

Simon Johnson Quality Foods
55 Queen Street, between Oxford & Moncur Streets, Woollahra (9328 6888/www.simonjohnson.com). Bus 389. **Open** 10.30am-7pm Mon-Fri; 9am-5pm Sat; 10am-4pm Sun. **Credit** AmEx, BC, MC, V. **Map** p313 E4/5.
Established and esteemed foodie Simon Johnson has set himself up as the nation's leading provider of Australian and imported gourmet foods. His produce comes from more than 50 key sources, all vetted for quality. This shop has a great upstairs kitchenware section, a pleasingly odorous cheese room and plenty of sweet offerings. **Other locations**: 181 Harris Street, Pyrmont (9552 2522).

Health foods

Bayside Natural Health Centre
30-36 Bay Street, between Cooper & Cross Streets, Double Bay (9327 8002). Ferry Double Bay/bus 324, 325, 327. **Open** 9am-6.30pm Mon-Fri; 9am-6pm Sat; 11.30am-5.30pm Sun. **Credit** AmEx, BC, DC, MC, V. **Map** p312 E3.
Lots of organic fresh and dried produce including bread and a small deli section. A few well-placed stone buddhas and oil burners create a calming ambience in which to splurge on the herbal remedies, natural skin-care cosmetics and therapeutic massages (book in advance) on offer.

Oriental

TQC Burlington Supermarket
Corner of Thomas & Quay Streets, Ultimo (9281 2777/www.tqc-burlington.com.au). CityRail Central/Monorail Haymarket/LightRail Central, Capitol Square or Haymarket. **Open** 9am-7pm daily. **Credit** AmEx, BC, MC, V. **Map** p311 B4.
A huge emporium of Chinese and other Asian groceries, including fruit and veg and a butcher.

Lucky Food Stores
36 Campbell Street, between George & Castlereagh Streets, Chinatown (9212 4743). CityRail Central/LightRail Capitol Square. **Open** 9.30am-6pm daily. **No credit cards**. **Map** p311 B/C4.

Eat, Drink, Shop

Only in Oz

Singing koala? Tick. Victoria Bitter foam stubbie holder? Tick. Yellow hopping-kangaroo road-sign fridge magnet? Tick. What else is there to take home to the folks? An awful lot, actually. Check out the following souvenirs for a taste of real Australia.

Akubra hats

Damn, those colonials were stylish! Nothing much has changed in the shape of the Akubra hat (above) since hatter Benjamin Dunkerley and his family set up business, first in Tasmania and later in Sydney, making felt hats from rabbit under-fur. Styles range from the traditional country hats (Coolabah and Coober Pedy, both around $150) to tophats and even 'the Croc' – the authentic Akubra made famous by Paul Hogan in *Crocodile Dundee*.
● Available from **David Jones** (*see p166*); **Gowings** (*see p176*); **RM Williams** (*see p177*); **Strand Hatters** (*see p181*).

Beach wear

Aussie surfwear has exploded into one of the country's most desirable exports. Sure, you can buy gear back home in the burgeoning number of concept stores, but on local turf you'll get the absolute latest designs. At the time of writing, top of the cool barometer is **Rip Curl** (right), **Roxy** (for girls) and perennial fave **Mambo** (top right). For a Bondi souvenir, and one that helps save lives, visit the excellent **Between the Flags** (*see p178*). All the gear you need, including bathers, deckchairs, umbrellas and special Bondi Nippers T-shirts, carries the Bondi Surf Bathers' Life Saving Club logo in some form or another. This is where to buy swimming trunks with BONDI on the bum, as worn by the lifesavers. Best of all, ten per cent of the retail cost goes to the BSBLSC.
● *See p177* **Surfwear & swimwear**.

Blundstone boots

Nicknamed 'Blunnies', the steel toe-capped versions were worn by the dance troupe Tapdogs for their sell-out shows. Originally made by English immigrant shoemakers to survive the harsh Tasmanian winters, Blundstones quickly became Australian for 'workboot'. With ranges called Yakka and Redback (after the lethal spider), this is tough, long-lasting, no-nonsense footwear. Recent additions include brightly coloured suede Blunnies for the kids. Expect to pay $80 for a basic brown budget boot and around $129 for a swankier suede pair.
● Available from **Gowings** (*see p176*) and **Platypus** (*see p181*).

Boomerangs

Quintessentially Australian, a boomerang works because of the effect of air pressure on two opposed surfaces (produced by the twist in the wood at the tips of the boomerang), combined with the spinning motion produced by the throw. Be warned that the majority of boomerangs you see in the shops are not the real deal, and there are lots of dos and don'ts when it comes to throwing. If you're really serious, visit **Duncan**

McLennan's Boomerang School (224A William Street, Kings Cross, 9358 2370, open 10am-6pm daily). McLennan has been working in the boomerang business for more than 40 years, and if you buy one of his boomerangs he'll give you a free lesson; he reckons the average person can grasp the basics in just five minutes. You learn on a beginner's model ($8), but McLennan also sells the traditional, more decorative boomerangs, which he commissions from Aboriginal craftsmen from all over Australia.

Didgeridoos

Probably the oldest instrument in the world, the droning sound produced by this long wooden flute was played by Aborigines thousands of years ago to represent as accurately as possible the sounds of nature: running water, trees creaking, the flapping of wings. Authentic didgeridoos are made from tree branches or trunks that have been hollowed out by termites. They are cleaned with hot coals and treated with oils and wax, and cut to an average of 1.3 metres (4.25 feet). You can buy them plain or painted and expect to pay anything from $100 to $2,000.
● Available from **Didj Beat Didgeridoos** (see p186) and **The Spirit of Downunder** (see p169).

Driza-Bone

The Driza-Bone was invented in the late 19th century by Scotsman E Le Roy, who discovered that the torn sails of a windjammer made excellent protective coating for sailors. When his sea days were over, he set up a thriving business manufacturing 'dry as a (sun-dried cattle-) bone' coats and adapting them for land use, with fantails for use in the saddle. The flammable paraffin once used as a waterproofer has long since been abandoned, but Driza-Bones' exact ingredients remain a well-kept secret. A short riding coat will set you back around $179, $215 for a long one.
● Available from **David Jones** (see p166) and **Gowings** (see p176).

RM Williams boots

Intrepid 'RM' was a boy with a taste for adventure, and when he left South Australia in his teens he began exploring some of the remotest parts of Australia, but always doing the hard yakka along the way. So when he crafted his first boot 60 years ago, he knew exactly the tough conditions a good boot (left) would need to face to 'last a lifetime.' A Yard Boot costs around $299.95, a Bushman $274.95 and a Yearling $349.95.
● Available from **David Jones** (see p166), **Gowings** (see p176) and **RM Williams** (see p177).

Uggs

Think Pamela Anderson on the set of *Baywatch*, cup of coffee in hand and woolly uggs (far left) on her feet. Ugg is the generic term for Aussie-made sheepskin footwear and they're traditionally worn barefoot. Prices start at $53 for scruffs (slip-on slippers without backs), $60 for slippers, $95 for a short boot and $119 for a full-length boot.
● Available from **Gowings** (see p176) and **Rocks Merino** (see p169 **The Rocks Centre**).

This is quite simply a fabulous store for Thai food-stuffs. Where else will you find ten brands of fish sauce? Plus 25kg bags of Thai rice, enormous bags of fresh beansprouts, pink and white lime paste and bottles of chilli paste with sweet basil leaves.

Tea

Taka Tea Garden
320 New South Head Road, between Manning & Kiaora Roads, Double Bay (9362 1777/www.taka teagarden.com.au). CityRail Edgecliff/ferry Double Bay/bus 323, 324, 325. **Open** noon-6pm Tue-Sat. **Credit** AmEx, BC, MC, V. **Map** p312 E3.
Taka Pan and Helen Kwok opened this sophisti-cated tea house in 1999. This is the only place in Australia to sell Japanese Chikumedio tea, a con-noisseur's green tea grown on the slopes of Mount Fuji. They also have Taiwanese and Chinese green teas, German herbal infusions and Ceylon black tea, which you can buy loose or taste in store with a slice of green tea cake.

Furniture

Visitors staying for a while will probably end up renting the Australian way – unfurnished (furnished lets are much more expensive). For reasonably priced, brand-new contemporary furniture, try **Freedom** (9313 8211, www. freedom.com.au), those clever Swedes **IKEA** (9313 6400, www.ikea.com.au) or **Fantastic Furniture** (9663 4588, www.fantastic furniture.com.au), all located in Moore Park's **Supacenta** (corner of South Dowling Street and Todman Avenue).

There are heaps of second-hand furniture emporiums, which sell (when you arrive) and buy (when you leave) all types of furniture from lamps to sofas, beds to washing machines. Two reliable outlets are **Bondi Furniture Market** (2 Jacques Avenue, Bondi Beach, 9365 1315) and **Peter Foley's Furniture** (93 Bronte Road, Bondi Junction, 9387 3144).

To rent white goods and/or furniture, look in the *Yellow Pages* under 'Hire Household Appliances & Furniture'.

Gifts & homeware

Also check out the great gift shops in the **Museum of Sydney** (*see p60*), **Museum of Contemporary Art** (*see p57*) and the **Powerhouse Museum** (*see p71*).

Abode
16 Hall Street, between Campbell Parade & O'Brien Street, Bondi Beach (9365 4706). CityRail Bondi Junction then bus 380, 381, L82/bus 380, L82. **Open** 9am-7pm daily. **Credit** AmEx, BC, DC, MC, V. **Map** p83.

Humour is the name of the game in this cool gift shop. You can choose from swinging hula-hula girls for your dashboard or cuddly swinging dice for the rear view mirror. Along with all of the silly stuff there are also great Levi handbags and tote bags, quality bath products, incense, photo frames, and plenty of fun things for the kids.

Arte Flowers
112 Queen Street, between Ocean & Oxford Streets, Woollahra (9328 0402). Bus 389. **Open** 9.30am-6pm Mon-Fri; 9am-6pm Sat; 10am-5pm Sun. **Credit** AmEx, BC, DC, MC, V. **Map** p313 E4/5.
This is a stylish European-feel homewares and gift shop on the busy antiques shop strip of Woollahra. You can just pop in for a coffee and browse the glossies at a big old wooden table at the back and then take in the delights of the designer furniture, glassware and jewellery, as well as Lulu Guinness bags, Prada stationery and decadent and lovingly designed gardener's gloves.

Didj Beat Didgeridoos
Clocktower Square Mall, corner of Argyle & Harrington Streets, The Rocks (9251 4289/ www.didjbeat.com). **Credit** AmEx, BC, DC, MC, V. **Map** p310 B1.
These people are serious about their didgeridoos and have hundreds of them. They consider themselves to be a music shop, rather than a souvenir place, and prices range from $100 to $2,000 – you're paying for size and design; they claim the sound quality of their superior stock is the same whatever the price. The 'how to play the didgeridoo' lessons on Sundays cost $30, which will be taken off the cost of the instru-ment if you go on to buy.

Dinosaur Designs
Strand Arcade, 412-414 George Street, between King & Market Streets, CBD (9223 2953/www. dinosaurdesigns.com.au). CityRail Martin Place or St James/Monorail City Centre. **Open** 9.30am-5.30pm Mon-Wed, Fri; 9.30am-8.30pm Thur; 10am-4pm Sat. **Credit** AmEx, BC, MC, V. **Map** p311 C3.
Dinosaur Designs stocks beautiful glowing resin bowls, vases, jugs, plates and other household items as well as big jewellery.
Other locations: 339 Oxford Street, Paddington (9361 3776).

Ecodownunder
584 Darling Street, between Victoria Road & West Street, Rozelle (9555 9991/www.ecodownunder.com). Bus 500, 501, 502, 504, 505, 506, 507, 508. **Open** 10am-6pm Mon-Fri; 9.30am-3.30pm Sat; 9.30am-2.30pm Sun. **Credit** AmEx, BC, DC, MC, V.
Everything in this store is organic and much of the stock is predominantly Australian-made. A recent change of owners has resulted in a shift in focus towards babies – 'it's when people have kids that they start to get interested in organic stuff,' says owner Tim Toft, and he's got a point – the most pop-ular product is the organic baby food, but there is plenty here to choose from.

Indian Cottage Emporium

108 King Street, between Missenden Road & Fitzroy Street, Newtown (9550 6710). Bus 422, 423, 426, 428, 352. **Open** 11am-6pm daily. **Credit** AmEx, BC, DC, MC, V.

This is a veritable Indian bazaar right in the middle of King Street. It's got hundreds of Ganesha and Shiva icons in every conceivable style, and the cheapest packs of incense in town. This is the place to buy your bindi – there are literally hundreds of them here– and gaudy Indian bracelets.

Made in Japan

437 Oxford Street, between Elizabeth Street & Jersey Road, Paddington (9360 6979/www.mij.com.au). Bus 378, 380, L82. **Open** 10am-6pm Mon-Wed, Fri, Sat; 10am-8pm Thur; 11am-4pm Sun. **Credit** AmEx, BC, DC, MC, V. **Map** p313 E4.

As it says on the sign, everything here is made in Japan, pleasingly displayed and of very good quality. There's lots of lacquerware, some exquisite (and pricey) kimonos, tea sets, lanterns, heavy wooden chests and oodles of chopsticks.

Morning Glory

The Galeries Victoria, 500 George Street, at Park Street, CBD (9286 3098). CityRail Town Hall/ Monorail Galeries Victoria. **Open** 9am-6pm Mon-Wed, Fri; 9am-8pm Thur; 10am-5pm Sat; 11am-5pm Sun. **Credit** (over $20) BC, MC, V. **Map** p311 B3.

Kitsch keyrings, mini models, Miss Kitty bags, and stationery, including erasers, tiny notebooks and highly coloured pencils fill the shelves in this cute little shop. The trinkets are mostly made in Korea and school kids devour them.

Other locations: 22 Goulburn Street, Haymarket (9267 7899).

Octopus Design

260 King Street, between Enmore Road & Watkin Street, Newtown (9565 4688/www.octopusdesign. com.au). CityRail Newtown. **Open** *Summer* 11am-7pm Mon-Wed, Fri; 11am-8.30pm Thur; 9am-6pm Sat; noon-5pm Sun. *Winter* 10am-6pm Mon-Wed, Fri; 10am-7.30pm Thur; 9am-6pm Sat; noon-5pm Sun. **Credit** AmEx, BC, DC, MC, V. **Map** p93.

This award-winning gift shop stocks a kitsch collection of novelties, funky ashtrays, photo frames, beach bags, clocks, drag-queen greetings cards and Lulu Guinness handbags.

Other locations: **Opus Designs** 344 Oxford Street, Paddington (9360 4803).

The Pop Shop

143 Oxford Street, between Crown & Flinders Streets, Darlinghurst (9331 7849/www.thepop shop.com.au). Bus 378, 380, L82. **Open** 9am-6pm Mon-Wed, Fri, Sat; 9am-7.30pm Thur; 10.30am-5.30pm Sun. **Credit** AmEx, BC, DC, MC, V. **Map** p311 C4.

Sydney's best queer gifts shop offers a wonderful selection of deeply camp merchandise, including kitsch clocks, colourful inflatables and, at the time of writing, the popular board game for the hit TV series *Australian Pop Idol*.

Punch Gallery

209 Darling Street, near Gladstone Park, Balmain (9810 1014/www.punchgallery.com.au). Bus 433, 443, 445. **Open** 10.30am-5.30pm Tue-Sat; 11am-4pm Sun. **Credit** AmEx, BC, DC, MC, V.

Punch is something of a success story, having recently celebrated its 14th birthday. It began life in a nearby back street, but now takes pride of place on Balmain's prestigious main drag, where it has been popular for years for its unusual jewellery, lamps and ceramics made by designers from all over Australia and the rest of the world. Everything here is bright, colourful and one-off.

Health & beauty

Beauty salons & body treatments

Ella Baché

236 Oxford Street, between Young & Ormond Streets, Paddington (9356 4611/www.ellabache. com.au/Paddington). Bus 378, 380, L82. **Open** 10am-7pm Mon-Wed; 10am-8pm Thur; 10am-6pm Fri; 9am-6pm Sat; 10am-5pm Sun. **Credit** AmEx, BC, DC, MC, V. **Map** p313 D4.

This place is beloved for its skin diagnosis with a Wood's Lamp (using a black light to highlight skin defects) followed by bespoke skin therapy programmes and a host of luscious treatments, from

Napoleon Make-up Academy. *See p188.*

massage to body bronzing, water therapy, waxing and body wraps – all are done using Ella Baché's many famous products.
Other locations: throughout the city.

Ginseng Bathhouse
First Floor, Crest Hotel, 111 Darlinghurst Road, between William & Macleay Streets, Kings Cross (9358 2755/www.thebathhouse.com.au). CityRail Kings Cross. **Open** 10am-10pm Mon-Fri; 9am-10pm Sat, Sun. **Credit** AmEx, BC, DC, MC, V. **Map** p312 D3.
Traditional Korean bath house offering steam treatments, ginseng baths, scrubs and masterly massage. Separate baths for men and women.

Complementary medicine

A Natural Practice
161A Glebe Point Road, between Mitchell & St John Road, Glebe (9566 4038/www.anaturalpractice. com.au). Bus 431, 432, 433. **Open** 10am-5.30pm Mon-Fri; 9am-4.30pm Sat. **No credit cards.** **Map** p311 A4.
Acupuncture, shiatsu, reflexology, remedial massage, naturopathy, osteopathy: you name it.

Phoenix Holistic Centre
31 Rowe Street, off Syd Einfeld Drive, Woollahra (9386 1225). CityRail Bondi Junction. **Open** 9am-5pm Mon-Fri; 9am-1pm Sat. **Credit** BC, MC, V. **Map** p313 F5.
Whether it's iridology, acupuncture, counselling, kinesiology, ayurvedic medicine, astrology readings, energy balancing through massage, Chinese medicine or herbs that you're in need of, you'll find it here.

Cosmetics

Jurlique
Strand Arcade, 412-414 George Street, between King & Market Streets, CBD (9231 0626/www.jurlique. com.au). CityRail Martin Place or St James/Monorail City Centre. **Open** 9am-6pm Mon-Wed, Fri; 9am-9pm Thur; 9am-5pm Sat; 11am-4pm Sun. **Credit** AmEx, BC, DC, MC, V. **Map** p311 C3.
Already selling overseas, this small company based in South Australia does a range of Oz aromatherapy products. They're not cheap though.
Other locations: 352A Oxford Street, Paddington (9368 7373); 573 Military Road, Mosman (9969 2155).

Napoleon Make-up Academy
74 Oxford Street, between Barcom Avenue & Glenmore Road, Paddington (9331 1737/ www.napoleoncosmetics.com). Bus 378, 380, L82. **Open** 9.30am-7pm Mon, Wed; 9.30am-6.30pm Tue, Thur, Fri; 9.30am-6pm Sat; noon-5pm Sun. **Credit** AmEx, BC, DC, MC, V. **Map** p313 D4.
Australian-owned and developed by Napoleon himself (not the French emperor, but a Hollywood make-up artist), this shop has its own brand of cosmetics and in-house professional make-up artists.
Other locations: Sydney Central Plaza, 450 George Street, CBD (9221 6277).

Exotic **Cambodia House**. *See p189.*

Perfect Potion
QVB, 455 George Street, between Market & Druitt Streets, CBD (9286 3384/www.perfectpotion. com.au). CityRail Town Hall/Monorail Galeries Victoria. **Open** 9am-6pm Mon-Wed, Fri, Sat; 9am-9pm Thur; 11am-5pm Sun. **Credit** AmEx, BC, MC, V. **Map** p311 B/C3.
These people are serious about their holistic aromatherapy, and so they have a good skin-care range made from essential oils, infused plant oils, cold pressed vegetable oils, organically grown herbal extracts and plant-derived ingredients. Those who believe in the benefits of such natural ingredients flock here in droves.
Other locations: Westfield Shopping Centre, 500 Oxford Street, Bondi Junction (9389 6120).

Hairdressers

In addition to the shops listed below, there's also a barber shop at **Gowings** (*see p176*) offering basic cuts for $15.

Barberia
323 Crown Street, between Campbell & Albion Streets, Surry Hills (9360 3452). CityRail/LightRail Central/bus 378, 380, L82. **Open** 10.30am-6pm Tue, Wed, Fri, Sat; 10.30am-9pm Thur; 10.30am-5pm Sat. **Credit** BC, MC, V. **Map** p311 C4.
Groovy barber-cuts by hip clubbers. Very local, very cool and always good chatter.

Muse

*First Floor, 4-6 Flinders Street, at Taylor Square,
Darlinghurst (9331 1188/www.musehair.com.au).
Bus 352, 373, 374, 377, 378, 380.* **Open** 9am-5pm
Tue, Wed, Fri; 9am-7.30pm Thur; 9am-3pm Sat.
Credit AmEx, BC, MC, V. **Map** p311 C4.
Popular with Sydney's girlie fashion set and always
up with the latest cut, this upstairs joint overlook-
ing Taylor Square has won numerous awards.

Music

The shops listed below are all good, but there
are always the megastores. **HMV** (Mid City
Centre, 197 Pitt Street Mall, 9221 2311,
www.hmv.com.au) and **Sanity** (Town
Hall Square, Town Hall Station, 9286 3541,
www.sanity.com.au) are both options. Check
the phone book for other locations.

Ashwood's Music & Books

*129 York Street, between Market & Druitt Streets,
CBD (9267 7745/www.ashwoods.com). CityRail
Town Hall/Monorail Galeries Victoria.* **Open** 9.30am-
6.30pm Mon-Wed, Fri; 9.30am-8pm Thur; 9.30am-
5pm Sat; noon-4pm Sun. **Credit** BC, MC, V.
Map p311 C3.
This basement music emporium opposite the QVB
is a great place to find obscure CDs or vinyl. It's also
good for second-hand music books and DVDs.

Birdland

*3 Barrack Street, at York Street, CBD (9299
8527/www.birdland.com.au). CityRail Wynyard or
Martin Place.* **Open** 10am-5.30pm Mon-Wed, Fri;
10am-7pm Thur; 9am-4.30pm Sat. **Credit** AmEx,
BC, DC, MC, V. **Map** p310 C2.
Birdland is the best jazz shop in the city – some
would say the best in the world.

Central Station Records

*46 Oxford Street, between Hyde Park and Crown
Street, Darlinghurst (9361 5222/www.central
station.com.au). CityRail Museum/bus 378, 380,
L82.* **Open** 10am-7pm Mon-Wed, Fri; 10am-9pm
Thur; 10am-6pm Sat; noon-6pm Sun. **Credit** AmEx,
BC, MC, V. **Map** p311 C3.
Whether you're a vinyl LP collector, a budding bed-
room DJ, someone off the street who wants to buy
that CD dance single you heard in the club last night,
or even the nightclub DJ who was playing that CD,
this is the shop for you. Central Station's vast basement store houses the very latest in import and
domestic dance, euro, house, hip hop, R&B and
Mardi Gras compilations. It even produces its own
compilation series – Wild and Skitz Mix.

Fish Records

*261 King Street, between Church & O'Connell
Streets, Newtown (9557 3074/www.fishrecords.
com.au). CityRail Newtown.* **Open** 9am-10pm
daily. **Credit** AmEx, BC, DC, MC, V. **Map** p93.
Next to the Dendy cinema, this Fish stocks mostly
Top 40 and dance music with a good soundtrack

section. The Balmain branch specialises in jazz,
while the George Street branch focuses on classical
music – both are excellent.
Other locations: 350 George Street, CBD (9233
3371); 289 Darling Street, Balmain (9810 8421);
Norton Plaza, Norton Street, Leichhardt (9560 0344);
468 Oxford Street, Bondi Junction (9388 9641).

Folkways Music

*282 Oxford Street, between Ormond & Elizabeth
Streets, Paddington (9361 3980). Bus 378, 380,
L82.* **Open** 9am-6pm Mon-Wed, Fri, Sat; 9am-9pm
Thur; 11am-6pm Sun. **Credit** AmEx, BC, DC, MC, V.
Map p313 D/E4.
Folkways is the standard bearer for folk and ethnic
music plus modern grooves.

Red Eye

*66 King Street, between George & York Streets, CBD
(9299 4233/www.redeye.com.au). CityRail Wynyard.*
Open 9am-6pm Mon-Wed, Fri; 9am-9pm Thur; 9am-
5pm Sat; 11am-5pm Sun. **Credit** AmEx, BC, MC, V.
Map p310 B2.
The biggest of the indie stores, Red Eye has an excellent selection of Australian bands and labels, as well
as a good selection of imports. The Pitt Street branch
specialises in second-hand merchandise.
Other locations: 370 Pitt Street, CBD (9262 9755).

Op shops

Op shops ('op' for opportunity) are the Australian
version of the UK's charity shops and the US's
thrift stores.

Cambodia House

*445 Oxford Street, between Elizabeth Street &
Jersey Road, Paddington (9328 6110). Bus 378,
380, L82.* **Open** 9.30am-5.30pm Mon-Fri; 9am-5pm
Sat; 10am-4pm Sun. **Credit** AmEx, BC, DC, MC, V.
Map p313 E4.
Woollahra fashion guru Mary Read established this
chic, not-for-profit business in 1999 to help poor
Cambodians, including survivors of landmine
injuries. The aim is to develop Cambodia's export
market and in so doing create income-generating
opportunities for the shop's suppliers. You'll find
pottery, richly coloured silk quilts, wraps, pillows
and cushions, footwear, handbags, candles, bowls
and wonderful greeting cards.

St Vincent de Paul

*292 Oxford Street, between Elizabeth & Underwood
Streets, Paddington (9360 4151). Bus 378, 380,
L82.* **Open** 9.30am-5.30pm Mon-Wed, Fri; 9.30am-
7.30pm Thur; 10am-5pm Sat. **Credit** AmEx, BC,
MC, V. **Map** p313 E4.
This Oxford Street store specialises in clothes, and
it's good enough that the turnover is quick. It's pos-
sible to find the current season's fashion and design-
er labels including Diesel jackets, Marcs jeans and
even CK T-shirts here. Proceeds go to St Vincent de
Paul hospitals and charity work.
Other locations: throughout the city.

Eat, Drink, Shop

Salvos Store St Peters

7 Bellevue Street, off Princes Highway, St Peters (9519 1513). CityRail St Peters. **Open** 8.30am-3.30pm Mon-Fri; 8.30am-1.45pm Sat. **Credit** BC, MC, V.

More department store than humble op shop, this vast store holds racks of clothes with regular specials, enough furniture to fill an apartment block, old computers, a good collection of records and cut-price household goods. Proceeds go to the Salvation Army (Salvos) – huge in Australia.
Other locations: throughout the city.

Opticians & eyewear

K Optica

432 Oxford Street, between George & Elizabeth Streets, Paddington (9331 3400). Bus 378, 380, L82. **Open** 9.30am-6pm Mon-Wed, Fri, Sat; 9.30am-8.30pm Thur; 11am-5.30pm Sun. **Credit** AmEx, BC, DC, MC, V. **Map** p313 E4.

A small but perfectly formed and popular eyewear shop with an ever-changing collection of the latest frames, including designer lines. There's also an on-site optician service.

Pharmacies

Non-prescription painkillers commonly available over the counter include Panadol (paracetamol), Disprin, Aspro Clear (aspirin), Nurofen (ibuprofen) and Panadeine (codeine/paracetamol). There are very few 24-hour chemists, but plenty of the chains trade into the evening, including:

Darlinghurst Prescription Pharmacy

261 Oxford Street, at South Dowling Street, Darlinghurst (9361 5882). Bus 378, 380, L82. **Open** 8am-10pm Mon-Sat; 11am-6pm Sun. **Credit** AmEx, BC, DC, MC, V. **Map** p311 C4.

Situated just up the road from St Vincent's Public & Private Hospitals, this friendly, well-stocked pharmacy has knowledgeable staff and a full prescription service.

Sport & outdoor

In addition to the shops listed below, *see also* **RM Williams** (*p177*) and **Gowings** (*p176*).

Kathmandu

Shop 35, Town Hall Arcade, corner of Kent & Bathurst Streets, CBD (9261 8901/www.kathmandu. com.au). CityRail Town Hall/Monorail Galeries Victoria. **Open** 9am-5pm Mon-Wed, Fri, Sat; 9am-8.30pm Thur; 10am-4pm Sun. **Credit** AmEx, BC, MC, V. **Map** p311 B3.

'Live the dream, ski it, sail it, run it, climb it, surf it, walk it, paddle it, explore it, skate it!' That's their motto and they mean it. They have everything in here – the gear, the clothes, the gadgets.

Paddy Pallin

507 Kent Street, at Bathurst Street, CBD (9264 2685/www.paddypallin.com.au). CityRail Town Hall/Monorail Galeries Victoria. **Open** 9am-5.30pm Mon-Wed; 9am-9pm Thur; 9am-6pm Fri; 9am-5pm Sat; 10am-4pm Sun. **Credit** AmEx, BC, DC, MC, V. **Map** p311 B3.

Excellent equipment shop catering to all your climbing and outdoor needs. The Parramatta branch opposite the post office is also excellent.
Other locations: 74 Macquarie Street, Parramatta (9633 1113).

Toys & games

Both **David Jones** and **Grace Bros** (*see p166*) have well-stocked toy departments.

Kidstuff

126A Queen Street, between Moncur & Ocean Streets, Woollahra (9363 2838). Bus 389. **Open** 9.30am-5.30pm Mon-Fri; 9am-5pm Sat; 9am-4pm Sun. **Credit** AmEx, BC, DC, MC, V. **Map** p313 E4.

Vast selection of quality and educational toys for all ages, including lots of Australian-made items and grandma-friendly wooden toys and doll's houses.
Other locations: 780 Military Road, Mosman (9960 5298).

Toy Villa – Toy Kingdom

455 New South Head Road, between Kiaora & Manning Streets, Double Bay (9327 7558/9327 1494). CityRail Edgecliff/ferry Double Bay. **Open** 9am-5.30pm Mon-Fri; 9am-5pm Sat; 10am-4pm Sun. **Credit** AmEx, BC, DC, MC, V. **Map** p312 E/F3.

Don't be put off by the shabby frontage, this is one of Sydney's more versatile toy shops with everything from cheap farmyard animals, yoyos, Lego and so on to the model kid's car that Double Bay junior might park next to his dad's BMW.

Travel agents

Flight Centre

18-32 Oxford Street, between Hyde Park & Crown Street, Darlinghurst (9331 0993/www.flightcentre. com.au). CityRail Museum/bus 378, 380, L82. **Open** 9.30am-6pm Mon-Fri; 10am-3pm Sat. **Credit** AmEx, BC, DC, MC, V. **Map** p311 C3.

You can bank on friendly, well-travelled, efficient staff in this ever-growing Australian chain. Great for good flight deals and also for putting together travel plans at home and overseas.

STA Travel

855 George Street, at Harris Street, Haymarket (9212 1255/www.statravel.com.au). CityRail Central. **Open** 9am-6pm Mon-Wed, Fri; 9am-7pm Thur; 10am-3pm Sat. **Credit** AmEx, BC, DC, MC, V. **Map** p311 B4.

Not just for students, this international chain is good on prices for travel in Australia and beyond.
Other locations: 9 Oxford Street, Paddington (9360 1822); Broadway Shopping Centre, Broadway (9211 2563).

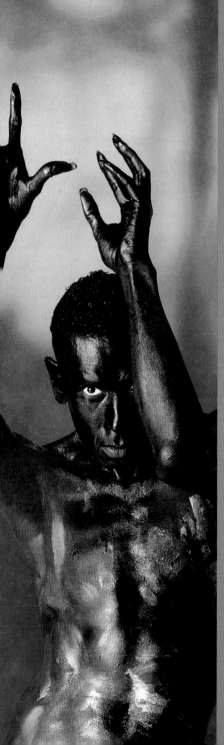

Arts & Entertainment

Features

Festivals & Events

Sydney's all grown up now – and it's got the parties to prove it.

In a city that is constantly trying to affirm its identity, festivals are very important, and as Sydney matures the number of festivals it holds is exploding. The result is that rarely a week goes by without a celebration of one kind or another, and each year the organisers try to make each event bigger and better than the previous one. Every festival comes with a huge party attached and, with one of the most beautiful backdrops in the world, the carousing usually takes place outdoors.

Events can broadly be divided into three categories: arty, sporty and multicultural. And many events – like the colourful **Carnivale** and the eclectic **Sydney Festival** – cross more than one category. Top of the charts for attendance – and events not to be missed if you're in town – are standards such as the **New Year's Eve** fireworks, the **Sydney Hobart Yacht Race**, the **Royal Easter Show** and the **Gay & Lesbian Mardi Gras**. But there are many other occasions that attract smaller, more manageable crowds.

For details of what's going on when, check out the **Sydney City Council website** at www.sydneycity.nsw.gov.au or the daily papers. For NSW public holidays, *see p293*.

Spring

Good Food Month

Various venues (http://gfm.smh.com.au/index.asp).
Date Sept.
You'll find every top chef and foodie in Sydney doing something at this *Sydney Morning Herald*-sponsored festival. There are masses of events, indoor and outdoor, including the Spring Picnic in Centennial Park, Night Noodle markets at the Royal Botanic Gardens and the Sydney Food & Wine Fair. Check the *SMH* (www.smh.com.au) for details.

Festival of the Winds

Bondi Beach (8362 3400/www.waverley.nsw.gov.au). CityRail Bondi Junction then bus 380, 381, 382, L82/bus 380, L82. **Map** p83. **Date** 2nd Sun in Sept.
Australia's largest free kite-flying festival is staged outside the Bondi Pavilion on Bondi Beach and in the park behind the beach, attracting up to 50,000 people. The kite competitions are only open to kite club members, but there are plenty of other events and activities for beginners and non-kite enthusiasts, including performers, multicultural musicians and masses of stuff for kids. The festival kicks off around 10am and finishes about 4.30pm.

Sydney Marathon Festival

8907 9460/www.sydneymarathon.org.
Date Sun in mid Sept.
This annual celebration of the 2000 Olympic Games is comprised of three road runs and open to all (entry rules permitting). The marathon, half-marathon and 10km (6.2-mile) Bridge run are the only community road races that close the Sydney Harbour Bridge and offer the opportunity to run across it. The marathon follows the famous 'blue line' used in the Olympics and charts a spectacular route, taking in the Sydney Opera House, the Royal Botanical Gardens, Centennial Park, Anzac Bridge and Sydney Olympic Park. All three races start in North Sydney.

Manly International Jazz Festival

Manly (9977 1088/www.manly.nsw.gov.au).
Ferry Manly. **Map** p104. **Date** last weekend in Sept/1st weekend in Oct.
Australia's largest and longest-running community jazz festival attracts crowds of up to 20,000 to hear artists from around Australia and overseas. Stages are erected along the Corso, on the beach, at the Manly Wharf Hotel and on the council forecourt opposite Manly Wharf. There are more than 60 free performances, plus various chichi pay-for events.

Sleaze Ball

Fox Studios Australia, Driver Avenue, Moore Park (9557 4332/www.mardigras.org.au). Bus 339, 373, 374, 375, 376, 377, 393, 395, 396. **Map** p313 D5.
Date last Sat in Sept/1st Sat in Oct.
A spectacular and, of course, sleazy dance party organised by the Gay & Lesbian Mardi Gras. For more information, *see p220*.

Carnivale

Various venues (9251 7974/www.carnivale.com.au).
Date Sept-Oct.
The country's biggest multicultural arts festival features artists from more than 140 ethnic backgrounds in an attempt to offer a snapshot of Australia's vibrant multiculturalism. Now supported by some hefty sponsors, the month-long festival is slicker and more diverse than ever.

Sculpture by the Sea

Along the cliff walk from Bondi to Tamarama (9357 1457/www.sculpturebythesea.com). CityRail Bondi Junction then bus 380, 381, 382, L82/bus 380, L82. **Map** p83. **Date** late Oct-early Nov.
Australia's largest outdoor free exhibition of contemporary sculpture – and what a location! For two or so weeks, around 100 works by local and overseas artists line the coastal cliff walk from Bondi

Beach down to Tamarama beach. Another 60 small works are on show in the Bondi Pavilion Gallery.

Glebe New Music Festival & Street Fair

Glebe Point Road, from Parramatta Road to Bridge Road, Glebe (9281 0024/www.glebenewmusic festival.com.au). Light Rail Glebe/bus 431, 432, 433, 434, 370. **Map** p311 A4. **Date** 3rd Sun in Nov.
Sydney's longest-running community carnival celebrated its 20th birthday in 2003 with a new focus on music. Around a kilometre of Glebe Point Road is closed to traffic and given over to stages, food stalls, wine-tasting booths, arts-and-craft stalls, stilt-walkers, clowns and bands. Foley Park is devoted to children's activities. Expect crowds of around 100,000.

Summer

Homebake

The Domain, Mrs Macquarie's Road, Royal Botanic Gardens, CBD (tickets 9266 4800/www.homebake.
com.au). CityRail Circular Quay or Martin Place/ ferry Circular Quay. **Map** p310 C2. **Date** late Nov/early Dec.
As the name suggests, this one-day concert features some of Australia's leading home-grown rock bands. Tens of thousands of revellers descend on the Domain for 12 hours of ear-splitting pleasure. Doors open at 11am. There are no age restrictions, but bring photo ID if you want to drink alcohol.

Carols in the Domain

The Domain, Mrs Macquarie's Road, Royal Botanic Gardens, CBD (www.carolsinthedomain.com). CityRail Circular Quay or Martin Place/ferry Circular Quay. **Map** p310 C2. **Date** week before Christmas.
Some 100,000 folk fill the Royal Botanic Gardens for an evening, singing traditional carols by candlelight and trying to bring some Victorian Christmas cosiness to steamy, multicultural Sydney. The public is buoyed along by the Sydney Youth Orchestra, a 150-strong choir and a chorus of local celebs. The small entry fee (which goes to charity) gets you a candle and a book of carols.

Pyros on parade

Sydney's bold, brash and spectacular firework displays at **New Year's Eve** have become an issue of pride. Each year the event promises to set a new world benchmark of sparky flamboyance and (weather permitting) usually succeeds. There are two pyrotechnic displays (aka pyros): the first, at 9pm, is for families; the second, at midnight, is for everyone else – and it's the late show that's the real jaw-dropper.

The city begins to shut down around noon on New Year's Eve in readiness for the big night ahead. Roads are closed throughout the centre and around vantage points; ferries stop running at 6pm; taxis charge a premium (and are very hard to find and even harder to book); diehards (and there's well over a million of them) stake out the best spots early on; and special public transport arrangements are in place throughout the night. Put simply: don't leave it until the 11th hour – claim your territory well ahead of time, and use public transport.

The *Daily Telegraph* (a sponsor) carries information in the weeks leading up to the big night, plus you can contact the City of Sydney on 1 300 651 301, or look at the excellent www.sydneynewyearseve.com.au, which is usually up and running by the beginning of December and has a guide to all the free vantage spots. Call the Transport Infoline on 131 500 for public transport arrangements.

SAFETY

Despite the size of the event, it's pretty safe at street level, thanks to plenty of police and the laid-back nature of the average Aussie reveller. The city's police are seasoned at keeping low-key but firm control. In 2002 heightened security levels were introduced, which at the time of writing are still in place. If you see anyone or anything suspicious you're advised to report it and, as with any night on the town, the best way to stay safe is to stick to the well-lit main areas with your friends. If you're going to an organised event, expect to have your bag searched.

VIEWS FOR CASH
On the water: cruises

Lots of private boats anchor around the harbour area and, if you're cashed up, many cruise companies offer scheduled New Year's Eve dos, complete with booze, nibbles and entertainment. Group and individual bookings are taken, but it's always cheaper if you're in a group. Alternatively, if money's no object, you can charter your own vessel.

Sydney Mainsail (9979 3681, www.sydney mainsail.com.au) charters catamarans for groups of up to 20 (for a whopping $5,000); **Captain Cook Cruises** (9206 1111, www.captcookcrus.com.au) offers a range of party packages, with prices starting at ▶

Christmas Day on Bondi Beach

Bondi Beach. CityRail Bondi Junction then bus 380, 381, 382, L82/bus 380, L82. **Map** *p83.* **Date** 25 Dec.

Thousands of travellers from around the world (especially Brits) gather at Bondi each year for an impromptu party. Since the council introduced an alcohol ban on the beach a few years ago, this traditional festivity has become more of a family affair.

Sydney Hobart Yacht Race

Sydney Harbour (9363 9731/www.cyca.com.au). **Date** 26 Dec.

Hundreds of keen yachtsmen and supporters turn out on Boxing Day for the 1pm start of the notoriously gruelling race to Hobart in Tasmania. Several sailors died during the 1998 race when wild seas tore yachts apart. The sight of hundreds of sails filling the harbour, as the racers make their way between North and South Head into the Pacific Ocean, is spectacular. The best viewing areas are North Head, in Manly, or coastal cliff spots around South Head such as Watsons Bay, Vaucluse and Diamond Bay.

New Year's Eve Fireworks

Sydney Harbour & Darling Harbour (9265 9757/ www.sydneynewyearseve.com.au). **Date** 9pm & midnight 31 Dec.

If you're in Sydney for New Year, you'll see the best fireworks in the southern hemisphere, and possibly in the world. For details of the best viewing spots, *see p193* **Pyros on parade**.

Darling Harbour Summer School Holiday Program

Darling Harbour (9240 8786/www.darling harbour.com). CityRail Town Hall/ferry Darling Harbour/Monorail Darling Park. **Map** *p310/311 B2/3.* **Date** Dec-Jan.

An annual show of glitzy entertainment including waterski displays, twilight concerts and fireworks, which usually take place every weekend in summer.

Sydney Festival

Various venues (8248 6500/www.sydneyfestival. org.au). **Date** Jan.

Launched in 1976 to celebrate the city and bring people into the CBD, this is now the leading cultural

---

▶ ## Pyros on parade (continued)

$400 per head; while **Budget Party Cruises** (9555 8822) aims for the younger crowd (at around $230 per head). A list of cruise companies is available from the **Sydney Visitor Centre** (*see p292*) or in the *Yellow Pages* under 'Boat Charter Services'.

In the harbour: the islands

The harbour islands – **Fort Denison** (Pinchgut), **Goat**, **Shark** and **Clark** – offer the next best thing to a cruise. The Fort Café on Pinchgut, close to the Bridge, is the ideal spot – if you can get one of the prized tickets, that is. These cost several hundred dollars and usually include food and alcohol; information is available in late November, with tickets on sale in December. The other islands are usually for BYO picnic-style partygoers. Tickets start at around $100 per head and there are usually 250 available for Clark Island, 750 for Shark and 1,000 for Goat. Ferry transport is provided for all islands.

For booking and information, contact the **NSW National Parks & Wildlife Service** (9247 5033, www.nationalparks.nsw.gov.au).

At the top: aerial views

Numerous restaurants offer stunning views over the harbour, with New Year's menus to match, but the revolving **Sydney Tower Restaurants** complex atop Sydney Tower

(100 Market Street, 8223 3800, www.sydney-tower-restaurant.com) has the edge. There are two restaurants here and on New Year's Eve both serve a five-course set menu including drinks and entertainment for $275 a head. **Map** *p311 C3.*

VIEWS FOR FREE
Mrs Macquarie's Point

The most spectacular vantage point for many Sydneysiders, and situated one inlet along from the Opera House, facing the Bridge. Together with the adjacent Domain, nearly 50,000 squeeze themselves in over this giant grassy knoll. You can bring a hamper but not alcohol, which is on sale. Access is from the Domain only (not from the Royal Botanic Gardens) and the site opens at 8am. **Map** *p310 D1.*

Sydney Opera House

You may not get anywhere near the great hall complex itself (usually reserved along with Bennelong restaurant and the Opera Bar for Sydney's glitterati), but the nearby walkway is priceless for sheer atmosphere (if you can handle the 10,000-strong crowds) and, of course, for the view. You can't bring in alcohol, but you can buy it here. Arrive early, as this spot is usually full by 5pm. **Map** *p310 C1.*

event in Sydney – and possibly Australia. Held over a three-week period, the festival showcases dance, theatre, visual arts, opera and music, with acts from home and abroad. Ticketed events are supplemented by a renowned free outdoor programme, including Symphony in the Domain. The festival culminates in boat races (such as the Ferrython; *see below*) and firework displays in Sydney Harbour. It ends on Australia Day.

Australia Day
Various venues (1 300 654 124/www.australiaday. com.au). **Date** 26 Jan.
Festivities take place all over the city (and the country) in the annual celebration of European settlement in Australia. The main Australia Day concert is usually held in the Domain. Other events include the Tall Ships Race on the harbour and excellent fireworks – weather (and bush fires) permitting – over Sydney Harbour.

Ferrython
Sydney Harbour (www.sydneyfestival.org.au). **Date** 26 Jan.

Although it's not an integral part of the Australia Day celebrations, this hilarious boat race is great fun to watch, with elaborately decorated ferries of all sizes racing from Circular Quay, around Shark Island and back to the Harbour Bridge. The spectacle is best viewed from Milsons Point, Millers Point, McMahons Point, the Botanic Gardens or Mrs Macquarie's Chair. The race starts at 11am.

Sydney Fringe Festival
Various venues (www.waverley.nsw.gov.au). **Date** Jan-Feb.
Fun, quirky and very inclusive, this two- to three-week festival is the alternative to the mainstream Sydney Festival and features what must be the city's campest sporting event – the Drag Race – and free shows (4-6pm daily) on Bondi Beach. Check the local press for more details.

Chinese New Year
Chinatown (1 300 651 301/www.sydneychinese newyear.com.au). CityRail Central Station/Light Rail/Monorail Haymarket. **Map** p311 B3. **Date** varies, usually Feb.

Blues Point Reserve
The north shore's best spot (along with Balls Head, at nearby Waverton) for a panoramic view; also, it's larger than many of the other local foreshore areas. If you're desperate to get even closer to the Bridge, head west towards McMahons Point, still further to Bradfield Park, Milsons Point, or to nearby Kirribilli (though space is extremely limited). You can take alcohol, but no glass.

Dawes Point Park
A crowd squeezer, and understandably so. Like Milsons Point, Dawes Point offers in-your-face views of the displays (it's right next to the Bridge). Its location, however, has one drawback: situated in the Rocks, it tends to attract lager-lout tourists. After 4pm you can only access the area from Lower Fort Street and Hickson Road (not from George Street). **Map** p310 C1.

Darling Street
An obvious hit with locals of the 'village', Balmain's main drag, Darling Street, beats nearby Milsons Point and Darling Harbour for its intimate atmosphere. There's green park space to the left and right of the ferry wharf, and you can also glimpse the action from the adjoining roads. **Map** p310 A1.

Bradley's Head
At the tail end of the long spit that leads up to Taronga Zoo, Bradley's Head in Mosman boasts an awesome view from the north shore. (The zoo itself and nearby Robertsons Point, Cremorne, offer similarly spectacular vantage points.) You can take alcohol, but access is limited, with Bradley's Head Road closed all day to vehicles. You should also take a torch, as there's very little light at this site.

Nielsen Park
Spend a few hours on Shark Beach during the day, then walk up the hill into the park and secure your spot early. There's room for 3,000 people, usually locals. You can take alcohol and, like Bradley's Head, you'll need a torch – there are no lights in the park. Whatever you do, don't climb the trees – they're protected.

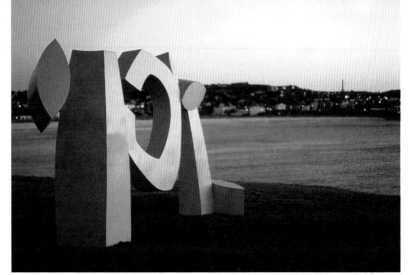

Phillip Spelman's *Ylang-Ylang*, part of **Sculpture by the Sea**. *See p192.*

Head to Chinatown for two days of traditional New Year's festivities, complete with dragon boat races, firecrackers, markets and a parade.

Autumn

Gay & Lesbian Mardi Gras Party

Various venues (9557 4332/www.mardigras.org.au).
Date Feb; ends on last Sat in Feb or 1st Sat in Mar.
For three or four weeks (plus recovery time), Sydney's gay and lesbian community gets the keys to the city. There's so much going on, it's impossible to catch the lot. For more details, *see p214* **Welcome to New Mardi Gras**.

Royal Easter Show

Sydney Showground, Sydney Olympic Park, Homebush Bay (9704 1111/ www.greataustralian muster.com.au). CityRail Olympic Park. **Date** from the Fri before Good Fri.
For two weeks the Royal Easter Show brings rural Australia to Sydney. Organised by the Royal Agricultural Society of NSW, it is held dear by many a grandma who remembers going as a lass to see the prize livestock. These days it's still a huge event attracting more than a million visitors. There are sheepdog trials, rodeos, showjumping, huge pumpkins and lots of rides and kids' activities.

Anzac Day March

Route: along George Street from Martin Place to Hyde Park. CityRail Circular Quay, Martin Place, Wynyard or Town Hall/ferry Circular Quay.
Map (Martin Place) p310 C2. **Date** 25 Apr.
Sydneysiders pay their respects to the Australian and New Zealand troops killed at Gallipoli and in other wars by turning out in their thousands to watch the parade of national heroes. The event starts with a dawn service at the Martin Place Cenotaph followed by a march (starting at 9am) along George Street and a service (12.30pm) at the Anzac Memorial in Hyde Park.

Sydney Writers' Festival

Various venues (9252 7734/www.swf.org.au).
Date May.
Budding and established wordsmiths wait with anticipation for Sydney's biggest literary event, involving a week of debates, discussions, book readings and the chance to meet authors. Local and international writers appear, and most events are free, although some require booking.

Biennale of Sydney

Various venues (9368 1411/www.biennaleofsydney. com). **Date** June-Aug.
Billed as 'the southern hemisphere's largest collection of contemporary art', the annual Biennale festival/exhibition takes itself very seriously. Each year explores a different subject or theme through the works of Australian and international artists.

Winter

Sydney Film Festival

Various venues (9280 0511/9660 3844/ www.sydneyfilmfestival.org). **Date** mid June.
Always controversial, either for being too mainstream or too daring, this fortnight will exhaust even the most ardent film buff. *See p204.*

City to Surf Fun Run

Hyde Park to Bondi Beach (1 800 555 514/ http://city2surf.sunherald.com.au). **Date** early Aug.
This 14km (8.75-mile) community fun run starts in Hyde Park in the city and finishes at Bondi Beach. Upwards of 50,000 runners participate, some world-class, but mostly amateur joggers, people in silly costumes, corporate publicity-seekers and walkers.

Children

From tots to teenagers, how to amuse the kids.

Crammed full of beaches, parks, waterways and all kinds of outdoor activities, and blessed with a generally sunny climate, Sydney is a fun and inspiring place for families. And if the kids show signs of boredom, distract them by jumping on a ferry for a journey across the harbour – it works every time.

Remember that hats and sunblock are essential protection from the strong and ever-present Australian sun, especially in summer. A good time to visit is in the spring (September to November), when the weather is not too hot, but still warm enough for a swim. Most local kids wear 'rashies' at the beach – long-sleeved body suits originally designed to go underneath wetsuits to prevent chafing. Hats are a compulsory accessory at all schools ('no hat, no play'); the legionnaire-style is recommended as it protects the head, neck and shoulders as well. You'll find both at most department stores and pharmacies.

Sydney's Child (www.sydneyschild. com.au) is an extremely useful – and free – monthly publication, full of information on activities and child-friendly excursions and events. It can be found in most libraries, museums and toy shops – or call 9484 5334.

For shops selling children's clothes, *see p177*; for toys, *see p190*.

Beaches

Manly (*see p103* and *p124*) offers surf and still-water beaches, walks and plenty of cheap places to eat. Head north from the Corso to find some great playgrounds at **North Steyne** and **Queenscliff**. Head south along the waterfront pathway, Fairy Bower, to swimming at **Shelly Beach**, and a paddling pool along the way. **Bondi Beach** (*see p82* and *p120*) tends to be too lively (and the surf too strong) for small kids, but there's plenty of space for rollerblading and skateboarding teens.

South of Bondi, sheltered **Bronte Beach** (*see p121*) has a large park with barbecues, a fantastic playground and a mini steam train, plus great cafés and a wonderful fish and chip shop. Also worth checking out is **Balmoral Beach** (*see p120*) on the north shore, which is great for picnics. Enjoy a cappuccino in the boatshed café while the kids play in the adjacent playground or swim in the netted area.

Of the northern beaches, **Dee Why Beach** has a great playground and a wide selection of child-friendly cafés and restaurants, while **Collaroy Beach** (*see p124*) has a paddling pool and a large playground with barbecue facilities. Further north, **Clareville Beach** (*see p107*) is a secluded and safe swimming beach on the Pittwater (western) side of the peninsula; the water's too shallow for adults, but it's ideal for little kids.

Whichever beach you decide to use, respect the surf and stay within the marker flags when swimming. For other family-friendly beaches, *see pp118-124*.

Museums

The **Australian Museum** (*see p63*) has lots of interactive exhibits for kids including the indoor play and discover area Kids Island. There's also an extensive activities programme in the school hols. Children enjoy exploring the ships and playground at the **Australian National Maritime Museum** (*see p70*), while the innovative **Powerhouse Museum** (*see p71*), set in a former power station, is filled with hands-on technological gadgetry.

Sydney Children's Museum

Corner of Pitt & Walpole Streets, Merrylands (9897 1414/www.sydneykids.org). CityRail Merrylands. **Open** 10am-4pm daily. **Admission** $5.50; $4.40 concessions; $20 family; free under-2s. **No credit cards.**
Aimed at kids from five to ten years old, this excellent museum of science and technology in Sydney's western suburbs is perfect for inquiring minds. The emphasis is on taking part, and interactive displays include a space maze, TV studio, plasma ball, ultra-violet room and giant kaleidoscope.

Parks & playgrounds

When you tire of water, head to **Centennial Park** in Paddington (*see p80*), an enormous open space buzzing with activity. Rollerblades, bikes and pedal cars can all be hired from **Centennial Park Cycles** (*see p283*), at the Musgrave Avenue entrance. The café in the park is right next to a toddlers' playground.

Darling Harbour (*see p70*) may be touristy, but it's a great central destination for kids, with an enormous playground at

Tumbalong Park surrounded by cafés. There's a fun water play area, paddle-boats and a merry-go-round, plus the Sydney Aquarium and the IMAX cinema. There are numerous attractions here, so it's easy to while away a few hours. On weekends and during school holidays you'll find lots of street entertainers and, quite often, open-air concerts.

Fox Studios Australia (*see p80*) in Moore Park has two large playgrounds, numerous cinemas and plenty of child-friendly restaurants. Other attractions include an ice rink, Lollipop's indoor play centre (9331 0811) and TV studio Channel V (teens love it). On weekends there's an excellent market and during school holidays you'll also find a fairground, a petting zoo and pony rides.

Services

Dial an Angel

9362 4225. Phone enquiries 8.30am-8.30pm daily. **Credit** BC, MC, V.
Offers an excellent nanny/babysitting service, 24 hours a day. All carers are carefully screened.

Tresillian

9787 5255. Phone enquiries 24hrs daily.
A counselling service for help with unsettled babies, breastfeeding and any other parenting problems. Call for details of rates.

Theatre & film

Children's concerts and pantomimes are on the agenda in the school holidays, especially at Christmas and during the **Sydney Festival** (*see p194*) in January; check the local newspapers and *Sydney's Child* for up-to-date details. At the **Sydney Opera House** (*see p60*), the Kids at the House programme gives children a hands-on introduction to the world of music, dance and theatre, with workshops, performances and other events; visit www.soh.nsw.gov.au for more information. The **IMAX cinema** (*see p203*) at Darling Harbour is always a good choice for a rainy day, while the Palace and Hoyts cinema chains both offer regular 'babes in arms' sessions for parents and infants.

The Rocks Puppet Theatre

Rocks Puppet Cottage, 77 George Street, at Kendall Lane, The Rocks (9247 9137). CityRail/ferry Circular Quay. **Shows** *School holidays* 11am, 12.30pm, 2pm daily. *Termtime* 11am, 12.30pm, 2pm Sat, Sun. **Admission** free. **Map** p310 C1.
The Rocks Puppet Theatre puts on shows for children daily during the NSW school holidays, and at the weekend the rest of the year. They also offer storytelling and a range of craft activities.

Wildlife

Sydney has two aquaria: **Sydney Aquarium** (*see p71*) in Darling Harbour and **Oceanworld Manly** (*see p105*). Both offer close encounters with sharks and stingrays, as well as hands-on experiences with starfish and sea urchins. Oceanworld Manly also features 'Dangerous Australian Animals', and offers an educational sleepover night for kids (minimum 20). Sydney Aquarium is a great place to see the huge range of Australian marine life including penguins and seals, and to take an underwater walk through a coral reef.

For native Australian animals and a wide range of exotics, visit harbourside **Taronga Zoo** (*see p99*). There are frequent animal shows and a fantastic water play area that will keep kids happy all day (remember to bring a change of clothes). The best way to get there is by ferry – a great introduction to the city – then catch the cable car to the main entrance at the top and work your way down the hill to the ferry again. For more Aussie creatures head west out of town to **Featherdale Wildife Park** (*see p112*) near Blacktown, where kids can hand-feed a kangaroo, wallaby or emu and have their photo taken with a koala (for free). The **Royal Botanic Gardens** (*see p65*) with its spacious grassy acres and colony of flapping fruit bats is also worth a visit. Kids also enjoy the 'trackless train' there.

If you want to get out into the bush, there are several very accessible walks in and around Sydney, in particular at **Berry Island Reserve** (*see p90* Sacred sites), where you'll find a short track with informative plaques about the area's Aboriginal heritage. **Manly Dam Reserve** off King Street, Manly Vale (catch a bus from Wynyard or Manly Wharf) has several easy and very scenic walks and safe swimming. The **NSW National Parks & Wildlife Service** runs Discovery walks, talks and tours for children (details on 1300 361 967, www.npws.nsw.gov.au).

Australian Reptile Park

Gosford exit of Sydney-Newcastle Freeway, Somersby (4340 1022/www.reptilepark.com.au). CityRail Gosford then 10min taxi ride. **Open** 9am-5pm daily. **Admission** $18; $9-$11.50 concessions; $46 family; free under-4s. **Credit** AmEx, BC, MC, V.
Head 60 minutes north to find plenty of cold-blooded critters and creepy-crawlies, as well a plethora of native animals, including koalas, echidnas, wombats and Tasmanian devils. There are lots of noisy, colourful birds too. Interactive exhibits include Spider World and the Lost World of Reptiles, and there are regular shows and talks. If you visit on Sunday, be sure to see Eric the saltwater crocodile being fed at 1pm.

Film

Stars, studios and sun: Sydney is Australia's Tinseltown.

There's no question that film is Australia's favourite artistic medium, and it's getting more popular every year. The latest statistics show that the average annual number of cinema admissions per head in Australia is a little over five – that's third in the world after the US and Iceland. In Sydney, Rupert Murdoch's film studio complex **Fox Studios Australia** (*see p80*) adds a Hollywood buzz to the city with local stars scoring supporting roles alongside Hollywood A-listers. International hits shot at Fox include the *Matrix* trilogy, *Moulin Rouge*, *Mission: Impossible II,* and Episodes II and III of *Star Wars.* Local wannabes can also try their luck at the studios' regular extras' castings.

What all this adds up to is a lot of love for the movie business. Hollywood has been quick to recognise the importance of the lucrative Aussie market and regularly sends its stars halfway round the world for red-carpet premières. Accordingly, Sydney's cinemas are slick, comfortable venues, suitable for viewing international blockbusters. Gaudy multiplexes are the place to go for action and teen flicks, but Sydney is no slouch when it comes to art house fare, and a clutch of festivals ensure that the experimental end of the market gets a showcase. The city's diverse ethnic mix means that foreign films, from Italy to China, are well patronised too.

Another boost to the local industry has been the growing international success of Australian actors. There's a vibrant and enthusiastic pool of local talent hoping to follow in the footsteps of Cate Blanchett, Russell Crowe, Toni Collette, Rachel Griffiths and Nicole Kidman and even more who are happy to stay on home turf and develop the industry here.

TICKETS AND INFORMATION

First-run movies open on Thursdays, with three or four premières every week. Unless it's a blockbuster, you can usually get a ticket without problem. Prices are around $14.50 for adults, with concessions for children, senior citizens, students and the unemployed. Monday or Tuesday nights are bargain nights, when all tickets are reduced to around $10.

There are daily cinema ads in the entertainment sections of the *Sydney Morning Herald* and *Daily Telegraph.* Session times are also available through **Cinema Information Line** (1902 263 456) for a premium call fee.

Cinemas

First-run

The multiplexes are the best place for Hollywood blockbusters and kids' movies. Christmas, September school holidays and the Easter long weekend are key periods for distributors, who often hold back movies to show at these times and battle for the greatest screen space. Many cinemas have been extensively refurbished and offer digital sound and good seating.

Hoyts on Broadway

Broadway Shopping Centre, Bay Street, at Greek Street, Broadway (9211 1911/www.hoyts.com.au). Bus 413, 431, 432, 433, 434, 436, 437, 438, 440. **Tickets** $14.50; $8-$11 concessions. **Credit** AmEx, BC, DC, MC, V. **Map** p311 A4.

Plonked on top of the inner west's temple to convenience shopping, this huge 12-screen complex (the largest with 379 seats) is scarily popular and oftens wilts under the pressure of numbers, particularly at weekends. Three screens are housed in 'cinemaxx' auditoria, meaning high-backed seats with perfect sight lines, super-large screens and digital surround sound. What the cinema can't promise is control of the rowdy, popcorn-munching kids who flock here for their teen-flick fix. Like the Palace chain's 'babes in arms' events, there are monthly 'mums and bubs' sessions for movie-craving parents/grandparents/carers/nannies and their infants.

Hoyts at Fox Studios

Bent Street, Fox Studios Australia, Driver Avenue, Moore Park (9332 1300/www.hoyts.com.au). Bus 339, 373, 374, 375, 376, 377, 393, 395, 396. **Tickets** $14.50; $8-$11 concessions. **Credit** AmEx, BC, DC, MC, V. **Map** p313 D5.

Part of the soulless Fox Studios complex, this 12-screen, 3,000-seat complex may be big and garish, but its huge screens, stadium seating and impeccably clean facilities are a refreshing change from the pushing, shoving and bus fumes of George Street. A classy extra, popular with first-time daters, is a package called La Premiere, available in five of the cinemas. For around twice the cost of a usual ticket, you get to watch the movie from a cosy, two-person sofa strategically placed to allow unobstructed views. You also get use of the La Premiere lounge with free soft drinks, tea, coffee and popcorn. There's booze to buy (and take into the cinema) and a free cheese platter with every bottle of plonk.

Enjoy art deco splendour at the **Hayden Orpheum**. *See p201.*

Hoyts-Greater Union
George Street Cinemas

505 George Street, between Bathurst & Liverpool Streets, CBD (9273 7431/www.hoyts.com.au). CityRail Town Hall/Monorail World Square. **Tickets** $14.50; $9.50-$11 concessions. **Credit** AmEx, BC, DC, MC, V. **Map** p311 B3.

This 17-screen development, popular with teens and out-of-towners, is the Hoyts-Greater Union flagship and shows pretty much every new commercial release as soon as it opens. It's a noisy place at the heart of George Street's garish entertainment strip and can get a little edgy at night, so hang on to your handbag. But you can't fault the state-of-the-art auditoria, which come with digital surround sound and comfortable seats.

Manly Twin Cinemas

43-45 East Esplanade, opposite Manly Wharf, Manly (9977 0644/www.manlycinema.com.au). Ferry Manly. **Tickets** $14.50; $8-$11 concessions. **No credit cards. Map** p104.

This smallish two-screen cinema offers first-run mainstream movies and the odd art house flick. Seats are adequate and the main screen has Dolby digital sound. Located next to the ferry wharf, it's patronised by Manly locals.

Reading Cinemas

Level 3, Market City Shopping Centre, 9-13 Hay Street, entrance on Thomas Street, Haymarket (9280 1202/www.readingcinemas.com.au). CityRail Central/LightRail/Monorail Haymarket. **Tickets** $14.50; $7.50-$11 concessions. **Credit** BC, MC, V. **Map** p311 B4.

After a bumpy start in the late 1990s the American-owned Reading chain has succeeded in getting a toehold in the lucrative Australian market. Its Chinatown five-screener is located directly above Paddy's Market and shows first-release mainstream and Hong Kong movies (in Cantonese with English and Chinese subtitles). Seats are perfectly comfy and all the cinemas have Dolby digital sound.

Ritz Cinema Randwick

39-43 St Paul's Street, at Avoca Street, Randwick (9399 7758). Bus 314, 372, 373, 374. **Tickets** $10; $5-$7 concessions. **Credit** BC, MC, V.

Built in 1937, the art deco Ritz has been restored twice in recent years, resulting in a 1,815-capacity, six-screen, movie-lovers' haven. Its eye-catching cream, green and red frontage is a Randwick icon, but don't expect arty stuff: the programme consists of quality mainstream fare including kids' flicks. The 833-seater Cinema One features plenty of art deco detailing and an excellent sound system. Signs on the door outline a series of rules – no alcohol/bare feet/smoking/laser lights/skateboards – and if you hit the place in the afternoon after school's out, you'll see why: the cinema is crammed with local youths loaded with attitude. In the evening it's a different crowd, including film geeks who seek out the Ritz for its great acoustics and old-fashioned flair.

Art house

Both the Dendy and Palace cinema chains have great-value membership schemes, which are well worth the investment if you plan to go to the cinema regularly.

Arts & Entertainment

Academy Twin Cinema

3A Oxford Street, between South Dowling & Verona Streets, Paddington (9361 4453/www.palacecinemas. com.au). Bus 352, 378, 380, 382. **Tickets** $14; $7.50-$10.50 concessions. **Credit** AmEx, BC, DC, MC, V. **Map** p311/313 D4.

Part of the Palace chain and one of the city's longest-running art cinemas, situated in the heart of the 'pink strip', the Academy is fittingly the main base for the Mardi Gras Film Festival (*see p204*). It presents an interesting programme of foreign and Australian movies, plus arty commercial releases. Its two screens have 434 and 294 seats and while production quality is great, the seats themselves are not for best in town and legroom is poor. Oh, and beware the queue in the ladies' loos.

Chauvel Cinemas

Paddington Town Hall, Oxford Street, at Oatley Road, Paddington (9361 5398/www.chauvel cinema.com.au). Bus 352, 378, 380, 382. **Tickets** $14; $8-$10 concessions. **Credit** BC, MC, V. **Map** p313 D4.

On the first floor of Paddington Town Hall, cine-buff Alex Meskovic presides over Sydney's best art house cinema, which operates under the slogan: 'If it's at cinemas everywhere… it's not on here!' Films screened in the two auditoria (seating 380 and 95) combine re-releases of masterpieces with exclusive first releases, short films, foreign films and documentaries. The spacious and sunny foyer has a great smokers' balcony and a decent bar. Inside, the seating is acceptable but the technology is not state of the art; still, it's the content that matters here. The Chauvel also runs the National Cinémathèque, which screens classic double bills on Monday nights and Saturday afternoons; you'll need to buy a membership pass ($30-$34 for four double sessions), but it's well worth it.

Cinema Paris at Fox Studios

Bent Street, Fox Studios Australia, Driver Avenue, Moore Park (9332 1633/www.hoyts.com.au). Bus 339, 373, 374, 375, 376, 377, 393, 395, 396. **Tickets** $14.50; $7-$10 concessions. **Credit** AmEx, BC, DC, MC, V. **Map** p313 D5.

A small but very smart art house cinema with four screens and a combined seating capacity of 600. Its setting, deep in the concrete jungle of Fox Studios, may not be typical for an art house cinema, but the selection of films is impeccable and it hosts several edgy film festivals.

Dendy Newtown

261 King Street, between Mary & Church Streets, Newtown (9550 5699/www.dendy.com.au). CityRail Newtown. **Tickets** $14.50; $8-$10.50 concessions. **Credit** AmEx, BC, DC, MC, V. **Map** p93.

Recently refurbished and expanded, the once drab Dendy Newtown is now a match for its Opera Quays sister (*see below*) in lusciousness. Showing quality first releases, its four screens (seating 562 in all) offer super-comfortable seats, big screens and Dolby digital surround sound; there's also a bar and

free parking for filmgoers in the Lennox Street car park behind the cinema – a definite plus in often jam-packed King Street.

Dendy Opera Quays

2 East Circular Quay, Circular Quay (9247 3800/ www.dendy.com.au). CityRail/ferry Circular Quay. **Tickets** $14; $8-$9 concessions. **Credit** AmEx, BC, DC, MC, V. **Map** p311 C1.

Housed under one of Sydney's most loathed structures (the so-called 'toaster' building), with views of Australia's most loved structure (the Harbour Bridge), this utterly luxurious three-screen complex seats a total of 579. It programmes a mix of middle-brow and art house fare, and is fully licensed, with good-quality wine to sup through the film. There is full disabled access to all screens.

Double Bay

377 New South Head Road, between Manning & Kiaora Roads, Double Bay (9327 1003/www.greater union.com.au). CityRail Edgecliff/bus 323, 324, 325. **Tickets** $10; $7-$9.50 concessions. **Credit** AmEx, BC, DC, MC, V. **Map** p312 F3.

Situated in the heart of well-heeled Double Bay, this Greater Union-owned cinema has two screens and a combined capacity of 852 seats. Its programme is geared towards the soft end of the market: costume dramas, quirky comedies and the odd sweet-natured foreign-language film – the kind of stuff its middlebrow, middle-aged audience lap up. It has Dolby digital sound in Cinema One.

Govinda's

112 Darlinghurst Road, between William & Hardie Streets, Darlinghurst (9380 5155/www.govindas. com.au). CityRail Kings Cross. **Tickets** $9.90; $18.90 with meal; $13.90 concessions. **Credit** AmEx, BC, MC, V. **Map** p312 D3.

Adored by its regulars, this Krishna-operated restaurant doubles as a quality art house cinema. After you've loaded up on the tasty vegetarian buffet, sit back and enjoy arty films, documentaries and classics. Or lie back if you prefer: the films, screened in a boutique cinema in 35mm large-screen format, are best watched in a horizontal position from one of the many upholstered bean bags and overstuffed cushions. You can watch and not eat, but diners are given preference and since there are only 65 seats in the cinema – roughly half the restaurant's capacity – it's best to buy your ticket early.

Hayden Orpheum Picture Palace

380 Military Road, between Winnie & Macpherson Streets, Cremorne (9908 4344/www.orpheum. com.au). Bus 143, 144, 151, 228, 229, 230, 243, 246, 247, 257. **Tickets** $14.50; $7-$11 concessions. **Credit** BC, MC, V.

They certainly don't make 'em like this anymore: Cremorne's exquisite art deco picture palace is a fantastic step back in time. It was built in 1935 by George Kenworthy, the top theatrical architect of the period, but what you see today is even glitzier than the original – the result of a $2.5-million restoration

AbOriginal Into the outback

In 1955 director Charles Chauvel made cinematic history with *Jedda*. It was the first Australian-produced film to be shot in colour, the first to go to the Cannes Film Festival and, more importantly, the first to use Aboriginal actors in lead roles. Set in the Northern Territory, *Jedda* was based on the true story of an Aboriginal child adopted by a white woman to replace her own baby, who had died. Named after a wild bird, Jedda is raised as a white girl, isolated from her cultural heritage. Her story is cruel and tragic and provided daring subject matter for the time; it was also an unexpected commercial and critical success in England and America.

It was an auspicious start, but in subsequent decades – despite the odd exception including Nicolas Roeg's *Walkabout* (1970), Peter Weir's *The Last Wave* (1977) and Fred Schepisi's *The Chant of Jimmie Blacksmith* (1978) – films about indigenous Australia became increasingly marginalised and 'Aboriginal issues' were widely considered box-office suicide. Then, in 2002, Australian director Phillip Noyce changed all that with *Rabbit-Proof Fence*, sparking a renewed cinematic interest in all things indigenous.

Like *Jedda*, *Rabbit-Proof Fence* was about the nation's 'stolen generation' and, like *Jedda*, it was based on a true, brutal story. Noyce had started his career with a road movie about a young Aborigine (*Backroads*) but then moved to Hollywood to make mainstream pics such as *Dead Calm* and *Patriot Games*. He used all his new big-screen tricks in *Rabbit-Proof Fence* including a soundtrack by Peter Gabriel and sweeping, romantic shots of the outback, but stayed faithful to the essence of this uniquely Australian story. Noyce's cast of indigenous actors included the incredible Everlyn Sampi in the lead (pictured), a young girl who had never been to a movie before, let alone starred in one.

Rabbit-Proof Fence became the most successful Australian film of 2002. But at that year's Australian Film Institute awards it was just one of three movies with Aboriginal themes in the limelight – the others being *Beneath Clouds* and *The Tracker* (for which David Gulpilil, probably the best-known Aboriginal actor, won the best actor award). Australia was ready to recognise its past.

Meanwhile, it's hoped that Noyce's international success will open up much-

Arts & Entertainment

funded by local TV celeb and owner Mike Walsh. Each of the six cinemas has its own colour scheme and decor, but the Orpheum is the true star of the show. It has 744 seats and a genuine Wurlitzer cinema organ, which rises out of a stage pit on weekend evenings, complete with flashing lights and a grinning organist. Programming mixes mainstream US, British and Australian fare, with some art house, special presentations and cabaret concerts.

Norton Street Cinema
99 Norton Street, between Marion Street & Parramatta Road, Leichhardt (9564 5620/ www.palacecinemas.com.au). Bus 436, 437, 438, 440, 445, 470, L38. **Tickets** $14; $7-$10.50 concessions. **Credit** AmEx, BC, DC, MC, V.
Located in the heart of Little Italy, this sophisticated operation is the cream of the Palace chain's trio of cinemas in Sydney. It opened in 1997 and, thanks to frequent carpet cleaning and a programme devoid of teen flicks, still looks brand new. There are four screens, the largest two seating 214 each. Seats are plush, the air con keeps you cool, and the sound and sight lines are excellent. Expect offbeat Hollywood releases, foreign (including an Italian Film Festival) and Australian art house fare. The 'babes in arms' sessions on Thursday mornings are popular with

local mums: lights are turned up, sound down and breastfeeding is everywhere. Martini, the trendy Italian (of course) restaurant and bar on the first floor, offers good movie/pasta/pizza deals.

Valhalla
166 Glebe Point Road, between Bridge Road & Hereford Street, Glebe (9660 8050/www.valhalla cinemas.com.au). Light Rail Glebe/bus 431, 432, 433, 434, 370. **Tickets** $14; $6-$10 concessions. No credit cards.
The Valhalla is a local institution, but its comfort levels leave a lot to be desired. But the Val isn't about soft seats. The 1937 art deco building, originally the Astor Theatre, was bought in 1979 by Chris Kiely, who converted it into an art house cinema – retaining the deco detail – and has kept it true to its arty ideals ever since. The programme consists of first releases of foreign-language and documentary movies and special film festivals, all serious stuff. The two cinemas seat 400 and 200 in stacked vintage chairs – that's wooden arms and unyielding seats – and are decidedly musty, but at least there's air con. Buffs flock to 'popcorntaxi', a midweek screening followed by a discussion with the film's director or star. Guests have included Dennis Hopper, Baz Luhrmann and Ewan McGregor.

Festival. In 2003 Aboriginal actor David Ngoombujarra won an AFI award for best supporting actor for his portrayal of a man wrongfully arrested for the rape and murder of a nine-year-old girl in Craig Lahiff's searching *Black and White*, based on a true story.

Stoking the flames for a fully indigenous cinema is the Australian Film Commission's Indigenous Film Unit. Set up in the early 1990s, the unit offers finance, workshops

needed funding for the growing number of talented indigenous filmmakers who want to tell their own stories from a black perspective. Directors such as Rachel Perkins, Tracey Moffatt, Leah Purcell and Ivan Sen have been beavering away in the background for years. In 1998 Perkins' *Radiance* charmed the critics; its star, Aboriginal Deborah Mailman, won the AFI best actress award. In 2001 Perkins released the bold musical drama *One Night the Moon*, and Ivan Sen's *Beneath Clouds* won awards at the 2002 Berlin Film

and assistance to indigenous filmmakers so that they have total control over their cultural heritage and the way they are portrayed. No more stereotypes, no more white lies, that's the idea – and it's already working.

The Sydney Indigenous Film Festival, held every July in Parramatta, is a proud and uplifting event that showcases the work of Aboriginal filmmakers and also offers discussion forums and the chance to meet industry players. Check the local press for details or visit www.parracity.nsw.gov.au.

Verona

17 Oxford Street, at Verona Street, Paddington (9360 6099/www.palacecinemas.com.au). Bus 352, 352, 380, 382. **Tickets** $14; $7-$10.50 concessions. **Credit** AmEx, BC, DC, MC, V. **Map** p311/313 D4.

The Verona is one of Palace Cinemas' three venues in Sydney and a mainstay for Paddington's intellectuals, arty crowd and pink scene. The four screens are a little on the small side and the seats not as soft as they could be, but the movies are an enticing combination of quirky commercial, sexy foreign and the best of Australian.

Drive-ins

Regrettably, changing tastes and rising land values have resulted in the near extinction of the drive-in. Two remain in Sydney's west: one in a field at Blacktown and a stunning one at Bass Hill. Both are run by Greater Union and usually screen double features, mainly new mainstream releases, with action blockbusters high on the agenda. Gates and snack bars at both venues open at 6.30pm, with the screening starting at 7.30pm.

Greater Union Drive-In Bass Hill

Johnston Road, between Arundle & Handle Streets, Bass Hill (9724 1289/www.greaterunion.com.au). **Tickets** $13; $7-$9 concessions. **No credit cards**.

Greater Union Drive-In Blacktown

Cricketers Arms Road, between Reservoir Road & M4 motorway, Blacktown (9622 4170/9622 0202/www.greaterunion.com.au). **Tickets** $13; $7-$9 concessions. **No credit cards**.

IMAX

IMAX Sydney

Southern end of Darling Harbour, Pyrmont (9281 3300/www.imax.com.au). CityRail Town Hall/ ferry Darling Harbour/Light Rail Convention/ Monorail Darling Park or Convention. **Tickets** $16; $11-$13 concessions; $34-$44 family. 3-D films $17; $12-$14 concessions; $38-$49 family. **Credit** AmEx, BC, MC, V. **Map** p311 B3.

You can't miss the huge, eye-shaped IMAX theatre right on the water in touristy Darling Harbour, but it's hardly a hot ticket. The 540-seat theatre screens around 12 movies a day from 10am to 10pm and is claimed to have the world's largest screen, some eight storeys high, but the docudrama fluff that tends to get projected on to it would barely rival an evening in front of the telly. That said, the visceral impact on first-time viewers (especially when the film is in 3-D) is undeniable.

Open-air

Sydneysiders love being outdoors, and open-air movies have become a firm fixture on the summer social calendar. There are two main venues – on the grass in Centennial Park or on stacked seats in the Domain. Weather permitting, both are great nights out.

Moonlight Cinema

Centennial Park (1900 933 899/www.moonlight. com.au). Bus 378, 380, 382, L82. **Tickets** $14.50; $10-$11.50 concessions. **Credit** AmEx, BC, DC, MC, V. **Map** p313 E5. **Date** late Nov-early Mar.
Classics are the mainstay here. Some, like *Grease* – at which a huge cheer always accompanies our Livvy's announcement that she's Sandy, from 'Sydney, Australia' – are enduring favourites. Films start at sunset (around 7.30pm) and entrance is via Woollahra Gate (Oxford Street) only. Tickets can be bought at the gate or through Ticketek (9266 4800). Bring a picnic, cushions and insect repellent.

Open-Air Cinema

Mrs Macquarie's Chair, The Domain, CBD (1300 366 649/www.stgeorge.com.au/openair). CityRail Circular Quay or Martin Place/ferry Circular Quay. **Tickets** (plus booking fee) $18; $16 concessions. **Credit** AmEx, BC, DC, MC, V. **Map** p311 C2. **Date** 3wks from early Jan.
A brilliant, dress-circle location with the Bridge and Opera House in the background and seating for around 1,700 people. Expect mainstream recent releases with a few classics thrown in. Films start at 8.30pm, but the gates open from 6.30pm, as do the bar and restaurant.

Festivals

Festival of Jewish Cinema

Date Nov.
Presented by the Melbourne-based Jewish Film Foundation, this annual gathering of international Jewish fare, at turns tragic, heartwarming and hilarious, is often the place to see next year's Oscar-nominated documentaries and features. Check the local press for details of venues and timings.

Flickerfest

Information: PO Box 7416, Bondi Beach, NSW 2026 (9365 6877/www.flickerfest.com.au). **Date** early Jan.
Australia's only competitive short film festival was recognised in 2003 by the American Academy of Motion Picture Arts & Sciences as an Oscar-qualifying festival. Thanks to that accolade, the nine-day Flickerfest is now considered a serious event on the world film calendar. It's one of the few forums in which local short filmmakers can directly compare their work with international fare. Films are shown at the Bondi Pavilion on Bondi Beach.

Mardi Gras Film Festival & queerDOC Festival

Information: Queer Screen, PO Box 1081, Darlinghurst, NSW 1300 (9332 4938/ www.queerscreen.com.au). **Date** *Mardi Gras* Feb. *queerDOC* Sept.
Queer Screen organises the annual Mardi Gras Film Festival as part of Sydney's month-long gay and lesbian jamboree (*see p214* **Welcome to New Mardi Gras**), with mainly international gay movies screened at the Academy Twin Cinema (*see p201*) and other venues around the city. Queer Screen also puts on the queerDOC festival, the world's first dedicated entirely to queer documentaries.

Sydney Film Festival

Information: Level 5, Suite 105, 414-418 Elizabeth Street, Surry Hills, NSW 2010 (9280 0511/9660 3844/www.sydneyfilmfestival.org). **Date** mid-June.
One of the oldest moviefests in the world, the Sydney Film Festival was started in the 1950s by buffs hungry for intellectually challenging cinema. It has evolved into a slick, high-profile, two-week orgy of international and Australian film, with up to 250 movies (opening on the Queen's Birthday weekend in early June). Regular highlights include major retrospectives and meet-the-filmmaker forums. The main venues are the grand State Theatre (*see p253*) and the Dendy Opera Quays (*see p201*).

Tropfest

Information: 62-64 Riley Street, East Sydney, NSW 2010 (9368 0434/www.tropfest.com.au). **Date** last Sun in Feb.
Instigated by local actor John Polson (*Mission: Impossible II*), this free, outdoor festival of short films is held every February for just one day at Polson's old hangout, the Tropicana Caffe in Darlinghurst, and simulcast on giant screens in the Domain to an audience that runs into the thousands (and to other cities around Australia). Heavily frequented by actors, directors and writers, the festival's judging panel usually includes A-list celebs who are working in town; Samuel L Jackson, Russell Crowe and John Woo have all performed judging duties in the past. All films are under seven minutes, made specially for the festival and has to contain a reference to that year's Tropfest Signature Item (past items have included a kiss, a coffee bean, chopsticks).

Women on Women

Information: PO Box 522, Paddington, NSW 2021 (9332 2408/www.wift.org). **Date** Oct, every 2yrs.
Women in Film & Television (WIFT) is a non-profit organisation committed to improving the lot of women in film. It organises the bi-annual Women on Women film festival, featuring short and feature-length work by new and established female talent. The 2002 WOW festival was held at Fox Studios.

Galleries

Welcome to Artstralia.

Find impressive works at **Martin Browne Fine Art at the Yellow House**. *See p208.*

Is Sydney the heart of visual arts in Australia? Not quite. A somewhat tired but persistent rivalry continues between Melbourne and Sydney for cultural and aesthetic supremacy, with Melbourne generally considered the more 'artistic' city. In recent years, however, impressive venues in Sydney such as the **Museum of Contemporary Art** (*see p57*) have brought the northern centre its own legitimacy. Both cities are now acknowledged as possessing similarly vibrant visual arts scenes, and it's not unusual for important established artists to be represented by galleries in both state capitals. And when Christie's (Australia) has an auction, there will be viewings in both Sydney and Melbourne. On an international level, artists from across the world have shown at the Sydney **Biennale** (*see p195*), while Australian artists have been featured at the Venice Biennale.

Familiar faces can be seen again and again at openings around town, especially in Paddington, which has more galleries than any other area. Here you'll find a blend of serious collectors as well as purchasers with somewhat less legitimate agendas (discussing, for example, whether a particular canvas is an appropriate buy or not, because it might clash with the furniture). Art is definitely a fashionable purchase in Sydney, with artworks increasingly present in restaurants and public buildings, and paintings common on the innumerable TV renovation shows. If the Sydney scene is currently lacking a particular movement in terms of theme, it's more than made up for in variety and daring.

Sydney's mix of public, commercial, artist-run and regional galleries keeps the city's art heart beating. Commercial galleries, such as **Eva Breuer** (*see p211*), deal in some of Australia's prominent artists and cater to more conventional media, such as painting. Installation-based and new media works can usually be seen at galleries like **Artspace** in Woolloomooloo (*see p76*), with works tending towards the experimental. (Expect nudity, violence and, occasionally, Mike Parr, the legendary performance artist who in 2002 sat at the gallery for two days with his arm nailed to the wall). Art also regularly blends

AbOriginal Art and galleries

Once dismissed and now hugely fashionable, Aboriginal art has proved popular from New York to London, even influencing the artistic efforts of Prince Harry. Prince Harry's use (or perhaps appropriation) of the form outraged many indigenous people, however, reflecting the many challenges facing those keen to embrace this complex and exciting art form.

Aboriginal art is probably the most vital and diverse – some would say the best – aspect of Australian art today. There are more styles, in more media, with more variations in content than even the most enthusiastic art lovers can fathom.

First, some basics: Aboriginal art has arguably the longest continuous tradition in the world, dating back at least 50 millennia. It is, however, probably the last great tradition of art to come to the attention of the world at large. The past 25 years have seen a surge in creative activity. For the first time, works of art are being made en masse, to be seen by a wider public in a variety of traditional and non-traditional media. The works are also proving incredibly lucrative – for owners and dealers, at least – with *Water and Bush Tucker Dreaming* by Johnny Warangkula Tjupurrula fetching US$78,145 ($117,000) at a Sotheby's auction in 2003.

For Aboriginal artists, however, the upsurge in interest and prices has not always brought financial gain. In an industry that is now worth

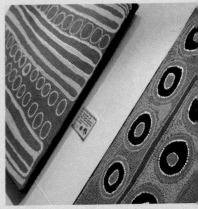

an estimated $200 million a year, only $50 million goes back to the artists, according to a 2002 report. Federal legislation to introduce resale royalties for artists might help matters, but buyers should be aware of the political and social context in which works are sold. 'Aboriginal art' is marketed in tourist shops all over Sydney, but to ensure authenticity it's best to buy from a specialist. Ask whether the gallery is endorsed by the **Australian Indigenous Art Trade Association** (visit www.arttrade.asn.au/index.cfm for more

with performance and installation at the **Performance Space** in Redfern (*see p252*), as alternative and offbeat galleries are hugely in vogue in Sydney. Artist-run spaces include **Phatspace** (*see p209*) and **Wren** (corner of Riley and Reservoir Streets, Surry Hills, 9280 2714), and are the best places to see work by emerging artists. Standards vary, but the scene is certainly worth a look.

One of Australia's most successful artists is **Tracey Moffatt** (represented by **Roslyn Oxley9 Gallery**; *see p211*). She's had more than 30 solo exhibitions overseas and has appeared in such major group shows as the Sydney, Venice and São Paulo Biennales. Moffatt's work celebrates and critiques indigenous culture, sexuality and gender in highly stylised photographic images, and has also been shown at the MCA.

Populist artist **Ken Done** has his own gallery (1 Hickson Road, The Rocks, 9247 2740, www.kendone.com.au). Done made his name

with childlike and colourful landscapes of Australia, sold at the gallery in frames or on tea towels and T-shirts. A hit with tourists, Done is not taken terribly seriously by Australian art critics. The late great **Brett Whiteley** also has his own gallery (*see p74*). In the 1960s and '70s Whiteley caught the public's attention through his bold use of colour and equally bold lifestyle; put crudely, he's Australia's Francis Bacon (though clearly unique) and his works also hang at the **Art Gallery of New South Wales** (*see p63*). Don't make any judgments about Australian art until you see a Whiteley.

INFORMATION AND OPENING HOURS

Art Almanac ($2.20, published 11 times a year) and *Art Gallery Guide Australia* ($3, published six times a year) both offer a great round-up of what's on around town, with the latter featuring a handy calendar of openings for those seeking a buzzy atmosphere. They are available at bookstores, galleries and newsagents.

Arts & Entertainment

information) or the **Australian Commercial Galleries Association**, and get paperwork on the artist and the work concerned.

Financial considerations aside, art remains central to traditional Aboriginal life. Why? It expresses relationships between people and the land; it activates the powers of ancestral beings, connecting people in the present with the Dreamings; and it is an expression of individual and group identity.

Be aware, though, that when a dealer tells you a given work should be interpreted as articulating such-and-such, it's rarely that simple. In Aboriginal culture, status is attained through knowledge; traditional hierarchies are maintained by means of a system of secrecy and initiation. It follows that the designs and symbols of Aboriginal art are imbued with layers of meaning and interpretation, so what makes basic sense to you is going to make a whole lot more sense to the initiated.

A themed exhibition in 2002 entitled 'Yilpinji: Love, Magic and Ceremony' at the **Outback Centre** (see p209) is a case in point. The paintings reflected fundamental cultural differences between Western and indigenous concepts of love: for example, pangs of love for the Warlpiri and the Kukatja peoples are felt in the stomach, not the heart. Ultimately, of course, we're also talking about

a visual medium – and the best contemporary Aboriginal artists are renowned precisely for their talent at creating visual excitement.

Once you've seen big barks by John Mawandjul, canvases by Rover Thomas, Emily Kame Kngwarreye, Michael Nelson Jagamarra or Mick Namarri Tjapaltjarri, or the more radically innovative designs by Ginger Riley, Judy Watson, Jimmy Pike or Ian Abdulla – chances are you're going to want to see and know more.

The best commercial galleries specialising in Aboriginal art are **Aboriginal & Pacific Arts**, **Hogarth Galleries** and **Utopia Art Sydney** (for all, see p209). All have changing exhibitions, as well as excellent stockrooms, with works that range from traditional to urban.Other spaces, including **Annandale Galleries** (see p211), **Sherman Galleries** (see p211), **Watters Gallery** (see p210), **Boutwell Draper Gallery** (82-84 George Street, Redfern, 9310 5662, www.boutwell draper.com.au) and **Kaliman Gallery** (10 Cecil Street, Paddington, 9357 2273, www.kalimangallery.com) have occasional exhibitions of Aboriginal art, and the list is growing annually.

Also keep your eye on the big public galleries, where some excellent surveys of Aboriginal art can be seen. The **Museum of Contemporary Art** (see p57) and the ▶

Many galleries are shut on Mondays, and many close for some period over Christmas and the New Year, so it's wise to call ahead if you're in town at that time. Admission is free unless otherwise stated.

Central Sydney

The ArtHouse Hotel
275 Pitt Street, between Park & Market Steets, CBD (9284 1200/www.thearthousehotel.com.au). CityRail Town Hall or St James. **Open** 11am-midnight Mon-Fri; 5-10pm Sat. **Credit** AmEx, BC, DC, MC, V. **Map** p311 C3.
Chic and impressive, the new bar of the ArtHouse Hotel doubles as a unique art gallery, curated by Michael Lenehan. Despite the less than conventional surroundings, the gallery has represented the likes of portrait painter Margarita Georgiadis, and up-and-coming artists such as photographer Jason Kimberley. The gallery also holds weekly drawing classes and a monthly short film festival.

Collins & Kent Fine Art
Shop 25, Opera Quays, 7 Macquarie Street, Circular Quay (9252 3993/www.collinskent.com.au). CityRail/ferry Circular Quay. **Open** 10am-8pm Mon-Sat; 10am-6pm Sun. **Credit** AmEx, BC, DC, MC, V. **Map** p310 C1.
Representing the top end of town, Collins & Kent sits beneath Sydney's famed eyesore, the toaster building. The gallery represents only the European masters, with original works by artists such as Giacometti, Miró, Rembrandt, Picasso and Matisse.

Gallery 4A
Asia-Australia Arts Centre, 181-187 Hay Street, at Parker Street, CBD (9212 0380). CityRail Central/Light Rail Capitol Square. **Open** 11am-6pm Tue-Sat. **Credit** AmEx, BC, DC, MC, V. **Map** p311 B4.
Monthly exhibitions at Gallery 4A feature works by Asian Australian artists, fulfilling the gallery's aim to show the dynamic and changing nature of Asian communities within Australia. The artists frequently experiment with media, and it's not unusual to see heads sculpted from leaves, say, or a

Art Gallery of New South Wales (see p63)

have particularly good track records. They're excellent places for acquiring a taste for Aboriginal art before purchasing, and to see the differences between traditional styles and more subversive, contemporary works (epitomised by the work of emerging artist Jonathan Jones).

To gain a thorough appreciation, read Contemporary Aboriginal Art: A Guide to the Rebirth of an Ancient Culture, by Susan McCulloch (1999), a thorough, illustrated and sensitive guide to Aboriginal art region by region, with a chapter on urban contemporary art and its significance. It also has a list of recommended galleries around Australia.

Aboriginal & Pacific Arts Gallery

Level 8, Dymocks Building, 428 George Street, between King & Market Streets, CBD (9223 5900). CityRail Town Hall or Martin Place. Open 10am-5pm Tue-Fri; 10am-2pm Sat. Closed mid Dec-early Jan. Credit MC, V. Map p311 B3.
Perched high above the city, this collective gallery is run by Gabriella Roy, who has been working in indigenous art since 1970. The gallery specialises in Arnhem Land barks and carvings. It also shows early (ie 1970s) Papunya works, which are done in the famed Western Desert 'dot' style.

Blackfella's Dreaming

239 Oxford Street, between Flinders Street & Darlinghurst Road, Darlinghurst (9331 8701/ www.blackfellasdreaming.com.au). Bus 378, 380, 382. Open 10am-6pm Mon-Thur; 10am-8pm Fri, Sat; noon-5pm Sun. Credit AmEx, BC, DC, MC, V. Map p311 C4.
Owner Gordon Syron believes this is the first Aboriginal art gallery in Sydney owned and run by an Aboriginal artist. Artists represented include Clifford Possum Tjapaltjarri, Abraham Dakgalawuy, Barry Bangarr and Syron himself. Shows have included talks by featured artists and elders, so call to check for special events.

Boomalli Aboriginal Artists' Co-op

55-59 Flood Street, between Marian & Myrtle Streets, Leichhardt (9560 2541/ www.culture.com.au/boomalli). Bus 435, 436, 437, 438. Open 10am-4pm Tue-Fri; 10am-4pm Sat during exhibitions. Closed 2wks from Christmas. Credit BC, DC, MC, V. Boomalli's programme ranges from single artist shows and thematic curated exhibitions to all-inclusive surveys. Similarly, the media used here range from traditional to the very contemporary. Many of Australia's most highly regarded Aboriginal artists are, or have been, closely associated with Boomalli, including Bronwyn Bancroft, Michael Riley and Jeffrey Samuels. You are less likely to find desert

unicorn constructed from shop window dummies. The new Asian wing at the Art Gallery of NSW also offers an excellent array of contemporary Asian and Asian Australian art.

Legge Gallery

183 Regent Street, between Boundary Street & Henderson Road, Redfern (9319 3340/www.legge gallery.com). CityRail Redfern. Open 11am-6pm Tue-Sat. Closed mid Dec-early Feb. Credit BC, MC, V.
Most of Legge Gallery's artists are painters and sculptors, with some ceramicists also represented. They are also generally young. The most charming exception to the rule is Beryl Wood, who was in her sixties when she began painting naïve scenes of football games and other essentially Aussie subjects.

Martin Browne Fine Art

22 Macleay Street, between Rockwall Crescent & Challis Avenue, Potts Point (9331 0100/ www.martinbrownefineart.com). CityRail Kings Cross/bus 311, 312. Open 10.30am-6pm Tue-Sun. Closed 2wks from Christmas. No credit cards. Map p312 D2.

Martin Browne can always be relied upon to have an impressive array of significant pieces by a stable of major contemporary Australian and New Zealand artists, but he also stocks up on works from earlier in the 20th-century and other historical pieces. It has a sister gallery (see below) just up the street.

Martin Browne Fine Art at the Yellow House

57-59 Macleay Street, at Challis Avenue, Potts Point (9331 7997/www.martinbrownefineart.com). CityRail Kings Cross/bus 311, 312. Open 11am-6pm Tue-Sun. No credit cards. Map p312 D2.
The Yellow House was once the headquarters of bohemian Kings Cross, which once provided a base for up-and-coming artists, such as the 1960s avant-garde pioneers Brett Whiteley and George Gittoes (the distinctive paintjob here was apparently inspired by Van Gogh's unfulfilled dream of having a base for artistic expression). The recently renovated house is now an exhibition venue for Martin Browne Fine Art and represents contemporary Australian and international artists.

artists from Western Australia and the Northern Territory here: Boomalli has a commitment to contemporary urban Aboriginal artists in the NSW area.

Coo-ee Aboriginal Art Gallery

Corner of Lamrock & Chambers Avenues, Bondi Beach (9300 9233/www.cooee art.com.au). CityRail Bondi Junction then bus 380, 381, 382, L82/bus 380, L82. **Open** by appointment. **Credit** AmEx, BC, MC, V. **Map** p83.

Coo-ee has existed in various forms since 1980 as an exhibiting gallery. Proprietors Adrian and Anne Newstead source artworks from various indigenous art communities in the Northern Territory, Western Australia and the Torres Strait Islands.

Hogarth Galleries

7 Walker Lane, between Liverpool & Brown Streets, Paddington (9360 6839/ www.aboriginalartcentres.com). Bus 378, 380, 382. **Open** 10am-5pm Tue-Sat. Closed 2wks from Christmas. **Credit** AmEx, BC, DC, MC, V. **Map** p313 D4.

Gallery director Melissa Collins shows a diversity of Aboriginal art from Cape York, the Central and Western Deserts, Arnhem Land and Western Australia.

Other locations: Aboriginal & Tribal Art Centre 117 George Street, The Rocks (9247 9625).

The Outback Centre

28 Darling Walk, 1-25 Harbour Street, Darling Harbour (9283 7477/www.outbackcentre. com.au). CityRail Town Hall/Monorail Darling Park or Garden Plaza. **Open** 10am-6pm daily. **Credit** AmEx, BC, DC, MC, V. **Map** p311 B3.

Part gift shop and travel bureau, the Outback Centre also houses a reputable art gallery, promoting artists from the Central and Western Deserts, Arnhem Land and the Kimberleys. The space is curated by Catriona Stanton, who has worked in Aboriginal art centres for the past ten years. A free 30-minute talk explaining the basics about Aboriginal art is given at 4pm Tuesday to Friday.

Utopia Art Sydney

Danks Street Depot, 2 Danks Street, at Young Street, Waterloo (9699 2900). Bus 301, 302, 303, 305, 355. **Open** 10am-5pm Wed-Fri; noon-5pm Sat. Closed mid Dec-mid Jan. **Credit** AmEx, BC, MC, V.

Utopia specialises in Aboriginal artists from Utopia and Papunya Tula in the Northern Territory, with some non-Aboriginal exceptions: proprietor Christopher Hodges, himself an artist, shows here, as does Sydney artist John R Walker and sculptor Maria Gazzard. This is a good place to pick up works by the celebrated Emily Kame Kngwarreye and other Utopia artists, such as Gloria Petyarre.

Mori Gallery

168 Day Street, between Bathurst & Liverpool Streets, CBD (9283 2903/www.morigallery.com.au). CityRail Town Hall/Monorail Garden Plaza. **Open** 11am-6pm Wed-Sat. **No credit cards**. **Map** p311 B3.

Mori Gallery has a well-earned reputation for showing fine contemporary artists. As well as representing an impressive stable of established young Australians – including such artists as Felicia Kan, Susan Norrie, Deborah Paauwe, Raquel Ormella and Tim Johnson – gallery director Stephen Mori is known among artists for always being receptive to new artists, and his successful and interesting choice of 'unknowns' over the years has demonstrated that his is a remarkably discerning eye.

Phatspace

Room 35, Level 2, 94 Oxford Street, at Crown Street, Darlinghurst (8354 0344/www.phat space.com). Bus 378, 380, 382. **Open** noon-6pm Wed-Sat. Closed Christmas-mid Jan. **No credit cards**. **Map** p311 C3/4.

One of Sydney's artist-run galleries, Phatspace opened in 2002 with the aim of presenting works by emerging and young artists. Shows vary in terms of quality, but the use of a wide variety of media make for exhibitions that are rarely dull. The gallery also holds a digital arts evening every six weeks called 'Chewing the Phat', at which an artist curates a night of video, digital and sound-based work.

Ray Hughes Gallery

270 Devonshire Street, between Bourke & Crown Streets, Surry Hills (9698 3200/www.rayhughes gallery.com). Bus 301, 302, 303, 305. **Open** 10am-6pm Tue-Sat. Closed 2wks from Christmas. **Credit** MC, V. **Map** p311 C4.

Ray Hughes is one of the most colourful characters in the Sydney art world, and was once a subject for the prestigious Archibald portraiture competition. (The annual Archibald Prize is a highlight of the arts calendar, with the winning entry a perennial source of heated debate and often derision.) His gallery shows some of the best Australian and Chinese work around, representing established to mid-career

Arts & Entertainment

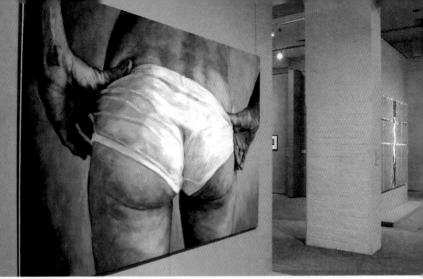

An unusual perspective at the **SH Ervin Gallery**.

artists such as Melbourne portrait painter Lewis Miller, landscape artist Joe Furlonger, sculptor Tom Risley, painters Lucy Culliton, Peter Cooley, Guo Jian and Michael Bell (whose work include images of farting dogs) and abstract artist Brett McMahon.

Sarah Cottier Gallery

585 Elizabeth Street, at Cleveland Street, Redfern (9699 3633/www.cottier.com.au). CityRail Central/ bus 308, 309, 310. **Open** *11am-6pm Wed-Sat; by appointment Tue. Closed Christmas & New Year.* **No credit cards. Map** p311 C4.

Since its inception, Sarah Cottier Gallery has worked with a small and focused group of artists, creating some of the most inventive and ground-breaking contemporary work in Australia. The gallery has maintained a vibrant exhibition programme, both in Australia and internationally, with artists such as Mikala Dwyer and Matthys Gerber.

SH Ervin Gallery

National Trust Centre, Watson Road, next to the Observatory, The Rocks (9258 0135/ www.nsw.nationaltrust.org.au/gall2002.html). CityRail Circular Quay or Wynyard/ferry Circular Quay. **Open** *11am-5pm Tue-Fri; noon-5pm Sat, Sun. Closed mid Dec-mid Jan.* **Admission** $6; $4 members. **Credit** AmEx, BC, DC, MC, V. **Map** p310 B2.

The National Trust gallery, initially the colony's first military hospital, is spectacularly situated on Observatory Hill. Specialising in Australian art, it has a small but high-quality collection of works on paper. Popular annual exhibitions include the 'Salon des Refusés', an alternative selection of some of the rejected works from the much-hyped Archibald and Wynne art prizes. Themed shows have also proved extremely popular, including La Serenissima, images of Venice by Australian artists such as Arthur Streeton and Lloyd Rees.

Watters Gallery

109 Riley Street, at Stanley Lane, East Sydney (9331 2556/www.wattersgallery.com). CityRail Museum. **Open** *10am-5pm Tue, Sat; 10am-7pm Wed-Fri. Closed Christmas & New Year.* **Credit** AmEx, BC, DC, MC, V. **Map** p311 C4.

In the 1970s, Watters was one of the most experimental spaces in town. These days, it represents a number of significant artists who have stayed loyal to the gallery throughout their careers – a rare thing in the fickle world of art. As a result, most of Watters' artists are at the mid-to-late stage of their careers; for example, acclaimed sculptor Robert Klippel, master surrealist painter James Gleeson and gestural painter Vicki Varvaressos. Also represented is the hugely popular Chris O'Doherty (aka Reg Mombassa), whose politicised, dazzling and hugely popular images bridge the worlds of fashion and art. He's also the man behind Mambo sportswear, although, unlike Ken Done, the commercialisation of his work has been less damaging to his reputation as a serious artist.

Eastern Suburbs

Australian Centre for Photography

257 Oxford Street, between Ormond & William Streets, Paddington (9332 1455/www.acp.au.com). Bus 378, 380, 382. **Open** *11am-6pm Tue-Sun. Closed Christmas-early Jan.* **Credit** AmEx, BC, MC, V. **Map** p313 D4.

ACP presents Australian and international photography, photomedia work and new image technologies over two galleries. A 'Project Wall' for emerging artists sits within the neighbouring restaurant, Bistro Lulu. The gallery also has darkroom facilities, a good bookshop, runs various courses and publishes the excellent *Photofile* magazine.

Eva Breuer Art Dealer

83 Moncur Street, between Queen Street & Jersey Road, Woollahra (9362 0297/www.evabreuer artdealer.com.au). Bus *380, 382, 389.* **Open** 10am-6pm Mon-Fri; 9.30am-5pm Sat; 1-5pm Sun. **Credit** AmEx, BC, MC, V. **Map** p313 E4.

Although it's the size of a chocolate box, Eva Breuer's gallery shows 20th- and 21st-century Australian art of a consistently high standard. The exhibition programme is a mix of solo shows by contemporary artists, mini-surveys of historical artists and arresting thematic shows.

Ivan Dougherty Gallery

Selwyn Street, at Albion Avenue, Paddington (9385 0726/www.cofa.unsw.edu.au/galleries/idg/news). Bus *378, 380, 382.* **Open** 10am-5pm Mon-Sat. **No credit cards. Map** p311/313 D4.

This gallery shares its premises with the University of NSW College of Fine Arts, but don't expect student work here. It specialises in international and Australian contemporary art, and stages some of the most fascinating exhibitions in Sydney. A recent show entitled 'Larrikins in London' centred on the artistic contributions of Australian artists who embraced 1960s London, including one-time artist Barry Humphries and Lewis Morley, the photographer behind the Christine Keeler portraits. You'll also find new media displays, diverse group exhibitions and, very occasionally, a mediocre show of work by art school staff.

Rex Irwin Art Dealer

1st Floor, 38 Queen Street, between Oxford & Halls Lane, Woollahra (9363 3212/www.rexirwin.com). Bus *380, 382, 389.* **Open** 11am-5.30pm Tue-Sat; and by appointment. **Credit** MC, V. **Map** p313 E5.

This smallish but smart gallery represents several of Australia's most bankable artists, including painting heavyweight Peter Booth, much-loved virtuoso printmaker Cressida Campbell and landscape artist Nicholas Harding. Rex Irwin also deals in works by Frank Auerbach, ceramicist Gwyn Hanssen Pigott, David Hockney, Lucian Freud, Picasso and the estate of Fred Williams, among many others.

Roslyn Oxley9 Gallery

8-16 Soudan Lane, off Hampden Street, Paddington (9331 1919/www.roslynoxley9.com.au). Bus *378, 380, 382.* **Open** 10am-6pm Tue-Fri; 11am-6pm Sat. Closed Christmas-early Jan. **Credit** AmEx, BC, MC, V. **Map** p313 E4.

Roslyn Oxley's gallery is one of the most beautiful spaces in town and arguably one of Australia's most prestigious galleries. She represents some of the biggest local names on the contemporary art scene, including artists such as Tracey Moffatt, the visual artist (with a penchant for found objects) Rosalie Gascoigne, indigenous photographer Destiny Deacon, internationally renowned photographer Julie Rrap, sculptor James Angus, installation artist Lindy Lee, multimedia artist and filmmaker David Noonan, videomaker and sculptor Patricia Piccinini and installation artist Fiona Foley.

Sherman Galleries

16-20 Goodhope Street, at Glenmore Road, Paddington (9360 5566/www.shermangalleries. com.au). Bus *380, 382, 389.* **Open** 10am-6pm Tue-Fri; 11am-6pm Sat. Closed mid Dec-mid Jan. **Credit** AmEx, BC, MC, V. **Map** p313 D4.

This highly regarded gallery opened in 1981 with a focus on contemporary Australian and international sculpture, but now also shows paintings and works on paper. Artists represented include sculptor and photographer Jacky Redgate and acclaimed indigenous artist Clinton Nain. The gallery also has a sculpture garden, something of a rarity in Sydney.

Stills Gallery

36 Gosbell Street, between Boundary Street & St Neild Avenue, Paddington (9331 7775/ www.stillsgallery.com.au). Bus *389.* **Open** by appointment Tue; 11am-6pm Wed-Sat. Closed mid Dec-Jan. **Credit** AmEx, BC, MC, V. **Map** p313 D3/4.

This bright, spacious, welcoming gallery shows a variety of contemporary Australian photographers, including gallery director Sandy Edwards' pieces. **Other locations: Stills South** Danks Street Depot, 2 Danks Street, Waterloo (8399 0611).

Inner West

Annandale Galleries

110 Trafalgar Street, at Booth Street, Annandale (9552 1699/www.annandalegalleries.com.au). Bus *370, 470.* **Open** 11am-5pm Tue-Sat. **Credit** AmEx, BC, MC, V.

Annandale Galleries represents a stable of mostly mid-career artists, many of whom are highly regarded; one of its most exceptional regulars is textural colourfield painter David Serisier. Also look out for work by contemporary international artists such as Leon Kossoff, William Kentridge and Maurice Cockrill, as well as graphic exhibitions by saleable masters including Marc Chagall and Joan Miró.

Danks Street Depot

2 Danks Street, at Young Street, Waterloo (9698 2201). Bus *301, 302, 303, 305, 355.* **Open** 7.30am-5pm Mon-Fri; 8am-5pm Sat. Closed Christmas-mid Jan Tue-Sat. **Credit** BC, MC, V.

This stunning new warehouse development has nine galleries, including internationals such as the Conny Dietzschold Gallery, photographic gallery Stills South and Aboriginal art centre Utopia Art Gallery (*see p209*). Topping it off is the Danks Street Depot café. This is a must-see venue, despite being located in a somewhat drab area (catch a cab there and back is the cautious advice).

Newspace

680 Darling Street, at Victoria Road, Rozelle (9555 6137). Bus *432, 433, 434, 440, 500, 502, 504.* **Open** noon-6pm Wed-Sat; noon-4pm Sun. **No credit cards.**

This artist-run gallery provides exhibition space for established figures (installation artist Nadia Pacheco) as well as students from Sydney College of the Arts .

Arts & Entertainment

Gay & Lesbian

Lesbian strippers, drag kings, brand-new Mardi Gras… it's all getting a bit queer.

There's no question that Sydney is one of the world's most welcoming gay capitals. A stroll down Oxford Street in pink central Darlo – aka 'The Strip' – lets you know who's in a minority round here, and it's not the queer folk. Sydney's Anglican and Catholic Churches may not welcome active homosexuals, but their bigotry is not felt in mainstream society. Frankly, businesses couldn't afford to turn their backs on the Sydney pink dollar and, to be fair, few want to. After all, the **Gay & Lesbian Mardi Gras Festival** (*see p214* **Welcome to New Mardi Gras**) and gay-friendly Sydney are a huge international tourist attraction, while Australian out-of-towners and country boys and girls constantly flock to the emerald city for fun and friendship. On the public platform there are many gay representatives from all walks of life who feel no need to hide their sexuality. In many ways, Sydney is about as egalitarian for gay people as it gets. Homosexuals in NSW are legally protected against discrimination, as are people living with HIV/AIDS and transgendered people. And same-sex sex is completely legal.

Sydney's gay scene clusters around two main areas: **Darlinghurst**, along Oxford Street, and **Newtown**, along King Street and stretching out to Erskineville and the famed **Imperial Hotel**, which was home of the shows that inspired *Priscilla, Queen of the Desert*. There are also a few venues around the Cross (Kings Cross), East Sydney and the edge of the city. Newtown has overtaken traditional dyke heartland Leichhardt with a plethora of flirty (and cheap) bars and pubs, while Oxford Street remains gay male central. Some places are exclusively gay or lesbian and most have security on the door, but the vast majority welcome anyone who's there for the vibe. In the more boysy clubs, women may still encounter the old 'no open-toed shoes' rule ('there could be broken glass'), actually a sly attempt to keep straight handbags out.

There has always been a lot of change on the gay scene, with venues opening and closing overnight, pubs changing direction and dance nights being cancelled, so check out the latest listings for details. Recently the scene has been hit by a worrying influx of drink spiking – keep

The **Colombian Hotel** – it's a jungle in here. *See p214.*

an eye on your glass – and police raids in search of drugs, a development that has caused temporary closure of some venues. Behind the scenes, though, is a community working hard to keep gay Sydney safe and happy. There are lots of groups covering every possible leisure activity, political bent, social cause or medical issue, so there's no need to be alone.

There has always been a strong and varied number of clubs for men, but the good news is that a spunky new class of gay girl is currently hotting up the lesbian scene. A clutch of dynamic drag kings – female-to-male cross-dressers – are taking Sydney by storm; **Gurlesque**'s raunchy 'lezzo strip nights' (*see p218*) celebrate the female form with explicit gay abandon; and the **Schmutzig** nights (*see p220*) pull crowds on to the dancefloor.

WHERE TO STAY

It can safely be said that any 'international' hotel (glass front, big lobby, expensive cocktails) in Sydney will be gay-friendly. A large chunk of staff at any of these places will be 'family', so you should have no hassles. If you want the full ghetto-accommodation experience, the place to enquire before arriving is the US-run **International Gay & Lesbian Travel Association** (IGLTA), and you can check its website at www.iglta.com. Other good online sites for travel to and within Australia, including gay-friendly accommodation lists, are **Silke's Travel** (www.silkes.com.au) or **Gay & Lesbian Tourism Australia** (www.galta.com.au).

PLAYING SAFE

While Sydney is one of the most tolerant places on earth for gays and lesbians, bashers and homophobes do still exist. At night, be sensible. Stick to well-lit streets with your mates, walk quickly and with a sense of purpose and, if you're intoxicated or just nervous, play safe and catch a cab. A 2003 report noted an increase in gay-related verbal abuse and violence, but the police say they are tackling it. The best bet is to do what the Sydney gays do – avoid Friday and Saturday nights when all the straight kiddies come out to play, and concentrate your partying around midweek and Sundays.

If you are in trouble or feel threatened, just look out for the pink triangle. The Safe Place Program started in 1993 after concerns about violence directed against gays and lesbians. Gay-friendly businesses now place the pink triangle stickers as conspicuously as possible outside, usually near the doorway.

Safe sex is a way of life – 'if it's not on, then it's definitely not on', as the local slogan goes. Sydney is the epicentre of Australia's

HIV/AIDS pandemic and while a decade of safe sex campaigns has hugely reduced the incidence of new infection, the evil lurgy is still out there. Condoms are available everywhere in gay Sydney – in bars, clubs – where there are often big bowls of them behind the bar – toilets, pharmacists and sex shops.

FURTHER ENLIGHTENMENT

For the latest on what's happening, ask the staff at the **Bookshop Darlinghurst** (*see p171*): they're approachable and their knowledge can't be bettered. Alternatively, wander into the **Sydney PRIDE Centre** (*see p286*), the city's queer community centre, which has recently moved to new premises in Erskineville.

Also check the queer press, available in gay outlets, bottle shops, newsagents, music venues and cinemas everywhere. The city's two free weekly gay newspapers, *Sydney Star Observer* and *SX* have full, up-to-the-minute what's on and venue guides. Dykes will find the free monthly news mag *Lesbians on the Loose* required reading. For gay community groups, helplines and support networks, *see p286*.

Nightlife

Most of the venues listed below are pretty gay from Monday to Thursday and on Sunday, but they become much more mixed (and crowded) on Friday and Saturday; many locals avoid the Darlo strip on these nights. Many of the bars and pubs have DJs and dancefloors and turn clubby as the night draws on. Others may have drag shows or themed entertainment, for which they may charge nominal entrance fees. Admission is free unless otherwise stated.

Bars & pubs

Packed with a mixed, cocktail-slurping crowd, the classy **Burdekin Hotel** (*see p134*) also hosts infrequent gay nights such as 'Back2Love', a mixed gay and lesbian soirée, and fundraisers for Mardi Gras.

Bank Hotel

324 King Street, between Newman & Wilson Streets, Newtown (9557 1692). CityRail Newtown. **Open** noon-late Mon-Sat; noon-midnight Sun. **No credit cards. Map** p93.

The Bank is extremely popular with a no-nonsense, butch crowd of girls, who stake their seats in Sleepers, the cocktail bar at the back. The cramped front bar, meanwhile, is preferred by passers-by and pool players. The hotel also draws big crowds on Wednesdays for 'Tasty', a cruisy night conducted by resident DJ Kelly Lynch, sometimes joined by guest DJ, Sydney's celebrated Kate Monroe. The bar's real treasure is the adjoining Sumalee Thai restaurant, which spreads out under trees and fairy-lights in the courtyard next door – just go down the side stairs under the mounted elephant head.

Civic Hotel
Corner of Pitt & Goulburn Streets, CBD (8267 3186). CityRail Central. **Open** 11am-late Mon-Thur; 11am-6am Fri; 1pm-6am Sat. **Admission** $10 after 10pm Fri, after 9pm Sat. **Credit** AmEx, BC, DC, MC, V. **Map** p311 B/C3.

In days gone by, the Civic was a legendary live venue, and that musical legacy lives on today with the bar's cracking selection of DJs, who spin in the hotel's three bars on Thursdays and throughout the weekend. Then there are the drag queens: Saturday night (unusually) is gay night and there are drag shows on the hour from midnight. The house stars are TV personalities Claire de Lune and Verushka Darling, two of Sydney's most talented performers. Just as showy is the decor: the building's deco exte-rior is reflected inside, where the aesthetic is classy and comfortable. There is also a noteworthy restau-rant in the upstairs Deco Lounge, and dancing into the wee hours in the basement.

Colombian Hotel
Corner of Oxford & Crown Streets, Darlinghurst (9360 2151). Bus 378, 380, 382. **Open** 10am-5am Mon-Fri; 7am-6am Sat, Sun. **Credit** AmEx, BC, DC, MC, V. **Map** p311 C3/4.

When the Colombian Hotel (formerly an old Westpac bank) opened its doors in the nick of time for the 2002 Gay Games, complete with a street-facing open-air bar, it paved the way for a new type of gay venue: one that's completely out and proud. Crowds are such that it's hard to appreciate the jungle-like decor: mirrors painted with parrots, plump leather sofas and animal-print pouffes. The management is keen to promote the place as a gay and lesbian venue that is straight-friendly, and it's certainly attracting the

Welcome to New Mardi Gras

Shock waves reverberated through the Sydney gay community when Mardi Gras went bust in 2002. By August of that year, the debt-ridden carnival organisers were forced into voluntary administration and a big question mark hung over the future of Sydney's most lucrative tourist magnet. In truth, a lot needed changing.

There had been rumbles of discontent and outspoken criticism from some of the community's most faithful for several years. The problem – aside from bad accounting – was one of perception: what exactly should Mardi Gras be about? On one level, it was a Sydney-tastic celebration of gay summer in the city. But what started in the winter of 1978 as a march in commemoration of the Stonewall riots was drowning under the weight of commercialisation and heteros trying to muscle in on the fun and the pink dollar. The good news is Mardi Gras has been reborn, thanks to four community-based organisations – the PRIDE Centre, Gay & Lesbian Rights Lobby, AIDS Council of NSW (ACON) and Queer Screen – who together have created New Mardi Gras.

To the tourist, New Mardi Gras looks pretty much the same as ever – especially the main public event, the parade, with its marching boys, drag queens in limos, disco lorries, dykes on bikes, masses of community help groups including PFLAG (Parents & Friends of Lesbians & Gays) and even the gay NSW police – but behind the scenes a lot more thought has goine into how the festival is run. New Mardi Gras has returned to the festival's roots, with a core aim of achieving equality for gay, lesbian, transgender, bisexual and queer people. But don't worry, it hasn't gone all serious: it's still very much a fun-filled, feathers-and-sequins affair.

WHAT AND WHEN
The Mardi Gras Festival takes place over three or four weeks, ending on the last weekend in February or the first weekend in March. Although it's the parade and party on the final Saturday that get the publicity, it's worth joining the locals at as many of the pre-parade events as you can fit in.

Events kick off with the **Festival Launch** (always on a Friday); it's free, attended by thousands and sets the tone for the festivities. The location varies, but in the past has included Hyde Park and the steps of the Opera House forecourt. Other celebrations include the **Mardi Gras Film Festival**, a number of art exhibitions, themed parties, and nightly cabaret performances and stage shows in venues all over Sydney. The **Fair Day** in Victoria Park, Camperdown (held on the Sunday a fortnight before the final weekend), attracts more than 60,000 people, and features an excellent high camp pet show. Meanwhile at **Shop Yourself Stupid**, Oxford Street shops hand over a percentage of their takings to the HIV/AIDS charity, the Bobby Goldsmith Foundation. And, down on the water, the **Harbour Party** (*see p218*), although not officially part of Mardi Gras, is always a big hit.

Arts & Entertainment

city's pretty people. There are two bars: the first-floor cocktail bar and ground-floor main bar, plus seating on a mezzanine level.

Imperial Hotel

35 Erskineville Road, at Union Street, Erskineville (9519 9899). CityRail Erskineville or Newtown. **Open** 3pm-midnight Mon-Wed; 3pm-late Thur; 3pm-6am Fri; 1pm-6am Sat; 1pm-midnight Sun. **Admission** $5 Fri, Sat. **No credit cards. Map** p93.
This beautiful art deco pub is quite schizophrenic: by day, it's a relaxed local; by night, it turns into one of Sydney queerest spaces. It's the home of the original 'Priscilla' shows (Thursdays, Fridays and Saturdays) and 'Le Velvet l'Amour', a new drag king show (Sundays), and is still the best place to see the city's most innovative drag. There are three bars, all open late: the front bar is mixed, often quiet and where the local dykes play pool; downstairs is mostly dancing boys, kind of cruisy and very dark; the back

bar, meanwhile, has the drag shows, the straight tourists and the crush. Get there early if you want any sort of a seat. On Tuesday evenings there's Bingay – that's bingo hosted by a drag queen.

Kinselas Middlebar

Kinselas Hotel, 383-87 Bourke Street, at Taylor Square, Darlinghurst (9331 3100). Bus 378, 380, 382. **Open** 8pm-3am Thur; 6pm-4am Fri; 7pm-4am Sat; 8pm-1am Sun. **Credit** AmEx, BC, DC, MC, V. **Map** p311 C4.
Located on the upper level of the Kinselas Hotel, the Middlebar is the place to be on a hot summer night, ideally while sipping one of its famous cocktails on the balcony overlooking Taylor Square. Being indoors has its advantages too: it's cool, great for posing and there are plush sofas, lots of mirrors and a New York-style bar. Middlebar has always been a popular gay haunt on Sunday nights, but recently the management has encouraged a mixed crowd of

The **parade** itself begins at sunset. It starts on the corner of Hyde Park and Whitlam Square, heads up Oxford Street to Flinders Street, and finishes at the party venue, Fox Studios in Moore Park. Half a million locals and tourists turn out to watch, many staking out their territory at least six hours before the parade. Numerous hotels and restaurants lining the route sell seats at ticket-only cocktail parties. Another comfortable option is the Bobby Goldsmith Stand on Driver Avenue, which seats 7,000 (for tickets and info, visit www.bgf.org.au or call 9283 8666). Many people head for Taylor Square, which is

a really bad idea, since the crush can get ugly. Instead, a good viewing spot is right at the end of the parade, opposite the BGF seating, but get there early because the police cordon off the streets, making access difficult.

After the parade comes the **party**. Attracting some 17,000 revellers, it features top DJs and performers whose identities are usually kept a guarded secret until the night – don't expect Kylie: she hasn't come for years. As well as the crammed dance halls and outrageous drag shows, there are plenty of different areas in the Fox Studios complex for drinking, eating and chilling. There's also a hefty medical presence, just in case your night goes wrong.

INFORMATION AND TICKETS

To keep abreast of what's happening, contact New Mardi Gras (9568 8600, www.mardigras.org.au) or get hold of the excellent, free official programme, available from January from gay-friendly venues around Oxford Street and Newtown. You'll need to book accommodation and tickets (at least for the major events) months ahead. Tickets for the main party ($120, $110 Mardi Gras members, $75 concessions) are available from mid December and usually sell out at least a month in advance, so don't wait until you hit Sydney to buy them. Tickets are limited to four per person and can be purchased from Ticketek (9266 4800, www.ticketek.com.au) and also through accredited travel agents (booking fees apply).

anyone who 'gets the vibe'. And the vibe is generally good, with DJs playing from 9pm. The latest Sunday craze is 'salsoul', a disco mix of salsa and soul.

Lord Roberts Hotel

Corner of Stanley & Riley Streets, East Sydney (9331 1326). Bus 378, 380, 382. **Open** 10am-midnight daily. **Credit** AmEx, BC, MC, V. **Map** p311 C3.

On Sundays the Lord Roberts' cocktail bar is home to the popular 'Better House and Beer Gardens', a gay night starting at 5pm and usually featuring some of the city's top DJs, plus a free barbecue. During the rest of the week a mixed, laid-back crowd is drawn by the outdoor balcony and restaurant.

Manacle

Basement, Taylor Square Hotel, 1 Flinders Street, between Patterson Lane & Taylor Square, Surry Hills (9331 2950). Bus 378, 380, 382. **Open** 7pm-3am Wed-Sat; 7am-3am Sun. **Admission** $5 7am-noon Sun. **No credit cards**. **Map** p311 C4.

Formerly the Barracks, a leather bar, the Manacle has had a lick of paint and some new furniture to go with its new name, but one thing hasn't changed: the guys still wear fetish gear. Despite the bar's new look, it remains pretty dungeon-like, so bears, leather and rubber devotees should feel right at home. A string of DJs pump out doof-doof heavy music on most nights, and on Sundays there's a full-day club, Bent, starting at (gasp) 7am and running all day and night. The entrance is on Patterson Lane.

Newtown Hotel

Corner of King & Watkin Streets, Newtown (9557 1329). CityRail Newtown. **Open** 10am-midnight Mon-Sat; 10am-10pm Sun. **No credit cards**. **Map** p93.

With its comfy assortment of leather chairs and doors that open right on to King Street, the Newtown Hotel is a great spot to sit and watch the world go by. Downstairs is the kind of place where customers feel at ease sitting on their own, either reading a paper or watching music videos on the large-screen TV. There's also an upstairs bar open at weekends and the management are planning to increase the hours. Thankfully, the well-stocked gaming lounge – known as Bar 2 – is enclosed in its own room, allowing audible conversation in the main bar. Drag shows run on Thursday, Friday and Saturday; the rest of the week is jam-packed with themed nights, dance nights and pool comps for the girls. In the back lies Linda's Backstage Restaurant.

The Oxford Hotel

134 Oxford Street, at Taylor Square, Darlinghurst (9331 3467). Bus 378, 380, 382. **Open** 24hrs daily. *Gilligans* 5pm-late daily. *Gingers* 6pm-late Fri, Sat. **No credit cards**. **Map** p311 C4.

The Oxford is a gay legend, probably because it's got one of the best sites in the city for pre- and post-clubbing drinking – right opposite Taylor Square on the corner of Bourke Street. At street level, it's a big 24-hour bar, almost universally male – it's the official meeting place for the Harbour City Bears – with lots of pokie machines and a huge video screen.

The vibe is quite sociable early on, but gets edgier as the evening wears on. Upstairs, past the beefy security, is Gilligans, also popular with Sydney's straight girls, who appreciate its comfortable banquettes, great views over Taylor Square and killer cocktail list. Upstairs again is Gingers – open to the public only on Fridays and Saturdays. At the time of writing the Oxford was in financial difficulties, but it's battling to stay open.

The Sly Fox

199 Enmore Road, between Cambridge Street & Stanmore Road, Enmore (9557 1016). Bus 423, 426, 428. **Open** 10am-4am Mon-Thur; 10am-6am Fri; 10am-5am Sat; 10am-midnight Sun. **No credit cards**.

From the outside the Sly Fox look like an average spit-and-sawdust Aussie pub, but get past security and you'll find one of Sydney's hottest lesbian bars. It's got a fabulous cocktail menu, cheap shots (7-9pm) and the big draw of drag king Sexy Galexy, who struts her stuff to a packed house every Wednesday night. The crowd goes wild as she sheds her foam boobs, stuffs them into her trousers and paints on a moustache with eyeliner. DJ Sveta also plays a combo of Madonna and Beyoncé to a fantastically friendly crowd, and there's even a female cop to arrest anyone 'not causing a disturbance'. And if you just want to play pool, they've thought of that too – there's a big table at the back and $100 bar tabs up for grabs if you win.

Clubs

Although not strictly a gay venue, megaclub **Home** (*see p235*) does host the odd gay dance party. Phone in advance for details and tickets.

ARQ

16 Flinders Street, between Oxford & Taylor Streets, Darlinghurst (9380 8700/www.arqsydney.com.au). Bus 373, 377, 378, 380, 382, 391, 394, 396. **Open** 9pm-9am Thur-Sun. **Admission** (after 10pm) $10 Fri; $20 Sat; $5 Sun. **No credit cards**. **Map** p311 C4.

The busiest club on the Sydney scene, housed in an old garage atop Flinders Street. Its big nights are Saturday and Sunday, with a very Oxford Street crowd of bare-chested pretty boys. Boasting two levels, with a mezzanine walkway, it holds around 900 people when full, which it always is on weekends. Drag queen and king shows (look out for 'Wet Pussy' on Fridays) are regulars in the downstairs bar, and are usually held earlier in the evening than in other venues; on nights when there is a cover charge, drag queens get in for free. *See also p233*.

The Exchange Hotel

34-44 Oxford Street, between Riley & Liverpool Streets, Darlinghurst (9331 1936). Bus 378, 380, L82. **Open** *General bar* 10am-late daily. *Lizard Lounge* 5-11pm Mon-Wed; 5pm-2am Thur, Fri; 5pm-10am Sat; 5pm-midnight Sun. *Phoenix Bar* 10pm-6am Fri, Sun; noon Sat-1pm Sun. *Q Bar*

Washboard lighting effects and bulging sounds at **Midnight Shift**.

9pm-late daily. *Stereo Bar* midnight-9am Fri, Sat. **Admission** *Q Bar* $15 Fri; $20 Sat. **Credit** AmEx, V. **Map** p311 C3.

There are four floors of fun in this decade-old gay favourite. The first-floor Lizard Lounge is a cocktail bar, sometimes redubbed Polly's Bar. Run by veteran drag queen and bar manager Polly, it offers drag shows on Thursdays and Fridays from around 9pm. On Sundays from 6.30pm there's the irreverent and unpredictable 'Polly's Follies' – a legendary drag talent show that been a launching platform for many of the strip's top queens (the show originated at the famed Albury Hotel, now closed). On Saturdays, Polly's Bar becomes Sound Lounge, with DJs and dancing. Downstairs in the basement is the Phoenix Bar, a small and sweaty box of a dance club. On the second floor are the Q Bar (*see p235*) with its daybeds, private booths and a unisex toilet. It is ideal for house music, often with live performances. Also on the second floor is the Stereo Bar, which, like the Q, is good for dancing until dawn with a mixed gay and straight crowd.

Icebox

2 Kellett Street, at Bayswater Road, Kings Cross (9331 0058). CityRail Kings Cross. **Open** 9pm-4am Wed; 10pm-6am Thur, Sat, Sun; 9pm-6am Fri. **Admission** $10 Thur, Sun; $16 Fri; $10 before midnight, $15 after midnight Sat. **Credit** AmEx, BC, DC, MC, V. **Map** p312 D3.

Icebox is a serious music lovers' dance club featuring the hottest DJs du jour. It's not exclusively gay, but often hosts girls' nights.

The Midnight Shift

85 Oxford Street, between Riley & Crown Streets, Darlinghurst (9360 4319). Bus 378, 380, 382. **Open** noon-4am Mon-Fri; 2pm-late Sat, Sun. **Admission** $5. **No credit cards. Map** p311 C4.

Another Sydney legend. At street level, it's a dark but friendly bar, with no cover charge, a wide range of punters and pool tables out the back. Upstairs is the packed dance club, which has an entry fee and a crowd of wall-to-wall men, who bump and grind both on and off the dancefloor. If you can take your eyes off the washboard stomachs and bulging biceps, there are great lighting effects and frequent drag shows, with the best production values in town.

Palms

124 Oxford Street, at Taylor Square, Darlinghurst (9357 4166). Bus 378, 380, 382. **Open** 8pm-3am Wed-Sun. **No credit cards. Map** p311 C4.

There was a time when Palms was a great spot to see cabaret-style drag, with lots of audience interaction. These days, the drag nights are occasional and it's more of a friendly, late-night drinking bar with a dancefloor and a Kylie/disco-diva soundtrack. It's an underground place located a few doors down from the popular and crowded Oxford Hotel (*see p216*), and has good air-con, which magically sucks out a lot of the hazy smoke.

The Stonewall Hotel

175 Oxford Street, at Taylor Square, Darlinghurst (9360 1963). Bus 378, 380, 382. **Open** 1pm-late daily. **No credit cards. Map** p311 C3.

A large, multi-level space, much loved and always busy. Downstairs there's a chatty, pub-style atmosphere with drag shows, karaoke contests and talent quests aplenty. Upstairs is a comfortable lounge with a groovy funk soundtrack and the occasional drag show. In late June it stages the hugely enjoyable ACON (AIDS Council of NSW) fund-raiser, 'Orgy of Drag', a marathon night of drag with turns by practically every drag queen in town. It's part of the annual Gay PRIDE Week in memory of the Stonewall riots in the States; regular events include Queer Screen's trivia night and the *Sydney Star Observer*'s PRIDE Awards ceremony.

The Taxi Club
40-42 Flinders Street, between Taylor & Short Streets, Darlinghurst (9331 4256). Bus 373, 377, 378, 380, 382, 391, 394, 396. **Open** 9am-5am daily. **Credit** BC, MC, V. **Map** p311 C4.
When everything else is closed, when desperation strikes, never fear – there's always the Taxi. This is the venue for night owls, serious drinkers or some combination of the two. It provides the cheapest drinks in queer Sydney and is open until 5am. Which is why it's a favourite with both drag queens – who stop here after a night's work – and some extremely intoxicated out-of-towners. There's also a restaurant and café on the ground floor, a gaming room, a TV area and lounge on the first floor, and a small dancefloor above that. It's a members' club, but you can get temporary membership on the door for free.

Venus Room
2 Roslyn Street, between Darlinghurst Road & Ward Avenue, Kings Cross (8354 0888). CityRail Kings Cross. **Open** 8pm-6am Mon, Wed-Sun. **Admission** $5 Fri, Sat. **No credit cards. Map** p312 D3.
A one-time DIVA best venue winner, this intimate, low-ceilinged bar with a small dancefloor and stage has drag shows from Thursday to Sunday, starting at around midnight. Arrive early to grab a table near the stage, or you're unlikely to get a decent view.

Dance parties & themed nights

If you want to get in with Sydney's in-crowd, you have to get into the dance party groove. The mainstays are the **Mardi Gras** party (*see p214* **Welcome to New Mardi Gras**), **Sleaze Ball**, **PRIDE's New Year's Eve** bash and, increasingly, the **Harbour Party**, but there are also many more to choose from throughout the year as the gay calendar is nonstop. Generally there's a party on every long weekend (that's one with a public holiday attached) as well as in the regular holiday periods. Ticket prices can be steep, but most of the events are charity fund-raisers. Preparing for and recovering from the party is just as important as the event itself. Clubs and bars host lavish pre- and post-parties and even post-post dos, known as 'post recovery' events.

There are also frequent themed party nights organised by enterprising individuals on the gay circuit. Currently, the most innovative is **Gurlesque** (*see below*), a lesbian strip night by girls for girls. For details of all these nights, look in Sydney's gay press or on billboards and fliers in bars and clubs.

Big Queer Nation
9206 2000/www.acon.org.au. **Date** wkend before 2nd Mon in June.
This used to be called the Hand in Hand, and is held annually on the Queen's Birthday long weekend in June. It's a huge dance party with guest DJs and drag queen hosts, and proceeds go to a good cause: it's the major fund-raiser for the AIDS Council of NSW.

Gurlesque
www.gurlesque.org.
Dancers Sex Intents and Glita Supernova formed Gurlesque, Sydney's no-holds-barred 'lezzo strip joint', ten years ago when they became tired of performing striptease for men and wanted to 'give it to the girls'. And the girls have been gasping for it ever since, with every show selling out. The troupe has also gone down well in Adelaide, Melbourne and overseas. With stunning costumes (just waiting to come off), decadent make-up and raunchy routines, Gurlesque has brought something unique and unrivalled to the girls' scene. Check the website or the lesbian press for performance details.

Harbour Party
Sydney Harbour Foreshore, The Domain, CBD (tickets 9266 4800/www.ticketek.com.au). CityRail Circular Quay or Martin Place/ferry Circular Quay. **Map** p310 D1/2. **Date** last wk of Feb/1st wk of Mar.
This outdoor dance party has one of the best locations in Sydney – on the harbour foreshore in the Domain, just around from Mrs Macquarie's Chair, with a fabulous view of the Opera House. It's become the hot ticket of the Mardi Gras Festival, although it's not officially part of it. The party is usually held on the Sunday before the Mardi Gras parade and starts early (around 6pm), owing to a midnight curfew imposed by the foreshore authorities. Those who can't nail (or afford) a ticket gather in the park above, within earshot of the music and with a bird's-eye view of revellers.

Inquisition
Horden Pavilion, Fox Studios Australia, Driver Avenue, Moore Park (9331 8608/www.sydney leatherpride.org). Bus 339, 373, 374, 377, 393, 395, 396. **Map** p313 D5. **Date** end Apr.
As the name suggests, Inquisition is all about leather and fetish. It's the closing party of Leather Pride Week and is hugely popular – too popular in fact. Purists from the Sydney Pride Leather Association (SPLA), which organises the event, want to ensure the party is dominated by diehard leather guys, not poseurs, and are currently taking steps to reorganise the event, so check the website for up-to-date info.

The main drag

It was really no accident that the world's quintessential drag queen movie, *The Adventures of Priscilla, Queen of the Desert*, was set partly in Sydney. The emerald city is arguably the drag queen capital of the world: there are almost as many drag shows per square mile as there are Thai restaurants. But Sydney queens do far more than put on some slap and tell old double-entendre jokes. This is drag as you've never seen it before: Hollywood-style production numbers with home-made costumes that knock feathers off of the best Broadway can offer. Innovative performers like Courtney Act (geddit?) and Wyness Mongrel Bitch are at the forefront of a scene that has become a trendsetter for drag queens the world over.

The current scene has its roots in the 1960s, when Sydney's most famous drag queen, Carlotta – now a full-blown TV personality, author and celebrity – headlined at drag supper club Les Girls in Kings Cross. It also evolved out of the back-room pub shows celebrated in Stephan Elliott's *Priscilla*. Since that classic film was released in 1994, drag has become more positively mainstream: queens like Claire de Lune and Verushka Darling host their own shows on pay TV, some drag queens took part in the closing ceremony of the 2000 Olympics and others are all the rage in TV commercials (advertising everything from coffee to the Rugby World Cup), and Courtney Act even made it to the final stages of the hit TV talent show *Australian Idol*.

Meanwhile, the **DIVAs** (Drag Industry Variety Awards), an annual AIDS fund-raiser, are the hottest tickets in town come August. The show is a veritable drag Oscars, with queens emerging from stretch limos on to the red carpet – scantily clad boys on arms as a 'handbag' – dressed to the nines in big wigs, fur collars and vertiginous stilettos. The glitzy event is a far cry from its inception in 1991, when 250 faithfuls squeezed into DCM nightclub on Oxford Street. In 2003, the 13th annual awards were held at the prestigious Randwick Racecourse, with an estimated audience of 1,000, along with five hosts and six production numbers.

Gongs traditionally go to 'Bitch of the Year', and 'Costume Designer of the Year', but the 2003 awards heralded an all-new category – Sydney's 'Favourite Drag King', celebrating the steady rise of female-to-male cross-dressing in the city's bars and clubs. The

trend first surfaced at New York's Casanova Club in the 1990s, but it has since taken off in Sydney, Brisbane and Melbourne. The 2003 winner, **Sexy Galexy** (pictured), is one of a number of drag kings who parody basic boy band stereotypes or specific pop stars, with Bryan Ferry being a favourite.

For the best drag shows in town, check out **ARQ** (*see p216*), the **Civic Hotel** (*see p214*), **Exchange Hotel** (*see p216*), **Imperial Hotel** (*see p215*), **Newtown Hotel** (*see p216*), **Sly Fox** (*see p216*), **Stonewall Hotel** (*see p217*) and the **Venus Room** (*see p218*). If you want a taste of dressing like a queen for the night, try **House of Priscilla** in Darlinghurst (first floor, 47 Oxford Street, at Pelican Street, 9286 3023), where the friendly staff are well versed in decking out drag artists and party boys. They also cater to specific drag fantasies: popular outfits include Barbie, Ken, Kylie, Geisha Girls and Wonder Woman, available to buy or rent.

Alternatively, you can always see Sydney through rose-tinted drag queen spectacles on a **Sydney by Diva** tour (*see p52*). This three-hour comedy bus tour of Sydney's tourist spots is hosted by one (or two) of the city's top divas and is an unforgettable ride. There are either economy ($60) or first-class ($80) fares, but be warned: if you choose economy, brace yourself for nonstop wisecracks.

PRIDE Party

9550 6188/www.pridecentre.com.au. **Tickets** $89;
$50 concessions. **Date** New Year's Eve.
This mammoth dance party brings in the New Year
with a bang. It's traditionally held at Fox Studios,
but there have been murmurings about moving to a
smaller venue to combat its huge production costs.
It's a fund-raiser for the PRIDE Centre.

Schmutzig

Date usually 4th Fri of the mth.
Local promoter Sarah Harris had reason to celebrate
in 2003 when girls' dance party Schmutzig defied all
odds to celebrate its first birthday. At only 23, Harris
had already launched other girls' nights, but faced
problems attracting a regular crowd. But the girls
are flocking to Schmutzig, where the excellent DJs
include Sveta (also a regular at the Sly Fox, *see p216*)
and the vibe and music are decidedly underground.
Schmutzig is currently held at the Phoenix in the
Exchange Hotel (*see p216*), but liable to change;
check the gay press for details.

Sleaze Ball

*Fox Studios Australia, Driver Avenue, Moore
Park (9568 8600/www.mardigras.org.au).*
Bus *339, 373, 374, 376, 377, 393, 395, 396.*
Tickets (plus booking fee) $90; $80 members;
$50 concessions. **Map** p313 D5. **Date** last Sat in
Sept/1st Sat in Oct.
The sister party to Mardi Gras is the aptly named
Sleaze Ball, a benefit event to raise funds for Gay &
Lesbian Mardi Gras. If Mardi Gras can be claimed
as mainstream, then Sleaze is very much a queer
bash and full fetish dress is encouraged.

Gyms & salons

Sydneysiders are obsessed with working out
and there are masses of gyms all over town.
Other gay favourites include **City Gym
Health & Fitness Centre** (*see p241*), which
has everything and is open round the clock.

Bayswater Fitness

*33 Bayswater Road, between Kellett Street & Ward
Avenue, Kings Cross (9356 2555). CityRail Kings
Cross.* **Open** 6am-midnight Mon-Thur; 6am-11pm
Fri; 7am-10pm Sat; 7am-9pm Sun. **Admission** $15.
Credit AmEx, BC, DC, MC, V. **Map** p312 D3.
Here you'll find an exhausting schedule of aerobics
classes as well as all the usual fitness facilities.

The Beauty Room

*220 Goulburn Street, between Riley & Crown Streets,
Darlinghurst (9212 4844).* **Open** 9am-6pm Mon,
Tue, Fri; 9.30am-9pm Wed, Thur; 9am-5pm Sat.
Credit AmEx, BC, MC, V. **Map** p311 C4.
When the shirts come off in Sydney's gay clubs, it's
easy to see who's been down to the Beauty Room.
This award-winning salon prides itself on serving
the gay community with waxing, tanning, tinting,
body treatments, manicures, pedicures and facials.
Go on, you're worth it.

Saunas & sex clubs

Sydney has plenty of men-only sex-on-premises
venues. Pick up any essential accessories at
your nearest **Tool Shed** (*see p177*).

Bodyline Spa & Sauna

*10 Taylor Street, at Flinders Street, Darlinghurst
(9360 1006/www.bodylinesydney.com).* Bus *378,
380, 382.* **Open** noon-7am Mon-Thur; noon Fri-
7am Mon. **Admission** $22; $11 noon-4pm Mon-Fri,
concessions. *Members* $15 Mon-Thur. **Credit** AmEx,
BC, DC, MC, V. **Map** p311 C4.
Bodyline was established in 1991 at a time when no
legal gay sex venues were owned by gay men. After
a landmark court case it became the first lawfully
established sex-on-premises gay venue in NSW, and
is still gay-owned and operated. It has a huge spa,
steam room and sauna on the lower ground floor; a
coffee lounge and cinema on the ground floor; private retreats, fantasy room, maze and video room on
the first floor; and a great sun deck and mini-gym
on the second floor. It's kept very clean. The motto
is 'Say yes with enthusiasm and no with courtesy'.

The Den

*1st Floor, 97 Oxford Street, between Crown &
Riley Streets, Darlinghurst (9332 3402/www.denin
ternational.com).* Bus *378, 380, 382.* **Open** 10pm-
late daily. **Admission** $13. **Credit** AmEx, BC, MC,
V. **Map** p311 C3/4.
The Den is now a gay mini-empire, with sex shops
and clubs scattered throughout NSW, Queensland
and New Zealand, but this location is the original.
You enter via a flight of stairs – dubbed the Den's
'stairway to heaven'. Inside are cubicles, fantasy sex
rooms, dark rooms and toilet blocks, plus a lounge
and coffee area to relax in between sessions. There's
no sauna or bar, but music is played throughout and
there are special themed evenings, such as circle
jerk, uniform and leather nights.

Headquarters on Crown

*273 Crown Street, at Campbell Street, Darlinghurst
(9331 6217/www.headquarters.com.au).* Bus *378,
380, 382.* **Open** 24hrs daily. **Admission** $5-$10
before 7pm Mon-Thur; $15 after 7pm Mon-Thur, all
day Fri-Sun. **Credit** BC, MC, V. **Map** p311 C4.
Specialises in 'fantasy play areas' (for example, a pig
pen, jailhouse and Alcatraz room), though only the
'Ute Room' is quintessentially Australian. There's a
coffee lounge and full air-con – thank goodness.

Ken's@Kensington

*83 Anzac Parade, opposite Ascot Street, Kensington
(9662 1359/www.kensatkensington.com.au).* Bus
373, 377, 392, 394, 396. **Open** noon-6am Mon-
Thur; noon Fri-6am Mon. **Admission** $20; $10-$16
noon-5pm Mon-Fri, concessions; $15 5-11pm Sun.
No credit cards.
Ken's has the usual steam, sauna and spa facilities,
plus an indoor swimming pool, gym, video and TV
lounges, private cubicles and theme rooms (complete
with free condoms and lube). DJs spin tunes on
Saturday and Sunday nights.

Music

The heart of rock 'n' roll (and jazz, too) beats on in Sydney.

Rock, Roots & Jazz

Rock

Sydney's rock scene has enjoyed a healthy renaissance since the 'pokie invasion' robbed bands of their essential grassroots venues in the lead up to the 2000 Olympics. Thanks to local lobbying – and the state government's reluctant realisation of the gambling monster they'd helped create – many pubs bowed to punter pressure and opted to shove said gambling dens into hitherto unknown corners, and reopen their main room for bands to re-strut their stuff. A case in point is the **Annandale Hotel** (*see p224*), which again serves as the prime inner-west testing ground for fresh talent from across Australia. Many pubs have followed suit with varying degrees of success, while others opted to become pub-grub, sports-TV drinking holes.

Historically, Sydney has always rocked. American servicemen helped usher in a musical revolution of sorts in local dives back in the war-torn '40s. By 1955, when the infamous 'Six O'Clock Swill' (when a 6pm close ensured mass-downings of beer) was dead and gone, Sydney was genuinely ready to embrace a homespun rock 'n' roll and ensuing teenage rebellion. The key year was 1957, when Johnny O'Keefe and Col Joye and the Joy Boys tore up the Town Hall for the inaugural Rock 'n' Roll Ball.

Australian TV programmes *Six O'Clock Rock* and *Bandstand* became a must-see for teens, while *Countdown* was the one to watch in the 1970s and '80s. But the music heart lay in the pubs, with the Angels, Cold Chisel, Radio Birdman, and Hunters and Collectors all blossoming in the beer barns that swelled with the music-hungry masses. After the post-punk pioneers had served their time and the likes of INXS had shot into orbit, the local scene suffered a recession as fire restrictions impinged and nightclubs took their place. The late advent of dance music threatened still further to finish off what was left, but thanks to power bands such as You Am I and, to a lesser extent, the Whitlams (both of which are still big players on the live scene), the mid to late 1990s saw a resurgence in band power.

Even with the very real threat of the poker machines, Sydney's band scene has proven ever-more resilient, serving up a host of daily gigs in dozens of venues. Another reason for Sydney's dominance of the national scene is that most record companies have their headquarters in the city; Sydney is also where the esteemed – and televised – ARIA (Australian Record Industry Association) awards are held every October.

The huge success of recent reality TV pop shows *Australian Idol* and *Popstars* have certainly awakened interest, in pop, at least – Guy Sebastian, the surprise *Idol* winner, announced at the end of 2003, has gone platinum four times with his number one album, and other finalists have scored record contracts. But it's too early to tell whether such programmes will have a lasting – or, indeed, positive – impact on the music scene.

The best Venues

For sweat and tears

The **Hopetoun Hotel** (*see p225*). When it's just about to heave, you won't want to leave. The very best of the local band showcase spots.

For the stars of tomorrow

Hot young things grace the fabled stage at the **Annandale Hotel** (*see p224*) before fame beckons. Say you saw them here first.

For muso-savvy bands

Mingle with the coolies at the **Metro** (*see p223*), while catching the big names getting intimate.

For jazzy-bluesy vibes

The **Basement** (*see p225*). Supper clubs never tasted – or sounded – so good. Small but sexy, this gets so cool it sometimes hurts.

For strings, brass and choirs

It's gotta be the **Sydney Opera House** (*see p230*). Unparalleled views in acoustic heaven ensure its iconic status.

Arts & Entertainment

Enmore Theatre: essential listening.

ABC's (Australian Broadcasting Corporation) national youth radio network Triple J (105.7 FM) still highlights new Aussie talent – past glories include Silverchair and Grinspoon, both still riding high in popularity. Annual festivals **Big Day Out** (www.bigdayout.com), held in Sydney and throughout Australia in January, and the all-Aussie **Homebake** (*see p193*), held in the Domain in December, pull in the talent for the young and young at heart.

Be aware, though, that music has famously played second fiddle to sport in Australia. But Sydneysiders do love their music, and will shell out for a great show. What's more, now the Aussie dollar is on a surer footing than its post-Olympic slump of 2002, overseas acts are back touring the country in ever-increasing numbers. And for the visitor wanting to catch a big-name show Down Under, tickets often sell out far less quickly than they do at home.

INFORMATION

For the latest and greatest info on what's hot, check out the free 'street press', *Drum Media* and the *Brag*, widely distributed in pubs and record shops across the city, they provide music news, reviews and listings. The *Sydney Morning Herald*'s Metro section on Friday includes full listings, and the pseudo-tabloid *Daily Telegraph* has the surprisingly good, youth-oriented SLM pullout every Wednesday. Newsstand mags are less local in content – Aussie versions of *Rolling Stone* and *Kerrang!* are the chief providers – but they serve as best they can in a small, dollar-pinched market.

You can book tickets for all major venues through agencies **Ticketek** (9266 4800/ www.ticketek.com) and **Ticketmaster7** (13 6100/www.ticketmaster7.com), but both charge booking fees.

Major venues

Enmore Theatre

130 Enmore Road, between Simmons & Reiby Streets, Newtown (9550 3666/www.enmoretheatre. com.au). CityRail Newtown. **Box office** 9am-6pm Mon-Fri; 10am-2pm Sat. **Tickets** $30-$90. **Credit** AmEx, BC, DC, MC, V. **Map** p93.

The most atmospheric of the few mid-scale venues in Sydney, this 1,600-seat, art deco-style theatre, dating from 1908, regularly plays host to established local talent, overseas acts and big-name stand-up and theatre. Queens of the Stone Age, Duran Duran and Nick Cave have all strutted their stuff here. The acoustics are first-rate and sightlines excellent, even if you're stuck up in the balcony. With removeable seats in the stalls, plus ultra-friendly door and bar staff, the Enmore can justifiably claim to be the muso experience par excellence.

Hordern Pavilion

Fox Entertainment Precinct, Driver Avenue, Moore Park (9383 4063/www.playbillvenues.com.au). Bus 339, 373, 374, 376, 377, 391, 392, 393, 395, 396. **Box office** (in person) 2hrs before show. **Tickets** $50-$120. **Credit** AmEx, BC, DC, MC, V. **Map** p313 D5.

A barn of a venue, yet with a typically relaxed Aussie vibe, the 5,500-capacity Hordern sits at the cool end of the Fox Studios complex. Built in 1924, it presents big-name local acts (Powderfinger, Cold Chisel) and overseas artists seeking financially viable intimacy (Ben Harper, Coldplay, the Strokes). With the floor area usually standing only and tiered seating behind and on both sides, it's ideal for those idyllic rock moments. It's also air-conditioned. Claim to greatness: Nirvana being besieged here by 10,000 raucous fans during 1992's Big Day Out festival.

The Metro

624 George Street, between Bathurst & Liverpool Streets, CBD (9287 2000/www.metrotheatre.com.au). CityRail Town Hall/Monorail World Square. **Box office** 10am-7pm Mon-Fri; noon-7pm Sat. **Tickets** $15-$70. **Credit** AmEx, BC, MC, V. **Map** p311 B3.

The coolest of the inner city's club-type venues, this 1,200-capacity theatre is more modest than its cousin, the Enmore. With a tiered, standing-only set-up – the stage is always in full view – the Metro is the archetypal muso hangout. Its central location, relatively intimate size and overwhelmingly vibey ambience keeps it constantly in demand. If a hot band's in town, chances are they'll sniff out the Metro first.

State Theatre

49 Market Street, between Pitt & George Streets, CBD (9373 6852/www.statetheatre.com.au). CityRail Town Hall. **Box office** (in person) 9am-5.30pm Mon-Fri; and until 8pm on show days. **Tickets** $25-$120. **Credit** AmEx, BC, DC, MC, V. **Map** p311 B/C3.

The first choice for older, more 'serious' artists (think Lou Reed, Bryan Ferry, Brian Wilson), this opulent entertainment palace, built in 1929, boasts massive chandeliers, abundant statuary, an imported marble staircase and enough gilt to challenge Versailles. It's a rococo-cum-deco delight, never short of atmosphere, and proudly plays co-host to the Sydney Film Festival (*see p204*) in winter when gigs are thinner on the ground. Holding comfortably in excess of 2,000, seating is mandatory, with dancing restricted to the side aisles – and only if security staff aren't looking. *See also p253.*

Sydney Entertainment Centre

35 Harbour Street, between Hay & Pier Streets, Darling Harbour (9320 4200/www.sydentcent. com.au). CityRail Central or Town Hall/Monorail/

Rock on

Given that this is the country that brought the world AC/DC and Kylie, you'll not be surprised to find that the music business in Australia is both big and varied. In general, Melbourne often leads the charge of talent, while Sydney lags a bit behind (the labels are mostly here, the talent less so). Aussie acts that have recently broken worldwide include the likes of the **Vines**, **Jet**, **Silverchair**, **Madison Avenue** and the **Avalanches**. Those that have not headlined in *NME* yet, but might soon, include straight-ahead rockers **Dallas Crane**, who have already made a name for themselves among other musicians, Perth's **Little Birdy** and Melbourne's folky **Architecture in Helsinki**.

Melbourne band **Something for Kate** may seem miserable and dour to many, but they comfortably fill big theatres on the east coast – such as the **Enmore Theatre** (*see p222*) – sell a pile of records, and supported Bowie on his Aussie tour. The **Sleepy Jackson** – Perth's biggest export of late, spearheaded by guitarist/vocalist Luke Steel – are carving a modern alt-country vibe all of their own and scoring hits with songs like 'Good Dancers' and 'Come to This'. Their 2003 album, *Lovers*, got cracking reviews overseas and they are increasingly hitting the big time.

Fur Patrol (pictured) hail from New Zealand, but live in Melbourne, and rock with a depth that belies their years. Claims to fame include supporting the Dandy Warhols in Oz, playing the Viper Room in LA and scoring platinum sales at home for their debut album Pet. If you're lucky, you might catch both them and the Sleepy Jackson at the **Annandale Hotel** (*see p224*). Also look out for the **Tremors**, the **Butterfly Effect** and **Sandrine**.

Arts & Entertainment

LightRail Haymarket. **Box office** 9am-5pm Mon-Fri. **Tickets** $60-$180. **Credit** AmEx, BC, DC, MC, V. **Map** p311 B3.

The aircraft hangar that roadies love and fans love to loathe, this 12,500-seater in Darling Harbour presents more A-list acts than any other. Built in 1983, it's where the biggest names perform, thanks to its ability to accommodate crowds easily and safely, its convenience for transport and accommodation, and its security and seating. But like most venues of this size, it falls well short on atmosphere, with heavy-handed security a regular hindrance if you feel the urge for a jig in the aisles. Radiohead, Bowie, Kylie and the like play here to packed houses, as do the few mega local acts who have graduated to arena status, such as Powderfinger.

The Basement: all-round fave. *See p225.*

Sydney Opera House

For listings, see p230.

The grandest of settings for any artist worth their salt. The Sydney icon's acoustics work better for introspective acts such as Jewel, Norah Jones and Michael Buble than louder, bombastic bands. That said, the powers that be have broadened the House's remit to a wider audience. As a result, the main Concert Hall now houses anything from the final telecasts of *Australian Idol* to avant-garde artistes, while the smaller Studio opts for intimate, often acoustic-based shows. Well worth visiting simply for the awe factor.

Sydney Superdome

Olympic Park, corner of Edwin Flack Avenue & Olympic Boulevard, Homebush Bay (8765 4321/ www.superdome.com.au). CityRail Olympic Park/ RiverCat Homebush Bay. **Box office** (in person) 1hr before show. **Tickets** varies. **Credit** AmEx, BC, DC, MC, V.

The young pretender of the large-scale venues – aside from the adjacent, but rarely used Stadium Australia, and the inner-city's Aussie Stadium – the Superdome boasts a whopping 20,000-seat capacity and multiple configurations for anything from rock, pop and rap (Korn, the Stones, Kiss, 50 Cent and, believe it or not, Cliff Richard have all played here) to big-scale dance parties, monster truck shows, equestrian events and even psychics. It was built for the 2000 Olympics, but bookings have not matched its initial super-hype status, leaving it open to cries of 'white elephant'. The Sydney Entertainment Centre (*see p223*) beats it hands down on all fronts, but the local council insists it will yet prove its worth. Don't hold your breath.

Pubs & clubs

There are literally dozens of pubs (aka hotels) and to a lesser extent clubs – Returned Services Leagues (RSL) – in Sydney, offering regular bands of all shapes and sizes. Having embraced, and in some cases, beaten, the national obsession for pokies, the following are the bigger inner-city players.

Note that RSL clubs have liquor laws that require all visitors, whatever their age, to show ID, so bring your passport and adhere to the dress code (no shorts, singlets or thongs) or you won't get in.

Annandale Hotel

Corner of Parramatta Road & Nelson Street, Annandale (9550 1078). Bus 413, 435, 436, 437, 438, 440, 461, L38, L40. **Open** 11am-midnight Mon-Thur; 11am-3am Fri, Sat; 3-10pm Sun. **Admission** $10-$25. **Credit** (phone bookings only) AmEx, BC, MC, V.

Reversing its pokie infestation of recent times, the legendary Annandale's main room is once again an intimate, low-key rock 'n' roll setting for the choicest Australian bands from the alternative scene. It's the best place to see bands from Melbourne and Perth who can't fill bigger venues, as well as Sydney bands on the rise. The sound is reasonable and the upper level at the rear is given over to tables and chairs for the terminally rocked out.

Bar Broadway
Corner of Broadway & Regent Street, Chippendale (9211 2321/www.barbroadway.com.au). CityRail/ LightRail Central. **Open** 10am-4am daily. **Admission** $10-$20. **Credit** AmEx, BC, DC, MC, V.
This blonde wood and stainless steel bar hosts everything from acoustic to ska and funk. The intimate upstairs space, with its low ceilings, cocktail bar and chat areas, doubles as a club. The downstairs bar has lighting dim enough to fake some prowess with a pool cue, and although poker machines still haunt the place, they're so far tucked away that you won't really notice them.

The Basement
29 Reiby Place, off Pitt Street, Circular Quay (9251 2797/www.thebasement.com.au). CityRail/ferry Circular Quay. **Open** noon-late Mon-Fri; 7.30pm-late Sat, Sun. **Admission** $15-$50. **Credit** AmEx, BC, DC, MC, V. **Map** p310 C2.
A hugely popular jazz and blues venue, the Basement boasts a supper club-style main area with tables, adjacent 'blue room' (remarkably, still a smoking area) and a bistro for cheap eats. Expect the likes of Tony Joe White or Roger McGuinn to turn up, along with world music maestros and established local jazz names. Intimate and warm, it's regularly used for TV and internet broadcasts.

Bridge Hotel
135 Victoria Road, at Wellington Street, Rozelle (9810 1260). Bus 500, 501. **Open** 24hrs Mon-Sat; until midnight Sun. **Admission** $15-$25. **No credit cards.**
Blues-oriented R&B acts and cover bands play the large room here (capacity 700), along with the odd thesp review. Retro discos spin into action on many nights after 11pm. Popular with meat-marketeers, birthday bashers and suburban gals.

Candy's Apartment
22 Bayswater Road, at Darlinghurst Road, Potts Point (9380 5600). CityRail Kings Cross. **Open** 8pm-6am Mon-Sat; 8pm-late Sun. **Admission** $10-$20. **No credit cards. Map** p312 D3.
Formerly a backpacker-favoured, sweat-soaked club, this basement venue now offers signed up-and-coming acts (Sandrine, Sunk Loto) as well as more obscure weekday offerings. Renovated with comfortable, muso-style ambience, it's proving to be the coolest space in the soon-to-be-banished red-light surroundings of Kings Cross. Media types often pop in for chance signings of new talent.

Cat & Fiddle Hotel
456 Darling Street, at Elliot Street, Balmain (9810 7931/www.thecatandfiddle.net). Bus 442, 443, 445, 446. **Open** 8am-midnight Mon-Sat; noon-10pm Sun. **Admission** $8-$15. **Credit** BC, MC, V.

Folk, bush, jazz and pop: all do the rounds at this seasoned, ever-reliable venue. Out-of-towners pick up plenty of work here, while old faves often play low-key shows for the faithful.

The Excelsior
64 Foveaux Street, at Bellevue Street, Surry Hills (9211 4945). CityRail/LightRail Central. **Open** 10.30am-midnight Mon-Thur; 10am-3am Fri, Sat; 2.30pm-midnight Sun. **Admission** free-$10. **Credit** (bar only) BC, MC, V. **Map** p311 C4.
A once-popular venue that's suffered an identity crisis in recent years (or perhaps just a lack of interest). Recently renovated under new management, it promises to continue the Surry Hills tradition of promoting local bands and those more established names out to rediscover their art. The band room is at the back, separated from the front bar, making for a comfortable drinking experience.

The Gaelic Club
64 Devonshire Street, between Chalmers & Elizabeth Streets, Surry Hills (9211 1687/www.thegaelicclub. com). CityRail/LightRail Central. **Open** noon-midnight Mon-Thur; noon-late Fri, Sat; noon-10pm Sun. **Admission** $5 membership fee; $20-$50. **Credit** AmEx, BC, DC, MC, V. **Map** p311 C4.
The Irish Society's challenge to the inner-city music scene has paid off in spades since the old Encore cinema was gutted for drinking, gigging and the screening of major sporting events. Another barn of a room, with capacity not far off the four-figure mark, it attracts local and international acts who can't – or don't want – to play the Metro. In under two years it's become the hottest venue in the once-thriving band centre of Surry Hills. The Darkness and Shane McGowan have both graced its stage.

Hopetoun Hotel
416 Bourke Street, at Fitzroy Street, Surry Hills (9361 5257). Bus 301, 302, 303. **Open** 2pm-midnight Mon-Sat; noon-10pm Sun. **Admission** $6-$15. **No credit cards. Map** p311 C4.
The quintessential pub venue in Sydney, the Hopetoun – like the Annandale Hotel (*see p224*) – succumbed to local pressure during the pokie boom to continue showcasing live local talent. The place is often so packed that the walls are literally streaming with sweat. A basement bar is open regularly at weekends for musos taking an audio break, plus there's an upper level for lunchtime snacks. Whether it's Melbourne favourites such as Even, Brisbane's George or Sydney's Lazy Susan, the Hopetoun is often the last stop as industry interest beckons. Highly recommended.

Lansdowne Hotel
2-6 City Road, at Broadway, Chippendale (9211 2325). Bus 426, 427, 428. **Open** 10am-midnight Mon; 10am-1am Tue; 10am-3am Wed-Sat; noon-10pm Sun. **Admission** varies. **Credit** BC, MC, V.
Struggling after it decided to embrace the poker machines, the Lansdowne was refurbished as a band venue, but it's still working on winning its punters

back. A good spot for a laid-back Sunday afternoon, when you can see three bands on the same bill, it may yet prove to be a serious contender. Convenient after a Saturday stroll around nearby Glebe.

Sandringham Hotel

387 King Street, at Enmore Road, Newtown (9557 1254). CityRail Newtown. **Open** 10am-midnight Mon-Wed; 10am-2am Thur-Sat; 10am-10pm Sun. **Admission** $5-$15. **No credit cards. Map** p93.
Rebooted as a band venue, the Sandringham's upstairs space is small but cosy, decked out in opulent red. Russell Crowe's missus Danielle Spencer played a regular Wednesday night set here for a while. Plenty of undiscovered talent rocks up to a receptive brigade hungry for fresh sounds.

The Vanguard

42 King Street, at Carillon Avenue, Newtown (9557 7992/www.thevanguard.com.au). Bus 422, 423, 426, 428, 352. **Open** 5pm-midnight Tue-Sat; 4-10pm Sun. **Admission** $10-$30. **No credit cards.**
The freshest of the recent band pubs, the Vanguard proves the inner west is pushing hard on the live music front. Opened in late 2003, it's already played host to a wide range of rock, jazz and blues acts, offering a cosy ambience and comfy surroundings. Recent faves include singer-songwriter Sandrine and jazz-flavoured vocalist Tina Harrod.

Jazz

The once-mooted Australian jazz renaissance has struggled to materialise beyond the regular inner-city wine-club sect. But there's still plenty on offer for the jazz conoisseur in and around the city limits, including overseas acts who fly in for intimate evenings.

Embracing the nu jazz movement, young experimentalists continue to work independently or in company with older but edgy players in the vein of Bernie McGann, Mike Nock, John Pochee, Mark Simmonds and Bob Bertles. These stalwarts helped bring an array of youngish bands to the fore, including Clarion Fracture Zone, Wanderlust, the Catholics, the Necks, Ute, Australian Creole, First Light, the Scott Tinkler Trio, Twentieth Century Dog and Engine Room, some of which achieved an enthusiastic reception overseas.

The continuing influence of the avant-garde lives on in many bands, adding bite and a degree of wildness to the prevailing world music influence. Many contemporary jazzers earn their living in rock, funk, Latin and blues bands and have allowed these influences to colour their playing and, in the case of Tina Harrod, their singing. Her jazz-funk leanings have now found their way on to a debut album, *Shacked Up in Paradise* (2003), which she is touting about to enthusiastic crowds with long-time collaborator Jackie Orszaczky.

That the up-and-coming jazz movement is possible at all is largely down to the Sydney Improvised Music Association (SIMA), which operates from the **Side On Café** (*see p229*). There's also the Jazzgroove Association, a musicians' co-op dedicated to promoting new

The Darren Jack Trio playing Newtown's latest, the **Vanguard**.

jazz talent. Recent artists to benefit from its efforts include the Gerard Masters Trio, Nicholas McBride and the Nick Bowd Quartet.

Jazz audiences remain loyal and continue to maintain the momentum. Eighties hero Vince Jones still sells out well in advance when he performs at the **Basement** (*see p225*). He croons over love gone wrong, sings uptempo, long-forgotten R&B numbers and between sets opines with a Brando-like whisper about deforestation and the like. Hard bop fans should catch Bernie McGann , a craggy veteran who wrings hugely emotional music from his alto sax and swings like a gorilla when hyped. Trumpeter James Morrison is very much the popular face of jazz in Australia. Technically he's brilliant, although good taste can give way to complex virtuosity.

More recent additions to the scene have helped to keep the oldies on their toes, and to keep the loyalists content. Saxophonists Mark Taylor, Dale Barlow and Tim Hopkins, vocalist Melanie Oxley, keyboardist Chris Abrahams and guitarist Ben Hughes show what can be done with melodies and instrumentation, while fans of hardcore free improvisers can get their kicks from multi-instrumentalist Jim Denley, turntable maniac Martin Ng, sound artist Rik Rue and ferocious noise combo Phlegm.

Possibly the best place to see the bulk of Sydney's jazz talent, and some top international acts besides, is the **Manly International Jazz Festival** (*see p192*). Held on the long weekend in early October, the festival has grown since it launched in 1977 along with its crowds – now up to 20,000. Its musical scope has also broadened to include swing, blues, funk, Afro-Latin and zydeco. The free outdoor **Jazz in the Domain** is also a popular fixture during January's **Sydney Festival** (*see p194*).

To get the scoop on what's happening jazz-time, tune into Eastside Radio (89.7 FM) to hear news, previews and the latest local music, and Jazz Perspectives (5-7pm, Saturday and Sunday) on ABC Classic FM (92.9 FM). Jim McLeod (aka 'Australia's high priest of jazz broadcasting') presents his Jazztrack programme on ABC Classic FM on weekends. For a full guide to jazz on local and national radio, visit www.jazzscene.com.au.

Venues

One of the hippest clubs on the jazz scene, the **Basement** (*see p225*) serves as the ideal forum for visiting artists and local talent with clout. New arrival the **Vanguard** (*see p226*) mirrors the modern-day vibe of the Basement in style and content. Expect a mix of roots, blues, jazz and acoustic-based melodies.

Jackie Orszaczky in the **Rose**. *See p228.*

Café Sydney

Level 5, Customs House, 31 Alfred Street, between Loftus & Young Streets, Circular Quay (9251 8683/ www.cafesydney.com). CityRail/ferry Circular Quay. **Open** *Summer* 10pm-midnight Fri. *Winter* 8.30pm-late Fri. **Admission** free. **Credit** AmEx, BC, DC, MC, V. **Map** p310 C2.

After the much-loved Harbourside Brasserie closed its doors to make way for the new Sydney Theatre building, this upmarket restaurant sprang up as a nearby alternative of sorts. But it lacks the Brasserie's friendly, pose-free vibe. Still, upcoming talent such as Carolinne Lynne, Emma Pask and Virna Sanzone have appeared here on Friday nights.

Opera Bar

Lower Concourse Level, Sydney Opera House, Bennelong Point, Circular Quay (9247 1666/ www.operabar.com.au). CityRail/ferry Circular Quay. **Open** 11.30am-late daily. **Admission** free. **Credit** AmEx, BC, DC, MC, V. **Map** p310 C1.

A mix of jazz and ambient DJs perform during the summer months in a setting that's hard to beat anywhere in Sydney. Expect to catch fresh nu jazz talent as well as mainstays such as Jackie Orszaczky throughout the week from 8.30pm, and at weekends from 2.30pm. *See also p134.*

The Rocks Market

George Street, at Playfair Street, The Rocks (www.rocksmarket.com). CityRail/ferry Circular Quay. **Open** 10am-5pm Sat, Sun. **Map** p310 C1.

Jazz acts feature regularly at this popular weekend market in the heart of the Rocks, to keep the tourist crowds jigging and grinning. Alto genius Bernie McGann has cropped up in the past, pouring his heart out to the passing punters. R&B, guitar duos, the occasional classical string ensemble or wandering street minstrels also mingle among the stalls. Lively afternoons are a given.

The Rose of Australia
1 Swanson Street, at Charles Street, Erskineville (9565 1441/www.roseofaustralia.com.au). CityRail Erskineville. **Open** 10am-midnight Mon-Sat; 10am-10pm Sun. **Admission** free. **Credit** AmEx, BC, DC, MC, V. **Map** p93.

A stayer in the jazz pub stakes, this low-key venue often has something going on. Resident funkmaster Jackie Orszaczky and younger talent Bernie Hayes squeeze into the tiny corner space weekly.

The Sackville Hotel
599 Darling Street, at Wise Street, Balmain (9555 7555). Bus 423, 441, 442, 445. **Open** 11am-midnight Mon-Wed; 11am-2am Thur, Fri; 10am-2am Sat; noon-10pm Sun. **Admission** free. **Credit** AmEx, BC, DC, MC, V.
The Sackville's Lime Bar is Balmain's main jazz venue. It offers possibilities for cross-pollination, with younger players getting some exposure alongside seasoned acts such as Dale Barlow.

AbOriginal Voice of a people

The indigenous peoples of Australia and its territories have long favoured music as a form of expression. Despite the white-dominated culture that threatened its very survival, indigenous music has gained some level of acceptance in today's Australia, even if a certain indifference among the masses continues to relegate it to the sidelines.

The bastions of indigenous music are **Vibe** (www.vibe.com.au), a Sydney-based multi-media organisation that promotes arts and sport, and **CAAMA** (Central Australian Aboriginal Media Association, www.caama.com.au), which caters for remoter country and desert areas. Both promote indigenous music through Aboriginal radio stations, online retail outlets and annual events. Vibe also publishes a monthly magazine and hosts the Deadly Awards, held every October at the Sydney Opera House. Effectively a black Australian of the Year show, the Deadlys celebrate their tenth birthday in 2004, and are now broadcast live on SBS television.

The indigenous music scene tends to strike a healthy balance between the traditional (such as didgeridoo star **Mark Atkins**), adult-oriented blues and country (must-see local legend **Jimmy Little**, country stars **Troy Cassar-Daley** and **Warren Williams**), jazz-flavoured artists (**Lexine Soloman**, **Liz Cavanagh**), and the hip-hop-cum-rap stars of urban life, including **Brothablack**, **NRS** and the metal-minded **Nokturnal**.

Add Central Desert boys **Spin.fx**, blending reggae, country, rock and blues, Arnhem Land stars **Saltwater Band** and **Yothu Yindi** (pictured), whose political song 'Treaty' was a huge hit in 1992. Indigenous music has also crossed into mass-market pop thanks to

female vocal duo **Shakaya** (their 'Stop Calling Me' was a massive breakout hit in 2002) and perennial TV fave **Christina Anu**.

However, the main stumbling block for all indigenous artists remains a dedicated performance space. In Sydney, many are left to vie for spots at local festivals, such as the Yabun concert in Redfern on Australia Day, or family-oriented summer events; you're more likely to come across street buskers aiming squarely at tourists than a regular roster of artists at any of the local venues.

The **ABC** shop chain (part of the Australian Broadcasting Corp) is a noteworthy source of indigenous music; there's a branch in the QVB (455 George Street, CBD, 9286 3726, http://shop.abc.net.au).

Side On Café

*83 Parramatta Road, between Johnston &
Trafalgar Streets, Annandale (9516 3077/
www.side-on.com.au). Bus 438, 440.* **Open** 7pm-
midnight Wed-Sun. **Admission** $10-$20. **Credit**
AmEx, BC, DC, MC, V.
This groovy little space is for those who like their
music mixed with a dash of film and art. Popular
with the musing city-centre crowd, Thursday nights
offer experimental music, while SIMA takes over on
Friday and Saturday nights, with regulars such as
Mike Nock, Bernie McGann and Sandy Evans.

Soup Plus

*383 George Street, between King & Market Streets,
CBD (9299 7728/www.soupplus.com.au). CityRail
Town Hall or Wynyard/Monorail City Centre.* **Open**
11.45am-midnight Mon-Sat. **Tickets** $8 Mon-Thur,
after 10pm Fri, Sat; $28 (incl 2-course meal) before
10pm Fri, Sat. **No credit cards. Map** p311 B3.
A long-standing trad jazz forum, the Soup presents
mainstream and bop stylists these days , as well as
jam sessions that can vary in quality, but are
invariably entertaining. Its central location and
restaurant layout mean that the music has to compete
with diners and office parties, but the last set
remains strictly for listening.

Wine Banc

*53 Martin Place, entrance on Elizabeth Street,
CBD (9233 5399). CityRail Martin Place.* **Open**
4pm-late Mon-Fri; 6pm-late Sat. **Admission** free.
Credit AmEx, BC, DC, MC, V. **Map** p310 C2.
This ultra-sophisticated wine and posing venue is,
after Café Sydney (*see p227*), the new kid on the
block of jazz. Trios and combos take the stage on
Tuesdays (from 9pm), Fridays and Saturdays (from
10pm). During the annual Sydney Festival (*see p194*),
the joint puts on nightly revels in the company of
local big names and lesser-known imports from the
US. *See also p134.*

Woollahra Hotel

*116 Queen Street, at Moncur Street, Woollahra
(9363 2782/www.woollahrahotel.com.au). Bus 389.*
Open 10am-midnight Mon-Sat; 10am-10pm Sun.
Admission free. **Credit** AmEx, BC, DC, MC, V.
Map p313 E4.
Not an ideal venue – it's stuck on the snobbier side
of the eastern suburbs and lacks the warmth of the
city centre's hallowed grounds – but its jazz-
flavoured servings can still surprise. Shows are on
Saturday (3-6pm) and Sunday (6-9.30pm).

Classical & Opera

Given that many Sydneysiders fancy
themselves as sports-mad outdoor types, they
can be surprisingly enthusiastic when it comes
to classical music. This is especially true when
it's laid on in an outdoor, picnic-style setting,
notably the big opera, symphony and carol-
singing sit-ins in the Domain. While those tend
to favour well-worn classics from Vivaldi and
Beethoven, the sweet strains of a symphony
orchestra, choir or opera production can be
heard inside the **Sydney Opera House**,
the principal classical venue, as well as the
CBD's young pretender, the **City Recital
Hall**. The **Eugene Goossens Hall** in Ultimo
is used for smaller events.

INFORMATION

Notices for concerts appear in the *Sydney
Morning Herald*'s Metro section on Friday and
48 Hours section on Saturday. ABC's TV and
radio stations often broadcast live relays of
opera performances, usually at weekends.
Leaflets listing forthcoming events are also
available from the Opera House box office,
most art galleries and good music venues.
For information on ticket agencies, *see p222.*

Venues

Sydney Town Hall (*see p69*) is used for
contemporary music, free organ recitals, the
SBS Youth Orchestra, the Sydney University
Musical Society and Sydney Festival events.
    Churches are also popular if irregular
venues for recitals, and a guide to church
music can be found in the *SMH*'s Metro section.
St Andrew's Cathedral (*see p69*) plays
host to the Cathedral Singers & Orchestra,
who perform choral classics, as well as jazz
choirs and guest chamber music groups. The
Sydney Conservatorium of Music (9351
1222/1342, www.usyd.edu.au/su/conmusic)
presents free Friday lunchbreak recitals during
termtime (March to June, August to October),
while the **Art Gallery of NSW** (*see p63*)
provides impressive occasional recitals to
complement exhibitions, usually on Wednesday
evenings when the gallery is open until 9pm.
    The **Sydney Festival** (*see p194*) alleviates
post-Christmas blues by running musical
events throughout January – including the
Sydney Symphony Orchestra's free **Symphony
in the Domain**. The other main outdoor event,
also free, is Opera Australia's **Opera in the
Domain**, on the last Saturday in January or
the first Saturday in February. The **Historic
Houses Trust of NSW** offers classical
(and jazz) performances in the ballroom at
Government House (bookings and info 1300 653
777/9518 6866, www.hht.net.au). Drinks are
served prior to the performances, giving you the
chance to stroll through the grounds at sunset.

City Recital Hall

*Angel Place, near Martin Place, CBD (admin 9231
9000/bookings 8256 2222/www.cityrecitalhall.com).
CityRail Martin Place.* **Box office** 9am-5pm

Mon-Fri; and 3hrs before show. **Tickets** free-$90.
Credit AmEx, BC, MC, V. **Map** p310 C2.
The biggest news of late has been the creation of the 1,200-seat City Recital Hall in the centre of the CBD, which has given Sydney's orchestras some room to roam, as well as hosting several international names including one David Helfgott. Created via a landmark deal with the AMP Corporation, the two-tiered, horseshoe-shaped hall has a colour scheme borrowed from a Latvian baroque church (soft grey, soothing aubergine and twinkles of gold), and the architecture and acoustics have been designed for both chamber orchestras and solo performers. The acoustics are even said to match such halls as Amsterdam's Concertgebouw, making it a must-visit venue for any classical enthusiast.

Eugene Goossens Hall

ABC Ultimo Centre, 700 Harris Street, between Ultimo & George Streets, Ultimo (8333 5790). CityRail/LightRail Central. **Box office** call for details. **Tickets** varies. **Map** p311 B4.
A less awesome space (seating a maximum of 500) in the ABC headquarters in Ultimo, often used by smaller ensembles playing contemporary music. Named after the British composer and conductor who first suggested the idea of the Opera House back in 1954, it has also hosted the Sydney Spring International Festival of Music, which showcases the Sydney Conservatorium Symphony Orchestra and young Australian composers.

Sydney Opera House

Bennelong Point, Circular Quay (box office 9250 7777/www.sydneyoperahouse.com). CityRail/ferry Circular Quay. **Box office** 9am-8.30pm Mon-Sat; and 2hrs before show Sun. **Tickets** $25-$50 Studio; $40-$140 Concert Hall; $50-$220 Opera Theatre.
Credit AmEx, BC, DC, MC, V. **Map** p310 C1.
The main venue here is the 2,700-seat Concert Hall in which, thanks to its purpose-built acoustics, symphonic music can be heard with a full, rich and mellow tone. Eighteen adjustable acrylic rings (the 'toilet seats' to local wags) are suspended above the orchestra platform to reflect some of the sound back to the musicians. The Concert Hall's Grand Organ is also noteworthy: it's the largest mechanical tracker action organ in the world with 10,500 pipes, and took a decade to build. Opera performances take place in the 1,500-seat Opera Theatre, while the Studio (capacity 300) showcases new music in keeping with the overall accessibility that the Opera House is at pains to promote. Whether it's rap artists, percussion bands, indigenous spoken-word shows, classical music or chamber opera company Music Theatre Sydney, the Studio has helped modernise the House's once-stuffy image. The two other spaces are used for drama productions (*see p253*).

Orchestras & groups

Australian Brandenburg Orchestra

9328 7581/www.brandenburg.com.au.

Australia's first period instrument group (baroque and classical) has played to sell-out audiences everywhere from Tokyo to Germany. Formed by artistic director Paul Dyer in 1990, the orchestra now puts on regular seasons at the City Recital Hall. Its concerts are fashionable events – rich mixes of visual and musical experience.

Australian Chamber Orchestra

8274 3800/www.aco.com.au.
Under the flamboyant artistic directorship of high-profile young violinist Richard Tognetti, the ACO has injected some excitement into classical music. Formed in 1975, the Sydney-based orchestra is relatively youthful – most performers are under 40 – and Tognetti's programming is always provocative. He likes to mix periods, offer rarely heard works and blend period instrument-playing soloists with contemporary instruments. A typical night might involve him lulling the audience with some Mozart before hitting them with something obscure before sending them home humming Haydn.

Musica Viva

8394 6666/www.musicaviva.com.au.
Musica Viva is the world's largest chamber music organisation, touring Australian and international groups around the country, as well as providing a school programme in Australia and Singapore. The outfit, which will celebrate its 60th anniversary in 2005, has broadened its brief of late, touring famous choirs and catering to a wider range of musical sensibilities. A roll-call of the world's best ensembles, including the Emerson Quartet, the Beaux Arts Trio and new Sydney stars the Tankstream Quartet, all appear on its impressive calendar.

Opera Australia

Opera Centre, 480 Elizabeth Street, between Devonshire & Belvoir Streets, Surry Hills (9699 1099/box office 9319 1088/tours 9318 8330/ www.opera-australia.org.au). CityRail/LightRail Central. **Open** *Box office* 9am-5pm Mon-Fri. *Tours* 10am, 11am (lunchtime tour), 2pm Mon-Fri. **Tickets** *Shows* $95-$220. *Tours* $18 incl tea; lunchtime tour $35 incl lunch. **Credit** AmEx, BC, DC, MC, V. **Map** p311 C5.
Australia may be far from the great European opera houses, but the country's divas have been disproportionately represented in the ranks of global opera stars – among them Nellie Melba, Joan Hammond, Joan Sutherland, Yvonne Kenny and Elizabeth Whitehouse. And Opera Australia has the third-largest programme (after Covent Garden and the Vienna Staatsoper) of any opera company in the world. The company performs in the Opera Theatre of the Opera House for seven months of the year; from April to May and November to December it ups sticks to Melbourne.

As is usual in big arts organisations, the backstage manoeuvering is often more interesting than what plays on stage. OA's bare-bones production budgets, and the costs of storing and restaging

Listen up – to the angelic acoustics at the **City Recital Hall**. *See p229.*

See p229.

productions from the past 30 years, have placed it under enormous financial stress. Conductor Simone Young was drafted in to prepare the company prior to the 2000 Olympics, but she immediately quarantined a substantial portion of the budget for her 'seriously undervalued and under-resourced' Australian Opera and Ballet Orchestra. A music-led revival occurred, with Young coaxing some remarkable playing from the previously disgruntled ensemble. Young also helped pile pressure on the Sydney Opera House Trust to improve the Opera Theatre's pit conditions, which she once described as 'gruesome'. Regrettably, even greater cost-cutting saw the departure of Young after three vibrant years in late 2003, but for the visiting punter such politics can be set aside. There are still 175 performances of more than a dozen operas in any given year, as well as 80 performances of four different ballets.

Visitors can also go behind the scenes at OA's headquarters in Surry Hills. The tour takes in the costume, millinery and wig-making departments, the props and storage departments, set design and building, and rehearsal spaces for singers and musicians. Tours are for groups (minimum 20 for the lunchtime tour, five for other tours), but if you call about two weeks ahead, they can usually fit you in.

Sydney Symphony Orchestra

9334 4600/www.symphony.org.au.

Under the new artistic directorship of conductor Gianluigi Gelmetti, following Dutch conductor Edo de Waart's departure after ten years, the SSO continues to be the flagship of a network of Australian state capital city orchestras. Established in 1932 as a radio broadcasting orchestra, the SSO has grown into the biggest and best in the country, attracting the finest musicians from Australia and abroad, including Britain's Nigel Kennedy. A subscription audience in 1936 of 500 people for its first annual concert programme has swelled into more than 400,000 people attending today's Sydney Symphony concert series, which includes more than 140 events per year. The annual outdoor concert, Symphony in the Domain, part of the Sydney Festival, attracts a crowd of well over 100,000.

Other ensembles

It's worth watching out too for the **Sydney Philharmonia Choirs** (9251 2024, www.sydneyphilharmonia.com.au), which has been going strong for 80 years and continues to stun audiences with a lusty *Carmina Burana* or luscious *Missa Solemnis* several times a year. Featuring six a cappella singers, the **Song Company** (9351 7939, www.songcompany.com.au) is Australia's premier vocal ensemble, performing early operas and oratorios in concert or partial costume. Other a cappella groups include Sydney's first world music choir, **Voices from the Vacant Lot**, while the **Sydney Gay & Lesbian Choir** (9360 7439) attracts an audience broader than its selection criteria might suggest. Local chamber groups **Macquarie Trio** and **Goldner String Quartet** are also highly regarded.

Nightlife

Is it a club? Is it a bar? The answer might show up in your wallet.

Just when you thought Sydney clubs had finished their mid-life nip and tucks, there they go again vamping up another level, glossed to go. Sydney is in credit crisis and we deeply suspect clubland has much to answer for. Now choking with even more chrome, lighting, leather and sound, venues have also upped their admission prices (blame **Home**, the über-club that kick-started the scene, *see p236*). An insider leaked one reason why clubland has gone all soft-serve: if it's comfy and cosy, punters will lounge around longer and drink more cocktails. And if you pitch the music harder than house, forget selling drinks: people will stomp on adrift on their BYO fuel.

Taking advantage of this new mood for smooth is the hermaphrodite-like explosion of bar/clubs. The line-up at King Street Wharf includes **Cargo Bar/Lounge** (*see p234*) and the **Loft** (*see p134*). It may have you wondering at dusk, but late into the night you'll have no doubt that despite their tiny dancefloors, their funky breaks and house (not to mention the DJs) are just as good as what's on offer at the best clubs – except that here admission is free.

This, of course, is proving a bonus with cash-strapped clubbers, who have all but let their fashion go to the wall. It's a sorry sight that the uniform *de jour* is low-slung denim (no matter what your size), little black top (no matter what the season), trainers or heels, fat white belt optional. This is playing havoc with the door policies of clubs, which have been forced to relax their precociously prickly bouncers. Those faded, ripped jeans could cost hundreds or come from a discount store – at a glance, who can tell?

Music too is having a bet each way, with bands that incorporate DJs finding their way into clubs – look out for the Herd and Good Buddha. Meanwhile, big-name international DJs and outdoor festivals running under their club names just keep coming as fast as the club nights themselves keep changing. The only way to navigate safely is to grab hold of the free, weekly, long-time club bible *3D World* magazine www.threedworld.com.au), available at inner-city bookstores and record shops. Note that admission to the venues below is free unless otherwise stated.

Join Sydney in going pool crazy at the **Beach Road Hotel**. *See p234 and p237.*

Arts & Entertainment

Bars & clubs

ARQ

16 Flinders Street, between Oxford & Taylor Streets, Darlinghurst (9380 8700/www.arqsydney.com.au). Bus 373, 377, 378, 380, 382, 391, 394, 396. **Open** 9pm-9am Thur-Sun. **Admission** (after 10pm) $10 Fri; $20 Sat; $5 Sun. **No credit cards. Map** p311 C4. The seven-tonne, million-dollar lighting rig is as much a part of the show as the people, who wear less, perhaps, than anywhere else in Sydney. It's a multi-level flesh show, and the music gets more desperately urgent the higher you go. Friday is an any-ones goes affair; Saturday and Sunday remain true to its original gay theme (*see p216*).

The ArtHouse Hotel

275 Pitt Street, between Park & Market Streets, CBD (9284 1200/www.thearthousehotel.com.au). CityRail Town Hall or St James/Monorail Galeries Victoria. **Open** *The Verge & Cocktail Bar* 11am-midnight Mon-Thur; 11am-3am Fri; 5pm-6am Sat. *Dome Lounge* 11am-10pm Mon-Fri; 5pm-midnight Sat. *Attic Bar* 5pm-late Wed-Sat. **Admission** $15. **Credit** AmEx, BC, DC, MC, V. **Map** p311 C3. Transforming this former 19th-century School of Arts into a 21st-century bar and clubbing outfit was ambitious. Perhaps they were banking on the mega-magazine stable (Kerry Packer's Australian Consolidated Press) around the corner being a cap-tive audience, and they were right – it's become the adopted hangout for media babes. The main bar, the Verge, touts its chapel beginnings, and all three 'club' bars stay true to their deco grandeur while

BEACH ROAD HOTEL.bondi

Don't miss # DJs

Enterprising rave-scene refugee Tim McGee, who manages the Australian arm of the UK's Ministry of Sound, has helped push Sydney's DJs up the celebrity ladder to crowd-worshipping glory. Having snaffled some of Sydney's top DJs into the recording studio, Tim – who himself plays techy house on Friday nights at *Yu* (*see p236* **Soho Bar**) and regularly at **Sounds on Sunday** (*see p236*) – knows those worth checking out. These are his picks:

Ajax
Music: whatever is ultra-hip at the moment to the fashion crowd.
Plays: Friday nights at **Moulin Rouge** (*see p235*).
Take-home CD: *Mashed* (Ministry of Sound).

Ken Cloud
Music: everything from techno to breaks.
Plays: Cloud performs so much that you'll have to read *3D World* magazine to keep up with him. He records/produces with Sameer at Poxy Music.
Take-home CDs: Green Velvet: *La La Land* remix (Ministry of Sound).

Mark Dynamix
Music: progressive house.
Plays: Friday nights at **Yu** (*see p236* **Soho Bar**); Saturday nights at **Moulin Rouge** (*see p235*).
Take-home CD: The *2003 Annual* (Ministry of Sound).

Goodwill
Music: mix of breaks, house and electro.
Plays: Saturday nights at **Home** (*see p235*). **Take-home CD:** *Alfresco Soiree 2* (Hussle Recordings).

Kid Kenobi
Has been voted number one DJ at the Australian Dance Music Awards for the past three years.
Music: breaks.
Plays: Thursday nights at **Globe** (*see p234*); Friday nights at **Home** (*see p235*); **Sounds on Sunday** (*see p236*).
Take-home CD: *Breaks 03: The Album* (Ministry of Sound).

Toby Neal
Music: US-style, jazzy disco house.
Plays: Saturday nights at **Tank** (*see p236*).

A night in the life of Sydney

Forget about hailing cabs, traffic jams and breathalysers, this is your walking street map to cover both the grunt and the glamour of Sydney. Best on a Friday or Saturday night.

6pm: Start the evening on the upper deck of **Cargo Bar/Lounge** (*see below*) on King Street Wharf. Kick off with a Red Bull Disco Juice while you recline under the setting sun and ogle the waterfront promenade. In winter, get to Cargo by 4.30pm to watch the sunset.

7.15pm: Walk south along Cockle Bay Wharf and turn left when you reach the end, before the Entertainment Centre. Shuffle uphill along Goulburn Street to the **Civic Hotel** (*see p214*) on Pitt Street. A slick take on an old-style Australian pub, this is a great pitstop for a quick G&T. If downstairs is after-work crowded, head to the discreet haven of the upstairs cocktail lounge.

7.45pm: Haul yourself out (this is a pitstop, remember?) and continue along Goulburn Street. Cross over Wentworth Avenue and head right up Commonwealth Street. Don't be pulled in by the fabulous crowd at Longrain prematurely. First, you need an injection of pure street cred, which can be found diagonally opposite, on the corner of Foster and Campbell Streets, at the **Hollywood Hotel** (*see p135*). One cheap beer – VB or Cascade – should be enough to intoxicate you.

8.10pm: Crossing back over Campbell Street, you go from grunt to glam in nanoseconds: **Longrain** is one of Sydney's most fashionable Thai restaurants (*see p148*). Join the slick crowd in the bar and sip a Caprioska while waiting to be called to your table for dinner (you've booked in advance, right?). Dinner for two with alcohol will cost around $120.

10.30pm: Climb further up Campbell Street. If you want the night crowd, turn left at Crown Street then right on to Oxford Street. If you've seen it all before, stay on Campbell Street, then turn left at Bourke Street and head for **Kinselas Middle Bar** (*see p215*) at Taylor Square. It's not officially a dance club, but the deep house music and a Slurpberry (made with fresh watermelon crushed with lime and raspberries, laced with tequila and

mixing in some sleek chrome and black. Saturday night's Kink brings international DJs to the turntable. The ArtHouse crowd ranges in age, but is always cosmopolitan. *See also p207.*

Beach Road Hotel
Corner of Beach Road & Glenayr Avenue, Bondi Beach (9130 7247). CityRail Bondi Junction then bus 380, 381, L82/bus 380, L82. **Open** 10am-11.30pm Mon, Tue; 10am-12.30am Wed-Fri; 9am-1am Sat; 10am-9.45pm Sun. **No credit cards. Map** p83.
Years of 'sexing-up' renovations have made Beach Road Hotel a viable club option, despite its 'school-night' closing times. The music selection begins with lounge on Monday night and moves through funky house on Wednesday to hip hop and live acts on Friday, before warming to a soul funk on Saturday and party disco on Sunday. While its changed decor now urges patrons to wear something more than a bikini top, Beach Road is a desperately needed post-beach dance option for those unwilling to make the trek into town. *See also p237.*

Cargo Bar/Lounge
52-60 The Promenade, King Street Wharf, Darling Harbour (9262 1777). CityRail Wynyard or Town Hall/Monorail Darling Park. **Open** noon-late daily. **Tickets** for special events; prices vary. **Credit** AmEx, BC, DC, MC, V. **Map** p310 B2.
Is it a bar? Is it a nightclub? Perhaps it's the music that decides. On the front row of this Gold Coast – sorry, King Street Wharf – strip, Cargo works hard to carry some music cred with its lolly-stick glamour. While the view speaks all languages by day, it gets extra pump with funky house and schmoozy international acts such as Dimitri. Fighting your way through the identikit crowd late on a Friday or Saturday night might mean all the difference between a dance at Cargo or a drink at one of the less-fancied venues nearby.

Gas Nightclub & Bohem Lounge
467-477 Pitt Street, between Eddy Avenue & George Street, Haymarket (9211 3088). CityRail/LightRail Central. **Open** 10pm-4am Thur; 10pm-6am Fri, Sat; 10pm-3am Sun. **Admission** $15 Thur, Sun; from $25 Fri; $25 Sat. **Credit** AmEx, BC, MC, V. **Map** p311 B4.
Gas has had a tricky time working out who it wants to attract, and has passed through various phases (none of them cool). One thing it's been a constant stickler for is neat, smart dress as part of an attempt to pull an older, more cashed-up crowd. Entry rules have relaxed somewhat; you no longer have to squirm through the original, gung-ho 'let's check for firearms' gauntlet. Once inside, music shifts from R&B to house and trance. Sexy is the mainstay.

Globe
Sydney Globe Hotel, corner of Park & Elizabeth Streets, CBD (9264 4844). CityRail Town Hall/Monorail Galeries Victoria. **Open** 10am-midnight Mon-Fri; 10am-late Sat; 10am-8pm Sun. **Admission** $10 Fri, Sat. **No credit cards. Map** p311 C3.

strawberries) will be enough to get jiggy to.
11.30pm Turn right on Oxford and left along
Darlinghurst Road. Stop off at the **Darlo Bar**
(*see p135*) on Liverpool Street, which hums
nicely to a quirky retro style. Here you can try
the unproven restorative powers of a shandy
before continuing.

Midnight: Blow the joint and push on along
Darlinghurst Road. The crowd gets a little
seamier as you inch towards Kings Cross.
Cross over the William Street Tunnel, then
take a left into Victoria Street and head
upstairs at the **Soho Bar** (*see p236*). Have
a game of pool and an Oceans 11 (muddled
fresh lime and mint with Jaggard, a beverage
made from native Australian lemon myrtle
leaves), while deciding whether or not to
spend $10-$20 on getting into the trendy
downstairs nightclub, Yu.

2am: If you're ready to be tucked in at this
stage, go back down Victoria Street and cross
into Bayswater Road, turning left at Kellet
Street. Wind around the corner and into
perennial late-nighter **Deans Café** (5 Kellet

Street, 9368 0953) for nachos and a comfy
hot chocolate. If you're in for the round trip,
however, here's where you get to cheat a
little: hail a cab to **Golden Century** restaurant
(*see p145*) in Chinatown. Brave the live fish
tanks and chow down with post-work chefs –
try a post-work pipis in XO sauce or salt-and-
pepper mud crab. Your next stop is...

3.30am: ...Home. No, not your hotel, the
nightclub. Still the biggest club in town, this
London-modelled hulk is worth a look, if only
for nostalgic reasons. To get there, turn left
out of Golden Century and back again into
Goulburn Street. Cross Harbour Street and
walk back along Cockle Bay Wharf until you
reach **Home** (*see below*). Friday nights are
hardcore house (perfect for trainer-wearing
walkers), while Saturdays play to a funkier
crowd. Make for the glass-fronted chill-out
room and watch the lights over the water.
If you dance for long enough you'll see the
sunrise reflected in the buildings across the
water. And, spookily enough, you're pretty
much back where you started.

Sexy and funky have been the guiding lights of the
revisioned Globe. Downstairs the tiny cave has been
extended to include a new room called the Kitchen
(what's with these domestic names in dance?), while
upstairs remains lounge. Funk, party and soul play
most nights but, for something different, you can try
Thursdays when Kid Kenobi gets into breaks and
bootleg mash-up which makes for a change.

Goodbar

*11A Oxford Street, at South Dowling Street,
Paddington (9360 6759). Bus 378, 380, L82.* **Open**
10pm-3am Wed-Sat. **Admission** $10-$15 Wed, Fri,
Sat. **Credit** AmEx, BC, DC, MC, V. **Map** p311 D4.
This club has been travelling in various forms since
the '80s, when it was called the Hip Hop Club. These
days, you'll find that downstairs has turned into a
disco lounge replete with a *Saturday Night Fever*-
style lit dancefloor. Hip hop still abounds on both
levels, whether it be underground or old skool, while
new skool hails live MCs.

Home

*Cockle Bay Wharf, Wheat Road, Darling Park
(9266 0600/infoline 9267 0674). CityRail Town
Hall/Monorail Darling Park.* **Open** *Club* 10pm-
7am Fri; 11pm-6.30am Sat. *Bar* noon-late daily.
Admission *Club* $25 Fri, Sat. **No credit cards**.
Map p311 B3.
Surviving the closure of UK Home, Sydney Home is
still one of this city's best large-scale experiences.
Spreading over three levels and four bars and with

room for up to 2,000, this is millennium clubbing –
with space-age lighting, a great view and chill-out
areas. Sublime @ Home on Friday spills over with
everything from house trance to drum 'n' bass, and
throws its finger at any critics by remaining the
longest-running club night in Sydney. Saturday's
Together @ Home caters to an older, funkier crowd.

Moulin Rouge

*39 Darlinghurst Road, at Springfield Avenue, Kings
Cross (8354 1711). CityRail Kings Cross.* **Open**
8am-6am Thur-Sat, occasional Sun. **Admission**
$7-$15. **Credit** AmEx, BC, MC, V. **Map** p312 D3.
Think *Moulin Rouge* the movie and you've got this
club – all gaudy red drapes, with the chutzpah of an
old stripper. Waitresses in corsets and fishnets are
only matched by the towering models this place
attracts – pretty, pretty, in skyscraper shoes. Masks
and feathers aren't unusual dress options, but the
owner insists the dress code is reasonably relaxed.
The dancefloor is almost a stage to the three split
levels rising above. It's a bit like having a nightclub
with a burlesque edge in your lounge – where you
can drink previously banned La Fee Verte absinthe
while listening to laid-back funky breaks and disco.

Q Bar

*Level 2, The Exchange Hotel, 34-44 Oxford Street,
between Riley & Liverpool Streets, Darlinghurst
(9360 1375/www.qbar.com.au). Bus 378, 380, L82.*
Open 9pm-late daily. **Admission** $15 Fri; $20 Sat.
Credit AmEx, BC, DC, MC, V. **Map** p311 C3.

The Exchange has been absorbed by Q – or is it the other way around? Nabbing old-stays such as the Lizard Lounge and Phoenix Club and remodelling them with slick little kinks that would please Hugh Hefner, Q Bar is just hanging in on the slick side of sleazy. What with daybeds, private booths and, worst, a unisex toilet, there's a slight nose-curling edge of 'what's been happening here' about the place. What's happening mostly is house music, often with live performances. But the free entry days of Q are well and truly over. *See also p237.*

Slip Inn

111 Sussex Street, at King Street, CBD (9299 2199). CityRail Town Hall or Wynyard. **Open** *Slip Bar* noon-2am Mon-Sat. *Sand Bar* 9pm-3am Fri, Sat. *Chinese Laundry* 10pm-4am Fri, Sat. *Cave* 11pm-4am Fri, Sat. **Admission** *Chinese Laundry, Cave* $5 before 10pm, $18 after 10pm Fri, Sat. *Sand Bar* $5 before 10pm, $18 after 10pm Sat. **Credit** AmEx, BC, DC, MC, V. **Map** p310 B2.

Chinese Laundry has been a big brother on the club circuit for years, and now it has a sibling, Cave. Friday night offers electro techno and drum 'n' bass, while Saturday add in funk and house. The Slip's Good Vibrations (Saturday) is becoming a marketable entity unto itself – watch for outside events. By the way, the Sand Bar is where Aussie real estate agent Mary Donaldson met the Prince of Denmark. With their wedding imminent, she's set to become a member of the Danish royal family. *See also p237.*

Sounds on Sunday

Greenwood Hotel, above Greenwood Plaza, 36 Blue Street, at Miller Street, North Sydney (9964 9477). CityRail North Sydney. **Open** noon-10.30pm Sun. **Admission** $15. **Credit** AmEx, BC, MC, V.

Don't call this a recovery party, since the touchy organisers call it a day/night dance festival (so there!). Sounds on Sunday transforms what is usually a suburban (former church) bar frequented by suits into a cool event. With three areas (the Courtyard, the Chapel, the Cocktail Bar) pumping everything from disco to trance, the only thing you have to worry about is daylight showing up your wrinkles – the crowd is mostly young.

Suzie Q's

169 Oxford Street, at Taylor Square, Darlinghurst (9331 7729). Bus 378, 380, L82. **Open** 10pm-6am Fri, Sat; 10pm-5am Sun. **Admission** $10 Fri, Sun; $15 Sat. **Credit** AmEx, BC, DC, MC, V. **Map** p311 D4.

Yep, it's another makeover and another namechange for this space, with Tantra evolving into Suzie Q's. The former 'don't touch me' white leather look has been replaced with a less intimidating brown suede, and the jailbait has gone, bringing in a older crowd to smooch to funky house, R&B, hip hop and old skool. Admission is also cheaper.

Tank

3 Bridge Lane, off Bridge Street, between George & Pitt Streets, CBD (9240 3094/www.tankclub.com.au). CityRail Circular Quay or Wynyard/ferry Circular

It's all cool blue at **Tank**.

Quay. **Open** 10pm-6am Fri, Sat. **Admission** $15 Fri; $20 Sat. **Credit** AmEx, BC, DC, MC, V. **Map** p310 C2.

Part of Justin Hemmes' Establishment complex, this high-columned über-club is the closest thing you'll get to a Studio 54 experience in Sydney. Big on style, the music has settled into a comfortable funky/jazzy house, which encourages cocktails as much as cruising. Brave the fashion-heavy door policy as much to see as to be seen. *See also p132 and p142.*

Soho Bar

171 Victoria Street, between Darlinghurst Road & Orwell Street, Potts Point (9358 4221/www.soho bar.com.au). CityRail Kings Cross. **Open** *Main bar* 10am-4am daily. *Soho Bar* 7pm-6am Fri, Sat, Sun. *Yu* 10pm-6am Fri-Sun. **Admission** *Yu* $15 Fri; $20 Sat; $10 Sun. **Credit** AmEx, BC, DC, MC, V. **Map** p312 D3.

The Soho Bar's ground-floor nightclub, Yu, has flashed itself up along with almost every other club in town, but this time the designers were thoughtful enough to include a sprung dancefloor into the comfortable style equation. The house and hip hop beats of Ear Candy (Friday) still attracts the shiny young set, while the funky breaks of After Ours (Sunday) is spreading the crowd. Feel the love. It's also got a stylish pool room; *see p237.*

UN

33 Oxford Street, between Brisbane & Pelican Streets, Darlinghurst (9267 7380). Bus 378, 380, L82. **Open** 10pm-4.30am Fri; 9pm-late Sat; 10pm-3am one Sun in the mth. **Admission** $20 Fri; $22 Sat; $5 Sun. **Credit** AmEx, BC, DC, MC, V. **Map** p311 C3.

Gay club DCM has gone, replaced by this ultra-vamped amber and fishtank sophisticate. Having hoicked itself up a style notch, it now (so they say) attracts the A-list crowd – TV celebs, rock stars and, heaven help us, racing car drivers. You'll find R&B on Friday nights and contemporary dance and house on Saturdays. On occasional Sundays it's 'farewell' to the old DCM gay stompers and 'hello' to the house recovery refugees.

Pool pubs

At first glance it would seem that Sydney is pool-mad. When you walk into almost any pub chances are the centre of attention, apart from the alcohol, is going to be a rectangle of green baize. The fascination must be waning slightly, though, as the number of pool tables per venue seems to be dropping.

Anyone is welcome to play but competition, even over friendly games, is intense, especially in inner-city pubs. Beginners are barely tolerated when the tables are full, particularly on Friday, which is universally regarded as pub night. Accordingly, competitions abound, and often for cash prizes. Although it's not unheard of for regular games to be played for cash in some joints, it's probably a good idea to get to know a place before putting money on the table. Rules vary from place to place, and are usually displayed near the tables. Don't make the mistake of assuming international rules: in most cases, it's the regulars who decide. And if you're just there for the beer, take care that you don't breeze past while a player's taking his shot – knocked elbows have been known to lead to brawls.

As well as the places listed below, the **Coogee Bay Hotel** (*see p137*) has eight pool tables, and its huge beer garden is a firm favourite with English backpackers.

Bar Cleveland

Corner of Cleveland & Bourke Streets, Surry Hills (9698 1908). Bus 301, 302, 303. **Open** 11am-2am Mon-Thur; 11am-4am Fri, Sat; 11am-midnight Sun. **Tables** 2. **Credit** AmEx, BC, MC, V. **Map** p311 C5.
Well, all right, with only two tables you might say why bother. But it's worth a game here to see just how classy old-style Australian pub decor actually was. Beautifully preserved and also updated with today's chrome, Bar Cleveland is one of the calmer environments for concentrating on the ball – except, perhaps, on weekends.

Beach Palace Hotel

Corner of Dolphin & Beach Streets, Coogee (9664 2900). Bus 372, 373, 374. **Open** *Basement* 11am-1am Mon-Thur; 11am-3am Fri, Sat; 11am-midnight Sun. **Tables** 7. **Credit** AmEx, BC, DC, MC, V.
This is bargain basement pool – and we do stress basement. While the upstairs level has some gob-smacking views over Coogee, the tables have been relegated to a windowless alcove in the downstairs bar. All blue tables are up for grabs at a tiny $1 per game on Monday and Tuesday, and the pool comp starts at 8pm on Tuesday. The weekday happy hour (5-7pm) make this a cheap backpacker night out.

Beach Road Hotel

For listings, see p234. **Tables** 8 upstairs, 5 downstairs.
The combination of bands, bar DJs and pool tables make this Bondi Beach venue a favourite throughout the week, and one of Sydney's best all-rounder pubs. Downstairs, the pool option still buzzes with a mix of backpackers and young indie beach refugees. Upstairs, the zushed-up pavilion bar points to more than a bikini, but the party atmosphere and cheapish drinks are hard to match.

Clock Hotel

470 Crown Street, between Foveaux & Arthur Streets, Surry Hills (9331 5333). Bus 301, 302, 303. **Open** 11.45am-midnight daily. **Tables** 4. **Credit** AmEx, BC, DC, MC, V. **Map** p311 C4.
The Clock Hotel's pool bar joins three smart bars, a gaming room and a restaurant in one of the more sophisticated multiplex entertainment developments popping up in town. Drift between pool and cocktails and lounge music all night.

Palace Hotel

122 Flinders Street, at South Dowling Street, Darlinghurst (9361 5170). Bus 378, 380, L82. **Open** 4pm-midnight Mon-Wed; 4pm-1am Thur-Sat; 4-11pm Sun. **Tables** 3. **Credit** AmEx, BC, DC, MC, V. **Map** p311 C4.
Pool doesn't come in more elegant surroundings than this art deco, two-storey pub. A Thai dining nook, a cool cocktail bar and one pool table sit below the main pool room upstairs.

Q Bar

For listings, see p235. **Tables** 5.
Q Bar, on level two of the Exchange Hotel, has undergone a major transformation, and that includes the pool tables. Surrounded by *Playboy*-pen glamour, pool players get to hover between cocktails, clubbing, arcade games and, of course, pool itself.

Slip Inn

For listings, see p236. **Tables** 2.
This entertainment hotspot has it all: three bars, the trattoria-style Ristorante and the basement club, Chinese Laundry. This winning mix pacifies both suits and street-threaded partygoers. It can get a bit crazy on the weekends, so visit on a weeknight if you're after a quiet game of pool.

Soho Bar

For listings, see p236. **Tables** 2.
The Soho Bar can be an expensive night of stick, but the quality tables and cues and upbeat music (commercial house, mainly) help to make it better than your average round of pool. This place is also a club with long queues on Friday and Saturday nights.

Arts & Entertainment

Sport & Fitness

Keen on the sporting life? You've come to the right place.

Sydney's biggest attraction is its seductive combination of splendid weather, natural beauty and urban sophistication. Everyone likes being outdoors – on the harbour, around the harbour, on the beach or in one of the many parks. And almost everyone is obsessed with sport – watching it, playing it, talking about it. So it is hardly a surprise to discover that the city has a wonderful range of sporting venues – especially since the 2000 Olympics.

Remember that rugby is called football and football is called soccer in Australia: rugby league dominates in Sydney, with rugby union and Australian Rules Football less popular. Apart from the continual cycle of football, there's a never-ending supply of cricket, swimming and just about every known sport under the sun. For the active visitor, Sydney offers an endless list of outdoor pursuits: from a gentle harbourside walk to the oceanic delights of surfing, sailing, swimming and scuba-diving, or the extreme thrill of a skydive, the choice is there for the taking. So take it.

Participation sports

Bowls

Lawn bowls is surprisingly hip in Australia and attracts an increasingly younger audience. Nearly every suburb has a bowling club and many offer lessons to beginners. You can even go 'Rock & Bowling', a bizarre mixture of rock, lessons and laid-back fun – expect groups in shorts and bare feet, with a beer in one hand and a bowl in the other. Some clubs even allow barbies and ghetto-blasters lawnside. Call the **Royal NSW Bowling Association** (9283 4555, www.rnswba.org.au) for more info.

Canoeing & kayaking

NSW Canoeing (9660 4597, www.nswcanoe. org.au) has information on the many places in Sydney for recreational canoeing, and also offers two-day skills courses. In the national parks that have rivers (such as Lane Cove and the Royal), you can hire canoes at low rates – an excellent way to pass a few leisurely hours. Harbour tours are offered by **Sydney Harbour Kayaks** (9960 4389, www.sydney harbourkayaks.com) in Mosman, while sea

kayaking adventures, either off the beaches or in Sydney Harbour, are run by **Natural Wanders & Sydney Kayaks** (9899 1001, www.kayaksydney.com).

Climbing

Rock climbing, abseiling and canyoning are all possible in the environs of Sydney, with lessons and tours available for beginners, plus hire shops for the experienced. Novices can get information from **Outward Bound Australia** (1800 267 999, www.outwardbound.com.au) or the **Australian School of Mountaineering** (4782 2014, www.asmguides.com).

Experienced climbers can ask for locations at an indoor climbing centre or at **Paddy Pallin** (*see p190*) equipment shop in the CBD. Indoor centres include **The Edge Adventure Sports** (Hudson Avenue, Castle Hill, 9899 8228, www.edge-adventure.com.au), and there are climbing walls at **Climb Fit** (12 Frederick Street, CBD, 9436 4600, www.climbfit.com.au) and **City Crag** at the back of Mountain Designs (499 Kent Street, CBD, 9267 3822).

For those who want the thrill of climbing combined with views of the coastline, try **Bush Sports** (9630 0587 www.bushsports. com.au), which tackles every adventure sport imaginable including climbing, abseiling, canyoning, rafting and caving. Most climbing is done in the Blue Mountains and Hunter Valley, but it is also possible to scale Sydney cliffs.

Cycling

With its undulating terrain and unrestrained drivers, Sydney is a rough place for cyclists and local councils have been slow to provide cycle tracks, although this is improving. Helmets are compulsory and be sure to take bottles of water with you on a hot day. Central Sydney's most enjoyable place for recreational riding is **Centennial Park** (*see p80*), which is threaded with roads and bike tracks.

Cycling NSW (9738 5850, www.nsw. cycling.org.au) can provide information on local clubs, rides and racing. **Bicycle NSW** (9281 4099, www.bicyclensw.org.au) is a recreational bike group with details on recommended cycle routes and paths; you can pick up its *Cycling Around Sydney* from bookshops for $30 or

Arts & Entertainment

they'll post you a copy. **BMX NSW** (6367 5277, www.bmxnsw.com.au) has information on bicycle motor-cross facilities and tracks.

For more advice on Sydney cycling and bike hire shops, *see p283*.

Fishing

Fishing is one of Sydney's biggest participation sports. The best up-to-date sources for where to fish are the weekend newspapers and tackle shops. To fish you need a recreational licence, which ensures you are aware of protected species and catch-bag allowances. You can buy a licence for three days ($5), one month ($10) or a year ($25) from hundreds of fishing shops and clubs, by phoning 1300 369 365 or online at www.fisheries.nsw.gov.au.

Fishabout Tours (9451 5420, www.fishnet. com.au/fishabout_tours) offer days out on the harbour; prices vary according to the number of people and the day you go, but start from around $140 per person. There are also several fishing charters based at Pittwater in the north and Botany Bay in the south. For gear and information, try the **Compleat Angler** in the CBD (Third Floor, Dymocks Building, 428 George Street, 9241 2080, www.compleat angler.com.au).

NSW is not as well known as Queensland for offshore fishing, but at certain times of the year – particularly autumn and spring – seriously big sporting fish, including marlin, can be caught. Captain John Wright of **Game & Sport Fishing Charters** (0414 542 548, www.gamefisher.com) is a marlin and tuna specialist operating out of Botany Bay. Prices range from $1,200 (up to six people) for game fishing and $900 (max six) for sport fishing. For parties larger than six, Game & Sport also works with **Abbott Boat Charters** (bookings 9929 0729, boat 0411 212 844, www.game fishingtours.com.au). No fishing licence is required when chartering these vessels.

Golf

Golf courses in Sydney are plentiful and relatively inexpensive. The best courses are private and you'll need a member's invitation to play, but most suburbs have a public course where the price of a round costs $25-$70; golf clubs can be hired for under $40 and lessons are around $50 per half hour. Public courses near the CBD include **Moore Park Golf Course** (Cleveland Street, 9663 1064, www.mooreparkgolf.com.au), which also has a three-level driving range, and the **Eastlake Public Golf Club** in Kingsford (Gardener Road, 9663 1374, ww.eastlakegolfclub.com.au).

Contact the **NSW Golf Association** (9264 8433, www.nswga.com.au) for more locations.

Gyms & sports centres

Weights, circuit training and aerobic classes are all available in Sydney, though the variation in standard and value for money between gyms is considerable, so it's worth shopping around. Annual membership can cost anything from $200 to $1,000, but monthly and short-term deals can be quite cheap and most places allow casual visits for around $12-$15. For gyms near the CBD, try the following:

Telstra Stadium. *See p244*.

Make a splash

From the striped headgear of bronzed lifesavers to small kids on boogie boards giggling in shallow surf to wreck-hunting divers – Sydney and the sea go together. The ocean is ingrained in the city's lifestyle: no matter who you are, when it's hot, everyone heads for the water. And of all water sports, surfing gets the prize. Probably because almost everywhere you look there are waves. Australian kids may take the waves for granted, but the rest of us have to be taught – or suffer the consequences. Fortunately, combining learning to surf with sightseeing is easy as the two most popular places to learn are Bondi and Manly.

A standard two-hour lesson in a group of six will give you tips on wave awareness and safety, and get you planting those pads in the right place. Equipment and a wetsuit is included. If jumping around on a practice surfboard on the sand in front of a bunch of strangers sounds too embarrassing, private lessons are also available. You'll have to pick up the lingo yourself (dude).

At **Manly Surf School** (9977 6977, www.manlysurfschool.com), Matt Grainger and his team of friendly instructors have been coaxing novices into the water for 17 years. There are beginner, intermediate and advanced courses, costing $50 a session for a two-hour group lesson and $80 an hour for one-to-one. A photographer is on hand to snap you riding your first wave. **Let's Go Surfing** in Bondi (128 Ramsgate Avenue, 9365 1800, www.letsgosurfing.com.au), charges $59 per person for a group class, three sessions for $140 or a private, one-to-one, 90-minute lesson for $110.

Surfing Australia (6674 9888, ww.surfingaustralia.com.au) also arranges courses in conjunction with local shops along the coast.

If being on top isn't your thing, how about being underneath? Scuba-diving around Sydney is spectacular: there's fabulous reef-diving and marine life – including sharks (safe ones, honest), sponge gardens and the unique, unbelievable, endemic 'weedy seadragon' – and plenty of wrecks. The sheer diversity around the Sydney foreshore will amaze, and it's an ideal place to get qualified before heading for the wonders of the Great Barrier Reef.

You can get a snapshot of the underwater world in just half a day, but you'll need longer if you want to get your PADI Open Water Certification (a minimum of three days), which will then allow you to dive pretty much anywhere in the world. This involves dive theory, pool sessions and a minimum of four ocean dives; if you have the time, it's wise to take a longer course (four or five days). A smart idea is to complete the theory and pool sessions at home or before you arrive and simply do the diving in Sydney to finish the certificate – who wants to study on holiday?

Pro Dive, one of the most experienced diving oufits in Australia, has scuba centres throughout Sydney, including ones in the city centre, Manly, Coogee and Cronulla – call 1800 820 820 to find your nearest shop or visit www.prodiveonline.com. Its full-time PADI course, aimed at complete novices, takes four days (starting on Monday) and costs $445 per person (less if there's two of you – check the website for specials). Alternatively, linked outfits **Dive Centre Manly** (10 Belgrave Street, 9977 4355) and **Bondi Dive Centre** (192 Bondi Road, 9369 3855) offer a variety of courses, for beginners to advanced. More details on www.divesydney.com.

If this all sounds too energetic, give snorkelling a go. Usually undertaken in calm, clear waters, snorkelling is an excellent way to see some underwater sights without effort. If you've never attempted it before, get a five-minute rundown from a local dive shop (where you can hire snorkelling equipment) – and make sure your mask fits snugly.

City Gym Health & Fitness Centre

107-113 Crown Street, between William & Stanley Streets, East Sydney (9360 6247/www.citygym. com.au). CityRail Kings Cross/bus 323, 324, 325, 389. **Open** 24hrs 5am Mon-10pm Sat; 8am-10pm Sun. **Admission** $13.50. **Credit** BC, MC, V. **Map** p309 C3.

This is a favourite with hardcore gym junkies and preeners buffing their six-packs.

Cook & Phillip Park

4 College Street, at William Street, CBD (9326 0444/ www.cookandphillip.com.au). City Rail Museum or St James. **Open** 6am-10pm Mon-Fri; 7am-8pm Sat, Sun. **Admission** *All facilities* $16; $8.50 concessions. *Pool only* $5.50; $3.50-$4 concessions. **Credit** AmEx, BC, MC, V. **Map** p309 C3.

This well-equipped aquatic/fitness centre has a 50m heated indoor swimming pool, a leisure pool with wave machine, hydrotherapy pools, basketball courts and a good gym. Various classes and team sports are available; the aqua aerobics classes are especially popular.

Hang-gliding, skydiving & paragliding

Beginners can experience the thrill of hang-gliding or skydiving in tandem with an instructor through **Adrenalin Club** (80 McDougall Street, Kirribilli, 9959 3934, www.adrenalin.com.au). Prices for hang-gliding start from $220 for a 45-minute flight and include membership in the Hang-gliding Federation for three months. Skydiving starts at $325; for an extra $120 you get a five-minute video and photos.

Tandem skydiving jumps for beginners are available at the **Sydney Skydiving Centre** (1 800 805 997, 9791 9155, www.sydneysky divers.com.au) based at Bankstown Airport. Jumps are over Picton, in Sydney's south-west, from 3,700 metres (12,000 feet) with an instructor; prices start at $275. They also offer accelerated freefall (AFF) courses, probably the most adrenalin-inducing thrill of all. The course consists of one day's training, followed by the jump on a second day at Picton. After a 40-second freefall (locked to an instructor) you pull the ripcord and have five minutes to enjoy incredible views of the coastline and Sydney. Prices start at $374.

For paragliding – jumping off a cliff with a parachute (and an instructor, should you wish) attached – try **Sydney Paragliding Centre** (4294 9065, www.sydneypara gliding.com) at Stanwell Park an hour south of Sydney, which offers tandem adventures from $195. Get more information from the **Australian Parachute Federation** (6281 6830, www.apf.asn.au).

Horse riding

The only place in central Sydney for horse riding is the old Sydney Showgrounds in Centennial Park. The **Centennial Parkland Equestrian Centre** (9332 2809, www.cp.nsw. gov.au) administers the site, and is located on the corner of Cook and Lang Roads, just past Fox Studios. Stables operating out of the centre include **Centennial Stables** (9360 5650, www.centennialstables.com.au), which offers individual one-hour lessons for $80, group lessons from $55 per person and casual rides around the park for $55 an hour.

Rollerblading (in-line skating)

The promenades of Manly and Bondi Beaches are popular for blading and Bondi has two half-pipes for in-liners and skateboarders. Centennial Park, with its flat roads and moderate traffic, is also a rollerblading haven. **Centennial Park Cycles** (*see p283*) hires out blades (including protective padding) at $12 for one hour, $18 for two and $25 for four. Skates can also be hired from some surf shops at the beaches.

Sailing

The **Charter Boat Information Service** (9552 1827) provides information on sailing, fishing and houseboats, as well as dinner cruises and party boat hire.

If you want to learn to sail, the **Pacific Sailing School** (9326 2399, www.pacific sailingschool.com.au) in Rushcutters Bay is one of the many schools in the Sydney Harbour, Middle Harbour and Port Hacking area. **Eastsail** (9327 1166, www.eastsail.com.au) also operates from Rushcutters Bay and offers courses in crewing and sailing. Beginners' courses (four three-hour practical sessions, one three-hour theory session and one club race) costs $465 each, with discounts for two or more people. Or try **Aussail** (9960 5451, www.ausailsydney.com.au), which operates from the Spit Bridge. The **Yachting Association of NSW** (9660 1266, www.nsw.yachting.org.au) can provide information on other companies and locations.

Scuba-diving

Sydney is a terrific place to dive and has many dive shops servicing almost every suburb. Manly (notably Fairy Bower) and Bondi/Coogee are probably the most popular places, with sheltered bays and marine reserves, but there are also excellent wreck and reef dives.

Arts & Entertainment

Learning to dive usually takes four to five days and costs around $425-$525; for more information, *see p240* **Make a splash**.

Surfing

Surfing is an integral part of Australian life, and Sydney is a fine spot for hitting the waves. Good surfing beaches include **Manly**, **Dee Why** and **Freshwater** (for beginners), **Bondi**, **Bronte**, **Cronulla** and any of the **northern beaches** (for intermediates and experts). Every beach of significance in Sydney has a surf lifesaving club and most hire surfboards and body boards for less around $15 an hour. If you've never stood on a board before, consider having some lessons first; *see p240* **Make a splash**.

For the latest surf conditions, visit www.coastalwatch.com or www.realsurf.com. Also look for the excellent *Wave-Finder* (published by the Hedonist Surf Company), a mini guide to beaches around Australia, available from surf shops and book stores.

Swimming

IN THE SEA

Beach swimmers are advised to swim between the red and yellow flags. These are cordoned-off sections (and they change every day) considered safe and patrolled by professional surf lifesavers. For more advice on beach safety, and details of Sydney's best beaches, *see pp118-124*.

IN OCEAN AND HARBOUR POOLS

Not everyone wants to brave the waves and many of Sydney's beaches have excellent tidal swimming pools. North Bondi has two small paddling pools, while south Bondi has the lane-marked Bondi Icebergs pool (*see p78* **Some like it cold**). Queenscliff, just north of Manly, has a nice 50-metre pool and Wylie Baths at Coogee is renowned as the best preserved of the seaside pools; there are also women-only baths about 200 metres south of Wylie. Collaroy, Bronte, Cronulla, Palm Beach and Dee Why beaches all have pools that become very busy in summer, mainly with children, women and older folk.

Some harbour beaches have enclosed swimming areas; good ones include those at Clontarf, Balmoral, Nielsen Park and the Redleaf Pool at Double Bay.

IN PUBLIC POOLS

Sydney International Aquatic Centre (*see p243*) is an Olympic venue open to the public outside competition times; it's a fantastic facility with wonderful play areas for kids. Closer to the city is the excellent 50-metre pool at **Cook & Phillip Park**(*see p241*). In the inner west, there are 50-metre pools in **Prince Alfred Park** (near Central Station off Chalmers Street, 9319 7045) and at **Victoria Park** (near Sydney University, between City Road and Broadway, 9660 4181). On the north shore, the **North Sydney Olympic Pool** (*see p98*) at Milsons Point occupies a fabulous position beside the Harbour Bridge, is heated during winter and has recently undergone an impressive refurbishment. The lovely **Andrew (Boy) Charlton Pool** (*see p63*) on the edge of the Domain is also a real gem.

For the location of other pools, contact the **NSW Swimming Association** (9552 2966, www.nswswimming.com.au).

Tennis

Public tennis courts are run by local councils and charge $12-$20 an hour. One of the best-known tennis centres in central Sydney is **White City Tennis Club** (30 Alma Street, Paddington, 9360 4113, www.whitecitytennis. com), where the Sydney International used to be held. Courts can be hired by non-members 10am-4pm Mon-Fri for $25 an hour.

For more information, call **Tennis NSW** (9763 7644, www.tennisnsw.com.au).

Windsurfing

Windsurfing, aka sailboarding, is very popular in Sydney. No doubt because of the great flat-water opportunities on Pittwater, the Narrabeen Lakes, Sydney Harbour, Botany Bay and Port Hacking, plus surf challenges at various beaches – notably Palm and Long Reef.

The **Balmoral Sailing School** (9960 5344, www.sailingschool.com.au) at Balmoral Beach is one of the best places to learn to windsurf. Courses range from introductory to advanced; prices start at $140. They also hire fully rigged windsurfers – $30 for beginners, $40 for advanced. Or try **Long Reef Sailboards & Surf** (www.longreefsailboards.com.au), which has two locations, north (1012 Pittwater Road, Collaroy, 9971 1212) and south (116 The Grand Parade, Brighton-le-Sands, 9599 2814). Both outfits also offer kite-surfing tuition.

Much of the enjoyment of sailboarding depends on weather and wind direction, so call the **boating weather forecast** (1 900 926 101) before going. For north-easterlies, the best spots are Pittwater at Palm Beach, Narrabeen Lake, Balmoral Beach, Rodd Point in the harbour and Botany Bay south of the airport. Silver Beach at Kurnell is good for westerlies,

The perfect place to learn to sail. *See p241.*

and southerlies favour the area around Captain
Cook Bridge in Sutherland. The **NSW
Boardsailing Association** (www.wind
surfing.org/nsw) has more information.

Spectator sports

Venues

Sydney's biggest sport venue is the **Telstra
Stadium** (formerly Stadium Australia), the
centrepiece of the Olympic Park site at
Homebush Bay. The stadium's advent has
marked a significant shift in Sydney's sporting
culture, taking some of the big events from
the **Sydney Cricket Ground** and **Sydney
Football Stadium**, both in Moore Park, and
moving them 20 kilometres (12.5 miles) west
to the city's demographic centre.

Most of the Olympic sites at Homebush
Bay continue to hold both elite and local
sporting events. The **Sydney Olympic Park
Visitor Centre** (1 Showground Road, 9714
7888, www.sydneyolympicpark.com.au) has
information on all venues.

TICKETS
Tickets for most of the big games must be
booked in advance through an agency.
Ticketek (9266 4800, www.ticketek.com) is the
main outlet for most sporting events in Sydney,
including those held at any of the Olympic
venues at Homebush Bay, but **Ticketmaster7**
(13 6100, www.ticketmaster7.com) sell tickets
for some soccer and rugby matches. Both have
booking fees. You can sometimes buy tickets
at the venue on the day, often for cash only.

Sydney Cricket Ground (SCG) & Sydney Football Stadium (SFS)
*Driver Avenue, Moore Park (1 800 801 155/9360
6601/tours 9380 0383/www.sydneycricketground.
com.au). Bus 372, 373, 374.* **Tours** 10am, 1pm Mon-
Fri. **Tickets** $19.50; $13 concessions; $52 family.
Map p311 D5.
Book ahead for a tour, which lasts two hours.

Sydney International Aquatic Centre
*Olympic Boulevard, Sydney Olympic Park, Homebush
Bay (9752 3666/www.sydneyaquaticcentre.com.au).
CityRail Olympic Park/RiverCat Homebush Bay
then bus 401.* **Open** 5am-8.45pm Mon-Fri; 6am-
6.45pm/7.45pm Sat, Sun. *Tours* noon, 1pm, 2pm
daily. **Admission** *Swim & spa* $5.80; $4-$4.60
concessions; $18.50 family. *Swim & gym* $10.50;
$8 concessions; *Tours* $17; $11 concessions; $47
family. **Credit** BC, DC, MC, V.
The centre, which hosted the swimming during the
Olympics, stages inter-school competitions and
high-quality international meets, and is also open to
the public – for swimming and tours.

Sydney International Athletics Centre
*Edwin Flack Avenue, Sydney Olympic Park,
Homebush Bay (9752 3444/www.sydneyathletic
centre.com.au). CityRail Olympic Park/RiverCat
Homebush Bay then bus 401.* **Open** 3-8pm Mon-Fri;
8am-1pm Sat; 9am-1pm Sun.

Sydney International Tennis Centre
*Rod Laver Drive, Sydney Olympic Park,
Homebush Bay (8746 0777/www.sydneytennis.
com.au). CityRail Olympic Park/RiverCat Homebush
Bay then bus 401.* **Open** 7am-10pm Mon-Fri;
9am-5.30pm Sat, Sun.

Sydney Olympic Park Sports Centre
*Olympic Boulevard, Sydney Olympic Park,
Homebush Bay (9763 0111/www.sports-centre.
com.au). CityRail Olympic Park/RiverCat Homebush
Bay then bus 401.* **Open** 7am-11pm daily.

Sydney Superdome
*Corner of Edwin Flack Avenue & Olympic
Boulevard, Sydney Olympic Park, Homebush
Bay (8765 4321/www.superdome.com.au).
CityRail Olympic Park/RiverCat Homebush Bay
then bus 401.*

Telstra Stadium

Olympic Boulevard, Sydney Olympic Park, Homebush Bay (8765 2000/guided tours 8765 2300/www.telstrastadium.com.au). CityRail Olympic Park/RiverCat Homebush Bay then bus 401.

The stadium's stands were moved in towards the main arena after the Olympics to improve sightlines and the overall atmosphere. It now has a seating capacity of 85,000. Crowds of around 40,000 are typical for regular rugby league games, while between 60,000 and 85,000 turn up for exhibition events. The biggest and most high-profile matches – rugby union tests, State of Origin rugby league games, the Rugby League Grand Final, plus the historic Rugby World Cup in 2003 – sell out. For information on tours, *see p111* **Sydney Olympic Park**.

Athletics

Sydneysiders love their athletics and are ardent supporters. The **Telstra Grand Prix Series**, the biggest annual event, with a smattering of international competitors, is held during the summer months in each of the state capital cities – in Sydney at the **International Athletics Centre** (*see p243*). For more info, contact **Athletics Australia** (03 9820 3511, www.athletics.org.au) or **Athletics NSW** (9552 1244, www.nswathletics.org.au).

Aussie Rules

Sydney's fickle relationship with Aussie Rules (aka Australian Football League) is symbolised in the fortunes of its local team. The **Sydney Swans** (9339 9123, www.sydneyswans.com.au) used to be the South Melbourne team, but were transplanted to Sydney in 1982, with initially poor results. However, they made it to the Grand Final in 1996 – their most successful season to date. Since then Sydney has become almost as fanatical as Melbourne and matches regularly sell out the 42,000-seat **Sydney Cricket Ground** (*see p243*).

The Swans play about a dozen matches at the SCG from March to September. The Kangaroos of Melbourne have been keen to make inroads into the Sydney market and usually play about five 'home' games at the SCG. *See also p245* **Aussie Rules**.

Baseball

Australian baseball is a relatively small but thriving sport with the local teams for just about every area playing in the Major League. There is also a beginners' league and under-18s competition. For details, contact the **NSW Baseball League** (9675 4522) or visit www.baseball.com.au.

Basketball

Sydney has two teams in the National Basketball League, the **Sydney Kings** and the **West Sydney Razorbacks**, and one women's NBL side, the **Sydney Flames** (9351 4960, www.sydneyflames.com), who play at Sydney University Sports Centre. The Kings (9281 1777, www.sydneykings.com.au) play at the **Sydney Entertainment Centre** (*see p223*). The Razorbacks, aka the 'Pigs' (9740 6259, www.razorbacks.com.au), are the newest boys of the NBL and play at Homebush's **Olympic Park Sports Centre** (*see p243*). Tickets start at $17.

For information, contact the **NSW Basketball Association** (9746 2969, www.nswbasketball.net.au).

Cricket

During the summer months, cricket enjoys a stranglehold on the sporting calendar, both as a spectator and participation sport. For well over 100 years, cricket has dominated the psyche of Australians, and fans of the 'gentleman's game' will tell you that a trip to the famous **Sydney Cricket Ground** (*see p243*) for an international match is a must for any visitor.

International matches involving Australia often play to sell-out crowds at the SCG, and also enjoy high TV ratings. The highlight of the year is the **Sydney Test**, played over five days against a touring side, usually in the first week of January. About five or six one-day matches are also played at the SCG in the afternoon and under lights in the evening. One-dayers are probably the best option for those not familiar with the sport as they are often played at a faster pace – and you're guaranteed a result. Getting tickets for the bigger matches can be difficult, but local games are usually not sold out. Ticket prices start from around $30 for a day's play. For information on matches, phone the SCG or visit www.baggygreen.com.au.

At state level, the New South Wales cricket team, the **NSW Blues**, plays about five matches at the SCG between October and March in the interstate Pura Cup competition, plus some one-day matches at the picturesque **North Sydney Oval**. The final takes place in early March – in Sydney, if NSW makes it. Meanwhile, hundreds of fields around Sydney host cricket matches of all levels and standards on summer Saturday afternoons.

For more information on fixtures and venues, contact **Cricket NSW** (9339 0999, www.cricketnsw.com.au).

Golf

Although Melbourne tends to get Australia's biggest golf events, Sydney usually hosts two or three major tournaments in the summer as part of the **Australasian Golf Tour**. The tour features the best golfers from Australia alongside a handful of overseas players.

The Sydney tournaments are shared between the **Lakes Golf Club** (King Street, Mascot, 9669 1311), the **Australian Golf Club** (53 Bannerman Crescent, Rosebery, 9663 2273, www.australiangolfclub.com), the **Royal Sydney Golf Club** (Kent Road, Rose Bay, 9371 4333, www.rsgc.com.au) or the **Terrey Hills Golf & Country Club** (116 Booralie Road, Terrey Hills, 9450 0155, www.terreyhillsgolf.com.au). Ticket prices range from about $30 to $150 per day's play. Youc an see up-to-date schedules at www.pgatour.com.au.

Greyhound racing

You can go to the dogs at **Wentworth Park** on Monday and Saturday evenings, with ten races each night.

Wentworth Park Greyhound Track

Wentworth Park Road, Glebe (9552 1799/ www.wentworthparksport.com.au). LightRail Wentworth Park. **Open** 6-11pm Mon, Sat. **Admission** $5.50. **No credit cards. Map** p309 A3.

Harness racing

'The trots' are held at **Harold Park** most Friday nights and Tuesday afternoons.

Harold Park Paceway

Wigram Road, Glebe (9660 3688/www.haroldpark. com.au). Bus 433. **Open** 1-5.30pm Tue; 7-11pm Fri. **Admission** $8. **No credit cards.**

Horse racing

On Saturdays and Wednesdays, all year round, there is a race meeting in Sydney. The **Australian Jockey Club** (9663 8400, www.ajc.org.au) runs meets at **Royal Randwick** and **Warwick Farm**, while the **Sydney Turf Club** (9930 4000, www.theraces.com.au) organises programmes at **Rosehill Gardens** and **Canterbury Park**. Night racing (on Thursdays and sometimes Saturdays) at Canterbury is a fixture on the racing scene from October to April.

The **Doncaster Derby Day** is Sydney's richest meeting – nine races with a total prize pool of around $9 million – and is traditionally held on Easter Saturday (though it moved to

Easter Monday for 2004). Other huge events are the $4-million **Golden Slipper** at Rosehill, usually held a week before Derby Day, and the **Spring Carnival**, held at Randwick on the public holiday weekend at the start of October.

Admission to normal meets is $10, to major races $30, with under-18s allowed in free.

Canterbury Park Racecourse

King Street, Canterbury (9930 4000). CityRail Canterbury then shuttle bus.

Aussie Rules

Very popular in Australia but almost unheard of elsewhere, Aussie Rules was invented in Melbourne around 1858. Played with an oval ball on an oval field, it shares similarities with soccer, rugby and Gaelic football. Teams consist of 18 players and the goals have four posts; you can run with the ball, punt-kick or hit it with your hand, but not throw it. It's fast, aggressive and involves lots of macho physical contact. It's utterly confusing to newcomers, but any fan will be delighted to enlighten you.

The game is more popular in Victoria, South Australia and Western Australia than NSW, but if you get the chance to see a match, take it – it's a cultural education. One thing you do not need to worry about is violence: Australian Rules is a family game, with kids in pushchairs kitted out in team colours. *See also p244.*

Rugby union World Cup 2003. Sorry, guys.

Rosehill Gardens Racecourse

Grand Avenue, Rosehill (9930 4000). CityRail Rosehill/RiverCat Parramatta then shuttle bus.

Royal Randwick Racecourse

Alison Road, Randwick (9663 8400). Bus 372, 373, 374.

Warwick Farm Racecourse

Hume Highway, Warwick Farm (9602 6199). CityRail Warwick Farm then shuttle bus.

Rugby league

Sydney is the only city in the world where rugby league is the biggest of the football codes – although rugby union does come a close second, especially after the success of the World Cup in 2003. The fact that the **NSW and Australian Rugby League** (9232 7566, www.nrl.com.au) is based in, and controlled from, Sydney has led to various upheavals

over the past few years, including a short-lived breakaway league set up by Rupert Murdoch. The current state of affairs is due to be reassessed in 2005.

The NRL was a 17-team competition in 1999, but that number was trimmed to 14 in 2000. Six clubs were forced to merge and one of the foundation clubs, South Sydney, was axed altogether. However, in July 2001, after a court ruling, the club was reinstated and returned in the 2003 season (so it's now a 15-team competition). Today, Sydney has nine teams, with the other six clubs hailing from Brisbane, Melbourne, Newcastle, Canberra, Townsville and Auckland.

The season runs from March to mid October, culminating in the finals at the **Sydney Football Stadium** (*see p243*) and **Telstra Stadium** (*see p244*). The big representative matches are the **State of Origin** series, when NSW takes on Queensland. Test matches, involving Australia, New Zealand, Britain or one of the Pacific nations, draw relatively little interest because Australia is rarely beaten and the sport is not widely known.

Tickets for Premiership matches cost $12-$50. For the State of Origin series, expect to pay around $30-$110 for a prime seat.

Sydney teams

Canterbury-Bankstown Bulldogs 9789 2922/ www.bulldogs.com.au
Cronulla-Sutherland Sharks 9523 0222/ www.sharks.com.au
Manly Sea Eagles 9938 3677/ www.mightyeagles.com
Parramatta Eels 9683 6311/www.parraeels.com.au
Penrith Panthers 4720 5555/ www.panthersworld.com.au
St George Illawarra Dragons 9587 1966/ www.dragons.com.au
South Sydney Rabbitohs 8306 9900/ www.souths.com.au
Sydney City Roosters 9386 3248/ www.sydneyroosters.com.au
West Tigers 8741 3300/www.weststigers.com.au

Rugby union

This is the other rugby code. Since Australia won its first Rugby World Cup in 1991, the sport has undergone a surge in popularity. When Australia won the World Cup again in 1999, it seemed everybody wanted to watch the Wallabies, the national team. The 2003 World Cup – staged throughout Australia – was a huge success, with every major game playing to capacity crowds. The nail-biting final between the Wallabies and England at Telstra Stadium only seemed to add to the country's enthusiasm, despite Australia's defeat, thanks to Jonny Wilkinson's last-minute drop goal.

The **Wallabies** play about six home internationals a year between June and September, of which two or three are usually in Sydney, at the **SFS** (*see p243*) or **Telstra Stadium** (*see p244*). From February to May, the **NSW Waratahs** play in the Super 12 competition against regional teams from Australia, South Africa and New Zealand; games are at the SFS. Tickets for club matches cost around $10, while Super 12 tickets start at $18 and test match tickets are $50.

More info is available from the **Australian Rugby Union** (9956 3444, www.rugby.com.au).

Soccer (football)

Soccer's popularity may be growing in Australia, with many kids playing the game at school, but it's still way below that of rugby league or union. Most serious football fans follow overseas soccer – particularly the UK competitions – more closely (via TV coverage) than the local action. Australia's national team plays occasional friendly internationals and World Cup qualifiers in Sydney at either the **Telstra Stadium** (*see p244*) or the **SFS** (*see p243*). The Socceroos, as they're known, have a history of failing to qualify for the World Cup, and until they do, soccer will remain in the shadow of rugby.

The National Soccer League is Australia's showcase of premium domestic soccer. It currently comprises 13 teams, stretching from Perth Glory in the west, over to Australia's east coast and across the Tasman Sea to the Football Kingz in Auckland, New Zealand. The season is from mid September to April, and tickets start at around $20. A full list of fixtures can be found at www.socceraustralia.com.au.

Sydney teams

Marconi Stallions 9823 6666/
www.marconifc.com
Northern Spirit 9970 7211/
www.northernspirit.com.au
Parramatta Power 9630 9777/
www.parrapower.com.au
Sydney Olympic 9560 4032/
www.sydneyolympic.com.au
Sydney United 9823 6418/
www.sydneyunited.com.au

Surfing

On almost every weekend in summer, surfing contests are held in Sydney, ranging from local intra-club meetings and regional junior tournaments to professional events attracting some of the world's top surfers. The World Qualifying Series tour normally holds one event at either Bondi or Manly. Contact **Surfing**

NSW (9349 7055, www.surfingaustralia.com.au) for info on events and locations.

SURF LIFESAVING

One of Sydney's clichéd images is the Bondi Beach lifeguard in brief Speedo-style bathers with an amusing tie-up skull cap. It's a stereotyped look derived from surf lifesaving competitions, which have been part of the Sydney scene for almost a century. The first lifesaving club was founded at Bondi in 1906; there are now more than 107,000 registered volunteer surf lifesavers in Australia, a small proportion of whom are professional lifeguards. Nearly every beach within range of a community has a surf lifesaving club (SLSC), and a structured series of competitions throughout the year is designed to develop and demonstrate the various skills of the lifesavers. Most clubs cater for 'nippers': kids as young as five or six join their local group to learn surf lifesaving, wave and beach skills.

Surf lifesaving events take place on most summer weekends, ranging from district to national competitions. All the skills of the lifesaving movement are on display – swimming and board races, sprint races and the popular Ironman event, which incorporates all three disciplines. For more information, contact **Surf Life Saving NSW** (9984 7188, www.surflifesaving.com.au).

Swimming

Swimming has always been incredibly popular with Sydneysiders – there are, after all, some breathtaking places to swim. Capitalising on its popularity, several World Cup swimming meetings are staged in summer in cities throughout Australia, including Sydney. The **International Aquatic Centre** (*see p243*) is the venue for most of the major local events.

It's also well worth catching the local Sydney beach swims – where up to 500 local and international competitors undertake one- to three-kilometre ocean swims from different beaches around Sydney. It is quite a spectacle.

More details are available from the **NSW Swimming Association** (9552 2966, www.nswswimming.com.au).

Tennis

The only world-ranked tennis event left in Sydney is the **Sydney International,** a warm-up event in January for the Australian Open in Melbourne, held at the **International Tennis Centre** (*see p243*). For details of upcoming tournaments, contact **Tennis NSW** (9763 7644, www.tennisnsw.com.au).

Arts & Entertainment

Theatre & Dance

Get your kicks at Sydney's varied performing arts scene.

On 4 June 1789, just over a year after the establishment of the Sydney colony, convicts put on the first stage production in Australia – George Farquhar's *The Recruiting Officer* – to honour the King's birthday and entertain the military elite in whose hands their fate rested. By the 1850s a hugely popular Australian version of melodrama was flourishing. Though much of the activity was focused on the gold-rush towns of Ballarat and Bendigo outside Melbourne, Sydney also enjoyed a thriving theatre scene with a strong local flavour. By the mid 20th century, however, an English sensibility had returned. To anyone with taste, Sydney was once again an outpost of the British Empire and home-made theatre gave way to tours of Shakespeare productions starring the likes of Laurence Olivier and Anthony Quayle.

Australian theatre experienced a renaissance during the 1960s; it was triggered in Melbourne but soon spread to Sydney with the birth in 1970 of the Nimrod Theatre. Melbourne has maintained its reputation as the best place in Australia for innovation, experimentation and subversive comment. Some call Sydney glitzy and shallow, but its mainstream theatre is better than Melbourne's and, on occasions, productions are world class.

Since the 2000 Olympics, a new vitality in the Sydney performing arts has lifted the standard of productions, from fringe to mainstream. The city's major company, the **Sydney Theatre Company**, opened its new venue, the **Sydney Theatre**, in January 2004 (*see p252* **Stage magic**). The company also has access to the **Sydney Opera House** and its own **Wharf Theatres** complex, which means it usually has several medium- to high-quality shows running concurrently. Sydney's other major group, **Company B**, mounts ambitious productions with a strong Australian flavour and attracts a loyal following. Its director, Neil Armfield, is probably the best in the country.

Fringe theatre is hot. The **Old Fitzroy Hotel** in Woolloomooloo has become the breeding ground for a new can-do generation of multi-talented artists that work across film, TV and their own brand of fresh, home-made theatre. The forms are not that challenging, the focus here is just on good writing and acting, but the productions are usually fun. The newly established **Darlinghurst**

Theatre is also used by many young artists, while the **Performance Space** in Redfern is home to cutting-edge performance art, diverse technologies and experimentation. Across the harbour at Kirribilli, the **Ensemble Theatre** continues its decades-long run of well-produced mainstream plays, appreciated by an older, discerning audience.

After an era of musical extravaganzas, including a deluge of mediocre, imported remounts, the musicals scene has been forced to regroup and lift its game. These days, there are fewer shows on offer, but the quality has improved; Australians love a good musical and the home-grown chorus lines are of an international calibre.

The dance scene tends towards the mainstream too. The more sophisticated choreographers – including Meryl Tankard, of Germany's Pina Bausch company fame – have been sidelined while those with more popular appeal remain in the top jobs. Graeme Murphy's **Sydney Dance Company** is the city's most popular contemporary dance group, and no wonder: sexy physicality is its trademark. If performing, the Aboriginal and Islander ensemble **Bangarra Dance Theatre** is definitely worth seeing. The Melbourne-based **Australian Ballet** has regular seasons at the Sydney Opera House for its largely old-fashioned repertoire.

TICKETS AND INFORMATION

In general, tickets obtained directly from theatre box offices offer the best deal; you can view the seating plan and choose your price range. Alternatively, you can use a telephone booking agency such as **Ticketek** (9266 4800, www.ticketek.com) or **Ticketmaster7** (13 6100, www.ticketmaster7.com), but both charge booking fees. Major productions use one or the other agency, but if you're budget-conscious and prepared to take a gamble, you could always head instead to the **Halftix** booth at the Darling Park Monorail station on Sussex Street, CBD (9387 7755, www.halftix.com.au; open noon-5pm Mon-Sat; phone bookings 9am-5pm Mon-Fri). It sells unsold tickets for half-price on the day of the performance (24 hours in advance for matinées).

For more information on what's on where, check the 'Entertainment' pages of the *Sydney Morning Herald*'s Saturday edition.

Theatre

Companies

Bell Shakespeare Company

9241 2722/www.bellshakespeare.com.au.
Actor-director John Bell almost single-handedly
created this remarkable company of young actors
which is devoted almost exclusively to the works of
William Shakespeare. The company focuses on bold
story-telling and clear speaking. All the productions
are enjoyable and accessible, and now and again
actually quite brilliant. Based in Sydney, with
regular seasons at the Sydney Opera House, the
company also tours all over Australia.

Company B

9698 3344/www.belvoir.com.au.
The most creative mainstream theatre company in
Australia, Company B specialises in bold readings
of the classics and new Australian plays. Artistic
director Neil Armfield's productions of Ibsen and
Patrick White (Australia's Nobel Prize-winning
writer) have been among the landmarks. Many of
Australia's best actors, including John Gaden,
Richard Roxburgh and Gillian Jones, have created
their best work in collaboration with Armfield. The
company also works with Australia's top Aboriginal
artists, producing works about the Aboriginal experience in contemporary Australia. Company B's
home is the Belvoir Street Theatre (*see p251*).

Ensemble Theatre Company

9929 8877/www.ensemble.com.au.
Founded in 1958 by American Hayes Gordon, the
Ensemble is the oldest surviving professional theatre company in NSW. Gordon introduced Method
acting to Australia, and his Ensemble school has
produced some excellent talent. To its credit, the
company remains successful without government
funding. Among its best recent productions have
been several Arthur Miller plays and premières of
work by the country's most successful mainstream
writer, David Williamson. It has its own theatre in
Kirribilli (*see p251*) and also hires out the Sydney
Opera House Playhouse a couple of times a year.

Griffin Theatre Company

9332 1052/www.griffintheatre.com.au.
If contemporary Australian theatre has a spiritual
home, this is it. In the early 1970s the Stables
Theatre (*see p253*), then known as the Nimrod, was
the crucible in Sydney for a renaissance in play-
writing with a bold Australian flavour. The theatre's
home-grown tradition continues today: the rustic
19th-century building now hosts the Griffin Theatre
Company, which is dedicated solely to developing
and producing new Australian work. This is partly
facilitated by the Griffin's annual $5,000 playwrit-
ing competition. In the past, winning scripts have
included Noelle Janacsewska's *Songket* (2002) and
Brendan Cowell's *Rabbit* (2003).

Belvoir Street Theatre. *See p251.*

New Theatre

9519 3403/www.newtheatre.org.au.
Established in 1932, the New Theatre was born of a
Workers' Theatre tradition. It has expanded its
repertoire from its early propaganda plays, as it has
staged works by Shakespeare, Arthur Miller and
Chekhov as well as contemporary shows by playwrights from Australia and around the world; in
2003, for instance, it staged Martin McDonagh's hit,
The Beauty Queen of Leenane. The New Theatre
also offers rental space to many a good independent
production at its Newtown base (*see p251*).

PACT Youth Theatre

9550 2744/www.pact.net.au.
Sydney's perennially edgy youth theatre is where
students experiment with their own emerging identities. It regularly turns out exciting, boundary-
breaking work at its Erskineville base (*see p252*).

Sidetrack Performance Group

9560 1255/www.sidetrack.com.au.
For more than 20 years, Sidetrack has produced
some of the most interesting contemporary plays in
the country at Studio 9 at The Centre (*see p253*). The

Australia's top indigenous dance company: **Bangarra Dance Theatre**. *See p254.*

group is multilingual, multicultural and multi-skilled. One of its best productions, and typical of its topical work, was about the ruinous effects of the new Sydney airport flight paths. The sound of the jets regularly thundering overhead was worked into the show wonderfully.

Sydney Theatre Company

9250 1700/www.sydneytheatre.com.au.
Sydney's leading theatre company has gone from strength to strength since artistic director Robyn Nevin took over in 1999. Nevin made her name as one of Australia's finest actors before taking up directing, and her respect for the actors' craft has lured the crème de la crème back to the company: Actresses Judy Davis and Cate Blanchett both made appearances in the STC's 25th anniversary 2004 season. About 80% of the group's income is derived from the box office and the company has had to depend on sure-fire hits to balance the books, most notably in the form of the witty social comedies of David Williamson. The opening of the brand-new, 850-seat Sydney Theatre (*see p252* **Stage magic**) opposite the company's home at the Wharf Theatres (*see p254*) should give it scope for ever larger, and more adventurous productions.

Urban Theatre Projects

9707 2111/www.urbantheatre.com.au.
Urban Theatre Projects works with Sydney's diverse cultures to make contemporary theatre. Based in western Sydney, work is produced through collaboration between artists and local residents with a focus on storytelling and use of multimedia. UTP can be found performing in warehouses, railway stations, schools and sometimes even in theatres.

Venues

The plush, 1,200-seat **Theatre Royal** in the CBD (MLC Centre, King Street, 9224 8444, www.mlccentre.com.au) once hosted major productions on a regular basis but is now regarded as uneconomical. It does see some action around Sydney Festival time, however. The art deco-styled **Enmore Theatre** in Newtown (*see p222*), better known as a rock venue, is also used for touring theatre shows.

Belvoir Street Theatre

25 Belvoir Street, at Clisdell Street, Surry Hills (9699 3444/www.belvoir.com.au). CityRail Central. **Box office** 9.30am-6pm Mon, Tue; 9.30am-7.30pm

Wed-Sat; 2.30-7.30pm Sun. **Tickets** *Company B productions* $42; $20-$27.50 concessions. *Other productions* varies. **Credit** AmEx, BC, MC, V. **Map** p311 C5.

This one-time tomato sauce factory is home to innovative Company B (*see p249*), which has exclusive use of the audience-friendly, 350-seat Upstairs Theatre. The more intimate, 80-seat Downstairs space hosts Belvoir's B Sharp fringe season and other productions. Belvoir Street attracts Sydney's most discerning theatre-goers: opening nights are like a family get-together as devotees mingle in the crowded foyer with actors and other arty types.

Capitol Theatre

13 Campbell Street, between Pitt & George Streets, Haymarket (9320 5000/www.capitoltheatre.com.au). CityRail Central/Light Rail Capitol Square. **Box office** 9am-5pm Mon; 9am-8pm Tue-Sat; 1-5pm Sun. No telephone bookings. **Tickets** varies. **Credit** AmEx, BC, DC, MC, V. **Map** p311 B4.

Completed in 1893, the interior of the Capitol – originally known as the Hippodrome – was designed by an American theatre specialist to create the illusion of sitting in a neo-baroque courtyard under a brilliant night sky. Once reduced to the status of a porn cinema, the world's first full-stage production of *Jesus Christ Superstar* brought life back to the venue in 1969, while an extensive restoration in the late 1990s has added to its appeal. Some might find the experience kitsch, but the orchestra pit is big, the acoustics are good and the staging is often spectacular. It still hosts such big-budget musicals as the *Lion King* and the odd Sydney Festival blockbuster.

Darlinghurst Theatre

19 Greenknowe Avenue, Potts Point (8356 9987/www.darlinghursttheatre.com). CityRail Kings Cross/bus 311, 312. **Box office** 6-10pm daily. *Telephone bookings* 10am-6pm daily. **Tickets** $27; $21 concessions. **Credit** AmEx, BC, MC, V. **Map** p312 D3.

This new fringe venue is located on the edge of Kings Cross. Situated in a former sports club, it has comfortable seats and a pleasant atmosphere. The theatre co-produces a variety of updated classics in collaboration with a range of local and touring independent companies. For the medium-to-low ticket prices, the quality is usually quite high.

Ensemble Theatre

78 McDougall Street, at Willoughby Street, Kirribilli (9929 0644/www.ensemble.com.au). CityRail Milsons Point/ferry Kirribilli. **Box office** 9.30am-4.30pm Mon; 9.30am-7.30pm Tue-Sat; 1.30-7.30pm Sun. **Tickets** $40-$59; $35 concessions. **Credit** AmEx, BC, DC, MC, V.

American Hayes Gordon transformed an old boatshed at Kirribilli into Sydney's first in-the-round experimental space in the late 1950s, and the city had never seen anything like it: close-up performances, Method acting and productions stripped of stage illusion. The space has since been redesigned to create a back wall and the steeply sloped seating

is now more comfortable. Ably run since 1986 by Sandra Bates, the theatre juts into Sydney Harbour like the nose of a ship, with lovely water views from the foyer, and a restaurant.

The Footbridge Theatre

University of Sydney, Parramatta Road, between Glebe Point Road & Ross Street, Glebe (9692 9955). **Box office** 9am-5pm (university holidays 10am-3pm) Mon; 9am-7pm Tue-Sat or until start of show. **Tickets** varies. **Credit** AmEx, BC, DC, MC, V. **Map** p311 A4.

The 700-seat Footbridge is in dire need of a facelift. Between long periods of darkness, it hosts international touring shows, local productions of variable quality and sometimes amusing student revues.

The Lyric Theatre

Star City Casino, Pyrmont Street, between Jones Bay Road & Union Street, Pyrmont (9777 9000/www.starcity.com.au). Light Rail Star City/ferry Darling Harbour/free Star City shuttle bus/bus 888. **Box office** 9am-5pm Mon-Sat; 11am-5pm Sun; later on show days. No telephone bookings. **Tickets** varies. **Credit** AmEx, BC, MC, V. **Map** p310 A2.

Purpose-built to attract major international productions and equipped with state-of-the-art facilities for music theatre, the cavernous Lyric, housed in the Star City Casino, seats about 2,000 people.

New Theatre

542 King Street, at Bray Street, Newtown (9519 3403/www.newtheatre.org.au). CityRail St Peters/bus 422, 308, 370. **Box office** from 1hr before show Thur-Sun. **Tickets** $22; $17 concessions. **Credit** (phone bookings) BC, DC, MC, V.

An intimate 160-seater that's home to the New Theatre (*see p249*), Australia's oldest continuously producing company. The ethos has shifted in recent years from a traditional Workers' Theatre perspective to a diverse range of low-budget projects. The 2003 season saw an outstanding production of Irish writer Tom Murphy's *The Gigli Concert*, staged by the O'Punsky's Theatre Company, starring Maeliosa Stafford and Patrick Dickson, directed by John O'May. All names to look out for.

NIDA Theatre

National Institute of Dramatic Art, 215 Anzac Parade, opposite University of NSW, Kensington (9697 7613/www.nida.edu.au). Bus 302, 303, 391, 392, 399. **Tickets** varies. **Credit** AmEx, BC, DC, MC, V.

Australia's most eminent drama school (and the alma mater of the likes of Judy Davis, Mel Gibson, Cate Blanchett) has built a monument to itself with the help of a large bicentennial federal grant and major private donations, including a million dollars from Gibson himself. Sadly, for all the whiz-bang gadgetry, the venue has little atmosphere. It's used mostly for student productions and is also hired out to visiting shows. Parking is a problem. Get tickets from Ticketek (*see p248*).

Arts & Entertainment

Stage magic

Back in 1984, the Sydney Theatre Company brought new life to a derelict area of Sydney Harbour when it took possession of one of the Walsh Bay wharfs on the western side of the Harbour Bridge. Over the years the area has been redeveloped and it is now home to a mix of Australia's best performing arts companies including **Sydney Dance Company**, **Bangarra Dance Theatre** (for both, *see p254*) and the Australia Theatre for Young People, plus the Sydney Writers Festival (an annual scribes get-together). Redevelopment has also resulted in an increase in plush waterfront apartments, smart offices and trendy coffee shops. Now it looks as though the STC is about to inject even more 'wow-factor' into the area with its sensational new $40m venue, which opened in January 2004.

In this centre, architect Andrew Andersons (who designed the below-sea-level concourse for the Sydney Opera House) has created an 850-seat theatre of thrilling intimacy incorporating elements found at the site with the best of the new.

The theatre's façade uses specially shaped bricks to ape the style of Hickson Road's tall, patterned brick buildings. It has an impressive main entrance arch, with a line of light bulbs across the front providing an elegant Broadway touch. The foyers, fly tower and raked auditorium, with its dramatic, horseshoe-shaped upper circle and side boxes, are housed in a space created by the demolition of a 1950s warehouse. Every seat in the theatre has an excellent, up-close view. Back-of-house facilities have been located in old Bond Stores – historically used as warehouses for Sydney's export wool trade – with many original items of equipment retained in situ to give the theatre building a sense of character and history.

The new theatre intends to draw together neighbouring companies for one annual programme, and provide a diverse mix of quality performing arts. Both Sydney Dance Company and the Australian Ballet have booked seasons, and the theatre will be hired out by major companies touring from

Old Fitzroy Hotel

129 Dowling Street, at Cathedral Street, Woolloomooloo (9294 4296/www.oldfitzroy.com.au). CityRail Kings Cross. **Box office** from 6.30pm on show days. **Tickets** $24; $18 concessions; $30 beer/laksa/show. **Credit** BC, MC, V. **Map** p312 D3.
Founded in 1997 by a hip collective of Sydney actors, and located under a charming old pub, the Fitz regularly programmes first-time playwrights, as well as contemporary takes on both classics and modern nuggets. With a laksa bar and popular trivia nights, it's the closest thing to a club that the young end of Sydney's entertainment industry has.

PACT Theatre

107 Railway Parade, between Swanson & Sydney Streets, Erskineville (9550 2744/www.pact.net.au). CityRail Erskineville. **Box office** 10am-6pm Mon-Fri. **Tickets** $15; $10 concessions. **No credit cards. Map** p93.
This old factory space is home to the often exciting PACT Youth Theatre (*see p249*) and occasionally hosts itinerant fringe companies.

Parramatta Riverside Theatres

Corner of Church & Market Streets, Parramatta (9683 2511/www.riversideparramatta.com.au). CityRail Parramatta/ferry Charles Street. **Box office** 9am-5pm Mon-Fri; 9.30am-1pm Sat; and 1hr before show. **Tickets** varies. **Credit** AmEx, BC, MC, V.

This nicely designed but somewhat unloved two-theatre complex attracts international and locally produced shows to the Parramatta CBD. Located 20km (12.5 miles) west of the Sydney Opera House, it also serves as a hub for the Sydney Festival.

The Performance Space

199 Cleveland Street, between George & Pitt Streets, Redfern (9698 7235/www.performancespace.com. au). CityRail Central/bus 372. **Box office** 10am-6pm Mon-Fri; and 1hr before show. **Tickets** $20; $12 concessions. **Credit** BC, MC, V. **Map** p311 B5.
An old dance hall with a surviving sprung floor, TPS is home to anything otherwise homeless – from fearless, boundary-breaking multi-techno feats to off-the-planet performance art.

Seymour Centre

Corner of City Road & Cleveland Street, Chippendale (admin 9351 7944/box office 9351 7940). Bus 422, 423, 426, 428. **Box office** 9am-5pm Mon-Fri; 11am-3pm Sat. **Tickets** varies. **Credit** BC, MC, V.
The Seymour Centre caters for a grab-bag of productions that have usually failed to find a better venue elsewhere in the city. The main stage was designed with Tyrone Guthrie's open-stage model in mind. It's a total flop and even good shows struggle to survive the venue. The two smaller spaces are a little more appealing, coming to life during the Mardi Gras Arts Festival and for Sydney University Drama Society productions.

interstate and overseas. With such big ideas and such a bonzer building, the theatre certainly deserves success, and it will need it – as it's the only theatre of this size in Australia expected to run without the support of a government subsidy. STC already covers 80 per cent of its costs from the box office. Sydney's newest will have to do even better.

Sydney Theatre
22 Hickson Road, opposite Piers 6 & 7, Walsh Bay (box office 9250 1999/ www.sydneytheatre.org.au). CityRail/ferry Circular Quay then 15mins walk/bus 430. **Box office** 9am-8.30pm Mon-Sat. **Tickets** $63; $51 concessions (not Fri, Sat). **Credit** AmEx, BC, MC, V. **Map** p310 B1.

Stables Theatre
10 Nimrod Street, at Craigend Street, Kings Cross (9250 7799/www.griffintheatre.com.au). CityRail Kings Cross. **Box office** 9am-8.30pm Mon-Sat; and from 1hr before show. **Tickets** *Griffin productions* $38; $20-£28 concessions. *Other productions* varies. **Credit** AmEx, BC, DC, MC, V. **Map** p312 D3.
Seating a closely packed audience of 120, this place isn't much to look at but it has lots of historic character. Home to the Griffin Theatre Company (*see p249*), it offers some of the best new Australian writing and close-up performances by Sydney's finest actors. They might not be household names, but the actors here do outstanding work.

Star City Showroom
Star City Casino, 80 Pyrmont Street, Pyrmont (9777 9000/www.starcity.com.au). Light Rail Casino/ferry Darling Harbour/free Star City shuttle bus/bus 888. **Box office** 6-9pm Mon-Fri; 2-9pm Sat; 2-5pm Sun. No telephone bookings. **Tickets** varies. **Credit** AmEx, BC, DC, MC, V. **Map** p310 A2.
If your idea of a show is something loud, lewd and Las Vegas-influenced, Star City's 900-seat, cabaret-style theatre might be the place for you. For phone bookings, call Ticketek (*see p248*).

State Theatre
49 Market Street, between Pitt & George Streets, CBD (9373 6852/www.statetheatre.com.au). CityRail Town Hall. **Box office** 9am-5.30pm Mon-Fri; and

until 8pm on show days. No telephone bookings. **Tickets** varies. **Credit** AmEx, BC, DC, MC, V. **Map** p311 B3.
Designed at the dawn of talking pictures, the overwhelming baroque interior of the State Theatre boasts a wild mix of faux-classical statuary, strident imperial symbols and the second-largest crystal chandelier in the world, weighing in at 4,000kg (9,000lb). The 2,000-seat auditorium hosts the annual Sydney Film Festival, major stand-up gigs, occasional musicals and the odd Kylie concert.

Studio 9 at The Centre
142 Addison Road, at Illawarra Road, Marrickville (9560 1255). Bus 428. **Box office** 10am-5pm Mon-Fri; and from 1hr before show. **Tickets** *Sidetrack productions* $30; $23 concessions. *Other productions* varies. **Credit** BC, MC, V.
Base camp for multicultural ensemble Sidetrack Performance Group (*see p249*), this corrugated iron barn (fully appropriate for the kind of urban, creative works for which the group is best known) is located right under the airport flight path – so expect bone-rattling roars for art's sake.

Sydney Opera House
Bennelong Point, Circular Quay (box office 9250 7777/www.sydneyoperahouse.com) CityRail/ferry Circular Quay. **Box office** 9am-8.30pm Mon-Sat; and 2hrs before show Sun. **Tickets** varies. **Credit** AmEx, BC, DC, MC, V. **Map** p310 C1.

Despite its iconic status, the Opera House gets mixed reviews from the opera and theatre companies that actually use the place – but if you haven't seen a show here, you haven't seen Sydney. Refits are finally under way supervised by leading Sydney architect Richard Johnson with the cooperation and some input (via Majorca) from the building's original designer, Jørn Utzon. Among the planned improvements are a larger orchestra pit for the Opera Theatre, better backstage facilities for artists, and improved amenities for audiences, including better disabled access. More women's toilets are also promised. In addition to the Opera Theatre and larger Concert Hall, there are three theatre spaces. The Drama Theatre is used by the Sydney Theatre Company (see p250), and the smaller Playhouse by the Bell Shakespeare Company, the Ensemble Theatre (for both, see p249) and touring productions. The underground Studio also has its own subsidised programme featuring experimental theatre, dance, music and cabaret.

Wharf Theatres

Pier 4/5, Hickson Road, Walsh Bay (9250 1777/ www.sydneytheatre.com.au). CityRail/ferry Circular Quay then 15mins walk/bus 430. **Box office** 9am-8.30pm Mon-Sat. **Tickets** $63; $51 concessions (not Fri, Sat). **Credit** AmEx, BC, MC, V. **Map** p310 B1.
A converted wharf and warehouse on the western side of the Harbour Bridge, this fantastic structure retains its industrial charm, complete with exposed iron beams and lots of wood. The complex houses Sydney Theatre Company's artistic, management and production staff, rehearsal space and a lovely restaurant, as well as two theatres. Wharf 1 presents the best of the STC's smaller productions; Wharf 2 is home to the STC's Blueprints season of new writing, the education programme and the Wharf Revue. The company's largest productions are now staged in the new Sydney Theatre across the road (see p252 **Stage magic**). A new bus service (the 430) has now made Walsh Bay more accessible, by linking it with Circular Quay, Wynyard and Town Hall.

Dance

In addition to the companies listed here, you might want to also keep an eye out for Gideon Obazarnek's groovy **Chunky Move** company. Based in Melbourne, it usually visits Sydney once a year and is well worth catching.

Australian Ballet

1300 369 741/www.australianballet.com.au.
Australia's national classical ballet company is based in Melbourne. It usually performs two seasons a year at the Sydney Opera House (see above) in April/May and November/December; tickets cost $20-$110. The company flourished under founding artistic director Peggy van Praagh (1962-74) – who attracted guest artists of the calibre of Rudolf Nureyev and Margot Fonteyn – and Maina Gielgud

(1983-96), who encouraged works by up-and-coming young Australian choreographers. Current artistic director David McAllister took over in 2001 after 17 years as a dancer with the company. Since then, more column inches have been devoted to the group's backroom squabbles than to its artistic output. In fact, at the end of the 2003 season another six dancers left to take up work elsewhere showing that tension is still an issue. While technical standards remain high, the company seems to have a problem finding a vital contemporary role; its staunchly conservative fan base has also hampered its efforts to take on a more modern repertoire.

Bangarra Dance Theatre

9251 5333/www.bangarra.com.au.
Bangarra is Australia's leading contemporary indigenous dance company. Under the artistic direction of Stephen Page since 1991, it has impressed audiences throughout Australia and abroad with its theatrical boldness and the intense spirituality of its work, merging timeless Aboriginal traditions with contemporary dance aesthetics. Based at the Wharf Theatres (see above), each year Bangarra performs a significant new work in Australia's main cities, as well as undertaking regional and international tours. The company played a major role in the opening ceremony of the 2000 Olympics.

National Aboriginal & Islander Skills Development Association

9252 0199/www.naisda.com.au.
Based in the Rocks, NAISDA has its roots in the early '70s movement that saw the development of programmes to help Australia's indigenous people establish control of their cultural heritage. AIDT (Aboriginal & Islander Dance Theatre) and NAISDA's student ensemble regularly perform their fusion of traditional and contemporary dance around Sydney. Often short of cash, NAISDA has recently been thrown a lifeline in the form of a gift from writer Patrick White's estate.

Sydney Dance Company

9221 4811/www.sydneydance.com.au.
In 1976, aged 26, Graeme Murphy was appointed artistic director of what was then the fledgling Dance Company of NSW, with dancer Janet Vernon (his partner) as associate director. In 1979 the name was changed to the Sydney Dance Company, and neither the troupe nor its artistic directors have looked back. The 18-strong ensemble has a huge local following and so it's no surprise that its long annual seasons at the Sydney Opera House (see above) often sell out. Murphy is a prodigious creator, and the boldness and over-the-top sensuality of his work accurately mirrors Sydney's brash physicality. While some prefer the large, narrative-based works, such as *Berlin* and *Tivoli*, others favour more abstract creations such as the recent *Ellipse*. The company has performed in more than 100 cities around the world; it also holds workshops and classes at its base at Pier 4 in Walsh Bay.

Trips Out of Town

Short Trips

You don't have to go far to find real Australian wilderness.

You could easily spend weeks in Sydney and still not experience everything on offer, but you'll be missing out if you spend all your time in the city. You can't head east, of course, unless you feel like swimming to New Zealand, so you'll just have to content yourself with the mountain scenery, historic towns and expanses of bushland to the west, or the pristine beaches, rainforest and national parks along the coasts to the south and north. Two hours' drive north of Sydney are the wineries of the Hunter Valley, while south lie the gentle rolling hills and the period villages of the Southern Highlands, and further on, the federal capital, Canberra.

Just about everywhere is easy to get to by car, and, where possible, we've included details of local trains, buses and internal flights. Unless stated otherwise, room rates are for a double room – weekday rates are often cheaper than weekend rates – and restaurant prices are for a main course at dinner, without drink. Journey times are from central Sydney.

INFORMATION

CountryLink (central reservations 13 2232, www.countrylink.info) operates trains and coaches in NSW, the ACT, Queensland and Victoria. Visit its **NSW Travel Centre** at Railway Concourse, Wynyard CityRail station (9224 4744, open 8.30am-5pm Mon-Fri) for details of its good-value, multi-day train and tour packages to destinations in NSW.

For general information on areas around Sydney, visit the **Sydney Visitor Centre** (*see p292*). **Tourism New South Wales** (9931 1111, www.tourism.nsw.gov.au/home) will direct you to a regional tourist office.

Heading West

The Blue Mountains region is top of the must-see list of destinations within striking distance of Sydney. It's a spectacular wilderness, so resistant to the city's westward sprawl that it can hide in its midst a species of tree (the Wollemi pine) that was thought to have been extinct for 150 million years. With dainty villages where portraits of Queen Elizabeth II crown mantelpieces and neat English gardens

vie with native plants and bushes, the area embodies the struggle by European settlers to tame the Australian landscape and recreate a little piece of home in cooler mountain climes.

The Blue Mountains – in reality a series of hills marked by dramatic gorges – are part of the Great Dividing Range, which cuts the seaboard off from the country's arid interior. In summer, with the eucalyptus oil rising off of the trees and refracting the sun's rays, the mountains really do look blue. The **Blue Mountains National Park**, which covers nearly 250,000 hectares (617,750 acres), is grouped together with six other nearby national parks to form the **Greater Blue Mountains World Heritage Area**.

The best way to explore the region is on one of the many signed bushwalks (ranging from a few minutes' to several days' trekking), or by trying a more challenging pursuit such as abseiling or mountaineering. Plenty of day tour operators provide a cursory look around; the smaller outfits (*see p258* **Top tours**) have a more intimate knowledge of the mountains. Another option is the double-decker **Blue Mountains Explorer Bus** (4782 4807, www.explorerbus.com.au). It leaves from outside Katoomba train station every hour from 9.30am to 4.30pm daily, stopping at 27 attractions, resorts, galleries and tearooms in and around Katoomba and Leura. You can get on and off as often as you want ($25, $12.50-$22 concessions, $62.50 family). You can also link the bus with a CityRail train from Sydney.

Of the 26 townships in the Blue Mountains, **Katoomba** is the most popular starting point, thanks to its proximity to attractions such as the **Three Sisters** rock formation near Echo Point, and the world's steepest rail incline, the **Scenic Railway**, and the equally giddy **Scenic Skyway** cable car, which travels on a six-minute return trip 300 metres (984 feet) above the Jamison Valley. If you've got some time, descend the precipitous 841-step **Giant Staircase** next to the Sisters, and then do the two-and-a-half-hour walk through the Jamison Valley to the foot of the railway.

Unfortunately, Katoomba itself has a high level of unemployment, and its attractions really don't extend beyond its art deco façades, the 1880s **Carrington Hotel** (*see p257*) and the intimate **Paragon Café**.

The **Scenic Skyway** cable car soaring above the **Three Sisters**.

Linked to Katoomba by a panoramic cliff drive is **Leura**, with its slightly snooty but comfortable guesthouses, shops, galleries and manicured gardens. Just down the road are the **Wentworth Falls**, another much-loved Blue Mountains attraction. The water has been known to flow upwards when strong winds blow up the valley. There's an excellent, if arduous, undercliff/overcliff walk nearby – count on about three to four hours' walking.

Further into the mountains beyond Katoomba, the **Hydro Majestic Hotel** (*see p258*) in Medlow Bath is popular for coffee with a view. More down to earth is the village of **Mount Victoria**, which is the starting point for many fine mountain hikes.

On the northern side of the mountains, off the Bells Line of Road above the Grose Valley, is the quintessentially English hamlet of **Mount Wilson**. This sweet little place is a riot of russet when the leaves change in the autumn, and its also where Nobel prize-winning author Patrick White once lived. His family's old summer house, **Withycombe** (built 1878), is now a classy guesthouse (4756 2106) with one of the many serene gardens in the area. For flora that's more native, continue on to the hushed **Cathedral of Ferns** at the end of the lane. But if it's European order you're after, head for the **Mount Tomah Botanic Gardens** (4567 2154, www.rbgsyd.gov.au).

You'll need to travel to the south-western edge of the Blue Mountains to reach the other main attraction in the area: the **Jenolan Caves** (Jenolan Caves Road, 6359 3311, www.jenolancaves.org.au). These are a tangled series of extraordinary underground limestone caverns within a large and peaceful nature reserve. They're open 9am to 5pm daily ($15-$27.50, $39 family). Some caverns are large and easily accessible; some, such as the **River Cave**, feature stalagmites and stalactites; others, such as the **Adventure Cave**, must be explored in helmet and overalls. Be aware of conditions before you enter – some involve a good deal of clambering around.

Scenic Skyway & Scenic Railway

Corner of Cliff & Violet Streets, Katoomba (Skyway 4782 2699/Railway 4782 2699). **Open** *9am-5pm daily.* **Tickets** *Skyway & Railway return trip $14; $7 concessions.* **No credit cards**.
The Skyway will be closed from May to November 2004 for renovations.

Where to stay & eat

Carrington Hotel

15-47 Katoomba Street, Katoomba (4782 1111/fax 4782 7073/www.thecarrington.com.au). **Rates** *B&B from $119.* **Credit** *DC, MC, V.*
A gorgeous, rambling, British Raj-style hotel with lots of antiques and oodles of charm.

Top tours

Plenty of tour operators run interesting and entertaining day trips in and around the Blue Mountains. Some of these tours start off in Sydney, while others leave from Katoomba. The following tour companies are recommended:

Australian School of Mountaineering

4782 2014/www.asmguides.com.
Based in Katoomba, ASM has provided outdoor training and guiding for more than two decades. It runs an impressive range of canyoning, rock climbing and abseiling trips; prices vary.

Fantastic Aussie Tours

4782 1866/1300 300 915/
www.fantastic-aussie-tours.com.au.
Rates from $75.
A day tour to Jenolan Caves from Katoomba, with cave entrance. Costs vary depending on the type of tour.

High 'n Wild

4782 6224/www.high-n-wild.com.au.
Rates from $85.
This Katoomoba-based adventure outfit runs canyoning expeditions involving swimming, wading, and squeezing through tight spaces.

Oz Trek Adventure Tours

9360 3444/www.oztrek.com.au.
Rates $54; $43 concessions.
A packed day trip from Sydney includes a visit to the Olympic site at Homebush, a tour of the major Blue Mountain sites and a one- to two-hour bushwalk.

Visitours

9909 0822/www.visitours.com.au.
Rates from $90.
The Blue Mountains tour from Sydney also includes a stop at Featherdale Wildlife Park and the Olympic Park. Learn to throw a boomerang and play the didgeridoo.

Wonderbus

9555 9800/www.wonderbus.com.au.
Rates from $70.
This group offers a range of tours to the Blue Mountains, including a day trip from Sydney that involves three hours of bushwalking and covers most of the area's main sites.

Hydro Majestic Hotel

Great Western Highway, Medlow Bath (4788 1002/
fax 4788 1063/www.hydromajestic.com.au). **Rates** from $175 midweek; $290 weekend. **Credit** AmEx, BC, DC, MC, V.
An upmarket, historic hotel with great views and a Victorian feel. If you don't stay the night, then at least come here for tea and scones.

Jenolan Caves House

Jenolan Caves (tel & fax 6359 3322/www.lisp.
com.au/~jenolan). **Rates** (per person) B&B from $95 midweek; $125 weekend. **Credit** AmEx, BC, DC, MC, V.
Part of the caves complex, this dark wood-panelled hotel with roaring fires has the feel of an English country house. Next door, the Gatehouse Jenolan offers four-bed dorms for $60 per room.

Katoomba YHA Hostel

207 Katoomba Street, Katoomba (4782 1416/
www.yha.com.au). **Rates** $20-$74 dorm; $64-$74 double; $108 family room. **Credit** BC, MC, V.
An excellent modern hostel in a historic 1930s building right in the centre of Katoomba.

Lilianfels Blue Mountains

Lilianfels Avenue, Echo Point, Katoomba (4780
1200/1800 024 452/www.lilianfels.com.au). **Rates** from $250 midweek; $400 weekend. **Credit** AmEx, BC, DC, MC, V.
This place is well known as the poshest accommodation in the mountains, with two famed restaurants and great views.

Getting there

By car

Springwood, Faulconbridge, Wentworth Falls, Leura, Katoomba & Mount Victoria
Take Western Motorway (Route 4) and/or Great Western Highway (Route 32). It's 109km (68 miles) from Sydney to Katoomba; journey takes about 2hrs.
Kurrajong & Mount Tomah
Take Great Western Highway (Route 32) or Western Motorway (Route 4); turn off to Richmond via Blacktown; then Bells Line of Road (Route 40). Mount Wilson is 6km (3.75 miles) off Bells Line of Road.
Jenolan Caves
Take Great Western Highway (Route 32) via Katoomba and Mount Victoria; then turn south at Hartley; its another 46km (29 miles) to the caves.

By train

Trains depart hourly from Sydney's Central Station. It's about 2hrs to Katoomba.

Tourist information

Blue Mountains Information Centre

Echo Point Road, Katoomba (1300 653 408/
www.bluemountainstourism.org.au). **Open** 9am-5pm daily.
Also check out website www.katoomba-nsw.com.

The long, lush, meandering path of the **Hawkesbury River**.

Heading North

Hawkesbury River

The Hawkesbury River, which for much of its length skirts the outer edges of Australia's biggest city, is a great greenish-brown giant, licking over 1,000 kilometres (620 miles) of foreshore as it curls first north-east and then, from Wisemans Ferry, south-east towards the sea, emptying into an estuary at Broken Bay. The river's fjord-like saltwater creeks and inlets are ideal for exploring by boat, and houseboating holidays are popular.

The town of **Windsor** retains many of its original buildings, as well as its waterwheel and charm. Among its stalwarts is the oldest inn in Australia still being used for its original purpose (the **Macquarie Arms**, built in 1815), Australia's oldest courthouse (1822), **St Matthew's Anglican Church**, built by convict labour from a design by convict architect Francis Greenway (also in 1822), and the oldest Catholic primary school still in use (1836). Also of note is **John Tebbutt's house and observatory**, with its outsized telescope.

It's worth taking a cruise with **Hawkesbury Heritage Discovery Tours** (4577 6882), as you'll get the enthusiastic low-down on the area's history from a local guide. Prices vary according to the tour and the size of the group.

Within easy reach of Windsor, there's more colonial architecture at **Richmond**, a tree-lined garden town whose railway station dates back to 1822, and **Ebenezer**, with Australia's oldest church (on Coromandel Road, built 1809).

The Hawkesbury's change of course is marked by an S-bend at **Wisemans Ferry**, another of the river's historic villages. It has the country's oldest ferry service, which still runs 24 hours a day (and is one of the few remaining free rides in New South Wales). On the far side of the ferry, to your right, is a section of the convict-built Great Northern Road, once 264 kilometres (164 miles) long, which shows just what sweat and toil really mean. In contrast, a pleasant place to hole up in, or to go for a hole-in-one on its riverside golf course, is the **Retreat at Wisemans** (*see p260*).

Up the road in the Macdonald River Valley, at the secluded hamlet of **St Albans**, is another colonial inn, the **Settlers Arms** (1 Wharf Street, 4568 2111) and two kilometres from here on Settlers Road in the Old Cemetery lies the grave of William Douglas, a First Fleeter who died in 1838. Strong rumours also suggest that St Albans was Windsor magistrates' preferred venue for illicit nooky over the years.

The lower reaches of the Hawkesbury are its most spectacular, with steep-sided forested banks and creeks branching off its wide sweep. Near the end of **Berowra Creek** (west of the Pacific Highway), at the foot of two deep, bush-covered hills, is beautiful **Berowra Waters**.

There's not much here apart from a small car ferry, a cluster of bobbing boats and a few restaurants offering fine cuisine (including Hawkesbury oysters). Much of the remainder of the river, as it makes its way to the sea, is equally tranquil – notably the slender fingers of water that make up **Cowan Creek** (east of the Pacific Highway). It's here, in the sweeping expanse of the **Ku-ring-gai Chase National Park**, that many people choose to cruise or moor for a spot of fishing.

If you haven't got time for houseboating, Australia's last riverboat postman may be the answer. The four-hour cruise from Brooklyn allows you to participate in the delivery of mail to such local personalities as the Pink Elephant, while taking in the scenery – giving you an inside view that few ever see. The boat leaves Brooklyn Wharf at 9.30am weekdays, excluding public holidays; details on 9985 7566.

Otherwise, you could always hike from Berowra railway station down to Berowra Waters along a fascinating, well-marked bush track (part of the Great North Walk). It takes about four hours round-trip.

Where to stay & eat

Able Hawkesbury Houseboats
River Road, Wisemans Ferry (4566 4308/1800 024 979/www.hawkesburyhouseboats.com.au). **Rates** from $440 (2 nights midweek). **Credit** AmEx, BC, MC, V.
Choose from seven different sizes of boat, ranging from 7.7m (26ft) to 14.5m (47ft) in length.

Berowra Waters Café
199 Bay Road, Berowra (9456 4665). **Main courses** $9-$15. **Credit** BC, MC, V.
A great setting with views across the water. Serves fish and chips in various guises. BYO.

The Court House Retreat
19 Upper Macdonald Road, St Albans (4568 2042/ fax 9871 0592/www.courthousestalbans.com.au). **Rates** from $180. **Credit** BC, MC, V.
B&B accommodation (four double rooms) in a historic sandstone building that once housed a courtroom, police station and lock-up.

The Retreat at Wisemans
Old Northern Road, Wisemans Ferry (4566 4422/ fax 4566 4613/www.wisemans.com.au). **Rates** from $99 per person. **Credit** AmEx, BC, DC, MC, V.
Comfortable rooms with views of the golf course or river. The Riverbend Restaurant, serving Mod Oz food, is recommended.

Ripples Houseboat Hire
87 Brooklyn Road, Brooklyn (9985 7333/ www.ripples.com.au). **Rates** from $500 (2 nights midweek). **Credit** AmEx, BC, MC, V.
Two kinds of boats, sleeping up to six or ten.

Getting there

By car
Richmond & Windsor
Via Hornsby Pacific Highway (Route 83) to Hornsby; Galston Road; then Pitt Town Road.
Via Pennant Hills Epping Road (Route 2) to Pennant Hills; then Route 40.
Via Parramatta Western Motorway (Route 4) to Parramatta; then Route 40.
It's 59km (37 miles) from Sydney to Windsor, and the journey takes between 60 and 90mins.
Wisemans Ferry & St Albans
Pacific Highway (Route 83) to Hornsby; Galston Road; then Old Northern Road.
Berowra Waters
Pacific Highway (Route 83); 12kms (7 miles) north of Hornsby, Berowra turn-off signposted. The Brooklyn turn-off is 12km (7 miles) further north.

By train
Richmond & Windsor
There's a regular train service to Windsor and the upper Hawkesbury River area on the Richmond line (via Blacktown) from Central Station. Journey time is around 1hr.
Berowra Waters
The main Sydney–Newcastle line from Central Station goes to Berowra Waters (via Berowra Station) and Brooklyn (via Hawkesbury River Station). The trip takes about 40mins (not all trains stop at both stations).

By bus
For details of coach services to the Hawkesbury region, contact the local tourist office (*see below*) or the CountryLink NSW Travel Centre (*see p256*).

Tourist information

Hawkesbury River Information Centre
5 Bridge Street, Brooklyn (9985 7947/ www.hawkesbury-river.com.au). **Open** 9am-5pm Mon-Fri; 9am-4pm Sat; 10am-3pm Sun.

Tourism Hawkesbury
Ham Common, Windsor Road, Clarendon (4588 5895/www.hawkesburyweb.com.au). **Open** 9am-5pm Mon-Fri; 10am-3pm Sat; 10am-2pm Sun.

Hunter Valley

The second most visited region in New South Wales after the Blue Mountains is the state's main wine-growing region, located two hours north of Sydney. You come here for one thing: wine and wine-tasting. The region around the main town of **Pokolbin** boasts more than 50 wineries (from the smallest boutiques to the big boys, such as Lindemans), which offer tastings and cellar-door sales of wine ranging from semillons and shiraz to buttery chardonnays.

Mingled among the vineyards are award-winning restaurants and luxury hotels – but there are plenty of cheaper options too.

While such wine-based indulgence has put the Hunter firmly on the tourist map, the area's personality is schizophrenically bound up with the vastly different industry of coal mining. The very waterway from which the region gets its name was originally known as the Coal River (it was renamed in 1797 after the then NSW governor, John Hunter), and the founder of the Hunter's wine-making industry, Scottish civil engineer James Busby, arrived in Australia in 1824 partly to oversee coal-mining activities in nearby Newcastle. But, while the Hunter Valley once boasted the largest shaft mine in the southern hemisphere, which held the world's record for coal production in an eight-hour shift (Richmond Main Colliery, now a museum and open irregularly), all but two of its mines have now shut down.

The wine industry, which originally sprouted from the humble beginning of little more than just a few hundred European vine cuttings, was introduced to the Hunter Valley in the 1830s, and has fared rather better. Seeing out the tough 19th century, then the Depression of the 1930s, and later fighting off competition from other antipodean wine regions, such as

South Australia, the Hunter made it to the 1970s wine-rush, and ever since then, it has done little but flourish.

Despite its small area – the main vineyard district north of the town of **Cessnock** is only a few kilometres square – the sheer number of wineries in the Lower Hunter Valley can present the wine tourist (as opposed to the expert) with a problem. Namely, where to start? Inevitably, familiarity leads many to the bigger, more established wineries, and this is a good way of gaining an insight into wine-growing traditions. Large family companies in Pokolbin, such as **Tyrrells** (Broke Road, 4993 7000), **Draytons** (Oakey Creek Road, 4998 7513) and **Tullochs** (Glen Elgin Estate Debeyers Road, 4998 7580) have been producing wine in the area for more than a century, while at **Lindemans** (McDonalds Road, 4998 7684) there's a museum exhibiting old wine-making equipment. Other big wineries, such as **McGuigan Brothers** (McDonalds Road, 4998 7402), offer full on-site facilities, including accommodation, a gallery, a restaurant and crumbly handmade cheeses from the Hunter Valley Cheese Company.

But it would be a shame to miss out on the smaller enterprises. Places such as **Oakvale** (set against the Brokenback Range, Broke Road,

Explore **Hunter Valley**'s many wineries.

he time and space for a more
nce of tasting. Many of these
...es are set within picturesque
...undings. The grounds of **Pepper Tree
Wines** (Halls Road, 4998 7539) incorporate a
former Brigidine convent, now the area's
swishest guesthouse (*see p263*), which was
moved lock, stock and barrel to the Hunter for
the purpose. Further afield, in Rothbury, the
40-hectare (100-acre) **Wandin Valley Estate**
(*see p263*) offers accommodation in villas,
and has its own cricket ground.

Look out for vintages produced in 1988, 2000
and 2003, for these were the best years in the
Hunter valley for decades.

Since the Hunter is reasonably flat and
compact, and the wineries never far apart, it's
a good place to ditch four-wheel transport.
Bikes are available from some guesthouses for
a small charge, while **Grapemobile** (0500 804
039, www.grapemobile.com.au) hires out bikes
and also runs enjoyable day and overnight
cycling and walking tours of the wineries from
Cessnock. Finally, if you're not high enough
already, see the regimented rows of vines
from above with a sunrise balloon flight;
try **Balloon Aloft** (Lot 1, Main Road,
North Rothbury, 4938 1955, 1800 028 568,
www.balloonaloft.com) – prices vary based
on the number of people and the season.

BARRINGTON TOPS

Although it's less than an hour's drive north of
the Hunter Valley, the Barrington Tops is as
different from the wine-growing district as it's
possible to be. A National Park with a World
Heritage listing, its upper slopes are thick with
sub-tropical rainforest containing thousand-
year-old trees, clean mountain streams and
abundant wildlife. With its swimming holes,
camping and bushwalking, the Barrington
Tops is a domain for out-there enthusiasts. The
area can also be explored with mechanical help:
try eco-specialist **Bush Track Tours** (9299
0991, www.bushtracktours.com, from $195 for
a full-day tour from Sydney).

Further south are green hillocks and greener
valleys, the sort of landscape that insists you
jump out of bed straight on to the back of a
horse or a mountain bike. If you have your
own transport and a three or four days to
spare, you might consider visiting the triangle
of attractions in this area – the Hunter Valley,
Barrington Tops and Port Stephens.

Wine tours

While many of the Hunter Valley vineyards
offer tastings at the cellar door, the local cops
rightly take exception to drink-driving, so the

best idea may be on an organised tour.
Wonderbus (*see p258* **Top tours**) runs a
wine trip, and the **Hunter Valley Visitor
Centre** (*see p264*) has details of other outfits.

Activity Tours Australia

9904 5730/www.activitytours.com.au. **Rates** $95;
$89 concessions.
Day trips from Sydney to the Hunter Valley, taking
in six wineries, a winery tour to see how wine is
made, and a cheese factory. Maximum 19 people.

Hunter Vineyard Tours

4991 1659/www.huntervineyardtours.com.au.
Rates $45; $65 with lunch.
Full-day tour in either 12- or 21-seat buses, taking
in five wineries (lunch optional) in the Cessnock area.
Pick up is from local hotels.

Trekabout Tours

4990 8277/www.hunterweb.com.au/trekabout.
Rates $28 half-day (Mon-Fri only); $44 full-day.
Half- or full-day winery tours for up to six people.
The shorter tour visits five to six wineries; the full-
day option gets to nine wineries. You'll need to get
yourself to the Hunter Valley – pick-up is from
hotels in the Cessnock/Pokolbin area.

Where to stay & eat

Most Hunter Valley guesthouses will not take
bookings for less than two nights, especially
over weekends. Rates are considerably cheaper
midweek. There are more – and cheaper –
hotels and motels in Cessnock. The first two
places are in the Barrington Tops region; the
rest are in the Hunter Valley.

Barrington Guest House

*2940 Salisbury Road, 30mins drive from Dungog
(4995 3212/fax 4995 3248/www.barringtonguest
house.com.au).* **Rates** (full board, shared bathroom)
from $95 per person. **Credit** AmEx, BC, DC, MC, V.
Interesting guesthouse-style accommodation and
luxury huts right on the edge of the rainforest. Semi-
tame kangaroos stretch out on the lawns and the
trees are thick with birdlife.

The Barringtons Country Retreat

*1941 Chichester Dam Road, 15mins from Dungog
(4995 9269/fax 4995 9279/www.thebarringtons.
com.au).* **Rates** (min 2 nights) from $60 per person.
Credit BC, MC, V.
If you like to flirt with rural surroundings safe in the
knowledge that modern comforts are close at hand,
try this place. Log cabins overlooking the valley, spa
baths and imaginative cooking at moderate rates.

Casuarina Restaurant & Country Inn

*Hermitage Road, Pokolbin (4998 7888/fax 4998
7692/www.casuarinainn.com.au).* **Rates** suite
$285 Mon-Thur, Sun; $310 Fri, Sat. **Credit** AmEx,
BC, DC, MC, V.

Wild thing

So you've gawped at the koalas in Taronga Zoo or Featherdale Wildlife Park, but where can you see some of Australia's amazing wildlife in the wild? Surprisingly, perhaps, Sydney itself is a good place to start, and there's more a little further afield.

Head to the rainforest area near the duck ponds in the **Royal Botanical Gardens** (see p65) and look up: you're sure to see some large, noisy, **grey-headed flying foxes** (aka fruit bats – pictured) hanging upside down. They're actually quite controversial Sydney residents; the locals love them, but they tend to strip the branches around the tops of their favourite roosting trees.

Also common are **sacred ibis**, funny-looking white birds with long, downward-curving black beaks. Australia's version of the urban pigeon, they strut around parks looking for scraps. **Sulphur-crested cockatoos** can be seen in the reserve alongside **Balmoral Beach** (see p120) and the southern beachside suburb of **Bundeena** (see p117). **Possums** are regular visitors to Sydney's suburbs too, but only come out at dusk.

If you're visit one of the national parks, you might come across a snake – probably a **red-bellied black snake**. They're poisonous, but usually prefer to make a dash for it. **Wallabies** are relatively common, but best spotted at dusk and dawn. Driving out of Sydney you might spot dead kangaroos and wombats alongside the road – yes, it's

unfortunate for them, but it also means that there's probably some healthy individuals out there. The best place to see **kangaroos** in the wild is at **Jervis Bay** (see p265), where you can even camp among eastern grey roos. An oddity is **Pebbly Beach** (see p266), 20 minutes south of Ulladulla, where kangaroos appear in the daytime, and have even been known to sunbathe on the sand.

Don't expect to see **koalas** in the bush around Sydney – they're getting pretty scarce. The best place is to the north, near **Port Stephens** (see p264). As for **emus,** you'll have to head to the arid lands in the south of the state. And **sharks**? Yes they're around, but, lucky for you, attacks are very rare.

Over-the-top themed suites are the thing here: pick from the Moulin Rouge, the Oriental, the Bordello, Casanova's Loft, the Mariner's Suite, Out of Africa, Edwardian, Palais Royale and, finally, Romeo's Retreat. Plus a pool, tennis court and a pretty good Mediterranean-style restaurant.

Hunter Valley Gardens Lodge
Next to McGuigan Brothers Winery, corner of Broke Road & McDonalds Road, Pokolbin (4998 7600/ fax 4998 7710/www.hvg.com.au). **Rates** B&B from $245 Mon-Thur, Sun; $543 Fri, Sat. **Credit** AmEx, BC, DC, MC, V.
A pleasant place to lay your head, right in the heart of the wine area. The associated Harrigan's Irish Pub also has pleasant rooms from $155.

Peppers Convent Guest House
Grounds of Pepper Tree Wines, Halls Road, Pokolbin (winery 4998 7539/convent 4998 7764/ fax 4998 7323/www.peppers.com.au). **Rates** from $328 Mon-Thur, Sun; $364 Fri, Sat. **Credit** AmEx, BC, DC, MC, V.

The ultimate indulgence, with lots of antiques and surrounding vineyards. Robert's restaurant (4998 7330), one of the country's classiest, is also here.

Wandin Valley Estate
Wilderness Road, Lovedale (4930 7317/fax 4930 7814/www.wandinvalley.com.au). **Rates** from $140. **Credit** AmEx, DC, MC, V.
Winery accommodation in four self-contained, well-appointed, villas five minutes from Pokolbin.

Getting there

By car
Lower Hunter Valley
Sydney to Newcastle Freeway (Route 1) to Freemans Interchange; then turn off to Cessnock (Route 82). Alternatively, leave Route 1 at Calga; head through Central Mangrove towards Wollombi; then turn off to Cessnock (Route 132). Journey time: 2hrs. The main wine-growing district around Pokolbin and Rothbury is about 12km (7 miles) north-west of Cessnock.

Barrington Tops

Direct route Sydney to Newcastle Freeway (F3/Route 1) to Maitland turn-off on New England Highway (Route 15); Paterson Road; then turn right for Dungog approx 5km (3 miles) beyond Paterson. **Via Hunter Valley** Follow signs from Cessnock to Maitland (via Kurri Kurri) then as above. The journey takes about 3hrs.

By train

Dungog, just south of Barrington Tops, is served by a few daily trains from Sydney (journey time just over 3hrs) via Newcastle (90mins). Some guesthouses will pick up from Dungog.

By bus

Rover Coaches (4990 1699/1800 801 012, www.rovercoaches.com.au) runs a daily service to the Hunter Valley from Sydney (departing at 7.30am, returning at 7.30pm), plus day and weekend tours of the region; call for departure points. Keans Travel (4990 5000, 1800 043 339) also operates a regular coach service (not Sat).

Tourist information

Gloucester Visitor Information Centre

27 Denison Street, Gloucester (6558 1408/ www.gloucester.org.au). **Open** 8.30am-5pm Mon-Fri; 8.45am-3.30pm Sat, Sun.
For information on the Barrington Tops.

Hunter Valley Wine Country Visitor Centre

111 Main Road, Pokolbin (4990 4477/www.wine country.com.au). **Open** 9am-5pm Mon-Fri; 9.30am-5pm Sat; 9.30am-3.30pm Sun.
You can also book accommodation here.

Port Stephens

The third pointer in a triangle of northern attractions that include the Hunter Valley and Barrington Tops, Port Stephens Bay is a beautiful stretch of water most famous for its whale and dolphin cruises. Two pods of dolphins – around 70 individuals – inhabit the bay, and your chances of getting up close to them are very high. Whales come into the calmer waters of the bay on their migration route from Antarctica.

The main town in the area is **Nelson Bay**, on the northern bank of the harbour, where you'll find hotels, restaurants and takeaways.

Several operators run good dolphin and whale-watching tours. Highly recommended is a cruise on **Imagine** (77 Sandy Road, Corlette, 4984 9000, www.portstephens.org.au/imagine) a luxury catamaran operated out of Nelson Bay Marina by Frank Future and Yves Papin. All year except June and July they offer a daily two-hour dolphin trip departing at 10.30am

($20 adults, $13-$16.50 concessions), and a range of longer cruises departing from D'Albora Marina. There's a boom net on board, which is lowered over the edge for thrill-seekers to lie in and get really close to the dolphins. They also operate humpback whale cruises from June to mid November (*see also p266* **Thar she blows!**).

You can also go looking for dolphins in a kayak with **Blue Water Sea Kayaking** (40 Victoria Parade, Nelson Bay, 4981 5177, www.seakayaking.com.au). **Wonderbus** (*see p258* **Top tours**) also runs daily tours from Sydney to Port Stephens that include wine-tasting in the Hunter Valley.

Another option for nature lovers is a visit to the **Tomaree National Park** (4984 8200, www.nationalparks.nsw.gov.au), which is on the southern shore of the inner harbour. Here, you can see low-flying pelicans skidding in to land on the water, and there's a large breeding colony of koalas at **Lemon Tree Passage**.

Where to stay & eat

Peppers Anchorage Port Stephens

Corlette Point Road, Corlette (4984 2555/fax 4984 0300/www.peppers.com.au). **Rates** $300 midweek-$596 weekends. **Credit** AmEx, DC, MC, V.
Part of the Peppers chain, this is a top-class resort right on the water. Private balconies offer sweeping views across the bay.

Port Stephens Motor Lodge

44 Mangus Street, Nelson Bay (4981 3366/fax 4984 1655). **Rates** $145. **Credit** AmEx, BC, DC, MC, V.
A motel-like place located a short stroll from the main township. There's also a swimming pool.

Salamander Shores

147 Soldiers Point Road, Soldiers Point (4982 7210/ fax 4982 7890/www.salamander-shores.com). **Rates** from $119 midweek. **Credit** AmEx, BC, DC, MC, V.
A pleasant hotel with standard motel accommodation, lovely rooms with balconies and sea views, and a pretty garden. There's a good restaurant too.

Getting there

By car

From Sydney, take Sydney Newcastle Freeway (F3 and also Route 1); it's a 2.5hr drive.

By train

CityRail trains run almost hourly from Central Station to Newcastle. Buses connect with the trains for transfers to Port Stephens.

By bus

Port Stephens Coaches (4982 2940, 1800 045 949, http://pscoaches.com.au) runs a daily service to

Nelson Bay, departing Eddy Avenue, Central Station, Sydney, at 2pm. It leaves Nelson Bay for the return trip daily at 9am. The journey takes 3.5hrs.

Tourist information

Port Stephens Visitor Information Centre
Victoria Parade, Nelson Bay (4981 1579/ www.portstephens.org.au). **Open** 9am-5pm daily.

Heading South

South Coast

According to most of the people who live there, particularly residents of the Shoalhaven region (which stretches 160 kilometres/99 miles south of the town of Berry), this is the area of New South Wales that has it all: wilderness galore (including large tracts of national park and state forest); beaches so long and white they make Bondi look like a house party at a sewage dump; some of the cleanest, clearest water in Australia; a bay 82 times the size of Sydney Harbour with pods of crowd-pleasing dolphins; easy access to magnificent mountain vistas; heritage and antiques; 'surfing' kangaroos at Pebbly Beach, just south of Ulladulla; and the best fish and chips in the country.

Travelling south from Sydney along the Princes Highway (Route 1), beyond the Royal National Park, the first region you encounter is Illawarra, the administrative centre of which is the city of **Wollongong**. It's perhaps unfair to view Wollongong as one of the two ugly sisters on either side of Sydney (the other being Newcastle), but as you approach its smoking industrial surroundings it's hard not to. Nevertheless, Wollongong does have a couple of decent city beaches, coastal views and a resident collection of Aboriginal and other Australian art at the **City Gallery** (corner of Kembla and Burelli Streets, 4228 7500, open 10am-5pm Tue-Fri, noon-4pm Sat, Sun, admission free).

It's not long before the road begins to slide prettily between the coast on one side and the beginnings of the Southern Highlands on the other (Illawarra comes from an Aboriginal word meaning 'between the high place and the sea'). You soon come upon the first of the seaside towns worthy of a stop, **Kiama**. The town's main attraction is the **Blow Hole** (set that freeze-frame camera option), which spurts spray up to 60 metres (197 feet) into the air from a slatey, crenellated outcrop next to a comparatively tranquil harbour (weather

permitting). Also by the harbour is a fresh fish market, while on the way into town there's a block of 1885 quarrymen's cottages, which have been renovated and turned into restaurants and craft shops. Nothing in Kiama, however, prepares you for the sign: 'Stan Crap – Funeral Director' (life's crap and then you die?) on the way out of town.

Kiama is a good base for exploring the subtropical **Minammurra Rainforest**, the **Carrington Falls** and nearby **Seven Mile Beach**. This undeniably impressive caramel arc, backed by a hinterland of fir trees, is best viewed from Kingsford Smith Lookout, just beyond Gerrigong.

An alternative base is the tree-lined inland town of **Berry**, a little further south. It's an entertaining hybrid of hick-town and quaint yuppie heaven, where earthy locals mix with weekending Sydneysiders in search of antiques and fine dining. The former are catered for by a couple of daggy pubs – in particular, look out for the priceless Bob Hawke wine flagon at the **Great Southern Hotel** – while many of the latter bed down at the **Bunyip Inn Guest House** (*see p266*).

JERVIS BAY
Undoubtedly the Shoalhaven region's greatest attraction, and the one that drives normally restrained commentators (and, it seems, the shopkeepers of Huskisson, the bay's main village) to reach for their superlatives, is **Jervis Bay**. A huge place, it encompasses the wonderful Booderee National Park and 56 kilometres (34 miles) of shoreline. It also has a history of close shaves. First, in 1770, Captain Cook sailed straight past it on the way towards Botany Bay, recording it only as 'low-lying wetlands', and missing entirely its deep, wide natural harbour (which made it an ideal alternative to Sydney as fulcrum for the new colony). Later, this ecologically sensitive beauty spot was mooted as a possible port for Canberra and the ACT. And in 1975, Murrays Beach, at the tip of the national park, was chosen as a site for a nuclear reactor (a project thankfully defeated by public protest).

These narrow escapes and a fortuitous lack of population growth around Jervis Bay mean that this coastal area remains one of the most undisturbed and beautiful in Australia. Divers testify to the clarity of its waters; swimmers are sometimes literally dazzled by the whiteness of its sands (Hyams Beach is said to be the whitest in the world). It's not just popular with people, and among its regularly visiting sea and bird life are fur seals, giant rays, whales (southern right, pilot and killer), sharks, sea eagles, penguins and many, many more.

Trips Out of Town

Thar she blows!

Each year, more than 3,000 humpback and southern right whales migrate north along the NSW coastline from their winter feeding grounds in the Antarctic to their summer breeding ground off the tropical Queensland coast. They are joined by a scattering of minke whales and pygmy killer whales. The migration starts in early June, and by the middle of the month has really hotted up. The peak month for the return trip is September, though you can still see stragglers up to mid November.

The best place to see whales from the land is where it juts out into deep water – notably such places as **Byron Bay** (in the north) and **Eden** (on the far south coast). Whales love to pop into sheltered bays too, to feed and rest; **Jervis Bay** and off **Ulladulla** are exceptional whale-watching spots. **Dolphin Watch Cruises** (*see p266*) run three-hour whale cruises to Jervis Bay in June, July and from mid September to mid November (departing at 9am, $40, $22-$35 concessions, $110 family).

Port Stephens is also on the migration route. **Imagine** (*see p264*) runs two daily cruises during June, July and the October school holidays (9.30am, 1.30pm, $49, $25-$41 concessions). From August to mid November, there's a cruise at 1.30pm. The trip lasts about four hours.

More and more whales are also coming right into **Sydney Harbour** itself these days, it seems. Diving specialist **Pro Dive** (www.whalewatch.prodiveonline.com) offers a three-hour trip from Sydney in June and July ($95, $85 concessions, not recommended for children under ten). You can call 1800 820 820 or 9281 6066 for more details.

A good way to get a feel for Jervis Bay and meet its resident dolphins is to go on **Dolphin Watch Cruises** (50 Owen Street, Huskisson, 4441 6311, www.dolphinwatch.com.au), which also run whale cruises (*see left* **Thar she blows!**). **Huskisson**, the launching point for the cruise, is one of six villages on the shores of the bay. It's got a couple of accommodation options, two dive shops – **Pro Dive** (64 Owen Street, 4441 5255, www.prodivejervisbay.com.au) and **Seasports** (47 Owen Street, 4441 5598, www.jbseasports.com.au) – wonderful fish and chips, and a pub with a bistro, the **Husky Pub** (4441 5001) on Owen Street. Just south of Jervis Bay there is excellent sailing, snorkelling and swimming on the trapped body of water at St George's Basin and fishing at Sussex Inlet.

There are a few places to stay in Huskisson itself, but it's well worth bringing a tent to get a proper feel for the **Booderee National Park** (admission $10 per vehicle per day), which is jointly managed by the local Aborginal community. The best place to camp is at **Caves Beach**, where you wake up to the calls of birds and Eastern Grey kangaroos. **Green Patch** has more dirt than grass, but better facilities and can accommodate campervans as well. The Christmas/New Year period sees a ballot for places. Book though the park's website or call 4443 0977.

ULLADULLA

Despite all the stunning scenery around Jervis Bay, it can be worth venturing further south to the sleepy fishing town of **Ulladulla** for somewhere to stay. Ulladulla's protected harbour may not quite recall Sicily, but the town has a sizeable Italian fishing community (guaranteeing decent local pizzas and pasta), and the **Blessing of the Fleet** is an annual event on Easter Sunday. From here it's easy to access wilderness areas to the west and further south – **Budawang** and **Murramarang National Parks** – plus yet more expansive beaches, such as **Pebbly Beach** (which is actually sandy) with its resident kangaroos.

Where to stay & eat

Bunyip Inn Guest House

122 Queen Street, Berry (4464 2064/fax 4464 2324). **Rates** from $60. **Credit** AmEx, BC, DC, MC, V.
A National Trust-classified former bank with 13 individually styled rooms, one with a four-poster bed. There's also a swimming pool.

Huskisson Beach Tourist Resort

Beach Street, Huskisson (4441 5142/www.huskisson beachtouristresort.com.au). **Rates** cabin from $68; camping from $24. **Credit** AmEx, BC, DC, MC, V.

This resort offers various cabins (including self-catering ones) as well as plenty of camping spots right opposite the beach. If other attractions pale, there's a pool too.

Jervis Bay Guest House

1 Beach Street, Huskisson (4441 7658/fax 4441 7659/www.jervisbayguesthouse.com.au). **Rates** from $130. **Credit** AmEx, BC, DC, MC, V.

This four-and-a-half-star guesthouse opposite a beach has just four rooms (with balconies overlooking the sea and the sunrise), and is a short walk to the shops and restaurants in Huskisson. All of this makes it very popular, so book early.

Ulladulla Guest House

39 Burrill Street, Ulladulla (4455 1796/1800 700 905/fax 4454 4660/www.guesthouse.com.au). **Rates** from $119. **Credit** AmEx, BC, DC, MC, V.

This is a popular five-star option with great service and lovely rooms. Along with those it also has a lovely saltwater pool, sauna, spa, small gym and an excellent French restaurant.

Getting there

By car

Take Princes Highway (Route 1). Allow at least 2hrs to Jervis Bay, 3hrs to Ulladulla and slightly longer to Pebbly Bay.

By train

For Wollongong, Kiama, Gerrigong, Berry and Bomaderry (for Nowra), there are regular trains from Sydney's Central Station via the South Coast line, changing trains at Dapto. It's 3hrs to Bomaderry; from there a limited coach service operated by Premier Bus Services (13 3410/www.premierms.com.au) continues on through Nowra as far as Ulladulla.

By bus

Interstate coaches travelling the Princes Highway (Route 1) between Sydney and Melbourne stop at many of the towns mentioned above. There are also local bus and coach services along the coast. Contact the local tourist offices for more details.

Tourist information

Booderee National Park Visitors Centre

Jervis Bay Road, Jervis Bay (4443 0977/www.deh. gov.au/parks/booderee). **Open** 9am-4pm daily.

Kiama Visitors Centre

Blowhole Point, Kiama (4232 3322/www.kiama. com.au). **Open** 9am-5pm daily.

Shoalhaven Tourist Centres

Corner of Princes Highway & Pleasant Way, Nowra (4421 0778/1300 662 808). **Open** 9am-4.30pm daily. *Princes Highway, Civic Centre, Ulladulla (4455 1269).* **Open** 10am-5pm Mon-Fri; 9am-5pm Sat, Sun. Also check out www.shoalhaven.nsw.gov.au/region.

Southern Highlands

The Southern Highlands, known by wealthy 19th-century Sydneysiders as the 'Sanatorium of the South' for its cool climes and fresh air, has recently experienced something of a renaissance as a tourist destination. It's easy to see why – just a two-and-a-half-hour train ride from Sydney, the area has well-preserved villages such as Berrima (founded 1831), fading stately homes like Ranelagh House in Robertson, and a range of cosy accommodation, all set in a gently undulating landscape so easy on the eye that it evokes a different country (even before the area was first settled, Governor Macquarie said it reminded him of England). This is the sort of place where you feel you're bound to bump into some maiden aunt (perhaps long since dead) taking cream tea in a drowsy teashop, or at least find her old knick-knacks in the countless antique shops.

There's some truth to the local saying that the Southern Highlands are mostly for 'the newlyweds and the nearly deads', but there is something here for most tastes: the Highlands encompass tropical and subtropical rainforest, the second-largest falls in NSW (Fitzroy) and the edge of **Morton National Park**, where you can walk on the wild side.

Of the many pleasant approaches by car, two leading from the main coastal road (Princes Highway) stand out. The first is to take the Illawarra Highway (from Albion Park) through **Macquarie Pass National Park**; the second is to take the tourist drive from just beyond Berry. The route from Berry – rising, bending and finally dropping towards the **Kangaroo Valley** – is often atmospherically thick with mist, but on even a partly clear day it affords luscious views of the countryside.

Kangaroo Valley Village, despite its iron roofs and sandstone-pillared Hampden Bridge (built in 1897) is a little disappointing, but the walking and camping nearby are excellent, as are canoeing and kayaking on the **Kangaroo River** (contact Kangaroo Valley Tourist Park near the bridge, 4465 1310, www.holiday haven.com.au/kangaroovalley).

Leaving Kangaroo Valley, the road rises and twists once more before leading you to the **Fitzroy Falls**. A short saunter (from the impressive **Fitzroy Falls Visitor Centre** (*see p269*) and you are amid scenery that's as Australian as Paul Hogan. There are five falls in the vicinity, but Fitzroy is the nearest and biggest, plummeting 81 metres (266 feet) into **Yarunga Valley**. Take any of the walks around the falls (the steep Valley Walk leads to its base) and you could encounter 48 species of gum tree, lyre birds and possibly a wombat.

Another way of exploring the top end of underrated Morton National Park is to use the town of **Bundanoon** as a base for bushwalking and cycling. Bundanoon, which means 'a place of deep gullies', is as Scottish in flavour as its name sounds. Every year in the week after Easter the town transforms itself into Brigadoon for a Highland gathering, featuring traditional games, Scottish dancing and street parades. Bundanoon was also once known as the honeymoon centre of the Southern Highlands – in its heyday it had 51 guesthouses – but these days the bedsprings rarely squeak, as it has largely fallen out of fashion. Slightly north of the forgettable town of Moss Vale is **Berrima**, considered Australia's finest example of an 1830s village. This is the town the railways forgot, so many of its early buildings remain in pristine condition. A highlight is the 1838 neo-classical **Court House** (corner of Wilshire & Argyle Street, 4877 1505, www.berrimacourthouse.org.au) with its sandstone portico and curved wooden doorways. Don't miss the reconstruction of the 1843 trial of the adulterous Lucretia Dunkley and her lover, particularly good is the judge's sentencing of the pair for the murder of her dull husband. Other historic buildings include **Harper's Mansion** and Australia's oldest continually licensed hotel, the **Surveyor General Inn** (*see below*), both built in 1834.

An unexpected delight on the long road to Bowral is **Berkelouw's Book Barn** (Old Hume Highway, 4877 1370, open 9.30am-4.30pm daily), a treasure trove of yellowing knowledge, containing some 200,000 books. Bowral itself is attractive enough, especially during the spring Tulip Festival, but its biggest claim to fame is as the town that gave Australian cricket the late Donald Bradman. The great man is honoured in the **Bradman Museum** (St Jude Street, 4862 1247, www.bradman.org.au, open 10am-5pm daily, $7.50, $3.50-$5 concessions, $20 family) on the edge of the lush Bradman Oval, opposite the old Bradman home. If cricket doesn't captivate you, then take a trip up to **Mount Gibraltar**, overlooking the surrounding countryside, and the view surely will.

There's not much more to the town of **Mittagong** than meets the eye, although **Lake Alexandra Reserve** (where the Mount Alexandra Walking Trail begins) is a pleasant spot for a picnic.

About 60 kilometres (37 miles) west of Mittagong (via part-dirt road), the mysterious and beautiful **Wombeyan Caves** are thought to be thousands of years old, and many feature a number of unique encrustations and deposits. You can take a guided tour, and there's on-site accommodation and camping; contact the

Wombeyan Caves Visitor Centre (Wombeyan Caves Road, Taralga, 4843 5976, www.jenolancaves.org.au, open 8.30am-5pm daily) for details.

Destined to become the area's most famous village, and all because of a talking pig, is the sleepy hollow of **Robertson**, where the film *Babe* was shot. Almost the entire cast is on the breakfast menu at **Ranelagh House** (*see below*).

Where to stay & eat

Bundanoon Country Hotel

Erith Street, Bundanoon (4883 6005/fax 4883 6745). **Rates** (per person) $55-$70. **Credit** AmEx, BC, DC, MC, V.
This creaky old hotel boasts a wonderful billiard table, Nea Hayes's famous pies and the occasional poetry reading.

Briars Country Lodge & Inn

Moss Vale Road, Bowral (4868 3566/fax 4868 3223/ www.briars.com.au). **Rates** from $145 midweek; $165 weekend. **Credit** AmEx, BC, DC, MC, V.
A country retreat with 30 contemporary garden suites set in beautiful parkland. Adjacent to the lodge is the historic Georgian Briars Inn (c.1845), which has a true country atmosphere, with intimate bars and renowned bistro food.

Grand Mercure Hotel Bowral Heritage Park

9 Kangaloon Road, Bowral (4861 4833/1300 656 565). **Rates** $200 midweek; $260 weekend. **Credit** AmEx, BC, DC, MC, V.
A posh hotel in leafy grounds, with a fitness centre.

Ranelagh House Guesthouse

Illawarra Highway, Robertson (4885 1111/fax 4885 1130/www.ranelagh-house.com). **Rates** (per person) from $66 midweek; $80 weekend. **Credit** AmEx, BC, MC, V.
This is the best place in the area to take a leisurely Devon cream tea. It also offers a country-style lunch and has a good dinner menu.

Surveyor General Inn

Old Hume Highway, Berrima (4877 1226/fax 4877 1159/www.highlandsnsw.com.au/surveyorgeneral). **Rates** (per person) from $60 midweek; $80 weekend. **Credit** AmEx, BC, MC, V.
The rooms are simple, with a brass bed and shared bathroom, but the inn oozes historical charm.

Getting there

By car

The inland route (120km/75 miles) is via Hume Highway (Route 31) and takes just under 2hrs. The coastal route is via Princes Highway (Route 60); then turn inland on Illawarra Highway (Route 48) by Albion Park. It's slightly longer (130km/81 miles) and slightly slower (just over 2hrs).

By train

Trains to the Southern Highlands depart from Sydney's Central Station every day. Most stop at Mittagong, Bowral, Moss Vale and Bundanoon. The journey takes about 2.5hrs.

By bus

Several companies serve the area, including Greyhound Pioneer (13 2030, www.greyhound.com.au) and Priors Scenic Express (1800 816 234, 4472 4040).

Tourist information

Fitzroy Falls Visitor Centre

Nowra Road, Fitzroy Falls (4887 7270). **Open** 9am-5.30pm daily.

Tourism Southern Highlands

62-70 Main Street, Mittagong (1300 657 559/4871 2888/www.southern-highlands.com.au). **Open** 9am-5pm Mon-Fri; 8.30am-4.30pm Sat, Sun.

Canberra

Canberra, sitting in its own Australian Capital Territory (ACT), was created in 1911 as the compromise choice of federal capital to end the squabbling between arch rivals Sydney and Melbourne. It's always been dogged by bad press. It's the city that people from other Australian cities love to hate – the New Zealand of intra-Australian jokes ('a waste of a good sheep paddock') – regarded by detractors as a sterile, low-level metropolis full of also-(Canber)rans, a mundane mecca for politicians and bureaucrats. For those Australians who have visited the city, Canberra can also evoke some less than favourable memories: of being escorted (by the ears if necessary) around endless exhibitions and galleries as a kid, or of being driven mad getting lost in the car among the city's eccentric circles.

Those clichés wouldn't exist if there wasn't some truth to them. Yet Canberra is also loved with a passion by many of its residents, who point to its space, tranquillity, clean air and proximity to unspoilt bushland. Interestingly, there were few trees on the plains around Canberra when white settlers came; hundreds of thousands have been planted since. New householders were given two trees to plant in front of their homes in exchange for not building walls or fences – perhaps a factor in the dreadful bushfires around Christmas 2002, when some 200 houses burned to the ground.

Whether you side with Canberra's detractors or its defenders is partly a matter of taste and partly a matter of perception. On a clear day, viewed from **Mount Ainslie**, the **Telstra Tower** (Black Mountain Drive, Acton, 6219 6111, 1800 806 718) or the basket of a hot-air balloon (try **Balloon Aloft**, 7 Irving Street, Phillip, 6285 1540, www.balloon.canberra.net.au), Canberra can appear stately, elegant and positively Washingtonesque. Back on the ground, the city may seem less disorienting from the saddle of a bicycle. In fact, compared with the murderous streets of Sydney, Canberra is a cyclist's heaven, with relatively flat terrain, plenty of cycle paths, negligible traffic (riding is permitted on pavements anyway) and most of the sights within easy pedalling distance.

Doing a circuit of the central, man-made **Lake Burley Griffin** (a two-hour ride) might even win you over to the vision of 'the city beautiful' that Canberra's architect, Walter Burley Griffin, originally had in mind. The **National Capital Exhibition** (Regatta Point, Commonwealth Park, 6257 1068, www.nationalcapital.gov.au, open 9am-5pm daily, free) is on a knoll overlooking the lake – near the submerged whale pretending to be a fountain. The exhibition provides further insights into Griffin's competition-winning design for Canberra, eloquently drawn by his wife Marion Mahoney. There is also a model of the city (with blinking lights indicating attractions), which makes it a good starting point for a tour.

Whatever Canberra's faults, as federal capital it can claim to have many of Australia's most important national monuments, buildings and galleries, the most significant (and visited) being **Parliament House**, the **Australian War Memorial**, the **National Gallery of Australia** and the new **National Museum of Australia** (Lawson Crescent, Acton Peninsula, 6208 5000, www.nma.gov.au, 9am-5pm daily, free). The latter, which opened in 2001, is the first official museum dedicated to the nation of Australia. It utilises state-of-the-art technology and hands-on exhibits to take visitors through Australian society and its history since 1788; the interaction of people with the Australian environment; and Aboriginal and Torres Strait Islander cultures and histories. It relies heavily on image and sound rather than actual objects, so might not be everyone's cup of tea.

Opened in 1988, **Parliament House** (6277 5399, www.aph.gov.au, 9am-5pm daily, free) might look like an oversized wigwam from afar – thanks to an 81-metre (265-foot) stainless-steel flagpole – but it's as imposing as it is humble, as human as it is functional. From its position on Capital Hill it still dominates Canberra's landscape, yet its turfed roof allows the people to stand above their elected representatives. The foyer, the Great Hall (an Arthur Boyd tapestry – one of the world's biggest – hangs here) and both chambers (Senate and House of Representatives) are airy and refreshingly

Parliament House (top left) and the **National Museum of Australia**. See p269.

bathed in natural light. Displays of Australian art and photos include portraits of the country's ex-prime ministers in the Members' Hall. There are some interesting free guided tours every 30 minutes from 9am to 4pm (try to join one early, before the coaches arrive). You can also view the goings-on in both chambers from the public galleries when parliament is in session.

Beneath this comparative baby of a building, but far from eclipsed by it, stands the **Old Parliament House** (6270 8222, 9am-5pm daily, $2), Australia's seat of democracy from 1927 to 1988. Opposite the main entrance is the **Aboriginal Tent Embassy** (see p272 **Protest point**), established in 1972. Old Parliament House is also home to the **National Portrait Gallery** (King George Terrace, Parkes, 1800 779 955, www.portrait.gov.au, 9am-5pm daily) and the **Australian Archives** (Queen Victoria Terrace, Parkes, 6212 3600, www.naa.gov.au). With leather sofas and film noir-ish frosted windows embossed in gold lettering, this place reeks of the machinations of Australia's political past. Just down the road, and reputedly once linked to Old Parliament House by a white line so that worse-for-wear politicians could find their way there at night, is the **Hotel Kurrajong** (6234 4444, www.hotel kurrajong.com.au). Once the Canberra home of prime ministers and other eminences, it's now a lovely boutique hotel.

Also located nearby is Australia's foremost art institution, the **National Gallery of Australia** (Parkes Place, Parkes, 6240 6411, www.nga.gov.au, 10am-5pm daily, free), which houses good collections of international, Australian, Aboriginal and Torres Strait Islander art, as well as major exhibitions from overseas that often bypass Sydney. Next door is the innovative **Questacon National Science & Technology Centre** (King Edward Terrace, Parkes, 6270 2800, www.questacon.edu.au, 9am-5pm daily, $14, $9.50 concessions, $42 family), with hands-on exhibits and a fairly realistic earthquake simulation.

On the other side of the lake stands the **Australian War Memorial** (Treloar Crescent, top of Anzac Parade, Campbell, 6243 4211, 10am-5pm daily, free). Commemorating as it does the country's 102,000 war dead from 11 international military involvements since 1860, this is obviously a poignant place – especially the Hall of Memory and the Tomb of the Unknown Soldier.

If you've ever wondered how Australia, with its relatively small population, is able to produce so many top-class athletes, a visit to the **Australian Institute of Sport** (Leverrier Crescent, Bruce, 6214 1111, www.ausport.gov.au) on the city's outskirts and its **Sports Visitor Centre** will shed some light. It's a sort of university for the country's elite sportspersons, and a tour ($13), led by one of its sleek and toned resident athletes, will probably leave you guiltily pondering your fat content.

The name Canberra is derived from an Aboriginal word for 'meeting place', and in the past local tribes used to gather to feast on bogong moths, which can end up here in their millions after being blown off course (they migrate from the grassy plains further north to high spots along the Great Dividing Range, where they hole up for the summer). While the range of Canberra's cuisine has obviously grown since then, it can still seem something of a ghost town after Sydney. However, in the suburb of Manuka, near the Parliamentary Triangle, you'll find the city's café culture alongside a cluster of clubs and restaurants.

The capital rarely gets overcrowded, except during the annual **Canberra Festival** (6207 2384, www.celebratecanberra.com), held over ten days in March. This colourful event marks the city's founding in 1913 and includes hot-air ballooning, exhibitions, theatre, music and dance. There's also **Floriade** (6205 0666),

which is a big and cheery yearly celebration of all things floral. It usually runs from mid September to mid October.

Where to stay & eat

Canberra has one of the highest room-occupancy rates in Australia, so book ahead.

Brassey Hotel
Belmore Gardens, Barton (6273 3766/fax 6273 2791/www.brassey.net.au). **Rates** from $132. **Credit** AmEx, BC, DC, MC, V.
A historic boutique hotel within walking distance of most attractions.

The Chairman & Yip
108 Bunda Streeet, Civic (6248 7109). **Main courses** $26. **Credit** AmEx, BC, DC, MC, V.
Popular with political bigwigs, Chairman & Yip serves modern Asian food, with lots of fish.

food@therepublic
20 Allara Street, Civic (6247 1717). **Main courses** $15. **Credit** AmEx, BC, DC, MC, V.
A top-class café offering great dining in a cutting-edge atmosphere.

Medina Classic Canberra
11 Giles Street, Kingston (6239 8100/fax 6239 7226/ www.medinaapartments.com.au). **Rates** from $149. **Credit** AmEx, DC, MC, V.
Just minutes from Parliament House in fashionable Kingston, the Medina has comfortable and very good-value one-, two-, and three-bedroom suites. There's a heated pool, spa and gym too.

Mezzalira
Melbourne Building, 55 London Circuit, Canberra City (6230 0025). **Main courses** $18-$26. **Credit** AmEx, BC, MC, V.
Smart modern Italian food in a converted bank.

Olims Canberra Hotel
Corner of Ainslie & Limestone Avenues, Braddon (6248 5511/1800 020 016/fax 6247 0864/ www.olimshotel.com). **Rates** from $145. **Credit** AmEx, BC, DC, MC, V.
Set in manicured lawns and just a short walk from the city, Olims has simple but comfortable enough rooms with a couple of pleasant dining options.

Rydges Lakeside Canberra
London Circuit, at Edinburgh Street, Canberra City (1800 026 169/fax 6257 3071/www.rydges.com). **Rates** from $240. **Credit** AmEx, BC, DC, MC, V.
This is the prime city address at which to stay, next to Lake Burley Griffin.

Tilley's Devine Café Gallery
Corner of Brigalow & Wattle Streets, Lyneham (6247 7753/www.tilleys.com.au). **Main courses** $7.50-$14.50. **Credit** AmEx, BC, MC, V.
A huge licensed bar and sidewalk café, and a major venue for touring music acts.

Trips Out of Town

Getting there

By air
Canberra has a small domestic airport about 15mins drive from the city centre. Both Qantas (13 1313) and Virgin Blue (13 67 89) fly there several times a day; the trip from Sydney takes 30-40mins.

By car
Canberra is 288km (179 miles) south of Sydney. Take M5 motorway connecting with the Hume Highway (Route 31); turn off to Canberra on Federal Highway beyond Goulburn. Journey time: 2.5hrs in a Ferrari, but allow up to 3.5hrs.

By train
CountryLink's very handy Xplorer train service (13 2232, www.countrylink.info) runs from Sydney's Central Station to Canberra and back again three times every day. The trip can generally be expected to take just over 4hrs.

By bus
Most major coach firms operate services to Canberra; try Firefly Express (1300 730 740, www.firefly express.com.au), Greyhound Pioneer (13 2030, www.greyhound.com.au) or McCafferty's (13 14 99, www.mccaffertys.com.au).

Tourist information

Canberra Visitor Centre
330 Northbourne Avenue, Dickson (1300 554 114/6205 0044/accommodation 1800 100 660/ www.canberratourism.com.au). **Open** 9am-5.30pm Mon-Fri; 9am-4pm Sat, Sun.

AbOriginal Protest point

The Aboriginal Tent Embassy in Canberra – a haphazard collection of tents, wobbly-looking structures hung with flags and a campfire – is an incongruous site among the manicured lawns, rose gardens and sweeping vistas of Old Parliament House. But its unimposing appearance is deceptive – various government schemes over the years to remove/replace/relocate the Embassy have proved fruitless.

On Australia Day (26 January) 1972, a small group of people planted themselves on the lawn of the then Parliament House, in protest against the government's refusal to recognise Aboriginal land rights. They described the site as an Embassy because of their sense of alienation from their own land. The spot was already significant because of a protest by Aboriginal elder Jimmy Clements at the opening of Parliament House in 1927.

In July, the tents that had sprung up were removed. Three days later, 200 protesters tried to re-establish the site, resulting in a violent confrontation with police. Over the next three decades the Embassy, which a detractor called an 'eyesore and a blight on the national capital', was rebuilt, demolished, blown down by a storm, rebuilt, briefly renamed, threatened by fire, relocated to Capitol Hill (the site of the current Parliament House) – then back again. Offshoots have sprouted in other locations in Canberra, at Mrs Macquarie's Chair in Sydney during the 1988 bi-centennial celebrations and at Victoria Park, Sydney, during the 2000 Olympics. In 2001 a delegation was sent to the Hague to start a case in the world court over Aboriginal land, genocide and crimes against humanity in Australia.

The site is even controversial within the Aboriginal community: some members of the local Ngunawal tribe have called it a 'disgrace'. For the many people who wish the whole thing would just go away there is little comfort. The site has acquired deep symbolic significance for both indigenous and non-indigenous people, and has been recognised by the Australian Heritage Commission for its historical importance ensuing its protection – and, no doubt, many more years of controversy.

Trip Planner

Big place, isn't it? Here's a short guide to the rest of Australia.

So you're going to Sydney, but what about the rest of the country? Australia is a huge continent – about 3,200 kilometres (1,900 miles) from south to north and 4,000 kilometres (2,490 miles) from east to west; roughly the same size as the contiguous US – and there's a lot to see. It lacks huge mountains, but otherwise has a great diversity of landscape, from the harsh red desert of the interior to the lush rainforests of the northern coast, plus such world-famous, must-see destinations as Uluru and the Great Barrier Reef.

Australia's vastness means that it can take a very long time to get anywhere, especially by road or rail – from Sydney to Perth, for instance, it takes five days by car, three days by train. Flying is often the best method, especially if your time is limited. Route-planning can be complicated, however; for example, you can fly to almost anywhere from Sydney, but only to certain major cities from Alice Springs. Pricing is also a minefield: discounts and special deals change frequently. Currently, Qantas's Boomerang Pass is a good bet for international travellers: it can only be purchased overseas and provides discounted rates on up to ten internal flights (you must buy at least two before you arrive in Australia). The newest airline, launched in 2004, is Jetstar, Quantas's budget carrier, which flies between Sydney, Melbourne, Brisbane and various destinations on the east coast.

Oz also has some superb, if pricey, long-distance rail journeys. Hot fave at the moment is the *Ghan*, which as of January 2004 has finally extended its route from Alice Springs to Darwin on the north coast, fulfilling a decades-old dream of railway enthusiasts; it starts in Adelaide, so you can now traverse the whole country from bottom to top. Budget-conscious travellers with an appetite for roughing it can take the bus.

Below we've listed (in alphabetical order) the main destinations outside Sydney, to give you some idea of what's where (for information on Canberra, *see p269*). Also visit Australia's official website **www.australia.com**. It's packed with information, including the useful Oz Planner, which suggests two-week themed itineraries around the country ('Sydney, Reef & Rock', for example, takes in Sydney, Alice Springs and Cairns).

Adelaide

Where is it?
The capital of South Australia is aptly positioned on the south coast of the continent. Its nearest large city neighbour is Melbourne, but that's 728 kilometres (452 miles) away along the scenic Great Ocean Road. It's also a 1,396-kilometre (867-mile) trek to Sydney. Just to the north is semi-desert country – the start of the Australian Outback.

What's there?
Nicknamed the 'City of Churches', Adelaide (population one million) is a genteel kind of place with a meandering river and an English gloss. It's pleasant enough for a couple of days, but the real attractions lie nearby: to the south is Kangaroo Island (the best place in Australia to see native animals without hassle); to the north-east the German-style wineries of the Barossa Valley are peaceful and popular; and to the north the craggy red ridges of the Flinders Ranges offer dramatic scenery and camel rides.

Ideal
If you want a taste of civilisation before setting out on an overland adventure.

Best time to visit
The arid lands make for some extremely hot days from December to February, when temperatures can reach 40°C (104°F). March and April are more pleasant, and October to November are warm too.

Getting there
By air: Qantas and Virgin Blue both fly direct to Adelaide from most state capitals.
By train: The famous *Ghan* travels between Adelaide and Darwin; the *Indian Pacific* between Sydney and Adelaide; and the *Overland* between Melbourne and Adelaide.
By bus: McCafferty's/Greyhound has regular services between Adelaide and Melbourne, and Adelaide and Sydney.

Alice Springs

Where is it?
Pretty much slap bang in the middle of Oz, in the Northern Territory at the heart of the Red Centre. It's a long way from nowhere: Darwin is 1,500 kilometres (930 miles) to the north,

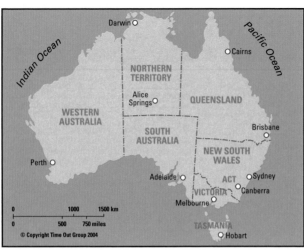

On the map: Darwin, Cairns, NORTHERN TERRITORY, Alice Springs, QUEENSLAND, WESTERN AUSTRALIA, SOUTH AUSTRALIA, Brisbane, NEW SOUTH WALES, Perth, Adelaide, ACT, Sydney, VICTORIA, Canberra, Melbourne, TASMANIA, Hobart, Indian Ocean, Pacific Ocean

0   1000   1500 km
0   500   750 miles
© Copyright Time Out Group 2004

Brisbane

Where is it?

On the coast, not far north of NSW. It's a fair distance from anywhere else of urban significance – Sydney is 1,100 kilometres (684 miles) to the south. Sparsely populated Queensland has some of the world's best beaches, and a receding hairline of tropical rainforests.

What's there?

With a population of 1.5 million, Brisbane's position in the humid subtropics on the banks of a languid river gives it a relaxed air, and there are plenty of trees to soften its historic sandstone centre. The river flows into beautiful Morton Bay, studded with hundreds of islands with long white beaches. The Gold Coast, an Australian icon, is an hour's drive south – it's a glitzy, overdeveloped sand strip edged with high-rises, nightclubs and theme parks. And two hours south lies the laid-back beachside mecca of Byron Bay, home of the very popular Blues & Roots Music Festival, held at Easter.

Ideal

To catch your breath before hitting the beaches, the rainforests and the Great Barrier Reef.

Best time to visit

Summer – roughly November to March – can be hot and humid, so bring your shorts. Winter – June to August – is much more pleasant.

Getting there

By air: Qantas and Virgin Blue fly to Brisbane. Both also fly to the Gold Coast from Sydney.
By train: Queensland rail operates long-distance trains between Brisbane and Cairns. It's a 14hr trip on a CountryLink train from Sydney to Brisbane.
By bus: It's 18hrs from Sydney with McCafferty's/ Greyhound. Take a good book.

Cairns

Where is it?

To the far north in Queensland and adjacent to the southern stretches of the Great Barrier Reef, 1,800 kilometres (1,120 miles) from Brisbane.

Adelaide the same distance to the south. The NT is also Australia's most barren and least populated region, and around 52,000 of its 190,000 inhabitants are Aboriginal.

What's there?

Most people visit Alice (population 25,000) because it's the jumping-off point for Australia's most famous natural monument, Uluru (Ayer's Rock), five hours to the south-west. Numerous companies offer organised trips to Uluru and nearby Kata Tjuta (the Olgas), and other desert highlights (Kings Canyon, the East and West McDonnell Ranges). The town itself is dusty and run-down, and has a frontier feel; still, there are some historical buildings, small museums, a base for the Royal Flying Doctor Service and a great Desert Park.

Ideal

If you want to get a feel for the untamed outback at Australia's arid heart or to pick up some Aboriginal art.

Best time to visit

Temperatures can be unbearably hot in the summer (November to March) and below freezing on winter nights (June to August). April to July are the most comfortable months.

Getting there

By air: Qantas and Virgin Blue both fly direct to Alice. Qantas also flies direct to Yulara (Uluru) airport (from Sydney, Perth and Cairns).
By train: Alice Springs is a major stop on the famous *Ghan* train route, which travels 2,980km (1,850 miles) from Adelaide to Darwin.
By bus: McCafferty's/Greyhound has daily services to Adelaide, Cairns and Darwin.

You can stay in Cairns or at nicer Port Douglas, a pleasant beachside resort just to the north.

What's there?
The Great Barrier Reef! It's more than 2,000 kilometres (1,240 miles) long, and even in just a few hours' snorkelling you can see dazzling coral, fish and other sealife. Cairns is close to the World Heritage-listed Wet Tropics Rainforest, including the magnificent 110-million-year-old Daintree Forest and Cape Tribulation. Cairns itself has a tropical feel and a sun-bronzed appeal, but no beach – unlike Port Douglas, which has a great sandy strip.

Ideal
If you want to experience the ultimate in snorkelling or diving (or even learn to dive), and stroll through rainforests rich with life.

Best time to visit
Temperatures are fairly stable all year round, but if you want to swim in the sea, go between May and September when the waters are free of box jellyfish, whose sting can be fatal.

Getting there
By air: Qantas and Virgin Blue fly to Cairns from Brisbane, Sydney and Melbourne. Qantas also flies from Darwin.
By train: The fast Tilt Train from Brisbane takes 25hrs; the Sunlander takes 32hrs.
By bus: McCafferty's/Greyhound travel from Brisbane, Alice Springs, Darwin and Townsville.

Darwin

Where is it?
On the central northern coast of Australia, within a day's drive of Kakadu National Park. Darwin is the capital of the Northern Territory, a huge, sparsely populated land arid in parts, and elsewhere burgeoning with rainforests. To the north-east of Darwin is Arnhemland, forests and riverlands owned by Aboriginals.

What's there?
With its gorgeous harbour, Darwin is lovely to visit, but it's largely a gateway to the attractions that surround it. Of these, Kakadu is arguably the most impressive, with a wetland wonderland of lily-clad lakes, birds and saltwater crocodiles. Waterfalls, dramatic red escarpments and Aboriginal art predominate. To the south is the Katherine Gorge, an orange-cliff canyon falling into a pristine green river.

Ideal
For an overland trip to Kakadu National Park, or inland to Katherine Gorge, where you can canoe among the crocs (careful – attacks do happen) or dot-paint with local Aborigines.

Best time to visit
Not during the wet season (mid October to April) as floods are common and the humidity is unbearable. Temperatures are comfortably warm in the 'dry' (late April to end of October).

Getting there
By air: Qantas flies to Darwin from most state capitals, and Virgin Blue from Sydney and Brisbane, with connections from Adelaide, Canberra, the Gold Coast, Melbourne and Perth.
By train: The *Ghan* travels once a week from Adelaide and back.
By bus: McCafferty's/Greyhound make the 20hr trip from Alice Springs. Greyhound also runs a daily service from Broome.

Transport tips

For car rental agencies, *see p283.*

Airlines
Qantas (13 1223, www.qantas.com.au) flies everywhere; **Jetstar** (13 1538, www.jetstar.com.au) serves the east coast; **Virgin Blue** 13 67 89, www.virgin blue.com.au) covers the eastern half of the country; **Regional Express (Rex)** (13 1713, www.regionalexpress.com.au) serves NSW, South Australia and Victoria; while **Alliance Airlines** (1300 130 092, www.allianceairlines.com.au) flies to/from Sydney and within Queensland. There are also smaller regional operators.

Buses
National carriers **McCafferty's** (13 1449, www.mccaffertys.com.au) and **Greyhound** Pioneer (13 2030, www.greyhound.com.au) are really one company; they have separate timetables and travel passes, but fares are identical and passes can be used on both services. Aimed at budget travellers, backpacker buses offer specific tours, sometimes with hop on, hop off services. Reliable oufits include **Groovy Grape** (1800 661 177, 08 8371 4000, www.groovygrape.com.au); **Oz Experience** (9213 1766, www.ozexperience.com) and **Wayward Bus** (1300 653 510, www.waywardbus.com.au).

Trains
Great Southern Railways (13 2147, www.gsr.com.au) operates the three major interstate services: the *Ghan* (Adelaide-Alice Springs-Darwin); *Indian Pacific* (Sydney-Adelaide-Perth); and the *Overland* (Melbourne-Adelaide).

Trips Out of Town

Hobart

Where is it?

On the south coast of Tasmania, straddling the Derwent River. Tasmania is larger than you might expect, and has a mountainous central spine with winding roads. Much of the west and north coasts are covered with wilderness and rainforests.

What's there?

Tasmania's capital (population 190,000) is a small town with a picturesque harbour dotted with sailing boats and ferries. On the waterfront, galleries, pubs and cafés peek out from colonial sandstone warehouses. Narrow lanes reveal historic cottages and small museums. Plenty of companies offer scenic trips along the river.

Ideal

If you want to experience a historic port town before setting off to see wildlife and the rugged green scenery of the interior.

Best time to visit

The weather is at its best between October and April. Winters (June to August) can be cold and harsh, especially in the high country.

Getting there

By air: Qantas flies from Sydney and Melbourne to Hobart and Launceston. Virgin Blue flies from Melbourne to Hobart and Launceston.
By ferry: Two car ferries, the *Spirit of Tasmania I* and *II*, make the 10hr crossing between Melbourne and Devonport (on the north coast) several times a week. The *Spirit of Tasmania III* makes the 20hr trip between Sydney and Devonport.

Melbourne

Where is it?

Right down south where the weather seldom gets sticky, in the state of Victoria and on the Yarra River. It's less than a two-hour flight or a nine-hour drive from Sydney (though most take the two-day coastal route).

What's there?

With its large green spaces, riverbanks, trams and imposing historic buildings, Melbourne (population 3.3 million) is reminiscent of central Europe. This is Australia's fashion and cultural heart, where image means everything. It's a cultural melting pot too, with large Greek, Italian and Vietnamese communities, and a great dining scene. Victoria is a small state, but packs a punch with mountains, long white beaches, stunning national parks and a thriving wine-growing region.

Ideal

For city-lovers. The capital of Victoria is a vibrant place, where culture, food and fashion are high on the list of priorities.

Best time to visit

Melbourne's weather is notoriously changeable. It can be cold and wet from June to August, but otherwise temperatures are usually warm enough for a T-shirt.

Getting there

By air: Qantas and Virgin Blue fly to Melbourne from most state capitals.
By train: The Sydney-Melbourne XPT train makes the trip in 10hrs. The *Overlander* travels between Melbourne and Adelaide.
By bus: McCafferty's/Greyhound buses take 12hrs to do the tri-weekly trip.

Perth

Where is it?

Located on the south-western coast, the capital of Western Australia is the most isolated city in the world. The nearest large metropolis is Adelaide, 2,712 kilometres (1,685 miles) away across the forbidding Nullarbor Plain, and it's a stonking 4,127 kilometres (2,565 miles) to Sydney, or four to five days of serious driving. Apart from a thin strip of coastal greenery, WA is rugged and cut off by deserts.

What's there?

Water, water, everywhere. Perth has some magnificent beaches and an expansive ocean outlook. It's an outdoors city with a relaxed vibe, and the sun always seems to shine. There are good museums here and in nearby sister city Fremantle. Just offshore is Rottnest Island, with good coral snorkelling and 10,000 quokkas (knee-high hopping marsupials). From September to November migrating whales appear in their hundreds off the coast.

Ideal

If you want to break in that swimming cossie and see a bit of nature on the side.

Best time to visit

With a Mediterranean climate, Perth can be sunny year round. Winters cool off to 18°C (64°F), and summers heat up to 30°C (86°F).

Getting there

By air: Qantas flies direct from all mainland capitals, while Virgin Blue flies from Sydney (a 4hr trip), Melbourne, Brisbane and Adelaide.
By train: The *Indian Pacific* takes three days to reach Perth from Sydney, twice a week.
By bus: McCafferty's/Greyhound runs daily from Sydney to Adelaide and once a week from Adelaide to Perth. There's also a daily service from Broome.

ey
orne
atta
ont Bay
arantine
ose Bay
Rydalmere
Shark Island
Taronga Zoo
Watsons Ba
Woolwich
Cruis
Cru

Directory

Features

Directory

Getting Around

By air

Sydney Airport (9667 9111, www.sydneyairport.com.au) is on the northern shoreline of Botany Bay, 11 kilometres (seven miles) south-east of the city centre. Opened in 1920, it's one of the oldest continuously operating airports in the world. Since its swanky upgrade for the 2000 Olympics, it's now among the world's best – and quite proud of it.

There are three terminals: **T1** is for all international departures on all airlines and for QF (Qantas) flights 001-399; **T2** domestic terminal for Virgin Blue, Regional Express and QF flights 1600 and above; **T3** Qantas terminal for QF domestic flights 400-1599.

The international terminal is a great place for shopping, with more than 100 outlets ranging from regular duty-free stores and international designer showcases to Aussie gear such as Mambo, Rip Curl and RM Williams, plus the excellent souvenir outlets selling Aboriginal artefacts and kitsch mementos.

GETTING TO AND FROM THE AIRPORT
The **AirportLink rail service** (www.airportlink.com.au) between Sydney Airport and Central Station was first introduced in 2000 to accommodate Olympic visitors, and runs an efficient service every ten minutes from both international and domestic terminals. The line is a spur of the green CityRail line, so serves all the main inner-city interchanges. It takes eight minutes to reach Central Station from the domestic terminals, 11 minutes from the international. Trains run from 5.09am to 11.45pm Monday to Friday, from 5.13am to 12.42am Saturday and Sunday. A single fare from the international terminal to Central Station costs $11.60 ($7.90 under-16s), $11 ($7.60 under-16s) from the domestic terminals.

The success of AirportLink made the State Transit-run Airport Express bus service redundant, but the excellent **KST Sydney Airporter** (9666 9988, www.kst.com.au) bus shuttle is still in steady operation. It runs a door-to-door service to all hotels, major apartment blocks and backpackers in the city, Darling Harbour and Kings Cross. A single costs $8 ($4 under-12s). Look for the blue and white buses outside McDonald's at T1 and directly outside both T2 and T3. You need to book three hours in advance for hotel pick-ups.

Each terminal has its own sheltered **taxi** rank, with supervisors in peak hours to ensure a smooth and hassle-free flow of taxis. You never have to wait for long, even in the vast sheep pen-style queuing system of the international terminal, where 190 vehicles are on call. If you have any special needs – wheelchair access, child seats, or a need for an extra large vehicle for any reason – just go to the front of the queue and tell the supervisor, who will call you a specially fitted taxi. It takes about 30 minutes to the city depending on the traffic and time of day, and costs around $25.

The main car rental companies all have desks at the airport; for more info on driving in Sydney, *see p281.*

AIRLINES: INTERNATIONAL
More than 30 airlines operate regular international flights into Sydney, including:

Air Canada 1300 655 767
www.aircanada.ca
Air New Zealand 13 2476
www.airnz.co.nz
Alitalia 9244 2400/www.alitalia.it
British Airways 8904 8800
www.britishairways.com
Cathay Pacific 13 1747
www.cathaypacific.com
Emirates 1300 303 777
www.emirates.com
Garuda Indonesia 1300 365 330
www.garuda-indonesia.com

JAL (Japan Airlines) 9272 1111
www.jal.co.jp
Malaysia Airlines 13 2627
www.malaysiaairlines.com.my
Qantas 13 1313
www.qantas.com.au
Singapore Airlines 13 1011
www.singaporeair.com
Thai Airways 1300 651 960
www.thaiair.com
United Airlines 13 1777
www.ual.com

AIRLINES: DOMESTIC
Alliance Airlines 1300 130 092
www.allianceairlines.com.au
Qantas 13 1223
www.qantas.com.au
Regional Express (Rex) 13 1713
www.regionalexpress.com.au
Virgin Blue 13 67 89
www.virginblue.com.au

By bus

There are a large number of bus companies operating throughout Australia; for details, *see p279.* Handily, they all use the Sydney Coach Terminal located in Central Station as their main pick up and drop off point.

By rail

The State Rail Authority's CountryLink (www.countrylink.info) operates out of Central Station with extensive user-friendly services to all main interstate and NSW destinations. For more details, *see p256.*

By sea

International cruise liners, including the QE2, dock at either the Overseas International Passenger Terminal located on the west side of Circular Quay, or around the corner in Darling Harbour.

Public transport

To get around Sydney you'll probably use a combination of trains, ferries, buses and perhaps the airborne Monorail or the chic LightRail streetcars. The government-run State Transit Authority (STA) operates Sydney Buses, as well as Sydney Ferries and the CityRail train network. The other transport services you will see around are privately run and therefore generally more expensive.

The centre of Sydney is so small that if you're in a large group, it's often cheaper to pool for a taxi.

Transport Infoline

13 1500/www.sta.nsw.gov.au. **Open** *Phone enquiries* 6am-10pm daily. A great, consumer-friendly phone line and website offering timetable, ticket and fare information for STA buses, Sydney Ferries and CityRail, plus timetabling (only) for cross-city private bus services.

Fares & tickets

There are several combination travel passes covering the government-run transit system, and they're worth buying if you plan extetnsive use of public transport.

TravelPass

Unlimited seven-day, quarterly or yearly travel throughout the zones for which it has been issued, on buses, trains and ferries. These passes are aimed at commuters, but can be useful if you're in Sydney for any length of time. To find the right TravelPass for you, check the STA website or ask at any train station or bus information kiosk. You can also buy TravelPasses at STA Sydney Buses Info Kiosks, ticket agents such as newsagents displaying a Sydney Buses Ticket Stop sign, CityRail stations, and ticket offices/vending machines at Circular Quay and Manly.

Passes are also available for a combination of buses and ferries, or for travel solely by bus, ferry or train. TravelPasses cannot be used on the STA premium Red Sydney Explorer and Blue Bondi Explorer bus services, Sydney Ferry harbour cruises, JetCats or private bus services.

SydneyPass

This one is specifically aimed at tourists. Unlimited travel on selected CityRail trains, buses (including premium services such as the Explorer buses) and on ferries (including premium services such as JetCats and cruises). Valid for any three or five days within a seven-day period, or seven consecutive days. Prices for a three-day pass are $90 ($45 concessions, $225 family); for a five-day pass $120 ($60 concessions, $300 family); and $140 ($70 concessions, $350 family) for a seven-day pass.

DayTripper

This pass offers unlimited one-day travel on buses, ferries and CityRail trains until 4am. It costs $15 ($7.60 under-16s) and is available on board buses, from STA offices and at Sydney Ferries ticket offices.

CityHopper

This pass has unlimited one-day bus and CityRail travel in the central city area bounded by Kings Cross, North Sydney and Redfern. It costs $6.80 ($3.40 under-16s) peak, $4.80 ($2.40 under-16s) off-peak.

BusTripper

A pass offering unlimited all-day travel on buses only – except for the premimum Explorer bus services. It costs $10.90 ($5.40 under-16s).

Buses

Buses are slow but also fairly frequent, and offer a better way of seeing the city than the CityRail trains, which operate underground within the centre. Buses are the only option for transport to popular areas such as Bondi Beach, Coogee and the northern beaches (beyond Manly), which aren't served by either train or ferry. Sydney is divided into seven zones; the city centre is zone 1. The minimum adult fare is $1.60 (80¢ under-16s), which covers two zones.

The bus driver will not automatically stop, so hold out your arm to request a ride. Pay the driver (avoid big notes) or validate your travel pass in the green machine at the door.

The bus route numbers give you an idea of where they go. Buses 131-193 service Manly

and the northern beaches; 200-296 the lower north shore (including Taronga Zoo) and the northern suburbs; 300-400 eastern suburbs (including Bondi, Darlinghurst, Sydney Airport and Paddington); 401-500 the inner south and inner west suburbs, including Leichhardt, Newtown, Balmain and Homebush; and 501-599 the north-west including Parramatta and Chatswood. In general, the 100s and 200s start near Wynyard Station and the 300s-500s can be found around Circular Quay.

Bus numbers starting with an 'X' are express services, which travel between the suburbs and major centres on the way into the city. Stops are marked 'Express'. Limited-stop or 'L' services operate on some of the longer routes to provide faster trips to and from the city (mainly for commuters).

Buses in the central and inner suburbs run pretty much all night, but services from central Sydney to the northern beaches stop at just around midnight. Nightrider buses operate hourly services to outer suburban train stations after the trains have ceased running, up until 5am.

STA also runs the tourist-oriented **Red Sydney Explorer** and **Blue Bondi Explorer** bus services. For full details of both these, and private bus tours, *see p51.*

CityRail

CityRail is the passenger rail service covering the greater Sydney region (and the sister company to CountryLink, covering country and long-distance routes within NSW). The sleek, double-decker silver trains run underground on the central City Circle loop – Central, Town Hall, Wynyard, Circular Quay, St James and Museum stations – and overground to the suburbs (both Central and Town Hall stations provide

Directory

connections to all the suburban lines). Although certainly quicker than the bus, trains are not as frequent as many would like and waits of 15 minutes, even in peak time, are not uncommon. For one of the best rides in Sydney, take the train from the city to the north shore – it passes over the Harbour Bridge and the views are spectacular.

CityRail tickets can be bought at ticket offices or vending machines at rail stations. Expect huge queues in rush hour. A single ticket anywhere on the City Circle costs $2.20 ($1.10 under-16s); an off-peak return costs $2.60 ($2.20 under-16s).

The newest addition to CityRail's electric fleet is the ultra-modern Millennium Train. It was introduced in July 2002, but within less than a year the four new trains had to be withdrawn for technical reasons. At the time of writing, the trains are gradually being reintroduced, but their future remains uncertain. That said, if you have the chance to go on one, it's well worth the ride. The comfort levels leave the old trains in the shade.

For more details of CityRail services, call the **Transport Infoline** (*see p279*) or visit **www.cityrail.info**. For a map of the CityRail city network, *see p316*.

Ferries

No trip to Sydney would be complete without clambering aboard one of the picture-postcard green-and-yellow ferries that ply the harbour and are used daily by hundreds of commuters. All ferries depart from Circular Quay ferry terminal, where Sydney Ferries operates out of wharves 2 to 5. These stately vessels are a great way to explore the harbour: there's plenty of room to take pictures from the outdoor decks or just to

sit in the sun and enjoy the ride. JetCats – sleek and fast catamarans – operate a service to Manly, taking 15 minutes, as opposed to 30 minutes on a regular ferry.

Ticket prices vary, but a one-way from Circular Quay to destinations within the Inner Harbour costs $4.50 ($2.20 under-16s). A single JetCat fare is $7.50. If you plan to use the ferries a lot, the FerryTen pass covers ten rides within the Inner Harbour and costs $28.50 ($14.20 concessions); and $42.90 ($21.40 concessions) to Manly (by ferry only, not the JetCat). A JetCatTen costs $62.50.

Tickets are sold at ticket offices and vending machines at Circular Quay and Manly. Tickets for Inner Harbour services can also be purchased from on-board cashiers. For a map of the ferry system, *see p315*. For details of Sydney Ferries cruises, *see p52*.

Sydney Ferries Information Centre

Opposite Wharf 4, Circular Quay (9207 3170/www.sydneyferries. nsw.gov.au). CityRail/ferry Circular Quay. **Open** 7am-5.45pm Mon-Sat; 8am-5.45pm Sun.

Metro LightRail

In 1997 Sydney welcomed back its streetcars. Trams were abolished in the early '60s, but the privately run Metro LightRail, operated by Connex (which is also in charge of the Metro Monorail), now provides a slick 14-station service from Central Station via Darling Harbour, Pyrmont and Star City casino to the inner west. It's especially useful for visiting Darling Harbour, Paddy's Market, the excellent Fish Markets, Glebe and the Powerhouse Museum.

Trams operate 24 hours, seven days a week between Central and Star City stations, and from 6am to 11pm Monday to Thursday and Sunday, 6am to midnight

on Friday and Saturday, from Central all the way out to Lilyfield in the west. Trams run about every ten minutes 7am to 9pm, and at longer intervals outside these hours. The line is divided into two zones. Single tickets for zone 1 cost $2.60 ($1.40 under-16s), and $3.60 ($2.60 under-16s) for both zones. A Day Pass offers unlimited trips for $8 ($6 under-16s). Tickets are available from Central Station or on board the train.

For more info, call 9285 5600 or visit **www.metrolight rail.com.au**.

Metro Monorail

Sydneysiders are not great fans of the noisy airborne monorail that runs anti-clockwise around the CBD at first-floor office level, but it's often the first thing tourists notice and does provide a fun, novelty ride between Darling Harbour, Chinatown and the city centre. It runs every three to five minutes, 7am to 10pm Monday to Thursday, 7am to midnight Friday and Saturday, 8am to 10pm Sunday.

The six station loop costs $4 (under-5s free) whether you go one stop or all the way. A Supervoucher Day Pass ($9) offers a full day of unlimited travel, plus some discounts on museum admissions. Tickets can be bought at station ticket offices or vending machines.

For more details, call 9285 5600 or visit **www.metro monorail.com.au**.

Taxis

It's quite easy to flag a taxi in Sydney and there are many taxi ranks in the city centre, including ones at Central, Wynyard and Circular Quay. Staff in a bar or restaurant will also call a taxi for you. A yellow light indicates the cab is free, and it's common to travel in the front passenger seat alongside the driver. Drivers will often ask which of two routes you want to follow, or whether you mind if they take a longer route to avoid traffic. But there are swags who don't know where they're going and will stop to check the address on a map; if this happens, make sure they turn off the meter. Tipping is not expected, but passengers sometimes round up the bill.

The standard fare is $1.45 per kilometre from 6am to 10pm (add an extra 20 per cent from 10pm to 6am), plus a $2.55 hiring fee and, if relevant, a $1.25 telephone booking fee. If a cabbie takes you across the Bridge, the toll will be added to the fare, even if you travelled via the toll-free northbound route.

Taxi companies
Legion Cabs 13 1451
RSL Cabs 13 2211
Silver Service Taxis 13 3100
Sydney's popular luxury taxi service; amazingly, the same price as a regular taxi, but often hard to book.
Taxis Combined Services 8332 8888
Wheelchair Accessible Taxis Service 1800 043 187

Water taxis

These are great fun, but expensive. The cost usually depends on the time of day and the number of passengers, but the fare for two from Circular Quay to Doyles fish restaurant at Watsons Bay, which takes ten to 12 minutes, is around $59. Both outfits listed below accept all major credit cards, and can be chartered for harbour cruises.

Beach Hopper Water Taxis
0412 400990/www.watertaxi.net.au.
If you want to be dropped off at a beach – literally on to the sand – call Sydney's only purpose-built beach-landing water taxi service.

Water Taxis Combined
9555 8888/www.watertaxis.com.au.
This company can pick you up from almost any wharf, jetty or pontoon

provided there is enough water depth, and, in the case of a private facility, there is permission from the owner. Smaller taxis take up to 12 passengers, the larger ones up to 28.

Driving

Driving in Sydney can be hair-raising, not so much because of congestion (Sydneysiders may complain, but it's not at all bad for a major city), but primarily because of the fast and furious attitude of locals.

Under Australian law, most visitors can drive for as long as they like on their domestic driving licence without the need for any special governmental authorisation. A resident must apply for an Australian driving licence after three months, which involves both a written and physical test. You must always carry your driving licence and your passport when in charge of a vehicle; if the licence is not in English, you need to take an English translation as well as the original licence.

Driving is on the left. The general speed limit in cities and towns is 60kph (38mph), but many local and suburban roads have a 50kph (30mph) limit. The maximum speed on highways is 100kph (60mph), and 110kph (70mph) on motorways and freeways. Speed cameras are numerous and there are heavy penalties for speeding. The legal blood alcohol limit is 0.05% for experienced drivers, zero for provisional or learner drivers. Seat belts are mandatory and baby capsules or child seats must be used for all children.

Fuel stations

Petrol stations are fairly plentiful, and particularly easy to find on all main roads, although you won't find nearly as many in central Sydney. At the time of writing, the cost of petrol (regular unleaded) was 96.5¢ per litre.

Parking

In central Sydney parking is a pain and not recommended. In some suburbs, such as tree-lined Paddington, the quality of the road surface is poor, and narrow one-way streets with parking on both sides compound the problem. Note: you must park in the same direction as the traffic on your side of the road.

Rates at city centre car parks range from $7-$15 for one hour to $34-$49 maximum day rate. 'Early Bird' special rates often apply if you park before 9am and leave after 3.30pm. Look under 'Parking Stations' in the *Yellow Pages* for more car parks.

Cinema Centre Car Park
521 Kent Street, between Bathurst & Liverpool Streets, CBD (9264 5867). **Open** 6.30am-1am Mon-Thur; 6.30am-2am Fri; 7.30am-2am Sat; 8.30am-1am Sun. **Credit** AmEx, DC, MC, V. **Map** p311 B3.

Secure Parking
155 George Street, at Alfred Street, CBD (9241 2973). **Open** 7am-10.30pm Mon-Wed; 7am-11pm Thur; 7am-1am Fri; 8.30am-1am Sat; 9am-10pm Sun. **Credit** AmEx, DC, MC, V. **Map** p310 C2.
Other locations: Clock Tower, The Rocks (9247 8747); Harris Street, Ultimo (9552 6318).

Tolls

The toll for the Harbour Bridge and Tunnel is currently $3 for cars heading south (free for northbound cars). The toll for the 'eastern distributor' is $4 for northbound cars travelling into the city, free for those heading out/south.

Vehicle hire

The major car rental firms are all situated near one another on William Street in Kings Cross, and also have outlets at Sydney Airport. Rates vary almost hourly and all offer discounted deals. What's

timeout.com

The online guide to the world's greatest cities

given below is the rate for the cheapest hire car available for a one-day period quoted on a given day. Rates drop if the car is hired for a longer period. We list a few of the major car hire companies below, but more companies are listed in the *Yellow Pages* under 'Car &/or Minibus Rental', although those offering ultra-cheap deals should be approached with caution – always read the small print.

You will need to show a current driver's licence and probably your passport. Credit cards are the preferred method of payment, but if you arrange it in advance some companies will accept travellers' cheques. A few firms will rent to 18-year-olds, but usually you have to be 21 and hold a full driving licence to rent a car in NSW. If you're under 25, you'll probably have to pay an extra daily surcharge, and insurance excesses will be higher.

Avis
200 William Street, at Dowling Street, Kings Cross (9357 2000/ www.avis.com.au). CityRail Kings Cross. **Open** 7.30am-6.30pm Mon-Thur, Sat, Sun; 7.30am-Fri. **Rates** (unlimited km) from $61 a day. **Credit** AmEx, DC, MC, V. **Map** p311 C3.
Other locations: Central Reservations (13 6333/9353 9000); Sydney Airport (8374 2847).

Budget
93 William Street, at Crown Street, Kings Cross (8255 9600/ www.budget.com.au). CityRail Kings Cross. **Open** 7.30am-5.30pm daily. **Rates** (unlimited km) from $63/day. **Credit** AmEx, DC, MC, V. **Map** p311 C3.
Other locations: Central Reservations (1300 362 848); Sydney Airport (9207 9160).

Hertz
Corner of William & Riley Streets, Kings Cross (9360 6621/ www.hertz.com). CityRail Kings Cross. **Open** 7.30am-6pm Mon-Thur, Sat, Sun; 7.30am-7pm Fri. **Rates** (unlimited km) from $56 a day. **Credit** AmEx, DC, MC, V. **Map** p311 C3.
Other locations: Central Reservations (13 3039); Sydney Airport (9669 2444).

Thrifty
75 William Street, at Riley Street, Kings Cross (8374 6177/ www.thrifty.com.au). CityRail Kings Cross. **Open** 7.30am-6pm daily. **Rates** (unlimited km) from $52/day. **Credit** AmEx, DC, MC, V. **Map** p311 C3.
Other locations: Central Reservations (1300 367 227); Sydney Airport (1300 367 227).

Cycling

Sydney's steep hills, narrow streets and chaotic CBD make cycling a challenge, even for the most experienced of cycle couriers. However, Centennial Park and Manly both offer safe cycle tracks with fine views from the saddle. Helmets are compulsory for all cyclists, including children being carried as passengers. During the day a bicycle must have at least one working brake and a bell or horn. At night, you'll need a white light at the front and a red light at the rear, plus a red rear reflector. There are lots of other road rules – cycles are considered to be vehicles – for full details, see **www.rta. nsw.gov.au**. You may get fined if you break the rules.

Cycle nuts are vocal in Sydney and are being heeded by the state-sponsored Bike Plan 2010, which promises the creation of a series of arterial cycle networks across NSW, resulting in 200 kilometres (125 miles) of bike ways being constructed across the state each year until 2010. The RTA provides 'Cycleways' maps for the Sydney metropolitan area. You can view them online at www.rta.nsw.gov.au or obtain hard copies by phoning 1800 060 607.

Centennial Park Cycles
50 Clovelly Road, between Avoca & Earls Streets, Randwick (9398 5027/www.cyclehire.com.au). Bus 339, 372, 377. **Open** 8.30am-5.30pm Mon-Fri; 8am-5.30pm Sat, Sun. **Rates** mountain bikes from $10/hr; children's bikes from $8/hr. **Credit** AmEx, MC, V.

Family-run, Sydney's largest cycle and rollerblade hire shop has been in operation for more than 30 years. They have everything here, from tandems to tricycles, pedal cars and scooters. They also provide a bicycle pick-up and delivery service. Credit card details and photo ID are required to hire equipment.

Manly Cycle Centre
36 Pittwater Road, at Denison Street, Manly (9977 1189/ www.manlycycles.com.au). Ferry Manly. **Open** 9am-6pm Mon-Wed, Sat; 10am-7pm Thur; 10am-5pm Sun. **Rates** $12/hr; $25/day. **Credit** AmEx, DC, MC, V.
Located a block from Manly Beach, this full-service bike shop hires out front-suspension mountain bikes, and even jogging strollers for ultra-fit mums and dads. Credit card details and photo ID are necessary.

Woolys Wheels
82 Oxford Street, at Greens Road, Paddington (9331 2671/www.woolys wheels.com). Bus 378, 380, 382. **Open** 9am-6pm Mon-Wed, Fri; 9am-8pm Thur; 9am-4pm Sat; 11am-4pm Sun. **Rates** from $33/day. **Credit** AmEx, MC, V. **Map** p313 D4.
A Paddo institution, hiring high-quality, 21-speed hybrid bikes, from one day up to a week. A $400 deposit is always required.

Walking

Walking is often the most practical way of getting around central areas, though there can be long waits for pedestrian lights. There are a number of marked scenic walks that you can do; ask at the **Sydney Visitor Centre** (*see p292*) for details. Free leaflets on the excellent **Sydney Sculpture Walk** are available from the City of Sydney (in the Town Hall complex offices), on 9265 9007 or via www.cityofsydney.nsw. gov.au. A number of harbour and beachside walks are detailed in the Sightseeing chapters of this guide; look for the **Walkabout** boxes.

For street maps of the centre of Sydney, *see pp304-16*. To buy street maps, travel guides and national park walking guides, visit **Map World** (*see p171*).

Directory

Resources A-Z

Addresses

Addresses begin with the house or apartment/unit number, followed by the street name. For example, Apartment 5, 50 Sun Street would be written as 5/50 Sun Street. This is followed by the locality and then by the state or territory – eg Paddington, NSW 2021. Many residents and businesses have post office box numbers instead of personalised addresses.

Age restrictions

It is legal to purchase and consume alcohol at 18. A learner's driving licence can be applied for at 16. A driving test can be taken at age 17, after which drivers must show a provisional 'P' plate for one year before being eligible for a full driving licence. Both gays and heterosexuals can have sex at 16 in NSW (laws vary from state to state). It is illegal to sell cigarettes to anyone under 18, but there is no legal minimum age for smoking.

Business

Conventions & conferences

Sydney Convention & Exhibition Centre

Darling Harbour (9282 5000/ www.scec.com.au). Ferry Darling Harbour/Monorail/LightRail Convention. **Map** p311 B3.
This integrated centre has 30 meeting rooms and six exhibition halls, plus two business centres, in-house catering and audio-visual services, 24-hour security and parking for more than 900 cars.

Couriers & shippers

Australia Post (13 1318/ www.auspost.com.au) has national and international courier services: **Messenger**

Post Courier is the national service, while **EMS International Courier** dispatches to more than 180 countries. Also try:
Allied Express 13 1373/ www.alliedexpress.com.au.
DHL Worldwide Express 13 1406/www.dhl.com.au.

Office hire & business services

The **Kinko's** chain has several branches around town, some of which are open 24/7 for internet access, self-serve computers, photocopying and printing.

Servcorp

Level 17, BNP Centre, 60 Castlereagh Street, CBD (9231 7500/www.servcorp.com.au). CityRail Martin Place. **Open** 8.30am-5.30pm Mon-Fri. **Credit** AmEx, DC, MC, V. **Map** p310 C2.
Servcorp offers prime business space in the CBD, North Sydney and North Ryde for the one- to ten-person company with full business services – and it claims to be cheaper than a secretary. Especially geared to foreign clients, with a multilingual support team.

Secretarial services

AW Secretarial Services

Suite 3, Level 5, 32 York Street, CBD (9262 6812). CityRail Town Hall. **Open** 8.30am-5pm Mon-Fri. **Credit** MC, V. **Map** p310 B2.
For all word processing, résumés and spreadsheets.

Translators & interpreters

Commercial Translation Centre

Level 20, 99 Walker Street, North Sydney (9954 4376/1800 655 224/ www.ctc.com.au). CityRail North Sydney. **Open** 9am-5pm Mon-Fri. **Credit** MC, V.
The worldwide CTC has 80 linguistic staff with languages that include Japanese, Chinese, Korean, Thai, Malay, French, German, Spanish, Dutch and Swedish.

Useful organisations

Australian Stock Exchange
20 Bridge Street, CBD (9227 0000/1300 300 279/www.asx. com.au). CityRail Wynyard. **Open** 8am-6pm Mon-Fri. **Map** p310 B2.
Australian Taxation Office
100 Market Street, CBD (13 2869/ www.ato.gov.au). CityRail St James. **Open** 8.30am-4.45pm Mon-Fri. **Map** p311 C3.
State Chamber of Commerce
Level 12, 83 Clarence Street, CBD (9350 8100/www.thechamber. com.au). CityRail Wynyard. **Open** 9am-5pm, Mon-Fri. **Map** p310 B2.

Consumer

The **NSW Office of Fair Trading**'s excellent and practical website offers advice for consumers on how to avoid 'shady characters, scams and rip-offs'. The **Traveller Consumer Helpline** (1300 552 001) provides a rapid response (including access to translators) for travellers who experience unfair employment schemes, problems with accommodation or car rental, faulty goods or overcharging.

NSW Office of Fair Trading

1 Fitzwilliam Street, Parramatta (9895 0111/www.fairtrading.nsw. gov.au). RiverCat/CityRail Parramatta. **Open** 8.30am-5pm Mon-Fri.

Customs

Before landing on Australian soil you will be given an immigration form to fill out, as well as customs and agriculture declaration forms. You will pass through either the Green (nothing to declare) channel or the Red (something to declare) channel. Your baggage may be examined – and more often than not, will be – by Customs, regardless of which channel you use.

Anyone 18 years or over can bring in $400 worth of duty-free goods ($200 for under-18s),

1,125ml of alcohol and 250 cigarettes or 250g of tobacco products. You must declare amounts of $10,000 or more.

Visitors can bring duty-free items such as computers into Australia, provided Customs is satisfied that these items are intended to be taken with them on departure.

UK Customs & Excise (www.hmce.gov.uk) allows returning travellers aged over 18 from outside the EU to bring home £145 worth of gifts and goods, 200 cigarettes or 250g tobacco, 11 bottles of spirits or 2l of fortified wine, 60ml perfume, 250ml toilet water. **US Customs** allows Americans to return from trips to Australia with goods valued at up to US$800 (www.customs.ustreas.gov).

Quarantine

You must declare all food, plant cuttings, seeds, nuts or anything made from wood, plant or animal material that you bring into the country. This includes many souvenirs and airline food. If you don't you could face an on-the-spot fine of $220, or prosecution and fines of $60,000. Sniffer dogs will hunt out the tiniest morsel as they roam the airport with their handlers.

Quarantine uses high-tech X-ray machines to check your luggage. Quarantine bins are provided for you to ditch any food and plants before you reach immigration. Check **www.aqis.gov.au** for details.

Australia also has quite strict laws prohibiting and restricting the export of native animals and plants. These include birds, their eggs, fish, reptiles, insects, plants and seeds. Products made from protected wildlife such as hard corals, giant clam shells, etc, are not allowed to be taken out of the country. If in doubt check with **Environment Australia** (6274 1900).

If you need to bring your medicine in or out of the country, it is advisable to have a prescription or doctor's letter. Penalties for carrying illicit drugs in Australia are severe and could result in a jail term. Check the **Customs National Information Line** (1300 363 263, www.customs.gov.au).

Disabled

It was not until 1992 that building regulations required that provisions be made for the disabled, so some older venues do not have disabled access. Restaurants tend to do better, as most have ramps.

New transport standards will require that people with disabilities have access to most public transport within 20 years. That said, many Sydney streets are far from wheelchair-friendly. Constant construction and the city's hills aside, the standard of pavement surfaces in the inner suburbs leaves a lot to be desired. Poor street lighting compounds the problem.

For more information, contact the excellent Disability Information service at the **State Library of NSW** (*see below*) or the following:

Disability Information & Referral Centre (DIRC)
Level 7, 35 Spring Street, Bondi Junction (9387 4199/www.dirc. asn.au). **Open** 9am-5pm Mon-Fri. Provides info and referral on all disabilities for the eastern Sydney area. Has a great, up-to-date database on eastern suburbs services.

Spinal Cord Injuries Australia
9661 8855/www.spinalcordinjuries. com.au. **Open** *Phone/internet enquiries only.*
This organisation provides consumer-based support and rehabilitation services to help people with physical disabilities participate fully in society.

State Library of NSW Disability Information
State Library of NSW, Macquarie Street, CBD (9273 1583/www.sl. nsw.gov.au/access). **Open** *Phone enquiries* 9am-5pm Mon-Fri. **Map** p310 C2.
Helpful info line that offers a great starting point for disabled visitors.

Drugs

Cannabis and hard drugs are illegal in Australia, but that hasn't prevented a huge drug culture – and problem – from developing. Imports from Asia ensure cheap and dangerously pure strains of heroin on the streets, while cannabis, ecstasy and cocaine are the chosen poison of the city's youth. Kings Cross is the epicentre of drug dealing in Sydney

---

Travel advice

For up-to-date information on travelling to a specific country – including the latest news on safety and security, health issues, local laws and customs – contact your home country government's department of foreign affairs. Most have websites that are packed with useful advice for would-be travellers.

Australia
www.dfat.gov.au/travel

Canada
www.voyage.gc.ca

New Zealand
www.mft.govt.nz/travel

Republic of Ireland
www.irlgov.ie/iveagh

UK
www.fco.gov.uk/travel

USA
www.state.gov/travel

Directory

and at the time of writing was undergoing a clean-up campaign by Sydney's mayor which could change things. The future of the 'shooting gallery' safe injection room in the area hangs in the balance, as right-wing nay-sayers and enthusiastic project supporters argue over its success rates. Still, come nightfall it's not uncommon for addicts to shoot up on the streets, in the parks and even on beaches. Needle disposal bins are everywhere.

Electricity

The Australian domestic electricity supply is 230-250V, 50Hz AC. UK appliances work with just a basic plug adaptor, but US 110V appliances will need a more elaborate form of transformer as well.

Embassies & consulates

Canada
Level 5, Quay West Building, 111 Harrington Street, at Essex Street, CBD (9364 3000/visa information 9364 3050/www.canada.org.au). CityRail/ferry Circular Quay. Open 8.30am-4.30pm Mon-Fri. Map p310 B2.

Ireland
Level 30, 400 George Street, at King Street, CBD (9231 6999). CityRail Wynyard. Open 9.30am-1pm, 2.30-5pm Mon-Fri. Map p310 B2.

New Zealand
Level 10, 55 Hunter Street, at Castlereagh Street, CBD (9223 0222/www.passports.govt.nz). CityRail Martin Place or Wynyard. Open 8.30am-5pm Mon-Fri. Map p310 C2.

South Africa
Rhodes Place, State Circle, Yarralumla, Canberra (6273 2424/www.rsa.emb.gov.au). Open 8.30am-5pm Mon-Fri.

United Kingdom
Level 16, The Gateway, 1 Macquarie Place, at Bridge Street, CBD (9247 7521/www.britaus.net). CityRail/ferry Circular Quay. Open 9am-5pm Mon-Fri. Counter hours 10am-12.30pm, 1.30-4.30pm Mon-Fri. Map p310 C2.

USA
Level 59, 19-29 Martin Place, CBD (9373 9200/www.usconsydney.org). CityRail Martin Place. Open 8am-5pm Mon-Fri. Map p310 C2.

Emergencies

For the fire brigade, police or ambulance, dial 000. It's a free call from all phones.

For hospitals, see below Health. For other emergency numbers, see p287 Helplines. You can contact the Poisons Information Centre (open 24 hours daily) at 13 1126.

Gay & lesbians

The quickest way to access gay Sydney is via the Sydney Star Observer newspaper (www.ssonet.com.au), the boysy SX, or, for women, excellent free mag Lesbians on the Loose (www.lotl.com). All are free from newsagents, clubs and bars all over town.

Help & information

For STDs, HIV & AIDS information, see p287.

Gay & Lesbian Counselling Service of NSW
8594 9596. Open 5.30-10.30pm daily.
Information and phone counselling.

Gay & Lesbian Tourism Australia
4787 7905/www.galta.com.au.
A non-profit organisation dedicated to the welfare of gay and lesbian travellers in Australia.

Sydney PRIDE Centre
Erskineveille Town Hall, 104 Erskineville Road, Erskineville (9550 6188/www.pridecentre.com.au). CityRail Erskineville. Open 10am-6pm Mon-Fri. Map p93.
Sydney's queer community centre is a great info resource.

Health

The Australian Medicare system has a reciprocal agreement with Finland, Italy, Malta, the Netherlands, New Zealand, Republic of Ireland, Sweden and the UK, entitling residents of these countries to necessary medical and hospital treatment. This agreement does not cover all eventualities (for example, ambulance fees or dental costs), and only applies to public hospitals and casualty departments.

If you have travel insurance, check the small print to see whether you need to register with Medicare before making a claim; if not, or if you don't have insurance, you can claim a Medicare rebate by taking your passport and visa, together with the medical bill, to any Medicare centre. For more information, phone or write to the information service below.

Health Insurance Commission (HIC) Postal address: PO Box 1001, Tuggeranong DC, ACT 2901 (6124 6333/www.hic.gov.au). Open Phone enquiries 8am-6pm Mon-Fri.

Medicare Information Service Postal address: PO Box 9822, Sydney, NSW 2001 (13 2011/www.hic.gov.au). Open Phone enquiries 9am-4.30pm Mon-Fri.

Accident & emergency

In an emergency, call 000 for an ambulance.

Prince of Wales Hospital Barker Street, Randwick (9382 2222). Bus 304.

St Vincent's Public Hospital Corner of Burton & Victoria Streets, Darlinghurst (8382 1111). CityRail Kings Cross/bus 380.

Royal Prince Alfred Hospital Missenden Road, Camperdown (9515 6111). Bus 412.

Royal North Shore Hospital Pacific Highway, St Leonards (9926 7111). CityRail St Leonards.

Complementary medicine

Australians are very open to complementary medicine and treatments; indeed, many GPs take a holistic approach and combine mainstream and complementary care. Look in the *Yellow Pages* under 'Alternative Health Services' for hundreds of practitioners. The following organisations may be of help.

Australian Traditional-Medicine Society *Postal address: PO Box 1027, Meadowbank, NSW 2114 (9809 6800/www.atms.com.au).*

Australian Natural Therapists Association *1800 817 577/ www.anta.com.au.*

Contraception & abortion

FPA Health (Family Planning Association)

For clinics and advice: 1300 658 886/www.fpahealth.org.au. **Open** 9am-5pm Mon-Fri.
Nurses provide free phone advice and practical assistance, including contraception and pregnancy testing.

Marie Stopes International

9764 4133/www.mariestopes.com.au. **Open** *Phone enquiries* 24hrs daily.
Offers counselling, pregnancy termination, advice on contraception and other health issues.

Dentists

Dental treatment is not covered by Medicare, and therefore not by the reciprocal agreement (*see p286* **Health**). Be prepared for hefty fees. It's advisable to ask locals for recommendations. Check the *Yellow Pages* for listings.

Doctors

For listings of doctors, see the *Yellow Pages* under 'Medical Practitioners'. If your home country is covered under the reciprocal Medicare agreement, and your visit is for immediately necessary treatment, you can claim a refund from Medicare. It's advisable to visit one of the increasingly rare 'bulk billing' medical practices, where your trip will be free. Otherwise you will only get back a proportion of the fee, which must be claimed in person.

Hospitals

Hospitals are listed in the *White Pages* at the front of the directory in the 'Emergency, Health & Help' section, with a location map. For hospitals with 24-hour A&E, *see p286* **Accident & emergency**.

Pharmacies

Standard weekday opening times for chemists are 9am to 5.30pm. Weekend opening times depend on the area, but are usually 9am to 5.30pm Saturdays, 10am to 5pm Sundays. Many convenience stores and supermarkets stock over-the-counter drugs. *See also p184.*

Prescriptions

In Australia, prescriptions cost $23.10 – but to get this price you must have a Medicare card or temporary Medicare card (which are available to visitors from nations with a reciprocal health care agreement) from any Medicare office, with your passport and visa.

STDs, HIV & AIDS

AIDS Council of NSW (ACON)

9 Commonwealth Street, Surry Hills (9206 2000/www.acon.org.au). CityRail Museum. **Open** 10am-6pm Mon-Fri. **Map** p311 C4.
An active organisation providing information, advice and support.

HIV/AIDS Information

9332 4000/after hours 9382 2222/www.sesahs.nsw.gov.au/albion stcentre. **Open** *Phone enquiries* 8am-7pm Mon-Fri; 10am-6pm Sat.
A statewide information service.

Sydney Sexual Health Centre

Sydney Hospital, Macquarie Street, CBD (9382 7440). CityRail Martin Place. **Open** *Phone enquiries* 9.30am-6pm Mon-Fri. *Open clinic* 9.30am-5pm Mon, Tue, Thur, Fri; 2-5pm Wed. **Map** p310 C2.
Government-funded clinic aimed at young people at risk, gay men and sex workers.

Alcohol & Drug Information Service *9361 8000/www. community.nsw.gov.au.* **Open** *Phone enquiries* 24hrs daily.
Crisis counselling, information, assessment and referrals.

Alcoholics Anonymous *9799 1199/www.alcoholicsanonymous. org.au.* **Open** *Phone enquiries* 24hrs daily.
Manned by volunteers who are recovering alcoholics.

Child Abuse Line *1800 066777/ www.community.nsw.gov.au.* **Open** 24hrs daily.
For immediate help, advice and action involving children at risk.

Domestic Violence Line *1800 656463.* **Open** *Phone enquiries* 24hrs daily.
Call 000 if in immediate danger, otherwise this service offers expert counselling and advice.

Gamblers Counselling Service *9951 5566/G-Line 1800 633 635/ www.wesleymission.org.au.* **Open** *Phone enquiries* 9am-5pm Mon-Fri. *G-Line* 24hrs daily.
A face-to-face counselling service plus 24-hour telephone helpline.

Kids Helpline *1800 551800/ www.kidshelp.com.au.* **Open** *Phone enquiries* 24hrs daily.
Confidential, non-judgmental support for youths aged five to 18. Counsellors available by email or for real-time web counselling.

Lifeline *13 1114.* **Open** *Phone enquiries* 24hrs daily.
Help for people in crisis.

Rape Crisis Centre *9819 6565.* **Open** *Phone enquiries* 24hrs daily.
Rape counselling over the phone.

Salvation Army *Salvo Care Line 9331 6000/Salvo Crisis Line 9331 2000/Salvo Youth Line 9360 3000.* **Open** *Phone enquiries* 24hrs daily.
Help for anyone in crisis or contemplating suicide.

Women's Information & Referral Service *1800 817227.* **Open** 9am-5pm Mon-Fri (answer service after hours).
Advice on rape, violence, legal referrals, work, accommodation, government services and health.

Getting some travel insurance is advisable, especially if you're aiming to stay in backpacker hostels, where thefts are common. Australia has reciprocal health care agreements with many countries; *see p286* **Health**.

Directory

Cybercafés are everywhere in Sydney. Look out for **Global Gossip**, which has locations all over town; try 770 George Street, CBD (9212 1466) or visit www.globalgossip.com for others. Most backpacker hotels have internet links, and most libraries will provide access for a small fee.

Language

Despite the country's history, contemporary vernacular Australian owes more to US English than UK English, so you may read about a 'color program', and 'pissed' means annoyed not drunk. Words that have peculiarly Australian meanings include arvo (afternoon), daks (trousers), thongs (flip-flops, not g-strings) and skivvies (polo neck jumper, not washerwomen). And take special care when talking about your roots ('root' means shag/bonk/sexual encounter – anything but your ancestry or blonde streaks in your hair).

And you will probably hear 'G'day, mate' and 'Fair dinkum', but often said with a knowing wink.

Nasty critters

Australia's array of mini-creatures is legendary. And Sydney, being temperate and humid, is the perfect breeding ground for all things cold-blooded or with six-plus legs. Most bugs, arachnids and reptiles are completely harmless, and most tend to bother residents rather than visitors in built-up areas, but there are a few nasties to look out for. The following are the critters you should be aware of.

SPIDERS

While many different types of spider tend to congregate in Sydney, there are two with a potentially fatal bite – the **funnel web** and the **redback**. The funnel web is a nasty, aggressive creature native to the Sydney bush. Reddish-brown and hairy, it lives in holes in the ground. If bitten, apply pressure and immobilise the wounded area, using a splint if possible, and get to a hospital (or dial 000) immediately. The redback, which is smaller and black with a red stripe on its body, lives mainly outside. Apply ice if bitten and seek immediate medical help.

SNAKES

Five of the ten most dangerous snakes in the world are said to live in Australia, with names like **king brown**, **taipan** and **tiger**. Most are more scared of you than you are of them, but a couple can be more aggressive – so it is sensible to play it safe: always wear boots when hiking through the bush, don't put your hands in any holes or crevices, and watch where you're walking. If someone with you is bitten, assume that the snake is venomous. Wrap the limb tightly, attach a splint and keep the victim still and calm, then seek immediate medical attention. Snake bites will not cause immediate death and antivenin is usually available.

COCKROACHES

They say the cockie will be the only thing to survive a nuclear holocaust – whether or not this is true, Sydneysiders will try anything short of Napalm to wipe them out. Despite being gross, the cockroaches (which seem to mutate to the size of frogs during summer – perhaps a response to the chemical warfare) are harmless.

FLIES AND MOSQUITOES

Flies and mozzies are a fact of Aussie life, but besides imparting an itchy bump (mozzies) and an irritable disposition (flies), they're harmless. There are also a couple of flies that bite, such as the **march fly** – but their bite is not poisonous, just a tad painful. Some people can experience nasty allergic reactions to bites – if this is you, try prescribed or over-the-counter antihistamines (ask the pharmacist for advice). Personal repellents, such as Rid, tend to be fairly effective, or you can buy coils to burn outdoors, or repelling candles. Mosquito nets and screens are a good idea in summer.

BUSHLAND BRUTES

If you plan to fit in a little bushwalking anywhere on Australia's east coast, there are a couple of creatures you need to watch out for besides snakes.

Ticks are very dangerous, if not removed immediately, as they excrete a toxin that can cause paralysis or, in extreme cases, even death. So each day after bushwalking check your body for lumps and bumps – they tend to like hairy areas, skin creases and ears – and slowly pull or lever any ticks out with sharp-pointed tweezers. **Leeches** are common bushland suckers – literally. However, they aren't dangerous and can be easily removed by applying salt or heat.

Left luggage

There are left-luggage lockers in the international terminal of **Sydney International Airport** (call 9667 0926 for information). They cost $8.75 per bag for up to 24 hours. At **Central Station** (call 9379 4876) there are lockers inside the entrance on the left-hand side. They cost $4, $6 or $8 for 24 hours, based on locker size.

Lost property

For belongings lost on State Transit public transport, try phoning the main STA switchboard on 9245 5777 (buses), 9207 3166 (ferries) or 9379 3000 (CityRail). For the Monorail, phone 8584 5268; for LightRail, phone 8584 5288. If you've left something behind in a cab, phone the relevant taxi company. For property lost on the street, contact the police on 9281 0000. For items lost at the airport, phone 9667 9583 or contact the airline.

Media

Newspapers

DAILIES

Sydney has two local papers, the broadsheet *Sydney Morning Herald* (owned by Fairfax) and the tabloid *Daily Telegraph* (owned by Rupert Murdoch). The *SMH* is an institution with an ego to match. Local stories prevail, with solid coverage of politics and events, but beware the comment columns. A recent addition has been *the (sydney) magazine*, a self-indulgent monthly freebie, filled with Versace and Porsche ads.

The *Daily Telegraph* puts out two editions, morning and afternoon, giving it the edge over the *SMH* for scoops. In true tabloid style, it also carries plenty of bitchy celebrity news in its 'Sydney Confidential' spread. The most recent addition here is *SLM*, a brash listings title with a great gig guide, but puerile humour, every Wednesday.

The two national newspapers the *Australian* (Murdoch) and the *Australian Financial Review* (Fairfax) are both based in Sydney, and both reveal their bias in their coverage. The *Australian* has been trying to

shake out its starchiness, but the result has been a rather bizarre mish-mash of armchair trendiness and what could be called a kind of 'gentle conservatism'. Along with all of this, the *Review* also offers excellent news coverage, plus business and politics.

WEEKEND

The Saturday *Sydney Morning Herald* is vast, mainly due to a surfeit of classifieds. The *Saturday Telegraph* is not as thick, but still contains added supplements. *The Australian* aspires to stylish minimalism, with a slick, svelte weekend broadsheet (published on Saturday), accompanied by a print-heavy magazine.

On Sundays, the *SMH* turns itself into a tabloid – the *Sun Herald* – which is designed to compete with the popular *Sunday Telegraph*.

Radio

AM stations

Radio National (ABC) 576 AM
The thinking person's radio station with intelligent, provocative talk shows, arts and current affairs.
NewsRadio (ABC) 630 AM
Rolling news service with strong international content and daytime coverage of parliament.
2BL (ABC) 702 AM
The Australian Broadcasting Corp's popular talk station features non-commercial, non-ranting, reasonably intelligent banter.
Radio 2GB 873 AM
Veteran talk show radio station that feeds off local whingeing, humorous tirades and chatty hosts.
2UE 954 AM
The home of Sydney's best-loved and -hated talk show kings. These big mouths – including John Laws and Stan Zemanek – have egos as large as their bank balances.
2KY 1017 AM
Racing, racing and more racing.
SBS Radio 1 1107 AM
Ethnic, multilingual programmes for Sydney's diverse multicultural communities.
2CH 1170 AM
Easy, yawn, listening.

FM stations

ABC Classic FM 92.9 FM
Classical music for non-purists, and some cool jazz.
MIX 106.5 FM
Celine Dion, Phil Collins, the Spice Girls, oh and is that Lionel Ritchie?
SBS Radio 2 97.7 FM
Special-interest ethnic programming.
2000FM 98.5 FM
Ethnic specialist with community-driven shows.

2DAY 104.1 FM
Made its name by taking women seriously. And the listeners flocked. Funny, that.
2MMM (Triple M) 104.9 FM
Rock, ads and then more rock.
Triple J 105.7 FM
Well-respected as the station most devoted to the discovery and spread of new music.

Television

The government-funded TV and radio networks are **ABC** (Australian Broadcasting Corporation) and **SBS** (Special Broadcasting Service). ABC has strong links with the BBC and tends to get first dibs on new BBC series. It also has a significant number of home-made shows and is good for documentaries and current affairs. SBS has a remit to support multicultural programming and is desperately underfunded. It features foreign subtitled films, has Australia's best world news at 6.30pm every night and is renowned for its documentaries.

The other three networks – **Seven**, **Nine** and **Ten** – are commercial and, for the most part, populist, featuring a large dose of US TV, and heaps of local lifestyle shows. Essentially it's a battle between the two Kerrys – Packer, who owns the richer Nine, and Stokes, who is constantly building on his empire at Seven. Ten sticks to its own niche youth market and is the home of *Big Brother*.

Pay TV (satellite and cable) is growing with (Murdoch-owned) **Foxtel** snatching the lion's share of the market, and **Optus Vision** lagging.

Money

In 1966 Australia went decimal and relinquished pounds, shillings and pence for the Australian dollar ($) and cent (c). Paper money comes in $100, $50, $20, $10 and $5 denominations. Coins come in bronze $2 and $1 pieces and silver 50c, 20c, 10c and 5c pieces. At the time of writing, the tourist exchange rate was approximately $2.45 to £1, $1.5 to US$1 and $1.72 to €1.

ATMs

There are 24-hour ATMs all over town – outside banks, and increasingly in pubs, bottle shops and convenience stores.

Most of the banks have reciprocal arrangements to accept each other's cards, but will charge a fee. Some ATMs accept credit cards – check the card logos displayed at the top of the cash dispenser. Be aware that withdrawing money on your credit card usually incurs interest straight away. Most ATMs also accept debit cards linked to international networks such as Cirrus, Connect and Barclays.

Banks

All the banks below have branches throughout the city.

ANZ

97 Castlereagh Street, CBD (13 1314). CityRail Town Hall. **Open** 9.30am-4pm Mon-Thur; 9.30am-5pm Fri. **Map** p311 C3.

Commonwealth

48 Martin Place, CBD (9378 2000). CityRail Martin Place. **Open** 9.30am-4pm Mon-Thur; 9.30am-5pm Fri. **Map** p310 C2.

National

300 Elizabeth Street, CBD (13 2265). CityRail Museum. **Open** 9.30am-4pm Mon-Thur; 9.30am-5pm Fri. **Map** p311 C3.

Westpac

60 Martin Place, CBD (13 2032). CityRail Martin Place. **Open** 9.30am-4pm Mon-Thur; 9.30am-5pm Fri. **Map** p310 C2.

Bureaux de change

American Express

105 Pitt Street, CBD (1300 139 060). CityRail Wynyard. **Open** 8.30am-5pm Mon-Fri. **Map** p310 C2. **Other locations:** can be found throughout the city.

Travelex

Harvey World Travel, 175 Pitt Street, CBD (9231 2523). CityRail Town Hall. **Open** 9am-5.15pm Mon-Fri; 10am-2pm Sat. **Map** p311 C3. **Other locations:** throughout the city.

Credit cards

MasterCard (MC), Visa (V), Australia and New Zealand Bankcard (BC), Diners Club (DC) and American Express (AmEx) are widely accepted. You can also use credit cards to get cash from any bank (take your passport), and some ATMs. To report lost or stolen cards, call (free) the 24-hour numbers below.

American Express 1300 132 639
Bankcard 1800 033 844
Diners Club 1300 360 060
MasterCard 1800 120 113
Visa 1800 805 341

Tax & tax refunds

GST (Goods & Services Tax) is charged on some goods, food and services. The tax is included in the display price and tourists can reclaim their GST on selected goods when leaving the country using the **Tourist Refund Scheme** (TRS). You can also reclaim the 14.5 per cent **Wine Equalisation Tax** (WET) on departure. The refund only applies to goods you take with you as hand luggage or wear on to the aircraft or ship when you leave.

The refund can be claimed on goods costing $300 (GST/WET inclusive) or more, bought from the same store no more than 30 days before you leave. You can buy lower-priced items from one store within the 30-day period provided the total store purchase is $300 or above. And you can buy items from several stores, provided each store's tax invoice totals at least $300.

To claim a refund, you must get a tax invoice from the store. You then claim your

refund at a TRS booth after passport control. Here you'll need to show your goods, the tax invoices, your passport and international boarding pass. Refunds are paid by cheque, credit to an Australian bank account or payment to a credit card. Customs aims to post cheque refunds within 15 business days, while bank and credit card refunds are issued within five business days.

Natural hazards

With a dangerously thin ozone layer, the sun is Sydney's biggest natural hazard. The best way to avoid it is to 'slip, slap, slop' – slip on a T-shirt, slap on a hat, and slop on some sun-cream, preferably SPF 30.

For information about Sydney's wildlife hazards, *see p288* **Nasty critters**.

Opening hours

Shops are usually open from 8.30am or 9am to 5pm or 5.30pm Monday to Saturday, and from 10am or 11am to 4pm or 5pm Sunday. Thursday is late-night opening (usually until 9pm). Some shops close at noon on Saturdays. Banks are usually open from 9.30am to 4pm Monday to Thursday, until 5pm on Friday, and closed at the weekend.

Police stations

To report an emergency, dial **000**. If it is not an emergency, call the police at **13 1444**. The **City Central Police Station** is at 192 Day Street, CBD (9265 6499). For more information, consult www.police.nsw.gov.au.

Postal services

According to Australia Post, about 90 per cent of letters within the metropolitan area arrive the next business day. Post is delivered once a day

Monday to Friday; there is no delivery on Saturdays or Sundays. Post to Europe takes four to ten days. Stamps for postcards to the UK, Europe and USA cost $1, those for letters cost $1.65, and all international aerogrammes cost 90c. Letters within Australia cost from a basic 50c to $2.45, depending on size and weight.

Most post office branches open from 9am to 5pm Monday to Friday, but the GPO Martin Place branch is open for longer. Stamps can also be bought at some newsagents and general stores. Suburban post offices will receive post for you; otherwise have it sent Poste Restante (general delivery) to the George Street branch. Most post offices also rent out PO boxes for a minimum of one month.

General Post Office
1 Martin Place, CBD (9244 3713). CityRail Martin Place. **Open** 8.15am-5.30pm Mon-Fri; 10am-2pm Sat. **Map** p310 B/C2.

Poste Restante
Hunter Connection Building, 310 George Street, CBD (13 1318). CityRail Martin Place or Wynyard. **Open** 9am-5pm Mon-Fri. **Map** p310 B2.

Religion

All religions are represented in multicultural Sydney. Consult the *Yellow Pages* under 'Churches, Mosques and Temples' for details of places of worship.

Safety

Sydney is a fairly safe city, although car theft, vandalism and burglary are on the increase. That said, you will frequently read about drug-related shootings, and racial tensionhas heightened since the Bali bombings (*see p11* **Terror in Bali**). The stereotype is for hot-blooded Aussie males to end an

alcohol-fuelled evening with a pub brawl. It's not the norm, but it does happen – so steer clear of drunken red-necks at closing time.

In an emergency, dial **000**.

Smoking

Sydney is heavily anti-smoking, although crowds of smokers will be spotted standing outside restaurants. Smoking is banned on public transport, in cafés and restaurants, and a wide range of enclosed spaces, such as theatres, shopping malls and community centres.

The NSW Workcover Occupational Health Act states that smoking should be eliminated from all indoor areas in the workplace, and you may not smoke on premises where facilities are being provided for children. Smoking is still allowed in pubs and clubs, but there is a move to ban it. There are fines for tossing cigarette butts out of car windows.

Study

Anyone can apply to study in Australia, but you must obtain a student visa before starting a course. For more details, see **www.immi.gov.au**. You'll be granted a student visa only for a full-time registered course.

Universities

University of NSW
Postal address: University of NSW, Sydney, NSW 2052 (9385 1000/ www.unsw.edu.au). Location: Anzac Parade, Kensington. Bus 302, 303, 391, 392, 393, 394, 395, 396, 397, 398, 399, 400, 410.
The UNSW is one of the leading teaching and research universities in Australia. Almost 9,000 of its 40,000 students are foreign.

University of Sydney
Postal address: University of Sydney, NSW 2006 (9351 2222/www.usyd. edu.au). Location: Parramatta Road, Camperdown. Bus 413, 436, 461, 480.

The University of Sydney, founded in 1850, is Australia's first uni. It has around 42,000 students, of whom 6,000 are international.

Macquarie University
Postal address: Macquarie University, NSW 2109 (9850 7111/ www.mq.edu.au). Location: Balaclava Road, North Ryde. Bus 288, 292.
Macquarie has more than 27,000 students. The university is set in bushland north of Sydney, offering a rural alternative to city universities.

Telephones

Dialling & codes

The country code for Australia is **61**; the area code for NSW, including Sydney, is **02**. You never need to dial the 02 from within the state. Numbers beginning 1800 are free when dialled within Australia.

Making a call

To make an international call from Sydney, dial the international access code – either **00 11** or **00 18** – followed by the country code, area code (omitting the initial 0 if there is one), and then the number. Telstra offers a choice of 0011 Minutes or 0018 Half Hours. The 0011 calls are for shorter chats, charged per second. The 0018 calls are for a long chat and you'll know exactly how much your call will cost upfront. Warning beeps tell you when your half-hour is almost up.

The country code for the UK is **44**, for New Zealand **64**, for the United States **1**, for the Republic of Ireland **353** and for South Africa **27**.

Standard local calls are untimed flat-fee calls between standard fixed telephone services within a local service area. To check if local call charges apply, call 13 22 00.

STD calls (national long distance calls) are charged according to their distance, time and day, plus a fee. Each call starts with five pip tones.

Directory

Public phones

There are plenty of public phones dotted around the city, as well as in bars, cafés, railway stations and post offices. You can also make long-distance and international calls at many internet cafés. Most public phones accept coins ($1, 50c, 20c, 10c). Some also accept major credit cards. Phonecards are available from newsagents.

Directory enquiries

Dial **12455** for national directory enquiries, and **1225** for international directory enquiries.

Operator services

For operator-assisted national or international calls, phone **1234**.

Mobile phones

Australia's mobile phone network operates on dual-band 900/1800 MHz (megahertz). In theory, this means that if you're coming from the UK you should be able to use your own mobile phone – but in many cases your phone will be locked to your service provider's network, and, in order to unlock it, you will need to get a code. In practice, this can be fraught with difficulties and it may be easier to buy or rent a phone. The good news is that there are plenty of Sydney companies offering competitive mobile phone rentals, for a minimum of three days, billed to your credit card.

If you're in Sydney for a longer period, you could buy a phone on a pre-paid package, or sign on to a fixed-term plan, usually 12 months minimum. Look under 'Mobile Telephones & Accessories' in the *Yellow Pages* or check out the following:

Paddington Phones

381 Riley Street, Surry Hills (9281 8044/www.paddington-phones. com.au). CityRail Central. **Open** 9am-5.30pm Mon-Fri; 9am-3.30pm Sat. **Map** p311 C4.
Rentals, pre-paid and fixed-term deals are all available.

Vodafone Rentals

Level 1, 50 Park Street, CBD (9267 0433/www.vodafone.com.au). CityRail Town Hall. **Open** 9am-5pm Mon-Fri. **Map** p311 B3.

Time

New South Wales operates on **Eastern Standard Time** (GMT plus 10 hours). Between October and March, Daylight Saving Time comes into operation and the clocks go back one hour. Australia has three time zones – the others are Western Standard Time (GMT plus 8 hours) and Central Standard Time (GMT plus 9.5 hours). Confusingly, Queensland doesn't recognise Daylight Saving Time.

Tipping

Tipping is appreciated, but not expected in restaurants and cafés, where ten per cent is the norm. Locals never tip in taxis.

Toilets

There are plenty of free, well-maintained public lavatories in Sydney – in department stores, shopping centres, rail stations, beaches and parks. It is frowned upon to use the toilet in a bar if not buying a drink.

Tourist information

Sydney Visitor Centre

106 George Street, between Argyle Street & Mill Lane, The Rocks (9255 1788/www.sydneyvisitorcentre.com). CityRail/ferry Circular Quay. **Open** 9am-6pm daily. **Map** p310 C1.
Other locations: *33 Wheat Road, Darling Harbour (9255 1788). Ferry Darling Harbour/City Rail Town Hall/Monorail Darling Park.* **Open** 10am-6pm daily. **Map** p311 B3.

This is the main information centre, with two locations – in the Rocks and in Darling Harbour.

Cadman's Cottage/ Sydney Harbour National Park Information Centre

110 George Street, between Argyle Street & Mill Lane, The Rocks (1300 361 967/9253 4600/ www.nationalparks.nsw.gov.au). CityRail/ferry Circular Quay. **Open** 9am-5pm Mon-Fri; 9.30am-4.30pm Sat, Sun. **Map** p310 C1.
Situated next door to the Sydney Visitor Centre.

Manly Visitor & Information Centre

The Forecourt, Manly Wharf, Manly (9977 1088/www.manly tourism.com). Ferry Manly Wharf. **Open** 9am-5pm Mon-Fri; 10am-4pm Sat, Sun. **Map** p104.

Parramatta Heritage & Visitors Information Centre

346A Church Street, Parramatta (8839 3300/www.parracity.nsw. gov.au). CityRail/ferry Parramatta. **Open** 10am-5pm Mon-Fri; 10am-4pm Sat, Sun.

Visas & immigration

All travellers, including children – except for Australian and New Zealand citizens – must have a visa or an **ETA** (Electronic Travel Authority) to enter Australia. An ETA is sufficient for tourists from EC countries (including the UK and Ireland), the USA, Canada and Japan (but not South Africa), who are intending to stay for up to three months.

ETAs, available for straightforward tourist and business trips, are the simplest to arrange: your travel agent or airline or a commercial visa service can arrange one on the spot if you give them details or a copy/fax of your passport (no photo or ticket is required).

You don't need a stamp in your passport: ETAs are confirmed electronically at your port of entry.

Alternatively, you can apply for an ETA online via **www.eta.immi.gov.au**. The service costs $20 and you can be approved in less than 30 seconds.

If your entry requirements are more complex or you want to stay longer than three months, you will probably need a non-ETA visa, which you apply for by post or in person to the relevant office in advance of your trip. For up-to-date information and details of the nearest overseas office where visa applications can be made, check **www.immi.gov.au**. For details on working visas, *see below* **Working in Sydney**.

Weights & measures

Australia uses the metric system.

When to go

Sydney has a moderate climate, with warm to hot summers, cool winters and rainfall all year round.

Spring brings blossoming flowers and clear blue days, with temperatures barely warm enough to shed the woollies, but clement enough

to enjoy a spell of sunlight. In summer, Sydneysiders live in shorts. In January and February the sun bakes the city, and temperatures can top 30°C (90°F). In autumn, the city is swept by strong winds, while winter mornings and nights mean low temperatures that can – but rarely do – dip down to 6°C (43°F). Winter daily maximums tend to hover between 14°C (57°F) and 18°C (64°F), and on occasion snow falls in the Blue Mountains.

NSW public holidays

New Year's Day (1 January), **Australia Day** (26 January), **Good Friday, Easter Monday, Anzac Day** (25 April), the **Queen's Birthday** (2nd Monday in June), **August Bank Holiday** (1st Monday in August), **Labour Day** (1st Monday in October), **Christmas Day** (25 December) and **Boxing Day** (26 December).

Women

Chauvinism may still be alive even in Sydney, but Australian women more than hold their own. The nation was the second country to give women the vote (in 1894 in South Australia). In real terms Australian women still do not earn the same as their male counterparts, and in many industries they're a long way off breaking the glass ceiling.

Sydney is pretty safe for women, but take care when leaving the hub of the city at night; you don't have to go far for it to feel remote.

Feminist Bookshop

Orange Grove Plaza, Balmain Road, Lilyfield (9810 2666). Bus 440. **Open** 10.30am-6pm Mon-Fri; 10.30am-4pm Sat. **Credit** AmEx, BC, MC, V.
Good stock of books, journals and mags by and about women.

Women's Information & Referral Service

1800 817 227. **Open** 9am-5pm Mon-Fri (answer service after hours).
Information on rape, violence, sex discrimination, legal referrals, work, accommodation, government services and health centres.

Working in Sydney

If you want to work while in Sydney, you'll need to have a visa that allows this. The **Working Holiday Program** provides opportunities for people aged 18 to 30 from some countries (including the UK, Canada, the Netherlands, Ireland, Japan, Germany, Denmark, Sweden, Norway) to holiday in Australia and supplement their funds through incidental employment. The visa allows a stay of up to 12 months from the date of first entry to Australia, regardless of whether or not you spend the whole time in Australia. You are allowed to do any kind of work of a temporary or casual nature, but you cannot work for more than three months with any one employer.

Working holiday visas can be obtained by making an application on the internet at **www.immi.gov.au**, or by lodging a written application at an overseas visa office.

If you do not fit the working visa mould, you may still be able to work if you are sponsored by a company or if you apply for residency. Be warned though, the latter option is complex, expensive and takes a great deal of time.

Average climate

Month	Temperature (°C/°F)	Rainfall mm/in
January	19-26/66-79	89/3.5
February	19-26/66-79	102/4
March	17-24/63-76	127/5
April	14-22/58-72	135/5.3
May	11-19/52-67	127/5
June	9-16/49-61	117/4.6
July	9-16/49-61	117/4.6
August	9-17/49-63	76/3
September	11-19/52-66	74/2.9
October	13-22/56-72	71/2.8
November	16-24/61-75	74/2.9
December	17-25/63-77	74/2.9

Directory

Further Reference

Non-fiction

Carlotta & McSween, Prue
I'm Not That Kind of Girl
From 1963 Carlotta was the Queen of Kings Cross in Sydney; the legend of Les Girls, the glamorous drag dance troupe. Born a boy in working-class Balmain, Carlotta was to undergo Australia's first sex change operation. This is her fascinating life story, told with trademark warmth, honesty and humour.
Clark, Manning *A History of Australia*
Six-volume history of the white settlement, with sympathy for the underdog.
Dalton, Robin *Aunts Up the Cross*
Dalton's affectionate memoir of life in Sydney's most raffish locale, Kings Cross, from the 1920s to the '40s.
Doyle, Alice *Doyles Seafood Cookbook*
A lavish update of Alice Doyle's 1979 cookbook contains recipes from the famous Sydney seafood restaurant and the full Doyles' history.
Evans, Matthew & Hudson, Lisa (eds) *The Sydney Morning Herald Good Food Guide*
The *SMH*'s annual round-up of the best restaurants, cafés and bars in Sydney and beyond.
Facey, Albert *A Fortunate Life*
Enormously successful autobiography tracing Facey's life from outback orphanage to Gallipoli, the Depression and beyond.
Foster, David & others
Crossing the Blue Mountains
Contemporary and historical accounts of epic journeys into the interior from Sydney, including that of Darwin in 1836.
Fraser, Dawn *Dawn: One Hell of a Life*
The autobiography from 1950s Australian swimming icon Dawn Fraser, a multiple gold medal winner over three consecutive Olympics.
Gill, Alan *Orphans of the Storm*
Shocking true story of the thousands of people who came to Australia in the 20th century as child migrants.
Halliday, James *Australia & New Zealand Wine Companion*
Informative guide to Australian and NZ wines – good to take with you on a tour of vineyards.
Hewett, Dorothy *Wild Card*
A writer and poet, Hewett was known for her outspoken views and unconventional life. She joined the Australian Communist Party in 1945 and later left her first husband to live in Redfern with her lover.

Hooke, Huon & Kyte-Powell, Ralph *The Penguin Good Australian Wine Guide*
This long-running annual guide to the Australian wine industry is aimed mostly at enthusiasts, but is still accessible to beginners as well, and thus very useful.
Hughes, Robert *The Fatal Shore*
Epic tale of brutal early convict life, by the Sydney-born New York art critic; made into a TV series.
Hughes Turnbull, Lucy
Sydney, Biography of a City
Authoritative tome from way back to now. Good reference material.
James, Clive *Unreliable Memoirs*
Britain's favourite Aussie casts his caustic eye over his own childhood in Sydney.
Ker Conway, Jill *The Road from Coorain*
Conway's courageous, moving account of growing up on a remote sheep farm on the western plains of NSW was made into a compelling TV series starring Juliet Stevenson. Her girlhood solitude, despair during an eight-year drought and dreams of a new destiny make for gripping reading.
Kersh, Jennice & Raymond
Edna's Table
Recipes from the famous Sydney restaurant with a reputation for using the best native Australian produce in the most innovative Mod Oz cooking.
Moorhouse, Geoffrey *Sydney*
A new look at the city's history by a distinguished travel writer.
Morgan, Sally *My Place*
Bestselling autobiography of a Aboriginal woman from Western Australia.
Pilger, John *A Secret Country*
Passionately critical account of Australia by the expat journalist.
Walsh, Kate *The Changing Face of Australia*
A pictorial chronology of a century of immigration, underlining the shift towards a multiculture.
Wheatley, Nadia *The Life and Myth of Charmian Clift*
A well-crafted biography of one of Australia's most undervalued writers, who, after a rich and extraordinary life, returned to Australia where she became a well-loved newspaper columnist.

Fiction

Carey, Peter *Bliss, Illywhacker, Oscar and Lucinda, The True History of the Kelly Gang*
Booker Prize-winning novelist who started life as an ad agent.

Courtenay, Bryce *The Power of One, The Potato Factory*
Australia's bestselling writer, though he doesn't always stick to Oz-related subject matter.
Franklin, Miles *My Brilliant Career*
Famous 1901 novel about a rural woman who refuses to conform.
Gibbs, May *Snugglepot and Cuddlepie*
The most famous of Gibbs's successful children's books about the gumnut babies.
Keneally, Thomas *Bring Larks and Heroes, The Chant of Jimmy Blacksmith*
Two novels about oppression – of convicts in the former, Aboriginals in the latter.
Lawson, Henry *Joe Wilson and His Mates*
Collection of short stories about mateship and larrikinism by the first Australian writer to be given a state funeral (in 1922).
Lindsay, Norman *The Magic Pudding*
Splendidly roguish children's tale – as Australian as a book can get. Made into a so-so movie.
Park, Ruth *The Harp in the South, Poor Man's Orange*
Tales of inner-city struggle, written in the 1940s. Park also wrote the wonderful children's book *The Muddle-Headed Wombat*.
Slessor, Kenneth *Selected Poems*
The quintessential Sydney poet. This collection contains 'Five Bells' and 'Groaning to God in Darlinghurst'.
Spender, Dale (ed) *The Penguin Anthology of Australian Women Writers*
Celebrating the work of female writers, past and present.
Stead, Christina *For Love Alone*
Evocative tale set in Sydney about a creative young girl from an unconventional family. Finally she satisfies her wanderlust and heads for London.
Winton, Tim *Cloudstreet, That Eye, The Sky*
The best from two times-winner of the Miles Franklin literary award.

Travel

Bryson, Bill *Down Under*
Amusing travel writer Bryson disects the Aussie character and explores the brown land.
Dale, David *The 100 Things Everyone Needs to Know About Australia*
Essential background reading; covers everything from Vegemite to Malcolm Fraser's trousers.

Drewe, Philip *Sydney Opera House*
An incisive and intellectual examination of Utzon's building as a piece of notable architecture.
Graham, Lorrie *Sydneysiders*
Photojournalist Lorrie Graham's warm and gritty album of the many different characters who make up contemporary Sydney.
Jacobson, Howard *In the Land of Oz*
Parodic account of Jacobson's travels Down Under. It's sharp and at times insulting, but nevertheless an entertaining read.
Lambin, Ann & Davies, Djida *Sydney for Children*
An excellent and comprehensive guide for parents, giving practical information on how to make the best of Sydney's child-friendly resources.
Morris, Jan *Sydney*
Personal and highly readable account of the city 'left on the shores of history by Empire's receding tide'.
Park, Ruth & Champion, Rafe *Ruth Park's Sydney*
Completely rewritten update of Park's 1960s classic companion *Guide to Sydney*. Covers the city from La Perouse to Manly.
Smith, Seana *Sydney for Under-Fives*
Solid reference book picking out the best of Sydney for babies, toddlers and pre-schoolers.
Sproule, Kristen *Sensual Sydney*
A little bit naughty and a little bit kitsch, but also a surprisingly useful guide to Sydney's more pleasurable exploits.

Film

See also pp199-204.
The Adventures of Priscilla, Queen of the Desert (Stephan Elliott, 1994) Terence Stamp joins Guy Pearce and Hugo Weaving in high heels for this gritty high camp tale of Sydney drag queens on tour in the bush.
Erskineville Kings (Alan White, 1999) Hugh Jackman in a gritty role in a flawed but powerful tale of two brothers and their abusive upbringing in a Sydney suburb.
He Died with a Felafel In His Hand (Richard Lowenstein, 2001) Noah Taylor (*Shine*) is great as a neurotic twentysomething who ends up in Sydney.
Lantana (Ray Lawrence, 2001) AFI award-winning thriller about marriage and relationships. Stars Aussie actors Geoffrey Rush, Kerry Armstrong and Anthony LaPaglia.
Looking for Alibrandi (Kate Woods, 2000) An Italian-Australian battles with her identity in Sydney's western suburbs. Local star Pia Miranda excels in the lead, with Greta Scacchi as her mum.

The Matrix/The Matrix Reloaded (Andy & Larry Wachowski, 1999, 2003) Keanu Reeves schlepped over to Sydney to film one of Fox Studios Australia's early successes and its violent sequel – action tales about a virtual world.
Mission: Impossible II (John Woo, 2000) Tom Cruise chose the home of his then wife (Nicole Kidman) to film the superspy sequel. The city features in a big way in the opening sequences.
Moulin Rouge (Baz Luhrmann, 2001) OTT love story for the MTV generation from local boy Baz Luhrmann, set in decadent, turn-of-the-20th-century Paris and filmed at Sydney's Fox Studios.
Newsfront (Phillip Noyce, 1978) Two rival news teams in 1950s Sydney battle to shoot the best film for cinema newsreels.
The Sum of Us (Geoff Burton & Kevin Dowling, 1994) A youthful Russell Crowe plays a gay plumber looking for love in Sydney.
Two Hands (Gregor Jordan, 1999) Bryan Brown plays an underworld Sydney crime boss, with Heath Ledger as the hapless lad who's entangled in his world. Watch out for a sparky Bondi Beach scene.

Music

See also pp221-231.

Classical

David Hirschfelder One of Australia's most successful modern composers. Combines classical world with contemporary styles. His film scores for *Shine* and *Elizabeth* were nominated for Oscars.
Dame Joan Sutherland Born in Sydney in 1926, she became one of the world's greatest operatic sopranos. She had her final performances in Sydney in 1990, playing Marguerite de Valois in *Les Huguenots*.

Rock & pop

AC/DC Angus Young's schoolboy attire became rock fashion, but the death of singer Bon Scott in London in 1980 came before their milestone work *Back In Black*.
Peter Allen Born in NSW, Allen was spotted by Judy Garland, who became his manager and took him to America. In 1981 he won an Oscar for 'Arthur's Theme' ('The Best That You Can Do'). He was a local star until he died of throat cancer.
INXS Sydney's ultimate rock star Michael Hutchence headed this internationally loved rock band of the 1980s/'90s until his untimely

and unseemly death in a Double Bay hotel room in 1997. Their most successful album was *Kick* (1988).
Nick Cave Enigmatic brooding vocalist from the Bad Seeds. The introspective, depressing *The Boatman's Call* (1997) is considered one of his finest works.
Delta Goodrem Latest popsicle to make the break from *Neighbours*. Writes her own stuff and plays the piano. First album *Innocent Eyes* (2003) released just before she was diagnosed with Hodgkin's disease.
Natalie Imbruglia After leaving soap *Neighbours*, Imbruglia moved to London and launched a smash music career helped by her winsome voice. Her debut single 'Torn' (1997) was a huge worldwide hit.
Ben Lee Released his solo debut in 1995 aged just 16. *Grandpaw Would* received such high praise from his peers that he was dubbed 'the greatest Australian songwriter of all time'.
Midnight Oil The band that began life as Farm in Sydney in 1971 became as famous for its political activities as its music. In 1976 they reformed as Midnight Oil, and played gigs to support Save the Whales and Greenpeace. But it was album *Black Fella, White Fella* (1986) about the plight of indigenous Australians that produced their most famous single, 'Beds Are Burning'.
Silverchair Australia's answer to Nirvana, fronted by Daniel Johns, the three-man band first performed in Europe in 1995. Now back in Sydney, they have a huge cult following. Worked with classical pianist David Helfgott (the subject of movie *Shine*) on a song taken from 1999 hit album *Neon Ballroom*.
The Whitlams Took a traditional path to rock 'n' roll stardom – years of crap venues and no money. After six years gigging around Sydney, frontman Tim Freedman begged, borrowed and finally scraped the funds for a last-ditch CD. Its single 'No Aphrodisiac' became the ARIA award-winning monster hit of 1998.

Websites

Backpackers Ultimate Guide
www.bugaustralia.com/sydney
Useful site for those travelling in Sydney on a budget.
Bureau of Meteorology
www.bom.gov.au
Get the latest weather forecast.
City of Sydney
www.cityofsydney.nsw.gov.au
Weekly update of events happening in the city, with full contact details.
City Search
www.citysearch.com.au
Guide to what's going on in Sydney and elsewhere in Oz, with events, restaurants and entertainment.

Directory

Index

Note Page numbers in **bold**
indicate section(s) giving key
information on a topic; *italics*
indicate photographs.

Advertisers' Index

Please refer to the relevant sections for contact details

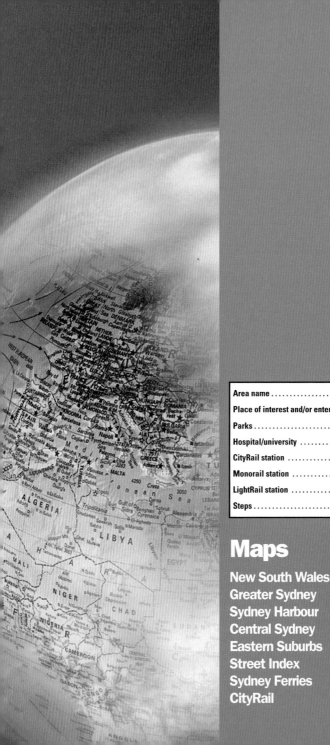

Area name	**PADDINGTON**
Place of interest and/or entertainment	
Parks	
Hospital/university	
CityRail station	⬅
Monorail station	Ⓜ
LightRail station	Ⓛ Ⓡ
Steps	

Maps

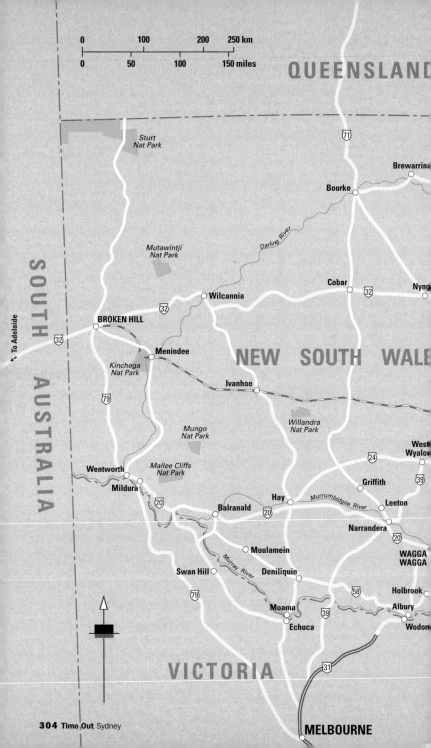

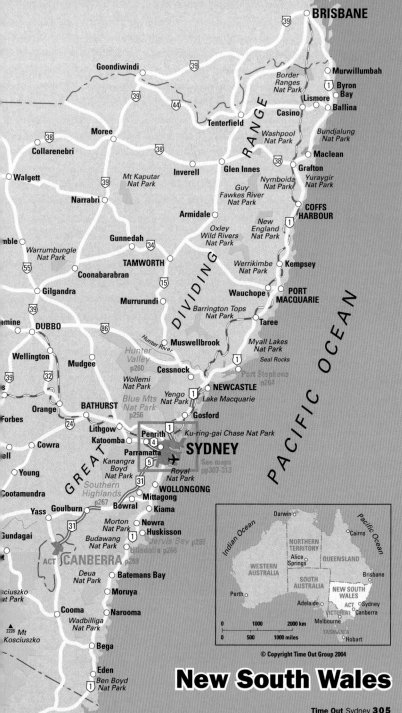

BRISBANE

39

Goondiwindi

39

39

44

Murwillumbah

Border
Ranges
Nat Park

Byron
Bay

Lismore

Ballina

Casino

Tenterfield

Washpool
Nat Park

Bundjalung
Nat Park

Moree

38

Maclean

Collarenebri

38

Glen Innes

Grafton

Inverell

38

Walgett

39

Mt Kaputar
Nat Park

Nymboida
Nat Park

Yuraygir
Nat Park

Narrabri

Armidale

Guy
Fawkes River
Nat Park

COFFS
HARBOUR

mble

Gunnedah

34

Oxley
Wild Rivers
Nat Park

New
England
Nat Park

1

Warrumbungle
Nat Park

55

Coonabarabran

TAMWORTH

15

Werrikimbe
Nat Park

Kempsey

Gilgandra

39

Murrurundi

Wauchope

PORT
MACQUARIE

mine

DUBBO

86

Barrington Tops
Nat Park

Taree

Wellington

Mudgee

Hunter River

Muswellbrook

Myall Lakes
Nat Park

39

32

Hunter
Valley
p260

Cessnock

1

Seal Rocks

Port Stephens
p264

Orange

BATHURST

Wollemi
Nat Park

Yengo
Nat Park

1

NEWCASTLE

Forbes

24

Lithgow

Blue Mts
Nat Park
p256

Lake Macquarie

Cowra

Katoomba

Penrith

Gosford

1

Ku-ring-gai Chase Nat Park

Young

4

SYDNEY

Parramatta

5

See maps
pp307-313

Cootamundra

Kanangra
Boyd
Nat Park

31

Royal
Nat Park

Yass

Goulburn

Southern
Highlands
p267

Bowral

WOLLONGONG

Mittagong

31

Kiama

Gundagai

Morton
Nat Park

Nowra

ACT **CANBERRA**

Budawang
Nat Park

Huskisson

1

Jervis Bay p265

Ulladulla p266

p263

sciuszko
at Park

Deua
Nat Park

Batemans Bay

Moruya

Cooma

Narooma

2228 Mt
Kosciuszko

Wadbilliga
Nat Park

Bega

Eden

Ben Boyd
Nat Park

1

PACIFIC OCEAN

GREAT DIVIDING RANGE

Darwin

Pacific
Ocean

Indian Ocean

Cairns

NORTHERN
TERRITORY

QUEENSLAND

Alice
Springs

WESTERN
AUSTRALIA

SOUTH
AUSTRALIA

Perth

Brisbane

NEW SOUTH
WALES

Adelaide

ACT Sydney
Canberra

VICTORIA

Melbourne

0   1000   2000 km

TASMANIA

0   500   1000 miles

Hobart

© Copyright Time Out Group 2004

New South Wales

Taking time off?
Take Time Out.

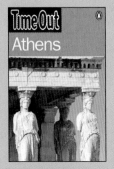
Time Out Athens

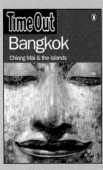
Time Out Bangkok
Chiang Mai & the islands

Time Out Buenos Aires

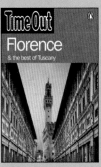
Time Out Florence
& the best of Tuscany

Time Out Havana
& the best of Cuba

Time Out Hong Kong
Macau & Guangzhou

Time Out Los Angeles

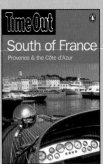
Time Out South of France
Provence & the Côte d'Azur

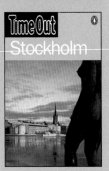
Time Out Stockholm

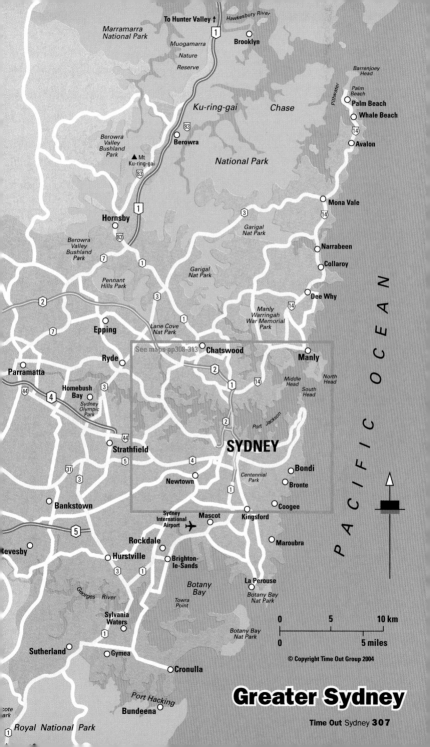

Greater Sydney

Time Out Sydney **307**

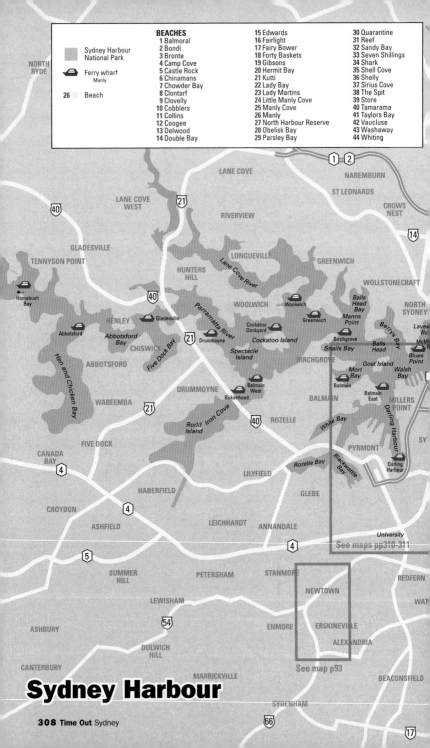

BEACHES

1 Balmoral	15 Edwards	30 Quarantine
2 Bondi	16 Fairlight	31 Reef
3 Bronte	17 Fairy Bower	32 Sandy Bay
4 Camp Cove	18 Forty Baskets	33 Seven Shillings
5 Castle Rock	19 Gibsons	34 Shark
6 Chinamans	20 Hermit Bay	35 Shell Cove
7 Chowder Bay	21 Kutti	36 Shelly
8 Clontarf	22 Lady Bay	37 Sirius Cove
9 Collins	23 Lady Martins	38 The Spit
10 Cobblers	24 Little Manly Cove	39 Store
11 Collins	25 Manly Cove	40 Tamarama
12 Coogee	26 Manly	41 Taylors Bay
13 Delwood	27 North Harbour Reserve	42 Vaucluse
14 Double Bay	28 Obelisk Bay	43 Washaway
	29 Parsley Bay	44 Whiting

Sydney Harbour National Park

Ferry wharf
Manly

26 Beach

NORTH RYDE

LANE COVE

NAREMBURN

ST LEONARDS

CROWS NEST

LANE COVE WEST

21

40

RIVERVIEW

14

GLADESVILLE

TENNYSON POINT

LONGUEVILLE

LANE COVE River

HUNTERS HILL

WOOLWICH

GREENWICH

WOLLSTONECRAFT

Homebush Bay

40

Gladesville

HENLEY

Parramatta River

Woolwich

Greenwich

Balls Head Bay

Manns Point

NORTH SYDNEY

Laven Be

Abbotsford

Abbotsford Bay

CHISWICK

21

Drummoyne

Cockatoo Dockyard

Cockatoo Island

Birchgrove

Berrys Bay

Balls Head

McM

ABBOTSFORD

Five Dock Bay

Spectacle Island

BIRCHGROVE

Snails Bay

Blues Point

Hen and Chicken Bay

WAREEMBA

DRUMMOYNE

Balmain West

Birkenhead

Goat Island

Mort Bay

Walsh Bay

FIVE DOCK

Rodd Island

Iron Cove

BALMAIN

Balmain

Balmain East

MILLERS POINT

CANADA BAY

4

21

40

ROZELLE

White Bay

Darling Harbour

SY

CROYDON

4

HABERFIELD

LILYFIELD

Rozelle Bay

PYRMONT

ASHFIELD

5

Blackwattle Bay

Darling Harbour

LEICHHARDT

GLEBE

SUMMER HILL

PETERSHAM

STANMORE

ANNANDALE

4

University
See maps pp310-311

REDFERN

LEWISHAM

NEWTOWN

WAT

ASHBURY

54

ENMORE

ERSKINEVILLE

DULWICH HILL

ALEXANDRIA

CANTERBURY

MARRICKVILLE

See map p93

BEACONSFIELD

Sydney Harbour

SYDENHAM

66

17

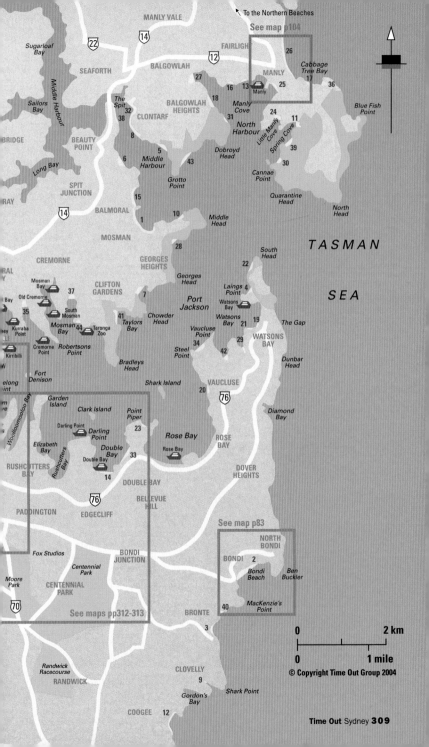

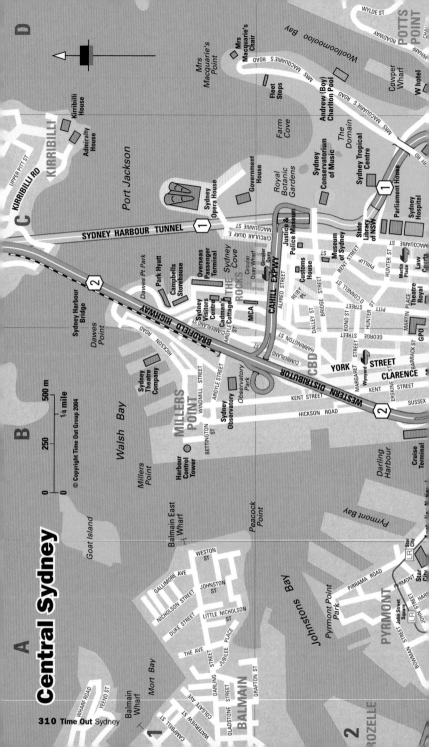

Central Sydney

A **B** **C** **D**

1

2

0   250   500 m
0   1/4 mile
© Copyright Time Out Group 2004

KIRRIBILLI

UPPER PITT ST
KIRRIBILLI RD

Kirribilli
House

Admiralty
House

Port Jackson

WYLDE ST
POTTS
POINT
CHALL

Woolloomooloo Bay

ROADWAY
WHARF
Cowper
Wharf
W hotel

Mrs
Macquarie's
Chair

Mrs
Macquarie's
Point

MRS MACQUARIE'S ROAD

Fleet
Steps

Andrew (Boy)
Charlton Pool

Farm
Cove

The
Domain

Sydney Tropical
Centre

Sydney
Opera House

Government
House

Royal
Botanic
Gardens

Sydney
Conservatorium
of Music

Government House

MACQUARIE ST E

Parliament House

State
Library
of NSW

Sydney
Hospital

MACQUARIE ST

Law
Courts

SYDNEY HARBOUR TUNNEL

CIRCULAR QUAY E

Justice &
Police Museum

THE ROCKS

Dawes Pt Park

Park Hyatt

Campbells
Storehouse

Overseas
Passenger
Terminal

Sydney
Visitors
Centre

Cadman's
Cottage

MCA

Sydney
Cove

Circular
Quay Wharf

Circular
Quay

Customs
House

Museum
of Sydney

BENT STREET

PHILLIP STREET

HUNTER ST

Martin
Place

Theatre
Royal

MARTIN PLACE

GPO

Sydney Harbour
Bridge

Dawes
Point

BRADFIELD HIGHWAY

HICKSON ROAD

ARGYLE STREET

CUMBERLAND ST

CAHILL EXPWY

ALFRED STREET

REIBY PL

DALLEY ST

CUMBERLAND ST

HARRINGTON ST

BRIDGE STREET

BOND ST

O'CONNELL ST

GEORGE STREET

PITT STREET

HUNTER STREET

BARRACK ST

CBD

YORK STREET

CLARENCE S

Walsh Bay

Millers
Point

Goat Island

Sydney
Theatre
Company

MILLERS
POINT

WINDMILL STREET

Observatory
Park

Sydney
Observatory

Harbour
Control
Tower

BETTINGTON ST

KENT STREET

HICKSON ROAD

WESTERN DISTRIBUTOR

MARGARET STREET

KENT STREET

Wynyard

ERSKINE STREET

SUSSEX

Balmain East
Wharf

Peacock
Point

Pyrmont Bay

Darling
Harbour

Cruise
Terminal

Mort Bay

Balmain
Wharf

WHARF ROAD
YEEND ST

WATERVIEW ST
CAMPBELL ST
COLGATE AVE
GLADSTONE STREET
DARLING STREET
GRAFTON ST
THE AVE
JUBILEE PLACE
DUKE STREET
NICHOLSON STREET
LITTLE NICHOLSON
JOHNSTON ST
GALLIMORE AVE
WESTON ST

BALMAIN

Johnstons Bay

Pyrmont Point
Park

PIRRAMA ROAD

PYRMONT STREET

BOWMAN STREET
JOHN STREET

John Street
Square

PYRMONT

Star
City

Star
City

LR

ROZELLE

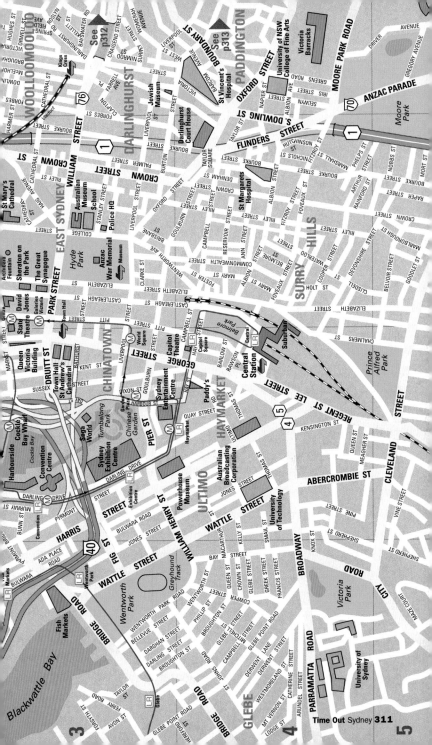

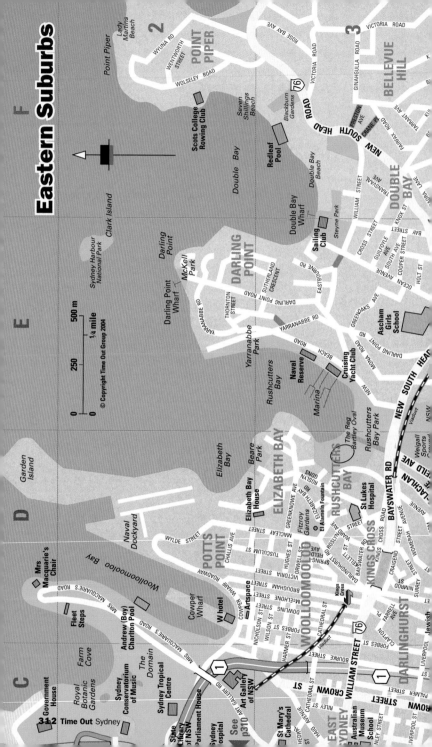

Eastern Suburbs

© Copyright Time Out Group 2004

0   250   500 m
0   ¼ mile

F

Point Piper

Lady Martins Beach

WYUNA RD

WENTWORTH STREET

WOLSELEY ROAD

POINT PIPER

ROSE BAY AVE

VICTORIA ROAD

Scots College Rowing Club

Seven Shillings Beach

Blackburn Gardens

NEW SOUTH HEAD ROAD

76

VICTORIA ROAD

GINAHGULLA ROAD

BELLEVUE HILL

PRESTON AVE

GROSVENOR

FAIRFAX ROAD

TARRANT AVE

Redleaf Pool

Double Bay

Double Bay Beach

DOUBLE BAY

WILLIAM STREET

CROSS STREET

KNOX ST

BAY STREET

OCEAN AVENUE

GUILFOYLE AVE

SOUTH AVE

COOPER STREET

HOLT ST

TRANSVAAL AVE

2

3

Double Bay

E

Clark Island

Sydney Harbour National Park

Darling Point Wharf

Darling Point Wharf

Darling Point

McKell Park

DARLING POINT

Double Bay Wharf

Steyne Park

Sailing Club

YARRANABBE RD

Yarranabbe Park

THORNTON STREET

SUTHERLAND CRESCENT

DARLING POINT ROAD

EASTBOURNE RD

GREENOAKS AVE

Ascham Girls School

DARLING POINT ROAD

MONA ROAD

NEW SOUTH HEAD

Rushcutters Bay

BEACH ROAD

Naval Reserve

Cruising Yacht Club

Marina

The Reg Bartley Oval

Rushcutters Bay Park

BAYSWATER RD

NEW SOUTH HEAD RD

LACHLAN AVE

Weigall Sports Ground

NSW

Viaduct

D

Garden Island

Naval Dockyard

Woolloomooloo Bay

Elizabeth Bay

Beare Park

Elizabeth Bay House

ELIZABETH BAY

POTTS POINT

WYLDE STREET

CHALLIS AVE

MACLEAY STREET

TUSCULUM ST

VICTORIA STREET

GREENKNOWE AVE

ELIZABETH BAY RD

ROSLYN GDNS

Fitzroy Gardens

El Alamein Fountain

WARD AVE

GREENKNOWE AVE

RUSHCUTTERS BAY

St Lukes Hospital

KINGS CROSS

SPRINGFIELD AVE

ROSLYN ST

BARNCLEUTH AVE

WARD AVE

ROSLYN ST

KINGS CROSS ROAD

CRAIGEND STREET

BAYSWATER RD

WOMERAH AVENUE

C

Mrs Macquarie's Chair

Fleet Steps

Royal Botanic Gardens

Farm Cove

Government House

MRS MACQUARIES ROAD

The Domain

Andrew (Boy) Charlton Pool

Sydney Tropical Centre

Sydney Conservatorium of Music

Cowper Wharf

W hotel

Artspace

COWPER WHARF ROADWAY

WOOLLOOMOOLOO

BROUGHAM STREET

McELHONE STREET

DOWLING STREET

FORBES STREET

CATHEDRAL ST

WILSON ST

NICHOLSON STREET

HARMER ST

BOURKE STREET

Kings Cross

WILLIAM STREET

76

State Library of NSW

Parliament House

Sydney Hospital

See p310

Art Gallery of NSW

ART GALLERY RD

1

St Mary's Cathedral

EAST SYDNEY

Australian Museum

National Art School

CATHEDRAL ST

RILEY ST

CROWN STREET

FORBES ST

PALMER STREET

DARLINGHURST

CROWN STREET

LIVERPOOL STREET

Jewish

1

FARRELL AVE

NIMROD ST

SURREY STREET

HARE AVE

NLEY STREET

BOURKE STREET

HEGE AVENUE

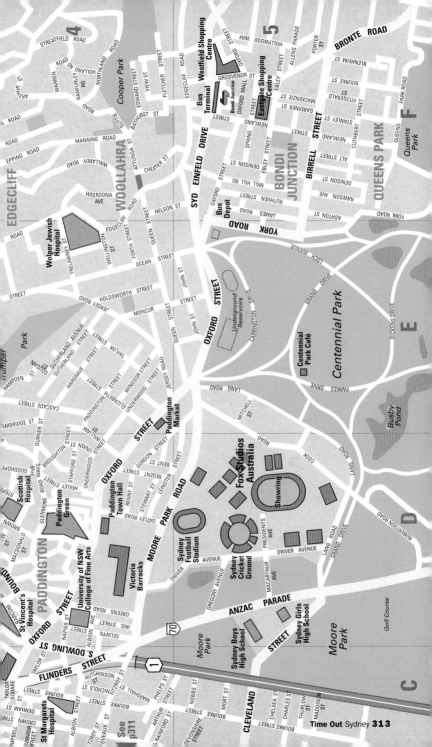

Street Index

Sydney Ferries

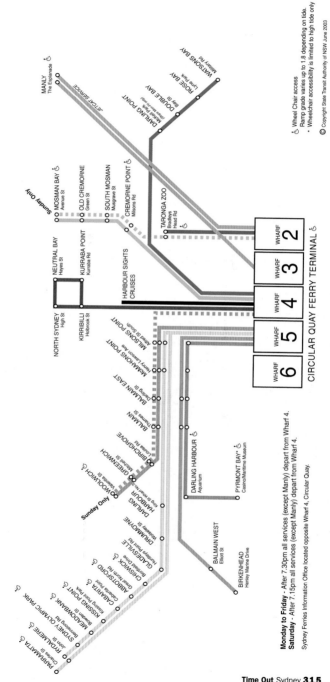

MANLY
The Esplanade

JETCAT SERVICE

DARLING POINT
McKell Park
(New Beach Rd)

ROSE BAY
Lyne Park

DOUBLE BAY
Bay St

WATSONS BAY
Military Rd

MOSMAN BAY
Avenue St

Sunday Only

OLD CREMORNE
Green St

SOUTH MOSMAN
Musgrave St

CREMORNE POINT
Milsons Rd

TARONGA ZOO
Bradleys
Head Rd

NEUTRAL BAY
Hayes St

KURRABA POINT
Kurraba Rd

HARBOUR SIGHTS
CRUISES

NORTH SYDNEY
High St

KIRRIBILLI
Holbrook St

WHARF 2

WHARF 3

WHARF 4

WHARF 5

WHARF 6

CIRCULAR QUAY FERRY TERMINAL

MILSONS POINT
Alfred St (South)

McMAHONS POINT
Henry Lawson Ave

BALMAIN EAST
Darling St

BALMAIN
Thames St

BIRCHGROVE
Louisa Rd

GREENWICH
Mitchell St

WOOLWICH
Valentia St

DARLING
HARBOUR
King St Wharf No.2

Sunday Only

DRUMMOYNE
Thompson St

GLADESVILLE
Punt Rd

ABBOTSFORD
Great North Rd

CHISWICK
Blackwall Point Rd

CABARITA
Cabarita Point

KISSING POINT
Bowden St

MEADOWBANK
Bank St

SYDNEY OLYMPIC PARK

RYDALMERE
John St

PARRAMATTA
Charles St

DARLING HARBOUR
Aquarium

PYRMONT BAY*
Casino/Maritime Museum

BALMAIN WEST
Elliot St

BIRKENHEAD
Henley Marine Drive

Monday to Friday - After 7.30pm all services (except Manly) depart from Wharf 4.
Saturday - After 7.15pm all services (except Manly) depart from Wharf 4.

Sydney Ferries Information Office located opposite Wharf 4, Circular Quay.

Wheel Chair access
Ramp grade varies up to 1.8 depending on tide.
· Wheelchair accessibility is limited to high tide only

© Copyright State Transit Authority of NSW June 2003

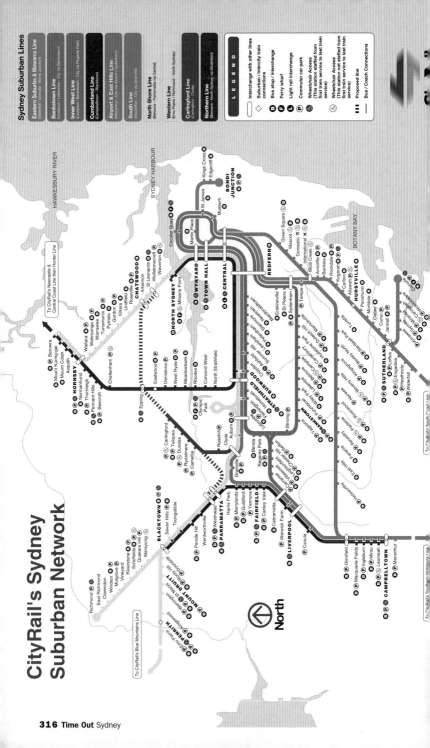

CityRail's Sydney Suburban Network

Sydney Suburban Lines

Eastern Suburbs & Illawarra Line
(Waterfall / Cronulla - Bondi Junction)

Bankstown Line
(Liverpool / Lidcombe – City via Bankstown)

Inner West Line
(Liverpool / Bankstown – City via Regents Park)

Cumberland Line
(Campbelltown – Blacktown)

Airport & East Hills Line
(Macarthur – City via Airport / Sydenham)

South Line
(Macarthur – City via Granville)

North Shore Line
(Berowra – Parramatta via Central)

Western Line
(Emu Plains / Richmond - North Sydney)

Carlingford Line
(Carlingford - Clyde)

Northern Line
(Berowra - North Sydney via Strathfield)

LEGEND

○ Interchange with other lines
◇ Suburban / Intercity train connections
Ⓑ Bus stop / Interchange
Ⓕ Ferry wharf
Ⓛ Light rail interchange
Ⓟ Commuter car park
Ⓧ Wheelchair Access (This station is staffed from first train service to last train service)
Ⓐ Wheelchair Access (This station not staffed from first train service to last train service)

▬▬▬ Proposed line
▦▦▦ Bus / Coach Connections